Real Estate Investment

Mary Alice Hines
University of Alabama

Real Estate

Investment

Macmillan Publishing Co., Inc.
NEW YORK

Collier Macmillan Publishers
LONDON

Copyright © 1980, Mary Alice Hines
Printed in the United States of America

All rights reserved. No part of this
book may be reproduced or transmitted
in any form or by any means, electronic
or mechanical, including photocopying,
recording, or any information storage
and retrieval system, without permission
in writing from the Publisher.

Macmillan Publishing Co., Inc.
866 Third Avenue, New York, New York 10022

Collier Macmillan Canada, Ltd.

Library of Congress Cataloging in Publication Data

Hines, Mary Alice.
   Real estate investment.

   Includes index.
   1. Real estate investment. I. Title.
HD1375.H594   1980   332.6'324   79-15719
ISBN 0-02-354490-2

Printing: 1 2 3 4 5 6 7 8   Year: 0 1 2 3 4 5 6

To John W. and Alberta E. Hines

Preface

Real Estate Investment can be used without a prior real estate course or previous real estate knowledge. However, it may also be used by a student who has had other real estate courses. The early portion of the book provides a quick review or summary of the fundamentals of real estate that the investor or student needs to recall or learn.

Several approaches to the topic of real estate investment are taken. Risk-return analysis is a part of the economic approach. The legal approach to the subject involves the coverage of possible ownership forms and property rights and limitations. The managerial approach is represented in the discussion of portfolio planning and tax analysis and forecasting related to real estate investment. The financial approach is represented in the cash flow and profit planning and investment return measurement. The review of the social and economic aspects of real estate investment represents the socioeconomic approach to the subject. Case illustrations also reflect the socioeconomic orientation of the text.

The three chapters of Part One present a review of real estate investment fundamentals. Since financing and appraising are strategic to real estate investment, these areas are discussed in Part Two. Part Three builds on this strategic foundation to examine personal and corporate portfolio strategies as they relate to real estate investment. The forms of ownership and their liability and tax status are considered. Investment risk is introduced. Reduction of this risk through diversification is also considered in this section. The section ends with three chapters on tax regulations affecting the three general stages of real estate development.

Part Four deals with real estate investment analysis. All investors want to be able to forecast and measure investment yields. The several methods of real estate investment yield analysis are summarized. Cash flow and profit analysis are vital to yield measurement, and they are introduced in Chapter 15. This chapter is immediately followed by discussions of discount cash flow analysis in Chapter 16 and of investment return measurement methods in Chapter 17. The most often used methods of yield analysis are combined with the suggested methods of net present value and discounted rate of return. The required interest tables are located in the Appendix of the book.

Part Five, the final section, analyzes investment in specific types of real properties, such as houses, apartment units, apartment projects, shopping centers, office buildings, industrial buildings, and so on. The unique investment characteristics of each type of property are surveyed along with the investment returns reported over recent years. If the reader finds any of the real estate terms unfamiliar and wants a capsule summary of the meaning of specific terms, there is a glossary in the back of the text.

This text and the instructor's manual have ample learning and teaching aids. For example, within the text itself may be found chapter introductions, chapter sections relating the particular chapter content to the content of previous and subsequent chapters, end-of-chapter summaries, and end-of-chapter Key Terms and Concepts. Questions for self-examination of the multiple-choice and true-false types are found at the end of each chapter. Problems are provided that can be done with or without the help of an instructor. Chapter appendices contain up-to-date illustrations and exhibits. The instructor's manual provides multiple-choice and true-false questions for each chapter. Three sample examinations are also provided.

Numerous people have influenced the writing of this book. Owen Meredith, Jr., CPM, ASA, of Owen Meredith & Sons of Tuscaloosa, Alabama, assisted the author through the preparation of the manuscript. As a real estate professional who is the owner of a diversified real estate company, this professional colleague provided encouragement and current sources of information about real estate investment and realized returns. This assistance was priceless. Another professional friend, James D. West, MAI, SRPA, has provided data on real estate investment and valuation. This professional colleague, who has also taught at the University of Alabama in the real estate area for a number of years, has provided general encouragement for the preparation of the manuscript. In addition, the enthusiasm for real estate investment of James Gibbons, MAI, SREA, of Garden City, New York—an instructor of Course VI, Real Estate Investment Analysis, offered by the American Institute of Real Estate Appraisers—influenced the completion of this textbook.

The finance faculty of Wright State University of Dayton, Ohio, assisted in the formulation and revision of the exhibits of Chapters 10 and 11. They also offered constructive criticism of the original drafts of several of the exhibits of those chapters.

Mary Alice Hines
Professor of Real Estate and Finance

Contents

PART ONE:
REAL ESTATE INVESTMENT FUNDAMENTALS

Chapter 1. Introduction *2*

Reasons for Studying Real Estate Investment *4*

Views on Real Estate Investment *5*
  The College Student   The Prospective Real Estate Investor   The Future Job Applicant

The Approaches to Real Estate Investment *5*

A Survey of the Text Contents *6*

The Significance of Real Estate Investment *7*
  Home Ownership   Housing Starts and Mobile Home Shipments   Investment in Private Housing Versus the Gross National Product   Growth in Real Estate Investment   Growth in Residential Mortgage Debt   Apartment and Commercial Building Construction and Mortgage Debt

Investment Alternatives *11*

Basic Terminology Associated with Real Estate Investment *13*
  Real Estate   Real Property   Personal Property   Real Estate Investment   Bank   Primary Mortgage Market   Secondary Mortgage Market   Mortgage   Cash Flow   Profit   Real Estate Appraisal

Summary *14*

Key Terms and Concepts *15*

Questions for Student Self-examination *16*

Problems *17*

Chapter 2. Social and Economic Aspects of Real Estate Investment *18*

The Relationship of This Chapter to Other Chapters of the Text *19*

Social Aspects of Real Estate Investment *19*
  The Social Acceptance of Home Ownership   Government Goals and Programs for

ix

Standard Housing for All Citizens   The Civil Rights Laws and Real Estate Investment
Joint Ownership to Facilitate Property Acquisition   Real Estate Investment and Population Characteristics

Economic Aspects of Real Estate Investment *24*
The Trend in Savings   Relative Sales of Existing Versus New Homes   Vacancy Rates of Rental Residential Units Versus Single-Family Houses   Second-Home Ownership   Rental Incomes of Americans

Economic Cycles and Real Estate Investment Returns

Disintermediation

Inflation and Real Estate Investment

The Movement of Mortgage Monies from Capital-Rich to Capital-Scarce Areas

The Trends in Home Ownership
Age Groups   Income Groups   Ethnic Groups   Geographic and Urban-Suburban Locations

Attributes of Real Estate Investment *31*
Inflation Protection   Marketability   Tax Shelter   Leverage   The Relative Yield on Real Estate

Summary *32*

Key Terms and Concepts *34*

Questions for Student Self-examination *35*

Problems *36*

Chapter 3. Property Rights and Limitations *37*

Introduction *38*

The Relationship of This Chapter to Other Chapters of the Text *39*

Freehold Versus Leasehold Estates *39*

Freehold Estate
Fee Simple Estate   Life Estate

Leasehold Estate
Leasehold Estate from Period to Period   Leasehold Estate for Years   Leasehold Estate at Will   Leasehold Estate at Sufferance

Marital Rights at the Death of a Spouse *42*
Dower Rights   Curtesy Rights

Zoning Ordinances *44*
The Relationship to the Master Plan for the Community   The Coverage of Zoning Ordinances

Environmental Controls *44*
Federal Environmental Controls   State Environmental Controls

Building Codes *46*

The Power of Eminent Domain *46*

Adverse Possession *47*

Joint Ownership Rights and Limitations *48*
Tenancy by the Entireties   Tenancy in Common   Joint Tenancy   Community Property

Summary *49*

Key Terms and Concepts *50*

Questions for Student Self-examination *51*

Problems *52*

PART TWO:
FINANCING AND APPRAISING

Chapter 4. Mortgage Financing and Leverage   54

Introduction   55

The Relationship of This Chapter to Other Chapters of the Text   56

The Importance of Mortgage Financing to the Investor   56
   The Effect of Leverage on the Investor's Return on Investment   Tax Effect of Mortgage Interest

The Effect of Mortgage Financing on Lender Rules of Thumb   60
   The Typical Breakeven Ratio   The Typical Loan-to-Value Ratio   The Typical Loan Amount per Unit   The Typical Debt Service Coverage Requirement

The Strategic Terms of a Mortgage   61
   A Relatively Long Mortgage Term   A Reasonable Interest Rate and Possible Lender Participation in Income   Low or No Prepayment Penalty   Interest-Only Amortization   A Good Overall Amortization Plan   The Assignment of Rents   The Provision for Further Subordinated Financing

The Types of Real Estate Loans on Houses and Income Properties   63
Financing of Residential Property
   Financing the Lot   Financing House Construction   Financing the Permanent Loan on a House
Income Property Financing
   Financing the Land   Financing Land Development and Construction   Gap Loans   Permanent Financing   Wraparound Loans

Summary   69

Key Terms and Concepts   70

Questions for Student Self-examination   71

Problems   72

Chapter 5. Loan Application and Analysis   73

Introduction   74

The Relationship of This Chapter to Other Chapters of the Text   74

Applying for a Mortgage Loan   75
   The System for Applying for a Mortgage Loan   Shopping the Market   The Personal Interview and Loan Application   Credit Investigation   The Appraisal of the Property

Ratio Analysis   79
Ratio Analysis and the Home Loan Application
   General Home Price and Mortgage Ratios   Commonly Used Credit Guidelines for Home Loans
Ratio Analysis and the Income Property Loan Application
   Usual Required Financial Documents   Common Financial and Credit Ratios

Summary   86

Key Terms and Concepts   87

Questions for Student Self-examination   88

Problems   89

Chapter 6. Sources of Mortgage Money 90

Introduction 91

The Relationship of This Chapter to Other Chapters of the Text 92

Sources of Mortgage Funds 92
  Lenders of Home Mortgage Money   Lenders of Other Types of Mortgage Money

Mortgage Lending and Portfolio Investment Practices of Selected Financial Institutions 96

The Primary Mortgage Market Institutional Lending Patterns
  Savings and Loan Associations   Commercial Banks   Life Insurance Companies   Mutual Savings Banks   Pension Funds   Finance Companies   Real Estate Investment Trusts   Credit Unions   Foundation and Endowment Funds

The Secondary Mortgage Market Institutional Lending Patterns
  Federal National Mortgage Association   Federal Home Loan Mortgage Corporation   Government National Mortgage Association

Summary 103

Key Terms and Concepts 104

Questions for Student Self-examination 105

Problems 106

Chapter 7. The Appraisal System of Analysis 108

Introduction 109

The Relationship of This Chapter to Other Chapters of the Text 110

The Nature of Real Estate Appraising 111

Some Basic Terminology 111
  Cost, Price, and Market Value   Reproduction Value Versus Replacement Value   Value in Use Versus Value in Exchange

Major Determinants of Value 112
  Location   Demand and Supply   Scarcity   Utility   Ability to Pay   Buyer Knowledge of Alternatives

The Principles of Real Estate Appraising 113
  Balance   Conformity   Change   Anticipation   Competition   Substitution   Supply and Demand   Contribution   Increasing and Decreasing Returns   Highest and Best Use

The Appraisal Process 116
  Definition of the Problem   Preliminary Survey and Appraisal Plan   Data Acquisition   Data Classification and Analysis   Reconciliation of the Values from the Three Approaches   Final Estimation of Value or the Value Range

Methods of Estimating Cost 118
  Quantity Survey   Unit in Place   Market Comparison   Builder's or Trade Breakdown

Accrued Depreciation 122
  Physical Deterioration   Functional Obsolescence   Economic Obsolescence

The Market Comparison Approach to Value 124

Property Characteristics Subject to Market Comparison
  Single-Family Dwelling   Apartment Building

Adjustment of the Sale Price of the Comparable to the Value of the Subject
  Types of Adjustments to Value

The Income Approach to House Appraising 126
  A Case Example

Summary *129*
Key Terms and Concepts *130*
Questions for Student Self-examination *131*
Problems *132*

Chapter 8. Income Property Appraising *133*

Introduction *134*
The Relationship of This Chapter to Other Chapters of the Text *134*
The Approaches to Value Used in Income Property Appraising *135*
The Principles of Appraising Emphasized in Income Property Appraising *135*
  Highest and Best Use   Substitution   Contribution   Balance
The Income Approach to Income Property Appraisal *136*
The Income Capitalization Method of Appraised Valuation
  The Method of Derivation of *I*, or Net Operating Income   Various Methods of Derivation of *R*, the Overall Capitalization Rate   The Application of Income Capitalization
The Gross Income Multiplier Method of Appraised Valuation
The Discounted Cash Flow Method of Appraised Valuation
  Income Stream of Uneven Cash Flows   Income Stream of Even Cash Flows
Summary *145*
Key Terms and Concepts *145*
Questions for Student Self-examination *146*
Problems *147*

PART THREE:
PORTFOLIO STRATEGY: PERSONAL AND CORPORATE

Chapter 9. Ownership Forms, Liability, and Taxation *150*

Introduction *151*
The Relationship of this Chapter to Other Chapters of the Text *152*
The Various Forms of Organization for Real Estate Investment *152*
The Proprietorship Form of Organization
  Liability Status of the Sole Owner   The Tax Status of the Proprietorship
The General Partnership Form of Organization
  Fund-Raising Ability   The Legal Nature of the General Partnership   The Liability Status of Each General Partner   The Tax Status of the Partnership and the Individual Partners
The Limited Partnership Form of Organization
  Fund-Raising Ability   The Legal Organization of the Limited Partnership   The Property Holdings of the Limited Partnership   The Liability Status of the Partners   The Tax Status of the Partnership and the Individual Partners
The Corporate Form of Organization
  The Tax Status of the Corporation and the Stockholder
Other Forms of Investor Organizations Similar to Partnership Agreements
  The Joint Venture   The Real Estate Syndicate   The Business Trust   The Land Trust   The Real Estate Investment Trust

Summary *160*
Key Terms and Concepts *161*
Questions for Student Self-examination *162*
Problems *163*

Chapter 10. The Numerous Avenues for Real Estate Investment *165*

Introduction *166*
The Relationship of This Chapter to Other Chapters of the Text *167*
The Broad Assortment of Real Estate Investment Opportunities *167*
   Stock Purchase   Commercial Paper, Note, and Bond Purchase   A Summary of Selected Investment Alternatives
Characteristics of Selected Real Estate Investment Alternatives *170*
   Building Construction   Purchase of a Lease for Subletting to a Tenant   Purchase of Stock   Purchase of Bonds or Other Debt Obligations
Summary *178*
Key Terms and Concepts *179*
Questions for Student Self-examination *180*
Problems *181*

Chapter 11. Diversification to Reduce Investment Risk *182*

Introduction *183*
The Relationship of This Chapter to Other Chapters of the Text *183*
Investment Risk *184*
   Land and Buildings for Owner or Tenant Occupancy   Leasing or Subletting   Land Development   Investment in a Construction Company   Stock   Bonds   Summary of Real Estate Investment Risks
Investment Goals and Typical Investor Situations *187*
   Liquidity   Profitability   Safety of Principal   Tax Shelter   A Few Typical Investor Situations
A Suggested Financial Foundation for Further Real Estate Investment *191*
Portfolio Strategy to Meet Investment Goals *191*
Summary *194*
Key Terms and Concepts *194*
Questions for Student Self-examination *194*
Problems *196*

Chapter 12. Taxation During the Planning Stage of Real Estate Development *197*

Introduction *198*
The Relationship of This Chapter to Other Chapters of the Text *199*
The Stages of Real Estate Development *199*
   Planning and Construction   Operation   Sell-off or Termination
The Possible Timing of the Three Stages of Development

The Tax Implications of Costs Incurred During the Planning Stage   201
  The Recent Tax Environment   Taxation of Planning Costs   Taxation of Recording Costs
  Taxation of Financing Costs
The Taxation of Construction-Related Costs Contracted During the Planning Stage
  Real Estate Taxes on Unimproved Land Holdings   Construction Loan Interest   Insurance
  Premiums
Limitations on the Deduction of Interest on Investment Indebtedness   205
The Tax Burden of Single and Married Real Estate Investors   205
The Federal Income Tax Burden of Corporations   207
Summary   207
Key Terms and Concepts   209
Questions for Student Self-examination   209
Problems   210

Chapter 13. Taxation During the Operating Stage of Real Estate Investment   212

Introduction   213
The Relationship of This Chapter to Other Chapters of the Text   214
Depreciation Guidelines and Regulations   214
  Depreciation of Personal Property Related to Real Estate Investment   Depreciation of
  Real Property Used for Business Purposes   Comparison of the Three Depreciation
  Methods   The Depreciation Period   Change in Depreciation Method   Recapture of
  Excess Depreciation   The Significance of the Depreciation Expense for Federal Income
  Tax Purposes
Investment Tax Credit   221
The Deductibility of the Cost of Repairs and Mortgage Prepayment Penalty   222
The Deductibility of Interest and Taxes   222
  The Capitalization and Amortization of Construction Period Interest and Taxes   The
  Current Deductibility or Amortization of Prepaid Interest   The Limitation on Investment
  Interest Deduction
The Minimum Taxes on Tax Preference Items   224
  The Regular 15 percent "Add-On" Minimum Tax   The New Alternative Minimum Tax
  Involving Capital Gains and Adjusted Itemized Deductions Preference Items   The Capital
  Gains Preference Item   Adjusted Itemized Deductions Preference Items
Special Allocation of Partnership Income, Loss, Gain, Deductions, or Credits   225
Summary   225
Key Terms and Concepts   226
Questions for Student Self-examination   226
Problems   228

Chapter 14. Taxation During the Termination Stage of Real Estate Investment   229

Introduction   230
The Relationship of This Chapter to Other Chapters of the Text   231
The Sale of a Property for Immediate, Total Payment   231
  Computation of a Gain or Loss on the Sale of the Property   The Establishment of the

Nature of the Gain or Loss   Computation of Overall Short- or Long-Term Capital Gain or Loss   Taxation of Individual Net Long-Term Capital Gains   Tax Treatment of Individual Net Long-Term Capital Losses   The Corporate Capital-Gains Treatment   Tax Treatment of Corporate Net Capital Losses   Taxation of Net Individual Short-Term Capital Gains and Losses   Capital-Gains Taxation in the Calculation of After-Tax Net Cash Proceeds at Resale   Recapture of Excess Depreciation

The Installment Sale of Real Property   *236*
Computation of First-Year Reportable Gain and the Percentage of Each Future Payment That Must Be Reported by the Seller as Gain

The Tax-Free Exchange of Business or Investment Real Estate   *237*
Like-Kind Property   Holding Period for the Property Acquired   The Basis for the Acquired Property   The Exchange of Mortgaged Properties   The Tax Consequences of the Exchange Involving Boot and Mortgages

Tax-Free Home Sales   *240*
The Sale of a Principal Residence and Its Replacement with an Equally or Higher Priced Residence   The Terminology and Conditions of the Transaction   Calculation of the Gain Recognized for Tax Purposes   Calculation of the Adjusted Basis for the New Residence

Summary   *242*

Key Terms and Concepts   *243*

Questions for Student Self-examination   *243*

Problems   *244*

PART FOUR:
REAL ESTATE INVESTMENT ANALYSIS

Chapter 15. Cash Flow and Profit Planning   *248*

Introduction   *249*

The Relationship of This Chapter to Other Chapters of the Text   *249*

Cash Flow Versus Profit   *250*
Pro Forma Statements and the System for Deriving Cash Flow to Equity

Forecasting Cash Inflows and Outflows   *254*
The Impact of Inflation   The Impact of the General Economic and Real Estate Cycles   The Complexities of Forecasting Future Cash Flows

Cash Flow Differences in Terms of the Basic Investment Forms   *256*

Cash Flows by the Stage of Real Estate Investment and Development   *256*
Cash Flows of the Planning Stage
   The Use of Leverage   The Loan-to-Value Ratio   The Debt Coverage Ratio
Cash Flows of the Operating Stage
   The Operating Ratio   The Breakeven Ratio
Cash Flows of the Termination Stage

Summary   *260*

Key Terms and Concepts   *261*

Questions for Student Self-examination   *261*

Problems   *262*

Chapter 16. Mathematics of Investment Analysis 264

Introduction 265

The Relationship of This Chapter to Other Chapters of the Text 266

The Components of Real Estate Investment Returns 266
   Amount of Equity Funds Invested   Amount of Borrowed Funds and Their Related Loan Terms   Net Operating Income and Sale Proceeds

Some Fundamental Concepts 268
   Mortgage Payment   The Mortgage Constant   The Mortgage Balance Due

Real Estate Investment as a Dynamic Process

The Use of Sensitivity Analysis

The Time Value of Money in Real Estate Investment Analysis
   The Future Worth of a Single Sum   The Future Worth of an Annuity   The Present Value of a Single Sum   The Present Value of an Annuity

Summary 283

Key Terms and Concepts 283

Questions for Student Self-examination 284

Problems 285

Chapter 17. Investment Return Measurement 286

Introduction 287

The Relationship of This Chapter to Other Chapters of the Text 288

Some Indications of Recent Real Estate Investment Yields 288
   Real Estate Values Versus Competing Asset Values   Rates of Return on Equity of Various Types of Real Property

Methods of Measuring Investment Yields 291
   Total Dollar Return   Broker's Method, or the Cash-on-Cash Return   Cash Payback   Net Present Value   Internal Rate of Return   Financial Management Rate of Return

Summary 299

Key Terms and Concepts 300

Questions for Student Self-examination 300

Problems 302

PART FIVE:
ANALYSIS OF INVESTMENT IN SPECIFIC TYPES OF PROPERTY

Chapter 18. Home Ownership for Occupancy and Rental Income 304

Introduction 305

The Relationship of This Chapter to Other Chapters of the Text 306

General House Investment Factors *306*
The Demand for Houses
  The Balance of Sales Between Existing and New Houses   The Trend in the Home-Buying Age Group   Regional Patterns of Home Sales   The Trend in Personal Incomes and Family Expenditures for Housing   Mortgage Assumption   Home Financing Programs
The Supply of Houses
  Housing Starts   The Availability of Loans   Methods of Construction   Cost of Construction
Owner-Occupied Housing *312*
The Traditional Single-Family Detached Dwelling
  Purchase and Investment Motivations   Construction-Cost Trends   The Demand for the Owner-Occupied Single-Family House   The Characteristics of the Traditional Single-Family House   The Investment Yield
Owner-Occupied Condominium and Cooperative Housing
Owner-Occupied Mobile Homes
Rental Housing *317*
  The Rented Single-Family Detached Dwelling   The Rented Condominium or Cooperative Unit Rental Mobile Homes
Summary *319*
Key Terms and Concepts *319*
Questions for Student Self-examination *319*
Problems *320*

Chapter 19. Apartment Building Investment *322*

Introduction *323*
The Relationship of This Chapter to Other Chapters of the Text *324*
Some Factors Creating the Momentum for Increased Apartment Investment *324*
  The Affordability of One-Family Homes   Second-Home and Condominium Demand Vacancy Rates for Rental Apartment Buildings   Gradual Rise in Apartment Rents Stable Mortgage Financing Terms   Rise in the Number of Households   Environmental Regulations
The Market Survey and Feasibility Analysis *326*
Apartment Construction Costs *328*
Trends in Apartment Building Income and Expenses *331*
The Appraisal of Apartment Projects *335*
The Financing of Apartment Buildings *336*
Investment Yield Analysis for Apartments *337*
Summary *338*
Key Terms and Concepts *339*
Questions for Student Self-examination *343*
Problems *344*

Chapter 20. Shopping Center Investment *345*

Introduction *346*
The Relationship of This Chapter to Other Chapters of the Text *346*
The Shopping Center *347*
  Neighborhood Shopping Center   Community Shopping Center   Specialty Shopping Center   Regional Shopping Center   Super-regional Shopping Center

The Trend in Shopping Center Development   348
Shopping Center Construction Costs   348
Cash Flow Analysis   349
  Revenue Sources   Expense Sources   Components of Cash Flow Analysis
Financing the Shopping Center   350
Shopping Center Investment Yields   352
  Shopping Center Investment as Inflation Protection   Return on Equity Realized
Summary   357
Key Terms and Concepts   366
Questions for Student Self-examination   366
Problems   367

Chapter 21. Office Building Investment   369

Introduction   370
The Relationship of This Chapter to Other Chapters of the Text   370
Recent Trends in Office Building Investment   371
The Future Trend in Office Space   371
  Demand Factors Related to Office Building Development   Supply Factors Related to Office Building Development
The Cost Trend in Office Building Construction   373
Income-Expense Relationships for Office Buildings   373
  Income Relationships   Expense Relationships
The Financing of the Office Building   375
Office Building Leasing and Management   377
Investment Yields on Office Buildings   378
Summary   380
Key Terms and Concepts   385
Questions for Student Self-examination   385
Problems   387

Chapter 22. Industrial Building Investment   388

Introduction   389
The Relationship of This Chapter to Other Chapters of the Text   389
The Trends in Industrial Building Expansion   390
Locational Preferences of Industrial Land Users   391
  An Overview of Site Selection Factors   The Principal Site Selection Factors and Their Relative Importance in the Various States
The Trend in Construction Costs and Land Prices   391
  Construction Costs of Industrial Plants and Warehouses   Industrial Land Prices   Acreage Prices in Industrial Parks
Financing Industrial Development   393
  The Three Basic Methods of Financing Industrial Development   State Tax Incentive and Financing Programs for Pollution Control
Investment Yields on Industrial Buildings   395

Summary *396*
Key Terms and Concepts *396*
Questions for Student Self-examination *397*
Problems *398*

Chapter 23. Other Income Property Investment *399*

Introduction *400*
The Relationship of This Chapter to Other Chapters of the Text *401*
Investment in Hotels and Motels *401*
Construction Costs and Their Trend *402*
Operating and Financing Characteristics of Hotels and Motels *402*
    The Management Organization   Operating Statistics for the Lodging Industry   Financing Characteristics of the Hotel-Motel Structures, Equipment, and Furnishings
Yields for Investors in Hotel and Motel Properties *403*
Investment in Mobile Home Parks *404*
    The Economies of Scale of the Mobile Home Park   Overall Construction Costs   Typical Sources of Operating and Financial Expenses and Revenues   Investment Yields on Mobile Home Parks
Investment in Planned Unit Developments and New Towns *407*
    Current Types of Planned, Large-Scale Developments   The Corporate and Institutional Investment Opportunities   The HUD-Sponsored New Town Program
Summary *409*
Key Terms and Concepts *411*
Questions for Student Self-examination *413*
Problems *414*

Appendix *415*

Glossary *433*

Index *467*

Part One

Real Estate Investment Fundamentals

Chapter 1
Introduction

Reasons for Studying Real Estate Investment
Views on Real Estate Investment
   The College Student   The Prospective Real Estate Investor   The Future Job Applicant
The Approaches to Real Estate Investment
A Survey of the Text Contents
The Significance of Real Estate Investment
   Home Ownership   Housing Starts and Mobile Home Shipments   Investment in Private Housing Versus the Gross National Product   Growth in Real Estate Investment   Growth in Residential Mortgage Debt   Apartment and Commercial Building Construction and Mortgage Debt
Investment Alternatives
Basic Terminology Associated with Real Estate Investment
   Real Estate   Real Property   Personal Property   Real Estate Investment   Bank   Primary Mortgage Market   Secondary Mortgage Market   Mortgage   Cash Flow   Profit   Real Estate Appraisal
Summary
Key Terms and Concepts
Questions for Student Self-examination

> **LEARNING OBJECTIVES** After studying this chapter, you should be familiar with
>
> The many reasons for studying real estate investment
> The significance of home ownership
> The trends in housing starts and mobile home shipments
> The portion of gross national product represented by private residential investment
> Growth trend in real estate investment and mortgage debt
> Trend in apartment and commercial building construction
> Investments that usually compete directly with real estate investment
> Recommended foundation for personal real estate investment
> Differences between the terms *real estate*, *real property*, and *personal property*
> Differences between the operations and participants of the primary mortgage market and the secondary mortgage market
> Nature of the mortgage
> Layman's definition of *bank* and its specific meaning
> Definition of *cash flow* and its difference from the definition of *profit*
> Nature of the real estate appraisal

Our civilization is associated with a long history of property ownership. Real estate investment has given a sense of security and economic well-being to individuals across the centuries.

Since the beginning of time, land holdings have been important to political, governmental, and economic systems. The Babylonian, Egyptian, Greek, and Roman empires were built on conquered lands and peoples. The conquered lands were added to their original land holdings in the development of empires. As property law developed, surveying techniques were perfected by the Egyptians, the recording of mortgages was established by the Babylonians, the Greeks added logical thought to the formulation of property law, and the Romans established mortgage law for the financial control of their vast land holdings. The protection of ownership rights has been important since the early civilizations.

As the Roman Empire crumbled, the Middle Ages set in. During this period, the feudal system allowed land ownership only to the sovereign power. All other persons living within the realm obtained the use of land in return for produce grown and handmade on the land and in return for military service. Real estate investment was nonexistent during this long period of European development. As William of Normandy conquered England at the end of the Middle Ages, he encountered English common law, whose foundations of thought led to the eventual formation of the private property or allodial system of land ownership. Private property rights were eventually protected so that people could pass their real estate holdings to their children and friends at their deaths. With the protection of the courts, property owners could enjoy private ownership and control of their property. Real property rights were established and then preserved by the courts. Finally, at this point, real estate investment became possible.

The system of private property ownership, or the allodial system, prevails today in the United States. Real property rights are held by private individuals, companies, and institutions. The government entities, at the same time, retain real property rights to extensive tracts of land and numerous structures for purposes of operating the government.

REASONS FOR STUDYING REAL ESTATE INVESTMENT

Students of real estate investment are motivated in a number of ways. Some students are merely interested in real estate investment as an economic and social phenomenon. Most people are affected by real estate investment in some way; we all must have a roof over our heads. The field of study interests such people in a general way; they seek to know about the general area of business activity and how they are personally affected by real estate investment.

Some students are required to take the real estate investment course as real estate minors and majors in college or university curricula. Other fields of major study may require the course in the suggested sequence of institutional courses. In an affiliated area, the real estate license requirements may require the completion of a course in real estate investment along with other specified real estate courses. Laws have recently been changing in many states, and this new tendency prevails. Other states merely require, as real estate license exam prerequisites, the successful completion of a certain number of separate real estate courses before the real estate salesperson's or broker's exam may be taken. The course work in real estate investment tends to add the necessary knowledge for passing the real estate license exams regardless of the type of exam administered by the state real estate board or commission.

Personal investment success is the motivation for some students of real estate investment. The student may already own property or may be contemplating future real estate investment. He or she will seek to increase profits from the holding or ownership of such investments. The student will be looking for new ideas about reducing risks and increasing yields. Also, the student will be looking for sources of investible funds and mortgage monies. The legal, tax, and appraisal aspects of real estate may have eluded the student previously; the student may now want to fill the gap in his or her knowledge, which may lead to greater financial success in real estate investment.

Employment opportunities exist in the area of real estate investment. Real estate investment counselors with or without legal or accounting proficiencies are needed by our society. For example, our financial institutions employ many investment counselors, analysts, and advisors. The loan officers of many financing institutions are essentially investment analysts and advisors for their own financial institutions. For example, the mortgage loan officer of a local savings and loan association is actually scrutinizing proposed mortgage loans for investment by the association. If the loan goes into default, the savings and loan association will have a real estate investment on its hands whether it wants it or not.

As the student proceeds through the study of real estate investment, he or she may see the various employment areas available to astute, well-prepared real estate students. Real estate attorneys are needed; architects who design successful income property developments are needed; real estate appraisers who assess the risk and current value of proposed real estate investments are needed; and government housing, planning, and mortgage insurance officers are needed to provide necessary land-use controls, investment regulations, and financial stability.

VIEWS ON REAL ESTATE INVESTMENT

Those who study real estate investment have various views on the subject. Their viewpoints depend on their motivations. As the course begins, the student may have a certain viewpoint, but when the course ends, that viewpoint may be totally different.

The College Student. The real estate investment course broadens the horizons of the college student. The course of semester or quarter length introduces to the college student investment information that will probably not be offered in any other college course. The student may realize that investment may not be possible immediately but that real estate investment may be planned for financially prosperous years.

The Prospective Real Estate Investor. When a student of real estate investment plans to invest in real property in the near future, that person is intensely motivated to gain as much knowledge from the course as possible. This prospective investor wants to avoid many of the mistakes that others have inadvertently made. This seriously motivated student wishes to realize the highest earnings from the best investment for his or her personal situation. The portfolio planning chapters at the end of the text will help the student gain perspective. After having identified his or her investment goals, the student will learn through the portfolio discussion which investment best fulfills these goals. Throughout the text, this student will be reading closely the material on legal rights and limitations, government financing programs, the nature of the appraisal process, the sources of mortgage funds, property taxation, and investment yield analysis.

The Future Job Applicant. Many students in business school courses are vocationally and avocationally oriented. At graduation, or perhaps before, a student may take a position directly or indirectly related to real estate. Even though the employment position in some cases is not associated with real estate investment, the person may seek to develop a well-diversified and balanced investment portfolio in his or her spare time. The income from the employment may be partially set aside to meet the investment goals of the individual and the individual's family. Part of that investment may be scheduled for real estate holdings.

Employment opportunities related to real estate investment may be found in the following fields: real estate marketing or sales, property management, real estate appraising, mortgage lending, real estate regulation and taxation, investment counseling, mortgage insurance underwriting, real estate law, and real estate development. These are but a few of the employment areas that the student might consider. Substantial salaries may be acquired from managerial positions in these areas.

THE APPROACHES TO REAL ESTATE INVESTMENT

To serve the interests of the various types of students—young, middle-aged, and elderly—several approaches to the study of real estate investment are taken. The text begins in Chapter 2 with the social and economic significance of real estate investment. This chapter gives an overall view of the relevance to society of this area of study. The extent to which homes are purchased and the volume of funds devoted to real estate investment and mortgage lending are surveyed briefly. The cultural approval of real estate investment is also discussed. For example, the culture heartily approves home ownership for social preservation and the protection of family units.

The legal aspects of real estate investment affect all types of students with their various motivations. Real estate is a very legally oriented commodity. Therefore, property rights and limitations are covered in Chapter 3 of Part I.

The discussion of mortgage financing, leverage, and governmental and private sources of mortgage funds in Chapters 4, 5, and 6 continues the economic approach to the subject of real estate investment. The financial characteristics of the FHA and VA programs and the secondary mortgage market organizations are also discussed. Therefore, the financial approach to investment is quickly summarized in the introductory chapters.

The economic approach to real estate investment continues with the discussion of real estate appraisal in Part II. The systematic appraisal process and its use of the principles of land economics show the economic derivation of the appraisal profession. The financial and legal approaches to the subject are continued in Part III as ownership forms, taxation, alternative investments, and portfolio diversification are considered.

Part IV, Real Estate Investment Analysis, deals with financial analysis as applied to real estate investment return measurement. Cash flow analysis and forecasting precede the measurement of investment returns. Several methods of investment return measurement may be employed. Part V covers the specific investment attributes of specific types of properties commonly considered by real estate investors.

A SURVEY OF THE TEXT CONTENTS

The orientation of the book is risk-return analysis of real estate investment. The various sides of real estate investment have to be reviewed in order to observe the risk of this type of investment. There is a legal framework to protect property rights. There is a governmental organization for the encouragement and promotion of standard housing in decent, safe, and sanitary environments for all American citizens. There is a well-developed appraisal system for risk evaluation and establishment of property value. The financial institutions have developed methods of risk analysis that precede any funding of loan applications.

The study of portfolio analysis takes into account the assumption of risk and the overall desired portfolio return. The assumption is made that real estate investment fits into personal and institutional portfolios where the property attributes meet the investment goals of the individual or company. Our tax system enters the cash flow picture of any investment and affects the after-tax yield for the investor. No matter what happens in the investment situation, the investor must meet the required mortgage payments and periodic tax commitments. Near the end of the text risk-return analysis is discussed in the context of individual types of real estate investments such as apartment projects, shopping centers, and office buildings.

The many changes facing us today are discussed. The energy situation is referred to in terms of its impact on real estate investment. Increased environmental controls are viewed in terms of favorable or unfavorable implications for real estate investment. Recent tax changes are incorporated into the overall discussion. The impact of inflation is discussed in light of the trend of construction costs, financial costs, property values, and the composition of investment returns. Recent and contemplated changes in the financial institutions are brought out. Many of these changes are forecasted to affect mortgage financing of real estate investment. The changes in the business and real estate cycle also influence investment yields and risks.

THE SIGNIFICANCE OF REAL ESTATE INVESTMENT

Home Ownership. Approximately two-thirds of all American residential units are owner occupied. This proportion has prevailed for several years (Table 1-1). The highest levels of home ownership are to be found in the North Central and Southern portions of our country. In 1970 black home ownership reached the 42 percent level for all black households; the highest black home ownership level was established in the South.

The average sale price of new one-family homes in early 1979 was $68,000; the average sale price of existing one-family homes at the same time approximated $60,000. Therefore, the overall sale price of a one-family home averaged $64,000 at that time.

Housing Starts and Mobile Home Shipments. Housing starts totalled over two million in 1971, 1972, 1973, 1977, and 1978 (Exhibit 1-1). Subsidized housing starts—those in which the federal government partially finances the investment—in the mid-1970s were approximately 7 percent of total starts. Therefore, the remaining 93 percent of housing starts were unsubsidized in total.

Mobile home shipments from 1970 through 1974 approximated 42 percent of total housing starts (Exhibit 1-2). By 1979 the percentage had dropped to 18 percent. This was a much lower level than occurred in the early 1970s. Relatively high interest rates and the lack of funds for mobile home financing slowed down production and sales in the latter 1970s. Single-family site-built homes absorbed an unusually high percentage of the mortgage funds available.

Investment in Private Housing Versus the Gross National Product. Even though private housing investment is only part of real estate investment, that part has repre-

Table 1-1. Home ownership, 1890-1975

Year	Occupied Units	Percentage Owned
1890	12,690,000	47.8
1900	15,964,000	46.7
1910	20,256,000	45.9
1920	24,352,000	45.6
1930	29,905,000	47.8
1940	34,855,000	43.6
1950	42,826,000	55.0
1960	53,024,000	61.9
1970	63,445,000	62.9
1975	72,523,000	64.6

Source: Bureau of the Census, quoted in *1978 Savings and Loan Fact Book* (Chicago: U.S. League of Savings Associations), p. 36.

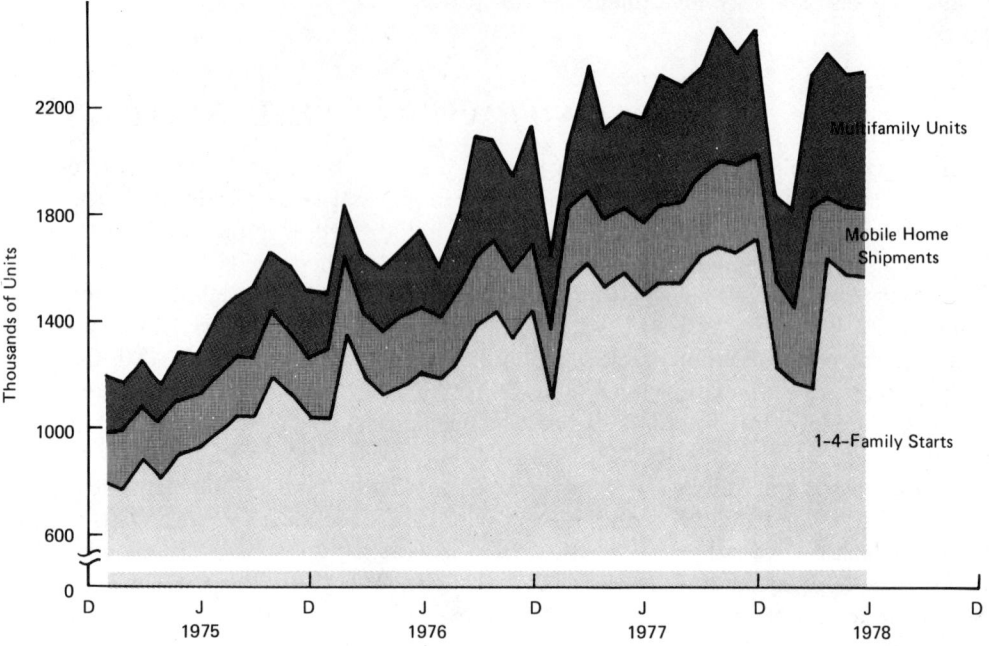

Exhibit 1-1. Total Shelter Production (Seasonally Adjusted Annual Rate)

Source: *Mortgage Banker* (September 1978), p. 40. With permission.

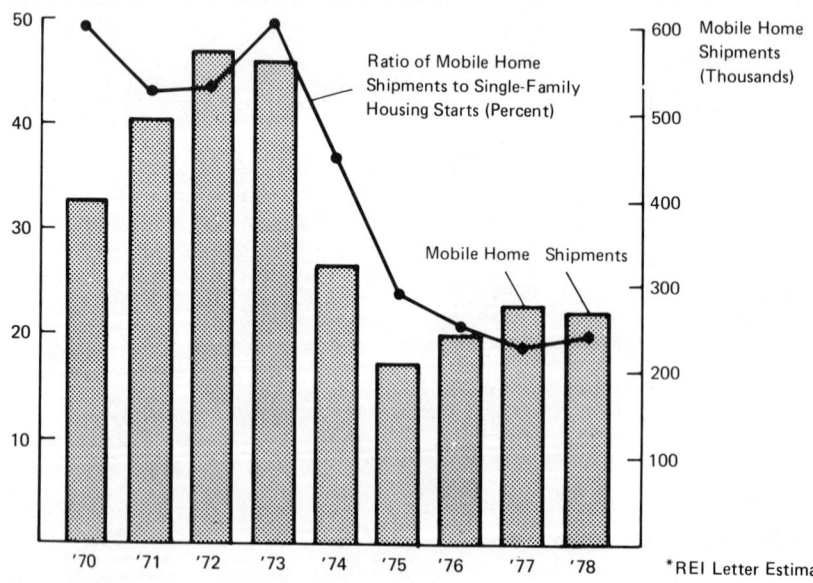

Exhibit 1-2. Mobile Home Shipments, 1970-1978

Source: Manufactured Housing Institute. With permission.

8 *Real Estate Investment Fundamentals*

Exhibit 1-3. The Relationship Between New Residential Private Investment and Gross National Product

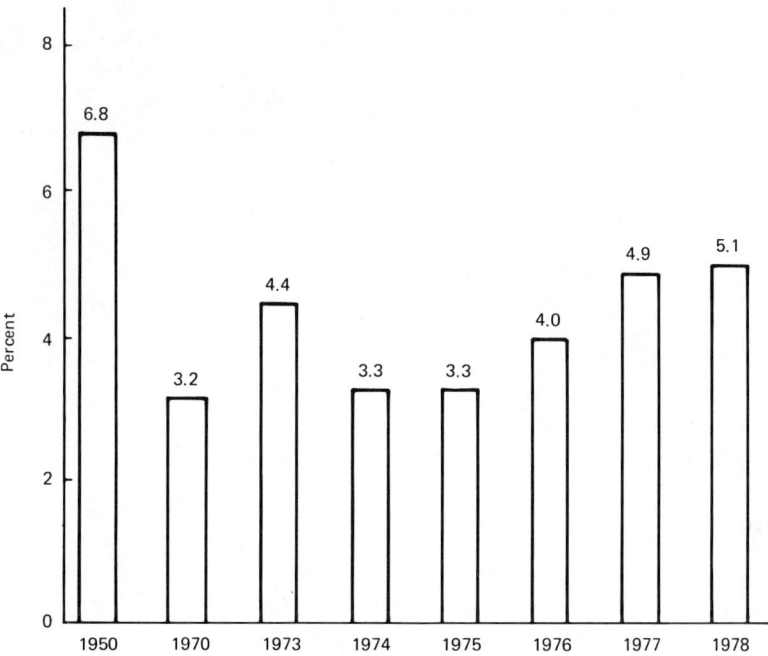

Source: *Federal Reserve Bulletin* (December 1975), p. A54; (November 1978), p. A52.

sented in the 1970s from 3 to 5 percent of the Gross National Product (otherwise called the GNP). In contrast, in 1950, private housing construction was valued at 7 percent of the GNP. In early 1979, residential private investment ($113.3 billion) approximated 5 percent of the GNP ($2,212 billion), according to the March 1979 *Federal Reserve Bulletin* (Exhibit 1-3).

Growth in Real Estate Investment. Real estate investment has grown steadily over the years since World War II (Table 1-2). Investment in nonresidential structures has shown steady growth, but investment in residential structures has been more fluctuating. In the late 1970s, though, there was phenomenal growth in investment in single-family dwellings. As this growth trend for real estate investment continues, the importance of real estate investment and the real estate industry in general continues.

In 1929, $5 billion was invested in nonresidential structures. The investment value of these commercial, industrial, and public utility structures declined during the 1930s and early 1940s. The growth pattern gained initial momentum in the late 1940s and during the 1950s. By 1970 the value of nonresidential structures reached $36 billion. By early 1979, nonresidential investment had more than doubled from the 1970 level to $85 billion. Half of this amount represented commercial and industrial structural investment. Admittedly, part of the investment growth in dollars must be attributed to inflation.

Growth in Residential Mortgage Debt. The lenders had only $24 billion invested in residential mortgage debt in 1945. By the late 1970s this amount had risen to $761 billion, reflecting the need for mortgage financing as investors purchased residential properties (Exhibit 1-4). Coupled with real estate investment trends, the trend in residential mortgage debt has steadily increased since World War II. Most single-family homes and apartment projects are mortgage financed to some extent.

Apartment and Commercial Building Construction and Mortgage Debt. Multifamily building starts fluctuate considerably. For example, in 1963, 589,000 two-or-more-family apartment units were started. By 1966 those starts were down to 386,000. In the early 1970s a peak was reached in 1972 of more than one million apartment unit starts.

Exhibit 1-4. The Trend During the 1970s of Residential Mortgage Debt

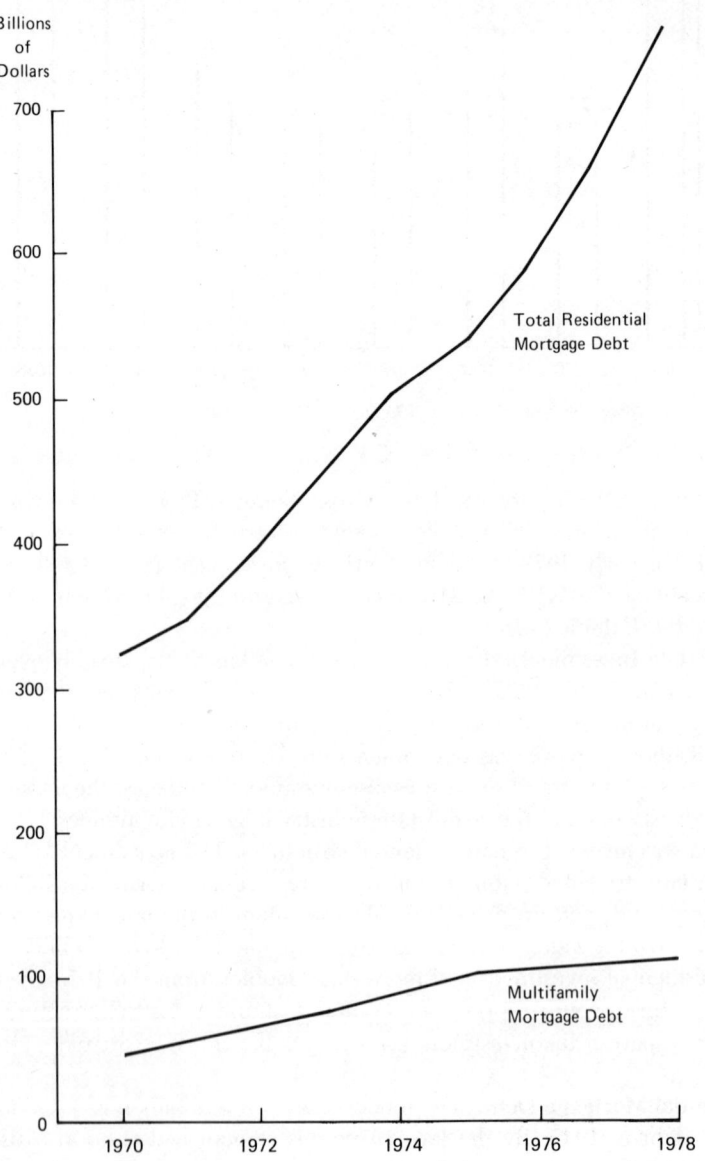

Source: *Savings and Loan Fact Book 1978* (Chicago: U.S. League of Savings Associations), pp. 31, 33. With permission.

Table 1-2. Investment in nonresidential and residential structures (given in billions of dollars)

Year	Nonresidential Structures	Residential Structures
1978	$84.6	$113.3
1977	63.9	91.9
1976	55.8	68.0
1975	52.9	51.5
1974	54.5	55.1
1973	47.0	57.2
1972	41.1	54.0
1971	37.9	42.8
1970	36.1	31.2
1969	34.2	32.6
1950	9.2	19.4
1941	2.9	3.9
1933	0.9	0.6
1929	5.0	4.0

Source: *Federal Reserve Bulletin* (October 1974), p. A56, and (November 1977 and March 1979), p. A52.

By 1974 the volume was back down to 450,000 starts. The volume of apartment starts went back up in 1978; the January 1979 starts declined to 520,000 on an adjusted annual basis.

In contrast, the multifamily mortgage debt has steadily increased from 1963 through the late 1970s. The mortgage debt outstanding on multifamily structures of five or more units was $21 billion in 1963 and gradually rose to $122 billion by 1978 (Exhibit 1-4). The financial institutions usually provide about 20 to 25 percent of the mortgage funds needed for multifamily building construction and investment. Individuals and other sources provide the remainder of the mortgage funds.

The value of newly constructed commercial and industrial buildings has steadily risen from $8 million in 1962 to $33 million in 1978 (Exhibit 1-5). In a similar pattern, the mortgage debt outstanding on commercial property has risen to $208 million. In other words, the investment in commercial and industrial buildings has steadily increased since the 1960s, and an increasing amount of mortgage debt has financed the investment. Most of the mortgage debt for these properties has come from the financial institutions; only 10 to 15 percent of the mortgage debt has come from other sources.

INVESTMENT ALTERNATIVES

A person with capital has many investment alternatives, of which real estate is only one. Before the investor enters on a discretionary investment program, however, he or she should have formed a basic foundation for investment. This recommended financial foundation generally consists of

1. Adequate provision for shelter, such as home ownership.
2. Adequate life and property insurance protection.
3. Adequate pension plan provisions.

Exhibit 1-5. *Value of New Private Industrial and Commercial and Public Construction Activity*

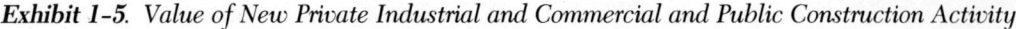

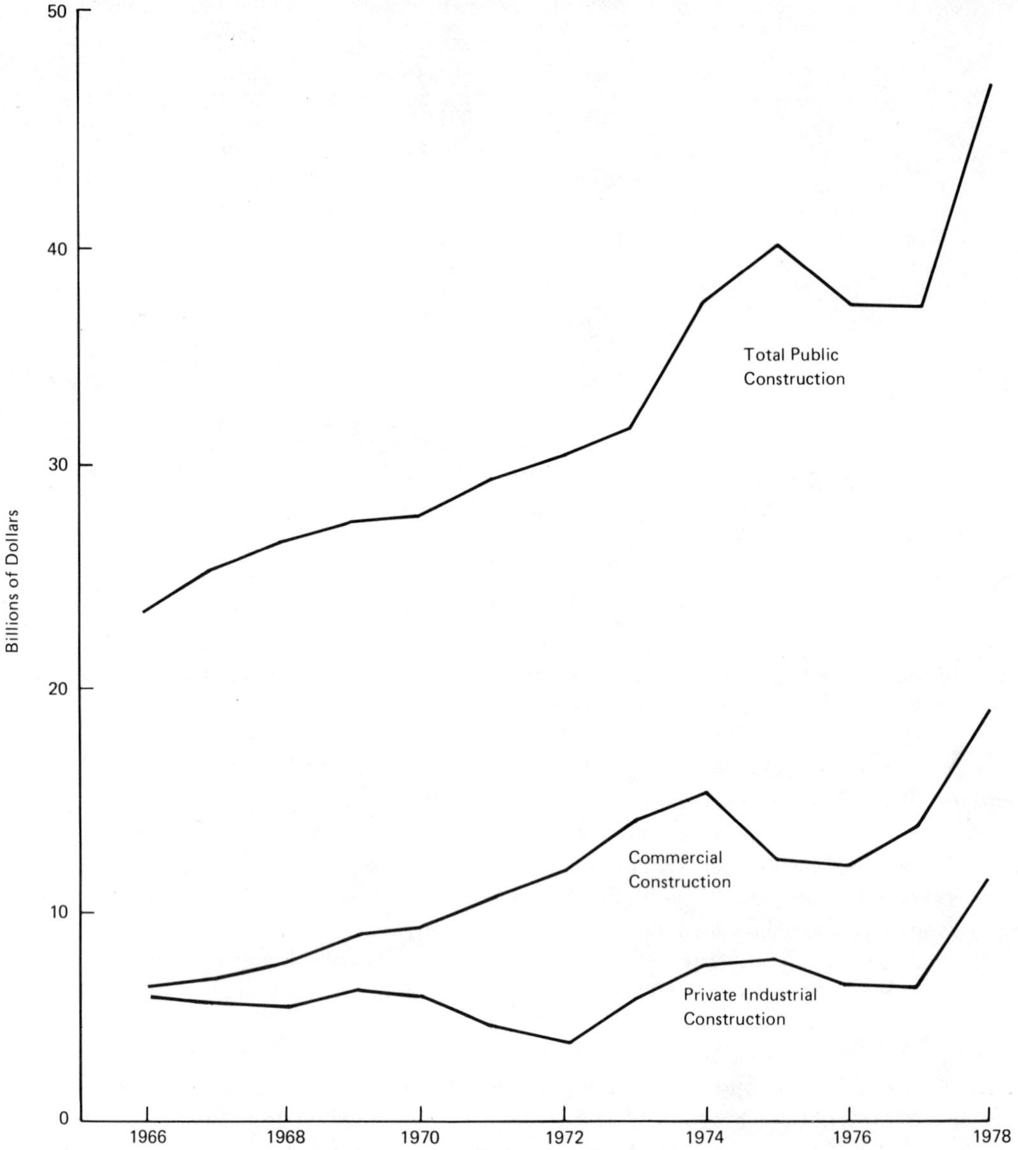

Sources: *Federal Reserve Bulletin* (November 1978), p. A50; (December 1975), p. A51.

4. Adequate transportation provisions, such as private car ownership to satisfy family needs.
5. Steady employment with chances for advancement.
6. A savings account with funds for a "rainy day."

After this prerequisite has been met, the investor may choose between the following:

Real estate interests: Mortgages
　　　　　　　　　　　　Mortgage-backed securities
　　　　　　　　　　　　Land contracts
　　　　　　　　　　　　Leases
Limited partnership shares
Corporate securities: Commercial paper
　　　　　　　　　　　 Debenture and convertible debenture bonds
　　　　　　　　　　　 Mortgage bonds
　　　　　　　　　　　 Common stock
　　　　　　　　　　　 Preferred stock
Financial institution securities: Regular savings accounts
　　　　　　　　　　　　　　　　 Time deposits, including certificates of deposit
Real estate investment trust securities: Shares of beneficial interest
　　　　　　　　　　　　　　　　　　　　Debenture and convertible debenture bonds
　　　　　　　　　　　　　　　　　　　　Commercial paper
Government securities:
　U.S. Treasury securities: Tax-anticipation Treasury bills
　　　　　　　　　　　　　　Regular Treasury bills
　　　　　　　　　　　　　　Treasury notes
　　　　　　　　　　　　　　Treasury bonds, such as savings bonds
　　　　　　　　　　　　　　"Flower" bonds
　Federal agency securities
　Municipal securities (state and local government securities):
　　Tax-exempt securities
　　Revenue bonds
　　General obligation bonds
Durable consumer goods, such as cars, furniture
Nondurable consumer goods, such as clothing
Equity in a small business
Franchise for a small business

BASIC TERMINOLOGY ASSOCIATED WITH REAL ESTATE INVESTMENT

Several terms are fundamental to the understanding of real estate investment. Investment relationships are often stated with these terms.

Real Estate. The term *real estate* means the land, everything that is attached to the land, and everything under and over the earth's surface. Real estate includes the physical aspects of the earth's surface, site improvements such as utility lines and landscaping, and buildings resting on the earth's surface.

Real Property. Whereas *real estate* refers to the physical aspects of land and its improvements, the term *real property* refers to the interests, benefits, and rights inherent in the ownership of the real estate. Real property is the bundle of rights with which the ownership of real estate is endowed. The property rights inherent in the ownership of real property generally include the right to sell, to give the property away, to use the property, to lease the property, to enter the improvements or to walk the land, and to refuse to exercise any of these rights.

Personal Property. Personal property refers to assets that are not real properties but are mobile and sometimes intangible. Personal properties may be described as furniture, other furnishings, office equipment, livestock, farm equipment, and stock and bond market securities. These items are not permanently attached as a part of the real estate. They may be removed without serious injury to the real estate or to the items themselves. Three factors are often considered as real property and must be separated from personal property. They are (1) the manner in which the property is attached, (2) the intention of the party who made the attachment, and (3) the purpose for which the premises are used.

Real Estate Investment. Real estate investment is the purchase of real property with the intent to receive a return or yield from the investment as well as the return of the purchase price. The purchaser of the asset usually wishes to acquire more than the physical real estate. Therefore, real estate investment implies the purchase of real property, not just real estate.

Bank. The term *bank* refers to the financial intermediary in the form of a commercial bank or a mutual savings bank. The bank takes in deposits and often invests in real estate mortgages and other real property interests.

Primary Mortgage Market. The primary mortgage market is the market within which mortgages are originated by lenders or lender correspondents with mortgagors. The lender underwrites the mortgage according to property and credit characteristics.

Secondary Mortgage Market. The secondary mortgage market is the market within which existing mortgages are traded. They are bought and sold by current mortgage holders and investors. The traditional mortgage lenders trade mortgages among themselves and with secondary mortgage market institutions. The secondary market institutions who buy and sell significant volumes of mortgages are the Federal National Mortgage Association, the Government National Mortgage Association, and the Federal Home Loan Mortgage Corporation.

Mortgage. The mortgage is a two-part financing agreement in which one part is a security agreement pledging real estate as collateral and the second part is a promissory note for the repayment of the mortgage debt.

Cash Flow. The most basic definition of cash flow is net operating income less mortgage interest and principal payment, but before federal income taxes. This amount is sometimes called *cash flow to equity*. When the federal income tax payment is subtracted from this amount or the tax savings are added to the amount, the *cash flow after taxes* results. This amount is sometimes called *spendable cash flow*.

Profit. Profit to accountants usually means taxable income or net profit. *Net profit* is defined as gross revenue minus bad debt loss, vacancy allowance, operating expenses, depreciation expense, and mortgage interest. Net profit can be expressed either on a before-tax or after-tax basis. The taxes deducted for an after-tax net profit would be federal income taxes. The term *net profit* often refers to the taxable income of the real estate investment.

Real Estate Appraisal. Real estate appraisal is the report of estimated value for a real property as of a given date. Normally the appraiser utilizes the cost, market, and income approaches to value in order to arrive at a final value estimate or a range of values.

SUMMARY

The chapter began with a historical summary of property ownership. Property ownership originated with early civilizations of the Middle East and the Mediterranean area of the world. In the United States, private property ownership thrives under the allodial system of private and public ownership of land and structures.

There are several reasons for studying real estate investment, including personal interest in the subject as a field of study, a college or university curriculum requirement, personal assistance with current and/or prospective real estate investments, and the search for good employment opportunities with a long-term challenge. The student viewpoints parallel their reasons for taking the real estate investment course. In general, they view real estate investment as interested college students, as prospective real estate investors, or as future job applicants.

A number of approaches—economic, social, legal, governmental, institutional, and financial—are taken to the study of real estate investment, as illustrated by the discussion of the various parts of this text.

The significance of real estate investment is pointed out in terms of home ownership patterns, the trends in housing starts and mobile home shipments, the proportion of the Gross National Product that investment in private housing represents, the growth in real estate investment, and the growth in residential mortgage debt.

The prospective real estate investor should have a good financial foundation before investigating investment alternatives. Investments that compete with real estate investments fall into the following categories: real estate interests that do not include direct real estate ownership, limited partnership shares, corporate securities, real estate investment trust securities, government securities, durable and nondurable consumer goods, equity investment in a small business, and franchises in small businesses.

The basic terminology associated with real estate investment includes the following terms: *real estate, real property, personal property, real estate investment, bank, primary mortgage market, secondary mortgage market, mortgage, cash flow, profit*, and *real estate appraisal*.

Key Terms and Concepts

Property law
Feudal system
English common law
Allodial system of land ownership
Private property rights
Real estate license requirements
Nonresidential structures
Multifamily mortgage debt
Mortgage-backed securities
Real estate
Primary mortgage market
Cash flow
Portfolio planning
Risk-return analysis of real estate investment
Institutional portfolios
The composition of investment returns

Investible funds
Financial foundation for investment
Real property
Secondary mortgage market
Profit
Housing starts
Mobile home shipments
Subsidized housing
Shelter production
Gross national product
Residential private investment
Personal property
Real estate investment
Bank
Mortgage
Real estate appraisal

Questions for Student Self-examination

Multiple-Choice Questions

1. As property law developed, surveying techniques were perfected by the
   a. Babylonians
   b. Greeks
   c. Romans
   d. Egyptians
2. The recording of mortgages was first established by the
   a. Babylonians
   b. Egyptians
   c. Romans
   d. Greeks
3. Approximately _____ of all American households own their own homes.
   a. one-third
   b. one-half
   c. two-thirds
   d. three-fourths
4. The highest levels of home ownership are to be found in the _____ portions of our country.
   a. Southwestern and Northeastern
   b. Northwestern and Southern
   c. Southern and Northeastern
   d. North Central and Southern
5. In 1970 the highest black home ownership level was established in the _____.
   a. West
   b. East
   c. North
   d. South

True-False Questions

T F 1. Under the feudal system, property owners could enjoy private ownership and control of their property.
T F 2. Today real property rights are held by private individuals, companies, institutions, and government entities.
T F 3. In the 1970s private housing investment represented from 20 to 25 percent of the Gross National Product.
T F 4. Since World War II, investment in nonresidential structures has shown steady growth, but investment in residential structures has been more fluctuating.
T F 5. Only a small portion of single-family homes and apartment projects is mortgage financed.
T F 6. The term *real property* refers to the physical aspects of land and its improvements.
T F 7. The secondary mortgage market is the market within which mortgages are originated by lenders or lender correspondents with mortgagors.
T F 8. A mortgage is a security agreement pledging real estate as collateral.
T F 9. Net profit can be expressed on either a before-tax or after-tax basis.
T F 10. A real estate appraisal is the report of estimated value for a real property as of a given date.

Answers
Multiple choice: 1d, 2a, 3c, 4d, 5d.
True–False: 1F, 2T, 3F, 4T, 5F, 6F, 7F, 8F, 9T, 10T.

Problems

1. If the yield on Money Market Certificates of the local thrift institution were 9.5 percent, the dividend yield on the stock of the local power company were 10 percent, and the normal cash flow yield or equity dividend rate on typical apartment projects were 6 percent, why might an investor select an apartment project for investment of his or her funds?
2. What has been the long-run trend in the proportion of home ownership? Based on the past and the economic predictions for the future, what do you forecast for the future of home ownership percentages? Explain your answer.
3. Is the ratio of private housing investment to the GNP significant? In what ways? For what reasons is it insignificant?
4. Real estate investments compete with other types of investments. What causes change in this competitive environment?
5. Does the growth of real estate investment imply a parallel growth in mortgage debt? Is the single-family housing situation different from the nonresidential investment situation?
6. Is there any difference between the factors impelling growth in apartment development and the factors contributing to the growth in commercial building development?

Chapter 2

Social and Economic Aspects of Real Estate Investment

The Relationship of This Chapter to Other Chapters of the Text

Social Aspects of Real Estate Investment
    The Social Acceptance of Home Ownership   Government Goals and Programs for Standard Housing for All Citizens   The Civil Rights Laws and Real Estate Investment   Joint Ownership to Facilitate Property Acquisition   Real Estate Investment and Population Characteristics: *The implications of the greater population mobility, The implications of smaller family size*

Economic Aspects of Real Estate Investment
    The Trend in Savings   Relative Sales of Existing Versus New Homes   Vacancy Rates of Rental Residential Units Versus Single-Family Houses   Second-Home Ownership   Rental Incomes of Americans

Economic Cycles and Real Estate Investment Returns

Disintermediation

Inflation and Real Estate Investment

The Movement of Mortgage Monies from Capital-Rich to Capital-Scarce Areas

The Trends in Home Ownership
    Age Groups   Income Groups   Ethnic Groups   Geographic and Urban–Suburban Locations

Attributes of Real Estate Investment
    Inflation Protection   Marketability   Tax Shelter   Leverage   The Relative Yield on Real Estate

Summary

Key Terms and Concepts

Questions for Student Self-examination

LEARNING OBJECTIVES After studying this chapter, you should be familiar with

The prevailing social acceptance of home ownership
Government goals and programs for housing all citizens of low, moderate, and middle incomes
The effect on real estate investment of the civil rights laws
Forms of joint ownership that facilitate property acquisition and development
Population characteristics that affect real estate investment
The trend of growth of real estate investment
The trend in savings in the United States
The portion of total home sales represented by sales of existing homes
Recent vacancy rates of apartments and single-family homes
The trend toward second home owership
The importance of rental incomes to American investors
General economic and real estate cycles
Conditions prompting disintermediation
Inflation's impact on real estate investment
The flow of mortgage monies from capital-rich to capital-scarce areas
Trends in home ownership related to age distribution, income distribution, preferred locations of ethnic groups, and geographic and urban area preferences
Five principal attributes of real estate investment

In Chapter 1 the student was introduced to real estate investment. It was discovered that real estate investment in nonresidential and residential structures is a sizable portion of the Gross National Product of the United States. It was also discovered that the trend for nonresidential and residential real estate investment has been rising steadily since World War II. The prices of new and existing homes have also risen over the years. In spite of the rising cost of homes, approximately two-thirds of all American families own their own homes. The student reviewed the definitions of some fundamental terms used in real estate investment.

THE RELATIONSHIP OF THIS CHAPTER TO OTHER CHAPTERS OF THE TEXT

In this chapter you will continue to observe the social and economic aspects of real estate investment. The broad framework is being laid in Part I for the remaining parts of the book. Since the financing and valuation aspects of real estate investment are fundamental to risk-return analysis, these are presented in Part II.

SOCIAL ASPECTS OF THE REAL ESTATE INVESTMENT

The Social Acceptance of Home Ownership. The American culture encourages home ownership. A high level of social approval is accorded the ownership of a single-family house. Associated with home ownership are the impressions of security, the evidence of ability to provide for the needs of the family, and the provisions of privacy for the owner-occupants.

Most homeowners are viewed as socially stable and good citizens of their community. They pay their share of property and other kinds of local taxes to support the local community and its government. They tend to be less transient than apartment dwellers and tend to live in a house longer than the same household would tend to live in a single apartment. Because of this reduced mobility and increased interest in the surrounding community, homeowners tend to exercise their rights of citizenship more frequently. They usually vote on election day on the current issues in which they tend to have an interest. As property taxpayers, homeowners typically have a more vital interest in the affairs of local and state government than do apartment occupants.

The house is seen to be a haven of security and a shelter for all the family members. The house should accommodate the lifestyles of each of its residents. If one family is well sheltered in the house, others in the marketplace may view the house as socially acceptable to them, so that the dwelling has good marketability.

If the house is not perfectly suited to the owners as they move into the premises, an owned home may be changed to suit the needs of the household, within the confines of the family budget. In contrast, the owner of rented space usually must approve changes to his or her investment property before the tenant may make those changes. Often the improvements to the rented property must remain with the property, and their benefits accrue to the landlord when the tenants move. In the case of an owned home, the value of the house in the marketplace may increase as improvements are made for the livability and usefulness of the household.

Government Goals and Programs for Standard Housing for All Citizens. Over the years Congress and the Secretary of the Department of Housing and Urban Development have often espoused the goal of standard housing in a decent, safe, and sanitary environment for all American citizens. A significant portion of the federal government housing programs are directed toward home ownership for low- and middle-income families; generally federal government housing programs are not oriented toward high-income families. Other programs are directed toward apartment project construction and rental occupancy. Many of the major FHA programs starting in 1961 had provisions for home ownership. The principal FHA program for unsubsidized middle-income single-family houses—the FHA 203(b) program—started in the mid-1930s. The Veterans Administration guaranteed home mortgage program commenced in 1944.

There are several socioeconomic groups of our society that are aided by government housing programs. Some of the groups receive home ownership assistance; others receive assistance in building residential structures for rental to the selected socioeconomic groups. The following are a few of the bases for government housing assistance:

Income level of the citizen.
Family size associated with the income level and wealth accumulation.
Involvement in the military service for an approved period of time.
College housing accommodations.
Physical disability.
Urban redevelopment.
Relocation from an original residential structure because of a government program.
Property improvement.

Generally, low-, moderate-, and middle-income groups benefiting from the FHA mortgage insurance and VA home mortgage guarantees move into (1) traditional single-family and multifamily ownership or rental property, (2) cooperative housing, (3) condominium housing, and (4) mobile homes.

The government methods of housing policy implementation fall into eight categories:[1]

1. *Insurance.*
   a. Mortgage insurance.
   b. Crime insurance.
   c. Flood insurance.
   d. Riot insurance.
2. *Grants and subsidies.*
   a. Disaster relief grants.
   b. Rent supplements.
   c. Interest subsidies.
   d. Land-price subsidies.
3. *Loan guarantees.*
   a. Veterans Administration loan guarantees.
   b. New town loan guarantees.
4. *Maintenance of the secondary mortgage market.*
5. *Employment in construction of persons of minority groups.*
6. *Tax relief.*
   a. Tax credits.
   b. Tax abatement.
   c. Federal tax deductibility of
      (1) Interest.
      (2) Depreciation.
      (3) Property taxes.
   d. Tax shelter for consolidated income.
   e. Homestead exemption.
7. *Regulations.*
   a. Building codes.
   b. Zoning.
   c. Mortgage interest rates.
   d. Interstate land sales.
8. *Counseling.*
   a. Foreclosure assistance.
   b. Housing management.

The Civil Rights Laws and Real Estate Investment. Since the Civil Rights Act of 1968 and subsequent amendments, persons of any race, religion, national origin, color, sex, or age may invest in real property in widespread locations. The whole spectrum of investment opportunities is available to any real estate investor. The property seller may not discriminate in approval of the property buyer on the basis of race, religion, color, national origin, sex, or age. The landlord may not discriminate on the same bases in the rental of space.

Congressional goals for integration are continuing to be carried out by various governmental agencies. The United States Department of Housing and Urban Development has sought housing integration on income, racial, and ethnic bases. Inner-city

[1] Mary Alice Hines, *Principles and Practices of Real Estate* (Homewood, Ill.: Richard D. Irwin, 1976), pp. 492-493.

and suburban residential areas have become integrated. Therefore, individuals and families have access to a wider variety of housing accommodations than was true in the past. Restrictive devices such as large-lot zoning and low-density standards may no longer restrict real estate investment of relatively exclusive areas to certain socioeconomic groups.

Joint Ownership to Facilitate Property Acquisition. Many joint-ownership forms are available for property acquisition. If a person needs additional financial resources, he or she may join with other parties to accumulate enough capital for the desired real estate investment. Partnership, trust, corporate, cooperative, condominium, joint tenancy, and tenancy-in-common forms of ownership are readily available for the joint financing of real estate investments. More is said about joint ownership in later chapters.

Real Estate Investment and Population Characteristics. Approximately 70 to 75 percent of those persons over 35 years of age own their own housing (Exhibit 2-1). With the decline in the birth and mortality rates, the population is growing older. Therefore, additional investment in homes will tend to take place as the population ages. The large group of young people of the 1960s and 1970s will become middle-aged during the 1980s and create a demand for single-family dwellings and condominiums.

Exhibit 2-1. Young People Rent, Older People Own Housing (1960-1971 Average)

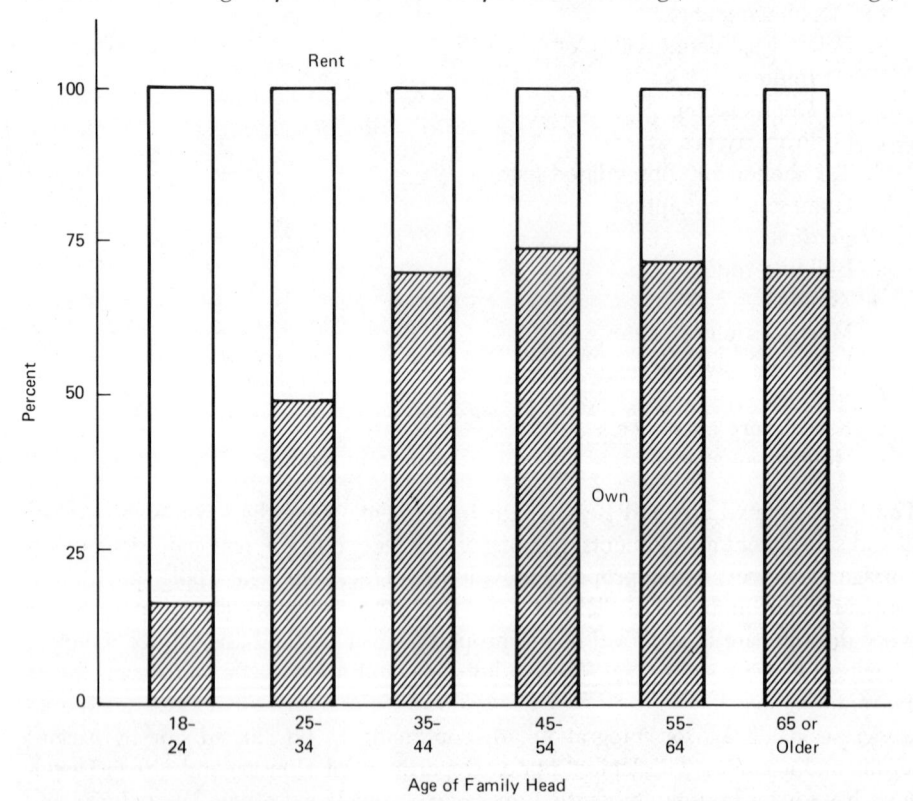

Source: Mortgage Bankers Association Economics and Research Department, adapted from *Survey of Consumer Finances, 1960-1971,* The University of Michigan. With permission.

The growing group of elderly citizens also implies an increasing demand for institutional retirement housing and traditional multifamily space. The growing senior citizen group will want planned retirement communities that serve ablebodied and active citizens as well as those that provide part-time and round-the-clock medical and nursing attention. Many elderly persons wish to have a private apartment independent of relatives where yard work and house maintenance are not required. Many elderly persons, therefore, desire rental, condominium, and cooperative apartment units. Real estate investors must realize the profit potential of this resident group.

Since 25 to 30 percent of those persons over 35 years of age rent their housing, the increased population of the United States implies an increased demand for rental space. A sizable portion of single people—divorced, widowed, and never married—desire rental apartment space. The same thing is true of childless married couples and married couples with perhaps one older child of school age. They may prefer rental multifamily living in the central city areas to single-family dwelling ownership in the distant suburbs. The real estate investor must observe these tendencies toward multifamily rental housing by sizable sectors of the urban population.

The implications of the greater population mobility. Increased personal and family incomes have tended to result in greater population mobility. That trend may result in more condominium and second-home ownership. Condominiums provide carefree living with federal income tax benefits from the deduction of mortgage interest and property taxes. The yard work and building maintenance are done by the employees of the condominium homeowners' associations.

The movement toward second homes was clearly discernible in the early 1970s. The recession of 1974 and 1975 dampened this trend. With the advent of the smaller household size, increased personal and family incomes, and the search for more varied recreation associated with a higher standard of living, the second-home movement may again prevail. The developers of second-home communities and resorts may again realize the profit potential of the trend toward more population mobility.

Population mobility also tends to favor rental single-family and multifamily development. A person or family who tends to move frequently tends to rent residential space rather than purchasing housing units. This housing decision is wise in many cases. A frequent mover may lose because the initial house ownership costs may not be covered by the increase in the house value over the term of house ownership. Inflation may cover the initial costs of home ownership if the owner occupies the space for a sufficient amount of time. A decision to rent a single-family dwelling or apartment unit may be financially shrewd. The real estate developer or investor should realize that this group exists and may become a profitable clientele.

The implications of smaller family size. The developer has already perceived the demand for smaller homes. The national trend toward smaller families, the higher cost of construction, the higher cost of mortgage money, and the higher prices of single-family homes have jointly created this type of demand. Fewer middle-income single-family homes have formal living rooms and family rooms or dens. The bedroom numbers and space per room have been reduced.

Smaller family size may mean a greater demand for townhouses and other multifamily buildings. If the family needs only two or three bedrooms, more housing alternatives may be considered. A large family requiring four or five bedrooms usually must seek single-family dwelling space. Multifamily housing that supplies four or five bedrooms is usually not affordable for the middle-income group. Usually only subsidized low-income and upper-income housing provides this much space in multifamily residential buildings. The small household may seek first the location that satisfies their wants, and then the form of housing tenure depends on what is available at that location. Most apartment building investors cater to the relatively small households who need residential space.

ECONOMIC ASPECTS OF REAL ESTATE INVESTMENT

Gross private domestic investment in structures continues to approximate 7 to 9 percent of the Gross National Product. The Gross National Product continues to expand. Likewise, gross private domestic investment in structures continues to increase. The final sales volume of all structures reached $244 billion in late 1978. In only five years this figure increased almost $97 billion, from $147 billion in 1974, an increase of 65 percent. From 1974 to 1978 the growth in residential investment was even stronger than the growth in nonresidential investment (Table 2-1).

The Trend in Savings. Even though the savings rate in the early 1970s approximated 8 percent, that rate had declined by the latter part of the 1970s to approximately 5 percent (Exhibit 2-2). The decline in the savings rate may have been a result of increased real estate investment, requiring high downpayments; consumer acceptance of continued high levels of inflation; and increased spending for consumer goods, including new automobile purchases. The lower rates of savings may depress real estate investment somewhat in future years.

Relative Sales of Existing Versus New Homes. Since existing home prices have been lower and mortgage terms subject to assumption have had lower interest rates, approximately five times more existing one-family homes have been sold recently than new homes. The multiple has approximated 3 to 5 over the last five years (Exhibit 2-3). The higher costs of construction and mortgage money have forced new home prices relatively high.

Vacancy Rates of Rental Residential Units Versus Single-Family Houses. House construction by developers has been encouraged by the continuing 1 percent vacancy rate nationwide for single-family houses. Recently the overall vacancy rate of 6 percent for residential rental units has tended to discourage apartment investment and construction somewhat. In many areas, though, the apartment vacancy rates have been steadily declining because apartment construction has been depressed since the recession of the 1970s, and the demand for space has increased.

Table 2-1. The percentage of the Gross National Product represented by the investment in structures

Year	Total Investment in Structures	Gross National Product	Percent of GNP
1978	$197.9	$2,212.1	8.9
1977	155.8	1,887.2	8.3
1976	123.8	1,700.1	7.3
1975	104.4	1,528.8	6.8
1974	109.6	1,397.4	7.8

Source: *Federal Reserve Bulletin* (November 1977; March 1979), p. A52.

Exhibit 2-2. Personal Savings as a Percentage of Disposable Personal Income

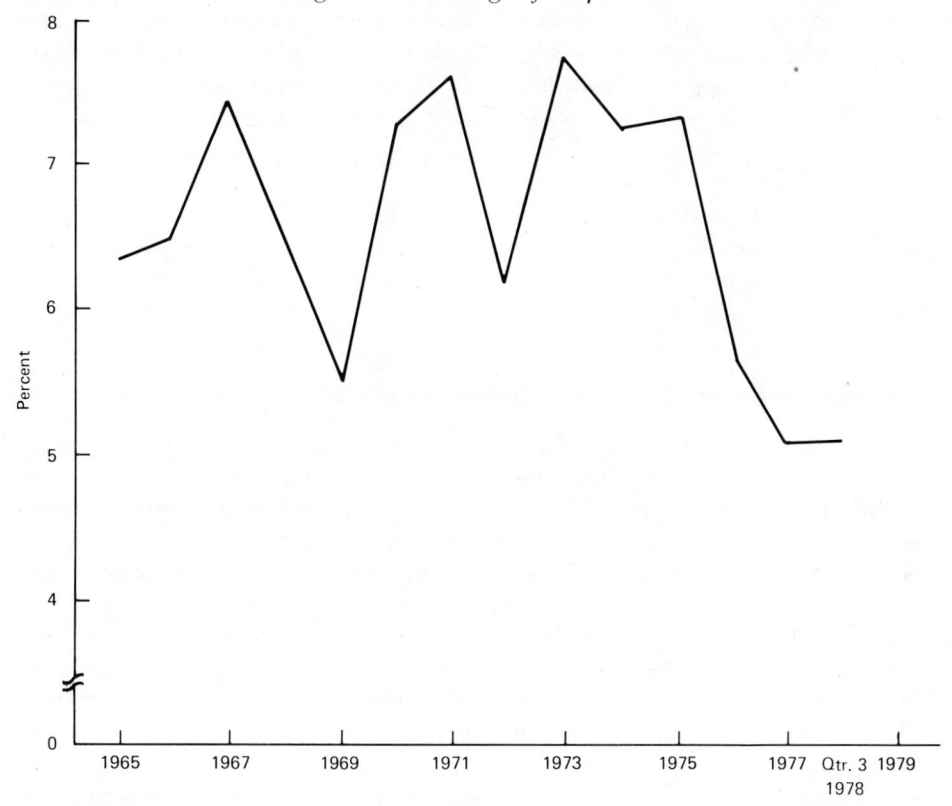

Source: *1978 Savings and Loan Fact Book* (Chicago: U.S. League of Savings Associations), p. 9. With permission. *Federal Reserve Bulletin* (Washington, D.C.: Board of Governors of the Federal Reserve System), p. A53.

Exhibit 2-3. The Relationship Between the Sales of Existing Homes and the Sales of New Homes

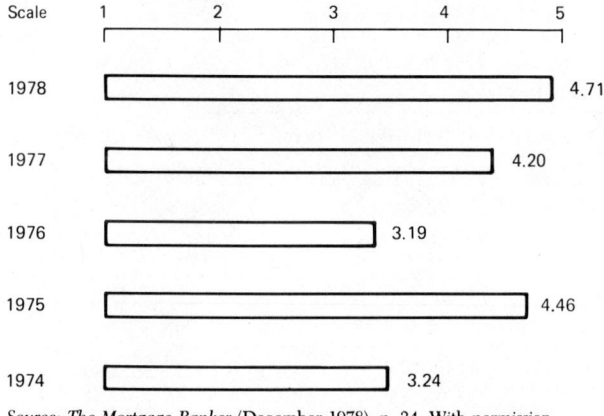

Year	Value
1978	4.71
1977	4.20
1976	3.19
1975	4.46
1974	3.24

Source: *The Mortgage Banker* (December 1978), p. 34. With permission.

Social and Economic Aspects of Real Estate Investment

Second-Home Ownership. Recent prosperity in the United States has led to the trend toward second homes for vacation, weekend, or holiday use. In 1970, 4.6 percent of all American households, or 2.9 million households, had second homes. A few of the second homes were jointly owned, since only 2.7 million second homes were owned. Two-thirds of the second homes were located in the Northeast and North Central regions. Usually the household invested in a second home within 200 miles of the primary residence.

Rental Incomes of Americans. The increased investment in real property in the United States has meant increased rental incomes. Rental incomes for persons in the United States rose from $21 billion in 1974 to $24 billion during the winter of 1978 (Table 2-2).

Economic Cycles and Real Estate Investment Returns

The real estate cycle in the United States is a part of the overall business cycle that our economy continues to experience. When business and personal incomes decline and unemployment rates rise, the real estate industry feels the impact. When business expands on a profitable basis, personal incomes rise, interest rates are relatively low, and mortgage money is plentiful, the real estate industry expands along with the rest of the economy.

The real estate cycle, like the business cycle, may be said to have four phases: expansion to a peak, equilibrium at the peak, contraction to a trough, and equilibrium at the trough or lowest point of the cycle. The duration of the full cycle has varied over previous centuries, but the periodic occurrence of the full real estate and business cycle persists.

During the expansion phase of the real estate cycle, structures are constructed while business and household prosperity exist. Homes are built and income property developments are planned and carried out. Mortgages are negotiated on reasonable terms with lenders who have an abundance of mortgage monies. Finally a peak is reached in the real estate expansion. The supply of space has outrun the demand for space. An *overbuilt condition* with relatively high vacancy rates occurs. Foreclosures begin to take place. Construction and financial costs often rise during the expansion phase. When the market becomes overbuilt, the high vacancy rates, the relatively high construction, operating, and financial costs, plus the impossibility of passing the higher costs on to the tenant create economic conditions that cause foreclosures.

Table 2-2. The trend in personal rental incomes

Year	Total Rental Income of Persons (Given in Billions)
1978	$24.4
1977	22.5
1976	22.5
1975	22.3
1974	21.4

Source: *Federal Reserve Bulletin* (November 1977; February 1979), p. A52.

During the contraction phase of the real estate cycle, construction slows down, lenders become more cautious about each loan they make, they start spending more time on foreclosed properties, and families and businesses tend to delay their real estate investment. A trough is reached when the vacancy rates tend to be so low that developers are finally enticed back into the market. Construction has reached such a low point that lenders finally start seeing some loan applications with normal risks, which they can finance with their accumulated investment funds. Mortgage funds become available for a few new developments; the real estate business starts to expand a little. At that time the real estate business moves out of the trough into the expansionary phase of the cycle.

Some say that the business cycle precedes the real estate cycle. Business and personal incomes must decline before the real estate industry declines. Coming out of a recession, business and personal fortunes usually tend to increase before the real estate business expands. There is little research proof of the relationship between the general business and the general real estate cycles.

Disintermediation

Disintermediation is associated with real estate recessions. The term *disintermediation* refers to the direct investment in short-term securities, rather than deposit of savings in institutional depository accounts, because the short-term security yields are higher than the deposit account yields. At the time of disintermediation, the yields on Treasury bills, commercial paper, and other short-term securities usually exceed the yields paid on the various types of short-term deposits of the traditional financial institutions. Investors, therefore, place their capital directly in Treasury bills, commercial paper, and other short-term securities rather than placing it in depository accounts for later investment by the financial intermediary.

When disintermediation occurs, the financial institution has less investible funds. Its profits are squeezed by the yields on their relatively low-yielding old loans and investments and their relatively high operating costs. New loans cannot be made without the new inflows of deposits or the sale of loans to secondary market institutions and investors. More specifically, disintermediation usually means a net outflow of funds at the thrift institutions—commercial banks, savings and loan associations, and mutual savings banks. These institutions are significantly responsible for the financing of real estate investment. Real estate investment usually must slow down or halt, if mortgage financing is required from the thrift institutions, during periods of disintermediation.

In recent periods of high interest rates, disintermediation has been alleviated because of the money-market certificates devised by the Federal Reserve Board and the Federal Home Loan Bank Board in mid-1978 for the use of the thrift institutions and the commercial banks. The yield on the short-term certificate requiring an investment of $10,000 or more is equal to the current six-month Treasury bill yield. As the short-term money market yields have increased to very high levels, investors have maintained and sometimes increased their deposits at the thrift institutions by way of the money-market certificates. The thrift institutions, therefore, have continued to supply mortgage monies to borrowers from this supply of depositor funds. Admittedly, when the yields on the certificates reach high levels, this cost of funds may equal or exceed mortgage yields. At that time, the institutions generally revise their offerings of money-market certificates. An individual institution may withdraw the offering of the certificates, reduce or eliminate the advertising of the certificates, or reduce the certificate yields.

Inflation and Real Estate Investment

Construction costs and the prices of properties have risen significantly because of inflation in the 1970s. Many prospective home and income property buyers have been forced out of the market by high prices and high money costs. In many cases personal incomes and yields from other investments have not kept pace with the inflation related to real estate investment.

In terms of 1967 prices, the purchasing power of the dollar was approximately 54 cents in 1978. The Consumer Price Index reached 205 in early 1979. This was an approximate increase of 13 percent over 1977. The rate of inflation has slowed somewhat from the rate of increase in the Consumer Price Index between 1973 and 1974 of 12 percent. At today's rate of inflation, it would take more than seven years for prices to double. As an indicator of future price changes, the Wholesale Price Index has risen at the same rate as the Consumer Price Index since the index year of 1967. The early 1979 index for the Wholesale Price Index was 207, based on an index of 100 in 1967.

Money costs have been relatively high in the mid-1970s. In 1979 the bank prime rate rose to 11.75 percent, while home mortgage rates have approximated 10.5 percent. The Treasury has been forced to pay 9 percent to investors in taxable Treasury bonds. Municipal tax-exempt Baa-rated bonds have been yielding about 7 percent.

Inflation has mixed effects with respect to real estate investment. Property owners realize substantial capital gains from the sale of their properties. In 1978 the homeowner may have realized a 20 percent gain (Table 2-3). When they turn to buy other

Exhibit 2-4. Price Inflation

(Percent Change, Year End to Year End)

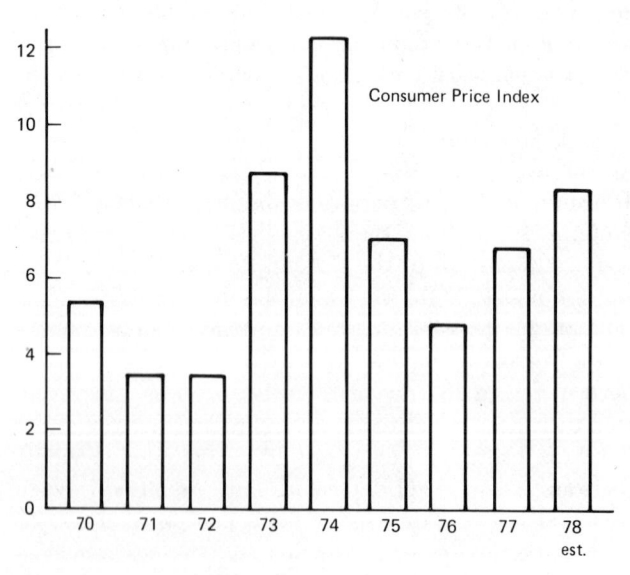

Consumer Price Index

Source: Bureau of Labor Statistics.

Table 2-3. Average house prices of units sold and annual rates of increase

Year	Prices of New Units	Percent of Annual Rate of Increase	Prices of Existing Units	Percent of Annual Rate of Increase
1979	$68,000		$59,800	
1978	67,200		58,100	
		23.5		21.3
1977	54,400		47,900	
		13.1		13.5
1976	48,100		42,200	
		13.1		8.1
1975	42,500		39,000	

Source: *Federal Reserve Bulletin* (November 1978 and March 1979), p. A50.

properties with the receipts from their property sales, they find other properties high in price and mortgage money high in price at the same time.

Rapidly rising construction prices for both materials and labor have forced building prices higher. But the cost of labor and materials has decreased as a portion of the house price, and the financing and land costs have increased in percentage terms (Exhibit 2-5).

The Movement of Mortgage Monies from Capital-Rich to Capital-Scarce Areas

Mortgage money cost is relatively high, even though capital does flow easily from capital-rich areas to capital-scarce areas. Without our current market mechanisms,

Exhibit 2-5. Amount of Housing Dollar Going for the Structure

Source: National Association of Home Builders. With permission.

mortgage monies would cost even more. Several aspects of the capital markets aid the flow of monies into areas where it is most needed. Institutional lenders have expanded their lending operations, so that loan officers scour the country for good mortgage loans and good investment real estate. Mortgage bankers scattered around the country assist their correspondents in finding good investments in all sections of the country. Even though the institutional lenders may have expanded their lending operations, they still tend to rely on mortgage bankers for additional investment recommendations. Private mortgage insurance, along with FHA mortgage on mortgage loans, permits the institutional purchase of mortgage loans from many sections of the country because of the standardized underwriting of the insured loans. The AMMINET market service maintained by the Federal Home Loan Mortgage Corporation for mortgage market making provides more information to the potential investor about the possible real estate and mortgage deals.

One of the biggest factors in the efficient allocation of mortgage and real estate investment monies is the secondary mortgage market system maintained by the Federal National Mortgage Association, the Government National Mortgage Association, and the Federal Home Loan Mortgage Corporation. These institutions buy and sell residential single-family and multifamily mortgage loans, which stabilizes the mortgage money flows and shifts monies to areas and developments of highest need.

The Trends in Home Ownership

Age Groups. The young are increasingly attracted to variable-rate, graduated-payment, and other types of nonstandard home mortgages. The young person with the prospect of a rapidly rising income, perhaps in a professional capacity, is a prime candidate, from the lender's point of view, for a nonstandard home mortgage. During the 1970s, the young person or head of a household was discouraged from home ownership by the large downpayment requirement and the large fixed monthly mortgage payments based on the current relatively high mortgage rates. As lenders continue to offer alternatives to our traditional, standard mortgages with fixed rates and maturities, more young people may have an opportunity to buy homes.

The elderly often wish to keep their own homes but, at the same time, need funds to pay ever-increasing property taxes and home maintenance and operating expenses. For this reason, lenders have been considering reverse annuity mortgage financing. A loan would be given the elderly homeowner, and the home would be assigned to the mortgagee at the death of the elderly borrower, for the payment of the outstanding obligation.

Income Groups. FHA mortgage insurance programs aid the low- and middle-income family in buying a home. Some federal housing subsidies are extended through the Section 8 Housing Assistance Program; some federal housing subsidies are extended through the rent supplement programs. Mortgages with less than market rates of interest are often purchased by the Government National Mortgage Association, since Congress authorized the use of tax monies for mortgage interest subsidies. Even though a low- or middle-income family may not be able to meet the regular underwriting requirements of the FHA program, that family may receive help through special assistance programs of the U.S. Department of Housing and Urban Development.

Ethnic Groups. Ethnic groups are being housed through FHA mortgage insurance programs in more widespread locations, and dense housing of ethnic groups in segregated neighborhoods is decreasing to some extent. As incomes rise through greater employment opportunities, the incidence of home ownership rises.

Geographic and Urban-Suburban Locations. Real estate investment opportunities are particularly available in the West, the Southwest, and the South. Therefore, investment is increasing in these areas. In the urban areas all over the United States, good sites for all kinds of real estate development are being sought in the suburbs. Business and industry wish to join forces in seeking good suburban locations rather than central business district or inner-city locations. Property taxes, payroll taxes, and relatively high land costs discourage site selection in central business districts and in the inner-city neighborhoods.

ATTRIBUTES OF REAL ESTATE INVESTMENT

Real estate investment has some important attributes that the investor considers seriously. These attributes are considered by the investor whether the investment topic is tax-exempt municipal bonds, Treasury certificates, or real estate investment. The attributes are inflation protection, marketability, tax shelter, leverage, and relative yield.

Inflation Protection. One of the best protections against inflation is real estate ownership. Not all real estate values rise constantly, but real estate values in the United States have a good growth record through recessions and prosperous periods. Land values may rise even though the buildings on the land do not rise in value. While real property values rise in most parts of an urban community from the population and business pressures and inflation, real property values may decline in other parts of the same urban community. Properties within declining neighborhoods may be declining in value. Properties whose road access is diminished by new freeway construction or urban redevelopment may decline in value. If the growth patterns of an urban area have turned away from the direction in which the owner's property lies, that property's value may stabilize or decline as a result of the whims of developers.

Income property values are not as recession-proof as house values may be. During a recession, a high vacancy rate of the income property in combination with high mortgage payments may force the income capitalized value of the property to a lower level than the property value before the recession. While the value estimated with the use of the appraiser's income approach may be lower during a recession, the market value from the appraiser's point of view may also decline because of the lack of buyers and the slow turnover of properties during a recession. If recession conditions cause relatively high unemployment and lower personal incomes in an urban area, housing values may be affected in a negative way. Unemployment and reduced incomes are not conducive to house buying and selling.

Most investors see real estate ownership as one of the best types of inflation protection. Proof may be seen in the average new house price of approximately $68,000 in today's market.

Marketability. In comparison with actively traded common stocks and industrial bonds, real estate has a relatively moderate or low degree of marketability. The characteristics of the real estate generally create the degree of marketability. If there is an active market for the particular type of income property or house, the property will sell quickly. A quick sale of a real property might be described as a sale within two or three months after the property is put on the market. Quick sales of some large income properties might be sales within six months to a year of the time the property was placed on the market. In contrast, actively traded stocks and bonds may be sold in minutes in a transaction on the New York or American Stock Exchange.

Just because a property may be readily sold does not mean that the sale will bring at least the amount paid for the real estate. Quite often, though, in today's market, a property bought a few years ago will easily sell for more than the purchase price.

Tax Shelter. Few investments have as many tax-shelter opportunities as income-producing real estate has. Depreciation may be deducted for federal income tax purposes. The depreciation expense is seldom invested in the property, so that income is sheltered from federal income taxation. Many investors wish good investment properties to show depreciation expense at least as much as mortgage amortization. In this way, the investor is developing an equity in the property through income sheltered from taxes by depreciation.

When the real property cash flow analysis shows a negative taxable income, that tax loss may be carried to other sources of income as a deduction for federal income tax purposes. Therefore, the tax loss from a real property may shelter otherwise taxable income.

Leverage. The investor may raise the return on an equity investment with the use of mortgage financing. As long as the cash flow yield on the overall property exceeds the effective rate of interest on the mortgage financing, positive leverage is being employed. The residual income to the equity investor after mortgage interest is paid from net operating income will give the investor a higher rate of return than if the property were not mortgage financed. The lower the cost of mortgage funds, the greater the impact of leverage on the return to the owner.

The Relative Yield on Real Estate. A number of studies have shown that real estate returns have, on the average, during most of the history of our country, outperformed investment returns from the stock and bond markets. Most studies show this general relationship to be true particularly since World War II. The cash flow yield of an income property may be as low as 6 to 8 percent, but the rest of the yield from equity buildup and capital appreciation will bring the total yield to a very competitive level.

SUMMARY

The American culture approves of home ownership. Most homeowners are viewed as socially stable and good citizens of their community. They tend to move less often than apartment dwellers and to vote on election day. The house is seen to be a haven of security and a shelter for all family members. The value of the house in the marketplace may increase as improvements to the house are made for the livability and usefulness of the property.

Federal government housing programs are designed to serve many socioeconomic groups of our society. The bases for government housing assistance include income level of the applicant, family size associated with the income level and wealth accumulation, involvement in the military service for an approved period of time, college housing accommodations, physical disability, urban redevelopment, relocation because of a government program, and property improvement. The government implements its housing policies through eight categories of assistance: insurance, grants and subsidies, loan guarantees, maintenance of the secondary mortgage market, employment in construction of persons of minority groups, tax relief, regulations, and counseling.

The civil rights laws have given widespread investment opportunities to all socioeconomic groups and have encouraged integration of income, racial, and ethnic groups in residential neighborhoods. When prospective property owners need additional funds for investment, many joint ownership forms are available for investment in property. The partnership, trust, corporate, cooperative, condominium, joint tenancy, and tenancy-in-common forms of ownership are available for joint ownership.

The general population characteristics have a bearing on real estate ownership. Approximately 70 to 75 percent of those persons over 35 years of age own their own housing. As the large group of young people of the 1960s and 1970s grows older, they will create a demand for homes and income-producing properties in the 1980s. The greater population mobility encourages the development of condominium and second-home communities. Smaller family size reduces the need for extraordinarily spacious homes and apartments. Some families desire only one living room and three bedrooms rather than a living room and a family room plus four to five bedrooms. The average overall square footage of the middle-income home is declining because of reduced family size, high construction costs, and relatively high mortgage payments.

Gross private domestic investment in structures continued to approximate 3 to 5 percent of the Gross National Product. In the mid-1970s the growth of investment in residential structures has far outpaced the growth in investment in nonresidential structures. The rate of savings has declined to approximately 5 percent from the earlier levels of 8 percent. Approximately five times more existing one-family homes are sold than new one-family homes. Vacancy rates for single-family homes still tend to be approximately 1 percent. Since vacancy rates for residential rental properties are coming down to normal levels in some markets, apartment construction is encouraged in those markets.

Second-home ownership is important in an economy of rising personal incomes and the increased leisure time created by shorter work weeks. Rental incomes of individual investors have been steadily increasing during the mid-1970s, to a total of $24.4 billion in 1978.

Economic and real estate cycles tend to persist. The real estate cycle periodically goes through the four phases of expansion, peak, contraction, and trough. Yields from real estate investment are best during the expansion and peak periods of the real estate cycle.

Disintermediation is a threat to the real estate industry. When investors take their funds out of thrift institution accounts and invest directly in short-term money market securities, the thrift institutions must cut back on mortgage lending and face reduced profits from rising operating costs and yields from existing mortgages. Disintermediation only occurs when the short-term money market rates are substantially above the deposit account and certificate rates at the commercial banks, savings and loan associations, and mutual savings banks.

Inflation affects the real estate industry in various ways. The property owner realizes relatively high prices for his or her property, but finds unusually high prices for properties that may be sought with the money from the prior sale. Inflation in construction costs and mortgage rates reduces property sales to some degree. This is true particularly in recessionary periods and periods of relatively high unemployment.

Mortgage rates have been relatively stable at a relatively high level in the late 1970s because of inflation in money costs and the efficient allocation system designed to move money from capital-rich areas to capital-scarce areas. Private and FHA mortgage insurance coverage of mortgages provides standardized underwriting and reduced risk to the mortgage market system. The secondary mortgage market institutions are active participants in the stabilization of money flows and interest rates.

Nonstandard mortgages are appealing to young people with good future income prospects. The elderly are attracted to reverse annuity mortgage loans to support their current housing and maintenance needs. As a result of government housing programs, all income groups have access to home ownership, with or without government subsidies. Ethnic groups are finding better home ownership opportunities in widespread locations, and the proportion of home ownership in these groups is increasing as incomes rise. Real estate investment opportunities are particularly attractive in the West, Southwest, and South. Suburban areas, rather than central city areas, still attract the homeowner.

Real estate investment generally provides excellent inflation protection, relatively low marketability, substantial tax-shelter opportunities, good opportunities for favorable leverage, and relatively good yields on investible funds.

Key Terms and Concepts

Mobility
Citizenship rights
Lifestyle
Government housing programs
FHA housing programs
Socioeconomic groups
Condominium
Age distribution
Gross private domestic investment in structures
Real estate cycle
Equilibrium
Trough
Money-market certificates
Purchasing power of the dollar
Bank prime rate
Mortgage money
AMMINET market service
Standard mortgages
Nonstandard home mortgages
Graduated payment mortgages
Inflation protection
Tax shelter
Recession
Mortgage amortization
Cash flow yield
VA home mortgage guarantees
Civil rights laws
Goals for integration
U.S. Department of Housing and Urban Development

Large-lot zoning
Joint tenancy
Second-home communities
Savings rate
Vacancy rate
General business cycle
Foreclosure
Expansionary phase
Depositor funds
Rate of inflation
Consumer Price Index
Municipal tax-exempt securities
Mortgage bankers
Federal Home Loan Mortgage Corporation
Reverse annuity mortgages
Section 8 Housing Assistance Program
Leverage
Declining neighborhood
Cash flow analysis
Equity buildup
Low-density standards
Joint ownership of property
Partnership
Trust
Corporation
Cooperative association
Tenancy in common
Family size
Existing home prices
Rental incomes

Real estate industry
Overbuilt market
Disintermediation
Mortgage yields
Wholesale Price Index
Money costs
Capital gains
Institutional lenders
Federal National Mortgage Association

Government National Mortgage
   Association
Variable rate mortgages
H.U.D. Special Assistance programs
Degree of marketability
Relative yield
Depreciation expense
Negative taxable income
Capital appreciation

Questions for Student Self-examination

Multiple-Choice Questions

1. The federal housing programs are not directed toward ____ families.
   a. low-income
   b. high-income
   c. middle-income
   d. all of the above
2. The principal FHA program for unsubsidized middle-income single-family houses is the ____ program.
   a. 235
   b. 232
   c. 221(d)(2)
   d. 203(b)
3. The following is not a basis for government housing assistance:
   a. income level of the citizen
   b. number of automobiles owned by the household
   c. family size associated with the income level and wealth accumulation
   d. physical disability
4. Generally, households benefiting from the FHA mortgage insurance and VA home mortgage guarantees move into
   a. traditional single-family houses
   b. mobile homes
   c. cooperative and condominium housing
   d. all of the above
5. Government insurance programs related to housing policy implementation do not include
   a. fire insurance
   b. mortgage insurance
   c. flood insurance
   d. crime insurance

True-False Questions

T F   1. The property seller may not discriminate in approval of the property buyer on the basis of race, religion, color, or national origin.
T F   2. The United States Department of Housing and Urban Development has sought housing integration on family size, income, racial, and ethnic bases.
T F   3. An individual with limited capital may invest in property even though sole ownership may not be possible.

T F 4. With the decline in the birth and mortality rates, the population of the United States is growing older.
T F 5. Even though the savings rate in the early 1970s approximated 8 percent, that rate had declined by the latter part of the 1970s to approximately 5 or 6 percent.
T F 6. In the late 1970s, approximately ten times more existing one-family homes have been sold than new homes.
T F 7. House construction by developers has been encouraged by the continuing 5 percent vacancy rate nationwide for single-family houses.
T F 8. Usually the family invests in a second home within 50 miles of the primary residence.
T F 9. The real estate cycle in the United States is a part of the overall business cycle.
T F 10. The real estate cycle is said to have five phases.

Answers
Multiple Choice: 1b, 2d, 3b, 4d, 5a.
True-False: 1T, 2F, 3T, 4T, 5T, 6F, 7F, 8F, 9T, 10F.

Problems

1. If the passbook savings rate of the local savings and loan association were 5.25 percent and the Treasury bill rate were currently 5 percent, is the investment climate conducive to disintermediation? If the Treasury bill rate were 9 percent, would the investment climate be conducive to disintermediation?
2. What impact would a recession probably have on the vacancy rates of apartment units and single-family houses?
3. As inflation causes construction costs and house selling prices to rise 12 percent a year, what market conditions are prone to develop?
4. The changes of what age and income groups are particularly strategic to the house real estate market? the commercial real estate market?
5. As the prospective investor analyzes a rental house listed at $25,000, what attributes of this real estate investment will probably appeal to the investor?
6. If a family of four maintains a stabilized annual household income of $50,000, what alternatives for a second home would be available to them?

Chapter 3
Property Rights and Limitations

An Introduction
The Relationship of This Chapter to Other Chapters of the Text
Freehold Versus Leasehold Estates
Freehold Estate
    Fee Simple Estate: *Defeasible fee*   Life Estate
Leasehold Estate
    Leasehold Estate from Period to Period   Leasehold Estate for Years   Leasehold Estate at Will
    Leasehold Estate at Sufferance
Marital Rights at the Death of a Spouse
    Dower Rights   Curtesy Rights
Zoning Ordinances
    The Relationship to the Master Plan for the Community   The Coverage of Zoning Ordinances
Environmental Controls
    Federal Environmental Controls   State Environmental Controls
Building Codes
The Power of Eminent Domain
Adverse Possession
Joint Ownership Rights and Limitations
    Tenancy by the Entireties   Tenancy in Common   Joint Tenancy   Community Property
Summary
Key Terms and Concepts
Questions for Student Self-examination

> **LEARNING OBJECTIVES** After studying this chapter, you should be familiar with
>
> Freehold and leasehold estates in general
> Difference between a fee simple estate and a defeasible fee estate
> The nature of the life estate
> Four general types of leasehold estates
> The significance of dower and curtesy rights for surviving spouses
> The usefulness of zoning ordinances and building codes
> The impact of environmental controls on real estate investment
> The nature of the power of eminent domain and its limitation on property ownership rights
> The rights of adverse possession and the requirements for title transfer
> Various joint ownership rights and limitations
> The differences between tenancy in common and joint tenancy

To conclude the section on real estate investment fundamentals, we will consider the rights and limitations of real estate ownership. The investor must be aware of his or her rights of ownership and the property rights of others. The limitations on ownership rights are also significant. As the investor seeks the highest yield from the investment, the limitations on his or her entrepreneurial position are strategic. The investor may have to recognize, work around, or overcome the limitations placed on yield attainment. The ultimate investment yield will reflect the utilization of the property rights inherent in the ownership and the restraints on investment maximization.

INTRODUCTION

The chapter deals with a number of property rights and limitations. The discussion begins with the differentiating features of freehold and leasehold estates. The fee simple estate is contrasted with the defeasible fee estate and the life estate. The various kinds of leasehold estates are surveyed: the leasehold estate from period to period, the leasehold estate for years, the leasehold estate at will, and the leasehold estate at sufferance. As the investor purchases real property rights, any of these existing estates may be encountered. The investor needs to know what rights may be capitalized on.

The marital rights associated with property ownership are important to the investor for two main reasons. The spouse of the investor assumes certain marital rights, the full extent of which are determined by individual state laws. The marital rights of the spouse of the seller of property rights are also noteworthy. If the spouse of the seller does not release full marital rights when the sale takes place, that spouse retains property rights that the investor may need to reach his or her investment goals.

Zoning ordinances and building codes limit the investor's prerogatives in development of land. Zoning ordinances restrict land use, and building codes control the construction features of the improvements to land. The investor must be cognizant of these restrictions imposed by local government. The current restrictions are always subject to change as local government deems necessary for the health, welfare, and environmental protection of its citizens.

Title to property is not permanently vested in the purchaser of real property. If certain conditions are met or public projects are authorized, the private property owner's rights may be partially or completely taken away through the rights of adverse possession or the exercise of the powers of eminent domain. The courts may convey the title to the real property from the recorded owner to the tenant of several years of the subject property if certain conditions of tenancy have been met. In other cases, a local authority may condemn a portion or a total property for acquisition by a public body for public land development purposes. The exercise of the power of eminent domain means the private property owner's rights are involuntarily taken in reasonable or just compensation.

A few of the more important property rights accruing to the investor are mentioned in this chapter, along with a number of the more strategic property limitations. More investor rights and limitations are discovered in later sections of the book.

THE RELATIONSHIP OF THIS CHAPTER TO OTHER CHAPTERS OF THE TEXT

The three introductory chapters establish the groundwork for further, more intensive exploration of real estate investment. Much of the basic terminology of real estate investment is introduced in these chapters. The other four sections of the book cover financing, appraising, portfolio strategy, yield analysis, and specific investment alternatives.

As investors from abroad find profitable real estate investment opportunities in the United States, they too must quickly realize the significance of real estate investment in the United States in terms of their own financial well-being and that of their countries. The capital of foreign real estate investors has, in recent years, become very important to the development of United States land. Foreign investors as well as domestic investors must be aware of the economics, sociology, and legal foundation of real estate in the United States. Both groups require knowledge of real property rights and limitations.

FREEHOLD VERSUS LEASEHOLD ESTATES

The investor may acquire either a freehold or a leasehold estate. The rights of the investor depend on the nature of the estate acquired. The investor acquires either a complete set of legal rights or a limited bundle of rights.

Freehold Estate

If the investor's property rights run indefinitely, he or she holds a freehold estate in property. In contrast, the leasehold estate has a definite termination date. There are several types of freehold estates, but each type has no definite termination date.

Fee Simple Estate. The fee simple estate is also called an *estate in fee* or *fee simple absolute*. The distinguishing features of the fee simple estate are (1) the indefinite duration of the estate, (2) the freely transferable or inheritable estate, and (3) the possession of the most absolute interest in property that is possible. The estate endures as long as the present owner wants to hold title to the property. When the present owner wishes to sell, lease, or give away the property, the title in fee simple is freely transferable. The property rights may be passed on freely to heirs, friends, and other interested parties. Inheritance rights are unrestricted.

All ownership rights accrue to the fee simple property owner. The owner may hold the title; give the property away; lease the property to others; sell the property; or refuse to give, lease, or sell the property to others. Only the government may encroach upon this almost perfect form of property ownership. In the case of any type of real property estate, the government may step in and limit the owner's rights in order to preserve the public good. For example, the local government usually imposes zoning restrictions on all privately and publicly owned property in order to further an orderly land-use pattern.

Defeasible fee. There are three kinds of fee simple estates that can be terminated by the happening of a specified event; these estates are called *defeasible fee estates:*

1. The *fee simple determinable estate* automatically terminates on the happening of a stated event and goes back to the grantor. For example, if a property donor gave land to a church on condition that the land be used only for church purposes, the donor might state in the deed conveyed that, once the land was converted to use for other than church purposes, the title would automatically revert to the donor or to the donor's estate. Since the fee simple estate of the church would be terminated upon the change in land use not related to church purposes and would automatically revert to the grantor, this would be an example of the fee simple determinable estate.

2. The *fee simple estate subject to a condition subsequent* depends on the exercise of the power of termination by the grantor or other such party to whom the estate has conditionally reverted. As in the case of the land donated to the church for church-related use, the donor or the grantor to whom the land title reverted upon the unapproved change in land use must take action to terminate the estate vested in the church. The grantor or other party who has succeeded to the grantor's interest must take the appropriate legal actions to regain title and terminate the church's estate.

3. The *fee simple estate subject to an executory limitation* is found where the occurrence of an event may automatically cause the transfer of the property title from the present holder to a third party. For example, if property in a divorce settlement is given to a spouse, the holding of title by the spouse may be invalidated by the spouse's remarriage. In the event of the spouse's remarriage, the fee simple deed may state that an only child born to the divorced couple would succeed to the property ownership. If the spouse does not remarry, the fee simple title would remain with the divorced parent indefinitely.

Life Estate. The life estate is a type of freehold estate whose duration depends on the length of life of the designated person or the lives of designated persons. The person whose life determines the duration of the life estate may be the grantee who has possession or is entitled to possession of the property, or it may be a third party. If, at the end of the designated lifetime, the title to the fee estate transfers to a third party rather than reverting back to the grantor or a successor, the third party is called the remainderman. If the remainderman is living at the time of the establishment of the terms of the life estate, the remainderman is said to be vested. If unborn heirs of the grantee are designated as remaindermen, the remainderman right is not vested but inchoate.

The holder of the life estate is entitled to the rents and profits from the land and improvements. The grantee may also alter or improve the premises, but such improvements will ultimately benefit the grantor or the reminderman, depending on who will receive the title at the death of the designated person. The grantee holds the property in trust for the grantor or the remainderman; the use or modification of the property must not detrimentally affect its value, since it is only temporarily owned by the grantee. The grantee, therefore, must keep the premises in good repair and pay the taxes placed on the property. The grantee may acquire the funds with the pledge of the life estate, but must meet the debt service payments in order to preserve the estate for the remainderman or the grantor.

The grantee may convey all rights owned by him or her that are part of the life estate. The new owner of the rights of the life estate is subjected to the terms of the original life estate; the new ownership ends at the death of the one designated in the original conveyance. The new grantee receives only those rights held by the original grantee. The reversion or residue of the life estate may still lie in the grantor. The fee of the grantor may also be conveyed, subject to the rights of the life estate holder.

An example of the conveyance of a life estate might be the conveyance by a son-in-law of a life estate in a property to his mother-in-law for the life of a sister of the son-in-law. At the death of the sister, the title to the property would be transferred to the heirs of the sister, perhaps so that the remaining children might continue to have shelter regardless of the other circumstances of the inherited estate. Another example would be the conveyance of a life estate by the son-in-law to his mother-in-law for her lifetime. At the death of the mother-in-law, the life estate would revert to the grantor or his successors or be merged with the fee estate held by the grantor or his successors.

The life estate can be created by will, by deed, or by operation of law. The term *by operation of law* refers to legal rights established by law, such as dower and curtesy. If the state statutes provide for dower and/or curtesy rights, a life estate is automatically established for the surviving spouse in perhaps one-third of the property rights held by the couple jointly at the death of the spouse.

Leasehold Estate

If the investor has property rights that are legally terminated at a specific time, the investor has a leasehold, or less-than-freehold, estate. Generally the leasehold estate is conveyed to the lessee (tenant) by the lessor (landlord) in return for periodic lease payments. The lessor, the landlord, retains the basic ownership rights and conveys the rights of possession and use temporarily to the lessee, the tenant. The leasehold estate held by the tenant does not run indefinitely; it usually terminates at a specific date.

In contrast to the freehold estates in real property, the leasehold estate is considered personal property by the courts. The leasehold estates fall into four categories: the leasehold estate from period to period, the leasehold estate for years, the leasehold estate at will, and the leasehold estate at sufferance.

Leasehold Estate from Period to Period. With the leasehold estate from period to period the lessee's estate continues from one designated period of time to another period of time of the same length. The period may be a week, a month, or a year. For example, when the lease for one year ends, the next period of the lease is one year. If the original lease period is one month, the subsequent lease periods each cover one month. On the other hand, if the original lease period is two years, the subsequent lease period is two years.

One example of the one-year lease that is renewable for another year is the apartment lease. Some apartment leases run for two- and three-year blocks of time after the first lease period is concluded. Some rooming houses lease sleeping rooms for one month at a time; once the tenant has completed one month's rental of the sleeping room, the landlord assumes the next space rental period to be one month.

Leasehold Estate for Years. The leasehold estate for years usually runs for a significantly long period of time. Often the leasehold estate for years runs for 10, 20, or perhaps 40 years. The shopping center storeroom that rents for an initial period of 10 years is an example of this type of lease. The ground lease that covers a 30-year period is another example. Leasehold financing is often based on this type of long-term leasehold estate.

Leasehold Estate at Will. If the investor wishes to permit a tenant to occupy his building space, the investor may allow the tenancy even though the tenant has not executed a lease and there is no agreement about the length of the permitted occupancy. The building owner merely permits the tenancy until he gives notice to the tenant to vacate the premises.

This type of leasehold estate may be created through an express agreement between the lessee and the lessor or by operation of law. The tenancy may continue as long as the landlord approves the occupancy; it may continue indefinitely. If the tenant entered the premises under the terms of a lease but the lease was never executed, the courts construe that a leasehold estate at will was created.

Either the tenant or the landlord may give notice of the impending termination of the leasehold rights. Notice must be given within a reasonable time before the termination date. The courts may construe a reasonable time to be 30 to 60 days in advance of the move from the premises.

Leasehold Estate at Sufferance. Once the lease between the lessee and the lessor has expired, the landlord may permit the lessee continued occupancy of the space. The occupancy may continue until the landlord notifies the tenant to move from the space, perhaps by an eviction notice. The landlord "suffers" the occupancy of the tenant. The lessor may enter into a new lease agreement with the tenant, the tenant may be treated as a trespasser, or the landlord may accept further rent with the recognition that he or she is renewing the tenancy agreement for the same period of time as the original agreement. The presumed renewal of the lease may cover only one month's occupancy if the original term of the lease was one month, or it may cover up to one year's occupancy.

MARITAL RIGHTS AT THE DEATH OF A SPOUSE

Dower, curtesy, and statutory substitutes for the marital rights extended by the various states affect the real estate investor. The investor—whether husband or wife—should consider the legal rights that vest in the surviving spouse in the property owned by the other spouse at his or her death. The investor also should realize the legal position of the other spouse when a purchase agreement is signed with only one spouse of a married couple.

Many states give dower, curtesy, and other such statutory rights to surviving spouses. The marital rights are seldom the same in any two states. Some states have rescinded both dower and curtesy; some states have substituted similar legislation within their inheritance laws; and some states have eliminated curtesy in favor of dower rights for both spouses.

Dower Rights. The dower right is usually the right to a life estate in one-third of the real property owned by a husband at his death, which is automatically conveyed to the surviving wife for her shelter and financial protection. Often the dower right is extended to the real property in which the wife did not release her dower interest that was transferred by the husband during his lifetime and the marriage. Some states have changed the right to a life estate to the right of the surviving wife to a fee simple interest in the real property owned by the husband at his death and in the real property transferred during the time of the marriage in which the dower interest was not released by the wife.

If the real properties owned by the husband at his death are easily divisible, the surviving wife assumes usually a one-third life estate in that total property. If the properties are not easily divisible, the surviving wife is automatically eligible to be the recipient of one-third of the rents flowing from the property; alternatively, the property can be sold and one-third of the proceeds paid to the surviving wife.

The dower rights are either inchoate or consummate. While real property is owned, the wife's right is inchoate, or unrealized or unvested, until the husband dies. The right is consummate at the death of the husband. The statutory provision automatically goes into effect. Dower is effective only if the following requirements are met:

1. A valid marriage is in effect at the husband's death.
2. The husband owned real property during the time of the marriage.
3. The husband died prior to the death of his wife.

Curtesy Rights. The right of curtesy usually extends to the husband at the time of his wife's death. This right, which becomes effective automatically at the wife's death, gives the surviving husband, in most states that preserve the right of curtesy, a life estate to a fractional part of the real property that was transferred to other parties during the marriage but in which the husband did not release his right of curtesy. Originally, according to old English law, the husband was entitled to a life estate in all the land owned by the wife during the marriage. Today the husband's share has been reduced by modern laws to a life estate in some fraction, perhaps one-third, of the wife's real property.

Originally, in some states in the United States, a child had to be born to the couple for the right of curtesy to arise. Of the dozen or so states that today provide for the rights of curtesy, this requirement has been abolished in Arkansas, Delaware, New Jersey, Oregon, Virginia, and perhaps other states.

In a manner similar to dower, curtesy is effective only if the following requirements are met:

1. A valid marriage is in effect at the wife's death.
2. The wife owned real property during the time of the marriage.
3. The wife died prior to the death of her husband.

In other words, if the couple is divorced, dower, curtesy, and other statutory substitutes are terminated. A divorce terminates only the dower or the curtesy rights of the spouse for whose fault the divorce is obtained in such states as Illinois, Massachusetts, Oregon, Rhode Island, and West Virginia.

The rights of dower and curtesy exist along with the other inheritance laws of each individual state. These rights supercede any disposition of the property by the deceased by will or by the estate administrator or executor. The minimum provisions established by curtesy, dower, and the basic inheritance laws must be met by the documents or private estate settlement.

As a practical matter, the investor may only acquire clear title with no inchoate right of curtesy or dower against the estate if the spouse of the contracting party also signs a release of curtesy or dower in the sales, financing, or lease agreement. At the same time, if the investor is married, the investor must realize the marital rights to property acquired that belong to the investor's spouse.

ZONING ORDINANCES

One of the police powers of local government is the power to zone property. Police power in general is the local government regulation for the preservation of the health, safety, and moral and general welfare of the citizens of the community. It is assumed that complete freedom of property use by the property owner is detrimental to the public interest. In the exercise of police power, no compensation is made for such interference by the government. It is assumed that the property owner is compensated as one of the many citizens of the community who benefit from the property regulations.

The Relationship to the Master Plan for the Community. Once the master plan for the community is drawn up and approved by the local government officials as representatives of the citizens of the community, zoning is developed to implement the master plan. The passage of new zoning ordinances generally does not affect the current land use but does help determine the land-use patterns of the future.

The Coverage of Zoning Ordinances. Since most urban areas are subject to zoning ordinances, we find that most urban areas are divided into districts whose land-use zones are regulated. Zoning ordinances involve (1) the land coverage ratio, (2) the land use, and (3) the development of the building lot. The land coverage ratio depends on the type of land use, the extent of scarcity of light and air, and the projected density of land use. The typical land-use categories that are a part of zoning ordinances include (1) residential, (2) agricultural, (3) commercial, and (4) industrial. Each one of these categories may be further broken down into more specific ones. For example, the residential zoning designation R-1 may refer to single-family residential zoning in which minimum frontage is 100 feet. At the same time, the residential zone designation RMF-1 may refer to multifamily residential zoning in which the maximum density permitted is 10 units per acre.

Zoning ordinances also involve the development of building lots. Setbacks from the front, rear, and side lines are usually specified in the zoning designation. The maximum building height is usually specified for the zoned area. This height restriction may be interpreted by the developer as the maximum floors in the structure to be designed. The use of the building lot may be further restricted. Storage of dangerous explosives may be prohibited. Animals other than commonly accepted domestic pets may not be permitted to be kept and cared for on the building lot. As an example, the zoning designation might not permit the keeping of goats, cows, or chickens.

ENVIRONMENTAL CONTROLS

Real property development is subject to environmental controls today. Federal environmental controls have existed since 1899, but most of them have been enacted only since the end of World War II. Each state issues environmental regulations as well.

Federal Environmental Controls. Water pollution and decent, safe, and sanitary housing were the chief focal points of the federal environmental legislation prior to World War II. Since the 1940s, the federal government has regulated air quality, highway and airport construction, water quality, noise pollution, coastal land use, and development in flood-prone areas (Table 3-1).

Since the National Environmental Policy Act was passed in 1969 and the Environmental Protection Agency was formed a few months later, real estate developers have been required to file environmental impact statements in advance of construction when a "major federal action" is involved that significantly affects the quality of the human environment. The environmental impact study and the resulting report to the EPA must usually cover (1) the description of the project, (2) the environmental description, (3) the environmental impact of the proposed development, (4) any adverse environmental effects that cannot be avoided if the proposed project is implemented, (5) mitigation measures proposed to minimize the impact, (6) the relationship between the local short-term uses of the environment and the maintenance or enhancement of long-term productivity, (7) any irreversible changes in the environment if the proposed development is implemented, and (8) the growth-inducing impact of the proposed

Table 3-1. Summary of federal environmental laws

1899	The Rivers and Harbors Act
1926	U.S. Supreme Court affirmed constitutionality of zoning and subdivision regulation
1933	National Planning Board, Department of the Interior—renamed National Resources Planning Board—stimulated formation of state planning boards
1934	National Housing Act of 1934—established the FHA—encouraged home construction (at that time there was no federal legislation or national plan for orderly land development)
1937	U.S. Housing Act of 1937—designed to provide decent, safe, and sanitary housing for low-income families through assistance to the states and their political subdivisions
1943	National Resources Planning Board abolished
1948	Federal Water Pollution Control Act (amended three times between 1970 and 1972)
1954	Federal Planning Assistance Program
1955	Clean Air Act (amended three times within period 1970-1974)
1956	Federal Aid Highway Act
	Airport and Airway Development Act
1967	Air Quality Act
1969	National Environmental Policy Act
1970	Water Quality Improvement Act (amended 1948 Act)
	Noise Pollution and Abatement Act
	Clean Air Act (amended 1967 Act)
1972	Noise Control Act
	Coastal Zone Management Act (Secretary of Commerce is authorized to make grants program administered by the National Oceanic and Atmospheric Administration of the Department of Commerce)
	Water Pollution Control Act
	Section 208, Areawide Waste Treatment Management Plans
1973	Flood Disaster Protection Act
1975	National Flood Insurance Program revised
1976	Federal Land Policy and Management Act

Reprinted by permission from Mary Alice Hines, *Real Estate Finance*, © 1978, p. 291. Reprinted by permission of Prentice-Hall, Inc., Englewood Cliffs, New Jersey.

development. Sponsors of sizable real estate developments—regardless of the area or location of the country—are subjected to EPA report requirements and EPA project approval.

State Environmental Controls. Most states enforce their environmental regulations through air pollution, water pollution, and solid wastes control agencies. Some states also maintain land-use control, occupational safety and health, coastal resources, noise control, hazardous waste control, and power plant siting agencies. Quite often, in each of the areas, the state agency controlling that area will require environmental impact statements, review and approve project plans, issue construction and operating permits, maintain enforcement power for their regulations, and regulate the indirect sources of pollution.

BUILDING CODES

For the protection of public health and safety, local government officials prepare and enforce building codes. The minimum construction and occupancy requirements set forth by the building codes supplement the basic state housing requirements, if such state requirements exist.

The building codes generally deal with permitted building materials and approved construction methods. For example, plastic water pipes may or may not be permitted in home constructions. Eave vents every four feet may be required for hip roofs of a specified length. If a bathroom has no access to outside ventilation, the code may require mechanical ventilation. If the city or county wishes to better control garbage collection, the building code may require installation of a compactor in every home. The compactor compresses the refuse into smaller units so that less space is needed for storage and disposal of refuse and less frequent garbage pickup is required by the public or private scavenger service.

The investor benefits from building code enforcement. The minimum requirements for building construction tend to assure stable property values and slower rates of depreciation and obsolescence.

THE POWER OF EMINENT DOMAIN

Even if the investor holds a fee simple title to the property—a title that guarantees the maximum private property rights—the local government may take the property through the use of the power of eminent domain if the public benefits from the taking. Part or all of the investor's property may be condemned for future public use. In contrast to situations involving the enforcement of the police powers of the local government, the service of the power of eminent domain requires reasonable compensation to the property owner for the portion of the property taken for public purposes.

Several common community-improvement projects involve the use of the power of eminent domain. When highways cut through the countryside or through urban areas, the condemning authority may first offer to buy the publicly and privately held property in its path. If the property owner is reluctant to sell, the local public agency can declare the property condemned, an appraised value is attached to the land, and payment may be made to the original property owner. When streets are broadened, condemnation proceedings may be necessary. If the master plan and the local urban renewal authority require land purchase, clearance, and sale so that desired urban redevelopment may take place, the power of eminent domain may be exercised when property owners refuse to sell their property rights on the terms established by the local urban renewal authority. Other common situations involving the powers of condemnation are the construction of a public library, a city park, or a new fire station. When power lines have to be stretched across the land, the power company is given the right of condemnation, since access to electric power serves the public benefit.

The power of eminent domain may only be utilized if an overall public benefit results. The local governing body must approve the public need for the project, which justifies the use of the power of eminent domain. In some instances, an agency related to the city or metropolitan area government may be given the power of eminent domain for the implementation of the desired project. In other instances, the state highway department or the public utility company may be given the power of condemnation to serve the public need.

The legal system assures the property owner of reasonable compensation for the condemned property. First the project managers determine the properties involved and the ownership of those properties and associated property rights. A value is set on each property by the agency appraisers or fee appraisers employed for the purpose. The owners are contacted for the purchase of their property rights. Some of the owners may settle immediately for a negotiated price. When other owners decline to sell on the terms offered, the property may be condemned. The property owner may file suit against the condemning authority for just compensation for property rights. The agency and the owner may each hire independent appraisers and attorneys to establish a fair market price for the property. When the court hears the case and decides on a fair price, the owner must accept this price and convey title to the condemning authority.

ADVERSE POSSESSION

In this modern era, the investor still faces the possibility of an occupant of the investment property taking title from the investor—the recorded title holder—once the statutory requirements of adverse possession are met. The illegal tenant of the property must convince the court that the requirements for title acquisition through adverse possession have been met. Those requirements include

1. Possession of the property by the claimant or his agent, licensee, or trustee.
2. Open and notorious possession by the tenant.
3. Exclusive possession by the illegal tenant and his or her heirs.
4. Continuous and uninterrupted possession.
5. Claim by the unlawful tenant of full ownership rights.
6. Possession for the statutory period set by the state legislature.
7. Payment of property taxes by the tenant-claimant, according to some states.

If the court is convinced that the illegal occupant has fulfilled the above requirements, the court may have the title to the property transferred from the recorded title holder to the tenant.

Private or public property ownership is subject to adverse possession rights. A "squatter" fulfilling the adverse possession requirements may file a claim for the title to privately or publicly owned property. If the publicly owned property is being used by the public body for their institutional purposes, the title cannot be taken under the rights of adverse possession. Otherwise, the title can be taken by the squatter.

The usual statutory period for the claimant to fulfill title requirements ranges from 10 to 30 years, depending on the particular state's statutes. If the tenant-claimant has paid the property taxes over the required period, the statutory period may be shorter than the usual range of time. In any case, over the statutory period, the title holder must not have approached the illegal tenant and given him or her notice to vacate the premises or pay rent, even though the tenant has in no way concealed the illegal tenancy. The tenant must have declared to neighbors, friends, and business associates his or her ownership of the property. The statutory period for possession may be fulfilled partly by the original tenant and partly by the heirs of the original tenant, as long as the exclusive, notorious, and continuous occupancy requirements are met. The requirements can also be met if the use of the property by the claimant is on a continuous seasonal basis.

JOINT OWNERSHIP RIGHTS AND LIMITATIONS

Without considering tax and financial liability and the organizational structures of business entities, which are discussed in a later chapter, the prospective investor should note the rights and limitations of common joint ownership forms for investment in real property. At this point we want to observe the rights and limitations of (1) tenancy by the entireties, (2) tenancy in common, (3) joint tenancy, and (4) community property.

Tenancy by the Entireties. About half the states provide for tenancy by the entireties for use by husbands and wives who jointly hold real assets. The co-owners under this joint ownership form must be husband and wife. They each have automatic survivorship rights at the death of the other spouse. When one spouse dies, therefore, the other spouse assumes the complete ownership of the jointly owned property. This right supersedes distribution rights of the state inheritance laws. If the state does not provide for this form of joint ownership for the married couple, the same survivorship relationship may be attained through the use of the joint tenancy or community property form. The joint tenancy form of property ownership is applicable to related and unrelated individuals. Tenancy by the entireties and community property may be considered special forms of joint tenancy, in which only husbands and wives are permitted as co-owners.

Tenancy in Common. Related and/or unrelated individuals may invest in property under the tenancy-in-common joint ownership form, in which two or more persons are owners of an undivided interest in a single estate. The partners may own equal or unequal fractional interests in the undivided estate and may contribute equal or unequal sums to the property ownership. For example, one of the partners may own one-tenth of the undivided property interest; another partner may own one-sixth of the property.

When a tenant wants to sell his or her interest in a property that cannot easily be divided, the purchaser becomes a tenant in common, in place of the original tenant. When a partition action is filed in court, and the property is subject to division, the purchaser may own separately a part of the property aside from the jointly held portion of the property. When the tenant in common dies, his undivided interest may pass to his heirs and assigns, depending on the provisions of the will. The new owner becomes a tenant in common with the remaining tenants in common.

Joint Tenancy. Joint tenancy gives survivorship rights to the joint owners. If one partner dies, his or her share of the undivided interest in the property is conveyed to the remaining joint tenants. As each partner dies, one partner may finally remain; this surviving partner will hold the entire undivided interest in the investment property.

The joint tenants must enter into the joint ownership entity at the same time with the same property interest, each with the right of possession under the same title. If any one of these requirements is not met, a tenancy in common results. The two or more persons are joint and equal owners of the same undivided interest. The joint tenant cannot dispose of his or her undivided interest at death through the provisions of a will; this interest is not subject to probate of the estate of the deceased joint tenant. If the joint tenant wishes to convey the ownership right to an heir or another person, or if the joint tenant wishes to sell his share of the jointly owned property, the court may be petitioned for a partitioning of the joint tenancy. After the partitioning of the individual interest, the recipient of the ownership share becomes a tenant in common with the joint tenants. The court may also require that the property be sold and the proceeds distributed to the individual joint tenants, including the joint tenant wishing to dispose of his interest.

Community Property. If the investor resides in a community-property state or if property is being purchased in a community-property state, community-property rights are significant to the investor. Property bought by a married couple during their marriage when they reside in a community-property state is assumed to be held by the couple jointly, each spouse holding an equal, undivided interest in the purchased property. (The community-property states are Arizona, California, Idaho, Louisiana, Nevada, New Mexico, Texas, and Washington.) The property owned by the spouses before they enter into marriage may be held separately after marriage; each spouse may acquire property during the marriage by inheritance, will, or gift, which may be owned separately. When property is purchased from a married couple subject to community-property laws, the investor should ascertain the ownership status of the property involved. Under most conditions, both spouses of the marriage should sign any documents related to the financing and conveyancing of the property.

SUMMARY

The real estate investor and the student should realize the rights and limitations inherent in joint ownership forms and in various estates in property. Governmental controls over private and public property rights should also be studied.

The freehold estates include the fee simple, the defeasible fee, and the life estates. The leasehold estates include the leasehold estate from period to period, the leasehold estate for years, the leasehold estate at will, and the leasehold estate at sufferance. Generally the leasehold estate terminates at a specific date; in contrast, the freehold estate runs indefinitely.

The spouse surviving the death of the other spouse is usually protected under state law by the rights of dower or curtesy. Dower or curtesy gives the surviving spouse a life estate in a fractional part of the property owned by the deceased spouse at the time of his or her death. The life estate may also cover the fractional portion of the property whose title was transferred to another person during the marriage, when the surviving spouse did not release dower or curtesy rights. Generally, the investor must be aware that the married sellers of property should both sign the conveyancing and financing agreements. The spouse of the investor also is entitled to the marital rights related to property ownership when the investor dies.

Zoning ordinances and building codes are local government regulations concerning the development, construction, and use of property within the local government's jurisdiction. Zoning ordinances establish permitted land uses, setbacks from property lines, maximum building heights, maximum land coverage ratios, minimum parking ratios, and maximum land-use densities. Building codes establish permissible building materials and construction methods.

The investor's property rights may be taken by condemning authorities whose exercise of the power of eminent domain is approved by local government bodies. When the public benefit overrides private property rights, the investor's property may be condemned for the public improvement, and the investor is paid a reasonable amount for the property. Many public works projects such as highway construction, library construction, fire station construction, and urban redevelopment employ the power of eminent domain to purchase, clear, and develop the land according to a publicly approved design.

An illegal occupant of a property owner's land and buildings may claim the rightful title to the property if the occupant meets the statutory requirements for transfer of title due to adverse possession. The court must determine whether the requirements are met for the lawful transfer of title from the recorded property owner to the tenant—and perhaps taxpayer—of many years.

When property is being bought and sold, knowledge of the nature of the joint ownership forms is necessary for the active participants in the market. Each of the individual joint ownership forms carries its own rights and limitations. Common joint ownership forms are tenancy by the entireties, tenancy in common, joint tenancy, and community property.

Key Terms and Concepts

Entrepreneurial position of the investor
Restraints on investment maximization
Defeasible fee estate
Power of eminent domain
Freehold estate
Estate in fee
Fee simple absolute
Remainderman
Reversionary interest
Dower rights
Ground lease
Leasehold financing
Community master plan
Environmental controls
Environmental impact statement

Adverse environmental effects
Building code enforcement
Notorious possession
Community property
Undivided interest
Life estate
Leasehold estate from period to period
Leasehold estate for years
Leasehold estate at will
Condemnation
Inheritance rights
Fee simple determinable
Fee simple subject to a condition subsequent
Debt service payments

Curtesy rights
Trespasser
Lease renewal
Land-use zones
National Environmental Policy Act
Growth-inducing impact
Obsolescence
Squatter
Tenancy by the entireties
Partitioning of an undivided interest
Leasehold estate at sufferance
Marital rights
Zoning ordinances
Building codes
Environmental protection

Foreign versus domestic real estate investors
Fee simple subject to an executory limitation
Reversion
"By operation of law"
Less-than-freehold estate
Inchoate rights
Consummate rights
Land coverage ratio
Environmental Protection Agency
Pollution
Adverse possession
Tenant-claimant
Spouse

Questions for Student Self-examination

Multiple-Choice Questions

1. Which of the following is not a freehold estate in real property?
    a. fee simple estate
    b. leasehold estate
    c. defeasible fee estate
    d. life estate
2. If the real estate investor's property rights have a definite termination date, the investor holds a _____ estate in property.
    a. leasehold
    b. fee simple
    c. life
    d. defeasible fee
3. Which is not a defeasible fee estate?
    a. fee simple determinable
    b. fee simple subject to a condition subsequent
    c. fee simple substitutable
    d. fee simple subject to an executory limitation
4. Which type of real property estate is described by the following statement: If the holding of the title depends on the occurrence of an event, the occurrence of the event may automatically cause the transfer of the property title from the present holder to a third party?
    a. fee simple determinable
    b. fee simple subject to a condition subsequent
    c. fee simple substitutable
    d. fee simple subject to an executory limitation
5. The life estate can be created
    a. by will
    b. by operation of law
    c. by deed
    d. all of the above

Property Rights and Limitations 51

True-False Questions

T F 1. Title to property is not permanently vested in the purchaser of real property.
T F 2. The investments of foreign real estate investors have, in recent years, remained relatively insignificant in the development of United States land.
T F 3. The real estate investor may acquire either a freehold or a leasehold estate.
T F 4. The government may step in and limit the real estate owner's fee simple right in order to preserve the public good.
T F 5. If the remainderman is living at the time of the establishment of the terms of the life estate, the remainderman is said to be inchoate.
T F 6. The holder of the life estate is entitled to the rents and profits from the land and improvements conveyed to him or her.
T F 7. The life estate grantee may convey all rights owned by him or her that are part of the life estate.
T F 8. The leasehold estate is considered real property by the courts.
T F 9. If the tenant entered the premises under the terms of a lease but the lease was never executed, the courts construe that a leasehold estate at sufferance was created.
T F 10. Some states have rescinded both dower and curtesy.

Answers
Multiple choice: 1b, 2a, 3c, 4d, 5d.
True-False: 1T, 2F, 3T, 4T, 5F, 6T, 7T, 8F, 9F, 10T.

Problems

1. If you want your children to inherit your real property but you want to house your mother-in-law during her lifetime, what title might you convey to your mother-in-law in the house that you own that suits her occupancy?
2. If you are a real estate officer for a major discount department store, what kind of leasehold estate will your boss prefer? Why?
3. If you are a married woman, what does the dower right promise you in your state? If you are a married man, what does the dower or curtesy right promise you by your state statutes?
4. If you are planning to develop a 100-unit apartment project, what effect will federal and state environmental regulations and controls have on your plans and the final development of the project?
5. If your $30,000 rental house lies in the path of a new highway, what effect will condemnation for the right of way have on your property ownership rights?
6. If you have not visited your distant property for 15 years and pay a visit to the property now and observe occupants there without your approval, what can you do to protect yourself from any rights of adverse possession?
7. If you and your spouse wish to hold the real property you just bought jointly with full survivorship rights for each of you, what forms of joint property ownership might you consider? Which form of joint ownership do you prefer? Why?

Part Two

Financing and Appraising

Chapter 4

Mortgage Financing and Leverage

Introduction

The Relationship of This Chapter to Other Chapters of the Text

The Importance of Mortgage Financing to the Investor
    The Effect of Leverage on the Investor's Return on Investment   Tax Effect of Mortgage Interest

The Effect of Mortgage Financing on Lender Rules of Thumb
    The Typical Breakeven Ratio   The Typical Loan-to-Value Ratio   The Typical Loan Amount per Unit   The Typical Debt Service Coverage Requirement

The Strategic Terms of a Mortgage
    A Relatively Long Mortgage Term   A Reasonable Interest Rate and Possible Lender Participation in Income   Low or No Prepayment Penalty   Interest-Only Amortization   A Good Overall Amortization Plan   The Assignment of Rents   The Provision for Further Subordinated Financing

The Types of Real Estate Loans on Houses and Income Properties

Financing of Residential Property
    Financing the Lot   Financing House Construction   Financing the Permanent Loan on a House: *Veterans Administration-guaranteed home mortgage loans, Federal Housing Administration-insured home mortgage loans, Conventional home loans*

Income Property Financing
    Financing the Land   Financing Land Development and Construction   Gap Loans   Permanent Financing   Wraparound Loans

Summary

Key Terms and Concepts

Questions for Student Self-examination

LEARNING OBJECTIVES After studying this chapter, you should be familiar with

The importance of mortgage financing to the typical real estate investor
The effect of leverage on the investor's return on investment
The decline in leverage over time from the periodic amortization of the mortgage
Tax deductibility of mortgage interest
Required breakeven ratios for mortgage financing
Typical loan-to-value ratios
Typical loan amounts per unit of space developed
Required debt service coverage ratios for mortgage financing
The strategic terms of a mortgage from the investor viewpoint
The methods of financing a house and its lot
The differences between VA-guaranteed, FHA-insured, and conventional home loans
The methods of financing land, construction, and permanent improvements of income-producing developments
The nature of the gap loan and its importance
Financing with wraparound loans

Few properties are bought with only cash. Few home buyers, for instance, purchase with all cash. They might prefer to buy with only cash, but their household finances do not permit it. On the other hand, few investment properties are purchased with all cash. Most income property investors do not intend to pay outright with cash, even if they can. These investors wish to tie up as little cash in the investment as possible. They realize that usually, the less cash they put into the real estate investment, the more their return on the investment increases. Therefore, mortgage financing or the use of leverage is vital to the real estate business.

INTRODUCTION

This chapter points out the significance of mortgage financing to the investor. Mortgage financing usually supplements the equity contributed by the investor and increases the return on that equity. The possibility of mortgaging out with a construction loan is mentioned as a possible favorable attribute of the financing.

It is pointed out that lenders have rules of thumb that they use in financing real estate. The debt financing the lenders permit or the leverage that they approve determines the level of the breakeven ratio, the overall loan-to-value ratio, the loan amount per unit, the debt service coverage, and the return on investment. The mortgage financing approved by lenders sometimes determines the extent of property development for energy conservation. For example, more than normal debt financing may be required for the installation of sufficient insulation and solar heating systems.

Certain terms of the mortgage must be scrutinized by the investor to insure that his or her best interests are being served by the mortgage. For example, the investor will negotiate with the lender for favorable prepayment and amortization plans. Interest-only provisions for the first few years of the mortgage and a balloon payment at the maturity of the loan may be desirable from the investor's point of view. If the lender demands a variable rate rather than a fixed rate of interest on the mortgage, the investor will attempt to forecast whether increasing rentals and net operating incomes will adequately cover any increase in debt service that comes about as a result of increases in money and capital market indices. The mortgage conditions associated with refinancing and the opportunities of subordinated financing with junior mortgages will also be investigated.

Various types of mortgage loans may be acquired for the purchase of homes and income properties. The typical terms of the various types of mortgage loans are summarized in terms of loan-to-value ratio, length of loan, relative level of interest rate, and the extent of mortgage insurance or guarantee.

THE RELATIONSHIP OF THIS CHAPTER TO OTHER CHAPTERS OF THE TEXT

This is the first chapter in Part II, which covers financing and appraising. These are both important to the investor. Since most investors require mortgage financing, this area of analysis has strategic importance. In order to receive the desired financing, the prospective property must be appraised so that the lender has a basis for a financing decision. Most institutional loan committees relate the amount of the desired mortgage loan to the amount of the appraised value (the loan-to-value ratio).

The important concept of leverage is studied in this chapter. The use of leverage may be favorable or it may be unfavorable. The degree of leverage ranges from a high degree—a high total loan-to-appraised-value ratio—to a low degree—a low total loan-to-appraised-value ratio.

The sources of mortgage monies, the usual portfolio composition, and the limitations and opportunities of the various institutional investment practices are set forth in Chapter 6. Since this chapter deals only with mortgage lending and the use of leverage in general, Chapter 6 points out the specific sources of funds and the lending conditions within which the institutions operate.

The last two chapters of Part II deal with real estate appraising. Many investors tend to informally appraise their own properties once they have learned the basic system of appraisal. Even though the investor may have a good idea of the appraised value, the lender will usually rely on the appraisal of a designated appraiser working in that community. Investors, in protecting their interests, should be aware of the basic appraisal system as set forth by the leading appraisal trade associations. Since considerable emphasis is placed on income property investment in this text, one complete chapter is devoted to income property appraisal. Only the basic income capitalization methods are needed for house appraisal, but a relatively complex system of analysis is required for income property valuation.

THE IMPORTANCE OF MORTGAGE FINANCING TO THE INVESTOR

Mortgage financing is important to the investor in four ways: the mortgage financing may supplement the investor's equity; it may eliminate the need for investment of equity by the investor; it can increase the return to equity; and the interest on the mortgage financing is tax deductible for federal income tax purposes.

If mortgage monies are available from a lender, the investor must contribute the difference between the purchase price and the mortgage funds.

Purchase price of a house	$60,000
(Purchase price = appraised value)	
Less mortgage amount	48,000
(80% of appraised value)	
Equity required	$12,000

If buildings are constructed, the developer-owner must put up equity in the amount of the difference between the total construction cost and the mortgage amount.

Total cost of office building construction	$1,000,000
Less mortgage amount	750,000
(75% of total construction cost)	
Equity required	$ 250,000

In the case of new construction, sometimes the investor contributes equity through the purchase of the land. The land cost is part of the total cost of the structures.

The investor may put up little equity when a large percentage of the total funds is raised in the form of mortgage money. An income property may have three or four mortgages on it; in this case, little equity may be needed to reach the total purchase price or the construction cost.

Purchase price of office building		$1,000,000
(Purchase price = appraised value)		
Less: First mortgage (75% of value)	750,000	
Second mortgage (15% of value)	150,000	
Third mortgage (5% of value)	50,000	950,000
Investor's equity required (5% of value)		$ 50,000

During some real estate and economic conditions, the construction loan amount may equal or exceed the total construction cost. This situation is possible if the appraised value of the completed structure far exceeds the total construction cost. The construction lender always appraises the construction project as if it were completed.

If the appraised value of the completed income property is $2,000,000, total construction costs are $1,400,000, and the lender can make a construction loan that is 75 percent of the appraised value of the completed structure, the investor would not have to spend any cash for the completion of the project.

Construction loan	$1,500,000
(75% of $2,000,000 appraised value)	
Less total construction costs	1,400,000
Surplus funds for investor	$ 100,000

Under such conditions, the investor-developer "mortgages out." The developer may be able to pocket money once the mortgage financing is arranged.

In the latter 1970s, little "mortgaging out" went on to the knowledge of the lenders. Lenders tended to be conservative in their lending practices following the real estate recession of 1974 and 1975. They wanted the developer to commit cash to the venture in order to reduce the lender's risk that the developer would take little interest in the financial success of the income property. If the developer "mortgages out," he or she has little incentive, with no personal or corporate investment in the project, to lease the space adequately and keep costs within reasonable operating limits.

The Effect of Leverage on the Investor's Return on Investment. The use of other people's money in order to increase the return on the owner's investment is often called leverage. The borrowed money is expected to generate a profit on the investment that exceeds the cost of the money to the investor. If the percent return on the total investment exceeds the interest rate on the borrowed money, favorable leverage will result; the percent return on the equity investment will surpass the return that would result from the use of only equity with no borrowed money. For example:

If the total investment is $1,000,000 and the return on the total investment is 10%, or $100,000

If mortgage money is borrowed at a rate of 8% and represents 80% of the total investment

Then return on total investment, or net operating income, is	$100,000
Less interest on the borrowed money, $800,000 × .08	64,000
Return to the equity, $200,000, is	$36,000
Return on the equity, $36,000/$200,000 = 18%	

If the $800,000 had not been borrowed from a mortgage lender, the return on equity would have been only 10% ($100,000/$1,000,000). The above illustration indicates favorable leverage. The return on the total investment exceeded the return required on the borrowed mortgage money. The return on equity increased because of the borrowed money, whose rate of interest was less than the return on the total investment. Continuing with the same example, if the total investment is $1 million and return on the total investment is 10%, or $100,000:

If mortgage money is borrowed at a rate of 12% and represents 80% of the total investment

Then return on total investment, or net operating income, is	$100,000
Less interest on the borrowed money, $800,000 × .12	96,000
Return to the equity, $200,000, is	$4,000
Return on the equity, $4,000/$200,000 = 2%	

This illustration indicates unfavorable leverage. The return on the total investment was less than the return required on the borrowed mortgage money. The return on equity declined because of the use of borrowed money whose rate exceeded the return on the total investment.

Table 4-1. How leverage declines over a period of time

Year	Original Investment	Mortgage Loan Balance	Equity Balance	Loan Principal Repayment	Interest Payment (10% Rate)
0	$1,000,000	$800,000	$200,000		
1		720,000	280,000	$80,000	$80,000
2		640,000	360,000	80,000	80,000
3		560,000	440,000	80,000	80,000

Continuing with the same example:

If the total investment is $1,000,000 and the return on the total investment is 10%, or $100,000

If mortgage money is borrowed at a rate of 10% and represents 80% of the total investment

Then return on total investment, or net operating income, is	$100,000
Less interest on borrowed money, $800,000 × 0.10	80,000
Return to the equity, $200,000, is	$20,000
Return on the equity, $20,000/$200,000 = 10%	

Leverage may not increase the return on equity. If the return on the total investment is the same as the interest rate on the borrowed money, the borrowed money may not increase or decrease the overall return on investment. In this case, the equity and mortgage funds are receiving the same return, 10 percent. This is no advantage in using mortgage monies.

The investor may finance an investment with a mortgage loan. The lender will probably want the borrower to repay the interest and principal over the life of the loan. As the debt service payments (payments on principal and interest) are made, the mortgage amount outstanding declines (Table 4-1). The leverage declines as the mortgage principal is repaid. The leverage may have been favorable when the mortgage loan was negotiated, but this situation changes as time passes. More equity is committed to the project, and less borrowed money is used at the given rate of interest.

The Tax Effects of Mortgage Interest. Mortgage interest is a deductible item for federal income tax purposes. That means that the effective mortgage interest expense is less than it appears. Let's look at two hypothetical situations where net operating income in both cases is $10,000.

Mortgage Interest Expense Not Tax Deductible		Mortgage Interest Expense Tax Deductible	
Net operating income without the deduction of mortgage interest expense	$10,000	Net operating income	$10,000
		Less mortgage interest expense	2,000
		Taxable income	8,000
Less taxes, assuming a tax rate of 40%	4,000	Less taxes, assuming a tax rate of 40%	3,200
After-tax income	$ 6,000	After-tax income	$ 4,800

Mortgage Financing and Leverage

Since mortgage interest expense is tax deductible, a short-cut method for determining how much tax expense is saved is the multiplication of the deductible amount times the tax rate. In this case, the reduction in taxes was $800; mortgage interest expense ($2,000) times 40 percent, the tax rate, equals $800. Therefore, the effective mortgage interest expense on an after-tax basis is $1,200. Taxpayers in the higher income brackets appreciate the lower effective expense of tax-deductible items. Many real estate investors fall into this category.

THE EFFECT OF MORTGAGE FINANCING ON LENDER RULES OF THUMB

When an investor is seeking mortgage funds, he or she finds that the lender has several financial rules of thumb that are the standards by which prospective mortgage loans are accepted or rejected. The lender can add mortgage financing to his project financing as long as the typical lender rules of thumb are not violated.

The Typical Breakeven Ratio. Lenders usually have a range of breakeven ratios that are pertinent to the financing of each type of income property. In the process, they normally define the breakeven ratio as operating expenses and debt service requirement divided by gross income. As the prospective owner finances his project, his initial breakeven ratio with only a first mortgage loan may be 75 percent. As a second mortgage is placed on the property, the breakeven ratio may rise to 85 percent, which may be acceptable to most lenders interested in financing the project. If the investor considers placing a third mortgage on the property, the breakeven ratio may rise to 90 percent, which may be outside a lender's range of permissible breakeven ratios. Too much leverage may repel the lender who is approached for more mortgage money.

The Typical Loan-to-Value Ratio. As a lender considers a mortgage loan on an investor's property, the lender considers the loan-to-value ratio established by previous mortgage financing. The loan-to-value ratio is defined, of course, as the ratio of the loan amount to the appraised value. The lender also considers the resulting overall loan-to-value ratio once the additional loan is placed on the property, particularly examining the margin of safety left in the appraised value for instances of higher than average vacancy rates, higher than average operating expenses, and lower than forecasted rental income. The additional mortgage financing may or may not leave a sufficient margin of value in the project to cover all contingencies.

The Typical Loan Amount per Unit. The investor must realize that the lender usually keeps track of the loan amount per unit of the project as a key element for the acceptance or rejection of additional financing. Excessive leverage would create a loan per unit in excess of acceptable limits. The use of a reasonable amount of leverage would create a loan per unit within an acceptable range for the lender.

The Typical Debt Service Coverage Requirement. The lender wants to know that the net operating income of an investment will more than cover the estimated debt service. Therefore, one rule of thumb is the debt service coverage.

$$\text{Debt service coverage} = \frac{\text{Net operating income}}{\text{Debt service}}$$

Lenders often expect this ratio to indicate a factor of 1.25 to 1.6. The danger of not meeting the required ratio lies in adding too much debt, so that the total debt service increases too much, while the net operating income remains the same. The debt service coverage factor is one of the limitations on the use of leverage.

THE STRATEGIC TERMS OF A MORTGAGE

Generally the real estate investor is vitally interested in negotiating for a good mortgage that fits the cash flow projections for the investment property. In general, the investor is looking for relatively long terms; a reasonable, fixed rate of interest; perhaps lender participation in a percentage of the gross or net income beyond a specified amount; no prepayment penalty; and amortization with interest only for the early years of the mortgage.

Certain clauses of the mortgage are often closely examined by the investor. Among these clauses are the provisions for a variable rate of interest, an assignment of rents, the approval of subordinated financing, and the amortization plan. The investor examines the need for a balloon payment at the end of the mortgage and the loan constant built into the mortgage repayment. In the next section the reader will find a few of these considerations dealt with at some length.

A Relatively Long Mortgage Term. Generally, the longer the term of the mortgage, the lower the periodic debt service payments. Before looking at some examples that illustrate this point, let us consider the definition of loan constant. A loan constant is a factor based on the interest rate and the term of the mortgage, multiplied by the number of thousands of dollars borrowed, to find the monthly mortgage payment due on a level-payment full amortization plan.

Turning to illustrations of the debt service requirements with regard to the mortgage rate and the mortgage term, we first observe that

> If the mortgage rate is 10% and
> the term of the loan is 10 years (120 months),
> the loan constant is 13.22.
> If the loan amount were $100,000,
> the monthly mortgage payment would be 13.22 × 100 = $1,322.
>
> If the only change were a 20-year term for the loan,
> the loan constant would be 9.66 and
> the monthly mortgage payment would be 9.66 × 100 = $966.
>
> If the loan were longer—say, a 30-year term—
> the loan constant would be 8.78 and
> the monthly mortgage payment would be 8.78 × 100 = $878.

As the mortgage payments decline, the return to the investor before and after taxes increases.

Reasonable Interest Rate and Possible Lender Participation in Income. Generally, the lender has a competitive rate in mind for the owner's mortgage. That competitive rate may be a fixed rate of interest or it may be a variable rate of interest. The variable rate usually is subject to change every six months if a money and capital market index indicates a change is needed. The index may consist of short-term money market and longer-term capital market rates.

If the lender is offering a fixed rate of interest on the mortgage, he or she may express an interest in participating in the success of the investment property. The lender may want a percentage of the gross or net income on a periodic basis to supplement the interest proceeds. Lender participation usually involves only a percentage of the gross or net income above a specified amount. Since the early 1960s the combination of fixed rate of interest and lender participation in profits has been in wide use. In the latter 1960s and the early 1970s, the variable-rate mortgage also became quite popular among the lenders as an inflation hedge.

Low or No Prepayment Penalty. This element of a mortgage tends to be more important to those who are financing a house than to those who are financing investment properties. As long as the revenue and net operating income cover debt service requirements, the investor usually has no reason to pay off the mortgage in advance of its maturity date. Homeowners, on the other hand, usually want to pay off the debt as soon as they can. They get tired of meeting high mortgage payments and want to reduce the amount of mortgage interest.

Some prepayment penalties seek penalties of several months' payments in advance. Some lenders will stipulate a percentage of the loan that must be paid as a penalty for early payment. The percentage of the loan established as a prepayment penalty usually declines the longer a mortgage has been in effect.

Interest-Only Amortization. Many income property owners desire interest-only amortization plans for the first few years of the mortgage. After the interest-only period, the higher-than-usual mortgage payments with principal repayment start. The mortgage payments that partially amortize the debt each payment period may completely repay the loan within the mortgage term, or a balloon payment may be required at the maturity of the loan. When an investor negotiates and receives terms that include a balloon payment at maturity, he or she usually faces lower-than-average debt service payments over the terms of the loan, and the sale proceeds are used to pay off the remaining loan balance. The mortgage may also be refinanced at a lower rate of interest or on better terms before the balloon payment is due.

A Good Overall Amortization Plan. In addition to an interest-only amortization schedule for the first few years, the prospective mortgagor should consider the following features of amortization plans:

1. There may be a lower-than-normal loan constant with a balloon payment at the end of the loan.
2. The term of the loan may vary:
   a. If the lender offers a fully amortized loan, the investor can negotiate for the longest term in order to reduce the debt service requirement.
   b. If the lender offers a relatively short-term loan, instead of high debt service payments on a fully amortized basis, the prospective investor may negotiate for a partially amortized loan with a balloon payment at the end of the loan.
3. There may be a step-up amortization plan in which the early loan payment schedule gradually moves from lower-than-normal debt service payments to normal or above-normal debt service payments within a 5- to 10-year period of a 30- to 40-year loan.

The Assignment of Rents. The lender often wants an assignment of rents clause in the income property mortgage. If the mortgagor should default on the loan, the assignment of rents causes the title to the property rents to be immediately transferred to the mortgagee. However, the mortgagor's best interests may not be served by this mortgage clause. In the case of loan default, the borrower may still want to collect the rents and apply the funds to the operating expenses in the best way possible. The lender may be afraid that the borrower will apply the rents from the subject property to other income properties owned by the investor-mortgagor.

The Provision for Further Subordinated Financing. The property owner may wish to further finance the property. Because of the capital constraints of the owner and the desire for favorable leverage from mortgage financing, the owner may wish to place several loans on the property. The owner should assure himself or herself that further financing will be permitted by the lender or mortgage insuror of the previous mortgage.

THE TYPES OF REAL ESTATE LOANS ON HOUSES AND INCOME PROPERTIES

Financing of Residential Property

Lenders grant different kinds of loans on houses from the ones they grant on income properties. Income properties require substantial sums for the various stages of real estate development. House lots are usually developed, so that the buyer merely finances the cost of the developed lot plus the construction or purchase of the house. Other development requires funds for land acquisition, land development, building construction, and permanent financing. Income property financing is far more complicated from the borrower's and the lender's points of view.

House financing may involve land loans, construction loans, and permanent loans. House loans can also be categorized by type of loan, such as Federal Housing Administration-insured, Veterans Administration-guaranteed, and conventional.

Financing the Lot. The buyer may not have enough cash or may not want to pay cash for the house lot or acreage. A few traditional lenders, such as real estate investment trusts, finance land loans. Landowners quite often finance the house lot that they sell. Usually the landowner finances the purchase with a purchase-money mortgage or a land contract. In either case, the landowner receives a return on the invested funds. The purchase-money mortgage calls for the immediate transfer of title to the land and the future repayment of the principal and interest over the term of the loan. The land contract does not provide for immediate transfer of title. In fact, the landowner may sell the land to several customers before a buyer pays enough on the contract to acquire equitable or normal title. When the buyer defaults on a land contract, the landowner regains possession and usually retains the mortgage monies previously paid. Since the landowner retains title to the land, he or she may again sell the land.

Financing House Construction. If a builder or an individual wants to build a house, several traditional lenders will make funds available. The savings and loan association often contracts with the borrower on the basis of a building-loan agreement. The savings and loan association, in this case, finances both the construction and the permanent loans under the same agreement. Commercial banks also finance construction loans for house construction. They treat construction loans as commercial loans rather than as mortgage loans. The real estate collateral is nonexistent until the construction job is finished; therefore, commercial banks think of construction loans as loans based on the credit of the owner or builder. Another department or subsidiary company of the bank finances permanent house loans. Mortgage companies finance construction and permanent loans with the funds from their mortgage loan correspondents. Often the lender correspondents want to invest in a sizable package of house construction and permanent loans. Many loan correspondents, such as life insurance companies, mutual savings banks, pension funds, and endowment funds, have substantial funds to invest continually. Therefore, they prefer relatively large investment packages of home mortgages.

Financing the Permanent Loan on a House. When the home buyer looks for permanent mortgage financing, he or she investigates the financing plans available. If the buyer is a veteran of the military service during specified military campaigns, three types of permanent home loans are available: Veterans Administration–guaranteed loans, FHA-insured loans for veterans, and conventional loans. If the home buyer has a low or moderate income or has had a house displaced by an urban renewal or other such public project, several types of FHA-insured permanent loan plans are available. VA-guaranteed loans are also available to the low- and moderate-income home buyer. If the home buyer is in the middle- or high-income bracket and has accumulated wealth, conventional home mortgage loans are available. Veterans Administration–guaranteed home loans are available to veterans of the military service of any income level. FHA-insured loan programs cater only to home buyers of low and middle incomes. Therefore, home buyers with middle incomes are usually eligible for VA-guaranteed, FHA-insured, and conventional home loans. Eligibility for individual loans depends on the mortgage loan program requirements, the lender's loan requirements, the requirements of the institutional regulatory agencies, and the credit status of the prospective mortgagor.

Veterans Administration–guaranteed home mortgage loans. The VA-guaranteed home loans usually require no downpayment. In most cases, if a lender makes the VA-guaranteed loan, the mortgagor gets 100 percent financing. The veterans with approved loan guarantee eligibility may pay some closing costs as part of the loan closing. Generally the veteran is not permitted to pay any required discount points; the seller or the builder usually must pay the "points." The mortgage interest rate is set at the current FHA–VA interest rate, established by the U.S. Department of Housing and Urban Development with the approval of Congress.

The lender considers the VA loan a low-risk investment, since the maximum loan guarantee is $25,000 on the top part of the loan. Usually, if the borrower defaults on the loan, the default occurs in the first two to three years. If the lender sustains a loss on the resale of the foreclosed property, the Veterans Administration will pay up to $25,000 of the proved loss. However, the guarantee on the loan is not necessarily $25,000. The guarantee is either 60 percent of the appraised value of the property at the time the loan is closed or $25,000, whichever is less.

The veteran may purchase more than one home on a VA-guaranteed basis. It depends on the increase over time of the Veterans Administration guarantee for veterans, the unused eligibility of individual veterans, and the repayment of the previous house loan. The veteran may permit a buyer of his or her property to assume a VA loan with the approval of the Veterans Administration and the lender of the funds. The Veterans Administration makes no monies available; a private lender must provide the funds to the mortgagor. The Veterans Administration sets no maximum loan limit, but the lenders often set such limits. The loan term is usually 30 years.

Federal Housing Administration–insured home mortgage loans. The U.S. Department of Housing and Urban Development has many home mortgage insurance programs for low- and middle-income home buyers and apartment developers. A few of these programs involve subsidized rent and interest payments. The most popular FHA-insured mortgage loan program over the years since 1934, the year of the establishment of FHA, has been the FHA 203(b) program for unsubsidized middle-income housing.

If the home buyer qualifies for an FHA 203(b) insured mortgage, the downpayment on the first $25,000 of the loan is 3 percent; the downpayment on the amount of the loan over $25,000 is 5 percent. According to the 1977 Housing and Community Development Act, the maximum FHA 203(b) loan is $60,000. The interest rate on the loan must be the FHA-VA administered rate. If this interest rate happens to differ from the market rate of interest, discount points may be required of the seller or the builder. Every discount point equals approximately 1 percent of the mortgage amount. To the lender, the payment of one point means approximately the addition of $1/8$ percent to the nominal yield. If points must be paid, the seller or builder pays the lender this interest in advance at the closing of the loan.

One-half of one percent of the outstanding average annual mortgage amount must be paid to the U.S. Department of Housing and Urban Development (HUD) each year. This annual sum insures the mortgage loan in favor of the lender. If the property owner defaults on the insured loan, HUD covers the loss of the lender, usually by paying the lender the loss amount in the form of interest-bearing bonds.

The mortgagor borrowing by means of a VA-guaranteed or an FHA 203(b) insured mortgage loan encounters the need for monthly payments into an escrow account of one-twelfth of estimated annual hazard insurance premium, the estimated annual property tax payment, and the annual FHA insurance premium. The payment into escrow each month is added to the regular mortgage payment covering interest and principal. The lender origination fees payable at loan closing are usually 1 percent of the loan amount for both FHA 203(b) and VA-guaranteed loans.

Since the 1977 Housing and Community Development Act, graduated payment mortgage insurance may be obtained under the FHA 245 program. Several graduated payment amortization schedules are available to the home buyer. Generally, the early payments are lower than normal payments. The payments are gradually increased in steps until, five to ten years into the mortgage term, the monthly payments rise above normal payments and stabilize on the final step of the payment schedule. These mortgages are designed for people with rapidly rising incomes, such as college graduates beginning their careers.

There are five plans available under the FHA 245 program:

Plan I.   Monthly mortgage payments increase 2.5% each year for five years. Beginning with the sixth year and through the thirtieth year, the monthly payments will remain basically the same.

Plan II.   Monthly mortgage payments increase 5% each year for five years. Beginning with the sixth year and through the thirtieth year, the monthly payments will remain basically the same.

Plan III.   Monthly mortgage payments increase 7.5% for five years. Beginning with the sixth year and through the thirtieth year, the monthly payments will remain basically the same.

Plan IV.   Monthly mortgage payments increase 2% each year for ten years. Beginning with the eleventh year and through the thirtieth year, the payments will remain basically the same.

Plan V. Monthly mortgage payments increase 3% each year for ten years. Beginning with the eleventh year and through the thirtieth year, the monthly payments will remain basically the same.

Of the five-year plans, Plan I requires the least downpayment and has the least deferred interest. Plan II requires more downpayment and has more deferred interest than Plan I. Plan III appears to be the most popular, as it affords the lowest initial principal and interest payment of any of the plans, thus enabling more purchasers to qualify. It does, however, require the most downpayment, the most deferred interest, and the greatest change in the principal and interest. Of the two ten-year plans, Plan IV has the least downpayment, deferred interest, and change in principal and interest. Plan V has the most downpayment, deferred interest, and change in principal and interest of the two ten-year plans.

The minimum downpayment under the FHA 245 program will, in most cases, be greater than that required under the standard FHA 203(b) mortgage program. Because payments in the early years of these plans frequently do not fully cover the amount of interest due on the loan, the outstanding principal will increase (negative amortization). The FHA 245 plan allows prospects who would not otherwise qualify to buy houses. For FHA mortgage loan insurance HUD requires that housing expense not exceed 35 percent of net effective income and that total fixed payments not exceed 50 percent of net effective income.

Conventional home loans. Any mortgage loan that is not guaranteed by the Veterans Administration or insured by the U.S. Department of Housing and Urban Development is usually called a conventional loan. This third type of home loan may be insured by a private mortgage insurance company. Typical downpayments on conventional noninsured loans are 20 to 25 percent of appraised value at the time the loan is closed. Higher ratio loans can perhaps be acquired, but private mortgage insurance coverage is usually required in such cases. The insurance premium schedule is more flexible than the FHA insurance program. A higher initial premium may be paid, and annual insurance premiums may last only 5 to 10 years of the mortgage term. A term of 20 to 25 years is common for conventional loans, in contrast to the typical 30-year VA and FHA loans. Most home mortgage loans are conventional loans (Exhibit 4-1).

Nonstandard variable-rate home loans fall into the category of conventional home loans. The variable elements tend to be the interest rate and the term of the loan. As these terms change, the monthly mortgage payment changes. If a money and capital market index moves sufficiently every six months, the associated mortgage interest rate is changed in the direction of the index change in six-month intervals. If the borrower, at the same time, prefers level mortgage payments, the length of the mortgage is changed, rather than the interest rate and the succeeding mortgage payments.

California state-chartered financial institutions and federally chartered savings and loan associations may offer variable rate mortgages. All federally chartered savings and loan associations in the country may offer graduated payment and reverse annuity mortgages, according to a ruling of the Federal Home Loan Bank Board in December 1978. The savings and loan variable-rate mortgages permit interest rate increases of .5 percent a year, with a maximum increase from the original rate of 2.5 percent. There is no limit on how far the variable rate may fall. Federally chartered savings and loan associations in California are limited in their variable rate mortgage investments to 50 percent of their home mortgage loans in a year. The state-chartered California financial institutions do not have this investment restriction.

Exhibit 4-1. *The Type of Financing in Terms of Percent of New Privately Owned Housing Units 1967-1975*

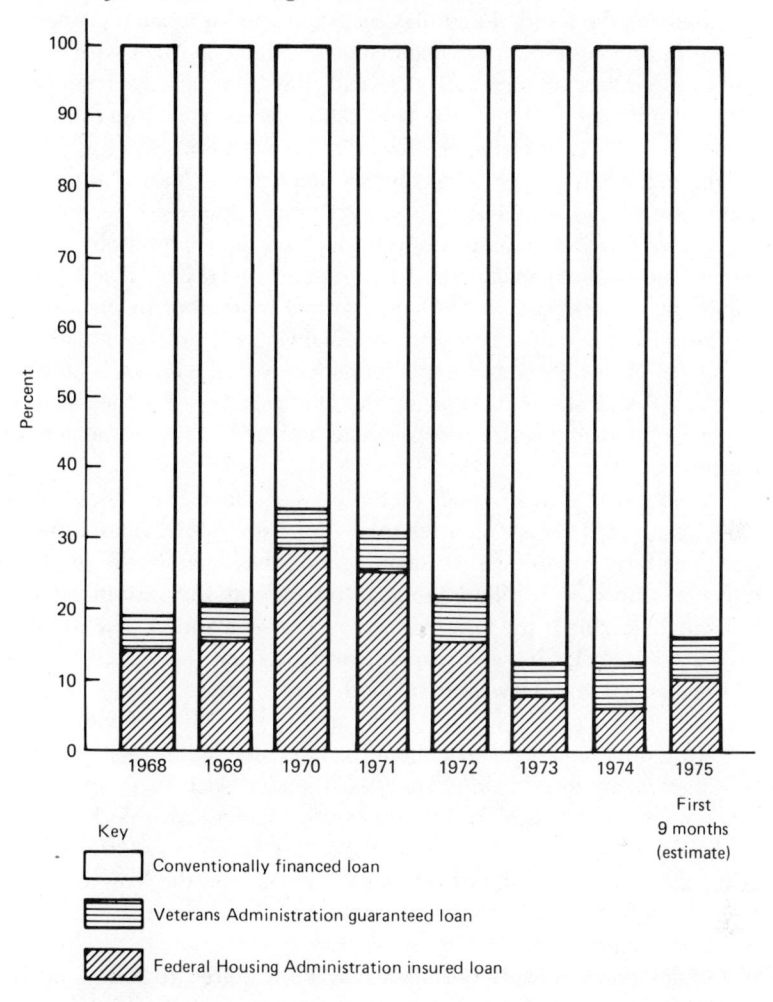

Key:
- Conventionally financed loan
- Veterans Administration guaranteed loan
- Federal Housing Administration insured loan

1975: First 9 months (estimate)

Source: 1967-1974: U.S. Dept. of Housing and Urban Development, *1974 Statistical Yearbook*, 1976, p. 243. 1975: Board of Governors of the Federal Reserve System, *Federal Reserve Bulletin*, November 1975, p. 714.

When a homeowner negotiates a reverse annuity mortgage from a federally chartered savings and loan association, the savings and loan agrees to make payments to the homeowner in return for a claim on the value of the home. The mortgage program appeals to older homeowners who have paid off their mortgages or who have large amounts of equity in their homes. The savings and loan gets a first lien on the property that is repaid when the homeowner sells the house or when the estate sells it after the owner's death.

Income Property Financing

Income property loans can be categorized by type of loan, such as FHA-insured and conventional loans. On the basis of the stage of real estate development, income property loans are classified as land, development, construction, gap, permanent, and wraparound loans.

Financing the Land. Land may be purchased for income property development by outright payment of cash, by negotiation of a land contract with the seller, by negotiation of a purchase-money mortgage with the seller, and by negotiation of a land loan with a traditional lender. If the land is bought outright, it may serve as the equity for the income property financing. This is often the case.

The seller may prefer land contract financing because of the delayed title transfer and the receipt of installment payments, which defer and spread out the capital gains tax burden. The seller retains title to the land until the purchaser has paid part or all of the land contract payments. Upon default, the seller retains title, and usually, the monies previously paid on the land contract by the borrower-buyer.

The land seller may agree to the financing of the buyer with a purchase-money mortgage. The seller conveys title immediately to the buyer. As the buyer finances the purchase, he or she is mortgaging the land in return for the financing. The periodic mortgage payments repay the principal and give an investment return to the seller-mortgagee.

A lender may provide funds on the basis of a land loan. For example, a commercial bank may provide funds on a relatively low loan-to-loan value ratio, high interest rate, and short-term basis. In case of loan default, the bank or other such lender might have difficulty immediately selling the land to recapture the outstanding capital. Land tends to be more salable if the improvements have been added. The primary sources of land loans have historically been commercial banks and real estate investment trusts.

Financing Land Development and Construction. As the developer adds streets, curbs, gutters, water, sewers, gas, electricity, and cable television lines to the land for later structural improvements, money is often needed. A relatively costly development loan may be acquired from a traditional lender, such as a commercial bank or a real estate investment trust. The interest rate is usually high—perhaps three to four points above the bank prime or commercial paper rate— the term is just long enough to cover the reasonable land development period, and the loan-to-value ratio may range from 70 to 80 percent. The typical loan-to-value ratios may permit total financing of the construction costs.

In addition, a construction loan may be acquired to follow up the land development. The same sources and general loan terms apply to this type of income property loan. The loan covers the normal construction period. If the land is being developed in phases, the development and construction loans earlier committed by the institution may be taken down in phases. When one phase is completed, the lender may release the next sum of money for the development of the next phase. Receipts from some land sales and ground rentals may be used to repay at least partially the development and construction loans. The primary source of funds for development and construction loan repayment is the permanent loan on the development.

Gap Loans. If the developer has difficulty getting a permanent loan, a gap loan might be acquired from a commercial bank or real estate investment trust, until a permanent commitment is obtained. If the lender who is not in a position to give the developer a permanent loan now might be interested in funding the permanent loan later, this lender might extend a gap loan at a relatively moderate rate of interest on a short-term basis, so that the developer has time to find good permanent financing. If the gap lender does not want to fund the permanent loan, this lender will charge relatively high rates for the standby loan and standby commitment to fund the permanent loan when the gap loan term runs out. In the latter case, the gap loan rate may be set several points above the bank prime.

Permanent Financing. Several permanent loans may be placed on an income property. The first mortgage loan is often 75 to 80 percent of value, runs for 20 to 30 years, has a variable yield to the lender, and is usually not insured by a private or public insurance organization. The lender may participate in the cash flow, in the gross revenue, or in the net profit. The interest rate may also fluctuate with the bank prime or commercial paper rate.

The permanent financing usually pays off the earlier negotiated loans on the development. Otherwise, if the investor is merely purchasing an existing investment property, the permanent financing provides a longer term loan for the gradual repayment of the principal and the interest. The investor may intend to hold the property for a few years or may plan to sell shortly and permit the buyer to assume the favorable permanent loans.

Wraparound Loans. If the investor needs more funds after the property has been held for some time, he or she may not find it advantageous to refinance the loans already on the property. The monies may be needed for structural improvements, additions, or further phases of development. The owner may approach an existing or a new lender and ask for more funds in the form of a wraparound loan. An additional junior loan—a wraparound loan—may be financed by the existing or new lender. The lender advances more funds and asks the mortgagor to pay a larger total amount in mortgage payments. Thereafter, the mortgagor pays the increased amount of debt service to the wraparound lender, who pays the first mortgage lender the amounts due and retains the residual amount. The residual amount gives the lender a substantial return on the new junior mortgage loan. The total new debt service may provide a good overall return to the existing lender and the new lender and would still be a lower yield than the mortgagor would have to give a lender who would refinance in total the original loan.

SUMMARY

Most investors need borrowed money in order to purchase or develop the properties that they are interested in acquiring. Mortgage financing, therefore, usually supplements the investor's equity. Sometimes mortgage financing eliminates the need for equity investment. If the lender's loan-to-value ratio applied to the appraised value results in a loan that equals or surpasses construction cost or acquisition cost, the investor needs to add no equity to the investment.

The use of leverage, or in other words, borrowed money, for real estate investment may magnify the investor's return on the equity investment. If leverage is favorable, the cost of borrowed funds is less than the overall return received on the total investment. On the other hand, if the cost of borrowed funds is equal to or more than the return on total investment, leverage is unfavorable, and the investor's return on equity declines through the use of borrowed money.

When a loan is amortized, the borrower periodically repays a part of the principal amount borrowed. Therefore, amortization of a loan means that leverage declines with time if more funds are not borrowed. Taking another view of leverage, we notice that mortgage interest is tax deductible for federal income tax purposes. Most investors in the higher tax brackets consider this a favorable aspect of borrowed money.

Mortgage lenders usually observe certain rules of thumb in making loans to prospective borrowers. Additional mortgage financing may create acceptable or unacceptable breakeven ratios, loan-to-value ratios, and loan amounts per unit. The investor needs to consider the lender's viewpoint in approaching the lender for additional funds.

When prospective income property mortgagors request a loan, they are usually looking for a relatively long mortgage term, a reasonable interest rate, reasonable lender participation in income if this is necessary, low or no prepayment penalty, interest-only amortization for the first few years of the loan, a good overall amortization plan, no assignment of rents in the event of default, and a provision permitting further subordinated financing.

Home financing often requires the financing of the lot and the house construction. A permanent loan is usually needed to repay the construction loan or merely to finance the purchase of the existing house. The three types of permanent loans for house financing are Veterans Administration-guaranteed loans, Federal Housing Administration-insured loans, and conventional home loans.

Income property financing often involves the financing of the land acquisition, land development, and building construction. If a permanent loan commitment from a lender is not immediately forthcoming, a gap loan may fill the time between the construction loan maturity and the eventual permanent loan commitment. Once permanent financing is acquired, a wraparound loan may be needed later, after the project has been successfully initiated, in order to develop additional phases of the undertaking or to make further improvements.

Key Terms and Concepts

Mortgaging out
Construction loan
Rules of thumb
Debt financing
Breakeven ratio
Loan-to-value ratio
Designated appraiser
Income property valuation
Prepayment penalty
Loan constant
Loan default
Real estate collateral
Subsidized rent
FHA 203(b) program
FHA 245 graduated payment mortgage insurance
Permanent loan commitment
Debt service coverage
Return on investment
Energy conservation
Solar heating systems
Prepayment plan
Interest-only amortization
Appraisal trade associations

Investor's equity
Tax deductibility
Variable rate of interest
Fully amortized loan
Capital constraints
VA loan eligibility
Subsidized interest payments
Escrow account
Private mortgage insurance
Land loan
Construction loan
Wraparound loan
Balloon payment
Net operating income
Money and capital market indices
Subordinated financing
Refinancing
Junior mortgages
Income capitalization methods
Favorable and unfavorable leverage
Lender participation
Assignment of rents
Step-up amortization plan
Purchase money mortgage

FHA-VA interest rate
Discount points
Hazard insurance premium

Land contract financing
Land development loan
Gap loan

Questions for Student Self-examination

Multiple-Choice Questions

1. In which way may mortgage financing be important to the investor?
   a. it may increase the return to equity
   b. mortgage interest is tax deductible for federal income tax purposes
   c. a and b
   d. none of the above

2. The construction loan amount may _____ the total construction costs.
   a. equal
   b. exceed
   c. be less than
   d. all of the above

3. Leverage _____ with time as the mortgage principal is repaid.
   a. stays the same
   b. increases
   c. decreases
   d. none of the above

4. Lenders normally define the _____ as operating expenses and debt service requirement divided by gross income.
   a. loan-to-value ratio
   b. debt service coverage
   c. breakeven ratio
   d. operating expense ratio

5. The lender often expects the debt service coverage to be _____ before funding the prospective loan.
   a. 0.25 to 0.35
   b. 2.6 to 4.2
   c. 0.62 to 0.65
   d. 1.25 to 1.6

True-False Questions

T F 1. The debt financing the lender permits determines the level of the breakeven ratio, the debt service coverage, and the return on investment.
T F 2. Mortgage financing usually supplements the equity contributed by the investor and decreases the return on the investor's equity.
T F 3. The relationship between the amount of the mortgage loan and the amount of the appraised value is called the loan-to-value ratio.
T F 4. The use of leverage may be favorable or it may be unfavorable.
T F 5. If buildings are constructed, the developer-owner must put up equity in the amount of the difference between the appraised value and the mortgage amounts.
T F 6. As in house financing, an income property has one mortgage on it.

T F 7. The construction lender always appraises the construction project as if it were completed.
T F 8. In the late 1970s, "mortgaging out" occurred frequently.
T F 9. A short-cut method for determining how much tax expense is saved is the multiplication of the deductible amount times the tax rate.
T F 10. The breakeven ratio is calculated by dividing debt service required into net operating income.

Answers
Multiple-Choice: 1c, 2d, 3c, 4c, 5d.
True-False: 1T, 2F, 3T, 4T, 5F, 6F, 7T, 8F, 9T, 10F.

Problems

1. If a prospective investor has $10,000 for a house downpayment, how may the rest of the money required for the $50,000 house be raised?

2. If the owner's return on total investment is 9 percent and the borrowed money requires interest payment at the rate of 11 percent, is the owner's leverage positive or negative? Is the owner's rate of return on investment increased or decreased by the borrowing of the money?

3. If the owner of a house has a taxable income of $15,000, makes an annual payment toward mortgage principal of $800, and makes an annual payment toward mortgage interest of $3,600, what is the taxable income once the deductible amounts associated with mortgage payments are subtracted?

4. If an apartment project is appraised for $360,000, was originally purchased for $400,000, and the mortgage amount is $270,000, what is the loan-to-value ratio?

5. If the annual net income available for the payment of debt service is $15,000 and the annual debt service is $12,000, what is the debt service coverage ratio or factor?

6. If an apartment net income is $28,000, the gross income $37,000, the operating expenses $9,000, and the debt service payment $10,000, what is the breakeven ratio of the apartment investment?

Chapter 5

Loan Application and Analysis

Introduction

The Relationship of This Chapter to Other Chapters of the Text

Applying for a Mortgage Loan
  The System for Applying for a Mortgage Loan   Shopping the Market   The Personal Interview and Loan Application: *Determination of the borrower's objectives, Determination of the borrower's capacity and intention to repay the loan, The nature of the home loan application, The nature of an income property loan application*   Credit Investigation   The Appraisal of the Property

Ratio Analysis

Ratio Analysis and the Home Loan Application
  General Home Price and Mortgage Ratios   Commonly Used Credit Guidelines for Home Loans: *FHA credit guidelines for nonsubsidized home mortgage loans, FHLMC credit guidelines, FNMA credit guidelines*

Ratio Analysis and the Income Property Loan Application
  Usual Required Financial Documents: *The balance sheet, The profit-and-loss statement, The flow-of-funds statement, The statement of changes in net worth*   Common Financial and Credit Ratios

Summary

Key Terms and Concepts

Questions for Student Self-examination

LEARNING OBJECTIVES After studying this chapter, you should be familiar with

The system for applying for a mortgage loan
The method of "shopping the market" for a mortgage loan
The method of taking a loan application through a personal interview
The nature of the credit investigation
The need for the appraisal of collateral property
Mortgage-lender ratio analysis
Commonly used credit guidelines for home loans
The usual company financial documents requested by mortgage lenders
Some of the financial and credit ratios examined from company statements

When the prospective investor starts to look for mortgage money, there is usually a lot of uncertainty about the current sources, the costs of each of the possible sources, and what the lenders' requirements are. The prospective borrower may not be up to date concerning mortgage market conditions and the availability of funds from local mortgage sources. Both first-time and experienced investors may want to review the process of loan acquisition in order to find the best mortgage financing. A better knowledge of current conditions and the relative costs of funds from various sources may mean a lower debt service, more funds, a more advantageous amortization plan, and fewer limitations built into the mortgage.

INTRODUCTION

This chapter reviews the loan acquisition process in terms of loan application and lender analysis. The system for finding suitable mortgage money and applying for it is discussed. Some stress is placed on shopping around before formal loan application. There is a review of the information about the prospective mortgagor that the lender usually must have.

Credit investigation is an important part of the loan review. The sources of credit information are surveyed. Later, in the discussion of ratio analysis, the information from the credit investigation is incorporated into loan ratio analysis for house and income property financing. Standard ratios for loan acceptance or rejection are used by many lenders and mortgage insurors, including the U.S. Department of Housing and Urban Development, the Federal National Mortgage Association, and the Federal Home Loan Mortgage Corporation. Some of the standard ratios affecting FHA, VA, and conventional loans are presented.

THE RELATIONSHIP OF THIS CHAPTER TO OTHER CHAPTERS OF THE TEXT

Since loan acquisition is an important subject to the real estate investor, four chapters of the text are devoted to the topic. After studying mortgage financing and leverage in Chapter 4, the reader surveys the loan application procedure and the lender's system of loan analysis in this chapter. Since these procedures and systems tend to apply to all mortgage lenders, Chapter 6 takes up institutional sources of funds and their relative costs.

Chapters 7 and 8 are devoted to real estate appraising, which is an important part of loan analysis and acquisition. The appraisal of the house or the income property may determine whether the loan will be made and, if the loan is accepted, what amount will be loaned. Since the investor should be familiar with the appraisal process, Chapter 7 is devoted to the principles of real estate appraising as applied to home appraisal. Chapter 8 is devoted to a brief review of income property appraisal principles and practices.

APPLYING FOR A MORTGAGE LOAN

Once the prospective investor has decided that mortgage funds are needed to proceed with the purchase of real property, he or she must scout the market for mortgage money and apply for a loan at the appropriate institutions or from the appropriate individual.

The System for Applying for a Mortgage Loan. In general, the prospective borrower should first "shop the market" for mortgage money. Then the most appropriate lenders should be approached. A personal interview may result in a loan application being taken. The prospective borrower may decline the offered mortgage terms, or the lender may reject the initial loan application. If the initial lender-borrower negotiation is favorable, the application will be completed by the lender running a credit check and employing a real estate appraiser to value the subject property. If the prospective borrower is a business entity, the borrower will be asked to submit audited financial statements for the past three to five years. From the financial data gathered, the lender engages in ratio analysis to determine whether the loan should be submitted to the institutional investment committee for acceptance or rejection. If the ratios justify the loan officer's submission of the loan to the investment committee, the committee can accept the desired terms, reject the terms, or accept the loan on modified terms.

Shopping the Market. To narrow down the group of possible lenders to the best one or two possibilities, the prospective mortgagor should shop the market. The prospective mortgagor might call friends and acquaintances for advice about the sources of the best loan terms for the type of investment at stake. A few sources of funds may stand out from the numerous possible sources. Then the prospective mortgagor can call or write the individual lenders who have been highly recommended. Each inquiry, with its specific questions about loan terms appropriate to the house or income property, will narrow the choice. Repeated calls or letters may be needed to investigate the sources before an appointment for a personal interview is made.

The Personal Interview and Loan Application. A lending institution usually requires a personal interview of the prospective mortgagor with a mortgage loan officer or other executive of the lending institution. The prospective mortgagor may or may not actually fill in a loan application. The loan officer may merely ask questions and make notes after the interview about the responses to the questions. Structured loan applications, sometimes even specifically designed for the individual lender, may be used.

Determination of the borrower's objectives. If a house loan is sought, the loan officer needs to determine whether the mortgagor will be an occupant or will be renting the premises. The lender may modify the loan terms if the mortgagor will not be an occupant. For example, FHA-insured loans usually are more stringent if the mortgagor will not be an occupant of the mortgaged property.

If an income property loan is sought, the loan officer must be sensitive to the principal investment motivations of the prospective mortgagor. If the mortgagor is a nonprofit entity, the tax consequences are irrelevant. If the borrower is subject to a high tax rate, the tax-shelter provisions of the investment may be most important. The tax-deductible mortgage interest and depreciation will have top priority in that investor's mind. If the mortgagor is subject to relatively high tax rates but already has enough tax shields, such as excess depreciation, the cash flow from the investment may be most important. If the borrower plans to expand the real estate project and refinance in perhaps five years, he or she will not want a prepayment penalty clause that will not permit this refinancing. Instead, the mortgagor will want the lowest possible prepayment penalty around the five-year point.

Mortgagors have personal preferences based on their egos, prejudices, and financial and social backgrounds. Maybe a relatively low interest rate is a "must" for the mortgagor. The lender might be able to accommodate with a below-market interest rate, but might ask for interest in advance in the form of discount points at the loan closing. Wraparound loans may be underwritten with relatively modest rates, but the junior lender's effective rate may be relatively high. The mortgagor can publicly quote, though, the relatively modest rate on the new wraparound loan.

Determination of the borrower's capacity and intention to repay the loan. The application for a house or an income property loan should establish the borrower's financial capacity and intention to repay the loan. The borrower's financial capacity is shown in several ways: (1) personal wealth; (2) current deposit balances at financial institutions; (3) stabilized annual income from wages, salary, rents, interest, and dividends; (4) stabilized normal living expenses, including total estimated housing expense; (5) any installment debt of more than eight months; (6) the downpayment required for the real estate purchase or construction; and (7) the property cash flow to equity each year before the payment of debt service and federal income taxes.

The buyer's intention to repay the loan being negotiated may be surmised indirectly. The lender may acquire previous repayment patterns from several sources, including the local credit bureau, credit card issuers, major department stores, previous and current mortgagees, Dun & Bradstreet reports, utility companies, associates, and supply houses. The previous and current payment pattern may be assumed to extend into the future if there are no indications of any changes in behavior.

The nature of the home loan application. The loan application should indicate, after the usual financial sources are contacted by the loan officer, the current financial position of the applicant. A forecast of future financial capability may be made by the loan officer from the questions asked and the information gleaned from the personal interview.

Once the future monthly housing expense is estimated from the application data—principal and interest payment, mortgage insurance periodic payment, periodic payment toward property taxes, periodic payment toward the annual hazard insurance premium, utility costs, and maintenance expenses—the lender can appraise the prospective borrower's financial ability to meet the mortgage payments.

Often the lender has a maximum limit set on the factor established by dividing the loan amount by the gross stabilized income of the prospective borrower. During the interview the loan officer would need to learn the gross stabilized income from the prospective borrower by asking tactful questions. Later the amount can be confirmed through investigation of current and past income with current and past employers.

In more specific terms, the loan application generally obtains the following information:

Ownership of the property

Description of the property

Information about the borrower
   Address and phone numbers
   Places of employment and regular and overtime payments
   Reputation for repaying debt obligations
   Financial capacity
     Credit reports
     Financial statements

Real estate appraisal
   Description of the property
   Neighborhood analysis
   Property utilities and restrictions
   The three approaches to values
   Reconciliation of the values derived
   Final value estimate

Photographs and maps

Plans and specifications
   Plans
     Plot plan
     Floor plan
     Wall sections
     Elevations
   Specifications
     Footings and foundations
     Exterior and interior walls
     Roof structure and finish
     Floors and floor finish
     Mechanical and electrical specifications
     Plumbing specifications
     On-site improvements
     Special features

Summary of the desired loan terms
   Loan amount
   Rate of interest
   Term of loan
   Escrow requirements
   Prepayment terms
   Real estate collateral and other security offered
   Type of security documents
   Property insurance coverage
   Mortgage insurance coverage

The nature of an income property loan application. If the prospective borrower negotiates directly with a possible lender, an application is made for the desired loan terms. However, the prospective borrower may often talk to a mortgage banker, who acts as a middleman and negotiates the terms for a loan application with a correspondent lender.

The application submitted to the correspondent lender for an income property loan requires more information than the home loan application. These additional items are included:

Description of security
   Assignment of leases
   Assignment of rents

Property management

Leases

Other items for summary of the desired loan terms
   Land value (per square foot)
   Building value (per square foot)
   Loan per square foot of building
   Gross income
   Expenses expressed as a percentage of gross income
   Net operating income
   Debt service and annual debt service constant
   Cash flow
   Breakeven point
   Debt service coverage
   Parking area and ratio to gross leasable area (GLA)
   Building efficiency or percentage of net rental to total gross rental area
   Square foot rental rates
   Land-to-building ratio

Exhibits related to the income property
   Vacancy surveys
   Feasibility studies
   Environmental impact studies
   Community survey
   Soil tests
   Building codes appropriate to the buildings
   Zoning requirements
   Area transportation maps
   Market studies

Credit Investigation. After the loan officer has personally interviewed the loan applicant, the financial aspects of the application are investigated more thoroughly. The investment committee of the institution will want to know:

   If the borrower will have the ready cash for the loan closing.

   If the borrower's income is sufficient in amount and stability to repay the loan according to the proposed amortization schedule.

   If the borrower has reserves for unforeseen emergencies such as hospitalization, tornado or flood damage, or unexpected unemployment.

The three basic areas of credit investigation are employment, credit rating, and savings and checking deposits. The present employer is asked to verify the nature of the current employment, the duration of the employment, the regular and overtime payment, and the trend in the employment relationship. The lender wants to know whether the work being done is satisfactory to the employer, whether the employee is looked on as a permanent employee and is being considered for further promotions, and whether the employee's salary has shown an upward trend in recent years. If the current employment relationship has been a short one, the loan officer may check with previous employers in ascertaining the same information. If the loan applicant or applicants are married, the employment history of each of the spouses is analyzed. If the spouse's employment is considered to be long-term, stable, and a substantial portion of the household income, the incomes from both spouses are analyzed with respect to loan repayment potential.

The credit rating report is scrutinized for slow or nonpayment of previous financial obligations. Evidence of personal or business bankruptcy, recent or long ago, is sought. If there is evidence of bankruptcy, was there satisfactory settlement of the claims of all parties involved, including the mortgage lenders? Frequently used sources of credit ratings are local financial institutions where the loan applicant has loans outstanding, credit bureaus, credit card issuers where the applicant has accounts, and tradespeople and retailers.

The mortgage lender also checks the current balances of the applicant's savings and checking accounts with local institutions. Distant financial institutions may be contacted if sizable accounts are maintained in these cities and little banking is done with local financial institutions. The lender is looking for evidence of enough capital and cash for the downpayment required on the purchase or the equity for the construction project and for the loan closing costs, which may amount to 2.5 to 3 percent of the mortgage.

The Appraisal of the Property. Since the lender bases the loan amount on a percent of the appraised value of the real property, the appraisal report is an integral part of the loan application or loan submission package. An appraisal report is needed whether the appraisal is made on the construction plans or the completed structure. The loan applicant usually pays a nominal sum for the report as part of the application costs.

By examining the appraisal report, the lender knows the estimated current value of the loan collateral. If the borrower defaults on the loan repayment, the lender will have to take title to the collateral and sell the property to recoup the amount owed by the mortgagor. The lender usually wants the best security possible for the loan. A good marketable property combined with a good, stable, continuing income in the hands of the mortgagor are the lender's best forms of loan security.

RATIO ANALYSIS

The mortgage lender is aware of the importance of ratio analysis in accepting and rejecting loan applications. There are rather general financial standards in terms of ratios used by the investment community, and there are rather specific financial standards established by individual mortgage lenders. The well-informed investor needs to be aware of these financial standards. At the same time, the investor should realize that the financial standards set by individual lenders tend to change with time and changes in institutional cash flows, mortgage demand, and economic conditions of the community, region, and nation.

When the prospective investor applies for a loan, the loan officer may calculate the credit and property cash flow ratios with a small, hand-held calculator. At the other extreme, though, the loan application may be run on the lender's computer system. The computerized ratio analysis may be encountered at the offices of large mortgage lenders who deal directly with prospective borrowers and at the offices of secondary mortgage market organizations who deal only with mortgage originator-sellers.

Once the basic ratios are calculated, the loan officer knows whether to pursue the loan application. Over the years of successful mortgage lending, loan officers and investment committees have established rules of thumb to distinguish between good and bad loans. Acceptable ranges of various ratios calculated from loan applications have been established by individual lenders for their current use. Once the ratios derived from a single loan application are compared against the current loan standards, the loan may be rejected, accepted, or investigated further. For example, the debt service coverage ratio of an income property loan application may be 1.05. If the acceptable range for the debt service coverage ratio for this type of property is 1.25 to 1.6, the loan might immediately be rejected or investigated further for unusual profit circumstances.

Ratio Analysis and the Home Loan Application

Only credit analysis by ratios is pertinent to home loan applications. In contrast, income property loan applications may be analyzed on the basis of both credit and cash flow ratios.

General Home Price and Mortgage Ratios. In the marketplace the investor may hear that the lender will permit a mortgage amount twice the gross income of the household (gross household income × 2 = affordable mortgage amount). At the same time, the investor may hear that a general rule of thumb of financial capacity is that the investor can afford to buy a house 2½ times his or her household income (investor income × 2.5 = affordable house price). In other words, if the investor's income is $25,000, a house priced at $62,500 could be purchased on a sound financial basis. According to the other rule of thumb, the investor would be able to support a mortgage of roughly $50,000. The resulting mortgage of $50,000 would be 80 percent of the house price. This loan-to-value ratio would characterize a conventional loan. The investor must be aware that these rules of thumb change with time.

One reason these general rules of thumb change is that interest rates and loan maturities change. If the loan constant on an 8 percent 25-year conventional home loan is 7.72, the debt service on a $50,000 mortgage would be 7.72 × 50, or $386 a month. The lender might approve of the lending factors of 2.5 and 2 mentioned above if the going rate on a 25-year loan were 8 percent. If the rate changed to 9.75 percent on a 25-year mortgage of $50,000, the loan constant would change to 8.92 and the debt service would be 8.92 × 50, or $446. The above-mentioned rules of thumb would probably not hold for households with incomes of $25,000. The income coverage for the debt service payment of $446 would probably be insufficient for lending purposes. The mortgage rule of thumb might drop to 1.6 times gross household income or some such factor. At the same time, the house-price rule of thumb would probably drop measurably. The investor must be aware of the current ratios and factors for loan analysis that the individual lenders are using in order to know what kind of home can be financed in the current market.

Commonly Used Credit Guidelines for Home Loans. Lenders and mortgage insurers have credit guidelines for home loans. Some of the most widely used credit guidelines are those of U.S. Housing and Urban Development Department, the Federal Home Loan Mortgage Corporation, and the Federal National Mortgage Association. The Federal Housing Administration-insured mortgage loans are subject to the guidelines set by the U.S. Department of Housing and Urban Development. The Federal Housing Administration was dismantled during the 1970s, when the cabinet department was reorganized, and its functions spread among the various divisions of HUD.

The FHA credit guidelines directly affect loan negotiations between the borrower and the lender. The FHLMC and FNMA credit guidelines indirectly affect the primary market negotiations. The originating lender cannot sell the home loan to either FHLMC (otherwise known as "The Mortgage Corporation") or to FNMA (otherwise known as "Fannie Mae") unless the loan fulfills the credit requirements established by those secondary mortgage market institutions.

FHA credit guidelines for nonsubsidized home mortgage loans. There are two credit rules of thumb: the 35 percent rule and the 50 percent rule. Both are expense-income ratios. Even though the basis is the net effective monthly income for both ratios, expense amounts are computed differently.

1. The 35 percent rule: Total monthly housing expense divided by net effective monthly income should be 35 percent or less.
    a. Total monthly housing expense: Total house payment, utility expenses, and maintenance expenses.

    >   Total monthly house payment
    > \+ Monthly utility expenses
    > \+ Monthly maintenance expenses
    >   Total monthly housing expense

    b. Net effective monthly income: Gross monthly income less monthly federal income tax.

    >   Gross monthly income
    > − Monthly federal income tax
    >   Net effective monthly income

2. The 50 percent rule: Total monthly fixed payments divided by net effective monthly income should be 50 percent or less.

    Monthly fixed payments: Total monthly housing expense plus state tax figured monthly, social security figured monthly, and installment debts of one year's duration or longer, due on a monthly basis.

    >   Total monthly housing expense
    > \+ State tax figured monthly
    > \+ Monthly social security payment
    > \+ Installment debts of one year's duration or longer, due on a monthly basis
    >   Monthly fixed payments

FHLMC credit guidelines. The Mortgage Corporation has two credit guidelines: a 25 percent rule and a 33⅓ percent rule.

1. The 25 percent rule. Monthly housing expenses, including principal repayment, interest expense, escrow expense for property taxes and hazard insurance, and

other expenses required to be paid under the mortgage, should not exceed approximately 25 percent of the borrower's stable monthly income.
2. The 33⅓ percent rule. The total amount of monthly payments including all installment debts having remaining terms of more than seven months should not exceed approximately 33⅓ percent of the borrower's stable monthly income.
   a. Stable monthly income: The borrower's gross monthly income from primary employment base earnings plus recognizable secondary income.
   b. Secondary income: Any borrower income such as bonuses, commissions, or overtime or part-time employment compensation.

FNMA credit guidelines. Fannie Mae has two credit guidelines: a 25 percent rule and a 33 percent rule. Both guidelines are based on gross allowable income.

1. The 25 percent rule. The house payment should not exceed 25 percent of the borrower's gross allowable income.
2. The 33 percent rule. The house payment plus debts of 10 months or longer, figured on a monthly basis, should not exceed 33 percent of gross allowable income.

Ratio Analysis and the Income Property Loan Application

In lender analysis of income property loan applications, the lender observes the credit and property cash flow ratios. The credit standing of the individual or business entity is

Exhibit 5-1. *Consolidated Balance Sheets: Assets of American Homes, Inc. (Rounded to Nearest Million)*

	1980	1981
Cash (includes certificates of deposit of $603,000 and $690,000 and restricted funds of $3,516,000 and $3,217,000)	$ 13,576	$ 13,388
Accounts, notes, mortgages, and escrows receivable ($16,476,000 and $12,519,000 due within one year), less reserve of $574,000 and $121,000 for doubtful accounts	24,188	16,758
Accumulated costs and profits on buildings in process, less advance payments of $41,919,000 and $45,257,000	23,234	24,785
Properties held for sale or investment and inventories, at the lower of cost or market		
Land held for investment or in process of development for sale	117,531	107,904
Single-family homes and condominiums completed or under construction	124,910	102,014
Income properties completed or under construction, less accumulated depreciation of $2,357,000 and $1,778,000	36,476	30,626
Building materials and supplies	3,603	3,104
Inventory of first mortgages receivable held for sale	5,850	7,013
Property, plant, and equipment, at cost, less accumulated depreciation of $4,240,000 and 43,355,000	12,610	11,286
Cost of investment in consolidated subsidiaries in excess of underlying book value ($2,911,000 in process of amortization), less accumulated amortization), less accumulated amortization of $186,000 and $109,000	10,728	9,301
Other assets and deferred charges (includes marketable securities of $549,000 and $380,000 at cost, which approximates market)	6,921	5,702
Total assets	$379,627	$331,881

scrutinized closely. In addition, the financial and operating ratios for the investment property are perused. Most lenders have established standard ranges of the strategic credit and cash flow ratios; they compare the loan ratios with the standard ratios before accepting a loan for investment.

Usual Required Financial Documents. The individual investor with substantial wealth will be asked to provide balance sheets and profit-and-loss statements for several years prior to the loan application. The incorporated investor will be asked to provide the following financial statements for several years prior to the loan application:

Balance sheet
Profit-and-loss statement
Flow-of-funds statement
Statement of changes in net worth

Exhibit 5-2. Consolidated Balance Sheets: Liabilities and Net Worth of American Homes, Inc. (Rounded to Nearest Million)

	1980	1981
Current liabilities:		
Short-term debt		
Unsecured bank financing	$140,000	$ 96,161
Other short-term financing	16,533	21,898
Current portion of long-term debt	23,227	24,534
Accounts payable	19,557	19,847
Customers' deposits, less related costs of $3,794,000 and $3,798,000	4,267	4,528
Other accrued liabilities	10,241	10,098
Federal and state income tax liability		
Current	4,349	5,133
Deferred	7,807	1,858
Total current liabilities	226,101	184,057
Long-term debt, less current portion	41,023	45,764
5½% convertible subordinated debentures	20,000	20,000
Commitments and contingencies		
Stockholders' equity:		
Preferred stock, $1 par value		
$5.50 cumulative convertible preferred stock, 14,100 shares authorized, issued, and outstanding	14	14
Undesignated as to series, 480,000 shares authorized, none outstanding		
Common stock, $.10 par value, authorized 15,000,000 shares, issued 9,504,604 shares (including 467,466 and 1,291,466 contingent shares issued in escrow)	950	950
Capital in excess of par value	45,594	44,582
Common stock warrants	1	1
Retained earnings	47,479	37,840
	94,038	83,387
Less treasury stock 754,958 and 72,920 shares of common stock, at cost	1,535	1,327
	92,503	82,060
	$379,627	$331,881

The balance sheet. The balance sheet of a company is the balanced financial accounting statement for assets, liabilities, and net worth for the company for one point in time. Assets usually balance with liabilities and net worth (Exhibits 5-1 and 5-2).

The profit-and-loss statement. The profit-and-loss statement shows the profitability of an organization over a period of time for which all incomes and expenses are accounted. The profit period is usually one year, and accounts are usually maintained on an accrual basis rather than on a cash basis (Exhibit 5-3).

The flow-of-funds statement. This statement of sources and uses of funds covers a specified period of time, usually a 12-month period. This is a capsule summary of the cash flows (Exhibit 5-4).

Exhibit 5-3. *Consolidated Statements of Income for American Homes, Inc. (Rounded to Nearest Million)*

	1980	1981
Sales	$350.520	$281.833
Revenues from rentals, utilities, and other operating properties	9.987	9.578
Total operating revenues	360.507	291.461
Cost of sales, excluding depreciation	278.109	217.459
	82.398	74.002
Expenses:		
Selling, general, and administrative	47.972	38.277
Depreciation	3.256	2.279
Interest	11.571	4.371
	61.799	44.927
Income from operations	20.599	29.075
Other income (expense):		
Interest income	2.578	1.359
Other, net	(0.790)	(0.081)
	1.788	1.278
Income before income taxes and extraordinary items	22.387	30.353
Provision for income taxes	11.318	14.416
Income before extraordinary items	11.069	15.937
Extraordinary items:		
Proceeds from officers' life insurance	----	1.000
Loss resulting from acquisition	----	(4.438)
	----	(3.438)
Net income	$ 11.069	$ 15.937
Earnings per share:		
Per common share and common equivalent share		
Income before extraordinary items	$1.13	$1.66
Extraordinary items	----	(0.36)
Net income	1.13	1.30
Per common share, assuming full dilution		
Income before extraordinary items	1.09	1.58
Extraordinary items	----	(0.33)
Net Income	$1.09	$1.25

Financing and Appraising

The statement of changes in net worth. This financial statement shows the change in net worth, usually as a result of a specified period of operations. If the company generated profits or sold stock during the specified period, for example, the net worth statement would show the change in total net worth (Exhibit 5-5).

Common Financial and Credit Ratios. Using the information divulged by the financial statements offered by the prospective borrower, the loan officer may examine certain ratios. Some of the commonly used ratios are return on total assets, return on stockholders' equity, times interest earned before taxes, return on sales, debt ratio, equity ratio, current ratio, and acid test ratio. Many mortgage lenders have compiled up-to-date standard and acceptable amounts for each of the ratios explored. Credit rating services like Dun & Bradstreet, Robert Morris & Associates, Standard and Poor, and Moody's provide the lender with some assistance in setting loan standards.

A sample of important financial ratios for 1980 and 1981 for American Homes, Inc. is given in Exhibit 5-6. Following the title of the ratio is an accounting definition of the numerator and denominator of each ratio. The ratios tend to show a stable and increasingly profitable real estate company, which is gradually reducing its liabilities while increasing its return on total assets, stockholders equity, and sales.

The illustrated financial statements show the complexity of statement analysis and the relative sources of the data for the financial and credit ratios. The loan officer must be familiar with statement construction, accounting conventions, and the significance of each of the accounts.

Exhibit 5-4. Sources and Uses of Funds Statement for American Homes, Inc. (Rounded to Nearest Million)

Funds provided by	1981	Funds applied to	1981
Funds generated from operations:		Fund utilized for other than operations during the current period:	
Net income before extraordinary items	$ 11.069	Repayment of unsecured revolving bank credit	$114.000
Add items not requiring funds		Reduction in long-term debt	25.988
Depreciation and amortization	3.504	Increase in properties held for sale or investment and inventories, excluding depreciation	39.197
Deferred income tax provision	4.705		
Funds generated exclusive of extraordinary items	19.278	Increase in accounts, notes, etc., receivable (net)	7.430
Proceeds from officers' life insurance	----		
Loss resulting from acquisition	----	Increase (decrease) in accumulated costs and profits on buildings in process	(1.551)
Funds (utilized) by extraordinary items	----		
Funds generated from operations	19.278		
Other sources of funds:		Property, plant, and equipment net increase (excluding depreciation of $1,768,000 and $1,319,000)	3.093
Marketable securities (increase) decrease	(0.169)		
Increase (decrease) in indebtedness			
Unsecured revolving bank credit	17.839	Payments of dividends	1.430
Unsecured open-line bank financing	140.000	Purchase of treasury stock and common stock warrants	0.150
Other short-term financing	(5.345)		
Long-term debt issued	19.940	Fair value of net assets acquired in connection with an acquisition	----
Common stock and treasury stock issued in connection with acquisitions	0.054	Increase in cost of investment in consolidated subsidiaries in excess of underlying book value	1.504
		Other net resources utilized (generated)	0.356
Total sources of funds	$191.597	Total funds used	$191.597

Exhibit 5-5. *Statement of Changes in Net Worth for American Homes, Inc. (Rounded to Nearest Million)*

	Preferred Stock		Common Stock		Common Stock Warrants		Treasury Stock		Capital in Excess of Par Value	Retained Earnings
	Shares	Amount	Shares	Amount	Shares	Amount	Shares	Amount		
Balance at December 31, 1981	0.014	0.014	9.50	0.950	0.020	0.001	0.073	(1.327)	44.582	37.840
Net income for the year	—	—	—	—	—	—	—	—	—	11.069
Cash dividends paid on preferred stock	—	—	—	—	—	—	—	—	—	(0.078)
Cash dividends paid on common stock	—	—	—	—	—	—	—	—	—	(1.1352)
Purchase of treasury stock	—	—	—	—	—	—	0.013	(0.150)	—	—
Treasury stock issued in connection with acquisition completed in prior years	—	—	—	—	—	—	(0.010)	0.010	0.044	—
Stock returned from escrow after final settlement of acquisition agreements	—	—	—	—	—	—	0.679	(0.068)	0.068	—
Tax benefit attributable to early disposition of stock acquired under qualified and restricted stock option and bonus plans	—	—	—	—	—	—	—	—	0.900	—
	0.014	$0.014	9.50	$0.950	0.020	$0.001	0.754	$(1.535)	$45.594	$47.479

Exhibit 5-6. *Financial Ratios for American Homes, Inc.*

Ratio	Method of Computation	1980	1981
Return on total assets	$\dfrac{\text{Net income + interest expense}}{\text{Investment in assets}}$	0.089	0.094
Return on stockholders' equity	$\dfrac{\text{Net income}}{\text{Stockholders' equity}}$	0.1197	0.152
Times interest earned (before taxes)	$\dfrac{\text{Net income before taxes and interest}}{\text{Interest expense}}$	6.495	11.57
Return on sales	$\dfrac{\text{Net income}}{\text{Total sales}}$	0.0316	0.0443
Debt ratio	$\dfrac{\text{Total debt}}{\text{Total assets}}$	0.756	0.753
Equity ratio	$\dfrac{\text{Stockholders' equity}}{\text{Total assets}}$	0.244	0.247
Current ratio	$\dfrac{\text{Current assets}}{\text{Current liabilities}}$	1.545	1.660
Acid test ratio	$\dfrac{\text{Cash, accounts receivable, notes receivable, marketable securities}}{\text{Current liabilities}}$	0.167	0.164

SUMMARY

When the prospective investor considers borrowing money, he or she should first shop the market for possible financing terms. After deciding that one or more lenders appear to be good sources for a loan, the prospective investor must apply for the loan, usually by making an appointment for a personal interview. During the personal interview with the loan officer, questions will be asked or answers volunteered about the borrower's investment objectives, capacity to repay the loan, and intention to repay the loan.

The home loan application requires less detailed financial information. The income property loan application requires property and debtor financial information in some depth. After the loan officer takes the application, either verbally or in written form, he or she makes a check of the data given. The loan officer verifies the employment information, the savings and checking account deposits, and the credit rating. The credit investigation is supplemented by an appraisal of the property.

Ratio analysis, whether on a sophisticated or a simple level, is generally a part of the analysis of the proposed loan. A computer may or may not be used for initial loan scrutiny.

Rules of thumb in ratio analysis—which change with changing economic and lending conditions—have been established by FHA, FHLMC, and FNMA. Standard home price-mortgage ratios also are compared against loan information. The figures for ratios needed in income property loan analysis generally originate from the prospective borrower's balance sheets, profit-and-loss statements, flow-of-funds statements, and statements of changes in net worth. A few of the widely used business credit ratios are the return on total assets, the return on stockholders' equity, the return on sales, times interest earned before taxes, the debt ratio, the equity ratio, the current ratio, and the acid test ratio. The results of the ratio calculations may be compared against industry standards, and the loan or investment committee may finally make a decision about the acceptability of the loan for investment of funds.

Key Terms and Concepts

Mortgage market conditions
Availability of funds
Lender-borrower negotiation
Loan application
Excess depreciation
Mortgagor's personal wealth
Savings and checking deposit verification
Hand-held calculator
Mortgage originator-sellers
Net effective monthly income
Gross monthly income
Gross allowable income
Balance sheet
Statement of changes in net worth
Times interest earned before taxes
Standard and Poor
Loan acquisition process
Credit investigation
Credit check
Principal investment motivations
Stabilized annual income
Overtime payment
Credit rating report
Computer system
Credit guidelines for home loans
Monthly fixed payments

Operating ratios
Profit-and-loss statement
Return on total assets
Return on sales
Debt ratio
Equity ratio
Moody's Investment Services
Ratio analysis
Standard ratios
Shopping the market for a loan
Tax shield
Financial capacity
Dun & Bradstreet reports
Employment history
Credit bureaus
Secondary mortgage market organizations
Total monthly housing expense
Secondary income
Cash flow ratios
Flow of funds statement
Return on stockholders' equity
Current ratio
Acid test ratio
Robert Morris & Associates
Liabilities

Questions for Student Self-examination

Multiple-Choice Questions

1. The borrower's intention to repay a loan is usually shown by
   a. personal wealth
   b. current deposit balances at financial institutions
   c. stabilized annual income from all sources
   d. previous loan repayment patterns

2. The following is usually not considered in estimating the future monthly housing expense of a prospective mortgagor:
   a. monthly principal and interest payment
   b. monthly country club dues
   c. monthly mortgage insurance payment
   d. estimated monthly maintenance expenses

3. Which is not one of the basic areas of credit investigation?
   a. real estate appraisal
   b. employment investigation
   c. credit rating report
   d. savings and checking deposit verification

4. FHA credit guidelines require that total monthly housing expense divided by net effective monthly income be
   a. 60 percent or less
   b. 90 percent or more
   c. 27.5 percent or more
   d. 35 percent or less

5. FHA credit guidelines require that total monthly fixed payments divided by net effective monthly income should be
   a. 95 percent or more
   b. 65 percent or less
   c. 30 percent or more
   d. 50 percent or more

True-False Questions

T F 1. FHA-insured loan terms are usually less stringent if the mortgagor will not be an occupant of the mortgaged property.

T F 2. Often the mortgage lender has a maximum loan limit set on the factor established by dividing the loan amount by the after-tax stabilized income of the prospective borrower.

T F 3. The mortgage loan application usually includes the appraised valuation of the property to be mortgaged.

T F 4. Loan closing costs may amount to 2½ to 3 percent of the mortgage amount.

T F 5. Under typical economic conditions, the house investor may hear that the lender will permit a mortgage amount four times the gross income of the household.

T F 6. Lender rules of thumb do not change with interest rates and loan maturities.

T F   7. According to the Mortgage Corporation's credit guidelines, monthly housing expenses, including principal repayment, interest expense, escrow expense for property taxes and hazard insurance, and other expenses required to be paid under the mortgage, should not exceed approximately 25 percent of the borrower's stable monthly income.
T F   8. According to FNMA credit guidelines, the house payment plus debts of 10 months or longer, figured on a monthly basis, should not exceed 33 percent of gross allowable income.
T F   9. The flow of funds statement shows the profitability of an organization over a period of time for which all incomes and expenses are accounted.
T F 10. A commonly used financial ratio is the return on stockholders' equity.

Answers
Multiple-choice: 1d, 2b, 3a, 4d, 5d.
True–False: 1F, 2F, 3T, 4T, 5F, 6F, 7T, 8T, 9F, 10T.

Problems

1. When a prospective mortgagor wishes to shop the market for mortgage terms, what does he or she usually do?

2. What are the FHA credit guidelines for nonsubsidized home mortgage loans? How are the strategic factors, such as total monthly house expense, defined?

3. If the gross household income is $25,000, what mortgage amount and house price could the household afford?

4. If the monthly housing expenses, including principal repayment, interest expense, escrow expense for property taxes and hazard insurance, and other expenses required to be paid under the mortgage, were approximately 35 percent of the borrower's stable monthly income, would the Mortgage Corporation approve this loan for purchase from the original lender?

5. If the house payment does not exceed 25 percent of the borrower's gross allowable income, would FNMA approve the loan for purchase from the original lender?

6. Name seven ways in which the prospective lender can ascertain the prospective mortgagor's financial capacity.

7. What is the difference between gross monthly income and net effective monthly income?

Chapter 6
Sources of Mortgage Money

Introduction
The Relationship of This Chapter to Other Chapters of the Text
Sources of Mortgage Funds
    Lenders of Home Mortgage Money   Lenders of Other Types of Mortgage Money
Mortgage Lending and Portfolio Investment Practices of Selected Financial Institutions
The Primary Mortgage Market Institutional Lending Patterns
    Savings and Loan Associations   Commercial Banks   Life Insurance Companies   Mutual Savings Banks   Pension Funds   Finance Companies   Real Estate Investment Trusts   Credit Unions   Foundation and Endowment Funds
The Secondary Mortgage Market Institutional Lending Patterns
    Federal National Mortgage Association   Federal Home Loan Mortgage Corporation   Government National Mortgage Association
Summary
Key Terms and Concepts
Questions for Student Self-examination

LEARNING OBJECTIVES   After studying this chapter, you should be familiar with

The general sources of mortgage funds
Lenders who make home mortgage money available
Lenders who make apartment and nonresidential mortgage money available
Savings and loan association lending patterns
Commercial bank lending patterns
Life insurance company lending patterns
Mutual savings bank lending practices
Pension fund lending practices
Finance company lending practices
Real estate investment trust lending practices
Credit union lending practices
Foundation and endowment fund lending practices
Lending patterns of the Federal National Mortgage Association
Lending patterns of the Federal Home Loan Mortgage Corporation
Lending patterns of the Government National Mortgage Association

Real estate lenders operating in the primary and secondary mortgage market serve real estate investors. Some of the lenders are individuals rather than institutions or lending organizations. Their lending activities are difficult to monitor; therefore, little information is available about individual mortgage lending, but we have the fullest knowledge about institutional lending policies and practices. This chapter, therefore, deals primarily with institutional sources of funds. Since institutional lending activity occurs on the loan negotiation level—the primary mortgage market—as well as on the loan sales and purchases level—the secondary mortgage market—the chapter deals briefly with the sources of funds in both levels of the mortgage market.

INTRODUCTION

This chapter first discusses sources of mortgage funds in general. The lending relationships for the financing of residential and nonresidential mortgages are reviewed. Then the chapter continues with an examination of the overall mortgage lending and portfolio policies of individual lenders.

We discover that special secondary mortgage market institutions exist whose mortgage lending practices vitally affect the investor. We also find that the same institutions that are operating in the primary mortgage market in directly negotiating loans with individuals and businesses also participate in the secondary mortgage market by selling existing loans to gain liquidity and by buying mortgage loans for investment.

The reader briefly reviews the activities of the Federal National Mortgage Association, the Federal Home Loan Mortgage Corporation, and the Government National Mortgage Association, institutions that lend mortgage monies on the secondary market level. There is also a review of the lending and portfolio practices of commercial banks, savings and loan associations, mutual savings banks, credit unions, finance companies, pension funds, life insurance companies, endowment funds, and real estate investment trusts.

THE RELATIONSHIP OF THIS CHAPTER TO OTHER CHAPTERS OF THE TEXT

The investor may realize that he or she needs to borrow mortgage money and may be familiar with the lending and loan application practices of the community, but the need still exists to actually acquire mortgage funds. The investor can conserve time and effort by knowing the basic lending patterns of individual institutional lenders.

This chapter concludes the financing section of part II. After analyzing the possible need for mortgage financing, the favorable attributes of the use of leverage, the information needed by the loan officer for a loan application, and the financial and credit ratios often observed by loan officers, we turn in this chapter to the primary and secondary market sources of mortgage funds. The remainder of the section is devoted to real estate appraising.

SOURCES OF MORTGAGE FUNDS

Historically, there has been a hierarchy of lenders, based on the volume of mortgage lending. The overall picture at the end of 1978 was indicative of the usual mortgage pattern among lending institutions (Exhibit 6-1). The savings and loan associations by far exceeded the other financial institutions and individuals in mortgage lending. Commercial banks ranked a distant second. Ranking third and fourth but close together in mortgage lending volume were individuals and households and life insurance companies. Mutual savings banks ranked fifth, in close proximity to the life insurance companies and individuals and households. The other institutions, which held significant volumes of mortgage loans but on a lesser relative scale than the lending mortgage lenders, were state and local retirement funds, finance companies, real estate investment trusts, private noninsured pension funds, credit unions, and foundations and endowments. Even the holders of the smallest portfolio of mortgages—foundations and endowments—held $1 billion worth of real estate mortgages at the end of 1978.

Lenders of Home Mortgage Money. Traditionally, the principal sources of mortgage money for home loans have been savings and loan associations, mutual savings banks, and commercial banks. In the 1970s the federal agencies entered the home mortgage market with billions of dollars of investible funds for home loans. These four home mortgage lenders have generally concentrated on first-mortgage loans. Individuals have also historically financed a substantial volume of first-mortgage loans. Finance companies, on the other hand, have usually concentrated their investible funds in junior mortgage loans on houses. The dollar-volume ranking of the home mortgage lenders, regardless of first or junior mortgage investment concentration, changes with time. At the end of the first quarter of 1978, savings and loan associations ranked first; commercial banks, second; and mortgage pools, third (Exhibit 6-2).

Lenders of Other Types of Mortgage Money. Life insurance companies for many years have been leading lenders on income property mortgages (Exhibit 6-2). Since the latter 1960s, life insurance companies have avoided investment in home mortgage

Exhibit 6-1. Outstanding Real Estate Mortgages of Significant Mortgage Lenders

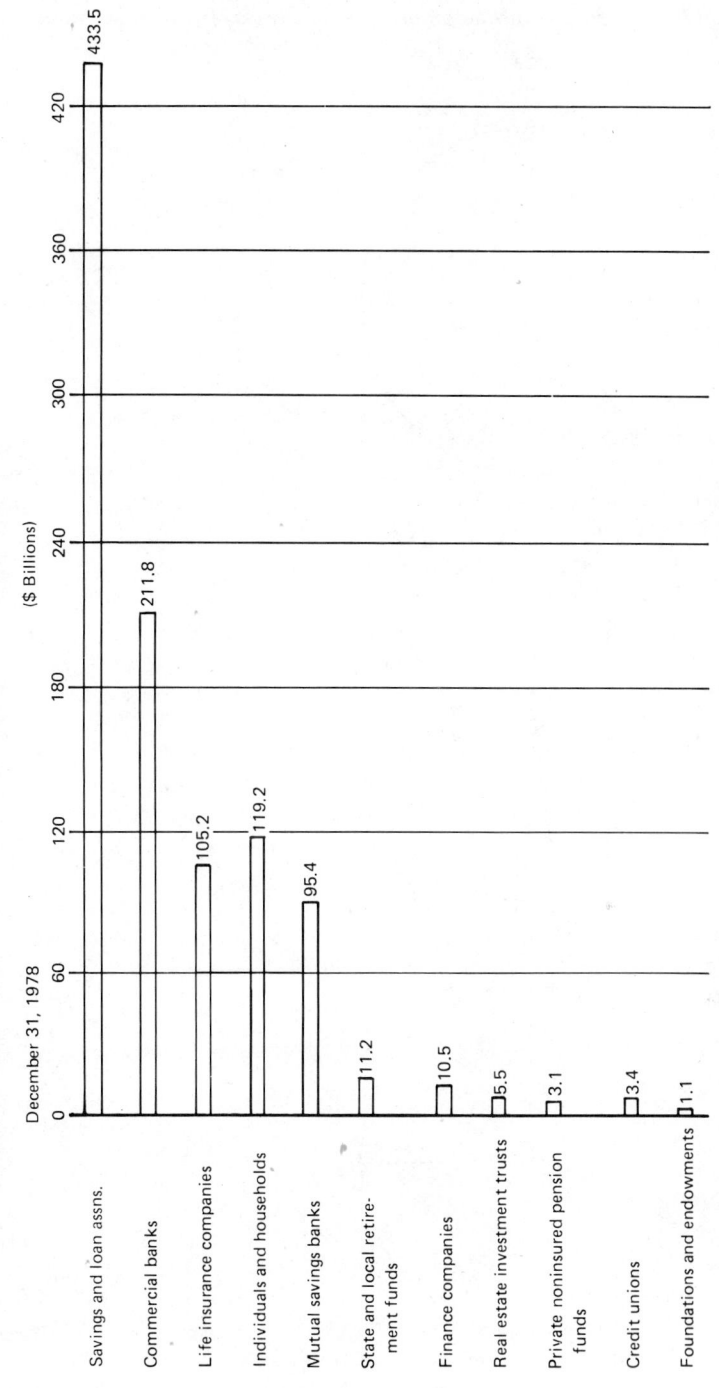

December 31, 1978
($ Billions)

Savings and loan assns.	433.5
Commercial banks	211.8
Life insurance companies	105.2
Individuals and households	119.2
Mutual savings banks	95.4
State and local retirement funds	11.2
Finance companies	10.5
Real estate investment trusts	5.5
Private noninsured pension funds	3.1
Credit unions	3.4
Foundations and endowments	1.1

Source: Henry Kaufman, James McKeon, Peter Chapman, *Prospects for the American Financial Markets in 1979* (New York: Salomon Bros., 1978), p. 19. With permission.

Exhibit 6-2. *Mortgage Market Net Flow of Funds (Institutional Shares)*

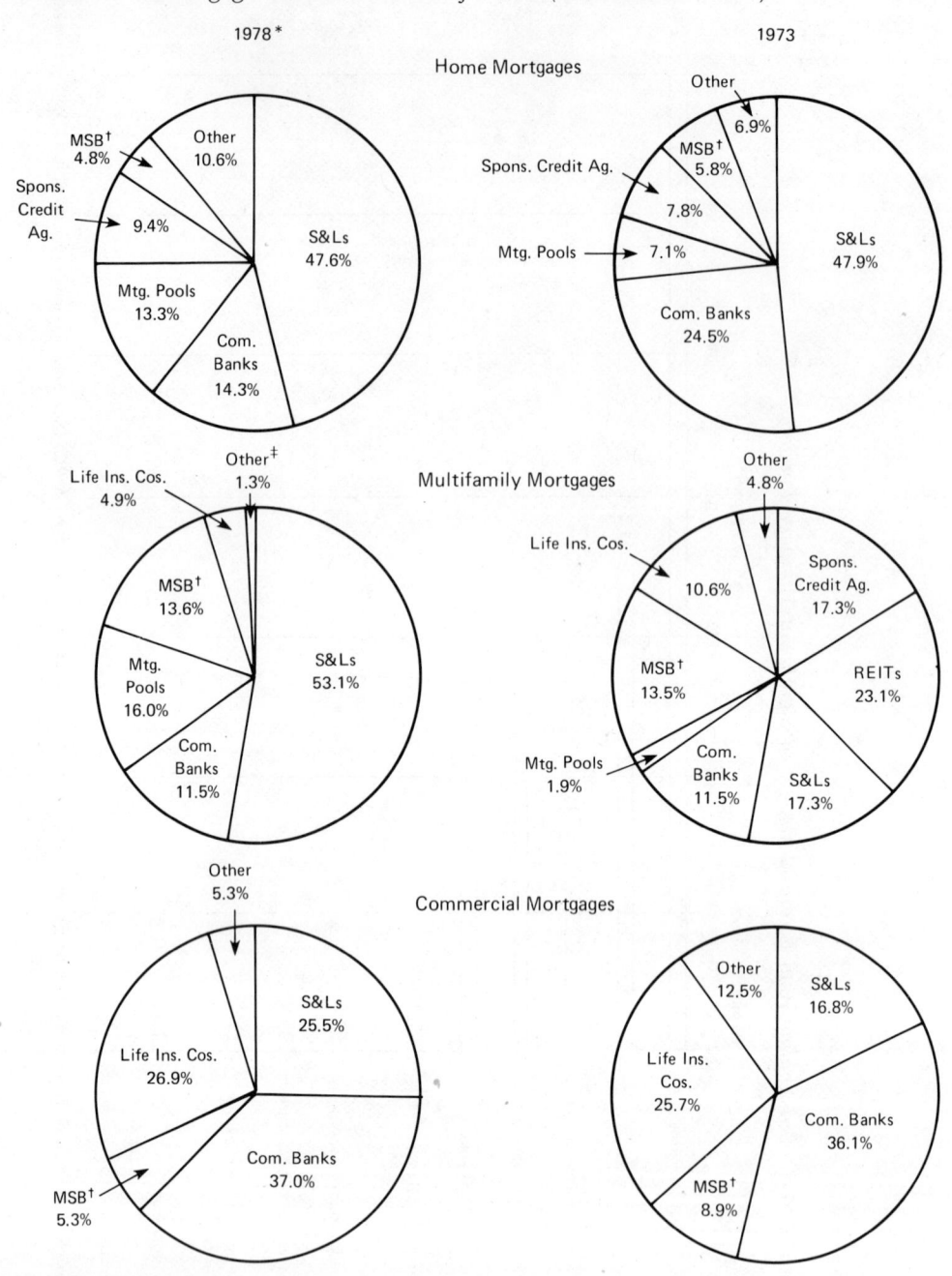

1978* — Home Mortgages
- S&Ls 47.6%
- Com. Banks 14.3%
- Mtg. Pools 13.3%
- Other 10.6%
- Spons. Credit Ag. 9.4%
- MSB† 4.8%

1973 — Home Mortgages
- S&Ls 47.9%
- Com. Banks 24.5%
- Spons. Credit Ag. 7.8%
- Mtg. Pools 7.1%
- Other 6.9%
- MSB† 5.8%

1978* — Multifamily Mortgages
- S&Ls 53.1%
- Mtg. Pools 16.0%
- MSB† 13.6%
- Com. Banks 11.5%
- Life Ins. Cos. 4.9%
- Other‡ 1.3%

1973 — Multifamily Mortgages
- REITs 23.1%
- Spons. Credit Ag. 17.3%
- S&Ls 17.3%
- MSB† 13.5%
- Com. Banks 11.5%
- Life Ins. Cos. 10.6%
- Other 4.8%
- Mtg. Pools 1.9%

1978* — Commercial Mortgages
- Com. Banks 37.0%
- Life Ins. Cos. 26.9%
- S&Ls 25.5%
- MSB† 5.3%
- Other 5.3%

1973 — Commercial Mortgages
- Com. Banks 36.1%
- Life Ins. Cos. 25.7%
- S&Ls 16.8%
- Other 12.5%
- MSB† 8.9%

*First quarter, seasonally adjusted annual rate.
†Mutual savings banks.
‡This "other" category includes REIT's and sponsored credit agencies.
Source: Board of Governors of the Federal Reserve System.

Financing and Appraising

loans because of the inferior yield from their investment standpoints. Unlike the situation with savings and loans, commercial banks, and mutual savings banks, their regulatory agencies have not encouraged investment in home mortgage loans.

Savings and loans invest some of their funds in income property mortgages, with an emphasis on apartment project loans. Federal agencies have also invested in apartment project loans, usually of the FHA-insured type. Individuals and households continue to invest in all types of mortgage loans, including income property loans. As of the end of 1978, mutual savings banks had approximately 45 percent of their mortgage portfolio devoted to income property mortgages (Exhibit 6-3). Historically, most of these loans have been apartment project loans. Pension funds continue to invest a small part of their funds in income property mortgage loans. The potential investment by pension funds is almost limitless in dollar volume. Pension fund contributions continue to increase each year; their investible funds are tremendous and increasing, and portfolio restraints are almost nonexistent.

When an investor wants money for a particular stage of real estate development, he or she finds that not all sources of income property mortgage money offer all kinds of real estate loans. Construction loans are normally acquired from commercial banks. Until the downfall of the mortgage investment trusts in 1974, commercial banks were also strong sources of construction funds. Life insurance companies and pension funds are in a position to lend junior mortgage money as well as to extend first-mortgage loans. Savings and loan associations, federal agencies, and mutual savings banks also offer first-mortgage monies; in fact, unlike pension funds and life insurance companies, they deal almost exclusively in first-mortgage loans.

Exhibit 6-3. The Principal Residential and Income Property Mortgage Lenders, Third Quarter, 1978 (in billions)

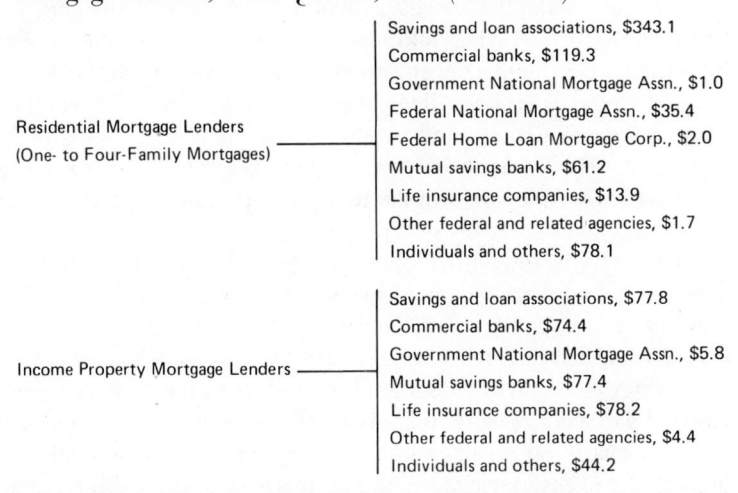

Residential Mortgage Lenders (One- to Four-Family Mortgages)
- Savings and loan associations, $343.1
- Commercial banks, $119.3
- Government National Mortgage Assn., $1.0
- Federal National Mortgage Assn., $35.4
- Federal Home Loan Mortgage Corp., $2.0
- Mutual savings banks, $61.2
- Life insurance companies, $13.9
- Other federal and related agencies, $1.7
- Individuals and others, $78.1

Income Property Mortgage Lenders
- Savings and loan associations, $77.8
- Commercial banks, $74.4
- Government National Mortgage Assn., $5.8
- Mutual savings banks, $77.4
- Life insurance companies, $78.2
- Other federal and related agencies, $4.4
- Individuals and others, $44.2

Source: Mortgage Debt Outstanding, *Federal Reserve Bulletin* (Washington, D.C.: Board of Governors, Federal Reserve System, February 1979), p. A41.

MORTGAGE LENDING AND PORTFOLIO INVESTMENT PRACTICES OF SELECTED FINANCIAL INSTITUTIONS

The mortgage lending and portfolio investment practices of several institutions in the primary mortgage market are reviewed here. Those institutions are savings and loan associations, commercial banks, life insurance companies, and mutual savings banks. They also include state and local retirement funds, finance companies, real estate investment trusts, private insured and noninsured pension funds, credit unions, and foundations and endowments.

The mortgage lending policies and practices of secondary mortgage market institutions are also discussed. These institutions are the Federal National Mortgage Association, the Federal Home Loan Mortgage Corporation, and the Government National Mortgage Association.

The Primary Mortgage Market Institutional Lending Patterns

Most mortgage lenders function in the primary mortgage market, where the borrower of mortgage funds negotiates directly with the lender or the lender's representative, the mortgage banker. At the end of 1977, the real estate mortgage holdings of primary market institutions represented 84 percent of total mortgage holdings. During 1978 primary market institutions financed 79 percent of all mortgages.

Savings and Loan Associations. State and federally chartered savings and loan associations make first and second permanent mortgage loans, construction and development first mortgage loans, and home improvement loans. Most investors are financing residential properties when they deal with savings and loan associations.

Savings and loan associations are first in general mortgage lending volume. They are also first in residential mortgage lending, which include one- to four-family-house loans. During 1977 savings and loans were second in income property mortgage lending. Their investment concentration in residential mortgage loans is encouraged by Federal Home Loan Bank Board regulations, by Federal Savings and Loan Insurance Corporation regulations, and by state department of banking or financial institutions regulations. The Internal Revenue Service also promotes their mortgage investment by reducing federal income taxation to a lower rate than regular corporate taxation when the savings and loan invests 82 percent or more of its assets in mortgage loans.

In addition to residential loans, savings and loans invest in income property mortgage loans, home improvement loans, loans on savings deposits for the financing of a home, and U.S. government securities. They hold federal government securities for liquidity and FHLBB reserves and cash for deposit withdrawals and contingencies. If the savings and loan is federally chartered, the charter is acquired from the Federal Home Loan Bank Board; this organization then regulates the association. Since all federally chartered savings and loans must insure their deposits with the Federal Savings and Loan Insurance Corporation, this organization also regulates their operations. When a state-chartered savings and loan insures its deposits through the Federal Savings and Loan Insurance Corporation, it is subject to FSLIC regulations.

Savings and loan associations make FHA-insured, VA-guaranteed, and conventional mortgage loans. Most of their business is confined to conventional lending on a permanent loan basis. The loan-to-value ratio usually ranges from 75 to 80 percent of appraised value. Loans for more than 80 percent of value may be made if the borrower pays for private mortgage insurance. The term of the loan ranges from 20 to 30 years, depending on the type of loan and the other circumstances pertaining to the loan. The interest rate on the conventional loan is usually the market rate; therefore, discount points are usually not required at the closing. Loans up to and including $60,000 may be made to fit into the normal residential portion of the savings and loan portfolio. Loans over $60,000 must fall within the FHLBB portfolio constraints, involving the 20 percent of assets set aside for miscellaneous investments. Single-family FHA 203(b) loans, regardless of the type of lender, may go up to $60,000; two-unit 203(b) loans, up to $65,000; and four-unit 203(b) loans, up to $75,000.

Commercial Banks. Commercial banks, the second most important mortgage lenders in terms of dollar volume, make all kinds of mortgage loans from their numerous departments and subsidiary companies. At the same time, commercial banks make all types of personal, commercial, and industrial loans. Their lending powers are the most diverse of all the institutional lenders, even though their regulations are the most stringent.

The commercial bank is second only to savings and loan associations in residential mortgage lending. In income property lending, the bank is second to life insurance companies. Its lending significance stems from real estate lending in perhaps three separate offices of the bank: the commercial loan department, the mortgage department or subsidiary company, and the bank-sponsored real estate investment trust. Most of the major banks have created a real estate investment trust to supplement their traditional real estate lending. The investor may acquire a construction and/or development loan for five years or less from the commercial loan department of the bank. From the mortgage department or company the investor may negotiate a permanent first- or second-mortgage loan, a gap loan, or a standby commitment. From the bank-sponsored REIT the investor may inquire about a development, construction, gap, wraparound, or permanent junior or permanent first-mortgage loan.

The commercial bank is stringently regulated by the appropriate agencies. A national bank is chartered and regulated by the Comptroller of the Currency and is further regulated by the Federal Reserve and the Federal Deposit Insurance Corporation. A state-chartered bank is regulated by the state department of banking; if its deposits are insured by the Federal Deposit Insurance Corporation, the bank is regulated by that body. The Federal Reserve regulations tend to cover the required reserves, loan rediscount rate, discount window operations, Open Market Committee functions, and savings deposit interest rate ceilings. The FDIC tends to regulate lending practices, whereas the Comptroller of the Currency is usually concerned with the granting of new charters and the approval or disapproval of impending mergers and consolidations.

The overall investment policies of the commercial bank revolve around safety of principal; community service; liquidity; and profitability, or return on investment. These objectives are pursued even though primary, secondary, and tertiary reserves are usually maintained by a bank to satisfy the Federal Reserve, to maintain adequate liquidity, and to maintain financial protection against contingencies. Mortgage lending fits in with these goals.

Commercial banks specialize in conventional mortgage loans. They do finance houses with FHA-insured and VA-guaranteed loans. Generally these home mortgage loans fall within the bank objectives of community service and safety of principal rather than bank profitability. The yields on home mortgage loans are usually considerably lower than the yields on personal, consumer, and business commercial loans.

Unlike the thrift institutions—savings and loan associations and mutual savings banks—commercial banks are depositories of checking and savings account monies; buyers of Treasury, federal agency, and municipal securities; and lenders of monies on the bases of unsecured consumer and business loans. Real estate loans are generally not principal investment media for commercial banks, even though banks are known for their construction lending. Savings and loans and mutual savings banks, on the other hand, are known for their permanent mortgage loan investments and for their higher yielding savings accounts, which permit more rapid accumulation of funds for the purchase or construction of a home or apartment building.

Life Insurance Companies. In total mortgage lending at the end of 1977, life insurance companies and individuals and households were almost equal; they ranked third and fourth in terms of dollar volume. The life insurance company ranking is primarily associated with commercial and industrial mortgage lending. Since the latter 1960s, most life insurance companies have shied away from one- to four-family mortgage loans because of lower-than-competitive yields in the marketplace. In the 1970s, income property loan yields have competed aggressively with corporate industrial and utility bond yields.

The state-chartered life insurance company may invest in all of the investments listed on the legal list established by the state insurance commission. Since most life insurance companies sell policies to residents of New York State, most life insurance companies, no matter where they are chartered, are subject to the modified legal list of the State of New York, set up by the New York State Insurance Commission. Since the modified legal list of New York State includes most types of traditional investment vehicles, the typical insurance company portfolio includes corporate bonds, common and preferred stocks of corporations, government securities, policy loans, real estate ownership, mortgages, and other types of assets.

In the real estate area of the portfolio are found sale-leaseback agreements, leasehold mortgage loans, first and junior mortgages on income properties, ground leases, and outright building ownership. Many life insurance companies have constructed and wholly invested in apartment projects of our major metropolitan areas.

Life insurance companies raise money through the sale of insurance policies—life, health, group, and industrial—and income from investments. The company must meet beneficiary payments, annuity payments, and operating expenses. Shareholders usually expect dividends from company operations and investments. Some policy loans result in a reduction of retained policy premiums, but the income flows back in from the repayment of the principal and the interest paid by the policy loan borrower.

Mutual Savings Banks. The second thrift institution that we want to consider is the mutual savings bank. The term *thrift institution* usually refers to the institution that acts as a depository for small savers who are often saving toward the purchase or construction of a home and that acts as a lender for prospective home buyers. Unlike savings and loan associations, mutual savings banks are not widely scattered around the country. Many Americans are less familiar with their savings account yields and mortgage lending because they are located in only 17 states. Most of these states are located in the Northeast and Middle Atlantic regions.

The savings banks are regulated by departments of the state governments in which they have been chartered; there are no federally chartered savings banks. If their deposits are insured by a state insurance corporation, regulation comes from that source; if their deposits are insured by the Federal Deposit Insurance Corporation, the FDIC regulates those savings banks.

Their portfolio regulations generally encourage the placement of investible funds in corporate industrial bonds and mortgages. The balance of mortgage-bond investment usually goes in favor of the investment yielding the highest return commensurate with acceptable risk. During the 1960s and 1970s, the portion of savings bank assets represented by mortgages approximated two-thirds.

According to the Federal Reserve, savings banks were fifth in mortgage lending as a whole in 1978, and they were fourth in residential mortgage lending in the same year (Exhibit 6-3). In income property mortgage lending in 1978, they ranked third. Usually they concentrate on permanent first and junior mortgage loans on residential and nonresidential property. On the average, 45 percent of their mortgage portfolio consists of one- to four-family home mortgage loans. Approximately 55 percent of the residential mortgage loans are conventionally financed. The rest are FHA-insured and VA-guaranteed. Their investments are nationwide in scope, even though savings banks exist in only 17 states. Mortgage bankers and mortgage brokers assist them in nationwide lending.

Pension Funds. Pension funds are providing more and more funds for the investment market. There are private insured and noninsured funds and state and local government retirement funds. In 1972, according to Salomon Brothers, these pension funds provided credit to the money and capital markets in the amount of $2.5 billion. In comparison, in 1977, they provided $22.5 billion in credit to the markets. Their assets are growing at a startling pace as a result of the 1974 Employee Retirement Income Security Act and the retirement plan coverage of more employees and companies. More and more company plans call for contributions from both the employer and the employee.

It is difficult to keep track of the pension fund assets managed by life insurance companies in their common investment funds. The pension plans managed by company investment managers, bank trust departments, and investment banking houses are more tractable. More and more companies with pension plans are hiring their own investment managers, according to *The Wall Street Journal*. The companies want their return on assets to outperform the general stock market as their pension liabilities increase.

The pension fund portfolio managers tend to determine the portfolio composition of a fund. There is little regulation of qualified tax-exempt retirement plans by the Internal Revenue Service; therefore, the portfolio managers have almost free rein. According to research studies, most portfolio managers have stock and bond backgrounds. Therefore, it is understandable why only $13 billion of the total $162 billion of pension fund assets found their way into mortgage investment in 1977. They have tended, though, to purchase mortgage-backed securities in the form of bonds. GNMA-guaranteed mortgage-backed securities, for example, are sold to pension funds in the bond-type and pass-through forms. In addition to the purchase of stock, bonds, and mortgages, pension fund counselors also advise the purchase of real estate directly. Some direct real estate ownership takes the form of sales-leaseback agreements covering land and/or structures.

Since the pension fund is tax-exempt and it must constantly invest substantial sums of money, real estate investment can absorb large quantities of funds at reasonably high expected yields. The same is true of pension fund investment in large blocks of mortgages, stock, and bonds. Large income property mortgages are particularly suitable for pension fund investment.

Finance Companies. In recent years finance companies have been investing a billion dollars a year in real estate mortgages. This type of investment has represented about 5 percent of their total credit extended per year. By the end of 1977 finance companies held $10 billion of one- to four-family mortgages in their portfolios, about 8 percent of their total assets of $127 billion. Other than residential mortgages, finance companies usually invest in business and consumer loans, cash, and other relatively liquid assets. They invest primarily in junior mortgage loans on residential property, to the exclusion of first-mortgage loans. As a financial institution, they are more conscious of yield and liquidity than are some of the other more traditional lending institutions. The sources of funds for their portfolio investment are traditionally the sale of commercial paper and the acquisition of short-term bank loans.

Real Estate Investment Trusts. The different types of real estate investment trusts (often called *REITs*) have different investment powers, depending on their individual declarations of trust. The business trust of which the REIT is one type requires the establishment of a declaration of trust at the trust's formation. The trust agreement declares the range of trust investment powers. Therefore, REITs take the form of short-term mortgage trusts, hybrid mortgage trusts, and equity trusts. The short-term mortgage trust invests primarily in short-term construction and development loans. The hybrid mortgage trust invests primarily in mortgages of various kinds and lengths of maturity, but may invest directly in real estate. The equity trust confines its investments predominantly to real estate ownership; some long-term mortgages may be originated or purchased for the portfolio as well.

The REIT usually finances commercial property. One- to four-family houses may be financed as a subdivision loan package with a subdivision developer. Otherwise, the REIT is generally interested in larger denomination loans and is not usually interested in originating or purchasing single-family home loans. The developer may acquire a short-term construction and development loan for the subdivision and/or a permanent first and/or junior mortgage loan. The REIT may be able to offer any kind of junior mortgage short-term or long-term loan, since only the Internal Revenue Service regulates the financial intermediary.

Otherwise, the REIT is unregulated and tax exempt. The Congress created the tax-exempt real estate *mutual fund* with the cooperation of the Internal Revenue Service in 1960. It is subject to net income distribution regulations and revenue source regulations in order to preserve the tax-exempt status.

The REIT raises its funds for investment via the sale of shares of beneficial interest, commercial paper, debentures, and convertible debentures. Otherwise, it negotiates with commercial banks for commercial loans to support the rest of the portfolio. Since the foreclosure of many loans during the real estate recession of 1974–1975, many REITs have had a difficult time paying off their creditors. Many outstanding mortgage trusts have become bankrupt or have experienced a serious decline in their asset values. Their declines in asset values and earnings per share have been reflected in depressed REIT stock prices and diminished sales of REIT securities on the market. Banks continue to be reluctant to loan any more funds to many of the REITs since previous REIT loans have ended in major loss of interest and principal. Most of the financial collapse has been linked to short-term mortgage trusts. The hybrid and equity trusts have continued to increase their earnings per share in the 1970s and to invest in real estate and long-term mortgages. Less mortgage monies, however, are available from the REIT industry now than a few years ago. Their mortgage investment policies have also become more conservative with the shakedown of the industry.

Credit Unions. One of the fastest expanding financial institutions, credit unions, has begun to offer mortgage loans along with consumer loans. These local institutions, who tend to take in deposits from the members of the group and give out loans to other members of the group, have in the past concentrated on investment in consumer loans. At the end of 1977 credit unions finally held 5 percent of their total assets of $50 billion in the form of one- to four-family mortgage loans. Seventy-four percent of total assets were still committed to consumer loans. The remaining assets were committed to cash, Treasury securities, federal agency securities, and other credit union shares.

Credit unions' mortgage loans tend to be only first mortgages, and the terms tend to be conservative in comparison with the local savings and loan association terms. Usually, only members or depositors of the credit union are eligible for mortgage loans.

The effective interest rate on the loan—mortgage or consumer—may tend to be lower than the market rate, and the yield on savings deposits may tend to be higher than the market yields because the credit union is exempt from federal income taxation. State-chartered credit unions may be subject to state excise taxes, and federally chartered credit unions may have to pay a fee to the National Credit Union Administration for supervision and regulation of the credit unions. The state-chartered credit unions receive their charters from the state banking department or state department of financial institutions and may choose to be regulated by the National Credit Union Administration (otherwise labeled the NCUA). Federally chartered credit unions must be regulated by the NCUA.

Foundations and Endowment Funds. Foundations and endowment funds, which are usually tax exempt, place substantial sums derived from contributions and accumulated personal and business wealth into real estate and mortgage investment. Salomon Brothers estimated that foundations and endowment funds had investments of $52 billion at the end of 1977. Two percent of this amount ($1 billion) was invested in mortgages. Two-thirds of the assets were placed in stocks and about 25 percent in corporate and foreign bonds. From statistics it is difficult to observe how much of these funds has been invested in land and buildings on sale-leaseback agreements. Considerable sums have been invested in income properties in selected areas, according to marketplace information.

The Secondary Mortgage Market Institutional Lending Patterns

Some lenders operate in the secondary mortgage market. At present, these sources of mortgage money are sponsored by the federal government or are regulated to a large extent by the federal government. Private secondary mortgage market organizations have existed but have been forced out of business by real estate recessions and by periods of high foreclosure rates. The remaining government or quasi-government agencies—the Federal National Mortgage Association, the Federal Home Loan Mortgage Corporation, and the Government National Mortgage Association—have a considerable impact on real estate investment. Even though they operate in the secondary mortgage market, where existing mortgages are traded, any of these lenders may be the principal source of funds for a real estate investor or developer.

Federal National Mortgage Association. The Federal National Mortgage Association (often called "Fannie Mae") is a source of funds for FHA-insured, VA-guaranteed, and conventionally financed residential mortgages. Since it deals only with mortgage originators, the individual real estate investor does not deal directly with FNMA. The principal mortgage originators who sell to and buy from FNMA are commercial banks and mortgage companies, even though other mortgage originators may be approved seller-originators.

If the mortgage seller wishes liquidity and wants to sell his or her mortgages to FNMA, this seller-originator must bid for FNMA money at the weekly auctions. One week the mortgage company or bank may bid for FHA and VA loan funds; the next week, for conventional loan funds. A fee must be paid for entering a bid; a fee must be paid when a bid for funds is accepted; and FNMA stock representing 1/10 percent of the average outstanding mortgage loan balance of the mortgages sold to FNMA must be purchased by the seller-originator.

In December of 1978 FNMA had invested $43 billion in residential mortgages. Of this amount approximately $21 billion was invested in FHA-insured mortgages; approximately $10.5 billion, in VA-guaranteed mortgages; and approximately $11.5 billion, in conventional mortgages. Approximately 85 percent of the money was invested in one- to four-family mortgage loans.

From a beginning as a federal government agency, FNMA became a private corporation with some federal government control in 1970. Today two types of stockholders are the owners of the corporation. Since FNMA common stock is listed on the national exchanges, part of the ownership lies in the hands of the public. The other part of the ownership is held by mortgage seller-originators. To finance the other portion of their mortgage operations, they sell bonds, discount notes, participation certificates, and GNMA-guaranteed mortgage-backed securities. This outstanding debt totaled $32 billion in January of 1978.

Federal Home Loan Mortgage Corporation. The Federal Home Loan Mortgage Corporation, a subsidiary of the Federal Home Loan Bank Board, buys and sells mortgages to savings and loan association members of its district Federal Home Loan Banks and to other financial institutions whose deposits are insured by an agency of the United States government. They, like FNMA, deal only in residential single-family and multifamily mortgages. In December of 1978 the Federal Home Loan Mortgage Corporation (otherwise known as "the Mortgage Corporation") held $3 billion in mortgages. Almost half of the investment consisted of FHA/VA mortgages; a little more than half of the portfolio consisted of conventional residential mortgages. About 80 percent of the mortgages represented one- to four-family mortgages.

The Mortgage Corporation, like FNMA, does not deal directly with the borrower. They buy mortgages from and sell mortgages to mortgage originators, who are usually savings and loan associations. When the savings and loan needs liquidity, it knows that it can sell its mortgages to the Mortgage Corporation. The Federal Home Loan Bank Board regulates the operations and financing of the Mortgage Corporation. The stock of the Mortgage Corporation is owned by the district Federal Home Loan Banks. Since the Federal Home Loan Bank system is a government-sponsored and controlled system, the Mortgage Corporation amounts to a federal government agency. This agency had outstanding mortgage debt amounting to $1.8 billion in early 1978. Like FNMA, the Mortgage Corporation raises funds for its operations by selling mortgages, participation notes, GNMA-guaranteed mortgage-backed securities, and other similar types of securities.

Government National Mortgage Association. While FNMA and the Mortgage Corporation invest in unsubsidized residential mortgage debt, the Government National Mortgage Association (otherwise called "Ginnie Mae") invests in subsidized residential mortgages. This government agency, which is a part of the U.S. Department of Housing and Urban Development, raises money to finance its mortgage operations by selling specially designed bonds to the U.S. Treasury and by selling to various institutions packages of mortgages, mortgage participations, and GNMA-guaranteed mortgage-backed securities in bond-type and pass-through forms. This government agency is charged with managing foreclosed government properties, guaranteeing mortgage-backed bonds that meet with its approval, and providing financial assistance to subsidized mortgage programs of the Department of Housing and Urban Development.

Of the $3.5 billion of GNMA mortgage debt outstanding at the end of 1978, about 70 percent was represented by multifamily mortgage debt. Mortgage pools or trusts established by GNMA for the sale of their mortgages involved $51 billion; one- to four-family mortgages made up about 95 percent of the mortgages in the pools.

If the individual or household wishes to borrow on the basis of a subsidized home or apartment project mortgage and meets the particular subsidized program requirements, the mortgage is originated by a local lender or mortgage banker. The loan is immediately sold to FNMA or the Mortgage Corporation, so it may proceed to sell the subsidized loan to GNMA. Both FNMA and the Mortgage Corporation usually invest only in unsubsidized mortgages; they usually do not hold any subsidized mortgages for resale. The interest rate or tenant rental subsidy can only be implemented if the mortgage is sold to GNMA. Part of the GNMA financing comes from tax monies received by the Treasury Department.

SUMMARY

When the investor needs mortgage money, he or she needs to consider the numerous sources for those funds. A great number of mortgage lenders exist to service prospective borrowers. Among them are savings and loan associations, commercial banks, life insurance companies, mutual savings banks, and pension funds. Also in the list of mortgage lenders are finance companies, real estate investment trusts, credit unions, and foundations and endowment funds.

More specifically, though, the prospective borrower must know what type of loan is needed and which lenders make that type of loan available. Not all lenders deal in all types of mortgage loans. The lenders tend to specialize. The principal home mortgage lenders are savings and loans, commercial and mutual savings banks, and federal agencies. Individuals, households, and finance companies also invest in home mortgage loans. Income property loans are negotiated by life insurance companies, savings and loan associations, and commercial banks. Federal agencies, households, mutual savings banks, and pension funds are also actively investing in income property loans.

When the borrower needs short-term construction and development loans for income properties, he or she goes to commercial banks, savings and loan associations, and real estate investment trusts. When a permanent loan is sought for an income property, the borrower goes to pension funds, life insurance companies, savings and loan associations, and mutual savings banks if a first-mortgage loan is sought. Finance companies are contacted if a second or more subordinated permanent loan is needed.

Savings and loans and mutual savings banks particularly concentrate in residential mortgage loans of all types. Commercial banks offer all types of mortgage loans from their commercial loan and mortgage departments and their REIT subsidiaries. Life insurance companies have such liberal regulation that they can make all types of mortgage loans, either from the company proper or from their REIT subsidiary. Since pension funds have little regulation over their lending and are generally tax exempt, they may lend on any kind of mortgage loan. They tend to want large loans on income properties or large real estate investments because of the constant flow of sizable pension contributions, which need immediate investment for the long term. Since finance companies focus on yield and turnover of their loans, they prefer to invest in junior mortgage loans of shorter maturities than typical first-mortgage loans. Real estate investment trusts have invested in every kind of mortgage loans and real estate that their individual declarations of trust permit. The individual trusts have tended to specialize and have been classified normally as mortgage trusts, hybrid trusts, or equity trusts. Credit unions have recently begun to invest in home mortgage loans to complement their consumer loan portfolios. Their mortgage lending may expand on a dollar basis and a percentage-of-assets basis. Foundation and endowment funds have historically invested in real estate and mortgage interests. These tax-exempt organizations usually have considerable sums to invest in income properties for the long run.

The secondary mortgage market lenders are the Federal National Mortgage Association, the Federal Home Loan Mortgage Corporation, and the Government National Mortgage Association. These lenders buy mortgage loans from mortgage seller-originators. FNMA and the Mortgage Corporation deal in unsubsidized single-family and multifamily mortgage loans. GNMA deals in subsidized single-family and multifamily mortgage loans exclusively. When the primary market lender originates a residential loan but does not have the investible funds at the time for the loan, this lender sells the complete loan to a secondary mortgage market lender. Commercial banks and mortgage companies usually sell unsubsidized loans to FNMA and subsidized loans to FNMA and to GNMA on a tandem plan. Savings and loans and mutual savings banks tend to sell their unsubsidized residential loans to the Mortgage Corporation and their subsidized loans to the Mortgage Corporation and to GNMA, also on a tandem plan basis.

Key Terms and Concepts

Institutional lending policies and practices
Loan negotiation
Primary mortgage market
State and local retirement funds
Federal Reserve
Loan rediscount rate
Interest rate ceilings
Liquidity
Secondary reserves
Safety of principal
Modified legal list
Sale-leaseback agreements
Annuity payments
Salomon Brothers
Bank trust departments
Investment managers
Internal Revenue Service
Bond-type mortgage-backed security

Pension fund counselors
Subdivision developer
Debentures
Treasury securities
National Credit Union Administration
Basic lending patterns
Sale of existing loans
Purchase of mortgage loans
Stage of real estate development
Real estate investment trusts
Federal Deposit Insurance Corp.
Discount window operations
Mergers and consolidations
Profitability
Tertiary reserves
State-chartered life insurance company
Leasehold mortgage loans
Thrift institution
Mortgage brokers

Investment banking houses
Portfolio managers
GNMA-guaranteed mortgage-backed securities
Short-term mortgage trust
Hybrid mortgage trust
Shares of beneficial interest
Convertible debentures
Federal agency securities
Mortgage seller-originator
Participation certificate
Regulatory agencies
Pension funds
Finance companies
Credit unions
Foundations and endowments
Comptroller of the Currency
Required reserves
Open Market Committee functions
Community service
Primary reserves
Contingencies
State insurance commission
Policy loans
Beneficiary payments
Mutual savings bank
1974 Employment Retirement Income Security Act
Qualified tax-exempt retirement plans
Pass-through-type mortgage-backed security
Equity trust
Commercial paper
Consumer loans
Credit union shares
Discount note
The Mortgage Corporation

Questions for Student Self-examination

Multiple-Choice Questions

1. Which institution does not lend mortgage monies on the secondary market level?
   a. Federal Reserve
   b. Federal National Mortgage Association
   c. Federal Home Loan Mortgage Corporation
   d. Government National Mortgage Association

2. In the late 1970s, which financial institution was not a principal source of first-mortgage money for home loans?
   a. life insurance companies
   b. mutual savings banks
   c. commercial banks
   d. savings and loan associations

3. Which financial institution usually concentrates its investible funds in junior mortgage loans on houses?
   a. life insurance companies
   b. commercial banks
   c. finance companies
   d. mutual savings banks

4. Which financial institution deals almost exclusively in first-mortgage loans?
   a. pension funds
   b. life insurance companies
   c. federal agencies
   d. all of the above

5. Which institution does not operate in the secondary mortgage market?
   a. National Credit Union Administration
   b. Federal National Mortgage Association
   c. Government National Mortgage Association
   d. Federal Home Loan Mortgage Corporation

True-False Questions

T F 1. Commercial banks by far exceed other financial institutions and individuals in mortgage lending.
T F 2. Savings and loan associations invest some of their funds in income property mortgages with an emphasis on shopping-center loans.
T F 3. Federal agencies invest in apartment project loans, usually of the FHA-insured type.
T F 4. All sources of income property mortgage money do not offer all kinds of real estate loans.
T F 5. In the secondary mortgage market the borrower of mortgage funds negotiates directly with the lender or the lender's representative, the mortgage banker.
T F 6. During 1978 primary mortgage market institutions did not finance 100 percent of all mortgages.
T F 7. Savings and loan associations hold federal government securities for liquidity.
T F 8. The usual conventional mortgage loan has a loan-to-value ratio of 45 to 50 percent of appraised value.
T F 9. The interest rate on the conventional mortgage loan is usually the market rate of interest.
T F 10. An investor may acquire a permanent first mortgage loan from the commercial loan department of a bank.

Answers
Multiple-choice: 1a, 2a, 3c, 4c, 5a.
True-False: 1F, 2F, 3T, 4T, 5F, 6T, 7T, 8F, 9T, 10F.

Problems

1. As Jim and Mary Crawford consider the financing of the house they want to buy, what financial institution near them would offer the highest probability of home mortgage money? In other words, what is the financial institution that leads year after year in home mortgage lending?

2. If Jim Sullivan had accumulated enough money to consider the construction of a small office building, where should he go in his community for a construction loan?

3. If a local shopping center developer, Jane Wilson, wishes to negotiate a sale-leaseback for her shopping mall, what financial institutions might she approach?

4. If Mark Stevens, a long-time employee of B. F. Goodrich Co., has been depositing his family's savings in the credit union of the company, what kind of loan might he expect to acquire from his credit union if the need arose?

5. If the Jackson Mortgage Company wishes to sell its mortgage loans to a secondary mortgage market institution, to which institutions may the company be eligible to sell loans?

6. If the Cook Mortgage Company packaged some mortgage-backed securities and wished to get a federal government guarantee for the package, what secondary mortgage market institution would the company officers approach?

Chapter 7

The Appraisal System of Analysis

Introduction
The Relationship of This Chapter to Other Chapters of the Text
The Nature of Real Estate Appraising
Some Basic Terminology
  Cost, Price, and Market Value   Reproduction Value Versus Replacement Value   Value in Use Versus Value in Exchange
Major Determinants of Value
  Location   Demand and Supply   Scarcity   Utility   Ability to Pay   Buyer Knowledge of Alternatives
The Principles of Real Estate Appraising
  Balance   Conformity   Change   Anticipation   Competition   Substitution   Supply and Demand   Contribution   Increasing and Decreasing Returns   Highest and Best Use
The Appraisal Process
  Definition of the Problem   Preliminary Survey and Appraisal Plan   Data Acquisition   Data Classification and Analysis   Reconciliation of the Values from the Three Approaches   Final Estimation of Value or the Value Range
Methods of Estimating Cost
  Quantity Survey   Unit in Place   Market Comparison   Builder's or Trade Breakdown
Accrued Depreciation
  Physical Deterioration   Functional Obsolescence   Economic Obsolescence
The Market Comparison Approach to Value
Property Characteristics Subject to Market Comparison
  Single-Family Dwelling   Apartment Building
Adjustment of the Sale Price of the Comparable to the Value of the Subject
  Types of Adjustments to Value
The Income Approach to House Appraising
  A Case Example
Summary
Key Terms and Concepts
Questions for Student Self-examination

LEARNING OBJECTIVES After studying this chapter, you should be familiar with

The nature of real estate appraising
The differences between cost, price, and market value
The difference between reproduction value and replacement value
The difference between value in use and value in exchange
The major determinants of value
The ten principles of real estate appraising
The nature of the appraisal process
Methods of estimating cost of construction
Methods of deriving the accrued depreciation of a structure
The differences between physical deterioration, functional obsolescence, and economic obsolescence
The nature of the market comparison approach to the determination of value
The nature of the income approach to house appraising

Investment is based on the appraisal of value. The complexity arises when different people place different values on the same property. They perceive different uses or functions for the property now and in the future. They approach the job of appraisal of property value from different viewpoints. Different methods are used in finding value.

Even if the real estate appraiser is designated by a professional appraisal organization and uses the appraisal methods promulgated by that professional organization, he or she may arrive at a value for investment purposes that will differ from the estimated value set forth by another designated appraiser. There are differences of opinion, and there are ranges of value that any one component of a property may assume. Even though the methods used for estimation of value may be the same among the group of appraisers asked to estimate the value of a property, six different values may be estimated for the property by six different real estate appraisers.

Appraising is partly an art and partly a science. The established methodology of real estate appraising is the portion of appraising based on the scientific approach and method. On the other hand, when the appraiser estimates the fluctuations in cash flows, including the future operating expenses and revenues, the appraiser is applying subjective judgment that originates from appraisal experience, knowledge of investment histories of properties, and intuition based on practical experience. The appraiser applies the art of forecasting and exercises innate judgment.

INTRODUCTION

The chapter begins with a definition of real estate appraising. The reader must know what is meant by real estate appraising before he or she can go further into the appraisal methods. Since the terms *cost*, *price*, and *market value* are often confused, these terms are differentiated. The same thing is true of the appraisal terms *reproduction value* and *replacement value*. The appraiser also distinguishes between *value in use* and *value in exchange*. The appraiser tends to distinguish between these terms; therefore, the reader should be familiar with the distinctions as the appraisal process is studied.

Several factors determine value. The interaction of demand and supply affect value. Property must be scarce to some extent in order to have value. Property must have utility for it to have value. The prospective purchasers must have the ability to pay in order for the desired property to have value in the marketplace. The prospective buyer's knowledge of alternatives in necessary to the establishment of relative values between property alternatives.

The leading appraisal organizations have established ten principles of appraising, upon which the appraiser relies in his or her everyday work. These fundamental principles are balance, conformity, change, anticipation, competition, substitution, supply and demand, contribution, increasing and decreasing returns, and highest and best use.

The appraisal process involves several steps. The appraiser first defines the problem of the client, he or she makes a preliminary survey of the data and work needed to make the desired appraisal, and the client receives an estimate of the appraisal delivery data and its cost. Then the work begins with data acquisition, classification, and analysis. The three approaches to the estimation of value—market, cost, and income approaches—are considered. Each approach is used if it is applicable. The value indicators from the three approaches are reconciled, and the client is given the final estimate of value.

Each of the three approaches to value involves a detailed system of analysis. The cost approach requires the derivation of the depreciated reproduction or replacement cost new. At least four methods of estimating cost may be considered: the quantity survey, the unit-in-place, the market comparison, and the builder's or trade breakdown methods. Depreciation must be estimated along three lines of analysis: physical deterioration, functional obsolescence, and environmental obsolescence. The curable and incurable elements are evaluated with a dollar amount. The market approach to value involves a grid analysis, in which adjustments to comparable properties are made element by element, in terms of dollars or percentages of the sale price of the individual comparable property. The commonly used features of comparison fall into the categories of time of sale, physical characteristics, location, and sale conditions. The income approach to valuation is illustrated in this chapter in terms of house appraising. The GRM, or Gross Rent Multiplier, approach, requires the derivation of an estimated market rent for the subject and the gross rent multiplier applicable to the subject. Sales prices and monthly rents at the time of sale for comparable properties are needed in calculating the appropriate gross rent multiplier.

THE RELATIONSHIP OF THIS CHAPTER TO OTHER CHAPTERS OF THE TEXT

We finish Part II with two chapters on appraising. Chapter 7 deals with the basic principles and practices of real estate appraising. Chapter 8 delves into the complexities of income property appraising. House appraising is used for illustrative purposes in Chapter 7.

We have already covered some of the financial relationships of which the investor should be aware. The investor needs a good knowledge of mortgage financing, the usefulness of favorable leverage, and the various sources of mortgage money and institutional specialties in mortgage lending. Now we observe that if the investor is a good appraiser, the investment returns may be greater. The investor should be able to arrive at the value of a property in general so that a good value will be received for payment. The methods of the professional appraiser may be useful to the professional or amateur investor. The investor may also check the appraisal work commissioned by the investor. Does the investor agree with the appraiser's findings? Is the appraiser's value dependent on the same assumptions that the investor is making?

THE NATURE OF REAL ESTATE APPRAISING

Before you can delve into any subject, you must first lay the basic groundwork. The reader should decide what real estate appraising is. Then there should be a basic understanding of at least a few of the principal terms of the real estate appraising business.

More than one definition of real estate appraising is espoused by practitioners in the trade. One of the commonly used definitions is that real estate appraising is the estimating of value of a real property interest as of a given date. A real estate appraisal, on the other hand, is the estimate of value of a real property interest as of a given date. The real estate appraisal report is the standard form or narrative research report that informs the client of the estimation of value that the appraiser derived from the use of the established appraisal process or system.

If the property being appraised is an income-producing property, the appraiser may say that real estate appraising is the estimating of present worth of future benefits from real property arising from ownership of property rights. When the investor receives revenue and incurs operating expenses associated with a property, his or her ideas of value are directly linked to the property's current and future net cash benefits.

SOME BASIC TERMINOLOGY

Some terms are emphasized by appraisers in their work. The appraiser, for example, differentiates between the terms *cost, price,* and *market value.* He or she also considers the differences between *reproduction value* and *replacement value* important. *Value in use* has an emphatically different meaning from *value in exchange* to the appraiser.

Cost, Price, and Market Value. To an appraiser the term *cost* means the dollar amount required for the acquisition of a property or the construction of an improvement. For example, it may cost $30,000 to build a house. To the appraiser the term *price* means the dollar amount paid to the previous owner by the new owner for the acquisition of title. At the time of sale the forces of supply and demand may have acted to bring about an equilibrium price, which means the forces of demand were equal to the forces of supply. On the other hand, price may not reflect the conditions of balanced demand and supply. A daughter may pay her father $200 for a house lot that he has been holding as an investment for a number of years; the market value of the lot at the time may be $10,000. The $200 is the price of the market transaction. Whereas *cost* is an accounting concept related to a dollar amount paid in a past transaction, *price* tends to reflect a current transfer of dollars to complete a transaction. The term *market value,* in contrast, may not represent the dollar amount exchanged to complete a past or present transaction. Market value is the highest price, estimated in monetary terms, that a property will bring if it is exposed for sale in the open market with a reasonable time allowed to find a purchaser. The purchase is made when the buyer and seller are under no unusual pressure; the purchaser buys with full knowledge of all the uses to which the property is adapted and the purposes for which it is capable of being used. Market value reflects an arm's-length transaction in which no relatives, close friends, or close business associates are transacting business. Price may or may not equal market value. Cost may or may not equal market value. It is said that the cost of house construction, including a reasonable profit for the builder, equals market value at the completion of the house. The price paid by a purchaser may be higher or lower than the cost or market value. Another example might be taken from the office building sector. The cost of constructing the office building, including the builder's profit, may be far less than market value. The price paid for the building may be far greater than market value or far less than market value. Cost might be $1 million; market value might be $1.25 million; the building might sell for $1.5 billion. For any number of reasons, the purchaser may be willing to pay over market value for the office building.

Reproduction Value Versus Replacement Value. If the subject property has been constructed, the appraiser has ready access to its reproduction value and uses it. The reproduction value is the cost of constructing the same physical structure at the present time. If the subject is a turn-of-the-century Victorian-style house, the reproduction value is the cost of replicating the exact structure today.

If the subject has existed for some time, the appraiser estimates the replacement value. The cost of replacing the functional utility in today's market is the goal of the appraiser. If the subject is a turn-of-the-century Victorian style house, the replacement cost might be figured on the construction cost of a three-bedroom ranch-style house with only one fireplace. Since most properties that are appraised have existed for some time, the appraiser is usually concerned with replacement value rather than reproduction value.

Value in Use Versus Value in Exchange. When a prospective investor negotiates with a satisfied owner-occupant of a property for a reasonable sale price, the investor finds a relationship that the appraiser often observes. The satisfied owner-occupant often perceives greater value in the subject property than the outside investor does. The value in use often surpasses the value in exchange. The value in exchange reflects the interplay of demand and supply forces at work in the marketplace. The outside investor appraises the functional, social, and economic utility of the subject property in terms of his or her business or household needs.

MAJOR DETERMINANTS OF VALUE

Property value is determined by many factors. A few of the more strategic determinants are location, demand and supply, scarcity, utility, ability to pay, and buyer knowledge of alternatives.

Location. Some real estate professionals say that the three determinants of value are location, location, and location. If a property has a "good" location, it will have a "good" value. If the property has a "bad" location, its value will be relatively low in comparison with properties with "good" locations. A "good" location usually has good transportation access, lies in the path of urban growth, experiences no adverse environmental influences, is situated near complimentary land uses, and is accommodated by all utility services needed by the building and its occupants.

A good location for a house generally requires proximity to good schools and fire and police protection. The employed workers of the household may prefer to be relatively close to their places of work. Public transportation access may be important to the resident of a major metropolitan area. All municipal and utility services needed by the household should be available. Property taxes for the site should be reasonable. Highways and streets should be relatively accessible, but the house should be located so that the adjacent streets are safe for children and household pets. Shopping, recreational, and religious facilities should be fairly close.

Demand and Supply. The balance of demand and supply tends to influence the trend of a property value. If the supply of a certain type of property far outruns the demand, the value tends to decline. If the market is flooded with 8- to 12-unit garden apartment buildings and many units are vacant, the value of such an apartment building will tend to decline. On the other hand, if apartment units in 8- to 12-unit garden buildings are in greater demand than the supply of units on the market, the value of the individual buildings will tend to rise as vacancies disappear. Value will remain stable if the supply of a certain type of building remains relatively in balance with the demand.

Scarcity. If a property is not scarce in any way, it does not have market value. An example of an asset that does not have market value is the air we breathe, which is not scarce in any way. If a potential home builder wants a relatively level, wooded lot, and if such house lots are quite scarce, the values of the qualifying lots may tend to be high because of the demand, which exceeds the scarce supply.

Utility. Building space that has a great deal of utility for a prospective business tenant has great value from the viewpoint of the tenant. Another building space with less utility for the prospective tenant has less value from the tenant's point of view. For example, a new office building with load-bearing exterior walls and no inner supporting columns may offer greater utility to the prospective corporate tenant than an older office building with supporting columns placed every so many feet across the office floor space. The utility of the new building increases its value in the marketplace.

Ability to Pay. A property has value if the prospective owner or investor has the ability to pay the price necessary to acquire the property. If an investor desires the location and the utility represented by the property, but does not have the funds for the downpayment and the future mortgage payments, this desire for the property is an ineffective demand.

Value is usually determined by the market exchange of comparable properties. If comparable units have not sold and those interested in the units do not have the ability to pay, the value of the subject cannot be determined.

Buyer Knowledge of Alternatives. The best indication of value comes from buyer knowledge of alternative properties available for sale. The prospective buyer balances the advantages and disadvantages of competing properties and ultimately places a value on each of the competing properties from his or her own viewpoint. The truest value for the subject property comes from the eventual sale price of each of the competing properties. Buyer knowledge of competing properties also stabilizes the value relationships between the properties.

THE PRINCIPLES OF REAL ESTATE APPRAISING

Over the years several principles of real estate appraising have been set forth. Ten principles or generalizations about property value have been delineated by the leading professional appraisal organizations.

Balance. When the four factors of production—labor, capital, land, and entrepreneurship—are represented in a balanced form in a developed property, the value of the property will reach its highest point. If any one of the factors of production gets out of balance with the other three, the value will tend to decline. For example, an office building ties up land, capital, labor, and entrepreneurship. If too many property managers are hired for the building or the right number of property managers are hired but they are paid excessive amounts, the labor factor may get out of balance with the other factors. The higher-than-normal property management expense will reduce the net operating income. When the appropriate capitalization rate is applied to the reduced net operating income, a lower value will result than if the optimal net operating income were received from the property.

Conformity. When the properties of a neighborhood generally conform to a pattern, each of the properties reaches its highest value. The properties do not have to be stereotyped or uninteresting in their conformity, but the general similarity results in the highest values for the individual properties in the neighborhood. The conformity might involve, for example, ranch-style homes with 150-foot frontage and approximately 3,000 square feet of livable area. If a small modern house with 75 feet of frontage were built in the neighborhood, the principle of progression would apply to the small house, which means that its value might increase beyond what would be its normal value in a neighborhood of other small houses. The principle of regression might also apply to the larger houses surrounding the small modern house. The values of the adjacent houses might decline from their normal level because of the nonconforming neighbor with smaller square footage, different architectural style, and lesser front footage.

Change. The real estate appraiser's work is subject to constant change. Property values fluctuate as changes take place in the community and as property buyer tastes and wants change. Stable values last until change occurs. For example, construction costs change, rents and operating expenses change, the demand for four-bedroom ranch houses changes, the general direction of new construction changes, retail centers' sales volumes change, and the size of the average household changes. Property valuation is based on the principle of change, since all these factors have an impact on property values.

Anticipation. Today's property value may be based on a forecast of future conditions. This is particularly true of income property values. The present value of the land and building is the value of the capitalized future net rental income. The income property is worth today only what it is expected to produce in net rental income and price appreciation in the future. The income and expenses of the future must be estimated and the appropriate capitalization rate based on expected future conditions must be derived. The future financing, property appreciation, investor yield requirement, and relative risk must be analyzed so that the capitalization rate will properly reflect the expected conditions. The appraiser must anticipate future conditions in light of professional competence and experience from past years.

Competition. Competition in the marketplace aids the establishment of value. The more competition for the purchase or rental of a property, the higher the value of the property. If there is a lack of competition for the acquisition of a property, the value of the property will tend to decline.

Since the value of an income property may be partly determined by the level of the capitalization rate, the competition for mortgage money is important to the determination of this rate. The more competition there is for a given amount of mortgage money, the higher the mortgage rates will tend to climb. As the mortgage rates rise, the capitalization rates for income properties tend to rise. As the "cap rate," as the capitalization rate is sometimes called, rises, the value of the property declines. The basic valuation formula is net operating income divided by an appropriate capitalization rate equals value.

$$\frac{NOI}{R} = V$$

Substitution. According to the principle of substitution, a prospective buyer with several alternative properties available, each of which would serve his or her needs, will select the property with the lowest price. Since most buyers do not want to spend any more than they have to, this appraisal principle fits the valuation of single-family houses in particular. The estimation of the market value of a house is based strategically on this appraisal principle. The recent sale prices of several houses comparable to the subject are acquired. The differences in the characteristics of the comparable properties from the characteristics of the subject property are examined in light of the recent selling prices.

Supply and Demand. The supply of various types of properties and the demand for them have an important impact on the value of property types in general and on the value of individual properties within the categories. For example, if office building space is scarce and demand for such space is strong, the values of office buildings tend to be relatively high. If high-class office space downtown is scarce relative to the corporate demand for this high-class space, the rental rate per square foot will tend to rise to relatively high levels. In contrast, if there is a surplus of office space with regard to current office space demand, the value of the buildings with surplus space will tend to decline.

If the supply of split-level houses is less than the demand for them, the market values of existing split-level structures will tend to rise until the home builders construct enough split-level houses to satisfy or to saturate the current market. Once the home builders construct too many of these houses, the market values of the split levels for sale will tend to decline. As the market demand for split levels is met or the market demand turns to other types of houses, the values on split levels decline.

Contribution. Two components of real property contribute to overall property value—the land and the buildings. The proportions of total property value contributed by the land and the buildings vary with the property situation. The land value may represent almost all the total property value. For example, the land under an economically obsolete building may contribute 95 percent of the property value. In other situations, the improvements may contribute most of the value. For example, a new, spacious, modern house in a rural area may contribute most of the value, since the land beneath the house may have a relatively low value and the costs of construction may have been relatively high.

Increasing and Decreasing Returns. Property value may be increased by improvements up to a point; improvements made after that strategic point is reached result in no increase in value or in a declining value, since the cost of the additional improvements is greater than the increase in value that is a result of the improvements. This principle applies to all areas of real estate, including home improvement and office building management. The investor may hire a full-time manager for an office building. The management and investment performance attained by the manager may reflect increased property productivity. However, if the owner hires two more property managers for the same building, individual productivity with respect to building value increase may decline markedly. At least one of the new managers may not contribute as much to investment value increase as his or her salary costs the owner.

Highest and Best Use. Appraisers tend to have two definitions of the principle of highest and best use. One definition is that the highest and best use of land is the use that produces the highest land value. The other definition is that the highest and best use is the land use that produces the highest present value for the land *and its improvements*. The highest and best use of the land is that use that is legally possible, appropriate to the site, and economically reasonable.

The highest and best use of a residential subdivision lot is probably the construction of a house. In a commercially zoned area, the highest and best use of a particular parcel of land may not be immediately determinable. Several commercial land uses might have to be explored, and an extensive analysis might be necessary in light of local market conditions. Perhaps a six-story office building might eventually be determined to be the highest and best use of the land.

THE APPRAISAL PROCESS

The appraisal profession tends to agree that the appraisal process encompasses a certain system of analysis, which takes place by means of an orderly progression of steps. The analytical process starts with the definition of the problem. It is followed by a preliminary survey of the data, personnel, and time requirements for the property valuation. A plan is developed for the completion of the valuation report. Then a data program is initiated. General and specific data associated with the subject property are gathered, then classified and analyzed. The use of the three appraisal approaches—cost, market comparison, and income—are considered in light of the type of property and its market conditions. From the values established from the three approaches, the appraiser reconciles the value indicators with respect to their applicability to the valuation problem and finally reaches an estimate of value or range of values (Exhibit 7-1).

Definition of the Problem. The client of the appraiser may have any one of several appraisal problems. The appraiser must inquire about the client's problem so that he or she can appraise the subject property for the right purpose. Typical problems needing an appraisal solution are

1. Value of condemnation purposes.
2. Value for mortgage lending purposes.
3. Value for property tax purposes.
4. Value for estate settlement purposes.
5. Value for hazard insurance purposes.
6. Value for corporate relocation of an employee.

When a condemning authority exercising the power of eminent domain wants to pay a reasonable price for property in the path of a publicly approved project, it seeks an appraisal, which usually emphasizes values from the market comparison and income approaches. The same thing is true of appraisal for mortgage lending, estate settlement, and corporate relocation of an employee. Property tax appraisals often reflect conservative fair market value and involve appraisal of similar properties in big blocks, either through the use of multiple regression statistical methods or hand calculation methods.

Exhibit 7-1. The Valuation Process

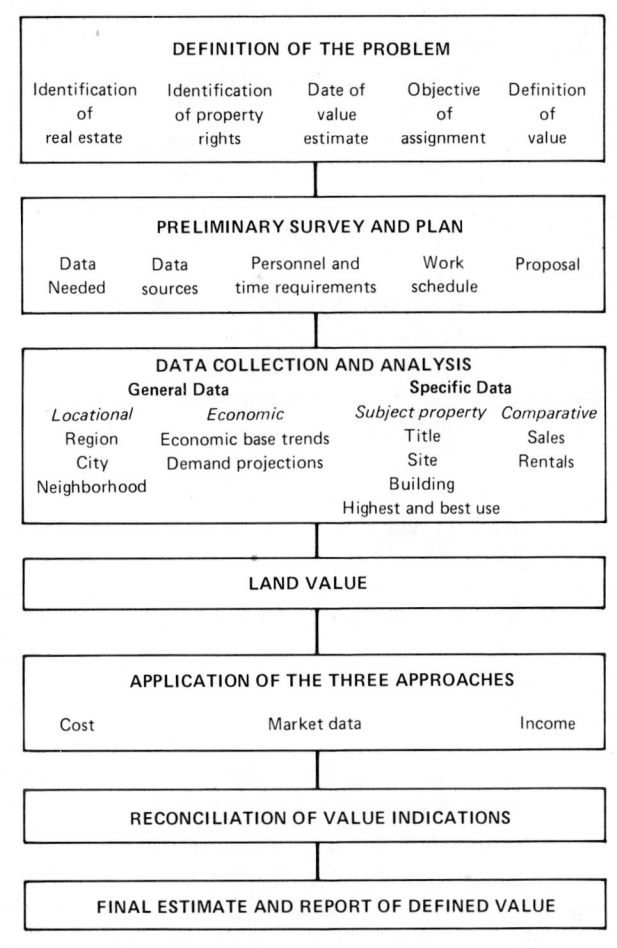

```
┌─────────────────────────────────────────────────────────────────────┐
│                     DEFINITION OF THE PROBLEM                       │
│                                                                     │
│  Identification   Identification    Date of     Objective  Definition│
│       of           of property       value         of         of    │
│   real estate        rights         estimate    assignment   value  │
└─────────────────────────────────────────────────────────────────────┘
                                   │
┌─────────────────────────────────────────────────────────────────────┐
│                     PRELIMINARY SURVEY AND PLAN                     │
│                                                                     │
│    Data        Data      Personnel and       Work                   │
│   Needed      sources    time requirements   schedule    Proposal   │
└─────────────────────────────────────────────────────────────────────┘
                                   │
┌─────────────────────────────────────────────────────────────────────┐
│                     DATA COLLECTION AND ANALYSIS                    │
│              General Data                Specific Data              │
│       Locational      Economic      Subject property   Comparative  │
│        Region     Economic base trends    Title           Sales     │
│         City       Demand projections     Site           Rentals    │
│      Neighborhood                        Building                   │
│                                    Highest and best use             │
└─────────────────────────────────────────────────────────────────────┘
                                   │
┌─────────────────────────────────────────────────────────────────────┐
│                            LAND VALUE                               │
└─────────────────────────────────────────────────────────────────────┘
                                   │
┌─────────────────────────────────────────────────────────────────────┐
│                  APPLICATION OF THE THREE APPROACHES                │
│                                                                     │
│        Cost               Market data                Income         │
└─────────────────────────────────────────────────────────────────────┘
                                   │
┌─────────────────────────────────────────────────────────────────────┐
│                  RECONCILIATION OF VALUE INDICATIONS                │
└─────────────────────────────────────────────────────────────────────┘
                                   │
┌─────────────────────────────────────────────────────────────────────┐
│              FINAL ESTIMATE AND REPORT OF DEFINED VALUE             │
└─────────────────────────────────────────────────────────────────────┘
```

Source: American Institute of Real Estate Appraisers, *The Appraisal of Real Estate,* 7th ed. (Chicago: American Institute of Real Estate Appraisers, 1978), p. 52. With permission.

Hazard insurance companies usually want depreciated cost. If the policy is written on the basis of current replacement value, the appraisal will tend to reflect current market value.

Preliminary Survey and Appraisal Plan. Before the appraisal job is accepted, the appraiser must consider the job requirements and how it fits into the appraiser's current schedule. In some cases a preliminary survey must be made before a bid can be made on a job. Whether or not a bid must be made, the appraiser must decide what the data, time, and personnel requirements are, so that a fee and a completion date can be established for the prospective client. The prospective client then can accept or reject the appraiser's terms.

If the client accepts the appraiser's terms, the client will expect the appraiser to meet the completion date. This may necessitate the appraiser's making a flow chart of jobs, either mentally or on paper.

Data Acquisition. Two types of data are necessary for the appraisal of an individual property: general data and specific data. The general data refer to the trends in business and real estate activity in the nation, region, metropolitan area, city, and neighborhood. Specific data relate to the site and its improvements. The titleholder must be determined, the site and improvements described, the zoning defined, and the real estate tax burden and trend determined.

Data Classification and Analysis. In order to determine the value of the subject from each of the three approaches, certain data must be acquired and classified. The data classified for use under each of the three approaches must be analyzed to establish a value from the cost approach, a value from the market comparison approach, and a value from the income approach. Each of the values relies on market data, whether it is cost information, rental and expense figures, or sale prices of comparable properties from the recent market.

Reconciliation of the Values from the Three Approaches. Once a value is determined from each of the three approaches to value, the appraiser examines the three values and evaluates their relevance to the current overall value of the property. The values may be very close or there may be a wide difference between the dollar amounts.

The appraiser may place more reliance on one of the values than on the others. One or two of the values may be better substantiated than the other one or two. The data from recent sales of comparable properties may be more reliable than the income-expense data for comparable income properties. If a house is being appraised, only one comparable house might have been found that had been rented at the time of sale. If the subject is a government property or a religious building, comparable buildings may not have been sold lately.

The professional appraiser is warned not to average the three value indicators in order to find the desired value. The appraiser finds it difficult to defend the adding of the three value indicators and dividing by three to find value. It is easier for the appraiser logically to defend individual and different weights for the individual value indicators. For example, if the market comparison data were weak, the value from the market comparison approach might be given a percentage weight of only 20 percent, while the value from the cost approach might be given a percentage weight of 50 percent. The value from the use of the income approach would be given the remaining weight of 30 percent, to bring the total to 100 percent. An expected value could be determined by adding together the weighted value indicators. The value from each approach would be multiplied by the percentage weight.

Final Estimation of Value or the Value Range. In today's market the appraiser may give the client a single value estimate or a range of value estimates. In most cases, admittedly, the appraiser reports a single dollar amount to the client. However, when significant sums of money are involved and when many estimates are made in order to arrive at overall property value, the appraiser often reports a range of possible values. For example, the valuation of large-scale income properties often results in a range of values because many estimates of future incomes and expenses must be made and the valuation result is not precise.

METHODS OF ESTIMATING COST

When the investor wants a value for the property from the cost approach, one of the four cost-estimating methods may be used. These four methods are often described as (1) the quantity survey, (2) the unit-in-place, (3) the market comparison, and (4) the builder's or trade breakdown methods. Each of the four methods has different degrees of usefulness.

Quantity Survey. The most comprehensive cost-estimating method is the quantity survey method. If the method were followed strictly, the cost-estimation procedure of the subcontractors and the contractor would be replicated. The quantity and quality of each type of material would be determined. The hours of labor of the specialized construction trades would be estimated. The unit costs for labor and material would be established. Finally a detailed reproduction cost would be derived for the subject property. Estimated direct and indirect costs for an apartment building using the quantity survey method are presented in Exhibit 7-2.

Unit in Place. While the elaborate detail of the quantity survey method of cost estimating may be required for certain special appraisal reports, some clients may be satisfied with the less detailed unit-in-place method (Exhibit 7-3). This cost-estimation method is based on the use of unit prices for the various building components. For example, the unit of cost may be associated with a linear foot of exterior wall, a square of roofing (100 square feet), a cubic foot or yard of concrete foundation, a cubic yard of excavation, or a ton of air conditioning. The unit of measurement depends on the cost practices of the particular building trade. Other building units—whose unit costs are figured—are plastering, plumbing, heating, and flooring. Each unit cost includes labor, materials, and overhead.

For example, the unit cost for a linear foot of brick veneer exterior wall is composed of the labor, materials, and overhead costs associated with that particular building unit. The costs of the stud framing, insulation, drywall, sheathing, and face brick for the linear foot must be determined. To find total unit cost, the number of linear feet is multiplied by the cost per linear foot.

Market Comparison. The most commonly used method of cost estimating is the market comparison method. The appraiser finds out from builders their square foot costs for recent construction of buildings similar to the subject. Adjustments are made for the extra features or the features lacking in the subject property. A cost figure is extracted from the various cost estimates of the various builders and applied to the cost estimation for the subject. For example, the builders may indicate that the cost per square foot of a 1,200-square-foot brick veneer house with standard fixtures is $22 to $23. If the subject has 1,150 square feet of livable space, the estimated reproduction cost of the house new might be figured by multiplying 1,150 times $22, which is $25,300. Once a lot value of $5,000 and patio and garage costs of $3,800 are added, the total reproduction cost of the house would be $34,100, or rounded off, $34,000. This estimation technique can be utilized by the appraiser for any type of property that has been recently constructed in the community.

Builder's or Trade Breakdown. This method of cost estimating is often used, particularly for income properties. The general contractor may make available his total cost estimate based on the subcontractors' bids. Each cost is generally the bid from a subcontractor. Then the general contractor adds his costs and overhead amounts. A sample cost estimate for a single-family dwelling based on the trade breakdown method is found in Exhibit 7-4.

Exhibit 7-2. Cost Estimate for an Apartment Building: Quantity Survey Method

Direct costs

Clearing the land	$ 1,400
Rough and fine grading	4,200
Footings	2,600
Cement slabs	17,400
Entrances	1,450
Interior stairs	2,800
Rough and finished carpentry	83,000
Doors (exterior insulated)	22,400
Windows (insulated glass)	8,700
Rough and finished hardware	4,740
Kitchen cabinets and bath vanities	21,200
Flooring	5,900
Refrigerators	4,500
Dishwashers	2,700
Electric surface units and hoods	1,800
Electric ovens	2,200
Draperies and hardware	4,900
Carpets and vinyl floor coverings	16,150
Painting	23,850
Insulation	11,125
Masonry	48,000
Drywall	32,300
Heating and air conditioning	21,125
Plumbing and fixtures	36,000
Electrical wiring and fixtures	18,000
Water mains	5,600
Water and sewer connections	2,840
Roofing, sheet metal, flashing, gutter and downspouts	11,300
Cleaning, general and contract	5,200
Landscaping	6,300
Fences	6,490
Temporary utilities	1,650
Concrete parking slabs	5,160
Service drive at rear	2,650
Storm and sanitary sewers	5,340
Supervision and timekeeping	18,250
Bathroom accessories	2,800
Wallpaper	3,600
Fireplace and chimneys	10,300
	485,920

Indirect costs

Permits	1,175
Builder's risk insurance	1,800
Economic studies, etc.	2,250
Surveys	1,200
Architectural design and supervision	25,000
Payroll taxes	9,400
Builder's overhead and profit	86,850
Total indirect costs	127,675
Total cost	$613,595

Source: Mr. Tom Farmer, chief engineer and cost estimator, Lloyd Wood Construction Co., Inc., Tuscaloosa, Ala. The cost figures reflect Southeast costs as of November 1978. With permission.

Exhibit 7-3. *A Typical Cost Estimation for a Two-Story Bank Building with Ground Floor Half Below Ground Level Using the Unit-in-Place Method*

Line	Component	Unit	Unit Cost	Total Unit Cost
1.	Job overhead, supervision, permits, insurance utilities, storage, etc.	13,300 sq. ft.	5.00	$ 66,500
2.	Common excavation	7,000 cu. yd.	1.75	12,250
3.	Foundation and concrete basement walls	6,700 sq. ft.	10.00	67,000
4.	Foundation wall waterproofing	5,200 sq. ft.	1.60	8,320
5.	Ground floor: slab, reinforcing, porous fill, and polyethylene waterproofing	6,700 sq. ft.	1.30	8,710
6.	Second floor: slab, reinforcing, metal form deck	6,600 sq. ft.	1.40	9,240
7.	Cash vault: reinforced concrete	360 sq. ft.	35.00	12,600
8.	Book vault: reinforced concrete	360 sq. ft.	23.50	8,460
9.	Exterior walls: 8-in. concrete blocks, 1-in. styroform wall insulation and brick veneer	6,150 sq. ft.	6.00	36,900
10.	Structural steel framework with steel joists at floor and roof	13,300 sq. ft.	3.40	45,220
11.	Steel fireproofing, sprayed on	13,300 sq. ft.	0.45	5,985
12.	Roof: metal deck, lightweight concrete, built-up roof with gravel, roof flashings	6,600 sq. ft.	4.15	27,390
13.	Exterior soffit and facia trim (plaster)	500 sq. yd.	18.00	9,000
14.	Exterior wall glass (insulation)	1,720 sq. ft.	13.35	22,962
15.	Floor cover: vinyl tile	240 sq. ft.	1.20	288
16.	Floor cover: ceramic tile	1,300 sq. ft.	3.50	4,550
17.	Floor cover: carpet	1,200 sq. yd.	14.00	16,800
18.	Interior wood doors and hardware	42 each	250.00	10,500
19.	Vinyl-coated sheetrock on wood stripping (on concrete walls)	5,800 sq. ft.	1.30	7,540
20.	Interior partitions: vinyl-coated sheetrock on metal studs	18,600 sq. ft.	1.40	26,040
21.	Millwork: bank teller cages, check desks, kitchen cabinets, storage shelving, some wall mouldings	13,300 sq. ft.	2.10	27,930
22.	Ceilings: ground floor, suspended acoustical tile (fire rated)	6,700 sq. ft.	0.75	5,025
23.	Celings: second floor, suspended acoustical tile (fire rated) with 6-in. insulation batts	6,600 sq. ft.	1.15	7,590
24.	Toilet partitions, metal	8 stalls	200.00	1,600
25.	Bathroom accessories (mirrors, paper and towel dispensers, waste receptacles, etc.)	4 baths	500.00	2,000
26.	Bank equipment: vault doors, safe deposit boxes, night depository, teller equipment, survey cameras, burglar alarm system, four drive-up windoes, etc.	13,300 sq. ft.	10.00	133,000
27.	Asphalt covering, parking lot, including curb and gutters	4,000 sq. yd.	11.00	44,000
28.	Painting	13,300 sq. ft.	0.60	7.980
29.	Plumbing: four toilet rooms, installation	20 fixtures	250.00	5,000
		13,300 sq. ft.	1.00	13,300
30.	Heating, ventilation, air conditioning	13,300 sq. ft.	7.00	93,100
31.	Electricity and lighting	13,300 sq. ft.	5.00	66,500
32.	Elevator, one only	13,300 sq. ft.	2.50	33,250
33.	Parking lot lighting	36,000 sq. ft.	0.25	9,000
34.	Furniture and drapes	13,300 sq. ft.	4.00	53,200
	Total cost using the unit-in-place method of cost estimating			$908,730
35.	Architect's fee	13,300 sq. ft.	4.50	59,850
	Total cost			$968,580

Source: Tom Farmer, Chief Engineer and Cost Estimator, Lloyd Wood Construction Co., Inc., Tuscaloosa, Alabama. The cost figures reflect Southeast costs as of November 1978. With permission.

Exhibit 7-4. *Cost Estimate for a Single-Family Residence: Trade Breakdown Method (Three-bedroom, 1600 sq. ft. heated, double carport)*

Cost component	Cost
Architect's fee	$ 350
Permits and utility connections	300
Site clearing	250
Excavation	200
Foundation	1,200
Fireplace and chimney, masonry	1,500
Exterior walls, brick veneer	3,100
Subflooring (material and labor)	1,050
Framing and finishing carpentry materials	12,000
Carpentry labor	2,400
Roofing	1,000
Windows and doors	1,875
Sheetrock	1,300
Floor covering	1,250
Cabinet work	1,400
Insulation, walls and ceiling	800
Painting	1,700
Plumbing	2,250
Heating and air conditioning	1,500
Electrical	1,000
Lighting fixtures	350
Insurance	150
Built-in kitchen appliances	700
Finished hardware	150
Termite treatment	75
Miscellaneous	200
Subtotal	38,050
Field overhead, 8 percent	3,044
Subtotal	41,094
Contractor's profit, 12 percent	4,931
Final total	$46,025

Rounded to $46,000
Cost per sq. ft. (1600) = $28.75

Source: Mr. Tom Farmer, chief engineer and cost estimator, Lloyd Wood Construction Co., Inc., Tuscaloosa, Ala. The cost figures reflect Southeast costs as of November 1978. With permission.

ACCRUED DEPRECIATION

The cost approach to value is based on the depreciated reproduction or replacement cost new. In estimating accrued depreciation, the appraiser focuses on three basic kinds of depreciation: physical deterioration, functional obsolescence, and economic obsolescence. Many existing properties exhibit elements of one or more of the three types of depreciation. Appraisers find that even new properties reveal evidence of certain types of depreciation. New structures may have elements of functional and/or economic obsolescence; usually the newness eliminates the possibility of physical deterioration.

Physical Deterioration. Physical deterioration is the loss in value of a property from wear and tear or from ordinary or extraordinary use; from deteriorating conditions from nonuse; and from the detrimental results of weather conditions. Examples of physical deterioration of a house are a leaking roof, cracked concrete sidewalks and driveways, inoperative air conditioning condenser, peeling outside paint, holes in window screens, and warped doors.

Any form of depreciation is curable if the increase in the value of the property after the defect is cured exceeds or equals the cost of curing the defect. The depreciation is incurable if the cost of curing the defect exceeds the increase in the property value resulting from the curing of the defect.

Some physically depreciated conditions must be cured immediately for habitability of the structure for business or residence purposes. Other defects are subject to deferred or postponed curability. For example, if the air conditioning system of a shopping center storeroom or of an office in the South is not working during the summer, this physical defect must be cured at once. If the roof has been on a house for three years and its normal life is ten years, the roof has partially depreciated through the wear and tear of weather conditions. The defect may be cured later, at the end of the useful life of the roof, rather than immediately.

Some physical depreciation cannot be cured physically or economically. If a house is settling on its foundation into a sink hole caused by an abandoned coal mine, this physical depreciation is usually not curable. If the slab foundation of a house cracks once the house is built and the carpet laid, the water seepage from the slab crack probably cannot be stopped entirely. A number of structural conditions fall into this category.

Functional Obsolescence. Functional obsolescence involves a loss in property value resulting from a lack of functional utility. An office building may show functional obsolescence if numerous columns that are used for building support are placed in the middle of office floors. The office layout is restricted and not flexible for growth and expansion of the operations and personnel. In the case of a house, if a closet with a full-length window faces outward on the front of the house, the functional utility of that closet is restricted. In like manner, functional obsolescence may be revealed when the full-length window of a bathroom is located on the front exterior wall of a house near the front door. The privacy of the bath is inadequate without further expensive installation of shutters or other window coverings.

Functional obsolescence may be shown in room layout, electrical wiring, storage space, closet space, kitchen counter space, room sizes, garage width and depth, access to light and air, and the operating capacity of air conditioning systems. Many types of structural defects fall under the category of functional obsolescence. New as well as existing structures may show elements of functional obsolescence. A builder may build functional obsolescence into a new house consciously or inadvertently. Functional obsolescence may appear in existing business and residential structures as business practices and operating methods change and as household needs and wants change.

Economic Obsolescence. Recently economic obsolescence has been labeled by some as "environmental obsolescence." An improvement to land may lose value because of adverse environmental changes. Generally this type of depreciation occurs as a result of forces outside the property and outside the power of the property owner. Therefore, economic obsolescence is usually called incurable. The property owner is usually powerless to counteract the unfavorable influence.

For example, a new freeway may cut through a neighborhood, leaving some properties without access to the main traffic arteries. The places of business may become relatively inaccessible to their usual clientele. Another example is the establishment of an industrial plant or factory in the neighborhood whose emissions pollute the air or water in the vicinity. The properties of the neighborhood that are affected may lose value on the basis of environmental obsolescence. Another example might be the loss in property value from the closing of a neighborhood elementary school when the residents of the neighborhood tend to have elementary school-age children who found the school convenient to attend.

THE MARKET COMPARISON APPROACH TO VALUE

When the investor wishes to finance or sell a property or the prospective investor wants to buy a property at the right price, the valuation of the property from the market comparison approach is important to the analysis. The market comparison approach to value utilizes properties sold recently that are very comparable to the subject property. Each of the three or four comparable properties is described in terms of strategic market elements and compared to the subject property. The sale price of each of the comparables is adjusted in terms of each of the strategic elements so that the adjusted price of each comparable is the value of the subject property. To reiterate, the value of each comparable is adjusted to reflect the value of the subject.

Property Characteristics Subject to Market Comparison

Single-Family Dwelling. When a single-family house is the subject, the appraiser often examines the following characteristics in terms of their effect on market value:

1. Time of sale.
2. Physical characteristics.
   a. Design and appeal to the typical buyer.
   b. Quality of construction.
   c. Condition.
   d. Gross living area.
   e. Basement and basement finished rooms.
   f. Functional utility.
   g. Air conditioning and heating.
   h. Garage/carport.
   i. Porches, patio, pool.
   j. Fireplace.
   k. Other: kitchen equipment, closet space, and other features.

3. Location.
    a. Proximity to subject.
    b. Site/view/trees.
    c. Corner versus inside lot.
4. Sale conditions.
    a. Motivations behind the sale.
    b. Sales or financing concessions.
    c. Type of financing.

Apartment Building. When an apartment building or project is the subject, the appraiser often considers the following characteristics of the comparables and the subject in relation to market value:

1. Time of sale.
2. Terms of sale.
3. Location.
4. Zoning and other public restrictions.
5. Age and condition of the improvements.
6. Residential amenities.
    a. Recreational facilities.
    b. Proximity of shopping centers.
    c. Views, lakes, wooded areas.
    d. Proximity of churches, day care centers, and entertainment media.
    e. Proximity of medical facilities.
7. Design and architecture.
8. Construction type and quality.
9. Income or rental level.

Commonly used units of comparison for apartment appraisals include

1. Sales price per apartment unit.
2. Sales price per room.
3. Sales price per square foot.
    a. Building area.
    b. Living area.
    c. Usable building area.
4. Rent per unit per month (or year).
5. Rent per room per month (or year).
6. Rent per square foot of living area per month (or year).
7. Gross rent multiplier (annual or monthly).
    a. Definition of annual gross rent multiplier: sales price/gross annual rent.
    b. Definition of monthly gross rent multiplier: sales price/gross monthly rent.

Adjustment of the Sales Price of the Comparable to the Value of the Subject

Once three or four recently sold properties that are comparable to the subject are found, the sales price of each of the comparables must be adjusted to the value of the subject. The data might be arranged as follows:

Comparative data for three comparable properties

Comparable Property	Sale Price	Time	Physical Characteristics	Location	Motivation Behind the Sale
1	$42,000	Two months ago	Inferior	Superior	Same as subject
2	$40,000	Nine months ago	Superior	Inferior	Need for immediate sale
3	$41,000	Five months ago	Superior	Inferior	Same as subject

Types of Adjustments to Value. As comparable sales prices are adjusted to the value of the subject, the adjustments may be made in terms of dollar amounts or percentages. In the following example, dollar adjustments are made. The adjustments could have been made in percentages of the sales price of the comparable or with a mixture of dollar and percentage adjustments. After the adjustments for the comparable elements are made, the adjusted sales price is stated in dollars.

The dollar adjustments required to value the subject property

Comparable Property	Sale Price	Time	Physical Characteristics	Location	Motivation	Sum of Adjustments	Adjusted Sales Price
1	$42,000	+ $ 100	+ $500	− $600	——	——	$42,000
2	$40,000	+ $1,000	− $500	+ $600	+ $1,000	+ $2,100	$42,100
3	$41,000	+ $ 500	− $500	+ $600	——	$ 600	$41,600

After the adjustments are made to the sales price of each comparable, the appraiser must reconcile the differences between the value indications for the subject. The appraiser may note the adjusted sales price of the comparable that required the least adjustment. In this case, the first comparable required no net adjustment to the sales price of $40,000. Since the adjusted values are so close together and the first comparable took no net adjustment, the appraiser would probably assign a value of approximately $42,000 to the subject from the use of the market comparison approach.

THE INCOME APPROACH TO HOUSE APPRAISING

The income approach to house appraising requires an estimated income stream and a multiplier or factor in order to arrive at value. From comparable properties that have sold recently while being rented, the appraiser must ascertain a rent per month suitable to the subject and a gross rent or income multiplier.

The gross rent multiplier is usually defined as the sale price divided by gross monthly rent, or

$$\text{Gross rent multiplier} = \text{GRM} = \frac{\text{Sale price}}{\text{Gross monthly rent}}$$

Financing and Appraising

The gross income multiplier is usually defined as the sales price divided by gross annual income, or

$$\text{Gross income multiplier} = \text{GIM} = \frac{\text{Sale price}}{\text{Gross annual income}}$$

To determine value, the estimated monthly or annual rent is multiplied by the appropriate multiplier:

Value = estimated gross *monthly* rent for subject × GRM

Value = estimated gross *annual* income for subject × GIM

A Case Example. The following case illustrates the use of the income approach in determining the value of a house [1]:

The subject is located on a street adjacent to lower priced property. It is a one-story, masonry, single-family, detached dwelling containing eight rooms, two and one-half baths and a panelled family room. The house has central heat, but neither air-conditioning nor a modern kitchen. There is a two-car attached garage with double doors. The general condition of the house is very good; no immediate repairs are required. The interior and exterior painting is excellent and we found no functional inutility.

Market research produced the following comparable rental/sales:

Rental/Sale No. 1. This property sold for $31,500; the monthly rent (unfurnished) was $215. This was a masonry house with a central air-conditioning system located in a superior neighborhood. In all other physical aspects, it was identical to the subject.

Rental/Sale No. 2. This masonry house sold for $32,400 with a monthly rent (unfurnished) of $225. It was located in a neighborhood superior to the subject, possessed a central air-conditioning system and a modern kitchen, which included an oven, range, dishwasher, disposal, and exhaust fan. The two-car attached garage was similar to the subject, and the balance of the physical description matched.

Rental/Sale No. 3. This masonry home sold for $29,750 with a monthly rent (unfurnished) of $200. Located in a superior neighborhood, it did have an air conditioning system, but no modern kitchen or garage. It was similar to the subject in all other respects.

Rental/Sale No. 4. This was a masonry home with a monthly rent (unfurnished) of $215 and a selling price of $31,400. Similar to the subject, the home had an air-conditioning system, modern kitchen, and two-car attached garage, but was in the same neighborhood as the subject and shared the locational problem.

Rental/Sale No. 5. This masonry home sold for $30,250, with a monthly rent (unfurnished) of $210. The property was located in a superior neighborhood to the subject. The home had central heat and air-conditioning and a modern kitchen, but did not have a two-car attached garage.

Rental/Sale No. 6. This home was of masonry construction and sold for $29,500 with a monthly rent (unfurnished) of $200. The property was in a superior neighborhood, but in all other respects was similar to the subject.

---

[1] J. R. Kimball, "How to Document, Justify, and Support," reprinted with permission from the November–December 1977 issue of *The Real Estate Appraiser*, published by Society of Real Estate Appraisers, Chicago, Illinois. No further reproduction is authorized; all rights reserved.

The next step in our analysis would be to arrange the data in a chart, such as [Exhibit 7-5].

We are now prepared to analyze the market variances through "paired" sales. This analysis is shown in [Exhibit 7-6].

Once the dollar amount of the adjustment is isolated by analyzing the market variances through paired sales, an adjustment chart [Exhibit 7-7] illustrates the appraiser's method of arriving at an estimate of market rent for the subject.

The indicated market rents for the subject property leaves little doubt that a rental of $190 per month is both logical and defensible.

Exhibit 7-5. Organizing Data for Comparison

Rental/Sale	Monthly Rental	Location	Air Conditioning	Built-In Kitchen	Garage
1	$215	Superior	Yes	No	Yes
2	$225	Superior	Yes	Yes	Yes
3	$200	Superior	Yes	No	No
4	$215	Similar	Yes	Yes	Yes
5	$210	Superior	Yes	Yes	No
6	$200	Superior	No	No	Yes

Exhibit 7-6. Analysis of Market Variances Through Paired Sales

Rental/Sales	Monthly Rental	Location	Air Conditioning	Built-In Kitchen	Garage
Analysis of location					
2	$225	Superior	Yes	Yes	Yes
4	215	Similar	Yes	Yes	Yes
Adjustment:	$ 10	Variance			
Location adjustment is $10					
Analysis of kitchen					
2	$225	Superior	Yes	Yes	Yes
1	215	Superior	Yes	No	Yes
Adjustment:	$ 10			Variance	
Kitchen adjustment is $10.					
Analysis of air conditioning					
1	$215	Superior	Yes	No	Yes
6	200	Superior	No	No	Yes
Adjustment:	$ 15		Variance		
Air conditioning adjustment is $15.					
Analysis of garage					
2	$225	Superior	Yes	Yes	Yes
5	210	Superior	Yes	Yes	No
Adjustment:	$ 15				Variance
Garage adjustment is $15.					

Financing and Appraising

Exhibit 7-7. *An Adjustment Chart for the Estimation of Market Rent for the Subject*

Major Value Factors	Subject	Sale 1		Sale 2		Sale 3		Sale 4		Sale 5		Sale 6	
Location	Poor	Superior,	−$10	Superior,	−$10	Superior,	−$10	Poor,	0	Superior,	−$10	Superior,	−$10
Air conditioning	No	Yes,	−$15	Yes,	−$15	Yes,	−$15	Yes,	−$15	Yes,	−$15	No,	0
Kitchen equipment	No	No,	0	Yes,	−$10	No,	0	Yes,	−$10	Yes,	−$10	No,	0
Garage	Yes	Yes,	0	Yes,	0	No,	+$15	Yes,	0	No,	+$15	Yes,	0
Net adjustment			−$25		−$35		−$10		−$25		−$20		−$10
Monthly rent			$215		$225		$200	$	$215		$210		$200
Indicated rent for subject			$190		$190		$190		$190		$190		$190

Exhibit 7-8. *Derivation of Gross Rent Multiplier*

	Sale 1	Sale 2	Sale 3	Sale 4	Sale 5	Sale 6
Sales price	$31,500	$32,400	$29,750	$31,400	$30,250	$29,500
Monthly rent	$ 215	$ 225	$ 200	$ 215	$ 210	$ 200
Gross rent multiplier	146.5	144.0	148.75	146.05	144.05	147.5

GRM analysis. Note in [Exhibit 7-8] that the gross rent multipler is computed on unadjusted sales/rental data. Documentation as to which GRM is selected and why it is chosen further demonstrates the analysis process used by the appraiser. . . . For purposes of the case example, a GRM of 148 is selected, since lower monthly rents command higher multiples than higher monthly rents. The GRM for Sale 3, with a rent of $200, is 148.75, and the GRM for Sale 6, with a rent of $200, is 147.5. The GRM multiplied by the selected monthly rent provides an indication of value by the income approach in single-family residential appraising. Therefore, the value indicated for the subject is $190 × 148, or $28,120. Rounded off, the estimated value of the house is $28,000, according to the income approach.

SUMMARY

When the prospective investor wants to know how much to pay for a property or when an owner wishes to finance or sell his or her property, that person must be able to appraise the property adequately or must be able to hire a good appraiser. Even though an appraiser is hired to value the property, the owner should be able to check the results of the appraisal job. Most investors recognize that they need to be knowledgable in real estate appraising.

Real estate appraising was defined as the estimation of property value as of a certain date. It was discovered that appraisers differentiate between the terms *cost, price,* and *market value. Reproduction value* is differentiated from *replacement value. Value in use* differs from *value in exchange.*

The reader found that the major determinants of value are location, demand and supply, scarcity, utility, ability to pay, and buyer knowledge of alternatives. The ten principles of appraising are balance, conformity, change, anticipation, competition, substitution, supply and demand, contribution, increasing and decreasing returns, and highest and best use.

The appraisal process starts with the definition of the problem. A preliminary survey and appraisal plan is made, and a fee commensurate with the difficulty of the job is quoted to the prospective client. Data is acquired, classified, and analyzed. The values from the three approaches to the appraised value are reconciled so that a final value or value range is determined.

Reproduction or replacement cost new is estimated through the methods of quantity survey, unit-in-place, market comparison, or builder's or trade breakdown. The three types of accrued depreciation are physical deterioration, functional obsolescence, and economic obsolescence. Physical deterioration and functional obsolescence may be curable; economic obsolescence is not curable, since outside forces normally cannot be changed by the individual property owner.

In the market comparison approach to the determination of property value, the subject and several comparable properties are characterized according to features closely related to market value. The recent sale prices of the comparable properties are adjusted to reflect the value of the subject property. Adjustments of each sale price may be made on the basis of dollars, percentages, or a mixture of dollars and percentages.

The income approach to house appraising involves estimation of a reasonable monthly rent for the subject, using several comparable rented properties that have sold recently. A gross rent or income multiplier must also be derived from the comparables. The value for the subject is arrived at from the multiplication of the estimated rent for the subject times the appropriate gross rent or income multiplier.

Key Terms and Concepts

Professional appraisal organization
Appraisal methods
Designated appraiser
Market value
Reproduction value
Market approach
Quantity survey method
Builder's or trade breakdown method
Incurable depreciation
Narrative report
Factors of production
Economically obsolete building
Estate settlement
Real estate tax burden
Linear foot
Dollar and percentage adjustments
Ranges of value
Subjective judgment
Cost
Price
Replacement value
Appraisal process
Cost approach

Unit-in-price method
Physical deterioration
Environmental obsolescence
Gross Rent Multiplier
Arm's-length transaction
Appropriate capitalization rate
Property productivity
Corporate employee relocation
Accrued depreciation
Gross Income Multiplier
Value in use
Value in exchange
Appraisal principles
Conformity
Substitution
Highest and best use
Income approach
Market comparison method
Functional obsolescence
Curable depreciation
Form report
Victorian-style house
Net operating income

Highest present value
Value indicators
Property tax appraisal

Comparable property
Subject property

Questions for Student Self-examination

Multiple-Choice Questions

1. Which of the following is not a method of estimating real property cost?
   a. quality survey
   b. unit-in-place
   c. market comparison
   d. trade breakdown

2. What is needed to calculate the appropriate Gross Rent Multiplier?
   a. construction costs and operating costs
   b. sale prices and annual rents
   c. operating costs and monthly rents
   d. sale prices and monthly rents

3. Which term is defined as the form or narrative research report that leads the client to the estimation of value that the appraiser derived from the use of the established appraisal process or system?
   a. real estate appraising
   b. a real estate appraisal
   c. a real estate appraisal report
   d. none of the above

4. Which of the following is not one of the four generally accepted factors of production?
   a. labor
   b. machinery
   c. land
   d. entrepreneurship

5. Which type of depreciation is usually considered in appraising to be incurable and never curable?
   a. physical deterioration
   b. functional obsolescence
   c. environmental obsolescence
   d. none of the above

True–False Questions

T F 1. Six different values may be estimated for a subject project by six different real estate appraisers.
T F 2. Appraising is partly an art and partly a science.
T F 3. Real property must have utility for it to have value.
T F 4. The first step in making an appraisal is to survey the data and the work needed to make the desired appraisal.
T F 5. The replacement value is the cost of constructing the same physical structure at the present time.

The Appraisal System of Analysis

T F 6. The value in use often surpasses the value in exchange.
T F 7. If the supply of a certain type of property far outruns the demand for that type of property, the value tends to rise.
T F 8. As the mortgage rates rise, the capitalization rates for income properties tend to rise.
T F 9. The basic valuation formula says that gross revenue divided by an appropriate capitalization rate equals value.
T F 10. The professional appraiser averages the three value indicators from the three appraisal approaches in order to find the desired value.

Answers
Multiple-Choice: 1a, 2d, 3c, 4b, 5c.
True-False: 1T, 2T, 3T, 4F, 5F, 6T, 7F, 8T, 9F, 10F.

Problems

1. If the owner of a house paid the builder $35,000 for its construction, if three or four prospective buyers would pay $40,000 for the house, and if the appraiser estimates the current value of the house to be $39,000, what is the cost? the indicated selling price? the market value?

2. If the appraiser must estimate the value of an antebellum house built in 1832 and finds that the cost to replace the existing structure would be $300,000 but that the cost to construct the functional equivalent of the house would be $60,000, what would the appraiser say the reproduction value was? the replacement value?

3. Which of the major determinants of value is said to be the most strategic in real estate valuation? (Note: three words are often used to describe the major determinant.)

4. If the house occupies approximately one-third of the house lot, which appraisal principle may apply to this observation by the appraiser?

5. If the appraiser is valuing an income property by projecting the cash outflows and inflows ten years into the future, what principle of appraising is being utilized?

6. If the prospective buyer observes that readily substitutable properties that suit his or her purposes can be bought for $55,000, what principle of appraising will affect the price that she or he pays for the property finally selected?

Chapter 8
Income Property Appraising

Introduction
The Relationship of This Chapter to Other Chapters of the Text
The Approaches to Value Used in Income Property Appraising
The Principles of Appraising Emphasized in Income Property Appraising
    Highest and Best Use   Substitution   Contribution   Balance
The Income Approach to Income Property Appraisal
The Income Capitalization Method of Appraised Valuation
    The Method of Derivation of I, or Net Operating Income   Various Methods of Derivation of R, the Overall Capitalization Rate: *The theoretical method, The market comparison method, The yield-recapture method, The band-of-investment method, The mortgage-equity method using the Ellwood formula*   The Application of Income Capitalization
The Gross Income Multiplier Method of Appraised Valuation
The Discounted Cash Flow Method of Appraised Valuation
    Income Stream of Uneven Cash Flows   Income Stream of Even Cash Flows
Summary
Key Terms and Concepts
Questions for Student Self-examination

LEARNING OBJECTIVES After studying this chapter, you should be familiar with

The importance of income property appraising
The principles of appraising as emphasized in income property appraising
How the appraiser applies the principle of highest and best use
The general nature of the income approach to value as applied to income properties
The income capitalization method of appraised valuation
The method for deriving net operating income
Various methods for derivation of the overall capitalization rate
How the market comparison method differs from the yield-recapture method when the value from the income approach is sought
Band-of-investment method of finding the capitalization rate
Ellwood formula
The gross income multiplier method of appraised valuation
The discounted cash flow method of appraised valuation

INTRODUCTION

Many income properties are needed in our economy to house the many businesses and service enterprises that maintain the economy and serve the needs of the citizens. The value of these income properties must be determined when the need arises. Income property appraisal is often needed for tax reasons, for condemnation reasons, for mortgage financing purposes, and for prospective buyer and seller information.

The real estate investor is entangled in this maze of reasons for income property appraisal. The investor either must appraise the property whose value is needed or contract with an appraiser to get the work done. The investor always wants to be in a position to supervise the quality of the appraisal work done. As large fees are paid for income property appraisal, the investor wants to be sure that a competent job was done.

THE RELATIONSHIP OF THIS CHAPTER TO OTHER CHAPTERS OF THE TEXT

This chapter concludes Part II, on financing and appraising. The early chapters of the section were devoted to mortgage financing, leverage, loan application and analysis, and institutional sources of funds. The latter chapters were concerned with real estate appraising. The first of the real estate appraising chapters introduced the reader to real estate appraising in general and to the appraisal of single-family houses. This chapter continues that discussion with application of appraisal techniques and methods to income properties rather than houses. As Part II ends, with income property appraising, the reader will move on to personal and corporate portfolio strategies in Part III.

THE APPROACHES TO VALUE USED IN INCOME PROPERTY APPRAISING

In an appraisal report, the client may read:

Value from the cost approach: $942,000
Value from the income approach: 975,000
Value from the market approach: 980,000

Therefore, since the values from the income and market approaches are most reflective of the value of the income property, the final estimate of value for the subject property is $975,000.

This typical excerpt indicates that all three approaches to value are used for income properties. For a profitable building, the appraiser expects the value from the income and market approaches to surpass the value from the cost approach. The structure is usually built so that more value is created than the cost as a result of the rental of the space in the structure. As the investors in the marketplace realize the profitability of the building, they will tend to bid relatively high prices for the building.

A fully occupied income property will indicate a relatively high gross monthly or annual rent. If a gross rent multiplier is derived from the recent sales of comparable income properties, this established multiplier times the relatively high gross rent per month will result in a relatively high value. Also, relatively high rent volume may mean a high net operating income, which may be capitalized with an appropriate rate to produce a high value.

$$\frac{\text{Net Operating Income}}{\text{Capitalization Rate}} = \text{Value}$$

Example: $$\frac{\$200,000}{0.10} = \$2,000,000$$

If the property has a high vacancy rate, a low amount of revenues, and a high amount of operating expenses, the values from the market and income approaches may be low and the value from the cost approach may surpass the values from the other two approaches.

THE PRINCIPLES OF APPRAISING EMPHASIZED IN INCOME PROPERTY APPRAISING

Four of the ten basic appraisal principles are particularly emphasized in income property appraising. The principle of highest and best use is foremost in importance. Close in importance to the principle of highest and best use is the principle of substitution. The principles of contribution and balance are also significant in income property appraising.

Highest and Best Use. When the appraiser has the job of estimating the value of an income property, he or she must first determine the highest and best use for the site. For appraisal purposes, the determination of highest and best use is not a formal, elaborate task requiring a great deal of time and money. The appraiser merely uses the rental, operating cost, and zoning data with which he is familiar to determine whether the current or proposed land use is the highest and best use. A formal highest and best use study would require a thorough analysis, which would require numerous hours of work and significant expense. For appraisal purposes, the real estate appraiser informally estimates the use of the land that would give the highest return. The appraisal reports this highest and best use, but may also state the value of the property as it is currently improved. The current improvements may not conform with the improvements that would afford the land its highest value. For example, an abandoned military base may rest on the land most suitable for a regional shopping center. The land would have the highest present value if the base were demolished and a shopping center developed.

Substitution. The principle of substitution applies to the determination of value for the income property from the cost, market, and income approaches. The cost of construction of new, readily substitutable properties is useful in determining the depreciated replacement cost of the subject. When the market value of the subject is sought, recent selling prices of substitutable income properties are sought, so that the market value of the subject may be estimated using various units of comparison. When the value of the subject from the income approach is sought, the histories of the revenues, operating expenses, and land and building appreciation are needed from substitutable income properties. The cash flow projections for present value analysis are built on historical operating data from substitutable properties. For example, a 10-year cash flow projection for a 12-unit apartment building is based on the operating experience of investors of comparable properties.

Contribution. In the appraisal of an income property, the appraiser must realize that part of the value is contributed by the land and part by the improvements to the land. Each component contributes to the total property value. For example, the land under an office building may be valued at $100,000; the office building resting on the land may be valued at $900,000. The total of the component values is $1,000,000.

Balance. The highest value of a property originates from a balance of the factors that contribute value. The economists would say that the highest value stems from a balance of the factors of production. The factors of production are labor, capital, land, and entrepreneurship. For example, the house and the house lot must be in balance in order for the property to achieve its highest value. In most areas, there is a preferred land-coverage ratio in terms of the market regardless of the land-coverage ratio established for the lot through zoning ordinances. If a sprawling house absorbs most of the house lot and the market objects to this extreme land-coverage ratio, the value of the property will decline. Too much capital is mixed with the land component.

Another example is the balance of labor in the office building investment mix. One full-time building manager may suffice to add adequate productivity so that an optimum cash flow may be realized from the office building. More than one full-time building manager may add more to operating costs than the increase in net revenue. Too much labor may throw the ideal balance of the factors of production out of kelter. Too much labor may result in a lower return on investment. An optimum balance of the factors contributing value must exist in order for the optimum return to the investor to be realized or for the overall property value to reach its highest level.

THE INCOME APPROACH TO INCOME PROPERTY APPRAISAL

The use of the income approach leads to the calculation of the present worth of anticipated net cash flows from the subject property. Three methods may be used to find the present value of the income property: (1) income capitalization, (2) gross income multiplier analysis, and (3) discounted cash flow analysis. Income capitalization and discounted cash flow analysis require discount or capitalization rates; the other method requires a multiplier or factor from market sales. All three methods require annual revenue estimates of various types. The income capitalization method requires an estimate of stabilized net operating income. The discounted cash flow method requires annual estimates of net cash flow. The gross income multiplier analysis requires a stabilized gross annual revenue. The appraiser uses the most appropriate method for the information available within the time frame of the appraisal job.

The Income Capitalization Method of Appraised Valuation

Valuation through the capitalization of income involves a general formula.

$$\text{Value} = \frac{\text{Net Operating Income}}{\text{Capitalization Rate}}$$

or

$$V = \frac{I}{R}$$

where

V = Value
I = Net operating income (first year of stabilized annual income)
R = Overall capitalization rate

The preceding formula requires an estimate of stabilized or first-year net operating income or net cash flow before depreciation and taxes plus an appropriate capitalization rate. The net operating income or cash flow may be estimated for any time period, including a month, a quarter, a six-month period, or a year. Usually income capitalization requires an annual cash flow estimate. The cash flow or net operating income estimate is the difference between the net cash inflows and the net cash outflows of the particular time period. Part of the cash inflow in the last year of the projection period would be the reversion value from the sale of the property or the refinancing proceeds.

The Method for Derivation of I, or Net Operating Income. Net operating income is derived by first estimating the gross potential income of the income property. The current contract rents may not reflect current market rental rates. Therefore, the gross potential income in light of current market rental rates should be estimated. Then an estimated amount of vacancy and bad-debt loss should be deducted from the gross potential income to find the effective gross income. From effective gross income should be deducted cash operating expenses to arrive at net operating income or net cash flow for the time period.

In summary, net operating income may be derived in the following way:

Step 1. Estimate gross potential income for the income property for the time period.

Step 2. Deduct the estimated vacancy and bad-debt loss for the time period.

Step 3. Subtract cash operating expenses to arrive at net operating income or net cash flow for the time period.

Various Methods for Derivation of R, the Overall Capitalization Rate. The overall capitalization rate can be found in a number of ways. Some of the most commonly used methods are (1) the market comparison method, (2) the band-of-investment method, (3) the yield-recapture method, and (4) the mortgage-equity method. The theoretical method of rate derivation could be used. The appraiser uses the method pertinent to the appraisal job and the information available.

If the appraiser has a lot of information from the client, including the client's expected yield and details about the mortgage financing, he or she will probably employ the most detailed method of finding the capitalization rate, the mortgage-equity method. The market comparison method is dependent on very similar income properties for the accuracy of its indicated capitalization rate. The band-of-investment method requires some information about the mortgage financing and information about the investor's expected yield; this method requires a little less information than the mortgage-equity method. The mortgage-equity method also requires an estimate of the sinking fund rate of interest and the percentage of property appreciation or depreciation expected over the investment holding period. The yield-recapture method requires only the investor's required yield and the economic life of the depreciable property. This produces a general rate for capitalization rate purposes. The theoretical method is a compilation of estimated interest rates with little relationship to reality. The market offers little evidence for the estimation of the various rate components needed for use of the theoretical method.

The theoretical method. When an appraiser wants to develop a capitalization rate by means of the theoretical method, he or she adds various interest components together. First a safe rate of interest is estimated. That interest rate may be an average rate for various maturities of Treasury bonds in the current market. It might also indicate the passbook savings rate of local commercial banks or savings and loan associations. An additional rate is needed to indicate the illiquidity of any real property. Any real property cannot be sold normally as quickly as highly marketable and liquid exchange-listed stocks and bonds. Another rate of interest needs to be added to compensate for the management required for real estate investments. Bonds and stocks can be held without active management, generally speaking, but real property needs management for its continual upkeep and rental. Another rate of interest may need to be added for the indicated investment risk in the real property; the real property investor always assumes a degree of financial risk. Sometimes the investment risk is minimal, such as the ownership and lease of a post office or other building that houses government offices. Sometimes the investment risk is significant, as in the ownership of a single-purpose resort property subject to seasonal swings in business and dependent on weather conditions.

To summarize, the derivation of a capitalization rate by the theoretical method involves

Safe rate of interest	i_s
Rate for illiquidity of investment	i_i
Rate for management required	i_m
Rate for risk involved	i_r
Overall capitalization rate	R

The market comparison method. To find the capitalization rate by the market comparison method, the appraiser needs recent sale prices of comparable properties and their net operating incomes at the time of sale. The rate of return on each of the comparable properties at the time of sale is used to estimate the rate of return or, in other words, the capitalization rate for the subject property. The market rate of return at the time of sale of each of the comparables is calculated in the following manner:

$$\text{Rate of return} = \text{Capitalization rate} = \frac{\text{Net operating income at the time of sale}}{\text{Sale price}}$$

The rates of return for the comparable properties are observed in estimating the subject's required rate of return or capitalization rate. The information on the comparable properties might appear as follows:

$$\text{Comparable A: } \frac{\text{Net operating income}_A}{\text{Sale price}_A} = \frac{\$10{,}000}{\$80{,}000} = 12\tfrac{1}{2} \text{ percent}$$

$$\text{Comparable B: } \frac{\text{Net operating income}_B}{\text{Sale price}_B} = \frac{\$20{,}000}{\$200{,}000} = 10 \text{ percent}$$

$$\text{Comparable C: } \frac{\text{Net operating income}_C}{\text{Sale price}_C} = \frac{\$12{,}000}{\$108{,}000} = 11 \text{ percent}$$

The appraiser would study the comparables to see which comparable most closely reflects the operating, rental, and selling characteristics of the subject. If all of the comparables are relatively the same with respect to the subject, the appraiser might estimate the appropriate capitalization rate for the subject to be 11 percent. This is rate determination by the market comparison approach.

The yield-recapture method. In order to derive a capitalization rate by the yield-recapture method, the appraiser must know the yield expected by the owner. If the owner or prospective owner is doing his or her own appraising, this person must consider his or her investment yield expectations. The economic life of the depreciable property that is going to be used for federal income tax purposes is also needed for the derivation.

The basic formula for rate determination is

Investor's yield requirement
+ Recapture rate
─────────────────────
Capitalization rate

1. *Straight-line recapture.* The recapture rate using a straight-line method is found by dividing one by the economic life of the depreciable property. This portion of the total investment in the depreciable asset is set aside each year until the total amount is recaptured at the end of the economic life of the property. The equal amount set aside each year is not assumed to be invested by the property owner. No interest accumulates on the amounts set aside.

For example, if the property has an economic life of 40 years, the straight-line recapture rate would be 1/40, or 0.025 per year. If the investor's yield requirement were 12 percent, then the capitalization rate would be

0.12 Investor's yield requirement
+ 0.025 Straight-line recapture rate
─────────────────────
0.145 Capitalization rate

2. *Annuity recapture.* The recapture rate using the annuity method assumes that the equal amounts set aside for investment recapture each year are invested as they are

Income Property Appraising

periodically set aside at the rate of interest reflecting the investor's yield requirement. If the investor's required yield is 12 percent and the economic life of the property is 40 years, the annuity factor at the investor's yield would be .001304. If .001304 of $1 is set aside each year and invested at 12 percent, $1 will be recaptured in 40 years. The capitalization rate under these circumstances would be

$$\begin{array}{l} 0.12 \text{ Investor's yield requirement} \\ + \ 0.001304 \text{ Annuity recapture rate} \\ \hline 0.121304 \text{ Capitalization rate} \end{array}$$

3. *Sinking-fund recapture.* The recapture rate using the sinking-fund method assumes that the equal amounts set aside for investment recapture each year are invested as they are periodically set aside at a "safe" rate of interest. This "safe" rate of interest is usually considerably less than the investor's required yield rate.

Let us continue to assume that the investor's required yield is 12 percent. If the economic life of the property is 40 years and the sinking-fund rate—the local short-term savings certificate rate—is 8 percent, the sinking-fund factor would be 0.003860. The capitalization rate under these conditions would be

$$\begin{array}{l} 0.12 \text{ Investor's yield requirement} \\ + \ 0.003860 \text{ Sinking-fund rate} \\ \hline 0.123860 \text{ Capitalization rate} \end{array}$$

In summary, use of the yield-recapture method of deriving the capitalization rate implies possible use of straight-line, annuity, or sinking-fund recapture rates. Since value, according to the $V = I/R$ formula, increases as the R decreases, the appraiser will reach a higher value for the property if the annuity recapture assumption is made. The next highest value for the property would be attained with the sinking-fund recapture assumption. The lowest property value would result from the straight-line recapture assumption.

The band-of-investment method. The general procedure for finding the appropriate capitalization rate by the band-of-investment method amounts to determination of the weighted cost of the sources of funds for the real estate investment. The percentage amount of mortgage funds provided by the first mortgage is multiplied by the loan constant for that mortgage. (The loan constant is the factor that is multiplied by the original mortgage amount to find the annual mortgage payment that meets the principal and interest requirements.) The percentage amount of mortgage funds provided by the second mortgage is multiplied by the loan constant for the second mortgage. The percentage amount of mortgage funds provided by each of the additional mortgages is multiplied by their respective loan constant. The percentage amount of equity investment is multiplied by the owner's yield requirement. The total of these weighted costs of funds makes up the capitalization rate for the valuation of the subject property.

An example may clarify the band-of-investment method for finding the capitalization rate. Assume that:

Loan-to-value ratio	= 75%
There is only one mortgage on the property.	
The loan constant	= 11%
The equity yield requirement	= 15%

Therefore according to the band-of-investment method:

Type of Funds	Percent of Total Funds	Cost of Funds	Weighted Average
First mortgage	75	× 0.11	0.0825
Equity investment	25	× 0.15	0.0375
	Capitalization rate	=	0.1200

The mortgage-equity method using the Ellwood formula. This method of deriving the capitalization rate employs detailed knowledge about the mortgage financing, the investor's yield requirement, the expected appreciation or depreciation in the property value over the expected holding period, the rate of interest to be received on periodic reinvestment of funds, the percent of the mortgage principal to be repaid at the end of the investment holding period, the loan constant for the full mortgage term, and the loan constant for the projection or holding period. Some short-cuts in finding the cap rate can be used when Ellwood tables are available.

$$R = Y - M \times C \begin{matrix} + \text{Dep} \\ - \text{App} \end{matrix} 1/S_n$$

where

R = overall capitalization rate (cap rate);
Y = equity yield rate (total investor yield requirement);
M = mortgage loan-to-value ratio;
C = mortgage coefficient, which can be found in the Ellwood tables in precalculated form for some types of mortgage financing;
Dep = percentage of depreciation in property value expected over the projection period;
App = percentage of appreciation in property value expected over the projection period;
$1/S_n$ = sinking fund factor for n periods at a selected safe rate of interest.

When C, or the mortgage coefficient, must be calculated, the formula is

$$C = Y + P\left(\frac{1}{S_n}\right) - f$$

where

C = mortgage coefficient;
Y = equity yield rate (mentioned above);
P = percentage of mortgage paid off at end of projection period (must be calculated);
$1/S_n$ = sinking fund factor (mentioned above);
f = loan factor used in determining the periodic mortgage payments that repay the principal and pay the mortgage interest over the mortgage term.

P, or the percentage of mortgage paid off by the end of the investment holding period, may be calculated by several formulas. One formula that may be used is

$$P = (\frac{f}{I} - 1)(S_p - 1)$$

where

S_p = the amount to which \$1 will grow with interest at the effective rate during the projection period;
I = nominal interest rate on mortgage.

Another formula that may be used is

$$P = \frac{f - I}{f_p - I}$$

where

f_p = loan factor used in determining the periodic mortgage payments over the projection period only;
f = loan factor used in determining the periodic mortgage payments over the entire mortgage period.

If an income property must be appraised for mortgage financing purposes, the appraiser may find out that the prospective 20-year mortgage can represent 75 percent of value and carry a 10 percent interest rate. The stabilized net operating income is estimated at \$20,000 a year. The owner expects to keep the property for five years because of the tax situation and expects to receive an overall yield on his investment of 15 percent. The appraiser expects the property to increase in value approximately 10 percent over the five-year holding period. The annual expected cash flow from the investment could be invested each year in savings certificates at the local bank at an investment return of 8 percent; this rate could be used for a sinking fund rate if the capitalization rate were derived by the Ellwood formula.

The Ellwood formula could be used to derive the cap rate, R. The appraiser would need to use the Ellwood tables or other compound interest tables that are available. The Ellwood formula would apply in the following way:

$$R = Y - M \times C \begin{matrix} + \text{Dep} \\ - \text{App} \end{matrix} \frac{1}{S_n}$$

In the case problem

$Y = 15\%$;
$M = 0.75$;
$C = 0.049316$, using the C Table from the *Ellwood Tables for Real Estate Appraising and Financing* (Cambridge, Mass.: Ballinger Publishing Company, 1977), p. 347.
App $= 0.10$;
$1/S_n = 0.021852$, using the sinking fund factor for 8% compounded annually *Ellwood Tables for Real Estate Appraising and Financing* (Cambridge, Mass.: Ballinger Publishing Company, 1977), p. 288.
$R = 0.15 - (0.75)(0.049316) - (0.10)(0.021852)$
$R = 0.110828$

$$V = \frac{I}{R} = \frac{\text{Net operating income}}{\text{Overall capitalization rate}} = \text{Value}$$

$$V = \frac{\$20,000}{0.110828} = \$180,459.81, \text{ or, rounded off, } \underline{\$180,500}$$

If the case problem had had an investment holding period of a number of years other than a multiple of 5, the C factor would have required calculation rather than extraction from an Ellwood table. C factor for 5, 10, 15, 20, 25, and 30 years, depending on the length of the mortgage amortization, may be found in the Ellwood tables.

The Application of Income Capitalization. Once the net operating income, I, and the capitalization rate, R, have been determined, value is derived by dividing the R into the I, as illustrated in the mortgage-equity case above. The value of $180,500 was determined by the division of 0.110828, the rate, into $20,000, the net operating income.

Income capitalization is useful when a stabilized annual cash flow or net operating income can be established reasonably or when only the first year net operating income can be used reasonably. If the net cash flows per year vary widely, the income capitalization method of finding property value is not particularly useful. The discounted cash flow or the gross income multiplier method may be more useful as an income approach to value. These two methods will be discussed in the next portion of the chapter.

The Gross Income Multiplier Method of Appraised Valuation

If comparable income properties have sold recently, the appraiser may look at the gross income multiplier reflected by the sale price. Of course, the appraiser must have access to the gross annual revenue amount that the property was generating when it was sold. The appraiser observes the following relationship for several recently sold comparable properties:

$$\frac{\text{Sale price}}{\text{Gross annual revenue}} = \text{Gross income multiplier} = \text{GIM}$$

Then the appraiser or prospective investor can apply the indicated multiplier to the gross annual income estimate for the subject property to arrive at the value of the subject. For example:

Comparable Property	Recent Sale Price	Gross Revenue at Time of Sale	Gross Income Multiplier
1	$3,375,000	$500,000	6.75
2	$3,038,750	$425,000	7.15
3	$3,036,000	$440,000	6.90

You might say the indicated gross income multiplier from the comparable properties is 7.0. If the subject property is generating an annual income of $450,000, then the estimated value using the GIM of 7.0 would be $3,150,000 ($450,000 × 7.0 = $3,150,000).

The Discounted Cash Flow Method of Appraised Valuation

An income property may also be appraised by the discounted cash flow method. This method requires estimated net cash flows per year and the investor's required rate of return as a discount rate. To derive total property value, the periodic income figure is the net operating income per year. As a review, the net operating income is derived in the following way:

Gross annual revenue
− Bad debt and vacancy loss

Effective gross income
− Cash operating expenses

Net operating income (cash flow to the mortgages and the equity investors before federal income taxes)

A difficulty is involved when the investor's required rate of return must be estimated. What would the typical investor require at the present time? That rate of return should be used as the discount rate.

Income Stream of Uneven Cash Flows. An example of the valuation method follows:

Expected Property Cash Receipts at Year End

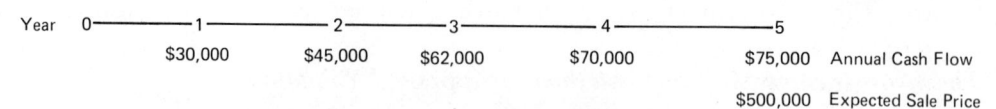

Year 0	1	2	3	4	5	
	$30,000	$45,000	$62,000	$70,000	$75,000	Annual Cash Flow
					$500,000	Expected Sale Price

The estimated investor's required rate is 15%.

Year	Cash Flow	Present Value Factor at 15%	Present Value of Cash Flow
1	$ 30,000	0.869565	$ 26,086.95
2	$ 45,000	0.756144	$ 34,026.48
3	$ 62,000	0.657516	$ 40,765.99
4	$ 70,000	0.571753	$ 40,022.71
5	$575,000	0.497177	$285,876.78
	Present value of property		$426,778.91

The estimated investor's required rate of return is 15 percent.

If the subject property is leased, an annuity table may be used. A lease is one type of annuity. An annuity is a periodic payment that is usually the same sum per time period, which draws interest at a given rate. An annuity table that may be used is a type of compound interest table. When the Ellwood tables label the present value of $1 table "present value reversion of 1," the present value of an annuity of $1 is labeled "present value, ordinary annuity 1 per period."

Income Stream of Even Cash Flows. If the subject property were leased for $20,000 a year for eight years, the expected property value at the end of the eight-year lease were expected to be $500,000, and the investor's required rate of return were 12 percent, the property value might be calculated in the following way:

Expected Property Cash Receipts at Year End

Year 0	1	2	3	4	5	6	7	8	
	$20,000	$20,000	$20,000	$20,000	$20,000	$20,000	$20,000	$20,000	Lease
								$500,000	Property Value

144 *Financing and Appraising*

Present value of ordinary annuity of $1 for 8 years at 12 percent: 4.967640

Present value of reversion of $1 (property value at end of eighth year is the reversion): 0.403883

Present value of property = $20,000, lease payment × 4.968, present value of annuity + $500,000, property value at end of eighth year × 0.403883, present value of reversion of $1
= $20,000 × 4.968 + $500,000 × 0.4039
= $99,360 + $201,950
= $301,310

SUMMARY

Since many properties are owned for the income they produce, these properties continually require appraisal for mortgage financing, tax, condemnation, and other purposes. In the appraisal of income properties, the principles of highest and best use, substitution, contribution, and balance are emphasized. The other appraisal principles apply to income property appraisal to a lesser degree.

There are three general approaches to income property appraisal: income capitalization, gross income multiplier, and discounted cash flow approaches. Income capitalization is based on value determination from the division of a capitalization rate into a net operating income figure. The net operating income amount is derived from a cash flow analysis over a number of periods of time. The capitalization rate may be derived by the theoretical, market comparison, yield-recapture, band-of-investment, or mortgage-equity method using the Ellwood formula.

The gross income multiplier method of finding the capitalization, or "cap," rate depends on recent sales and revenue figures from comparable properties. Once a gross income multiplier is estimated for the subject from comparable properties that have sold recently, it may be applied to the estimated gross revenue for the subject. The estimated multiplier times the estimated annual gross revenue results in the value of the subject.

The discounted cash flow method of finding value of an income property is dependent on the net cash flow projections for the investment holding period, the estimated reversion value at the end of the holding period, and the investor's required rate of return. The projected cash flows per time period of the future are discounted to present value. This total value represents the property value. The discounting method may be used whether the cash flows are even or uneven over the periodic intervals of the investment holding period.

Key Terms and Concepts

Discounted cash flow analysis
Effective gross income
Gross potential income
Market rental rates
Mortgage coefficient
Band of investment method
Yield-recapture method

Mortgage-equity method
Investor's yield requirement
Sinking fund factor
Straight-line recapture
Annuity recapture
Sinking fund recapture
Ellwood formula

Questions for Student Self-examination

Multiple-Choice Questions

1. Which method is used to find the present value of an income property?
   a. income capitalization
   b. discounted cash flow analysis
   c. gross income multiplier analysis
   d. all of the above

2. The _____ method of finding the capitalization rate requires an estimate of the sinking fund rate of interest and the percentage of property appreciation or depreciation expected over the investment holding period.
   a. theoretical
   b. yield recapture
   c. market comparison
   d. none of the above

3. The recapture rate using the _____ method assumes that the equal amounts set aside for investment recapture each year are invested at the rate of interest reflecting the investor's yield requirement.
   a. straight-line recapture
   b. annuity recapture
   c. sinking fund recapture
   d. none of the above

4. The _____ recapture method assumes that the equal amount set aside each year is *not* invested by the property owner for interest accumulation.
   a. straight-line recapture
   b. annuity recapture
   c. sinking fund recapture
   d. none of the above

5. The general procedure for finding the appropriate capitalization rate by the _____ method amounts to determination of the weighted cost of the sources of funds for the real estate investment.
   a. theoretical
   b. yield recapture
   c. market comparison
   d. none of the above

True-False Questions

T F 1. For a profitable building, the appraiser expects the value from the income and market approaches to surpass the value from the cost approach.

T F 2. If the property has a relatively high vacancy rate, low amount of revenues, and high amount of operating expenses, the value from the cost approach may surpass the values from the other two approaches.

T F 3. The principle of balance is foremost in importance in income property appraising.

T F 4. The cost of construction of new, readily substitutable properties is useful in determining the depreciated replacement cost of the subject.

T F 5. The highest value of a property stems from a balance of the factors of production.

T F 6. The income capitalization method of deriving property value requires an estimate of monthly stabilized net operating income.
T F 7. The value of a property may be found by dividing net operating income by the appropriate capitalization rate.
T F 8. Part of the cash inflow in the last year of the projection period is the reversion value from the sale of the property or the refinancing proceeds.
T F 9. In using the market comparison method of deriving the capitalization rate, the gross revenue at the time of sale is divided by the sale price for each of the comparable properties.
T F 10. The loan constant is that factor that is multiplied by the original mortgage amount to find the annual mortgage payment that meets the principal and interest requirements.

Answers
Multiple-Choice: 1d, 2d, 3b, 4a, 5d.
True-False: 1T, 2T, 3F, 4T, 5T, 6F, 7T, 8T, 9F, 10T.

Problems

1. If an old, dilapidated fruit stand occupies the corner of a major intersection on land zoned for commercial use, what questions would you have about the highest and best use of the land as you appraised the site and the improvements?

2. If an apartment building generated $20,000 in net operating income and the appropriate capitalization rate for the property were 10 percent, what would be the value of the apartment building?

3. If an income property generated $50,000 in net operating income and comparable properties exhibited the following data, what would you estimate the value of the subject to be?

Comparable Property	Net Operating Income at the Time of Sale	Selling Price
1	$40,000	$400,000
2	50,000	600,000
3	20,000	220,000

4. If the income property sold recently for $1,000,000, the mortgage loan on the building were $800,000, the appropriate loan constant were .12, and the investor's required rate of return were 10 percent, what would be the appropriate capitalization rate for the appraisal using the band of investment method?

5. If the appraiser were using the yield-recapture method of capitalization rate determination and the investor's required rate of return were 10 percent, the economic life of the property were 25 years, and the mortgage interest rate were 11 percent, what would be the appropriate capitalization rate?

6. If the subject has a gross annual income of $50,000 and the following data were available from comparable properties that have sold recently, what would be the appraised value of the subject using the GIM method of valuation?

Comparable Property	Recent Selling Price	Gross Income at the Time of Sale
1	$1,000,000	$160,000
2	280,000	40,000
3	360,000	60,000

Part Three

Portfolio Strategy: Personal and Corporate

Chapter 9

Ownership Forms, Liability, and Taxation

Introduction
The Relationship of This Chapter to Other Chapters of the Text
The Various Forms of Organization for Real Estate Investment
The Proprietorship Form of Organization
    Liability Status of the Sole Owner   The Tax Status of the Proprietorship
The General Partnership Form of Organization
    Fund-Raising Ability   The Legal Nature of the General Partnership   The Liability Status of Each General Partner   The Tax Status of the Partnership and the Individual Partners
The Limited Partnership Form of Organization
    Fund-Raising Ability   The Legal Organization of the Limited Partnership   The Property Holdings of the Limited Partnership   The Liability Status of the Partners   The Tax Status of the Partnership and the Individual Partners
The Corporate Form of Organization
    The Tax Status of the Corporation and the Stockholder
Other Forms of Investor Organizations Similar to Partnership Agreements
    The Joint Venture   The Real Estate Syndicate   The Business Trust   The Land Trust   The Real Estate Investment Trust
Summary
Key Terms and Concepts
Questions for Student Self-examination

LEARNING OBJECTIVES After studying this chapter, you should be familiar with

The investment, liability, and tax status of sole proprietorships
The fund-raising ability of general partnerships
The legal nature and liability and tax status of the general partnership and its individual partners
General investor considerations concerning limited partnerships
The advantages and disadvantages of the corporate form of organization
The nature of the joint venture
The nature and usefulness of the real estate syndicate
The characteristics of the business trust
The unique characteristics of the land trust for real estate investment
The characteristics of the real estate investment trust

When a person or business contemplates a real estate investment, many tax, liability, financial, and yield factors should be considered. The real estate investment will become a part of the investment portfolio of the person or business. The new investment may or may not fit advantageously into the existing portfolio. The greatest benefit will be received from the new investment if the investor will study the many factors that affect the benefits from the new and existing investments.

The new investment may have many benefits in and of itself, but does the investment complement and supplement the existing investments of the person or business? The investor needs to study the cash flow, the federal income tax burden, the means of raising additional investible funds, the personal or corporate liability, and other such factors in light of the characteristics of the present and planned future investments. The new purchase needs to fit into the overall present and planned portfolio so that the portfolio return is increased while the investment risk remains tolerable.

The investor must always analyze the investment and the portfolio characteristics with a balanced return and risk goal in mind. If the investor sets a high yield as the goal, he or she will probably have to settle for a high degree of financial and legal risk. If a more reasonable yield is sufficient, the investor's overall risk in attaining that goal may be set at a moderate level. If the investor wants to assume little risk, a relatively low yield may be achieved. With these risk-return relationships in mind, the investor must decide what goal must be set for the overall investment portfolio and what goal must be attained by the new real estate investment.

INTRODUCTION

This chapter on ownership forms, liability, and taxation begins Part III, "Portfolio Strategy: Personal and Corporate." The prospective real estate investor may first want to decide on the investment ownership form that fits the risk-return goals for the portfolio and the current investment. This chapter deals first with the pros and cons of real estate investment for a sole proprietor or individual investor not associated with any other individuals or business entities. The legal form, the liability status, and the general federal income tax status of the ownership form are considered. This discussion is followed by a survey of the same factors in relation to the general partnership form. The subsequent discussion deals with the limited partnership form of real estate ownership. Finally, the advantages and disadvantages of the corporate, joint venture, and syndicated form of property ownership are explored. This limited topic is a part of overall portfolio strategy. The ownership form has a major impact on the risk-return relationship of the investment and the portfolio.

THE RELATIONSHIP OF THIS CHAPTER TO OTHER CHAPTERS OF THE TEXT

Chapter 9 opens Part III, which deals with portfolio strategy. Part I dealt with real estate investment fundamentals; Part II set the foundation for real estate investment in terms of mortgage financing and real estate appraisal. The concepts of leverage and value, which are strategic to investment analysis, were introduced. The reader has surveyed some fundamental real estate relationships and learned how to employ "other people's money," how the professionals appraise real property, and how to value property so that wise offers for property can be made. The next step is organizational, portfolio, and tax planning. Part IV goes further into cash flow and profit planning and investment yield measurement.

THE VARIOUS FORMS OF ORGANIZATION FOR REAL ESTATE INVESTMENT

Federal and state laws permit several types of business organizations for real estate investment. State laws set the requirements for organizational chartering and registration for the operation of business and investment, for security sales, and for tax and license fee collection. Federal laws tend to pertain to the federal income taxation, interstate securities sales, and financial liability when investors come from more than one state of residence.

Among the various forms of business organization permitted for real estate investment are the sole proprietorship and the general partnership. Two of the often-used forms of business organization are the limited partnership and the corporation. Other forms of organization commonly in use are the joint venture, the real estate syndicate, the business trust, the land trust, and the real estate investment trust. Each of these organization forms has its distinct financial, legal, and tax characteristics, which serve certain types of investors and properties. This chapter identifies the basic characteristics of each of these forms of organization.

The Proprietorship Form of Organization

If an individual wishes to own property with no partners and no other complications, that individual may invest as a sole proprietor. Usually the state does not require registration of the business entity and requires no payment of chartering or license fee. The income tax authorities—the Internal Revenue Service and the State Department of Revenue—may or may not intercede while the real estate investment is treated as a personal asset and the property income is merged with personal income from other sources.

Here's a case example:

A full-time real estate appraiser—a fee appraiser associated with a federally chartered savings and loan association—is divorced and paying support for five children and alimony to a former wife. The savings and loan association has a retirement fund, but the appraiser wishes to supplement that expected retirement income. The appraiser purchases a house that can be remodeled into apartments for rental to students and working townspeople. A relatively short-term loan was acquired so that the purchase can be made with a relatively low downpayment. The property was acquired for $15,000, and remodeling was begun. One thousand five hundred dollars was required for the paneling of some of the rooms, partitioning for the separate apartments, lowered ceilings, additional kitchen and bathroom fixtures, a new roof, used air conditioning units and space heaters, paint, and some furniture.

The appraiser expected a return from the excess of the rent payments over the loan payments and other owner costs plus the tax shelter from the property depreciation. Of course, the appraiser expected capital gains from the sale of the property after a 12-month period, which would be taxed at the capital gains rate rather than at his ordinary federal income tax rate.

The sole owner of property can invest in property up to the maximum that can be financed on his or her wealth, annual income, and credit standing. Most individual property owners find this a limiting feature. Fund-raising for real estate investment is limited. On the other hand, the sole owner of real estate can make management and financial decisions without consultation with partners or other stockholders. Decisions can be made quickly to enhance the profitability of the real estate and the investor's total portfolio.

Liability Status of the Sole Owner. The sole owner of real estate has total and unlimited liability for any developments associated with the owned property. The investment in the real estate can be sacrificed; the other assets of the sole owner are subject to confiscation. In other words, the real estate liability extends to the other business and personal assets of the owner. Insurance protection—fire, theft, tornado, water, personal injury, as well as other types of coverage—limits the financial liability of the owner when the insurance policies are purchased and maintained.

The Tax Status of the Proprietorship. Any earnings or capital gains of the real estate held by a sole owner are blended with the earnings and capital gains of the owner that are derived from other sources.

> Net profit from the real estate
> + Net profit from salaries and other sources
> Taxable income of the individual, taxed at the individual's ordinary income or capital gains tax rate

The combined income is taxed once; the individual investor is not subject to double taxation. However, since the incomes from the various real estate and non-real estate sources are combined, the individual's ordinary income tax rate may be relatively high.

The individual's combined income may be reduced by the depreciation and other tax deductions permitted on the real estate owned. Such tax-deductible items "flow through" to the individual's taxable income. If an accelerated depreciation method is permitted and the individual investor takes advantage of the method, his or her taxable income may be reduced significantly in the first years of the real estate investment.

The General Partnership Form of Organization

When an individual joins with one or more other investors, a general partnership may be formed for investment in real property or real property interests. No longer does one individual make all the decisions and assume all the financial liability. Under a general partnership agreement registered with the state, all general partners have equal rights to make decisions for the general partnership and all general partners share the financial liability of the real estate investment. Here is a case example:

> An attorney and two builders decided to form a general partnership to develop a heavily wooded residential subdivision in a prime urban area. The builders had been affiliated in the same company for four years; one had been the chief assistant to the other. The attorney had purchased the land several years ago, and the builders each had funds to contribute to the land development and construction of homes. The attorney had an established clientele and found time on his hands since his wife had just died.
>
> The three partners had lived in the same community and had known each other for most of their lives. The possible capital gains on the land sales, the building profits, the reduction in outside legal costs for the development, and the possible provision of legal services to the purchasers of the building lots and houses enticed the three partners.

Fund-Raising Ability. Generally an individual investor joins with others in order to generate more investible funds than a sole investor can generate. Each of the general partners may contribute funds to the enterprise, even though their contributions may be unequal. A general partner may not contribute funds, but may contribute legal, land development, property management, or other forms of expertise. Among the other general partners, though, a significant amount of equity funds may be raised. These funds may serve as the equity basis for loan acquisition in the form of mortgage or commercial loan financing. Therefore, the equity funds may be multiplied several times through borrowing. The more equity funds, usually, the more funds that can be borrowed.

As new partners are permitted or encouraged to join the general partnership, more funds can be acquired for real estate investment—equity and borrowed funds. The general partnership agreement may be amended any time that the existing general partners wish to admit additional general partners.

The Legal Nature of the General Partnership. The general partnership is usually established when an attorney draws up an agreement that is satisfactory to all partners. The state usually requires the recording of this agreement. Its usual contents are

1. The contributions—monetary or nonmonetary—of the individual partners.
2. The responsibility for the management of the real estate investment.
3. The contracting authority for the partnership of each individual partner.
4. The distribution system for the partnership profits, depreciation, and cash flows.
    a. Periodic profits, depreciation, and cash flows.
    b. Refinancing proceeds.
    c. Sale proceeds.
5. The distribution system for the partnership losses and financial liabilities.
6. The provisions for the dissolution of the partnership agreement.
    a. The entrance of new partners.

    b. The death or withdrawal of existing partners.
    c. The change in the distribution of gains and losses.
    d. Final termination of the partnership agreement.

The Liability Status of Each General Partner. Each general partner has unlimited liability for the financial obligations of the general partnership. If assets of the partnership will not fully meet the obligations of the general partnership, the personal assets of each of the general partners may be attached to meet the general partnership obligations. For this reason, many general partners in recent years have incorporated to reduce their personal liability in partnerships. In fact, the general partnership may be comprised completely of incorporated general partners.

While each general partner has unlimited financial and legal liability, each of these partners may individually obligate the general partnership by entering into contracts in the name of the partnership. One general partner, without the approval of the other general partners, may bind the partnership to a contract. Therefore, the general partners should have faith in each other's integrity, managerial ability, and responsibility before they enter into the general partnership agreement.

The Tax Status of the Partnership and the Individual Partners. The income of the general partnership is not taxed. When the partnership income is distributed to the individual partners in the manner prescribed by the partnership agreement, this income, combined with each partner's other income from various sources, is taxed at the partner's ordinary and/or capital gains tax rates. Therefore, there is single taxation of general partnership income.

In a manner similar to that of the sole proprietorship, depreciation deductions for partnership property may flow through to the individual partners. The depreciation amounts may be distributed in an equitable manner among the general partners in the prevailing partnership agreement. Some partners may wish more depreciation deductions and less distribution of partnership cash flow because of their tax brackets. Other partners with lower tax brackets may wish less depreciation and more cash flow to be distributed to them. The partnership agreement should establish equal or unequal distributions of partnership depreciation deductions.

The Limited Partnership Form of Organization

Many aspects of the limited partnership form of organization are similar to that of the general partnership. More funds can be raised for investment because more partners are involved. Each partner represents a source of investment expertise and/or a source of investible funds.

Fund-Raising Ability. The limited partnership organization permits the sale of limited partnership interests. The limited partnership general partners and the security salespeople may set financial qualifications for new limited partners, but the partnership is subject to expansion at any time. To some degree, the fund-raising capability of the partnership is unlimited. Here is a case example:

> A new motel chain, the Royal Motel, solicited for new limited partners by running ads in selected newspapers in Indiana and Ohio, which offered limited partnership interests for a minimum investment of $25,000. The net worth requirement for any interested investor was $100,000 or more. The motel chain continued to expand its location as it sold the limited partnership interests.

The Legal Organization of the Limited Partnership. The limited partnership has two types of partners—general partners, who invest the partnership funds and manage the operation, and limited partners, who contribute the funds for investment, expecting a return but having no active role in the investment or management of the partnership property. There may be one or more general partners and one or more limited partners. The general partners may contribute funds to the real estate enterprise just as the limited partners do or they may individually contribute legal services, tax accounting services, development expertise, or other needed services.

The Property Holdings of the Limited Partnership. A limited partnership may hold one or more properties, and these properties may represent one or more categories of land use. For example, a limited partnership may have enough funds to invest in three apartment buildings in various sections of Sacramento, California. Another limited partnership may hold a single office building of 40 floors as their real property investment.

The Liability Status of the Partners. The general partners actively seek the appropriate properties for investment, and they actively manage those properties for the investment return of all partners in the organization. This classification of partner retains an unlimited legal and financial liability, while the limited partner has legal and financial liability only to the extent of his or her investment. By statute, if a limited partner takes an active role in the partnership organization beyond the contribution of funds, that limited partner becomes a general partner with unlimited financial liability and general partner responsibilities. To reduce the actual liability of a general partner, he or she may incorporate and gain limited financial liability in that manner.

Only the general partners may contract for the limited partnership. Limited partners may expect a return on their contributed capital, but they cannot contract for the organization.

The Tax Status of the Partnership and the Individual Partners. The limited partnership is subject to single taxation. The partners pay federal income taxes on their income distributed from the partnership earnings; the partnership entity pays no federal income taxes on its earnings. The deductible items, such as depreciation, are passed through the partnership to the individual partners. On their individual tax returns they deduct the amounts that are distributed by the partnership agreement. Deductible amounts, such as depreciation, may be unequally distributed among the various general and limited partners.

The Corporate Form of Organization

The corporation is an impersonal organizational entity with an indefinite life. The articles of incorporation are supplemented by by-laws, rules, and regulations. The board of directors makes policy for the day-to-day management group to accomplish. The owners of the organization's assets are the stockholders, who have liability limited only to their investments.

Since the corporation usually is subject to public disclosure, many types of taxation and fees, and accountability for profits for the stockholders, it requires a sophisticated accounting system for the itemization, accounting, and control of corporate revenues and expenses. Incorporation is accomplished according to the laws of the state in which the corporation is chartered. Legal costs must be incurred for the incorporation process.

Once the organization is incorporated, the corporate officers who are approved by the board of directors may contract in the name of the corporation. Therefore, when the company wishes to finance its property through a mortgage, the corporation is the mortgagor, since an officer signs the mortgage in the corporation's behalf.

When the corporation seeks to raise more money for investment in real estate, it may sell more stock and borrow more funds on the strength of the corporation's net worth. It actually may sell more than one class of stock in order to raise more money: preferred and common stock. Common stock usually retains the voting right, whereas the preferred stock retains the first right to dividends or preferred dividend status. Here is a case example:

> The Federal National Mortgage Association, which became a private corporation in 1970, sells common stock, discount notes, loan participations, and GNMA-guaranteed mortgage-backed debentures in order to purchase mortgages and mortgage participations from approved seller-servicers. The common stock must be purchased by the seller-servicers in order to sell mortgages and to bid for money from FNMA. The common stock is also traded on the New York Stock Exchange, so that stockholders retain liquidity and marketability of their interests in FNMA.

The Tax Status of the Corporation and the Stockholder. The owner of corporate stock is subject to double taxation. The profits of the corporation are taxed at the corporate rate. Then the profits distributed to the stockholders in the form of dividends are taxed at the shareholder's tax rate.

If the corporation is a personal holding company and not publicly owned, an excess accumulation of earnings may be taxed. The Internal Revenue Service safeguards against tactics of company owners to avoid federal income taxation. The owners may not wish to distribute company earnings since the dividends would raise the tax rate of the stockholder to exorbitant levels. Most of the dividend might be taxed away.

Corporation federal income tax rates may be lower than the stockholder's federal income tax rate. Of course, the reverse may be true. When the individual reaches high income levels, the corporate tax rates may easily be less than the individual tax rates. As of 1979, corporation taxable income was subject to a 17 percent rate for federal income tax purposes on the first $25,000 of taxable net income. On the next $25,000 of taxable net income, the corporation was subject to a 20 percent rate of federal income taxation; on the next $25,000, a 30 percent rate; and on the next $25,000, a 40 percent rate. Taxable net income over $100,000 was subject to federal income taxation at a 46 percent rate. At the same time, the stockholders were subject to a maximum federal income tax rate on earned personal income of 50 percent. The maximum federal income tax rate on other nonearned personal income was 70 percent. Incorporating for real estate investment may be financially advantageous from a tax standpoint even though the corporate stockholder is subject to double taxation.

If the corporation has a limited amount of assets and only a few shareholders, the Internal Revenue Service will allow this corporation to be taxed as a partnership if the requirements are met for a Subchapter S corporation. The corporation's profit is subject to only single-income taxation. The corporation's taxable net income flows through to the stockholders as personal income, which is taxed at each stockholder's personal tax rate.

Other Forms of Investor Organizations Similar to Partnership Agreements

Other commonly used forms of real estate investor organization are the joint venture, the real estate syndicate, the business trust, the land trust, and the real estate investment trust. Each of these organizational forms tends to have a special use.

The Joint Venture. The joint venture is usually employed for joint ownership of a single, large-scale real estate development by widely differing investors and lenders. The single project usually requires an immense amount of investment and borrowed capital, plus real estate development and management expertise. The key professional companies and financial institutions form a joint venture or special partnership agreement to develop and hold in portfolio the real estate venture. Here is a case example:

> The John D. Gilreath Development Co. of Nashville recognized a potentially profitable real estate opportunity for land on the southwest corner of the metropolitan area. Land could be purchased, sold to a financial institution, and leased back for a regional shopping center in a location surrounded by middle- and upper-middle-income suburban housing. John Gilreath approached the Security National Bank of Nashville and the Phoenix Mutural Life Insurance Company of Hartford, Connecticut, about forming a joint venture to invest in and finance the potentially profitable project. The Security National Bank was asked to provide the land-development and construction loans as well as to invest some of its trust department funds in the venture. Phoenix Mutual was asked to provide some equity and a lot of long-term debt capital in the shopping center. The development company was offering the land under option, which could be purchased by Phoenix Mutual and leased back to the joint venture.
>
> The three companies would be partners in the single-project joint venture and receive their agreed-upon distributions of the cash flows generated by the shopping center. In addition, of course, the bank would receive the normal interest income on its short-term land-development and construction loans and the life insurance company would receive interest on its leased land and the long-term permanent loans. The development company would work for its usual development, architectural, leasing, and management fees.

Each of the parties to the joint venture is usually incorporated. Therefore, its financial liability is reduced to its investment. The income received by each partner in the various forms is taxed at the partner's usual rates for the type of income; each partner's individual capital gains and ordinary tax rates would apply to the income he or she individually receives per time period. In the case example, the developer would be interested in the depreciation flowthrough in order to reduce his tax burden on the corporate schedule. The commercial banks and the life insurance company are both subject to federal income tax rates that are considerably lower than the corporate rates applicable to the real estate developer. The trust department investment return would be subject to relatively low tax rates, so depreciation flowthrough would be of minimal interest to the institutional investors.

The Real Estate Syndicate. A real estate syndicate is usually a "closed-end" real estate partnership, in which the syndicator—the general partner—sells limited partnership interests and invests the funds in suitable real estate and real property interests. Usually only a single offering is made by the syndicator, but additional offerings may be made by the syndicator to the syndicate members in the future if the syndicator thinks more property should be purchased for the profitability of the membership.

Therefore, the fund-raising capability of the real estate syndicate tends to be restricted to the single offering of syndicate shares. The syndicator's liability is unlimited unless the syndicator is incorporated, and the syndicate member's liability is usually limited to the member's contribution. The net cash flow and taxable deductions flow through to the syndicate members as in any other form of real estate partnership. Here is a case example:

> Bill Roulac, of a widely diversified real estate company of Berkeley, California, observed that three or four good citrus farms in the Sacramento Valley were for sale. The investment capital required was beyond the funds of any one investor currently in the market in the Berkeley area. The California real estate syndicate experience in citrus farms had been good in recent years. Roulac also could obtain another source of income as syndicate manager if sufficient syndicate investors could be found for the purchase of those or other even more profitable citrus farms.
>
> Roulac studied the syndication laws of the state of California and sought investors from California with sufficient combined investment capital. (Interstate syndicate offerings are always subject to Securities and Exchange Commission regulations, which are more stringent than state laws and regulations.) When enough syndicate members were located, Roulac sought and obtained options on the farms and mortgage money to make the investments in the name of the United Farm Syndicate of California.

The Business Trust. One of the earliest forms of partnership in the United States was the business trust. Several states encouraged the joint ownership of real property under the business trust organization, in which a board of trustees holds the title to the property for the holders of beneficial interest. Those who hold the shares of beneficial interest are the owners or the stockholders of the business trust. The board of trustees may also actively manage the assets of the trust, or it may employ a management group, which will receive a fee for its services.

Many properties are still under the business trust arrangement. Massachusetts is one state that has long fostered this type of business organization for the joint ownership of real estate.

The Land Trust. A few states, including Illinois, have permitted the formation of land trusts. Real property is owned by a number of investors, who employ a representative of their interests. On the public records only the name of the representative of the land trust is shown. There is no way of tracing the individual owners of the land trust other than through information given by the attorney or other such representative of the trust. It is sometimes called a *blind trust*. In Chicago, for example, many land trusts hold numerous apartment buildings around the city.

The Real Estate Investment Trust. The real estate investment trust was created by Congress in 1960, through changes in the Internal Revenue Code, to provide a real estate investment medium for small investors. The REIT (pronounced "rēēt") was designed to be a real estate *mutual fund* for small investors who wish to participate in diversified real estate ownership. Most REIT declarations of trust, filed in various states encouraging business trusts, permit REIT ownership of real estate, mortgages, and other loans related to real estate. The small investor could gain diversified real estate ownership by joining with other owners of shares of beneficial interest of a real estate investment trust.

The relatively new type of real estate organization, which is tax exempt if it meets IRS requirements for distribution of income, is a business trust committed to ownership of real property and real property interests, which publicly discloses its owners and management. The shares of many REITs are listed on the New York and American Stock Exchanges. The REIT is not a land trust per se because of its public disclosure.

The REIT is a partnership with one class of shareholders, a board of trustees that holds the title to the assets and makes overall policy, and a management group for daily asset and liability management. The partners—the holders of shares of beneficial interest—have liability limited to the amount of their investment just like corporate stockholders. The earnings distributions are taxed at the shareholders' personal tax rates as the REIT dividends are received. When shareholder dividends represent investment repayment or capital distribution, those dividends are tax free for federal income tax purposes. Depreciation and other tax-deductible items do not flow through to the individual shareholders as in a regular partnership.

In order for the trust to retain its tax-exempt status, at least 75 percent of its gross income must be derived from real estate investment sources, namely:

1. Rents from real property.
2. Real estate mortgage interest.
3. Gains from the sale of real property, or interests therein, on real estate mortgages.
4. Dividends from and gain on the sale of shares in other qualified REITs.
5. Real estate tax abatements and refunds.
6. Charges for customary services to tenants, even though billed separately.
7. Incidental rental of personal property, if 15 percent or less of total rent is attributable to the personal property.
8. Commitment fees.

The 75 percent requirement excludes income from the sales of securities. Until January 1, 1980, at least 90 percent of gross income had to come from the above real estate investment sources, plus

1. Dividends.
2. Other interest.

After January 1, 1980, the latter requirement changed to 95 percent. If the REIT fails to meet any of the required percentage tests, disqualification will generally result, and the REIT will be taxed on the income at the corporate tax rates. If fraud and willful intent to defraud are not present, some leniency is permitted.

After January 1, 1980, at least 75 percent of the income must be paid to shareholders before year end, or a nondeductible 3 percent excise tax is imposed. Deficiency dividend procedures are available to avoid disqualification as a result of adjustments made by the Internal Revenue during REIT examination. Ninety days are permitted after the IRS determination of an adjustment for the REIT to pay a deficiency dividend and retain its qualified tax-exempt status. If a REIT intentionally disqualifies, it generally cannot requalify until after a five-year wait. As of the Tax Reform Act of 1976, a REIT can use the corporate form.

SUMMARY

An important part of real estate investment is the form of legal organization available for the investor. Several investment forms exist. Each has its distinctive characteristics, fund-raising capability, liability ramifications, and tax regulations. The real estate investor should select the form of organization that benefits him or her most during the expected investment holding period. The investor must integrate the liability and tax implications of the new business form with the investor's existing portfolio of assets and their liability, tax, and risk implications.

If the investor wants to be the sole owner of the real property, the sole proprietorship form would suffice. The investor would retain full liability, limited fund-raising capacity, and taxation of combined real estate and other incomes at the investor's personal tax rates. The investor also might incorporate as a personal holding company, but other officers of the company would have to be declared, even though they were not providing investment capital.

Joint ownership of real estate may be accommodated by the general partnership, the limited partnership, the public corporation, the joint venture, the real estate syndicate, the business trust, the land trust, and the real estate investment trust forms of organization. Each of these forms has its distinctive combination of liability, taxation, and fund-raising features from which the investor can select. Only one class of owner or shareholder is involved in the general partnership, the joint venture, the real estate syndicate, the business trust, the land trust, and the real estate investment trust. The limited partnership and corporation provide for two or more classes or owners; each class has its own benefits and restrictions. The general partner of the limited partnership has full liability, whereas the limited partner has liability to the extent only of his or her investment. The corporation may have two classes of owners with limited liability: preferred and common stockholders. The preferred stockholders have a prior right to earnings distributions, and the common stockholders have voting rights regarding management policies.

If the investor wants limited liability but still wants a managing, general partnership interest, the investor may incorporate as a general partner. Without incorporating, the investor may gain limited liability by investing as a limited partner, a stockholder, or a holder of beneficial interest. If the investor wants to avoid double taxation, he or she will shy away from the corporate form of organization. If he or she wants the flow-through of depreciation and other tax-deductible items, the investor will select the proprietorship, the general partnership, the limited partnership, the joint venture, the real estate syndicate, and the business and land trust forms of organization. The real estate investment trust and the corporation do not permit flowthrough of depreciation and other tax-deductible items.

Key Terms and Concepts

The legal form
Liability status
Federal income tax status
Limited partnership
State Department of Revenue
Capital gains tax rate
Contracting authority
Distribution system
Management group
Preferred stock
Double taxation

Syndicate members
Blind trust
Qualified tax-exempt status
Joint venture
Real estate syndicate
Security registration
Business trust
Insurance protection
Flow-through deductions
Refinancing proceeds
Articles of incorporation

Stockholders
Dividend rights
Subchapter S corporation
Syndication state laws
Real estate tax abatements
Organizational chartering
Sole proprietorship
General partnership
Land trust

Ordinary income tax rate
Accelerated depreciation
Sale proceeds
By-laws
Common stock
Personal holding company
Management fees
Securities and Exchange Commission
Deficiency dividend procedures

Questions for Student Self-examination

Multiple-Choice Questions

1. Usually the state does not require registration of the _____ and requires no payment of chartering or license fees.
   a. corporation
   b. limited partnership
   c. land trust
   d. sole proprietorship

2. Corporation federal income tax rates may be _____ the stockholder's federal income tax rate.
   a. lower than
   b. higher than
   c. equal to
   d. all of the above

3. If the corporation has a limited amount of assets and only a few shareholders, the Internal Revenue Service will allow this corporation to be taxed as a partnership if the requirements are met for a _____ corporation.
   a. Chapter 10
   b. Subchapter S
   c. Chapter 11
   d. Subchapter C

4. The _____ is usually employed for joint ownership of a single, large-scale real estate development by widely differing real estate investors and lenders.
   a. real estate investment trust
   b. proprietorship
   c. general partnership
   d. joint venture

5. The fund-raising capability of the _____ tends to be restricted to the single offering of shares.
   a. real estate investment trust
   b. real estate syndicate
   c. proprietorship
   d. corporation

True-False Questions

T F 1. Federal laws set the requirements for organizational chartering, registration for the operation of business, registration for security sales, and registration for license fee collection.

T F 2. The sole owner or proprietor of real estate has total and unlimited liability for any developments associated with the property owned.

T F 3. The sole proprietor-owner of real property is subject to double taxation just as an incorporated investor is.

T F 4. Under a general partnership agreement registered with the state, one general partner has the right to make the decisions for the general partnership, and all the general partners share the financial liability of the real estate investment.

T F 5. A general partner may not contribute funds, but may contribute legal, land development, property management, or other forms of expertise.

T F 6. Many general partners in recent years have incorporated to reduce their personal liability in partnerships.

T F 7. The income of the general partnership is not taxed.

T F 8. The limited partnership is permitted to hold only one real property in its portfolio.

T F 9. The owners of the corporation's assets are the bondholders, who have liability limited only to their investments.

T F 10. The articles of incorporation are supplemented by by-laws, rules, and regulations.

Answers
Multiple-Choice: 1d, 2d, 3b, 4d, 5b.
True-False: 1F, 2T, 3F, 4F, 5T, 6T, 7T, 8F, 9F, 10T.

Problems

1. If Mr. Crawford wants to retain complete control of his income property and wants to take all profit as his personal income, what form of business organization should he select for his investment?

2. If Ms. Johnson has $20,000 to invest in a small office building and wants to attract capital from those who want an investment without management obligations, what kind of business organization might be used advantageously for the investment?

3. If the investor is in a 62 percent marginal tax bracket and wishes the depreciation to flow through the business organization for the real estate investment to his personal income, which business form would be preferable for the investor? Why?

4. If the investor is in a 62 percent marginal tax bracket, what benefits would she derive from the corporate form of business organization?

5. If the Equitable Life Assurance Society of America and the First National Bank wanted to invest jointly in an income property development as partners, what form of investment organization would be appropriate for them and their other partners?

6. If the investor seeks an outlet for investible funds in which low share prices usually exist, dividend yields may be substantial from the returns from organizational investment in real estate and mortgages, and the investment vehicle is tax exempt, what type of investment outlet should the investor seek? What other investment advantages may accrue from that form of real estate investment?

Chapter 10
The Numerous Avenues for Real Estate Investment

Introduction
The Relationship of This Chapter to Other Chapters of the Text
The Broad Assortment of Real Estate Investment Opportunities
  Stock Purchase   Commercial Paper, Note, and Bond Purchase   A Summary of Selected Investment Alternatives
Characteristics of Selected Real Estate Investment Alternatives
  Building Construction   Purchase of a Lease for Subletting to a Tenant   Purchase of Stock: *Shares of beneficial interest of a REIT, Stock of a building construction company or housing manufacturer, FNMA stock, Savings and loan association stock, Shares of a real estate syndicate, Shares of a real estate limited partnership*   Purchase of Bonds or Other Debt Obligations: *Debt obligations of real estate companies and institutions, Mortgage bonds, Mortgage-backed securities*
Summary
Key Terms and Concepts
Questions for Student Self-examination

LEARNING OBJECTIVES After studying this chapter, you should be familiar with

The broad assortment of real estate investment opportunities
Types of real estate stock that can be purchased
Types of real estate debt obligations that can be purchased
The characteristics of investment in building construction
Real estate investment by means of purchase of a lease for subletting of the space to an occupant
The investment characteristics of shares of beneficial interest of a REIT
The risk factors of investment in stock of construction companies or housing manufacturers
The risk factors of investment in FNMA stock
The risk factors associated with purchase of savings and loan association stock
The risks of investment in shares of a real estate syndicate
The investment risks of the general and limited partners of a real estate limited partnership
The investment risk factors of debt obligations of real estate companies and institutions
The investment characteristics of mortgage bonds
Mortgage-backed security investment

When a person, family, or business invests money, the investments often include real property and real property interests. These investments are combined with other nonreal property investments to form the individual, family, or business investment portfolio. As the investor plans the portfolio appropriate to the current economic circumstances, the stage in the family or individual life cycle, current and future needs for cash, investment objectives, and the amount of investible funds, the investor wants to know what investment opportunities are available at the time.

Since a number of investment opportunities are available in the real estate area, this chapter surveys the major investment alternatives and their comparative characteristics. Direct investment in real estate by one individual or company is always possible. In other circumstances, an investor may join with others in real property investment. In contrast to real estate ownership, a group of investors may join together to own interests in real property, such as mortgages or leasehold estates.

INTRODUCTION

Before we go further into Part III, we should survey the various avenues for sole or joint investment in real property or real property interests. The principal focus of the text is direct ownership of real property by an individual or group of investors, but there are several other avenues for investment in real property or real property interests. First, securities of companies and government agencies primarily engaged in real estate transactions may be purchased. In some cases common stock—and perhaps preferred stock—may be purchased by an investor. Bonds and other types of shorter term liabilities may be available for purchase. The stock and debt obligations may be listed and traded on the national and regional stock exchanges. Conversely, they may not be listed on the exchanges; the trading may only take place over the counter. These securities may be sold for the financing of real estate companies, financial institutions dealing largely in real property interests, and government agencies primarily involved in mortgage investment and trading.

Second, the investor may acquire leased land or buildings and sublet them to others for an investment return. Third, the investor may develop the available land and construct land improvements for a profit. This investor may not take a long-term position or a position as the developer of an income-producing property. Most of the text is devoted to investment in residential space and development and investment in income properties, which would be a fourth category of investment in real property or real property interests.

THE RELATIONSHIP OF THIS CHAPTER TO OTHER CHAPTERS OF THE TEXT

The first chapter of Part III, "Portfolio Strategy," dealt with direct real estate ownership on an individual or group basis. The liability and tax aspects of several ownership forms were surveyed. This chapter surveys ownership of real property interests on an individual or group basis. The investor has numerous avenues for investment in the real estate business.

After the consideration of alternative individual and group forms of investment in real property and real property interests, Chapter 11 deals with diversification of typical investment portfolios for the reduction of risk and the optimization of investment return. Since direct investment in real property usually fits into contemporary investment portfolios, the remaining chapters of Part III deal with the federal income tax aspects of the planning, operating, and termination stages of real estate development and investment. Then Part IV deals specifically with real estate investment yield analysis. The groundwork is laid for the comprehension of this section in the chapters of Part III on portfolio strategy. Diversification of the portfolio is necessary to reduce the investor's risk, but yield on the individual investments must be calculated in detail and merged into an overall portfolio yield commensurate with the risks assumed.

THE BROAD ASSORTMENT OF REAL ESTATE INVESTMENT OPPORTUNITIES

When the person with some savings or the company with retained earnings looks to real estate for investment opportunities, a broad assortment of possibilities present themselves. Purchase of land and buildings for occupancy or rental is only one of the investment possibilities. Land development is another. Purchase of a lease is an alternative. Building construction for immediate sale is one more investment avenue. Then there are many ways of investing with others in real estate and real estate interests.

Joint investment in real estate and real estate interests may be accomplished through the purchase of stock and bonds. The stock and bonds take various forms, but they still may represent indirect investment with others in real estate and real estate interests.

Stock Purchase. Some of the types of real estate stock include stock of real estate investment trusts (shares of beneficial interest); stock of building construction companies; and stock of real estate holding companies that may deal in real estate brokerage, insurance, appraising, and property management. The stock of the Federal National Mortgage Association may also be purchased through the New York Stock Exchange members and associated stockbrokers; FNMA trades in residential mortgages in the secondary mortgage market. The stock of a thrift institution may be purchased. In other words, the equity shares of stockholder-owned savings and loan associations may be purchased if the shares are traded publicly or if the officers of the privately held savings and loan offer stock to the potential investor. Along a different line, the shares of a real estate syndicate or a real estate limited partnership may be purchased if the potential investor meets the financial requirements and gains the approval of the syndicate manager or the other general and limited partners of the limited partnership. Exhibit 10-1 shows the assortment of possible stock purchase alternatives.

Commercial Paper, Note, and Bond Purchase. The potential investor can look over the possible investment returns from several types of commercial paper, notes, and bonds issued by real estate companies and financial institutions that generate mortgages and invest in real estate. The person or company can invest in the various types of indenture agreements issued by real estate investment trusts, diversified real estate holding companies, the Federal National Mortgage Association, and the Federal Home Loan Mortgage Corporation (otherwise called "The Mortgage Corporation"). Bonds representing long-term financing for a real estate development may be purchased. For example, mortgage bonds issued by the owners of an office building may be purchased by investors. Many issues of mortgage-backed securities, guaranteed or not guaranteed by the Government National Mortgage Association, are available periodically for investor examination and possible purchase. Exhibit 10-2 summarizes the types of real estate bonds that may be available for purchase. Exhibit 10-3 shows the relative yields from 1975 to 1978 on FNMA FHA/VA mortgages, GNMA securities, and prime commercial paper.

Summary of Selected Investment Alternatives. Before we go on to consider the characteristics of various real estate investment alternatives, let us observe the assortment of alternatives just mentioned. The purchase of stock, commercial paper, notes,

Exhibit 10-1. Types of Real Estate Stock

Shares of Beneficial Interest of a Real Estate Investment Trust
Stock of a Building Construction Company
Stock of a Real Estate Holding Company
FNMA Stock Listed on the NYSE
Savings and Loan Association Stock
Shares of a Real Estate Syndicate
Shares of a Real Estate Limited Partnership

Exhibit 10-2. *Types of Real Estate Bonds*

Commercial Paper, Notes, and Bonds of Real Estate Investment Trusts

Commercial Paper, Notes, and Bonds of Real Estate Holding Companies

Commercial Paper, Notes, Mortgage Participations, and Bonds of FNMA

Commercial Paper, Notes, Mortgage Participations, and Bonds of the Mortgage Corporation

Mortgage Bonds

Mortgage-Backed Securities

Exhibit 10-3. *Selected Yields: Yields on FNMA/FHA/VA Mortgages, GNMA Securities, and Prime Commercial Paper*

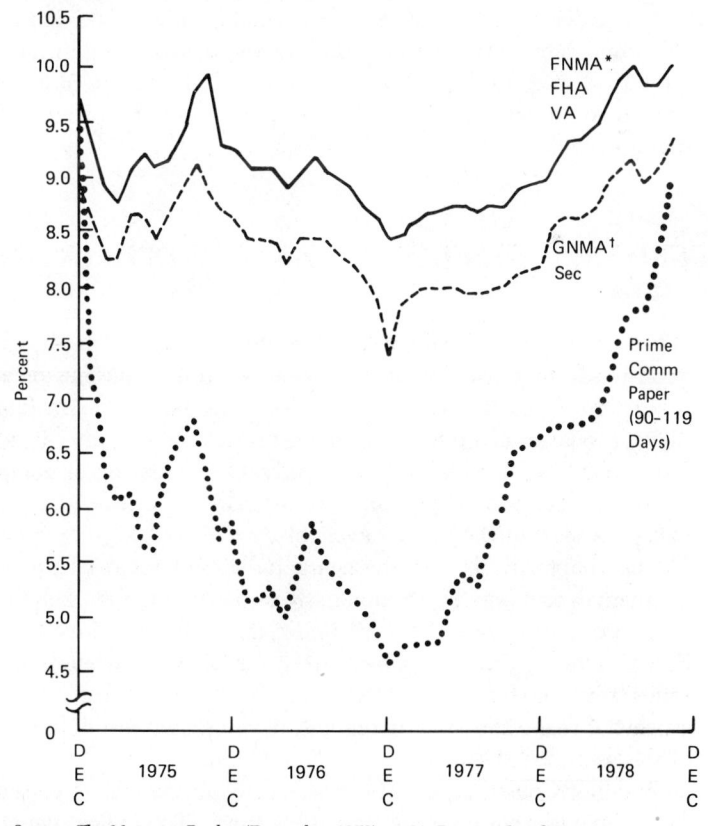

Source: *The Mortgage Banker* (December 1978), p. 36. Reprinted with permission.
*Weighted average gross yields for accepted bids of all FNMA free market auctions during that month.
†Survey of three New York security dealers' securities for immediate delivery.

The Numerous Avenues for Real Estate Investment

Exhibit 10-4

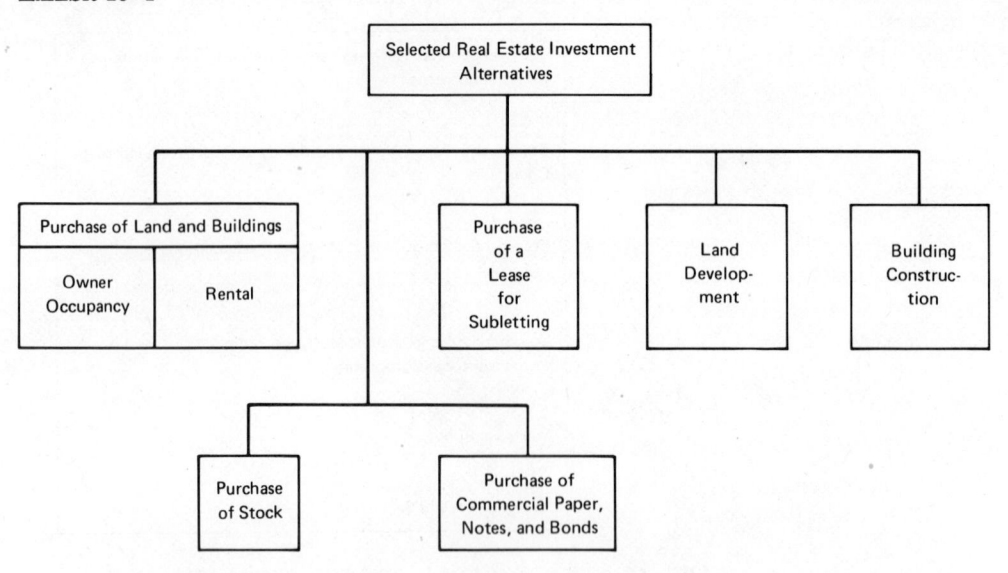

```
                    ┌─────────────────────────┐
                    │ Selected Real Estate    │
                    │ Investment Alternatives │
                    └─────────────────────────┘
         ┌──────────────┬─────────────┬─────────────┬──────────────┐
  ┌──────────────────┐ ┌──────────┐ ┌──────────┐ ┌──────────────┐
  │ Purchase of Land │ │Purchase  │ │  Land    │ │   Building   │
  │  and Buildings   │ │of a Lease│ │ Develop- │ │ Construction │
  │ ┌──────┬───────┐ │ │   for    │ │   ment   │ │              │
  │ │Owner │Rental │ │ │Subletting│ │          │ │              │
  │ │Occup.│       │ │ │          │ │          │ │              │
  │ └──────┴───────┘ │ └──────────┘ └──────────┘ └──────────────┘
  └──────────────────┘
              ┌────────────────┬─────────────────┐
        ┌──────────┐    ┌────────────────────┐
        │Purchase  │    │ Purchase of        │
        │of Stock  │    │ Commercial Paper,  │
        │          │    │ Notes, and Bonds   │
        └──────────┘    └────────────────────┘
```

and bonds of real estate entities was only a part of the picture. Previous chapters of the text considered direct real estate ownership; let us add the purchase of a lease for subletting, land development, and building construction to the overall panorama. Exhibit 10-4 gives us a quick view of selected investment alternatives. The reader may wish to add other alternatives that are pertinent to his or her individual objectives and that are available in the investor's locale.

CHARACTERISTICS OF SELECTED REAL ESTATE INVESTMENT ALTERNATIVES

Whether the prospective investor is a physician, a bricklayer, an attorney, a teacher, a dentist, a factory assembly-line worker, or a retired businessperson, he or she wants to review the alternates available for the investment of extra funds. It may have been difficult to accumulate the investment capital. On the other hand, the excess investible funds may have been inherited recently. Or the person or company may have experienced windfall profits by chance. At any rate, the prospective investor usually wants to make the most of the monies available.

This chapter deals with the characteristics of some selected real estate investment alternatives that are very common investments in the marketplace. Since Part IV deals with cash flow analysis, profit planning, and real estate investment return analysis, and Part V covers investment returns from the direct ownership of specific types of properties, this chapter covers other common types of real estate investments. The tax aspects of real estate investment and development are deferred to the latter chapters of this section and Part IV.

Building Construction. The prospective investor may consider building construction as an outlet for his or her investible funds. The building contractor invests funds in office maintenance, office personnel, accounting and legal services, sale of construction services through advertising and promotion, leased construction equipment, supervisory personnel, and other construction-related expenses. The general contractor maintains working relationships with subcontractors in the building trades so that the accepted building contracts may be completed on schedule. Time and effort are often expended in the preparation of a bid for a construction contract for a publicly or privately financed development. The bid may be accepted or rejected by the party who plans to erect a land improvement. The general contractor usually must consider the continuity of the employment of affiliated subcontractors as he or she bids continuously for jobs.

The contractor often borrows short-term bank funds on the basis of his or her equity in the business. The profit on the job must cover the interest and principal repayment on these borrowed operating funds, or working capital, as well as the other construction expenses incurred by the general contractor.

The general contractor may receive a return on his or her money in the following ways:

Profit built into the construction contract.
Building for the general contractor's own account and receipt of profit from the sale of the improvement, such as a single-family dwelling.
Speculative purchase of land for future building construction to gain a profit on the sale of the land.

Purchase of a Lease for Subletting to a Tenant. If the investor wants to be a *sandwich lessee*, he or she purchases an existing lease or sublets from an existing lessee. This investor then leases the space to a tenant, who will pay a rent that will provide a profit to the new sandwich lessee. The sandwich lessee buys out the existing lease or pays rent to the existing lessee. Then he or she collects rent from the sublessee, who actually leases from the sandwich lessee and occupies the space. The differential between the rent paid the existing lessee and the rent received from the sublessee is the gross profit to the sandwich lessee. If the lease is purchased, the rent payments from the sublessee-occupant must cover the sandwich lessee's investment in the lease and give the sandwich lessee a return on his or her money over the period of the sublessee's rental agreement. This type of investment occurs quite often in large cities, where major income properties have one or more sandwich lessees. Manhattan office buildings are often financed by means of prime lessees, sandwich lessees, and sublessee-tenants.

Purchase of Stock. Shares of several kinds of real estate companies and real estate-oriented financial institutions may be purchased, including shares of beneficial interest of a real estate investment trust, stock of a building construction company, stock of a real estate holding company, stock of the Federal National Mortgage Association, stock of a stockholder-owned savings and loan association, shares of a real estate syndicate, and shares of a real estate limited partnership. In each instance, the investor looks for two basic kinds of returns from the stock: periodic dividends and a capital gain from the rise in the stock price over the investment holding period. The investor will tend to watch and periodically calculate the dividend yield determined by dividing the current market price of the stock into the estimated or most recent annual dividend payment. The investor also examines the difference between the purchase price of the stock and the current market price in order to establish the unrealized capital gain. This type of capital gain calculation assumes that the stock purchase price was not financed through a brokerage house margin account or other means of financing. The financing would have to be taken into account in figuring the potential capital gain.

Shares of beneficial interest of a REIT. One class of stock may be sold by a real estate investment trust (often called a REIT) according to the usual declaration of trust recorded in the state of domicile. Most REIT shares of beneficial interest are offered to the public through the medium of the national and regional stock exchanges. REIT dividend yields have often been characterized by generous payouts similar to preferred stock yields. For this reason, the investor clientele tends to be the type that is normally attracted to preferred stock rather than common stock. The clientele is often composed of small, individual investors who seek periodic cash flow in the form of dividends; bank trust accounts; and pension funds of smaller companies.

The share price index of the REIT industry has been in the doldrums since the recession of 1974, which spelled decline in overall REIT earnings and asset volumes. Exhibit 10-5 shows some price increase since the low point in the price index in 1974. Some REITs, particularly the equity and hybrid equity-mortgage REITs, have tended to flourish, even though the short-term mortgage REITs have suffered major declines, many bankruptcies, and conversions to corporations and other forms of business enterprise. Exhibit 10-6 illustrates the recent financial data on ten selected REITs that

Exhibit 10-5. *NAREIT Share Price Index (January, 1972 = 100)*

	1972	1973	1974	1975	1976	1977	1978
January	100.00	103.27	62.36	24.17	21.04	24.36	26.39
February	101.22	96.33	63.23	21.23	22.93	24.13	26.72
March	101.42	94.59	57.81	23.57	21.58	24.03	28.00
April	100.38	90.01	47.38	20.79	21.15	24.73	28.44
May	99.08	84.15	41.66	20.92	20.29	24.29	
June	94.00	84.39	35.99	22.50	20.40	25.03	
July	93.89	85.39	33.45	21.47	20.74	26.03	
August	95.86	81.17	24.42	20.30	20.89	26.28	
September	96.94	87.44	23.44	18.01	21.05	25.94	
October	100.01	85.89	23.87	17.14	20.81	25.20	
November	103.32	69.23	20.53	17.02	21.89	27.81	
December	102.47	61.28	16.87	18.01	24.30	27.46	

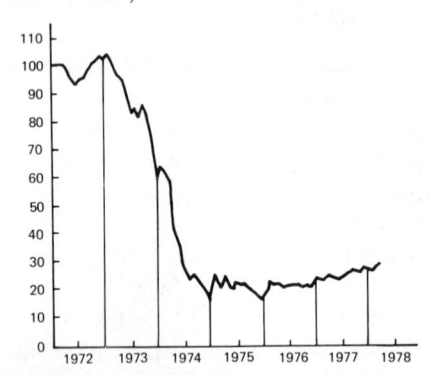

Source: The month-end price of REIT's traded on the New York Stock Exchange, American Stock Exchange, and the national O.T.C. market. Quoted in *REITs Quarterly*, Vol. IV (May 1977), p. 2. Reprinted with permission.

Exhibit 10-6. *Recent Financial Data on Selected Real Estate Investment Trusts*

REIT	Report Date	Assets ($ mil.)	Dividend Last Divd. Date	Dividend Last Divd. Amt.	Share Prices May 1978	Share Prices Year Ago
Equitable Life	1/78	$384.5	5/78	$0.50	$20.75	$24.75
General Growth	12/77	316.6	4/78	0.37	25.625	22.75
Connecticut General	12/77	322.4	5/78	0.40	18.50	19.25
Lomas Nettleton	12/77	246.8	5/78	0.43	19.75	15.75
Hubbard Real Estate	1/78	94.2	4/78	0.33	17.375	17.00
Continental Illinois Property	1/78	310.5	4/78	0.32	15.50	16.50
Real Estate Investment Trust of America	2/78	48.7	4/78	0.30	16.25	14.75
Northwestern Mutual Life	12/77	237.4	4/78	0.25	11.625	12.50
Massachusetts Mutual Mortgage	1/78	193.0	4/78	0.32	14.25	13.875
Wells Fargo	12/77	183.5	5/78	0.30	13.00	13.25

continue to be strong, profitable companies offering competitive investment returns. Many of these REITs are sponsored by life insurance companies such as Equitable Life, Connecticut General, Northwestern Mutual, and MassMutual Mortgage. A large California commercial bank sponsors Wells Fargo Mortgage Investors. Hubbard Real Estate Investors is a corporate subsidiary of the Merrill Lynch, Pierce, Fenner & Smith brokerage house. Lomas Nettleton, the largest mortgage company in the United States, which is headquartered in Dallas, sponsors a REIT that has had continuing business success.

Stock of a building construction company or housing manufacturer. The stock of a building company or a mobile home or modular home manufacturer may be listed on the major stock exchanges or traded over the market. For statistical purposes, the many companies in the buildings and housing manufacturing business may be divided into (1) smaller builders—under $25 million in sales, (2) large builders—$25 to $100 million in sales, (3) major builders—over $100 million in sales, (4) manufactured housing, and (5) Canadian homebuilders. Exhibits 10-7 through 10-12 indicate the exchange where the stock of selected companies is listed; the stock price history; the sales and earnings history; the current price-earnings ratio; the current volume of assets and equity; the equity portion of the company assets; the current percentage return on sales, assets, and equity; and the current asset turnover. Many opportunities for investment in real estate stocks are obvious to the reader.

Exhibit 10-7. Key Housing Stocks in 1979, 1978, 1977, and 1976

	Exchange	May 2 1979	July 14 1978	Dec. 30 1977	Dec. 31 1976
Building Companies					
Centex Corp.	NY	26 3/4	18 1/2	13 7/8	12 1/8
Cenvill Communities	AM	16 1/4	17 1/8	18 5/8	12 1/2
Kaufman and Broad	NY	8 5/8	8 1/2	6 1/8	8 3/4
Presley Cos.	AM	11 3/8	12 1/8	10 1/4	9 3/4
Pulte Home Corp.	AM	11 1/8	10 1/4	8	6 1/4
Ryan Homes	NY	18 3/4	18	16 1/2	19 7/8
Shapell Industries	NY	28 3/4	24 3/4	18	19
U.S. Home Corp.	NY	12 3/8	8 1/8	7 3/8	8 1/4
Mobile Homes & Modules					
Champion Home Builders	AM	1 3/4	2 1/4	1 7/8	3 7/8
Coachman Industries	NY	7 1/4	10 5/8	13 1/2	16 3/8
Golden West	AM	8	20 3/8	19	19
Mobile Home Industries	NY	2 1/8	2 7/8	2 3/8	4 3/8
Oakwood Homes	AM	12 1/4	11 7/8	10 7/8	10
Redman Industries	NY	4 1/2	4 7/8	4	3 3/8
Shelter Resources	AM	3 1/8	6 1/8	2 1/8	2 1/4
Skyline	NY	10 1/8	12 3/4	14 3/4	18 5/8
Zimmer Homes	AM	8 7/8	13 1/4	9 3/4	7 3/8
Land Developers					
Deltona Corp.	NY	12 1/2	10 1/4	5 3/4	5
GDV Inc.	NY	10 1/2	8 7/8	7 1/2	5 3/8
Horizon Corp.	NY	3 3/4	3 5/8	2 1/8	1 7/8

Sources: *The Wall Street Journal*, July 14, 1978 and May 2, 1979; *Housing* (February 1978), p. 14.

Exhibit 10-8. Sales for Smaller Builders

Smaller Builders—Under $25 Million Sales

Company—Location	Year (Interim)	Sales Mil.$	Sales % Chng.	Earnings Mil.$	Earnings % Chng.	Earn./Share	%Gross Margin	Profit % 1977	Profit % 1976	Stock Listed	P/E[a] Ratio	Mil.$ Assets[x]	Mil.$ Equity[y]	Equity % of Assets[x]	% Return on Assets[y]	% Return on Equity[y]	Asset Turns[y]
Braewood Devel., Tucson, Ariz.	June '77	$16.30	Not cal.	$1.29[a]	Z	$0.61[a]	12.5%	7.9%	NA	OTC	1.9	$14.2	$2.1	14.8%	8.4%	159.3%	1.06
Bresler & Reiner, Washington, D.C.	Dec. '77	13.50	+72.0%	0.06	+150.0%	0.05	1.2	0.4	0.3%	OTC	20.0	42.4	11.4	26.9	0.1	0.5	0.29
Christiana Cos., Santa Monica, Cal.	June '77	24.37	+13.1	1.98	+50.0	0.74	20.8	8.1	6.1	ASE	5.9	31.8	16.1	50.4	5.4	13.2	0.67
Carl M. Freeman Ass., Silver Spring, Md.	Dec. '77	10.01	−10.8	0.43	Z	0.30	17.1	4.3	[d]	OTC	14.7	24.6	9.7	39.5	1.8	4.6	0.42
Hunt Bldg. Corp., El Paso, Tex.	Aug. '77	13.28	−44.0	0.26	−43.5	0.27	Neg.	2.0	1.9	OTC	NA	5.9	2.3	39.4	2.7	9.6	1.38
Key Co., Greensboro, N.C.	Oct. '77	13.65	+26.7	0.68[a]	Z	0.83[a]	22.0	5.0	[d]	ASE	7.7	14.6	6.0	40.9	4.9	12.9	0.98
Landmark Land, Oklahoma City	Dec. '77	21.23	+36.5	1.04[a]	+8.3	0.29[a]	NA	4.9	6.2	ASE	18.2	36.9	13.9	37.5	3.4	8.1	0.70
McCarthy Co., Anaheim, Cal.	Dec. '77	10.12	−53.1	1.99[a]	+24.4	1.50[a]	NA	19.7	7.4	OTC	1.3	10.0	[d]1.0	Neg.	41.2	[d]	2.10
MCD Holdings, Seabrook, Md.	Sept. '77	24.30	+7.4	0.38	−63.5	0.09	19.7	1.6	4.6	OTC	16.7	48.9	17.9	36.7	0.8	2.2	0.52
H. Moller & Sons, Plantation, Fla.	Dec. '77	13.90	+46.5	0.73	+78.0	1.22	22.4	5.3	4.3	ASE	7.8	20.2	11.2	55.7	4.0	7.0	0.76
Realty Industries, Richmond, Va.	Oct. '77	14.06	+7.7	0.26	−40.9	0.24	42.1	1.8	3.4	OTC	10.9	40.1	5.9	14.7	0.7	4.6	0.36
Robino-Ladd, Miami, Fla.	Dec. '77	14.98	−51.8	0.22[ax]	NA	0.13[a]	15.3	1.5	NA	OTC	13.6	41.1	4.8	11.7	0.5	4.6	0.36
Seligman & Assoc., Southfield, Mich.	July '77	14.12	+63.0	[d]0.60	Z[d]	0.31	8.9	[d]	[d]	ASE	[d]	31.8	5.1	16.1	[d]	[d]	0.42
Tital Group, Paramus, N.J.	Dec. '77	20.23	+528.3	2.58[b]	+7.1	0.50[b]	NM	1.2	0.8	OTC	4.5	92.1	22.7	24.6	2.9	11.4	2.49
Totals		$209.07	+19.1%	$11.08[c]	+62.9%	—	18.2%†	5.0%	4.0%		10.3†	$456.6	$121.8	26.8%	5.9%	19.8%	0.89

[*]Price/earnings ratio based upon latest 12 months' earnings and price in April 1977. Earnings per share are for fiscal year shown.
[†]Gross profit margins and price/earnings ratios are averages of ratios shown; all other group averages are weighted averages of totals.
[a]Based on year-end assets and equity; totals and averages are for companies with data shown.
[y]Based on assets and equity at beginning of year, not shown separately. Asset turns is number of times beginning assets converted into sales. Data for interim reports are annualized.
[z]Not calculated, loss in one or both years.
[d]Deficit. NA—Not available or meaningful. Neg.—Negative.
[a]Extraordinary items in 1977 as follows: Braewood Devel., $818,000 or 34¢/sh. NOL benefit; Key Co., $355,000 or 43¢/sh. NOL; Landmark Land, $210,000 or 7¢/sh. NOL; McCarthy, $1,014 million or 76¢/sh. NOL; Robino-Ladd, $1.19 million or 70¢/sh. NOL and asset swap gains.
[b]Housing sales only for Titan Group; Net Income, profit margins, total assets consolidated for all lines.
[x]Sales and earnings of Robino-Ladd excluded from totals because of large asset swap gains in 1976.
Source: *Housing* June, 1978, pp. 52-53.

Exhibit 10-9. Financial Data on Major Builders

MAJOR BUILDERS	5-yr. Price Change Per- cent	1974–78 Price Range	Price Jan. 1979	Shares Out- stand- ing (Mill.)	Total Mkt. Value (Mill.)	Latest 12-Mo. Earnings per Share	Price Earnings Ratio	Indi- cated Annual Divd.	Curr. Yield	Growth in EPS, 5-yr. Aver., Per- cent	Growth in Sales, 5-yr. Aver., Per- cent	Ret. on Eq., 5-yr. Aver., Per- cent	Ret. on Eq., Latest 12 mo., Per- cent	Ret. on Capital, Latest 12 mo., Per- cent
Del E. Webb	324.1	38–2	15 3/8	9.3	143	1.58	10	$0.20	1.3	7.7	4.9%	10.1%	15.1%	8.0%
U.S. Home	79.5	13 1/8–2	8 3/4	11.0	97	2.31	4	0.32	3.7	– 3.5	16.6	9.5	21.7	5.0
Ryan Homes	48.8	25 5/8–5½	16	6.5	104	2.39	7	1.00	6.3	13.9	14.9	20.4	19.2	17.6
Kaufman & Broad	–47.3	14 3/4–2¼	6 1/8	15.8	97	1.14	5	0.20	3.3	–19.6	9.5	3.1	11.4	9.1
Centex	—	—	—	—	—	—	—	—	—	9.6	16.9	15.5	20.1	7.6

Source: "Who's Where in Profitability, Who's Where in Growth, and Who's Where in the Stock Market," *Forbes*, Vol. 123, No. 1, Jan. 8, 1979. Reprinted with permission.

FNMA stock. Part of the stock of the Federal National Mortgage Association (often labeled "FNMA") may be purchased by the general public; part of the stock is reserved for approved mortgage originator-sellers. As the mortgage originators sell mortgages to FNMA, they must purchase FNMA stock, which represents a small percentage of the dollar volume of the mortgages sold FNMA. The other publicly held stock has been listed on the New York Stock Exchange since the establishment of FNMA as a private corporation in 1970. As a private corporation, FNMA buys and sells residential mortgages as an important institution in the secondary mortgage market.

FNMA stock prices fluctuate with the general securities market. At times the margin requirement for the purchase of FNMA stock has been as low as 10 percent for the investor. A 10 percent margin requirement means that the investor need put down only 10 percent of the purchase price as the downpayment; 90 percent of the purchase price could be financed. This low margin requirement has encouraged individual and institutional purchase of FNMA stock.

Savings and loan association stock. If a savings and loan association has stock that is publicly held and if the savings and loan is a profitable one, the prospective investor might look into the yield characteristics of the stock. Some stock of savings and loan

Exhibit 10-10. Financial Data for Manufactured Housing Companies

	Jim Walter	Boise Cascade	Insilco	Evans Products
5-Year Price Change, %	103.6	84.6	67.1	—
1974–78 price range	44 1/4–13 3/8	33 3/4–9 7/8	17 1/4–4 5/8	—
Price, Jan. 1979	28	25 3/8	12 1/8	—
Shares outstanding (Mill.)	14.5	27.0	9.8	—
Total market value (Mill.)	407	685	118	—
Latest 12-Mo. earnings per share	5.05	4.80	2.18	—
Price-earnings ratio	6	5	6	—
Indicated annual dividend	1.60	1.25	0.94	—
Current yield, %	5.7	4.9	7.8	—
Growth in earnings per share, 5-yr. aver., %	16.4	deficit to profit	8.7	—
Growth in sales, 5-Yr. aver., %	12.0	4.7	4.9	—
Return on equity, 5-yr. average, %	17.4	11.9	15.5	8.3
Return on equity, latest 12 mo., %	16.6	13.5	16.5	21.0
Return on capital, 5-yr. average, %	11.5	8.5	9.2	12.6
Return on capital, latest 12 mo., %	9.7	10.4	9.9	6.0

Source: "Who's Where in Profitability, Who's Where in Growth, and Who's Where in the Stock Market," *Forbes*, Vol. 123, No. 1, Jan. 8, 1979. Reprinted with permission.

Exhibit 10-11. Financial Data for Mobile Home Manufacturers

	Fleetwood Enterprises	City Investing (Guerdon)	Skyline	Champion Home
5-yr. price change, %	169.7	38.8	−5.7	−38.5
1974-78 price range	20 7/8-3 7/8	18 1/4-4	26-9 1/2	6 3/8-1 3/4
Recent price, Jan., 1979	11 1/8	13 7/8	10 3/8	2
Shares outstanding (Mill.)	11.4	22.5	11.2	35.4
Total market value (Mill.)	126	312	116	71
Latest 12-Mo. earnings per share	1.77	4.11	1.37	−0.10
Price-earnings ratio	6	3	8	deficit
Indicated annual dividend	0.52	1.00	0.48	none
Current yield, %	4.7	7.2	4.6	none
Growth in earnings per share, 5-yr. aver., %	4.1	4.9	——	profit to deficit
Growth in sales, 5-Yr. aver., %	19.2	11.4	——	5.5
Return on equity, 5-yr. aver., %	12.1	——	——	deficit
Return on equity, latest 12 mo., %	19.5	——	——	deficit
Return on capital 5-yr. average, %	12.1	——	——	deficit
Return on capital, latest 12 mo., %	19.5	——	——	deficit

Source: "Who's Where in Profitability, Who's Where in Growth, and Who's Where in the Stock Market," *Forbes*, Vol. 123, No. 1, Jan. 8, 1979. Reprinted with permission.

associations is privately held and may only be acquired if the partners in the closely held corporation offer the stock to the individual investor. Many savings and loan associations are mutually owned rather than owned by stockholders. The stock of a profitable savings and loan may be as widely sought after as the stock of a profitable commercial bank in the community.

Shares of a real estate syndicate. The investor may prefer joint ownership of real estate or real property interests through purchase of shares of a real estate syndicate. The syndicate members may share in the ownership rewards of a single or many real estate investment properties. The manager selects the properties to be syndicated,

Exhibit 10-12. Financial Data for Industrial Corporations with Housing and Real Estate Subsidiaries

	IC Industries	Weyerhaeuser	Aetna Life and Casualty	Alcoa
5-yr. price change, %	16.7	−32.9	——	−5.7
1974-78 Price Range	32 1/2-10 3/8	49 5/8-20 3/4	——	61 1/4-25 7/8
Price, Jan., 1979	24 1/2	26 1/4	——	45 3/4
Shares outstanding (Mill.)	14.7	123.9	——	35.0
Total market value (Mill.)	360	3,253	——	1,600
Latest 12-mo. earnings per share	4.28	2.61	——	7.32
Price-earnings ratio	6	10	——	6
Indicated annual dividend	1.68	1.00	——	2.00
Current yield, %	6.9	3.8	——	4.4
Growth in earnings per share, 5-yr. aver., %	8.7	10.1	15.8	10.8
Growth in sales, 5-yr. aver., %	14.6	13.7	12.2	12.3
Return on equity, 5-yr. aver., %	8.0	16.2	15.7	——
Return on equity, latest 12 mo., %	8.8	15.8	23.5	——
Return on capital, 5-yr. aver., %	5.4	11.6	14.2	——
Return on capital, latest 12 mo., %	5.8	11.1	20.6	——

Source: "Who's Where in Profitability, Who's Where in Growth, and Who's Where in the Stock Market," *Forbes*, Vol. 123, No. 1, Jan. 8, 1979. Reprinted with permission.

advertises the syndicate shares through promotional plans and the printed security offering, manages the purchased properties, accounts for the earnings and cash flows of the syndicate, and distributes the generated cash flow and depreciation amounts to the syndicate members at the end of accounting periods.

The syndicate membership may have minimum financial requirements, such as minimum net worth requirements, for the prospective investor. The minimum investment for a share may be $10,000, $25,000, or some similar dollar amount. With the investment, the investor becomes essentially a limited partner in the syndicated venture.

Shares of a real estate limited partnership. Limited partnership shares give the investor the opportunity to own real estate jointly with other general and limited partners. The limited partnership share usually gives the investor financial liability that is limited to his or her financial contribution to the partnership. There are circumstances, though, in which the other assets of the limited partner will be drawn upon to cover the losses of the partnership. For instance, if debt is incurred in the partnership name on a recourse rather than a nonrecourse basis, the individual partners are liable for the debt repayment if the partnership income is insufficient. Nonrecourse debt confines the financial liability to the partnership income sources rather than the personal income sources of the individual partners beyond their financial contributions to the partnership.

Since partnership income and expenses flow through to the individual general and limited partners, the partners each receive periodic distributions of proportionate shares of cash flows, taxable income or loss, depreciation, and other noncash tax-deductible expense. The general partners estimate the future returns for the limited partners as they consider investment in shares of the limited partnership. As time goes by and the investments yield operating results, the actual cash flows are distributed to the partners. The preliminary prospectus or forecast of future investment yields may or may not parallel actual partnership receipts.

If the prospective investor enters into the limited partnership as a general partner, he or she will have complete financial and legal liability for the day-to-day management of the partnership property. In the partnership agreement, the general partners may each receive management fees plus distributions of cash flows and depreciation. Unless the general partner is incorporated, the losses of the partnership may be partially covered by the personal assets of the general partners. The limited partners may have to assume part of the operating or capital loss.

Purchase of Bonds or Other Debt Obligations. To the investor, the purchase of bonds or other indenture agreements of a real estate company or institution usually means a periodic, taxable interest payment and perhaps a capital gain at the end of the investment holding period if the period exceeds one year. According to the Tax Reform Acts of 1976 and 1977, the holding period for the calculation of capital gains after January 1, 1978, is one year and a day or more. Capital gains taxation is covered in later chapters of this section. Generally speaking, the capital gain is the positive difference between the price paid for the debt obligation and the selling price of that security. A capital loss—the negative difference between the price paid and the selling price—may be experienced particularly in times of rising interest rates. To increase the current yield to maturity on a debt obligation as the market yields increase, the price of the debt obligation in dollars adjusts downward. The current investor, therefore, receives the market yield on the price paid in the current market.

Debt obligations of real estate companies and institutions. Incorporated real estate companies and real estate investment trusts tend to issue several types of debt obligations in order to finance their businesses. The prospective investor may analyze the future expected returns from the commercial paper, notes, and bonds of

- Real estate investment trusts.
- Real estate diversified holding companies.
- The Federal National Mortgage Association.
- The Federal Home Loan Mortgage Corporation.
- Other real estate-oriented companies and financial institutions.

Mortgage participations may also be purchased from the Federal National Mortgage Association, the Federal Home Loan Mortgage Corporation, the Government National Mortgage Association, mortgage lenders originating loans in the primary mortgage market, and mortgage companies originating loans in the primary mortgage market for correspondent and other investor portfolios.

A mortgage participation is a security representing the partial ownership of a large mortgage. Commercial paper is the debt obligation, usually of no longer than 270 days, that is sold by the borrower through commercial paper dealers. A note is a debt obligation of the borrower that is longer in maturity than commercial paper and shorter in maturity than a bond. The maturity of a note may range from a year to five years. A bond usually has a longer term to maturity. In the traditional structure of the money and capital markets, the yield to maturity of the shorter-term debt obligation is less than the yield to maturity of the longer-term debt.

Mortgage bonds. In order to finance an income property under current market conditions, it may seem wise to the owner to finance the property by means of mortgage bonds rather than by means of traditional mortgages through one or two mortgage lending institutions. The necessary mortgage debt for the financing of a large income property, such as an office building, may be sold by splitting the mortgage obligation into numerous mortgage bonds of denominations to fit the needs of current investors in the marketplace. The bonds may be traded later over the counter at local or regional brokerage houses. The mortgage bonds may be privately placed with numerous investors and may promise competitive returns to the individual investors.

The prospective investor should examine the current and projected financial data on the income property to ascertain the future profitability of the income property whose cash flows will repay the mortgage bondholders their principal and will cover the interest obligations. The cash flows projected for the property must be sufficient to cover the operating expenses of the property, as well as the mortgage bond debt service, over the term of the mortgage bonds and beyond. The yield to the bond investor should approximate the yield to the traditional mortgage lender on a single mortgage covering the entire financing.

Mortgage-backed securities. The investor may be interested in the yields on pass-through or bond-type mortgage-backed securities. The Government National Mortgage Association may guarantee the principal repayment and interest installments on the mortgage-backed security. A mortgage lender may not ask GNMA to guarantee the security, but may put twice or three times as much mortgage debt as the par value of the security into a mortgage pool behind the security. The good credit rating of the issuer substitutes for the GNMA guarantee in the sale of the mortgage-backed security.

Most of the mortgage-backed securities sold in the decade of the 1970s were characterized by the pass-through type security. Monthly payments made by the mortgagors of the individual mortgages in the mortgage pool are collected by the issuer; an

Exhibit 10-13. Sample Yields on GNMA-Guaranteed Mortgage-Backed Securities, May 1978

Date	Yield According to GNMA Securities Bid
May 1, 1978	8.84%
May 8, 1978	8.86
May 15, 1978	8.89
May 22, 1978	8.98
May 30, 1978	9.04

Source: *The Mortgage Banker* (July 1978), p. 34.

underwriting and management fee is collected by the issuer from the mortgage payments; then the issuer makes interest payments to the holders of the mortgage-backed securities. The additional funds collected by the issuer from the individual mortgagors are accumulated for the principal repayment at the maturity of the mortgage-backed security. The mortgage monies pass through the issuer on their way to the investors. If a GNMA guarantee is not acquired for the issue, the issuer pledges repayment of principal and interest payment to the investor. Some sample GNMA mortgage-backed security yields are indicated in Exhibit 10-13.

SUMMARY

The chapter shows the broad assortment of real estate investment opportunities. Direct ownership of real estate is de-emphasized, since that subject is treated at length in the other chapters of the book. The emphasis of the chapter is partially on the investment in stock and debt obligations of real estate companies and real estate-related financial institutions. The emphasis is also on investment in real estate via ownership of a building construction and/or development company and investment in an existing lease for subletting to a tenant. Stock related to the real estate industry is issued by real estate investment trusts, building construction companies, housing manufacturing companies, stockholder-owned savings and loan associations, real estate syndicates, and real estate limited partnerships. Bonds related to the real estate industry are also issued by real estate companies and real estate-oriented financial institutions. Mortgage bonds and mortgage-backed securities can be analyzed and purchased by the investor seeking yields from operations of the real estate industry.

Key Terms and Concepts

Family or individual life cycle
Investment objectives
Sole investment
Joint investment
Indenture agreement
Subletting
Sale of construction services
Subcontractor

Speculative land purchase
Dividend yield
Housing manufacturer
Real estate stocks
Privately held stock
Minimum investment requirement
Principal repayment
National and regional stock exchanges

Over-the-counter transactions	Land development
Planning stage	Building construction
Operating stage	Syndicate manager
Diversified real estate holding companies	Mortgage bonds
Supervisory personnel	Windfall profits
Building trades	General contractor
Sandwich lessee	Working capital
Unrealized capital gain	Sublessee
Price-earnings ratio	Share price index
Margin requirement	Asset turnover
Syndicate shares	Institutional purchase or sale
Nonrecourse debt	Printed security offering
Tax Reform Acts of 1976 and 1977	Preliminary prospectus
Termination stage	Yield to maturity
Portfolio strategy	

Questions for Student Self-examination

Multiple-Choice Questions

1. Hubbard Real Estate Investors is a corporate subsidiary of _____.
   a. Equitable Life
   b. Lomas Nettleton
   c. Merrill Lynch, Pierce, Fenner & Smith
   d. Northwestern Mutual

2. As a private corporation _____ buys and sells residential mortgages as an important institution in the secondary mortgage market.
   a. GNMA
   b. FHLMC
   c. FNMA
   d. none of the above

3. Which form of organization does not sell commercial paper, notes, and bonds?
   a. real estate investment trusts
   b. real estate diversified holding companies
   c. joint ventures
   d. Federal National Mortgage Association

4. Mortgage participations may not be purchased from _____.
   a. real estate investment trusts
   b. Federal National Mortgage Association
   c. Federal Home Loan Mortgage Corporation
   d. Government National Mortgage Association

5. Most of the mortgage-backed securities sold in the decade of the 1970s were characterized by the _____ type security.
   a. stock
   b. bond
   c. pass-through
   d. none of the above

True-False Questions

T F 1. The stock of the Federal National Mortgage Association may only be purchased over the counter, not on the stock exchanges.
T F 2. The shares of a real estate syndicate or a real estate limited partnership may be purchased.
T F 3. All mortgage-backed securities are guaranteed by the Government National Mortgage Association.
T F 4. The contractor often borrows long-term bank funds on the basis of his or her equity in the business.
T F 5. If the investor wants to be a sandwich lessee, he or she purchases an existing lease or sublets from an existing lessee.
T F 6. The difference between the rent paid the existing lessee and the rent received from the sublessee who occupies the space is the gross profit to the sandwich lessee.
T F 7. The dividend yield is determined by dividing the current market price of the stock into the estimated or most recent annual dividend payment.
T F 8. The investor examines the difference between the purchase price of the stock and the most recent annual dividend payment in order to establish the unrealized capital gain.
T F 9. Only one class of stock may be sold by a real estate investment trust.
T F 10. The REIT investor clientele tends to be that clientele normally attracted to common stock rather than to preferred stock.

Answers
Multiple-Choice: 1c, 2c, 3c, 4a, 5c.
True-False: 1F, 2T, 3F, 4F, 5T, 6T, 7T, 8F, 9T, 10F.

Problems

1. If an investor in the 55 percent marginal tax bracket wants capital gains from a real estate investment, what type of real estate security should be purchased? Explain.

2. If an investor wants a fixed rate of return of 8½ percent from a real estate security, what alternatives are available among real estate securities? Would the alternatives offer any possibilities for capital appreciation?

3. How does the purchase of FNMA stock differ from the purchase of local savings and loan association stock?

4. What differences exist for the investor between investment as a member of a real estate syndicate and investment as a limited partner in a real estate limited partnership? What similarities exist for the investor in the 50 percent marginal tax bracket?

5. What differences would the investor realize between investment of $100,000 in mortgage bonds and investment of $100,000 in mortgage-backed securities?

6. What differences in risk exist between investment in construction as a general contractor and investment in a lease for subletting to a lessor-occupant?

Chapter 11

Diversification to Reduce Investment Risk

Introduction
The Relationship of This Chapter to Other Chapters of the Text
Investment Risk
    Land and Buildings for Owner or Tenant Occupancy   Leasing or Subletting   Land Development   Investment in a Construction Company   Stock   Bonds   Summary of Real Estate Investment Risks
Investment Goals and Typical Investor Situations
    Liquidity   Profitability   Safety of Principal   Tax Shelter   A Few Typical Investor Situations
A Suggested Financial Foundation for Further Real Estate Investment
Portfolio Strategy to Meet Investment Goals
Summary
Key Terms and Concepts
Questions for Student Self-examination

LEARNING OBJECTIVES After studying this chapter, you should be familiar with

The four general kinds of investment risk
Risks associated with the purchase of land and buildings for owner occupancy
Investment risks for tenant-occupied land and buildings
Risks associated with the purchase of a lease for subsequent subletting
Land development risks
Construction company risks assumed by the investor
Risks inherent in stock purchase
Risks inherent in bond purchase
The various liquidity positions of alternative investments
The extent of profitability of the various types of real estate investments
The extent to which investment principal is protected in the various types of real estate investments
The significance and existence of tax shelters for real estate investments
The suggested financial foundation for further real estate investment
General portfolio strategy to meet investment goals

All investors need to assume an investment risk that they individually can tolerate. The tolerance level for risk-taking among the various types of investors varies widely. The risk assumption that an M.D. with a continuous flow of high income and a penchant for risk-taking can tolerate might be intolerable for a middle-income father with six school-age kids and a conservative outlook on risk-taking. This chapter deals with investment risk, investment goals, and opportunities for short-term and long-term investment yields. It also deals with a suggested financial foundation for real estate risk-taking, types of investments associated with various investment goals, and the hierarchy of investment risks in real estate investment of various forms. Diversified real estate investment portfolios for selected types of investors are also suggested.

INTRODUCTION

In this chapter investment goals are viewed in light of risk assumption. The normal investment goals related to cash flow, tax shelter, and capital gains are translated into forms of real estate investment that further these goals. As the investment needs and goals of widely varying investors are considered, a number of alternative real estate investments are mentioned for possible inclusion in each investor's portfolio. The chapter does suggest, though, that the investor should have a basic financial foundation before embarking on investment in income-producing properties and real estate-related securities.

THE RELATIONSHIP OF THIS CHAPTER TO OTHER CHAPTERS OF THE TEXT

Portfolio strategy was introduced in Part III by the opening chapter on ownership forms, liability, and taxation. The last chapter covered some possible avenues for real estate investment. This chapter involves portfolio diversification in order to reduce risk. General tax objectives are considered in light of portfolio objectives. Specific tax provisions are relegated to the next chapters of this section.

INVESTMENT RISK

Four kinds of risk are associated with investment: inflationary, financial, interest rate, and liquidity risk. Real estate investment in general provides protection against inflationary risk as property values generally increase. A high level of financial, interest rate, and liquidity risk is usually associated with real estate investment.

Not all real estate investments are profitable. For example, the ownership of an apartment complex may result in a negative cash flow and profit position. Not all real estate companies and financial institutions operate in the black. Some end up operating in the red or taking a loss. The risk of financial failure or, in other words, the default risk, is quite visible in real estate investment; mortgage default, operating losses, and sale of securities at a loss are common occurrences.

Interest rates change constantly. The real estate industry hinges on the interest rate structure and the movement of the key rates. For example, the capitalized value of an income property may decline sharply with the increase in long-term mortgage rates. The property owner must demand a higher rate of income from the property to maintain a market yield. When the operating income is divided by a higher capitalization rate, reflecting the higher owner yield expectation, the property value declines. In the sales arena, properties tend to sit on the market for long periods when mortgage rates get abnormally high. In this instance the builder takes the risk of completing the structure and then not being able to sell it in a normal period of time. The builder assumes an interest rate risk, just as the income property owner inadvertently assumes the interest rate risk. The mortgage lender also assumes the high level of interest rate risk. His portfolio declines in value as current mortgage yields increase; his portfolio increases in value as interest rates decline in our inflationary era.

All parties in the real estate industry tend to assume the liquidity risk associated with real property and real property interests. Real estate securities listed on national and regional exchanges and traded actively may reveal only a moderate level of liquidity risk. Other real properties and real property interests tend to reflect high levels of liquidity risk. Real properties, particularly income properties, tend to be slow to sell. Even the normal selling time for a middle-income suburban home in the summer peak selling season may be three months after building completion. This situation reveals a low degree of liquidity. Mortgages and mortgage participations may sell easily if the usual wealthy investors and financial institutions are interested in the properties being financed and the yields of the loans. There may be a ready market for these real property interests. On the other hand, if the mortgages or mortgage participations do not fit the market demand, these investments reflect a low degree of liquidity as they "sit on the mortgage banker's shelf" for an unreasonably long period. Loan warehousing costs may absorb more money than the eventual profit in the mortgage or mortgage participation sale.

Therefore, we conclude that the real estate investment picture has mixed images regarding risk assumption. There is generally a low degree of inflationary risk as property value increases surpass the rise in property operating costs, but there is generally a high degree of financial, interest rate, and liquidity risk connected with any real estate investment.

In the last chapter we were concerned with various forms of real estate investment. Among the forms were (1) purchase of land and buildings for owner or tenant occupancy; (2) purchase of a lease or subletting; (3) land development; (4) building construction; (5) purchase of stock from various issuers; and (6) purchase of commercial paper, notes, and bonds of real estate-related companies and institutions. Each of these categories of real estate investment has its risk dimensions with respect to inflation, financial, interest rate, and liquidity risk.

Land and Buildings for Owner or Tenant Occupancy. If the land and buildings tend to increase in value with the pattern of inflation, the purchase of land and buildings for owner or tenant occupancy has a low degree of inflationary risk. Many properties do conform to this situation; some properties have declined in value, even though inflation has continued. A high degree of financial risk is involved as tenants periodically vacate the premises of income properties, as tenants fail to meet their rental payments and other space obligations, as tenant-companies fail and declare bankruptcy, and as the landlord-mortgagors fail to meet their mortgage obligations. Direct ownership of property also tends to be associated with a high degree of interest rate risk. As interest rates rise, the property value declines as a result of the necessary discounting of future net cash flows with a higher and higher discount rate. The investor's yield requirement increases with the level of interest rates in general and the level of long-term mortgage rates in particular. Since property tends to be slow to sell at the end of the desired investment holding period, a high level of liquidity risk is associated with direct real estate ownership.

Leasing or Subletting. A fixed rental rate on the purchased or existing lease assures the investor of fixed income; however, the fixed subletting rental payment is not inflationary protection as inflation continues. If the subtenant pays a variable rental payment based on gross income participation to the sandwich lessee, the sandwich lessee has fixed costs and some protection against inflated prices in the lease receipts. Under these conditions, the inflation risk is relatively low. The financial risk is relatively high, since the sublessee can move out of the premises or cease paying the monthly rental, and the landlord can default on the ground-lease or land loan payments. The financial risk is high because the financial status of three concerned parties in the investment is uncertain.

Landlord—Prime lease—Sandwich lessee—secondary lessee—Space occupant
(Lessor)   (Lessee)   (Sublessee)

Business conditions, business profitability, and the management practices of the three parties can undermine the sandwich lessee's expected return.

The interest rate risk is high when the investor invests in order to sublet. The movement of the interest rates up or down cause the value of the sandwich lessee's estate to go down or up in a reverse relationship. If rates go up, the investor must expect a higher, competitive return. The value of the sandwich lease estate declines when the sublessee's rental payments are capitalized by a higher rate of interest. The reverse situation,

$$\text{Value} = \frac{\text{Net operating income}}{\text{Capitalization rate}}$$

is also true. The value of the leasehold estate goes up if interest rates fortuitously go down. Of course, the investor cannot control the market yields and the general interest rates.

If the sandwich lessee wishes to sell his or her leasehold interest, the sale probably would take a fairly long period of time. Real estate interests generally do not sell quickly in comparison with listed and actively traded stocks and bonds.

Land Development. If the developed land sells or leases quickly, land development gives the investor a low degree of inflation risk. The marketability and subsequent value rise is excellent protection against the inflationary trend. There is a high degree of inflation risk in land development if the developed land, with or without structures, sells or leases abnormally slowly.

Land development usually has a high degree of financial, interest rate, and liquidity risk. If the development does not sell or lease, or if it sells or leases very slowly, the developer might not get back the cost of development, or those development costs might be recouped over an uneconomically long period of time. The holding costs might surpass any minor profit received over the long investment period. Interest rates may rise and drive down the value of the development. The change in interest rates affects the value of the land development substantially. High interest rates, in addition, may result in high mortgage payments and low marketability of the project. Depending on the sales or leasing success, the liquidity of land development may be extremely good, moderate, or nonexistent.

Investment in a Construction Company. The risks of investment in a construction company are similar to the risks associated with a land development company. The level of materials costs, labor costs, and financial costs are strategic to the profitability and risk exposure of the construction company. The marketability of the completed land improvements substantially determines the degree of inflation, financial, and liquidity risk. A high degree of interest rate risk is always present. Financial costs rise and fall with the change in the interest rate structure. As costs increase without a corresponding increase in revenues, profits usually decline.

Financial risk is also dependent on the financial security of the client with whom the construction is contracted. The contractor's overall risk is affected by the financial stability and profit position of the subcontractors on the job. If a subcontractor goes out of business or goes bankrupt, the general contractor must replace the subcontractor. During the time of the replacement, the construction job may be stopped or at least slowed down. Since weather conditions affect construction profitability, this factor, which is uncontrollable, also contributes to the high degree of financial risk.

Stock. Stock purchase may provide a high degree of inflation protection, financial risk, and interest rate risk. The price per share may rise with the pattern of inflation, thus giving the stock a low degree of inflation risk. Since the issuer of the stock will not be a government agency or government institution whose securities are backed by the full faith and credit of the federal government, the issuer that exhibits financial risk will always sell stock that is not quite guaranteed or safe with regard to regular dividend payout. There is always a chance that the stock issuer will generate a loss or a lower level of earnings than when the stock was purchased, and the issuer may not be able to support the purchase price of the stock with earnings.

Since stock dividend payout ratios tend to follow bond yields, the change in the interest rate structure is important. If fixed income securities in the marketplace offer higher yields, the stock prices will have to fall so that the dividend payout ratio can rise.

$$\text{Current dividend payout ratio} = \frac{\text{Last 12 months' dividends paid}}{\text{Current stock price}}$$

Therefore, stock displays a high degree of interest rate risk no matter who the issuer is.

If the stock is listed on regional and national stock exchanges and is actively traded, it has a low degree of liquidity risk. Otherwise, the stock reflects a moderate to high degree of liquidity risk. The investor would have trouble getting his or her investment out of the stock within a reasonable selling period if the stock is not actively traded.

Bonds. The prices of bonds generally do not move up with inflation. Bond prices move so that the current bond yields reflect market rates of yield for competitive investments. Therefore, bonds give little inflation protection. They are subject to a high degree of interest rate risk.

The financial risk of bonds is low if the bonds are guaranteed by the federal government or its agencies, such as the Government National Mortgage Association. If the real estate-related bonds are paid from the net proceeds or cash flow generated by an income property, the bonds tend to exhibit a high degree of financial risk. The building may never be fully rented at the end of its construction. The vacancy rate may remain high for a lengthy period. The gross income from the building may not be high enough to cover operating and financial expenses plus a reasonable profit. Most income properties reflect substantial financial risk.

Bonds, like stock, may be listed on regional and national bond exchanges and may be traded actively. These bonds have a low degree of liquidity risk. If the bonds have an inactive market and are traded occasionally over the counter rather than constantly in high volume on a major bond exchange, the bonds have a relatively high degree of liquidity risk associated with them.

Summary of Real Estate Investment Risks. A summary of the risk exposure of selected categories of real estate investment is shown in Table 11-1. The inflation risk may be of relatively low degree, whereas the financial, interest rate, and liquidity risks are usually fairly high for most of the investment categories.

The overall risk category of selected real estate investments may be summarized. Table 11-2 illustrates the investments that generally have the lowest overall risk, a medium risk stature, and a high overall risk status.

INVESTMENT GOALS AND TYPICAL INVESTOR SITUATIONS

Investors usually want to balance out certain goals for their investments so that they can optimize their financial positions. Many investors do not really seek to maximize their financial positions with real estate investment because they do not wish to engage in property management, heavy mortgage financing, and major risk-taking. They will settle for optimization of four general investment goals:

Liquidity.
Profitability.
Safety of principal.
Tax shelter.

Maximization of investment return might require a minimal level of liquidity, investment for capital gains and not periodic income, no safety of principal, and accelerated depreciation. The individual investor might settle for optimum investment return,

Table 11-1. Degrees of risk of selected real estate investments

Type of Investment	Type of Risk			
	Inflation	Financial	Interest Rate	Liquidity
Purchase of a house				
Owner occupancy	Low degree, as the price goes up with inflation	Generally low degree; house loan default ratio very low	Low degree, if high rates do not decrease marketability	High degree, if house is readily marketable
Rental	Low degree, as the price goes up with inflation	Moderate degree, since vacancies may occur	Moderate degree, since the value of house changes with interest rates	High degree, if house is readily marketable
Purchase of an income property	Low degree, if value rises with inflation	Low degree, unless rents will not cover debt service	Relatively high degree, since value of building changes with rates	Relatively low degree, since income properties are usually slow to sell
Purchase of land	Low degree, as the price goes up with inflation	Moderate degree; some buyers fail to meet all payments	Low degree, if high rates do not decrease marketability	Relatively low degree, since land may be slow to sell
Purchase of lease or subletting	Low degree, if a percentage lease	Relatively high degree, except for AAA tenants	High degree, since value of lease changes with investor yield requirements	Relatively low degree, if lease is slow to sell
Land development	Low degree, if a marketable development	Usually high degree, if developer does not have a high credit rating	High degree, since value changes with interest rates	Generally low degree, if sales are slow
Building construction	Low degree, if buildings are marketable	Relatively high degree, unless the developer has a high credit rating	High degree, since value changes with rates and yields	Generally low degree, if sales are slow
Purchase of real estate stock	Low degree, if price parallels inflation	High degree, if issuer does not have high credit rating	High degree, since stock price changes with level of interest rates	High degree, if stock is actively traded
Purchase of debt obligations	Low degree, if security income varies with inflation; high degree, if a fixed income is paid	High degree, unless issue is guaranteed by federal government or high-credit issuer	High degree, since price changes with general interest rates	High degree, if security is highly marketable

Table 11-2. Risk hierarchy for real estate and related investments

Investments with Lowest Overall Risk
  Bonds
    GNMA-guaranteed mortgage-backed bonds—active over-the-counter trading
    Bonds of high-credit-rated financial institutions or real estate corporations listed on bond exchanges
  Land purchase and lease to high-credit-rated tenants, such as regional shopping center corporation
  Building purchase and lease to high-credit-rated tenants, such as Postal Service
Investments with Medium Overall Risk
  Stock
    FNMA stock
    Stock of a well-established, profitable savings and loan association
    Stock in an insurance company offering homeowner's and personal property insurance
  Direct real estate ownership
    House for owner occupancy
    Regional shopping center with good, thorough feasibility analysis in advance of commitment
    Community shopping center with good, thorough feasibility analysis in advance of commitment
  Debt obligations of medium-credit-rated real estate companies and REITs
  Mortgage-backed securities not guaranteed by GNMA
Investments with High Overall Risk
  Stock
    Shares of beneficial interest of a REIT
    Shares of real estate syndicates
    Shares of real estate limited partnerships
    Stock of land development, housing manufacturing, or construction company
  Mortgage bonds
  Direct real estate ownership
    Rental house
    Small commercial building, such as a retail building or office building
    Duplex, triplex, or fourplex apartment building
    Land for speculation, such as a house lot or raw land in outlying semirural area

which would cause less mental strain and put more money in the investor's pockets currently.

Liquidity. Most real estate investors require some liquidity in their investments. A very profitable investment opportunity may arise quickly. The investor may want to free his or her cash from an earlier investment and invest that money—and perhaps some new money—in the new venture. The marketability of the existing real estate investment is important at that juncture. In another instance, the investor may be faced with more tax obligations than had been anticipated. Some property holdings may need to be sold to acquire cash for tax payment. A family emergency, such as a fire or an individual's hospitalization, may cause an immediate need for cash that must be acquired from the sale of property. There are numerous reasons why some liquidity in a real estate investment is usually an investment goal.

It is said, though, that there are some real estate investors who do not require liquidity of their holdings. Pension funds, life insurance companies, and endowment funds tend to fit into this category. They may wish to invest sizable sums in real estate interests, such as pools of mortgages or real estate ownership on a direct basis, because the investible funds need continual long-term investment at good yields where little investment management is required. These investors tend to keep the long-term maturity dates of their portfolios staggered so that their financial obligations are covered at the time the payments are due the beneficiaries.

Profitability. Most investors seek profitability, or a reasonable return on their money. Cash flow or earnings distributions may be sought on a periodic basis over a short- or long-term period. Some investors plan to live on their periodic dividends or interest payments. Whether periodic cash flow, capital gains at the end of the holding period, or both types of return are sought, the investor wants a reasonable return on his or her money.

Safety of Principal. Many investors want to protect their investment principal from erosion or outright loss. Some real estate investments promise safety of principal; others do not. GNMA-guaranteed mortgage-backed securities have guaranteed principal repayment. This is 100 percent safety of investment principal as long as there is a viable federal government. Stock prices of a real estate company may decline to very low levels or climb to very high levels. The investment principal in the form of the stock price paid is not protected from decline in value or disappearance with the bankruptcy of a real estate company or institution. If the stock issuer has a high credit rating, the safety of principal may be moderately risky.

Tax Shelter. If the investor faces a relatively high individual or business tax rate, tax shelter is a goal of that individual or business investor. If a real property investment can be depreciated, this—perhaps noncash—expense may be deducted from otherwise taxable income for federal income tax purposes. If accelerated depreciation is approved by the Internal Revenue Service for the type of real property held, the investor may shelter a substantial amount of taxable income acquired from sources other than the real estate project. Even straight-line depreciation may shelter enough otherwise taxable income that the sheltered income may meet the mortgage principal or amortization payments. Once the taxpayer finds that the deduction of the depreciation no longer shelters the amortization payments of the mortgage, the real property is often sold. Tax shelter tends to be an investment goal of high priority for high-income individuals and businesses.

A Few Typical Investor Situations. *A young professional person who is single:*

Possible investment goals:
  Build an estate
  Save for the purchase of controlling interest in a company
  Accumulate retirement fund
  Save for more luxurious car or boat
  Save for the downpayment on a condominium or house
  Save for extensive travel and recreation

Middle-aged blue-collar worker with a family:

Possible investment goals:
  Provide apartment or single-family detached homes for adult children and elderly relatives
  Receive additional income from investment receipts such as cash flow distributions and capital gains
    for early retirement

for deferred luxuries, such as a good-sized boat or an extra car for hunting season
Shelter income from taxes when children leave the family homestead
Capital gains for tax relief

Well-established physician with an extensive clientele and a family:

Possible investment goals:
Shelter income from federal and state income taxes
Gain a return on excess funds
  Preference for capital gains
  No need for more current or periodic income
Provide for a comfortable retirement
Need accumulated funds
  Children's college education or private high school or professional school tuition
  Set up newly married children with homes and businesses
Care of elderly relatives

A SUGGESTED FINANCIAL FOUNDATION FOR FURTHER REAL ESTATE INVESTMENT

Since real estate investment tends to have substantial elements of risk, the prospective real estate investor should secure his or her everyday financial position, provide funds for emergency situations, and provide funds for "good buys" that may suddenly appear before placing money in income-producing property or real estate securities. Table 11-3 shows some asset holdings that the investor probably should have before investing in real estate.

There are tax-shelter aspects of this suggested financial foundation. The home mortgage interest payments and property taxes are fully deductible for federal income tax purposes. The pension fund contributions may be made on a tax-deferred plan.

PORTFOLIO STRATEGY TO MEET INVESTMENT GOALS

The individual or business investor must decide on appropriate investment goals before portfolio strategy is mapped out. Let us assume that the investor has the necessary financial foundation for further real estate investment. First, the investor should select short- and long-term investment goals. For the short term, liquidity and profitability in terms of periodic cash returns may be the pertinent goals. For the long term, profit from periodic cash distributions, capital gains, and tax shelter may be the overriding goals of the investors. Different types of investments meet such short- and long-term goals in different ways. Listed real estate shock and bonds may meet short-term goals, whereas direct real estate ownership, investment in shares of a real estate syndicate or limited partnership, and land speculation may meet long-term goals.

Looking at the investor's goals in terms of cash flow return, tax shelter, and capital gains, we see from Table 11-4 that selected investments meet each of these individual goals. For example, the lease of land usually means periodic receipt of cash. Depreci-

Table 11-3. *Suggested asset holdings before investment in income-producing property and real estate securities*

1. Stable employment with a promising future of salary increases and increasing responsibilities
2. Life insurance adequate for individual or family protection
    a. Individual policies
    b. Group policies
3. Health insurance
    a. Individual
    b. Group
        (1) Hospitalization
        (2) Out-patient care
4. Shelter for the family
    a. Apartment with personal property and liability insurance coverage
    b. Home ownership with home owner's all-risk insurance
5. Automobiles adequate for the individual or family members with auto insurance
    a. A car for each full-time employed family member
    b. A car for each older child for school and work transportation
6. Checking account balance maintained at usual operating expense level and adequate to cover unexpected expenditures when goods and services are found at a good price
7. Savings account balance adequate to cover emergencies and unforeseen future financial needs
8. Pension plan for gradual accumulation of retirement funds, such as the Keogh plan

Table 11-4. *Investments for selected objectives*

Cash flow objective
    Lease of land owned
    Lease of building owned
    Stock with consistently high dividend payout, such as shares of beneficial interest of a real estate investment trust or savings and loan association shares
    Bonds with reliable interest payments
        GNMA-guaranteed mortgage-backed securities
        Bonds and other debt obligations of FNMA and FHLMC
    Subdivision and development of land for residential or industrial purposes for immediate sale or lease

Tax-shelter objective
    Depreciation deductions for building owned for rental income
    Mortgage interest deductions, such as heavily financed (levered) property ownership
    Lease deductions, such as sale-leaseback with option to purchase

Capital gains objective
    Land speculation, such as shoreline, suburban farm land, house lot
    Building for renovation and speculation, such as rental house or apartment building
    Owner-occupied house
    Construction of a speculative income property
    Development of an amusement park while holding adjacent land for speculation

ation deductions on buildings owned for rental income may meet tax-shelter goals. Land speculation may result in the desired capital gain.

With the investment possibilities and characteristics in mind, the investor will want to constantly review her or his objectives and decide how much inflation, financial, interest rate, and liquidity risk to assume in a diversified portfolio. A portfolio concentrated on one type of real estate investment magnifies the total risk from all risk sources that are attributable to the investment type. Diversification is wise for most investors—individual or business. There is more assurance of safety of principal.

To follow up the cases of the three typical real estate investors, their individual portfolios should reflect their goals and the appropriate risk assumption for each one's financial status and stage in their individual life cycle. Possible real estate investment portfolios for each of the three investors follow.

A young, single professional person:
Possible real estate investment portfolio
　Rental house
　　Possible requirements: Maintenance work by the owner
　　　　　　　　　　　　Payment of property management fee and payment for repairs when needed
　Home ownership
　　Single-family dwelling
　　Duplex or fourplex—live in and let other tenants contribute toward the mortgage debt service and operating expenses
　Small commercial property—perhaps joint ownership
　Speculation on a house lot in a new subdivision
　REIT shares—low price, good dividend yield, possible capital gain

Middle-aged blue-collar worker with a family:
Possible real estate investment portfolio
　House lot next door or in the same area
　Home ownership
　Small commercial property housing small business
　Share of a real estate limited partnership that owns a large apartment building or apartment complex
　Four-to-eight-unit apartment building
　Condominium in a warm region for early retirement and current rental

Well-established physician with an extensive clientele and a family:
Possible real estate investment portfolio
　Share in a real estate syndicate holding three or four apartment projects
　Share in a real estate limited partnership that owns a medical office building near the hospital
　Joint ownership in a limited partnership of a nursing home near the hospital
　Land speculation for capital gain
　Stock in a land development company
　Stock in a local savings and loan association
　FNMA stock using a margin account
　Sale-leaseback of the medical office building that the doctor is currently using

SUMMARY

Inflation, financial, interest rate, and liquidity risks are part of real estate investment analysis and portfolio planning. Various real estate investments exhibit various degrees of each of these four types of risk. The risks associated with direct real estate ownership, land development, building construction, and stock and bond purchase were analyzed systematically in the chapter.

Typical investment goals relate to liquidity, profitability, safety of principal, and tax shelter. Three typical investors were presented in light of their financial circumstances and social obligations. Portfolios of diversified real estate investments were suggested for each of the three typical investors. It was assumed that each of the investor types first established a basic financial foundation to cover current operating expenses, emergency situations, and associated liabilities before engaging in further real estate investment.

Certain investments were suggested for meeting short-term goals; other investments were suggested for the advancement of long-term goals. Selected real estate investments were divided into categories that advanced cash flow, tax-shelter, and capital gains goals. It was suggested that most investors desire diversified rather than concentrated investment portfolios to assure safety of principal and optimum investment yield.

Key Terms and Concepts

Hierarchy of investment risks in real estate investment
Short-term investment yields
Long-term investment yields
Investment goals
Interest rate risk
Investor's psychological makeup
Straight-line depreciation
Owner-occupied house
Financial risk
Liquidity risk
Inflationary risk
Default risk
Loan warehousing costs

Risk assumption
Triplex
Fourplex
Deferred luxuries
Speculative income property
Risk dimensions
Inflationary trend
Marketability
Overall risk
Fixed income securities
Dividend-payout ratio
Investment management
Pools of mortgages
Lease deductions

Questions for Student Self-examination

Multiple-Choice Questions

1. If the land and buildings tend to increase in value with the pattern of inflation, this investment form has a _____.
    a. low degree of financial risk
    b. high degree of inflationary risk
    c. low degree of inflationary risk
    d. high degree of financial risk

2. Which of the following indicates a low degree of financial risk?
   a. tenants periodically vacate the premises of income properties
   b. tenant companies fail and declare bankruptcy
   c. tenants fail to meet their rental payments and other space obligations
   d. landlord-mortgagors regularly meet their mortgage obligations

3. Which situation tends to be true? Land development has a _____.
   a. low degree of financial risk
   b. high degree of financial risk
   c. low degree of liquidity risk
   d. none of the above

4. Which statement tends to be true? Bonds usually have a _____.
   a. low degree of inflationary risk
   b. low degree of interest rate risk
   c. low degree of liquidity risk
   d. none of the above

5. Which is an investment with high overall risk?
   a. stock
   b. land purchase and lease to high-credit-rated tenants
   c. building purchase and lease to high-credit-rated tenants
   d. bonds

True-False Questions

T F 1. Real estate investment does not provide protection against inflationary risk because property values generally decline with inflation.
T F 2. In general, a low level of financial and liquidity risk is associated with real estate investment.
T F 3. Generally speaking, all real estate investments are profitable.
T F 4. The capitalized value of an income property may increase sharply with the increase in long-term mortgage rates.
T F 5. The mortgage lender's portfolio declines in value as current mortgage yields increase.
T F 6. The normal selling time for a middle-income suburban home in the summer peak selling season may be nine months after building completion.
T F 7. Direct ownership of property tends to be associated with a low degree of interest rate risk.
T F 8. The value of the leasehold estate goes up if interest rates go down.
T F 9. Real estate interests generally sell just as well as listed and actively traded stocks and bonds.
T F 10. As costs increase without a corresponding increases in revenues, profits usually decline.

Answers
Multiple-Choice: 1c, 2d, 3b, 4c, 5a.
True-False: 1F, 2F, 3F, 4F, 5T, 6F, 7T, 8T, 9F, 10T.

Problems

1. As Mark Johnson, a college real estate graduate, ponders investment in an apartment building, what risks should he consider and how should he view these risks in light of an apartment building investment?

2. Joan Black, a landowner whose property was located on the outskirts of a metropolitan area of 100,000 people, considered subdivision development. What is the nature of the risks that she would assume?

3. Joe Brown, a local real estate and insurance man, considered entering the construction business by setting up a subsidiary of his existing company. What risks would he possibly encounter as the principal owner of the construction company? Consider the four kinds of risk usually associated with investment.

4. If a local property manager, Ruth Jones, invested her hard-earned funds in real estate stock, what risks would she take? What benefits would she acquire?

5. If a physician making $80,000 a year from her medical practice sought to invest some funds, what goals would she probably have in mind? What common investment goals would she probably place less emphasis on?

6. Before Joe Barnes, a leading brick mason of the community, invests money in an income property, what financial foundation should he provide for himself and his family?

Chapter 12

Taxation During the Planning Stage of Real Estate Investment

Introduction

The Relationship of This Chapter to Other Chapters of the Text

The Stages of Real Estate Development
 Planning and Construction   Operation   Sell-off or Termination

The Possible Timing of the Three Stages of Development

The Tax Implications of Costs Incurred During the Planning Stage
 The Recent Tax Environment   Taxation of Planning Costs: *Fees for preliminary economic and engineering studies, Organizational legal expense, Syndication sales fees, Advertising and sales promotion costs*   Taxation of Recording Costs   Taxation of Financing Costs: *Incidental home financing expenses, Insurance premiums for fire, storm, theft, liability, and other coverage, Discount points or prepaid interest, Service charges for loans*

The Taxation of Construction-Related Costs Contracted During the Planning Stage
 Real Estate Taxes on Unimproved Land Holdings   Construction Loan Interest   Insurance Premiums

Limitations on the Deduction of Interest on Investment Indebtedness

The Tax Burden of Single and Married Real Estate Investors

The Federal Income Tax Burden of Corporations

Summary

Key Terms and Concepts

Questions for Student Self-examination

LEARNING OBJECTIVES After studying this chapter, you should be familiar with

The three stages of real estate development
The planning and construction stage of development
The operating stage of real estate development
The sell-off or termination stage of real estate development
The possible timing of the three stages of real estate development
The current tax environment
Taxation of planning, recording, and financing costs during the planning stage
Taxation of construction-related costs contracted during the planning stage
Limitations on the deduction of interest on investment indebtedness for federal income tax purposes
The general tax burden of single and married real estate investors
The federal income tax burden of corporations

The investor is concerned with the tax burden during the various stages of real estate development. As he or she makes cash flow projections over the life of the investment from the planning stage through the operating stage to the sell-out or termination stage, taxes are an important cash outflow that must be recognized in light of the property owner's tax position. The real estate investor usually plans to keep the tax outflows at the lowest possible amount. The investor knows that he can realize a return on any money that would normally be paid in taxes but is deferred in some way.

The control of tax outflow is in the same investment arena as the control of utility costs, management fees, and repair costs. The tax outflow is usually associated with federal income tax and property tax payment. Both periodic tax payments may be considerable, but the federal income tax burden is usually the greater of the two. Therefore, real estate investment analysis hinges on the federal income tax position of the property and the owner over the projected holding period.

INTRODUCTION

The three stages of real estate development are introduced separately. Then the overlapping of the stages is considered. The reader will first consider the use of the terms *front-end costs* and *soft costs* in the planning stage of real estate development. The prospective investor must become familiar to some extent with the terms bandied about by the real estate industry. The importance and duration of the planning stage is indicated by the expenses usually incurred and their time consumption. Then the tax implications for the investor are considered. Some expenses may be totally deducted for federal income tax purposes during the year they are incurred. Other expenses must be capitalized for federal income tax purposes. The 1979 tax-rate schedules for single and married taxpayers are introduced at the end of the chapter.

Some of the expenses with tax consequences for the developer during the planning stage are the fee for the market study, the fee for the feasibility study, the fee for the environmental impact studies for federal and state authorities, and appraisal fees. There may be an origination fee due the mortgage banker or mortgage lender for the securing of a land development, construction, or permanent loan. Discount points may need to be paid if an FHA-insured loan is obtained for a multifamily residential project. Brokerage costs may be involved for selling land or leasing space. Organizational legal expenses may be incurred that require immediate payment to an attorney. Other closing costs may be incurred, such as the title insurance premium, the deed recording fee, and the mortgage recording fee.

Some other expenses that affect the tax burden are mortgage interest payment during construction on the construction loan, payment of property taxes during construction, payment for hazard and liability insurance during construction, advertising costs, and the creation costs for promotional literature and news releases.

THE RELATIONSHIP OF THIS CHAPTER TO OTHER CHAPTERS OF THE TEXT

Tax considerations are an integral part of portfolio planning and strategy, whether for personal or business purposes. Since Part III is concerned in total with portfolio strategy, this chapter on taxation during the planning stage of real estate development is a significant portion of Part III. The tax consequences of the various *front-end costs* are important to the investor. The investor wishes to know how much out-of-pocket money is required for the *soft costs* incurred in the planning stage of the development. The investor knows that part of his or her investment in the project is consumed for expenses incurred in the planning stage. These expenses are not covered by loan proceeds or property net rentals during this period, so the investor must commit working capital to these preliminary and necessary costs of development.

Since the planning stage of the development precedes the operating stage of the project, this chapter precedes Chapter 13, on taxation during the operation of the development. This second stage is followed by the sell-out or termination stage of the investment. Chapter 14, therefore, in this series relates to the taxation incurred by the investor at the time of sale. The chapters on tax implications of the various stages of development wind up the section on portfolio strategy.

THE STAGES OF REAL ESTATE DEVELOPMENT

If real estate development is examined rather closely, one may observe that there are three stages involved: Planning and construction, operation, and sell-off or termination.

Planning and Construction. The planning and construction stage involves the preliminary studies, showing the forecasted profitability of the project, the value of the proposed project, and its environmental impact. During the planning stage various fees are paid for the acquisition of money, the organization of the investor group, and the recording of documents. Fees are also paid for loan origination, legal assistance and advice in setting up the investor organization, and deed and mortgage recording. Insurance premiums are paid during the planning stage for title insurance and hazard and casualty insurance for the construction period. Brokerage commissions are paid for the sales of land and the leasing of space. Fees are paid for advertising over the radio, on billboards, and in newspapers. Fees are paid for public relations and promotional articles and for printed literature.

During construction, mortgage interest must be paid as the money is drawn down for payment of workers and supply houses. Property taxes must be paid during the construction period as well.

In summary, here are some of the (1) planning, recording, and financing costs and (2) construction-related costs. The following are some planning, recording, and financing costs:

Fees for preliminary studies: market, feasibility, environmental impact.
Real estate appraisal fee.
Loan origination fee.
Attorney's fee for setting up the legal organization.
Deed and mortgage recording.
Insurance premium for title insurance.
Brokerage commissions.
Advertising and sales promotion costs.

These expenses are often called the soft costs or the front-end costs because their payment may precede the receipt of the construction loan money.
Construction-related costs include

Insurance premiums for hazard and casualty insurance coverage for construction.
Construction loan interest.
Property taxes.

Operation. After the construction of the building and the rental of the space, the operation of the real estate development begins. Taxes must be paid on taxable income and capital gains realized during the operating stage. Refinancing of the property during the operating stage may result in tax-free income.

Net operating income is reduced by depreciation and mortgage interest deductions in order to arrive at taxable income. This calculated income is subject to ordinary income tax rates where capital gains are subject to the appropriate capital gains rate. The method of depreciation used for the various depreciable assets has a great bearing on the amount of the taxable income.

Sell-off or Termination. When the investor decides to end the investment for tax or other reasons, there may be recapture of excess depreciation at ordinary income tax rates. Capital gains tax rates may have to be applied to realized capital gains net of capital losses. There may be wholly or partially deferred taxation when the principal residence of the owner is replaced within a statutory period by another principal residence, or when the original property is exchanged for another property on a tax-deferred basis.

The Possible Timing of the Three Stages of Development

The three stages of a commercial real estate development may be portrayed in the following way:

Exhibit 12-1. The Possible Timing of the Three Stages of Commercial Real Estate Development

Planning and Construction Stage	Operating Stage	Sell-off or Termination Stage
Possibly 3–4 Years	Possibly 7–8 Years	Possibly 6 Mo.–One Year

The timing of the stages would differ for single-family house investment. The stages might occur as follows:

Exhibit 12-2. *The Possible Timing of the Three Stages of Construction and House Investment*

Planning and Construction Stage	Operatiang Stage	Sell-off or Termination Stage
Possibly 6 Mo.	Possibly 7-8 Years	Possibly 4-9 Mo.

When a real estate project is developed in multiple phases, the stages of development of the various phases tend to overlap. As the first phase of development goes into the operating stage, another phase will probably be in the planning and construction phase. The other phases of development dovetail in a similar manner. The overlapping stages of development and the timing of the cash flows can be seen in Exhibit 12-3.

THE TAX IMPLICATIONS OF COSTS INCURRED DURING THE PLANNING STAGE

Let us consider the tax implications of the planning, recording, and financing costs before the tax implications of the construction-related costs. Generally, the taxation of the particular expense depends on whether the expenses are incurred for personal use or business property.

Exhibit 12-3. *Possible Timing of the Three Stages of Development When Multiple Phases of Real Estate Development Are Involved; Example Apartment Project Development*

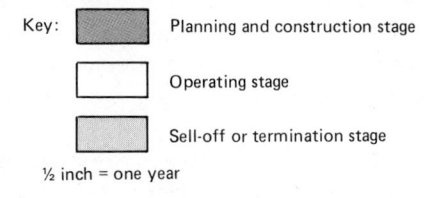

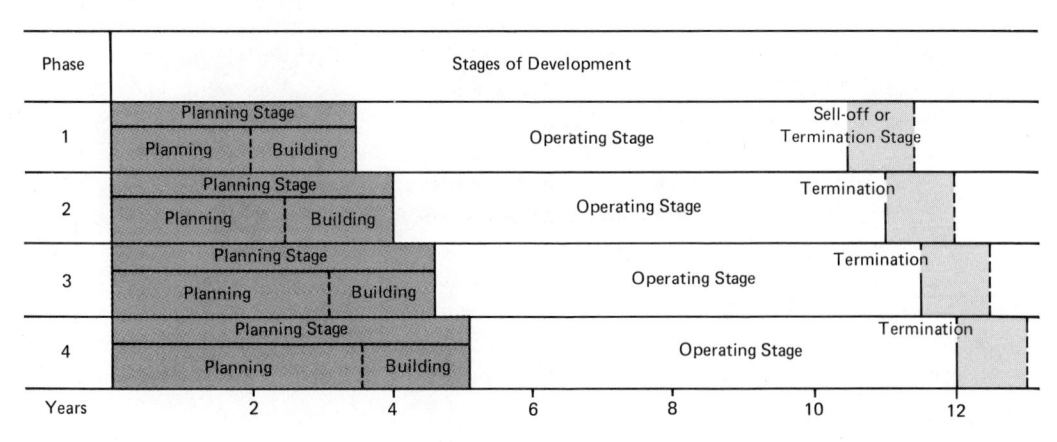

The Recent Tax Environment. If the tax legislation in a particular area has changed recently, that new tax plan usually calls for capitalization of the expense rather than immediate write-off. The legislation of 1976 started the era of "closing the loopholes" and conservative tax policies. In the mid-1970s, the tax surcharge was eliminated from personal income tax rates and corporate income tax rates were reduced. The standard deduction for households and individuals was increased, whereas the social security tax rates and base were raised. Congress has repeatedly considered eliminating real estate tax shelters and the capital gains tax rates. Accelerated depreciation benefits have been reduced for the various types of real estate development. Only the owners of new residential rental properties may now use 200 percent declining balance or sum-of-the-years'-digits methods of accelerated depreciation. Arbitrary allocation of partnership "income" is restricted as of the Tax Reform Act of 1976 and the Revenue Act of 1978. In other words, partnership investment in order to gain extra tax shelter and less cash flow is restricted. Reasonable allocations of depreciation on an economic basis are required for the partnership distributions per year.

Taxation of the various expenses differs according to Internal Revenue Service regulations. The 1979 Federal Tax Handbook, published by Prentice-Hall, indicates the following regulations currently in effect.

Taxation of Planning Costs. Planning costs include fees for preliminary economic and engineering studies of various types, organizational expense, syndication sales fees, and advertising and sales promotion costs.

Fees for preliminary economic and engineering studies. When fees for preliminary economic and engineering studies are considered ordinary and necessary business expenses, they may immediately be deducted for federal income tax purposes by the income property owner-developer. If the engineering studies are associated with a personal-use property, the fees for these studies are added to the home's basis and aid in reduction of the taxable gain when the house is eventually sold or exchanged.

Organizational legal expense. The costs of organizing a business entity, such as a partnership or corporation, must be *capitalized* rather than *expensed*. The term *capitalized* means that the cost is added to the basis of the income property and the cost is recaptured over a lengthy period of time with the rest of the property investment. The term *expensed* means immediate deduction for federal income tax purposes. The net operating income from the property is reduced immediately by the item, which is immediately written off the tax purposes.

The organizational expense must be capitalized and amortized over a period of not less than 60 months. The organizational expense for perhaps the creation of a corporation or a partnership must be incurred before the end of the first tax year in which the organization is in business. Organization costs are those that are (1) incurred for the creation of the business entity, (2) chargeable to the capital account, and (3) of a character that would be amortizable over the life of the business entity if its life were limited by its charter. The actual costs may include the expenses of temporary directors, organizational meetings, state fees for incorporation or chartering privileges, accounting costs related to the organization of the entity, and legal costs. The legal expense may include the expense of drafting documents, writing the minutes of organizational meetings, and establishing the terms of the original stock certificates or partnership interests.

Syndication sales fees. The costs of selling partnership interests or syndication shares must be capitalized and amortized over a period of not less than 60 months.

These costs are incurred to promote the sale of, or to sell interests in, the partnership. A syndicate is a form of partnership.

Advertising and sales promotion costs. Regular advertising and sales promotion costs for business purposes are immediately tax deductible. These promotional expenses are generally in addition to the expenses of selling syndicate and partnership interests.

Taxation of Recording Costs. The costs of recording mortgages and deeds are immediately deductible if they are ordinary and necessary business expenses. Such costs for personal-use properties are not deductible. This personal expense is added to the house's basis for the calculation of gain when the property is disposed of.

Taxation of Financing Costs. The following are some financing costs, which are listed along with their tax treatment:

Incidental home financing expenses. Appraisal fees, legal fees, transfer taxes, and other loan closing costs are considered personal expenses and are not deductible. These costs are added to the house's basis for tax purposes in the termination stage of the investment.

Insurance premiums for fire, storm, theft, liability, and other coverage. If the insurance premiums are associated with income properties, the premium expense is deductible as an ordinary and necessary business expense. If the insurance premiums are associated with personal-use property, the expense is not deductible as personal expense.

Discount points or prepaid interest. In house financing, if discount points are paid from separate funds of the borrower and not from the loan proceeds, the points paid to obtain a mortgage are deductible. If interest is prepaid beyond the end of the taxable year when a house is financed, that prepayment is tax deductible when paid. In the case of income property financing, the interest prepaid beyond the end of the taxable year is no longer deductible when paid, but is deductible in the year to which it relates, according to the 1976 Tax Reform Act.

Service charges for loans. Service charges or loan origination fees that do not represent prepaid interest are immediately tax deductible if these charges can be proven ordinary and necessary business expenses. Therefore, loan origination fees on personal-use property or houses are not deductible.

The Taxation of Construction-Related Costs Contracted During the Planning Stage

Real Estate Taxes on Unimproved Land Holdings. Generally, for federal income tax purposes, the property owner may deduct state and local real property taxes. If the taxpayer is using the accrual method of accounting, the tax payment may be deducted when the taxes are accrued or as they become a personal liability of the taxpayer. If the taxpayer is using the cash method of accounting, the tax payment may be deducted when the taxpayer pays the real estate taxes.

Following the Tax Reform Act of 1976, taxes paid or accrued during the construction period of a project must be capitalized according to the following time schedule:

By 1978 for nonresidential real property if construction started after December 31, 1975, and for residential real property except for the taxpayer's personal residence.

By 1982 for low-income housing.

These construction period taxes must be capitalized and amortized over a specific period of time—eventually 10 years. The first year's amortization may be claimed for the year in which the taxes were incurred. The second year's amortization may not be claimed until the construction is completed and available for rental or sale.

The gradual implementation of this tax plan involves the following: the type of property being constructed, the year in which the taxes are paid or incurred, and the prescribed amortization period related to the first year that taxes are paid or incurred (Exhibit 12-4).

Construction Loan Interest. Construction loan interest on nonresidential and residential real property is no longer immediately deductible for federal income purposes. This interest must be capitalized and amortized according to the table of Exhibit 12-4. Mortgage interest during construction is treated the same way as taxes during construction, as of the Tax Reform Act of 1976. The tax plan gradually goes into effect for the construction loan interest for the three types of property—nonresidential, low-income residential, and other housing.

Insurance Premiums. During the construction of an income property, the insurance premiums paid for fire, storm, theft, liability, and other insurance coverage are deductible as ordinary and necessary business expense. If the building being constructed is a house or other personal-use property, the insurance premiums are not tax deductible.

Exhibit 12-4. The Amortization Periods for Taxes and Mortgage Interest Paid or Incurred During the Construction Period

Type of Property	Year Interest or Taxes Paid or Incurred	Amortization Period
Nonresidential real property	1976	½ in 1976 remainder over 3 years
	1977	5 years
	1978	6 years
	1979	7 years
	1980	8 years
	1981	9 years
	1982 and later	10 years
Residential property	1978	4 years
	1979	5 years
	1980	6 years
	1981	7 years
	1982	8 years
	1983	9 years
	1984 and later	10 years
Low-income housing	1982	4 years
	1983	5 years
	1984	6 years
	1985	7 years
	1986	8 years
	1987	9 years
	1988 and later	10 years

Source: *Tax Reform Act 1976;* (Provisions Affecting Individuals). New York: Price Waterhouse & Co., 1976, p. 151. Reprinted with permission.

LIMITATIONS ON THE DEDUCTION OF INTEREST ON INVESTMENT INDEBTEDNESS

Currently the deduction of post-1975 interest on investment indebtedness is generally limited to

$10,000 plus net investment income.
Plus an additional $15,000 deduction for interest paid on funds borrowed to acquire stock or a partnership interest in a 50 percent owned corporation or partnership.

Any amounts of interest not currently deductible for federal income purpose because of these limitations can be carried forward indefinitely for deduction in future years.

The current deduction of post-1975 interest paid on a pre-September 1975 note to finance the acquisition of a specific income property is subject to a certain limitation in effect for years prior to 1976. The limitation on the deduction is the sum of the following:

$25,000 plus net investment income.
Net long-term capital gains in excess of net short-term capital losses (but the 50 percent capital gain deduction is lost to the extent that the interest deduction is increased).
One-half of any investment interest in excess of the preceding amounts.

THE TAX BURDEN OF SINGLE AND MARRIED REAL ESTATE INVESTORS

At this point it is worth stopping to consider the current tax burdens of single and married real estate investors. These schedules point out the importance of deductibility of project expenses on a federal income tax basis.

According to the 1979 tax rates for single individuals (Exhibit 12-5) the single taxpayer reaches a marginal tax rate of approximately 39 percent when he or she makes a taxable income of $25,000. Considerably more than this amount would be made on a gross income basis, because taxable income is net of all deductible items. The 49 percent marginal tax bracket is reached when the person's taxable income is $34,100. When the single taxpayer generates a taxable income of $50,000 a year, the marginal tax rate rises to approximately 55 percent.

Turning to the 1979 tax rates for married individuals filing joint returns (Exhibit 12-6), it may be observed that the married taxpayer filing jointly is subject to only an approximate 32 percent marginal tax rate at a taxable income of $25,000. When the married taxpayer filing jointly reaches a taxable income of $45,800, the marginal tax rate reaches 49 percent. When this married taxpayer makes $50,000 of taxable income a year, the person is subject to the same approximate rate of 54 percent as the single taxpayer would be at the same taxable income. In the other lower income cases, the single taxpayer was subjected to higher marginal rates than the married taxpayer filing jointly.

The married taxpayer filing separately (Exhibit 12-7) is subjected to marginal tax rates that are higher per given level of taxable income than the single taxpayer or the married taxpayer filing jointly. If the taxable income is $30,000, the single person pays according to a marginal rate of 44 percent, the married taxpayer filing jointly is sub-

Exhibit 12-5. *Tax Rates for Single Individuals Beginning December 31, 1978 (Other Than Surviving Spouses and Heads of Households)*

Taxable Income	Tax
Not over $2,300	No tax
Over $2,300 but not over $3,400	14% of excess over $2,300
Over $3,400 but not over $4,400	$154 plus 16% of excess over $3,400
Over $4,400 but not over $6,500	$314 plus 18% of excess over $4,400
Over $6,500 but not over $8,500	$692 plus 19% of excess over $6,500
Over $8,500 but not over $10,800	$1,072 plus 21% of excess over $8,500
Over $10,800 but not over $12,900	$1,555 plus 24% of excess over $10,800
Over $12,900 but not over $15,000	$2,059 plus 26% of excess over $12,900
Over $15,000 but not over $18,200	$2,650 plus 30% of excess over $15,000
Over $18,200 but not over $23,500	$3,565 plus 34% of excess over $18,200
Over $23,500 but not over $28,800	$5,367 plus 39% of excess over $23,500
Over $28,800 but not over $34,100	$7,434 plus 44% of excess over $28,800
Over $34,100 but not over $41,500	$9,766 plus 49% of excess over $34,200
Over $41,500 but not over $55,300	$13,392 plus 55% of excess over $41,500
Over $55,300 but not over $81,800	$20,982 plus 63% of excess over $55,300
Over $81,800 but not over $108,300	$37,677 plus 68% of excess over $81,800
Over $108,300	$55,697 plus 70% of excess over $108,300

jected to a rate of 37 percent, and the married taxpayer filing separately faces a 54 percent rate.

The maximum ordinary income tax rate on earned income for individuals is 50 percent. In contrast, the maximum tax rate on taxable income from investments is 70 percent.

Exhibit 12-6. *Tax Rates for Surviving Spouses and Married Individuals Filing Joint Returns. Taxable Years Beginning After December 31, 1978*

Taxable Income	Tax
Not over $3,400	No tax
Over $3,400 but not over $5,500	14% of excess over $3,400
Over $5,500 but not over $7,600	$294 plus 16% of excess over $5,500
Over $7,600 but not over $11,900	$630 plus 18% of excess over $7,600
Over $11,900 but not over $16,000	$1,404 plus 21% of excess over $11,900
Over $16,000 but not over $20,200	$2,265 plus 24% of excess over $16,000
Over $20,200 but not over $24,600	$3,273 plus 28% of excess over $20,200
Over $24,600 but not over $29,900	$4,505 plus 32% of excess over $24,600
Over $29,900 but not over $35,200	$6,201 plus 37% of excess over $29,900
Over $35,200 but not over $45,800	$8,162 plus 43% of excess over $35,200
Over $45,800 but not over $60,000	$12,720 plus 49% of excess over $45,800
Over $60,000 but not over $85,600	$19,678 plus 54% of excess over $60,000
Over $85,600 but not over $109,400	$33,502 plus 59% of excess over $85,600
Over $109,400 but not over $162,400	$47,544 plus 64% of excess over $109,400
Over $162,400 but not over $215,400	$81,464 plus 68% of excess over $162,400
Over $215,400	$117,504 plus 70% of excess over $215,400

Exhibit 12-7. Tax Rates for Married Individuals Filing Separate Returns Taxable Years Beginning After December 31, 1978

Taxable Income	Tax
Not over $1,700	No tax
Over $1,700 but not over $2,750	14% of excess over $1,700
Over $2,750 but not over $3,800	$147 plus 16% of excess over $2,750
Over $3,800 but not over $5,950	$315 plus 18% of excess over $3,800
Over $5,950 but not over $8,000	$702 plus 21% of excess over $5,950
Over $8,000 but not over $10,100	$1,132.50 plus 24% of excess over $8,000
Over $10,100 but not over $12,300	$1,636.50 plus 28% of excess over $10,100
Over $12,300 but not over $14,950	$2,252.50 plus 32% of excess over $12,300
Over $14,950 but not over $17,600	$3,100.50 plus 37% of excess over $14,950
Over $17,600 but not over $22,900	$4,081 plus 43% of excess over $17,600
Over $22,900 but not over $30,000	$6,360 plus 49% of excess over $22,900
Over $30,000 but not over $42,800	$9,839 plus 54% of excess over $30,000
Over $42,800 but not over $54,700	$16,751 plus 59% of excess over $42,800
Over $54,700 but not over $81,200	$23,772 plus 64% of excess over $54,700
Over $81,200 but not over $107,700	$40,732 plus 68% of excess over $81,200
Over $107,700	$58,752 plus 70% of excess over $107,700

THE FEDERAL INCOME TAX BURDEN OF CORPORATIONS

The Revenue Act of 1978 reduced the corporate federal income tax burden. Before the 1978 tax law, corporations were subject to taxation of 20 percent on the first $25,000 of taxable income, 22 percent on the next $25,000, and 48 percent on the corporate taxable income above $50,000. The new tax schedule established by the Revenue Act of 1978 has five steps. The schedule follows:

Taxable Income	Tax Rate
$0 to $25,000	17%
$25,000 to $50,000	20%
$50,000 to $75,000	30%
$75,000 to $100,000	40%
Over $100,000	46%

SUMMARY

This chapter introduced the three chapters of Part III that are concerned with taxation. This chapter dealt with the deductibility or capitalization of certain expenses normally incurred during the planning stage of real estate development. Chapters 13 and 14 deal with tax effects of normal expenses incurred during the operation and termination stages of development.

When we observe the timing of the three stages of real estate development, we notice that the three stages run in tandem when only one phase of development is involved. When multiple-phase development is underway, the three stages of each individual phase overlap the same general stages of development of the other phases. For example, some residential subdivisions are built in five or six phases. Each one of these phases takes planning and construction and involves operation and eventual termination of the investment holding.

The planning stage of development usually involves planning, recording, financing, and construction-related costs. Each of the expenses must be handled individually from a federal income tax standpoint. If the costs are related to an income property, they are handled for tax purposes differently than the costs that are related to houses or personal-use properties.

A great many tax changes have occurred in the middle and latter parts of the 1970s. In a few ways tax-shelter investments, such as income property investments, have been restricted by more stringent tax regulations. The use of accelerated depreciation has been restricted to some extent. Syndicate and partnership regulations have become more stringent and less beneficial to various types of real estate syndicate members. Corporation tax rates have been reduced; so have personal income tax rates. The tax surcharge was taken off personal income tax rates around 1975, and standard deductions were increased. In 1976 and 1977 social security tax bases and rates increased as the standard deductions increased.

If a house is planned and constructed, most of the expenses in that stage of development are not tax deductible. The costs are merely capitalized or added to the basis of the property, so that if there is a capital gain at the time the property is sold or exchanged, the difference between the sale price and the basis is less for capital gains tax purposes. Therefore, the additional costs of the planning stage must be capitalized and not expensed for federal income tax purposes.

If an income property is developed, some of the planning-stage expenses may be expensed for tax purposes and some must be capitalized and amortized or recaptured over a relatively long period of time. Syndication sales costs and organizational costs must be amortized and capitalized over at least 60 months. Since the Tax Reform Act of 1976, mortgage interest and taxes payable during construction must be capitalized and amortized over several years. The Internal Revenue Service established an amortization table, which depends on when the construction takes place and the type of property involved. The interest that can be paid on investment indebtedness is limited. Insurance premiums and loan origination fees of financial institutions can be expensed or immediately deducted for federal income tax purposes. Fees for preliminary economic and engineering studies are also deductible in the year paid. Advertising and sale promotion costs and recording costs are deductible. Interest prepaid on an income property loan beyond the end of the taxable year is no longer deductible when paid, but it is deductible in the year to which it relates.

At the time that the individual considers real estate investment, that person's tax position has become burdensome. The single taxpayer's marginal tax rate exceeds that of the married taxpayer filing jointly until a taxable income of $50,000 is reached. At that taxable income, both categories of potential real estate investors hit the 54–55 percent marginal tax bracket. When both categories attain a taxable income of $25,000, the single taxpayer is subject to a 39 percent marginal rate, whereas the married taxpayer filing jointly faces only a 32 percent marginal rate. The tax rates for married taxpayers filing separately tend to be higher than the rates for single taxpayers or married taxpayers filing jointly. The maximum marginal rate for annual earnings gained by means of salaries or wages, regardless of marital status and type of tax filing, is 50 percent; the maximum rate applied to income from investments is 70 percent.

The corporate tax burden was lightened by the Revenue Act of 1978. The maximum federal income tax rate of 46 percent is reached when taxable income exceeds $100,000. Five graduated steps in the tax schedule are employed, versus three steps that were used prior to January 1, 1979.

Therefore, the real estate investor usually is subject to a relatively high tax rate, and the tax status of the various development and investment expenses are important to the investor. The higher the investor's tax burden, the more conscious he or she is of the tax consequences of alternative investments. Investors quickly discover that real estate investment has many tax-shelter advantages.

Key Terms and Concepts

Front-end costs
Soft costs
Sell-out or termination stage
Tax-rate schedules
Mortgage recording fee
Promotional literature
200 percent declining balance
Sum-of-the-years digits
Loan closing costs
Accrual method of accounting
Market study fee
Feasibility study fee
Environmental impact study fee
Appraisal fee
Construction loan interest

News releases
Revenue Act of 1978
Capitalized versus expensed
Ordinary and necessary business expense
Loan origination fee
Brokerage costs
Organizational legal expenses
Title insurance premium
Deed recording fee
Advertising costs
Tax surcharge
House's basis
Syndication sales fees
Prepaid interest

Questions for Student Self-examination

Multiple-Choice Questions

1. Which term does not fit a commonly accepted stage of real estate development?
    a. operating stage
    b. financing stage
    c. planning stage
    d. termination stage

2. Which kind of costs are usually associated with the planning stage of real estate development?
    a. hard costs
    b. medium hard costs
    c. soft costs
    d. none of the above

3. What is the source of payment for the front-end costs of real estate development?
   a. loan proceeds
   b. investor's working capital
   c. property net rentals
   d. none of the above

4. Net operating income is reduced by _____ in order to arrive at taxable income.
   a. depreciation
   b. mortgage interest
   c. mortgage principal
   d. a and b

5. Which type of real estate development is permitted 200 percent declining balance or sum-of-the-years'-digits depreciation schedule?
   a. used residential rental property
   b. new nonresidential property
   c. new residential rental property
   d. used nonresidential property

True-False Questions

T F 1. The real estate investor usually plans to keep the tax outflows to the lowest possible amount.
T F 2. The real estate investor usually finds that the property tax burden is greater than the federal income tax burden.
T F 3. At the completion of the construction job, the owner pays the principal and all the interest on the construction loan.
T F 4. Front-end costs are expenses that must be paid before the receipt of the construction loan money.
T F 5. Capital gains rates apply to the recapture of excess depreciation at the time of property sale.
T F 6. Refinancing of the property during the operating stage may result in tax-free income.
T F 7. The tax legislation of the latter 1970s increased the accelerated depreciation benefits for various types of real estate developments.
T F 8. If insurance premiums are associated with income properties, the premium expense is deductible as an ordinary and necessary business expense.
T F 9. Loan origination fees on personal-use property or houses are not tax deductible.
T F 10. Construction loan interest must be capitalized and amortized.

Answers
Multiple-Choice: 1b, 2c, 3b, 4c, 5c.
True-False: 1T, 2F, 3F, 4T, 5F, 6T, 7F, 8T, 9T, 10T.

Problems

1. As David Aronov contemplates the development of University Mall, a regional shopping center with four major department stores, how many distinct phases of the development can be foreseen?

2. As the architects draw up plans for Park View Office Complex, what activities and jobs will John McCormick encounter in the planning and construction stage of the office park development? What tax consequences will result?

3. In the operating stage of the Rockefeller Apartment development, what tax problems will arise for John Rockefeller?

4. In an apartment development of several phases, how do the three stages of real estate development blend together?

5. According to the tax law of 1978, how would John Rockefeller handle the real estate taxes, construction loan interest, and insurance premiums paid during the construction stage of his apartment development for tax purposes?

6. How do the tax rates for individuals and corporations relate to each other as of the tax law of 1978? Which form of organization—proprietorship or corporation—would be taxed the least when the taxable income was $50,000? $100,000?

Chapter 13
Taxation During the Planning Stage of Real Estate Investment

Introduction

The Relationship of This Chapter to Other Chapters of the Text

Depreciation Guidelines and Regulations
    Depreciation of Personal Property Related to Real Estate Investment   Depreciation of Real Property Used for Business Purposes: *Straight-line depreciation, Declining balance depreciation, Sum-of-the-Years'-Digits Depreciation*   Comparison of the Three Depreciation Methods   The Depreciation Period   Change in Depreciation Method   Recapture of Excess Depreciation   The Significance of the Depreciation Expense for Federal Income Tax Purposes

Investment Tax Credit

The Deductibility of the Cost of Repairs and Mortgage Prepayment Penalty

The Deductibility of Interest and Taxes
    The Capitalization and Amortization of Construction Period Interest and Taxes   The Current Deductibility or Amortization of Prepaid Interest   The Limitation on Investment Interest Deduction

The Minimum Taxes on Tax Preference Items
    The Regular 15 percent "Add-On" Minimum Tax   The New Alternative Minimum Tax Involving Capital Gains and Adjusted Itemized Deductions Preference Items   The Capital Gains Preference Item   Adjusted Itemized Deductions Preference Items

Special Allocation of Partnership Income, Loss, Gain, Deductions, or Credits

Summary

Key Terms and Concepts

Questions for Student Self-examination

> **LEARNING OBJECTIVES** After studying this chapter, you should be familiar with
>
> The general depreciation guidelines and regulations
> The depreciation of personal property related to real estate investment
> The depreciation of real property used for business purposes
> The depreciation methods allowed for specific types of income properties
> The methods of calculating depreciation expense under the allowed methods
> The differences and similarities of the three depreciation methods
> The depreciable life
> The possible change in depreciation method
> The recapture of excess depreciation
> The significance of depreciation expense for federal income tax purposes
> Investment tax credit
> The deductibility of the cost of repairs and the mortgage prepayment penalty
> The deductibility of interest and taxes for federal income tax purposes
> Minimum taxation on tax preference items
> Special allocation of partnership income, loss, gain, deductions, or credits

A variety of tax regulations affect real estate investment and development during the operating stage. The investor must be prepared to meet the tax liabilities when they are due. On the other hand, the investor should know the rules concerning the tax deductibility of certain significant investment expenses. Usually the investor does not wish to pay more federal income taxes than absolutely necessary. Therefore, the tax-deductible items are significant to financial planning.

INTRODUCTION

Even though many real estate investors employ tax accountants and tax attorneys to handle their tax matters and to advise them, the investor remains ultimately responsible for the tax calculations and payments due the Internal Revenue Service. The tax accountants and tax attorneys can be wisely employed for the complicated tax accounting required for income-producing property. Some investors even employ these specialists for the tax accounting for their owner-occupied homes and for the preparation of their regular company tax returns. The tax specialist tends to recognize tax opportunities for the individual or company investor and tends to pass the tax-saving tips on to the investor.

Once the investor learns of the tax regulations, he or she may make intelligent decisions about the investment areas subject to tax regulation. For example, once the investor learns the depreciation deductibility rules, he or she can decide whether straight-line depreciation is preferable, in terms of the cash flow, to accelerated depreciation. Is the fast write-off of accelerated depreciation with the later taxation at ordinary rates of the excess depreciation preferable to the use of straight-line depreciation? How much mortgage financing is preferable in light of limitations on the amount of mortgage interest that is tax deductible? How much new and used equipment should be purchased for the real estate project in light of the current investment tax credit regulations? There are many questions that may arise in the mind of the investor after the more significant tax regulations are reviewed.

THE RELATIONSHIP OF THIS CHAPTER TO OTHER CHAPTERS OF THE TEXT

This chapter adds more tax considerations to Part III. Chapter 12, "Taxation During the Planning Stage of Real Estate Development," is now complemented by this chapter on taxation during the operating stage of real estate investment and development. The entire span of the real estate investment holding period is covered by the tax review in Chapters 12-14.

This chapter focuses on the tax deductibility of depreciation, the cost of repairs, any prepayment penalty charged by a mortgage lender, and mortgage interest. The applicability of the investment tax credit is surveyed. Attention is given to the limitations on the losses deducted by investors involved in tax-sheltered activities. The reader also notes that a minimum tax is exacted from all taxpayers who normally have many tax-preference items on their tax returns.

DEPRECIATION GUIDELINES AND REGULATIONS

The depreciation of personal and real property is important to the real estate investor. Depreciation expense for each tax period is deductible for federal income tax purposes. The amount of taxes paid is related to the amount of depreciation written off for federal income tax purposes. If the taxpayer falls into the 50 percent marginal tax bracket, each dollar of depreciation expense will result in tax reduction equal to 50 percent of the depreciation expense.

Depreciation of Personal Property Related to Real Estate Investment. If the investor owns real property that has personal property in the total investment package, depreciation regulations apply to the personal property. Generally, the personal property may be depreciated by classes of personal property or by components. In an industrial plant, equipment of the same category and the same general economic life may be grouped in asset classes and depreciated as a group. Each item of personal property may be depreciated separately on the component depreciation plan. See Table 13-1 for an example of the estimated asset lifetimes of personal property that condominium and other homeowners' associations may need to depreciate.

There is a special first-year depreciation allowance for business personal property. Twenty percent of the cost of business personal property may be deducted for federal income tax purposes in the year of purchase, but the deduction is limited to $2,000 for an individual taxpayer and $4,000 if the taxpayer files a joint return. A partnership for real estate investment is subject to the $2,000 limit; this deduction must be divided among the various partners as their individual shares of the tax deduction.

Many investment properties have personal property that is depreciable by the owner. An apartment project with unfurnished apartment units for rent usually has carpeting in the hallways and in the interiors of the apartment units; appliances for each unit in the form of refrigerators, stoves, sink disposals; main lobby furnishings; cleaning, repair, and maintenance equipment and tools; electric carts for manager

Table 13-1. Asset lifetimes

Item	Renovation/Replacement Lifetime (Years)
Swimming pools	4.5
Repainting	4- 5
Poolside furniture	3- 7
Filters and other equipment	8-10
Basic structure	30
Pool surface and deck	5- 8
Community centers	
Painting	5
Reroofing	15-20
Furnishings	5-10
Basic structural renovations	30
Tennis courts	
Resurfacing	5- 7
Structural repairs	25
Lighting	15
Tot lots	5- 7
Asphalt pathway repaving	15
Multipurpose (basketball) court	20
Recreational vehicle storage yard	
Gravel base	5
Chain link fence	15
Repaving of private asphalt roadways	8-10
Repainting of unit exteriors	4- 9
Reroofing of units	15-25

Source: *Financial Management of Condominium and Homeowners' Associations* (Washington, D.C.: ULI-The Urban Land Institute, 1975), p. 71. Reprinted with permission.

Note: These lifetimes may vary significantly with climate and level of usage.

surveillance of the property; other vehicles such as station wagons and trucks for property maintenance and repairs; individual or central air conditioning and heating units; elevators; bookkeeping equipment; and swimming pool maintenance equipment. Office buildings have similar personal property, which is depreciable by the owner. The carpeting of the hallways and lobbies, lobby furniture, elevators, maintenance equipment and vehicles, air conditioning and heating units, and office equipment are tax deductible on a class life or component basis.

Depreciation of Real Property Used for Business Purposes. As of 1978, only new residential rental property where 80 percent of the gross rents come from nontransient residents is eligible for double declining balance or sum-of-the-years'-digits depreciation. (Double declining balance depreciation is the same as 200 percent straight-line declining balance depreciation). In contrast, if the investor purchases an existing commercial or industrial property, only straight-line depreciation may be used for tax purposes. The allowable depreciation methods for all types of properties, including rehabilitated properties for rental to low-income tenants, are listed in Table 13-2.

Table 13-2. Allowable depreciation methods for all types of investment properties

Type of Property	Allowable Depreciation Methods
New residential rental property where 80% of gross rents are derived from nontransient residential tenants	200% straight-line declining balance method Sum-of-the-years'-digits method
Used residential rental property having a remaining economic life of 20 years or more	125% straight-line declining balance method
New nonresidential property	150% straight-line declining balance
All properties not listed above	Straight-line depreciation
Rehabilitation costs of low-income rental housing not exceeding $15,000 per unit, excluding cost of building acquisition	Amortization over a five-year period, using straight-line depreciation

The calculation methods for straight-line, declining balance, and sum-of-the-years'-digits methods of depreciation are different. Therefore, in this portion of the chapter the reader can quickly review the computation methods and some examples.

Straight-line depreciation. The depreciation expense using the straight-line method is uniform for every year of the economic life of the depreciable asset. The cost of the asset less salvage value is deductible in equal annual amounts over the estimated economic life. The real property may not be depreciated below its salvage value.

To find the fixed proportion of the asset basis that represents the annual depreciation, divide into 100 percent the number of years of the estimated economic life of the asset.

Example: Assume a swimming pool has an economic life of 40 years.

$$\text{The depreciation percent expense per year} = \frac{100\%}{40 \text{ years}} = 2.5\% \text{ per year}$$

To find the amount of depreciation per year, multiply the fixed ratio of depreciation per year times the depreciable cost of the asset. If the swimming pool has a depreciable cost of $20,000, then

$$\begin{array}{ccc}\text{Depreciable cost} \times \text{fixed ratio of depreciation} & = & \text{fixed depreciation per year} \\ \$20,000 \qquad\qquad 2.5\% & & \$500 \end{array}$$

At the end of the depreciation period, the property cost has been written down to the estimated salvage value through constant annual deductions for depreciation expense. The depreciation example of Table 13-3 illustrates the annual charges and the cumulative charges for a property with a useful life of 10 years using the straight-line method.

Assume that a newly acquired asset with a depreciable basis of $50,000 has an estimated useful life of 10 years and a negligible salvage value. The following table shows the annual depreciation allowances and the accumulated depreciation under the 10% straight-line rate, the 200% declining balance rate, and the sum-of-the-year'-digits method, so the reader can compare the results under each.

Declining balance depreciation. The depreciation expense under the declining balance method is computed by taking a fixed percentage of the undepreciated asset

Table 13-3. Depreciation

Year	Straight-Line, 10% Annual Charge	Cumulative	200% Declining Balance, 20% Annual Charge	Cumulative	Sum of the Years' Digits Annual Charge	Cumulative
1	$5,000	$ 5,000	$10,000.00	$10,000.00	$9,090.91	$ 9,090.91
2	5,000	10,000	8,000.00	18,000.00	8,181.82	17,272.73
3	5,000	15,000	6,400.00	24,400.00	7,272.73	24,545.46
4	5,000	20,000	5,120.00	29,520.00	6,363.64	30,909.10
5	5,000	25,000	4,096.00	33,616.00	5,454.55	36,363.65
6	5,000	30,000	3,276.80	36,892.80	4,545.45	40,909.10
7	5,000	35,000	2,621.44	39,514.24	3,636.36	44,545.46
8	5,000	40,000	2,097.15	41,611.39	2,727.27	47,272.73
9	5,000	45,000	1,677.72	43,289.11	1,818.18	49,090.91
10	5,000	50,000	1,342.18	44,631.29	909.09	50,000.00

balance. The fixed percentage may be 125 percent, 150 percent, or 200 percent of the percentage calculated under the straight-line method of depreciation. If the 150 percent declining balance method is selected, the first year's depreciation expense would be found by multiplying the straight-line percentage of depreciation by 150 percent and then multiplying the resulting percentage by the depreciable cost. The salvage value is not subtracted from the depreciable cost, but the property is only depreciated down to the estimated salvage value. The second year's depreciation expense is found by multiplying the calculated percentage times the remaining undepreciated balance. An example follows.

If the depreciable asset has a depreciable basis of $50,000, an estimated useful life of 10 years, and a negligible salvage value.

Straight-line depreciation percentage = $\frac{100\%}{10 \text{ years}}$ = 10% per year

150% declining balance depreciation percentage − 10% × 150% = 15%

Therefore, the first year's depreciation = 15% × $50,000 = $7,500

The remaining undepreciated balance: $50,000 Beginning balance
−7,500 First year's depreciation
$42,500 Undepreciated balance at end of first year

The second year's depreciation: 15% × $42,500 = $6,375

The remaining undepreciated balance: $42,500 Balance at end of first year
−6,375 Second year's depreciation
$36,125 Undepreciated balance at end of second year

An illustration of the computation of 200 percent declining balance may be found in Table 13-3. The center columns show the annual and cumulative charges, based on a fixed depreciation rate of 20 percent.

Sum-of-the-years'-digits depreciation. Depreciation expense under the sum-of-the-years'-digits method permits substantial depreciation expense in the first year of the ownership of the property and steadily declining depreciation expense over the remaining years of the depreciation period. The percentage of the depreciable basis less estimated salvage value changes every year. The first year's depreciation ratio is the fraction of the total years of depreciation divided by the sum of the numerals representing each of the years of the estimated useful life (sum of the years' digits). The ratio for depreciation expense for the succeeding years is the fraction of the years remaining in the depreciable life divided by the sum of the years' digits. An example follows.

If the asset has a depreciable basis of $100,000, a negligible salvage value, and an estimated useful life of five years, the first year's depreciation expense is

$$\frac{5}{\text{sum of the years' digits}} \times \$100,000$$

The sum of the years' digits = 5 + 4 + 3 + 2 + 1 = 15.

Therefore,

The first year's depreciation $= \frac{5}{15} \times \$100,000 = \$33,333.33$

The second year's depreciation expense $= \frac{4}{15} \times \$100,000 = \$26,666.67$

The third year's depreciation expense $= \frac{3}{15} \times \$100,000 = \$20,000.00$

The fourth year's depreciation expense $= \frac{2}{15} \times \$100,000 = \$13,333.33$

The fifth year's depreciation expense $= \frac{1}{15} \times \$100,000 = \$6,666.67$

Total depreciation expense taken over the five-year period:

First year	$ 33,333.33
Second year	26,666.67
Third year	20,000.00
Fourth year	13,333.33
Fifth year	6,666.67
	$100,000.00

Another illustration of the use of the sum-of-the-years'-digits method of depreciation may be found in Table 13–3.

Comparison of the Three Depreciation Methods. Using the straight-line and the sum-of-the-years'-digits methods, the entire depreciable amount down to the estimated salvage value may be written off. Table 13–3 also shows that the depreciable amount cannot be entirely written off by the 200 percent declining balance method; only $44,631.29 of the $50,000 was depreciated through the use of this depreciation method.

If the real property is held over two or three years, the sum-of-the-years'-digits method of depreciation provides the fastest write-off or the maximum depreciation expense for the time period. It is generally considered the fastest accelerated depreciation method. Even though this may be true and the method of depreciation may be allowed by the Internal Revenue Service for the investor's property, the investor may or may not wish to depreciate the property this quickly. The investor balances out the depreciation schedule with the amortization schedule and the taxation of excess depreciation when the property is sold.

The Depreciation Period. The depreciable asset must be depreciated over the estimated useful life of the asset, the amount of time that it will probably be actually used

Table 13-4. The range in asset depreciation periods for selected assets

Type of Asset	Lower Limit	Asset Guideline Period	Upper Limit
Office furniture, fixtures, and equipment	8	10	12
Data-handling equipment, except computers	5	6	7
Automobiles	2.5	3	3.5
Light general-purpose trucks (less than 13,000 pounds)	3	4	5
Land improvements, not including structures		20	

Source: *1979 Federal Tax Handbook* (Englewood Cliffs, N.J.: Prentice-Hall, 1979), p. 288. Reprinted with permission.

Table 13-5. Internal Revenue Service guidelines for depreciation

Group	Life Years	Straight-Line Percentage
One: Assets used by business in general		
Land improvements		
Apartments	40	2.5
Banks	50	2.0
Dwellings	45	2.222
Factories	45	2.222
Garages	45	2.222
Grain elevators	60	1.667
Hotels	40	2.5
Loft buildings	50	2.0
Machine shops	45	2.222
Office buildings	45	2.222
Stores	50	2.0
Theaters	40	2.5
Warehouses	60	1.667
Two: Class 1(d), farm buildings	25	4.0
Three: Class 17(d), gasoline service stations	16	6.25

Reproduced with permission from *1978 Depreciation Guide*, Vol. 65, No. 31, published and copyrighted by Commerce Clearing House, Inc., Chicago, Ill.; July 11, 1978, pp. 171-172.

by the taxpayer and not over the longer period of its physical life, according to the Internal Revenue Service. There are guidelines for the depreciation period for various types of assets. The Urban Land Institute issued the table of asset lifetimes shown in Table 13-1. Some additional asset guidelines are shown in Table 13-4, which are published in the *1979 Federal Tax Handbook*. The income property guidelines for depreciable life of specific types of land improvements are shown in Table 13-5. These guidelines are merely indicators that have been published over a period of years; the investor may wish to negotiate with the Internal Revenue Service for shorter, more reasonable useful lives for specific types of investment properties.

Change in Depreciation Method. Without the consent of the Internal Revenue Service, the taxpayer can change from declining balance methods to the straight-line method. This is true whether the property is new or used. Toward the end of the depreciation period, many taxpayers elect to change from accelerated methods to the straight-line method in order to maximize the remaining depreciation expense on an annual basis.

Recapture of Excess Depreciation. With the passage of recent tax laws, accumulated depreciation beyond the amount that would be accumulated under the straight-line method is subject to the taxpayer's ordinary federal income tax rate when the property is sold. This is called *recapture of excess depreciation*. For example: If the taxpayer's ordinary income tax rate was 50 percent, the taxes paid on the excess depreciation would be $27,500 × 0.50, or $13,750. The excess depreciation is also subject to regular 15 percent minimum taxation.

Accumulated depreciation expense using the sum-of-the-years'-digits method	$50,000
Accumulated depreciation expense using the straight-line method	− 22,500
Excess depreciation	$27,500

The Significance of the Depreciation Expense for Federal Income Tax Purposes. The depreciation expense is usually calculated for tax purposes. It may or may not represent cash outflow for the repair and modernization of the property. Many real estate analysts assume that, at least in relatively new buildings, the depreciation expense is a noncash expense of the taxpayer. The depreciation expense is considered a tax-shelter feature of income property investment. An example follows, which shows the difference between the federal income tax liability with and without the deduction of depreciation expense that requires no cash flow.

		No Depreciation Expense		Depreciation Expense
Net operating income before depreciation		$50,000		$50,000
Depreciation (noncash expense)			55,000	
Mortgage interest	10,000	10,000	10,000	65,000
Net taxable income (loss)		$40,000		($15,000)

The depreciation deduction may be the difference between the payment or nonpayment of federal income taxes. This type of deduction usually means that the payment of federal income taxes will be lower than it otherwise would be.

INVESTMENT TAX CREDIT

The investment tax credit is a credit against federal income tax, which is allowed in general for 10 percent of qualified investment in tangible personal property. There is a $100,000 limitation on the cost of used personal property that qualifies. The Revenue Act of 1978 permanently established the 10 percent investment tax credit and the $100,000 limit on used property.

The 10 percent tax credit only applies to qualified property that has a useful life of seven years or more. If the asset's useful life is at least five years and less than seven years, only $2/3$ of the cost of the asset is taken into account. If the useful life of the asset is at least three years and less than five years, $1/3$ of the cost is taken into account. To summarize:

Useful Life	Part of Investment Qualifying for Credit
Less than three years	None
At least three years but less than five years	$1/3$
At least five years but less than seven years	$2/3$
At least seven years	All

The investment tax credit may not be used if the property purchased is associated with property rehabilitation or child-care facilities, where rapid amortization is being used. The full 10 percent investment tax credit and five-year amortization period may apply to new pollution-control facilities acquired or constructed after December 31, 1978, that have useful lives of at least five years. If the useful life of the facility is less than five years, less than a 10 percent investment credit is applicable.

The investment tax credit may not exceed the tax liability of the investor. If the investor's tax liability exceeds $25,000, the tax credit may not exceed $25,000 plus 90 percent of the tax liability over that amount. The increase of the percentage from 50 percent, which was applicable when the Revenue Act of 1978 was signed by the President, to 90 percent was phased in by 10 percent a year, starting with the 1979 tax year. Any unused tax credit resulting from the limitations mentioned may be carried back three years and carried forward seven years.

Some of the items affected by the investment tax credit that are associated with real estate investment follow:

Elevators
Boiler facilities
Display racks and shelves
Neon and other signs
Refrigerators
Roadways within a manufacturing complex
Fire extinguishers
Golf course watering systems, including pumps and portable sprinklers
Office equipment
Wall-to-wall carpeting
Window-washing equipment
Special-purpose structures used for livestock, such as pigpens
Special-purpose structures used for commercially sold horticultural products, such as greenhouses

If a building has been in use 20 years or more, and it has been rehabilitated after November 1, 1978, the investment credit may be claimed by the taxpayer if the property qualifies. The investment credit may be claimed for only one renovation of a given building during any 20-year period. Existing buildings used in all types of businesses or production activities tend to qualify, even though apartment buildings (permanent lodging) do not qualify. For example, the following types of existing buildings are eligible for the credit: factories, warehouses, office buildings, and retail and wholesale stores. Transient lodging in the form of hotels and motels does qualify for the credit. The qualification for the investment tax credit is dependent on the use of the property after the rehabilitation. For example, the rehabilitation expenses for an apartment building that is renovated for subsequent use as an office building would qualify.

The expenditures must be treated as capital costs for the building that has a useful life of five years or more. The full 10 percent investment tax credit is available if the improvements attributable to the rehabilitation expenditure have a useful life of seven years or more. If the useful life is at least five years but less than seven, the qualifying expenditures are entitled to only two-thirds the full investment tax credit.

THE DEDUCTIBILITY OF THE COST OF REPAIRS AND MORTGAGE PREPAYMENT PENALTY

The cost of repairs to property used in a trade, business, or profession, or repairs to property held for the production of income, is deductible as an ordinary and necessary business expense. The repairs to an owner-occupied residence are a personal expense and therefore are not deductible for federal income tax purposes.

If an investor prepays a mortgage on an investment property or on an owner-occupied residence, the penalty paid is fully tax deductible.

THE DEDUCTIBILITY OF INTEREST AND TAXES

Generally, taxes and interest are deductible to the extent to which they are directly attributable to a trade, business, or property from which rents or royalties are derived. For example, property taxes paid or incurred on real property used in a trade or business are deductible.

The Capitalization and Amortization of Construction Period Interest and Taxes. Individuals, Subchapter S corporations, and personal holding companies can no longer deduct in the current year the interest and taxes paid or accrued during the period that a real property is under construction, according to the Tax Reform Act of 1976. Such construction-period interest and taxes must be capitalized in the year in which they are paid or accrued and must be amortized over a 10-year period. This ruling resulted from the closing of some of the tax-shelter loopholes that were previously permitted.

The transitional rules established to phase in the amortization program began operating in 1976. Transitional rules applied to nonresidential and residential real property and low-income housing in particular. The schedule follows:

Type of Property	Year Interest Paid or Incurred	Amortization Period
Nonresidential real property	1976	½ in 1976; remainder over 3 years
	1977	5 years
	1978	6 years
	1979	7 years
	1980	8 years
	1981	9 years
	1982 and later	10 years
Residential real property	1978	4 years
	1979	5 years
	1980	6 years
	1981	7 years
	1982	8 years
	1983	9 years
	1984 and later	10 years
Low-income housing	1982	4 years
	1983	5 years
	1984	6 years
	1985	7 years
	1986	8 years
	1987	9 years
	1988 and later	10 years

The Current Deductibility or Amortization of Prepaid Interest. Taxpayers who calculate their tax obligations on a cash basis rather than on an accrual basis must deduct prepaid interest for business and investment purposes over the loan period. In other words, prepaid interest on a loan for investment purposes must be amortized over the term of the loan. If the prepaid interest or points are associated with a mortgage for the purchase or the improvement of the taxpayer's principal residence, the points are generally deductible. (A point, or a discount point, represents 1 percent of the original mortgage amount. Points are paid at the closing of the loan and amount to prepaid interest.) To be currently deductible, the payment of such points on a home mortgage must be common in the geographical area where the loan is made and the number of points charged should be common to the area.

The Limitation on Investment Interest Deduction. Effective in the taxable years after 1975, the deduction by noncorporate taxpayers for interest on investment indebtedness is limited to $10,000 per year plus the taxpayer's net investment income. Investment interest, according to the Internal Revenue Service, is the interest paid or accrued on indebtedness incurred or continued to purchase or carry property held for investment. Net investment income means the excess of investment income over investment expenses. Investment income may be derived from interest, dividends, rents, royalties, net short-term capital gains attributable to the disposition of property held for investment, and any depreciation recapture treated as ordinary income. Investment expense includes all ordinary and necessary business expense.

The calculation of deductible interest involves the following:

Gross investment income	$_____	
Less investment expense	_____	
Net investment income	_____	
Add exemption	10,000	
Limitation on deductible interest		$_____

Deductible interest is the lesser amount of the actual interest or the limitation, as calculated above. The interest deductions that cannot be taken in any one year may be deducted in an unlimited number of future years, subject to the annual limit.

THE MINIMUM TAXES ON TAX PREFERENCE ITEMS

The Regular 15 Percent Add-On Minimum Tax. The Revenue Act of 1978 retained a modified version of the previously used 15 percent minimum tax on some tax preference items. A deduction is permitted for whichever is greater, one-half the regular tax paid for the year, or $10,000.

The items of tax preference covered by the regular add-on minimum tax include:

Excess intangible drilling costs (intangible drilling costs in excess of oil income).
Excess accelerated depreciation over straight-line depreciation (leased personal property and real property).
Exercise of qualified stock options (generally those granted before May 21, 1976).
Depletion.
Rapid amortization on railroad rolling stock, child-care, and pollution-control facilities.

The New Alternative Minimum Tax Involving Capital Gains and Adjusted Itemized Deductions Preference Items. The alternative minimum tax is applicable to taxable income plus capital-gains preference items and adjusted itemized deductions preferences, less a $20,000 exemption.

Taxable income
+ Capital gains preference item
+ Adjusted itemized deductions preference item
− $20,000
Amount taxed by the alternative minimum tax

The alternative minimum tax rates are

10% on the first $40,000.
20% on the next $40,000.
25% above $80,000.

These rates went into effect in 1979.

Taxpayers must figure their regular tax liabilities, including any regular minimum tax, less all nonrefundable credits, including the foreign tax credit. Then the taxpayer figures the alternative minimum tax and pays the *higher* of the two amounts.

The Capital Gains Preference Item. The amount of the taxpayer's capital gains tax preference item is equal to 60 percent of the net capital gain that was deducted before the computation of capital gains taxes due. For the purposes of the alternative minimum tax, the amount of the gain from the sale of a principal residence is not included in the capital gains preference item.

Adjusted Itemized Deductions Preference Items. Beginning January 1, 1979, the adjusted itemized deductions for alternative minimum tax purposes do not include medical and casualty loss deductions or state and local tax deductions. The amount of the preference item is the total of itemized deductions—except medical expenses, casualty losses, and state and local tax deductions—in excess of 60 percent of adjusted gross income.

SPECIAL ALLOCATIONS OF PARTNERSHIP INCOME, LOSS, GAIN, DEDUCTIONS, OR CREDITS

Normally the partnership agreement specifies the method of allocation of items of income, loss, gain, deduction, or credit to the individual partners. The allocation often is made in accordance with the proportionate interests of the individual partners in the partnership.

Special allocations of partnership items may be made unless the allocations are made in an attempt to avoid or evade income tax. Now such special allocations of overall income or loss are subject to a stricter test; the allocation must have "substantial economic impact" on the partners. First, the special allocation of income or loss must have a valid business reason other than mere tax advantage. Second, if a loss is allocated on a special basis to a partner, the partner must bear a reduction of his or her interest in the partnership properties in the amount of the loss. This substantial economic effect must occur, or the allocation of the partnership income and loss will be assumed by the Internal Revenue Service to be allocated in accordance with the partner's interest in the partnership.

SUMMARY

Taxation during the operating stage of real estate investment involves the current deductibility of repairs and the prepayment penalty on a mortgage. The tax regulations also relate to the current tax deductibility of depreciation. Certain methods of accelerated depreciation are permitted for certain types of income properties. When accelerated depreciation methods are utilized, the excess depreciation is usually taxed at the taxpayer's ordinary income tax rates when the property is sold.

The property owner, as a taxpayer, may take advantage of the investment tax credit. The purchase of many items associated with property ownership is subject to partial or total coverage by the authorized investment tax credit. If the item of personal or real property meets the requirements for the employment of the entire tax credit, the taxpayer may deduct from his or her otherwise taxable income 10 percent of the cost of the item. Normally, to justify the full 10 percent credit, the personal or real property must have a useful life of seven years or more.

As of the Tax Reform Act of 1976, personal investors in real property must capitalize and amortize the construction period interest and taxes. If discount points or prepaid interest are required for a mortgage on an income property, the prepaid interest must be amortized over the term of the loan. Prepaid interest on home mortgage loans may be deducted when incurred.

The real estate investor is also hamstrung by other limitations. The investment interest deduction is limited. There is a minimum tax of 15 percent on certain tax preference items. The Revenue Act of 1978 added an alternative minimum tax on selected tax preference items. Therefore, it is difficult to escape the payment of federal income taxes entirely.

Partnership distribution of income, loss, gains, deductions, or credits to individual partners is limited to distribution methods with valid business purposes and where the distributions have a "substantial economic impact" on each partner. Special allocations of partnership losses to individual partners in particular are limited. Two tests must be met before the Internal Revenue Service will concur with the reasonableness of the distribution system.

Key Terms and Concepts

Excess depreciation
Accelerated depreciation
Component depreciation
Asset lifetimes
Special first-year depreciation allowance
Class life basis
Tax-shelter loopholes
Intangible drilling costs
Pollution-control facilities
Partnership allocations
Double declining balance depreciation
Sum-of-the-years'-digits depreciation
Rehabilitated properties
Salvage value
Tax credit

Royalties
Depletion
Alternative minimum tax
Foreign tax credit
Cumulative charges
Estimated useful life
Internal Revenue Service
Urban Land Institute
Master Tax Guide
Qualified investment
Tangible personal property
Interest accrued
Railroad rolling stock
Nonrefundable credits
"Substantial economic impact"

Questions for Student Self-examination

Multiple-Choice Questions

1. Double declining balance depreciation is the same as
   a. 125 percent straight-line declining balance depreciation
   b. sum-of-the-years'-digits depreciation
   c. 200 percent straight-line declining balance depreciation
   d. class life depreciation

2. Which type of property is eligible for double declining balance or sum-of-the-years'-digits depreciation?
   a. existing residential rental property
   b. new residential rental property
   c. existing nonresidential property
   d. new nonresidential property

3. The depreciation expense using the _____ method is uniform for every year of the economic life of the depreciable asset.
   a. straight-line
   b. 125 percent declining balance
   c. 150 percent declining balance
   d. sum-of-the-years'-digits

4. Rehabilitation costs of low-income rental housing, not exceeding $15,000 per unit, excluding the cost of the building acquisition, may be amortized over a _____ period using straight-line depreciation.
   a. 30-year
   b. 25-year
   c. 10-year
   d. 5-year

5. Depreciation expense under the _____ method permits the highest depreciation expense in the first year of the ownership of the property and steadily declining depreciation expense over the remaining years of the depreciation period.
   a. sum-of-the-years'-digits
   b. 150 percent declining balance
   c. 200 percent declining balance
   d. straight-line

True-False Questions

T F 1. Many real estate investors employ tax accountants and tax attorneys.
T F 2. If accelerated depreciation may be used for the investor's property, the investor must utilize accelerated depreciation methods rather than straight-line depreciation.
T F 3. Depreciation expense is not deductible for federal income tax purposes.
T F 4. Construction period interest and taxes are immediately deductible for federal income tax purposes.
T F 5. Prepayment penalties are fully tax deductible for federal income tax purposes.
T F 6. If the taxpayer falls into the 50 percent marginal tax bracket, each dollar of depreciation expense will result in tax reduction equal to 50 percent of the depreciation expense.
T F 7. General personal property may be depreciated by classes of personal property or by components.
T F 8. A depreciable asset must be depreciated by the taxpayer over the remaining physical life of the asset.
T F 9. Without the consent of the Internal Revenue Service, the taxpayer can change from declining balance methods to the straight-line method.
T F 10. With the passage of the recent tax laws, accumulated depreciation beyond that which would be accumulated under the straight-line method is subject to the capital gains tax rate of the taxpayer when the property is sold.

Answers
Multiple-Choice: 1c, 2b, 3a, 4d, 5c.
True-False: 1T, 2F, 3F, 4F, 5T, 6T, 7T, 8F, 9T, 10F.

Problems

1. If you just purchased an apartment building with kitchen equipment built into each apartment, how can you depreciate this personal property?

2. If you just purchased an existing office building, what depreciation method is permitted for the building?

3. If you just developed a low-income apartment project, what depreciation methods are permitted for you, the developer-owner, to use?

4. If Phil Jones built a new rental apartment building, what method of depreciation is permitted for his use in tax accounting?

5. If an investor analyzed the difference between the first-year depreciation expense on a new rental apartment building, figured on both the double declining balance method and on the sum-of-the-years'-digits method, which method would give the highest tax-deductible expense?

6. If the owner of the John Hancock office building in Boston had to replace the broken glass of the exterior glass wall of the building, how would the repair expense be treated for tax purposes?

Chapter 14

Taxation During the Operating Stage of Real Estate Investment

Introduction

The Relationship of This Chapter to Other Chapters of the Text

The Sale of a Property for Immediate, Total Payment
   Computation of a Gain or Loss on the Sale of the Property   The Establishment of the Nature of the Gain or Loss   Computation of Overall Short- or Long-Term Capital Gain or Loss   Taxation of Individual Net Long-Term Capital Gains   Tax Treatment of Individual Net Long-Term Capital Losses   The Corporate Capital-Gains Treatment   Tax Treatment of Corporate Net Capital Losses   Taxation of Net Individual Short-Term Capital Gains and Losses   Capital-Gains Taxation in the Calculation of After-Tax Net Cash Proceeds at Resale   Recapture of Excess Depreciation

The Installment Sale of Real Property
   Computation of First-Year Reportable Gain and the Percentage of Each Future Payment That Must Be Reported by the Seller as Gain

The Tax-Free Exchange of Business or Investment Real Estate
   Like-Kind Property   Holding Period for the Property Acquired   The Basis for the Acquired Property   The Exchange of Mortgaged Properties   The Tax Consequences of the Exchange Involving Boot and Mortgages

Tax-Free Home Sales
   The Sale of a Principal Residence and Its Replacement with an Equally or Higher Priced Residence   The Terminology and Conditions of the Transaction   Calculation of the Gain Recognized for Tax Purposes   Calculation of the Adjusted Basis for the New Residence

Summary

Key Terms and Concepts

Questions for Student Self-examination

LEARNING OBJECTIVES After studying this chapter, you should be familiar with

The sale of a property for immediate, total payment
Computation of a gain or loss on the sale of property
Establishment of the nature of the gain or loss, short- or long-term
The current capital gains holding period
Taxation of net long-term capital gains
Corporate capital-gains treatment
Tax treatment of net long-term capital loss
Taxation of net short-term capital gains and losses
Recapture of excess depreciation
Installment sale of real property
The reasons for the use of the installment sale
The nature of the required installment payments
Computation of the reportable gain for the first and subsequent years
Tax-free exchange of business or investment real estate
The reasons for exchanging real property
The general requirements for a tax-free exchange
The tax consequences of the exchange involving boot and mortgages
Tax-free home sales
The sale of a principal residence by an individual 55 years of age or older

The termination stage of real estate investment involves the sale, exchange, or trade of currently owned property. There are considerable tax ramifications of a sale, an exchange, or a trade. As usual, the chapter deals primarily with federal income tax regulations and their implications for real estate investors.

INTRODUCTION

In this chapter the reader reviews the system for computation of after-tax net cash proceeds from a sale of property. The system of calculation involves computation of the taxable gain, recapture of excess depreciation, ordinary and capital-gains tax rates, and knowledge of the balance outstanding on the existing mortgages. The gradual lengthening of the capital-gains holding period is considered, as is the increase in the capital loss deduction. The method of determining the net long-term or short-term capital gain or loss is illustrated.

When the investor wishes to terminate the particular investment, she or he may decide to sell the property at once or to take another avenue of disinvestment. The property may be sold on an installment basis, or it may be exchanged on a fully or partially tax-free basis for another real property. If the current property is the owner's residence, the ordinary or capital-gains taxes may be currently avoided and the tax payment deferred by the sale of the property and repurchase of another existing property within 18 months of the sale of the original property. Alternatively, the original property may be replaced by a newly constructed residence. The construction of the new house must start within 18 months before or after the sale of the original house, and the dwelling must be completed and lived in within 24 months of the original property's sale. Once in a lifetime, according to the federal tax measure of 1978, a taxpayer 55 years of age or older may sell her or his principal residence, which has been lived in the required number of years, and have excluded from taxation the gain up to and including $100,000. Trade-in plans permit the taxpayer to delay taxation on gains indefinitely.

Taxes on the gain on the sale may be deferred, perhaps by borrowing money on the property before the sale, by placing the property under option, and by long-term leasing of depreciable property.

THE RELATIONSHIP OF THIS CHAPTER TO OTHER CHAPTERS OF THE TEXT

This chapter concludes the discussion of taxation of the three stages of real estate investment and development. It also concludes Part III, which covers portfolio strategy from the viewpoint of tax deductions, tax deferral, and tax payment. The assumption of risk from portfolio concentration or diversification, the possible return from a well-designed portfolio for the individual investor, and the tax implications of alternative actions were considered. Next we study real estate investment analysis in detail in Part IV.

THE SALE OF A PROPERTY FOR IMMEDIATE, TOTAL PAYMENT

The sale of a property for total payment at the closing involves:

   Calculation of the after-tax net cash proceeds.
   Calculation of the adjusted basis.
   Calculation of the sale price net of selling costs and expenses for property preparation in advance of the sale.
   Computation of the net capital gain or loss.
   Calculation of any excess depreciation.
   Tax liability on the transaction.

Computation of a Gain or Loss on the Sale of the Property. When an investment property is sold, a gain, a loss, or no change is realized. Quite often in our inflationary environment, a gain is realized because of the rise in market selling prices. The gain or loss on the property sale can be calculated, and then the nature of the gain—short or long term—can be recognized on the basis of the holding period.

To establish the net gain, the net loss, or the evidence of no change since the purchase, the adjusted basis is subtracted from the adjusted sale price (Exhibit 14-1). The adjusted sale price results from the subtraction of selling expenses from the value of the cash, mortgages, and notes given to pay the purchase price. The adjusted basis is derived from subtracting the depreciation deductions from the total cost of the improvements sold. The cost may amount to a total of the original cost of a structure and its site improvements plus the cost of later improvements to the property. The depreciation amount may have been calculated over time by any of the allowable depreciation methods for the property. Finally, the net gain, loss, or lack of change on the sale is found by subtracting the adjusted basis from the adjusted sale price.

Exhibit 14-1. The Computation of a Gain or Loss on a Sale of Property

Sale price		
Cash	$15,000	
Purchase-money mortgage	10,000	
First mortgage	50,000	
	75,000	
Less selling expenses	4,000	
Adjusted sale price		71,000
Adjusted basis		
Cost (basis)	55,000	
Improvements	3,000	
	58,000	
Less depreciation deductions	10,000	
Adjusted basis		48,000
Net gain on the sale		$23,000

The Establishment of the Nature of the Gain or Loss. The short- or long-term nature of the capital gain or loss from the sale is determined by the current regulation concerning the length of the holding period for capital-gains treatment. The type of gain or loss in the investor's total portfolio is determined after the property sale proceeds are integrated into the overall portfolio results.

Property must now be held for more than one year by the investor in order for the gain or loss to be treated as long term. Since this established period for capital-gains treatment has changed over the last decade, changes may occur in the future. The recent changes have been in the direction of a longer holding period. The period has gradually been changed from more than 6 months—which held for many years—to more than 9 months and now to more than 12 months.

Computation of Overall Short- or Long-Term Capital Gain or Loss. If the investor has more assets than the single real property investment, the net cash proceeds of the property sale will be integrated into the overall computation of net annual short- or long-term capital gain or loss for her or his portfolio and for federal income tax purposes. The long-term capital losses are first subtracted from the long-term capital gains (Exhibit 14-2). Then the short-term capital losses are subtracted from the short-term capital gains. Either the short- or the long-term positions or both may reflect net losses.

The computation of capital gains or losses may result in one of four possible outcomes:

Excess net short-term capital gain.
Excess net short-term capital loss.
Excess net long-term capital gain.
Excess net long-term capital loss.

Each of these possible outcomes tends to be treated differently for federal income tax purposes. (Corporate capital gains and losses are usually treated differently from individual capital gains and losses. As an exception, though, net short-term gains, whether corporate or individual are taxed at the taxpayer's ordinary rate.)

Exhibit 14-2. *Computation of Net Long-Term Capital Gain*

Long-term capital gain	$15,000
Long-term capital loss	(10,000)
Net long-term capital gain	5,000
Short-term capital loss	(3,000)
Short-term capital gain	500
Net short-term capital loss	(2,500)
Excess net long-term capital gain	$ 2,500

Taxation of Individual Net Long-Term Capital Gains. Individual net long-term capital gains are taxed at the investor's ordinary tax rate on 40 percent of the net long-term capital gain; the remaining 60 percent is taxed by the minimum tax rules. The minimum tax rules were discussed in Chapter 13.

The calculation of capital gains and losses may result in an excess net long-term capital gain. Exhibit 14-2 shows that an excess net long-term capital gain of $2,500 may result from a net long-term capital gain and a net short-term capital loss. Sixty percent of the $2,500 may be deducted as a capital-gains preference. The remaining 40 percent of the $2,500 gain is taxed at the taxpayer's regular tax rate. If the taxpayer's regular "marginal" tax rate were 70 percent, 40 percent of the net long-term capital gain would be taxed at the 70 percent rate. If the taxpayer's regular rate were only 14 percent, 40 percent of the net long-term capital gain would be taxed at the 14 percent rate. Forty percent of $2,500 would be $1,000, the amount taxable as a capital gain. This amount times 14 percent would result in a tax expense of $140.

Tax Treatment of Individual Net Long-Term Capital Losses. As of the Tax Reform Act of 1976, the maximum deduction from ordinary income for excess individual long-term capital losses is $3,000. Only half of the excess net long-term capital loss is currently deductible. The deduction from ordinary income may be as high as $3,000. Therefore, if the taxpayer calculates an excess net long-term capital loss of $6,000, a deduction of $3,000 may be made. Half of any loss under $6,000 is deductible. If the capital loss exceeds $6,000, the maximum deduction may be taken in the current year and the balance carried over to future years until that balance is used up.

Suppose that the taxpayer's ordinary income is $50,000, when the following financial situation occurs:

Long-term capital loss	$12,000	
Long-term capital gain	7,000	
Net long-term capital loss		5,000
Short-term capital gain	5,000	
Short-term capital loss	2,000	
Net short-term capital gain		3,000
Excess net long-term capital loss		2,000
		× .50
Amount currently deductible		$1,000

The $1,000 may be deducted from the ordinary income of $50,000, which reduces the ordinary income subject to taxation to $49,000. The other $1,000 of excess net long-term capital loss may not be deducted now or carried over to later years.

The Corporate Capital-Gains Treatment. Taxes are payable on corporate net long-term capital gains on the basis of the lesser of two methods of figuring the tax obligation. By the first method, the corporate net long-term capital gains are added to the regular corporate taxable income and the taxes are calculated using the applicable corporate tax rates. By the second method, the corporate net long-term capital gain is taxed at the alternative rate of 28 percent and the other corporate taxable income is taxed at the corporation's ordinary rates. The taxpayer may pay the lesser of the two amounts calculated.

Net short-term capital gains are taxed at regular corporate rates. Corporate capital gains are also subject to the regular 15 percent minimum tax, which was discussed in Chapter 13.

Tax Treatment of Corporate Net Capital Losses. The corporate net short-term loss is deductible dollar for dollar from corporate ordinary income. The adjustment cannot create a net operating loss, however. If there is an excess net short-term loss for the current tax year, this excess loss may be carried back to the three prior tax years and then ahead for the next five tax years. The same thing is true for corporate net long-term losses.

Taxation of Net Individual Short-Term Capital Gains and Losses. Excess net short-term capital gains are taxed dollar for dollar at the ordinary income tax rate of the

Exhibit 14-3. Calculation of After-Tax Net Cash Proceeds at Resale

1. Taxable gain

   Sales price (estimate) $ _____ $ _____
   Less:
     Acquisition cost   _____
     −Depreciation taken   _____
     Adjusted basis   _____

2. Excess depreciation

   Depreciation taken   _____
   −Straight-line depreciation   _____

   Excess depreciation   _____

3. Tax liability

   Income Taxed at Ordinary Rate
     Ordinary income taxed at ordinary rate $ _____ X . _____ = $ _____
     Excess depreciation taxed at
       ordinary rate   _____ X · _____ = _____

   Capital gains taxed at ordinary rate $_____

4. After-tax net cash proceeds of resale

   Sales price (net of commissions, prorated expenses, etc.)   _____
   Less:
     Balance outstanding on the mortgage   − _____

   Net cash reversion before tax (equity position)   _____
   Less:
     Tax liability   − _____

   After-tax net cash proceeds $ _____

taxpayer. Excess net short-term capital losses are deductible dollar for dollar from ordinary individual income, up to a maximum of $3,000. Any remaining balance may be carried over to future tax years until the excess net short-term capital loss is used up.

Capital-Gains Taxation in the Calculation of After-Net Cash Proceeds at Resale. The short- and long-term capital gains and losses enter into the investor's overall tax picture. Exhibit 14-3 shows a brief method of calculation of after-tax net cash proceeds from the sale of property, including the computation of the tax liability. The ordinary income subject to the ordinary tax rate is net of excess net capital losses.

Exhibit 14-4 summarizes briefly the taxation of corporate and individual short- and long-term capital gains and losses.

Recapture of Excess Depreciation. At the time of property sale, the amount of depreciation used to figure the adjusted basis may reflect the use of accelerated depreciation rather than straight-line depreciation throughout the investment holding period. The depreciation in excess of the amount of depreciation calculated under the straight-line method must be taxed at the taxpayer's ordinary income tax rate (Exhibit 14-3).

For example, the depreciable cost of an income-producing property might have been $1,000,000, and its economic life when new might have been estimated at 50 years. The taxpayer may have depreciated the property on the allowable method of double declining balance over the five years preceding the sale.

Exhibit 14-4. Taxation of Capital Asset Transactions

Individuals	
Net long-term gain:	40% of gain treated as ordinary income
	60% of gain treated as a tax preference item subject to minimum tax rules
Net long-term loss:	Offset against ordinary income 50 cents on the dollar, with a maximum deduction per year of $3,000; balance carried over to future years until it is used up
Net short-term gain:	Taxed at regular rates
Net short-term loss:	Up to $3,000 deducted in the tax year incurred against ordinary income dollar for dollar; balance carried over to future years until it is used up
Corporations	
Net long-term gain:	Taxed at 28% rate or taxed with other ordinary income at regular rates, whichever is lower
Net long-term loss:	Offset against ordinary income dollar for dollar; adjustments to ordinary income cannot create a net operating loss
	Balance subject to three-year carryback and then five-year carryover
Net short-term gain:	Taxed at regular rates
Net short-term loss:	Offset against ordinary income dollar for dollar; adjustments to ordinary income cannot create a net operating loss
	Balance subject to three-year carryback and then five-year carryover

The amount of depreciation using the double declining balance method:

First year: $1,000,000 \times \left(\dfrac{1}{50} \times 2\right)$, or $1,000,000 \times 0.04$ = $ 40,000.00
Second year: ($1,000,000 − $40,000) × 0.04, or $960,000 × 0.04 = 38,400.00
Third year: ($960,000 − $38,400) × 0.04, or $921,600 × 0.04 = 36,864.00
Fourth year: ($921,600 − $36,864) × 0.04, or $884,736 × 0.04 = 35,389.44
Fifth year: ($884,736 − $35,389) × 0.04, or $849,347 × 0.04 = 33,973.88
Total depreciation using the double declining balance method = $184,627.32

The amount of depreciation using the straight-line method:

$1,000,000 \times \dfrac{1}{50} \times 5$ = $100,000.00
Excess depreciation subject to ordinary income tax rates = $ 84,627.32

THE INSTALLMENT SALE OF REAL PROPERTY

Taxes on the profits from the sale of property may be deferred through the installment sale of real property. If real property is sold for a single payment, the taxes on the gain may be very significant. If the property is sold through the payment of a sum in the year of sale and further payments over the succeeding years, so that the total payments equal the sale price, tax payments are spread over the period of years of the payments, and the total tax payment may be lower than the payment of taxes on the single payment.

The buyer may prefer payments over a period of years rather than full payment for the purchased property immediately. In other words, property may be more marketable through installment sales. Also, when a long-term capital gain is deferred into the future, the gain may be matched against a loss that may be realized in the future. Taxes may be lowered as the gain offsets the loss. A gain that is deferred may become payable in a year when the taxpayer's rate bracket is lower than today's bracket.

Two or more payments for the installment sale are required. If only two payments are involved, each of the payments should be required in separate taxable years. The installment sale should be reported to the Internal Revenue Service in the year that the title was closed. The initial payments made in the year of the sale should not exceed 30 percent of the total selling price. The selling price is usually the gross contract price. Even though commissions and other selling expenses that reduce the net profit on the sale may have been incurred, the gross contract price is not reduced by these amounts.

Payments in the year of sale include all payments made by the buyer in the year the sale is closed, whether in cash or property, and all payments made by the buyer in the year prior to the title transfer, when the sales contract may have been signed but the title not conveyed. If a note of the buyer comes due in the year of the sale and title closing, the amount of the note becomes part of the initial payment. If the buyer's note comes due in subsequent years, the amount becomes a part of the installment payment received by the seller in the year the note becomes due and not part of the initial payment of the installment sale.

If a buyer assumes a mortgage of the seller as part of the initial payment, the amount that the mortgage exceeds the seller's basis for the property sold becomes a part of the payment received in the year of sale. If the buyer gives readily marketable bonds or debentures issued by a corporation, a government agency, or other government entity as part of the purchase price, the seller must consider the payments received in the year of sale as a part of the initial payment.

Computation of First-Year Reportable Gain and the Percentage of Each Future Payment That Must Be Reported by the Seller as Gain. The reportable gain in the first year depends on whether the gain is eligible for capital gains or ordinary income tax treatment. The percentage of the future payments that are reportable as gains depends on the ratio of total profit to the contract price. The contract price is defined by the Internal Revenue Service to be the entire amount the seller will receive, excluding any assumed mortgages. If the assumed mortgage exceeds in value the seller's cost basis for the property, the excess becomes part of the contract price.

For example, the selling price of a property may be $30,000 and its cost basis $20,000. The buyer agrees to assume an existing $6,000 mortgage and gives his own mortgage for $17,000. The purchase-money mortgage is payable over a 20-year period. The downpayment is $7,000, and the payments in the first year total $1,500.

Thirty percent of the selling price of $30,000 would be $9,000. Since a total of $8,500 was received in the year of sale, and $8,500 is less than 30 percent of the selling price ($9,000), the sale qualifies for installment reporting.

The first year's calculations follow:

Selling price	$30,000	
Cost basis	20,000	
Gain	10,000	
Payments received		8,500
Selling price	30,000	
Less mortgage assumed	6,000	
Contract price	$24,000	
Profit percentage: $10,000 divided by $24,000, or 42%.		
Reportable gain since long-term capital gains are involved (42% × $10,000)		$4,200

The $4,200 is subject to capital-gains taxation in the year of sale. Each of the future installment payments is subject to capital-gains taxation on 42 percent of each payment. The transaction qualified for installment sale reporting, since the $8,500 received in the year of sale was less than 30 percent of the selling price.

THE TAX-FREE EXCHANGE OF BUSINESS OR INVESTMENT REAL ESTATE

The owner of real property used in a trade or business or held as investment property may exchange her or his property for other property of like kind and avoid immediate payment of taxes that would normally result from the direct sale of the property. The exchange of business or investment real estate may be tax free. If the exchange is tax free, taxes will eventually be paid as the property acquired in the exchange is sold. Then taxes figured at the capital gains or ordinary rate of the taxpayer will be collected by the Internal Revenue Service.

The owner of property may wish to acquire new property and avoid current taxation on the sale of existing income-producing property. If new income-producing property is acquired immediately through the use of a property exchange, income and time are not lost between the sale of the existing income property and the acquisition of the next property. The cash flow to the property owner is continuous and not interrupted by the time taken in the search for a new income property.

When mortgage money is scarce, it may be difficult for the property owner to find a buyer who can pay for the equity in cash. It may be difficult for the prospective buyer to find mortgage money to supplement his or her cash in order to acquire the equity of the property being sold. In a direct sale, the seller would probably have to provide financing to the buyer through a purchase-money mortgage. As the seller attempts to buy another property, the seller might find that an insufficient amount of cash was immediately available to acquire another property immediately. The exchange may permit the trade of the existing equities in the traded properties and not require purchase-money mortgage financing by the seller.

Like-Kind Property. A tax-free exchange of property must involve exchange of like-kind properties. A property held for productive use in a trade or business or for investment can be exchanged tax free for a property held for productive use in a trade or business or for investment. Property held for productive use in a trade or business can be exchanged tax free for a property held for investment. The reverse is also true. An acquired property cannot be used for a residence in a tax-free exchange. The properties subject to tax-free exchange must be of like-kind with regard to their nature or character, but not with regard to their grade or quality. For example, city real estate may be exchanged for ranch or farm property; real property may be exchanged for a leasehold estate with 30 years or more to run; improved real estate may be exchanged for unimproved real estate; and so on.

Holding Period for the Property Acquired. After the exchange, the property acquired must be held for a reasonable period of time before it may be resold, in order for the exchange to be treated as tax free. If a real estate dealer makes the exchange with the purpose of immediate resale, the exchange will not be considered tax free.

The Basis for the Acquired Property. If a property is exchanged for another with the same value, the basis of the original property is assumed for the acquired property. For example, the taxpayer who owns real estate with a value of $70,000 and a basis of $20,000 may exchange it tax free for another like-kind property with a value of $70,000. The taxpayer would pay no capital gains or ordinary income taxes on the transfer at the time of the exchange. When the acquired property is sold later, after the taxpayer has held the property as an investment for a reasonable period of time, the sale of the acquired property would result in taxation on the difference between the basis of $20,000 assumed from the original property and the net sale price. If the taxpayer sold the property later for $70,000, a taxable gain of $50,000 ($70,000 sale price − $20,000 basis for the acquired property) would be realized and taxed at the appropriate rate. In contrast, if the taxpayer sold the original property outright, the taxable gain of $50,000 would be taxed immediately.

The Exchange of Mortgaged Properties. When mortgaged properties are exchanged, the amount of gain recognized for tax purposes is the lesser of (1) the gain realized or (2) the total value of the unlike property received in the exchange. The gain realized by each party must be determined. At the same time, the value of the unlike property received by each party to the exchange must be noted. The following example illustrates the computations involved:

Jones owns a building worth $150,000. The basis of his property is $25,000, and the building is subject to a $100,000 mortgage. Smith owns a building worth $200,000; its basis is $20,000. Smith's property is subject to a mortgage of $150,000.

Jones exchanges his building for Smith's building plus $40,000 in cash. Each party figures his gain in the following manner:

Jones received		
Value of Smith's property	$200,000	
Cash payment	40,000	
Mortgage on the old property	100,000	
Total amount received	340,000	
Jones gave		
Adjusted basis on the old property	25,000	
Mortgage on the new property	150,000	
Total amount given	175,000	
Jones' realized gain		$165,000

Smith received		
Value of Jones' property	$150,000	
Mortgage on the old property	150,000	
Total amount received	$300,000	
Smith gave		
Adjusted basis of the old property	20,000	
Cash paid	40,000	
Mortgage on the new property	100,000	
Total amount given	160,000	
Smith's realized gain		$140,000

According to the stated tax rules, the amount of gain recognized for tax purposes is the lesser of (1) the gain realized or (2) the total value of the unlike property received in the exchange. Therefore, Jones would recognize for tax purposes only $40,000 of gain, since the gain realized ($165,000) is more than the value of the unlike property received ($40,000). The $40,000 is the lesser amount of the two.

Smith gave up a mortgage of $150,000 on his original property and received a mortgage of $100,000 on the property he acquired. The net mortgage relief was $50,000. Since he paid $40,000 in cash, the net amount of the unlike property, or boot, was $10,000. Only $10,000 of the realized gain of $140,000 is currently taxable.

The Tax Consequences of the Exchange Involving Boot and Mortgages. When real estate is exchanged by two or more parties to a transaction, quite often boot and mortgages are involved. The term *boot* applies to money or property that is not of like-kind to the property exchanged. In contrast, mortgages are financing contracts between the mortgagor and the mortgagee. The tax code generally says that the adjusted basis of the old property is increased by the amount of the gain recognized, decreased by the amount of the loss recognized, and decreased by the amount of boot received. The tax regulation for this purpose provides that the amount of the mortgage on the property exchanged is treated as boot received, even if the mortgage is assumed by the other party.

In determining the basis of the property involved in a tax-free exchange, we can use the following formula:

Start with:	Adjusted basis of the older property	
Add:	Boot paid	
	Mortgage on the new property	
	Recognized gain	
Subtract:	Boot received	
	Mortgage on the old property	
Total:	Basis for the new property	

An example of the use of this formula follows (the Jones–Smith example is used):

	Jones		Smith	
Adjusted basis of the old property	$ 25,000		$ 20,000	
Add:				
Boot paid			40,000	
Mortgage on the new property	150,000		100,000	
Recognized gain	40,000		10,000	
Total		215,000		170,000
Subtract:				
Boot received	40,000			
Mortgage on the old property	100,000		150,000	
Total		140,000		150,000
Basis for the new property		$ 75,000		$ 20,000

TAX-FREE HOME SALES

There are two situations in which home sales may be tax free: (1) when the homeowner sells her or his principal residence and replaces it with an equally valued or more expensive principal residence within a specified period of time and (2) when the homeowner is 55 years of age or older and sells her or his principal residence, on a once-in-a-lifetime basis, after that residence has been lived in by the taxpayer three years out of the five years immediately prior to the sale. Once in a lifetime, according to the Revenue Act of 1978, a taxpayer at least 55 years old may exclude up to $100,000 of the gain realized on the sale of a principal residence, after July 26, 1978. Before July 26, 1981, a taxpayer aged 65 or older who made such a sale or exchange could exercise the one-in-a-lifetime tax provision, if the taxpayer lived five of the eight years immediately prior to the sale in the principal residence. The tax break is available only once during the lifetimes of the taxpayer and spouse. Short, temporary absences from the home for vacation and other seasonal occasions are not excluded from the required period of use.

The Sale of a Principal Residence and Its Replacement. If a taxpayer sells his or her home, generally speaking, any gain must be recognized for tax purposes. If the taxpayer replaces his or her principal residence with the sale proceeds and the new home is equal in value or exceeds in value the adjusted sale price of the original residence, all of the federal income taxes ordinarily due to the sale are deferred. The new existing home must be purchased within 18 months before or after the sale of the original home, or the new house under construction must be completed and lived in within 24 months of the sale.

The Terminology and Conditions of the Transaction. If the cost of the replacement home equals or exceeds the adjusted sale price of the former residence, no tax is due. Otherwise, a gain may be recognized for tax purposes. The *adjusted sale price* of the original home is the selling price of the old residence, less the selling and fix-up expenses incurred. The fix-up expenses must be incurred within 90 days before the sale and must be paid within 30 days after the sale. The cost of the new residence is the amount paid plus the sales commissions and other purchasing expenses. The sale and purchase prices include the mortgages on the properties.

The individual taxpayer may sell his or her existing home and replace it with a new home to take advantage of the tax break any number of times, but the required time between two such transactions is 18 months, unless the sales are related to the person's employment. If an employer requires the sale of the property before 18 months has expired and a replacement house must be purchased at another employment location, a tax-free sale is permitted the taxpayer. Only the principal residence of the taxpayer is involved in the tax regulation, even though the taxpayer may own two or more homes at any time. The term *residence* encompasses traditional single-family dwellings, mobile homes, cooperative or condominium apartments or houses, and houseboats.

Calculation of the Gain Recognized for Tax Purposes. In order to arrive at the gain recognized for tax purposes—if there is any—the amount realized on the sale, the capital gain realized on the sale, and the adjusted sale price must be calculated. An illustration is given below.

A taxpayer sold his residence, which had a basis of $50,000. In order to sell it quickly, he painted the outside at a cost of $500 in July 1981. He paid for the painting when the work was done. In August 1981, he sold the house for $72,000. Brokerage commissions and other selling expenses were $3,600. In December 1981, the taxpayer bought a new home for $65,000. The following calculations were required:

Selling price	$72,000
Less commissions and other selling expenses	3,600
Amount realized	68,400
Less basis of the old home	50,000
Gain realized	18,400
Amount realized	68,400
Less fix-up expenses	500
Adjusted sale price	67,900
Cost of purchasing the new home	65,000
Gain recognized for tax purposes	$ 2,900

Calculation of the Adjusted Basis for the New Residence. As the original home is sold and replaced by the new residence, the taxpayer needs to know the adjusted basis of the new residence. Taxes will be due in the future on this sale, but they will be paid on the difference between the sale price of the new residence and its adjusted basis. The adjusted basis for the new residence is calculated below.

Gain realized	$18,400
Less gain recognized	2,900
Gain realized but not recognized for tax purposes	15,500
Cost of the new residence	65,000
Less gain realized but not recognized	15,500
Adjusted basis of the new residence	$49,500

SUMMARY

Tax provisions vitally affect the termination stage of real estate investment, just as they strategically affect the planning and operating stages. When a property is sold and total payment is expected immediately, the gain or loss must be computed on the sale and the nature of the gain—capital gain or ordinary gain—determined. A property must be held 12 months or more before its sale in order for the gain to be considered a capital gain. As the investor's overall gain or loss position is assessed, the net long-term gain or loss position must be weighed against the net short-term gain or loss position. If a net short-term gain results, this gain is taxed at the taxpayer's ordinary income tax rate. If a net long-term gain results, 40 percent of the capital gain is taxed at the taxpayer's ordinary rate. The 60 percent of the net long-term gain is a capital-gains preference item, which is subject to the regular minimum tax or the alternative minimum tax, whichever results in the highest tax payment.

If tax regulations permit accelerated depreciation of the taxpayer's investment property, the taxpayer may decide whether to use straight-line or accelerated depreciation up to the maximum limit. If the investment property is sold after accelerated depreciation has been utilized, the taxpayer must pay income taxes at the ordinary rate on the excess depreciation taken over the straight-line depreciation amount.

If the taxpayer wishes to defer income taxes, real property may be sold by the installment plan, whereby the seller receives no more than 30 percent of the sale price in the initial year of the sale. The tax payment the first year depends on the nature of the gain on the sale. If a long-term capital gain is recognized, 40 percent of the gain received in the first year is subject to taxation at the taxpayer's ordinary rate. If the sale results in a short-term capital gain, the principal amount received is taxed in total at the taxpayer's ordinary rate. Each of the future installment payments is subject to capital-gains taxation on a portion of each of the payments. The portion is calculated by dividing the overall gain on the sale by the contract price of the sale, which is the difference between the selling price and the mortgage assumed.

Taxes may also be deferred through the exchange of business or investment real estate. If equally valued properties are exchanged with no boot or mortgages involved, the exchange may be totally tax free if the holding period and like-kind property requirements are met. If boot or mortgages are involved in the exchange, the payments received in these forms may be subject to taxation.

If a principal residence is sold and replaced within 18 months with an existing home or within 24 months with a newly constructed home, capital-gains taxes on the sale may be deferred. Generally, the newly acquired property assumes the basis of the original property, and the gain that is taxable on the future sale is the difference between the original basis and the sale price. If a principal residence of a taxpayer 55 years of age or older is sold after the home has been lived in for three years out of the five years immediately prior to the sale, the taxpayer may exclude, on a once-in-a-lifetime basis, up to $100,000 of the gain realized on the sale after July 26, 1978. If the taxpayer is 65 years of age or older and wants to use the tax benefit before July 26, 1981, the taxpayer may satisfy the requirement by living in the house five out of the eight years immediately preceding the sale. The capital gain is the difference between the adjusted sale price and the basis of the property at the time of sale.

Key Terms and Concepts

Installment sale
Property exchange
Tax deferral
Selling expenses
Tax-free exchange
Tax code
Adjusted sale price
Adjusted basis
Net gain on a sale
Marginal tax rate

Gross contract price
Like-kind property
Mortgage assumption
Cost of new residence
Long-term capital loss
Net cash reversion before tax
After-tax net cash proceeds
Realized gain
Boot
Recognized gain

Questions for Student Self-examination

Multiple-Choice Questions

1. When an investor wishes to terminate a particular real property investment, she or he may decide to
   a. sell the property on an installment basis
   b. exchange the property for another property
   c. sell the property outright
   d. all of the above are possibilities

2. Taxes on the gain on the sale of property may be deferred by
   a. borrowing money on the property before the sale
   b. use of escrow arrangements
   c. long-term leasing of depreciable property
   d. all of the above

3. When an investment property is sold, (a) _____ is realized.
   a. gain
   b. loss
   c. no change
   d. any of the above

4. The adjusted basis is derived from subtracting _____ from the total cost of the improvements sold.
   a. selling expenses
   b. depreciation deductions
   c. mortgages
   d. notes given to pay the purchase price

5. In 1978 and subsequent years, property must be held for more than _____ by the investor in order for the gain or loss to be treated as long-term gain or loss.
   a. 3 months
   b. 6 months
   c. 9 months
   d. 12 months

True-False Questions

T F 1. The capital gains holding period gradually shortened with the tax laws of the 1970s.

T F 2. If the current property is the owner's residence, the ordinary or capital gains taxes may be currently avoided and the tax payment deferred by the sale of the original property and purchase of another such property within two years of the sale of the original property.

T F 3. The nature of the capital gain—short- or long-term—can be recognized on the basis of the holding period and tax regulations.

T F 4. Adjusted sale price results from the subtraction of selling expenses from the value of the cash, mortgages, and notes given to pay the purchase price.

T F 5. The total cost of an improvement sold may amount to a total of the original cost of a structure and its site improvements plus the cost of later improvements to the property.

T F 6. The net gain, loss, or lack of change on a property sale is found by subtracting the adjusted sale price from the adjusted basis.

T F 7. For federal income purposes, long-term capital losses are first subtracted from the long-term capital gains.

T F 8. If the investor calculates an overall net short-term capital gain, that gain is taxed at the investor's ordinary income tax rate.

T F 9. If the property owner sells the property on an installment basis and wishes to defer taxes, the initial payment made in the year of the sale should not exceed 20 percent of the total selling price.

T F 10. The exchange of business or investment real estate may be tax free.

Answers
Multiple-Choice: 1d, 2d, 3d, 4b, 5d.
True-False: 1F, 2F, 3T, 4T, 5T, 6F, 7T, 8T, 9F, 10T.

Problems

1. What is the adjusted sale price if the buyer pays $10,000 in cash, receives a purchase-money mortgage of $15,000 from the seller, and mortgages the property with a savings and loan association for $40,000? The seller incurs selling expenses of $5,000.

2. What is the adjusted basis if the building cost $80,000, the improvements after purchase cost $15,000, and the depreciation deductions so far are $25,000?

3. What was the net gain on the sale price if the total sale price was $100,000, the adjusted sale price was $75,000, the depreciation deductions were $20,000, and the adjusted basis was $62,000?

4. If the investor held an apartment building seven months before selling it, would the possible gain be considered short- or long-term for federal income tax purposes?

5. If the net long-term capital gain is $10,000, the short-term capital loss is $2,000, and the short-term capital gain is $1,000, what is the overall status of the capital gain or loss?

6. If the investor has a net long-term capital gain of $10,000, how much of the gain is taxed at half of the investor's ordinary tax rate? How much is taxed by the minimum tax rules?

7. If the corporation's net long-term capital gains are $20,000 and the corporate taxable income is $30,000, how much would be paid in taxes on the net long-term capital gain?

Part Four

Real Estate Investment Analysis

Chapter 15
Cash Flow and Profit Planning

Introduction
The Relationship of This Chapter to Other Chapters of the Text
Cash Flow Versus Profit
    Pro Forma Statements and the System for Deriving Cash Flow to Equity
Forecasting Cash Inflows and Outflows
    The Impact of Inflation   The Impact of the General Economic and Real Estate Cycles   The Complexities of Forecasting Future Cash Flows
Cash Flow Differences in Terms of the Basic Investment Forms
Cash Flows by the Stage of Real Estate Investment and Development
Cash Flows of the Planning Stage
    The Use of Leverage   The Loan-to-Value Ratio   The Debt Coverage Ratio
Cash Flows of the Operating Stage
    The Operating Ratio   The Breakeven Ratio
Cash Flows of the Termination Stage
Summary
Key Terms and Concepts
Questions for Student Self-examination

LEARNING OBJECTIVES After studying this chapter, you should be familiar with

The differences between cash flow and profit
Derivation of pro forma statements
The system for deriving cash flow to equity
Forecasting cash inflows and outflows
The impact of inflation on cash flows
The impact of the general economic and real estate cycles on cash flow forecasting
Cash flow differences in terms of the basic investment forms
Cash flows of the planning stage of real estate development
The favorable use of leverage
The importance of ratio analysis during the planning stage
Cash flows of the operating stage of real estate development
The importance of ratio analysis during the operating stage
Cash flows of the termination stage of real estate development

Cash flow estimation and profit planning are both important to the real estate investor. Profit projections enable the investor to estimate future tax obligations or cash outflows for the payment of taxes. Cash flow estimates give the investor an idea of the possible return on the cash invested and how much cash is needed at specific intervals to cover net outlays.

INTRODUCTION

Chapter 15, the first chapter of Part IV, "Real Estate Investment Analysis," deals with cash flow planning and analysis. While the focus of the material is on cash flows, the concept of profit and its relevance are placed in perspective from the real estate investment viewpoint.

Cash flows are related to the three stages of real estate investment—the planning, operating, and termination stages. The variations in cash flow distributions with regard to the basic investment forms—acreage investment, land subdivision and sales, and land development and sales—are also acknowledged.

The focal points of five- to ten-year cash planning are noted. A sample 22-year projection is presented so that the reader may see the overall trend in projected annual and accumulated cash flow, taxable income, after-tax cash benefits, and the permanent loan balance. The cash outflows for construction, operating costs, and mortgage amortization are indicated, along with the cash inflows from building rental and refinancing.

THE RELATIONSHIP OF THIS CHAPTER TO OTHER CHAPTERS OF THE TEXT

This chapter introduces the section on real estate investment analysis. As the chapter distinguishes between cash flows and profits, the raw material for investment return analysis is observed. Chapter 16 takes the cash flows generated by an investment and analyzes their future and present values in terms of single sums and annuities. Chapter

17 identifies the methods of investment return measurement most commonly utilized. Each method requires the availability of specific profit and cash flow measures.

The previous three parts of the text have introduced real estate investment fundamentals, the principles and practices of property financing and appraising, and portfolio strategies in terms of investment goals, risk assumption, portfolio diversification, and tax regulations. The last part of the text analyzes the investment conditions related to specific types of properties.

CASH FLOW VERSUS PROFIT

The real estate investor tends to be concerned with the cash flow from an investment and how the after-tax flow relates to the cash investment. In order to calculate the expected cash flow per period, the net profit from the investment must be determined, so that the federal income tax payment can be figured. The investor usually wants to know the cash *throw-off*—or cash flow—to equity after the payment of federal income taxes. Therefore, the definitions of *cash flow* and *profit* are important.

The term *profit* applies to the taxable income from an investment. An investment may generate either a profit or a loss, depending on the balance between revenues and costs. If the revenues exceed the costs, the investment generates a profit. In real estate investment analysis, taxable income, or net profit, arises from the surplus of effective gross income over operating expenses, mortgage interest, and depreciation expense. Another way of calculating net income, or taxable income, is illustrated below.

   Net operating income
 − Mortgage interest
 − Depreciation
 ─────────────────────
   Taxable income (negative or positive)

The Internal Revenue Service permits the deduction of mortgage interest and depreciation expense from net operating income for federal income tax purposes. The bottom-line amount is the taxable profit from operations.

After-tax income is found by subtracting the required federal income tax payment from the net profit or taxable income.

   Taxable income (profit)
 − Federal income tax payment
 ─────────────────────────
   After-tax income

If there is a loss rather than a profit generated from the operations, tax savings may benefit the investor. If the real estate investor realizes a tax loss from the real estate investment and, at the same time, receives taxable income from other sources, the loss from the real estate investment may be applied to the other taxable income. A tax savings results. Therefore, the tax savings resulting from a real estate loss equals.

   Tax loss
 × Federal income tax rate
 ─────────────────────────
   Tax savings

For example, if real estate operations result in a tax loss of $5,000, and the investor's tax rate is 40 percent, the tax savings for the investor would be $5,000 times 40 percent, or $2,000.

Cash flow, generally speaking, means the dollar difference between the cash inflows and the cash outflows associated with a real estate investment. Noncash expenses are not deducted from the cash inflows in order to derive the net cash flow. Noncash expenses are those expenses that are deducted from operating income for federal income tax purposes but that are actually expenses for which no cash is spent. For example, depreciation is often considered a noncash expense, since the tax deduction may be taken but no property depreciation may be experienced. No cash may be expended to maintain, repair, or modernize the property.

Cash flow may be figured on a before- or after-tax basis. On a before-tax basis, net cash flow is calculated in the following way:

Rental income
− Cash operating expenses
− Mortgage debt service (interest and principal repayment)
Net cash flow before federal income taxes (positive or negative)

Another way of calculating net cash flow before federal income taxes is

Taxable income (negative or positive)
+ Depreciation
+ Mortgage interest
Net cash flow before debt service and federal income taxes (positive or negative)

Exhibit 15-1. *Five-Year Pro Forma Statement of Income and Cash Flow American Real Estate Investors, Ltd.*

	Year 1	Year 2	Year 3	Year 4	Year 5
Income:					
Gross rents	$32,400	$34,200	$36,000	$37,000	$39,600
Less 5% vacancy	1,620	1,710	1,800	1,890	1,980
Net rental income	30,780	32,490	34,200	35,910	37,620
Other income: laundry	364	364	364	364	364
Effective gross income	31,144	32,854	34,564	36,274	37,984
Expenses:					
Management and rental fee (7% of gross income)	2,180	2,300	2,419	2,539	2,659
Other operating expense	5,903	6,257	6,632	7,030	7,452
Interest on mortages	14,190	14,019	13,834	13,633	14,415
Depreciation	9,500	9,025	8,574	8,145	7,738
Total expenses	31,773	31,601	31,459	31,347	31,264
Taxable income	(629)	1,253	3,105	4,927	6,720
Depreciation	9,500	9,025	8,574	8,145	7,738
Mortgage principal	(2,070)	(2,240)	(2,440)	(2,650)	(2,870)
Net cash generated after debt service and before taxes	$ 6,801	$ 8,038	$ 9,239	$10,422	$11,588

Exhibit 15-2. Cash Flow and After-Tax Cash and Benefits Chart for Proposed Office Development

	Year 1	Year 2	Year 3	Year 4	Year 5	Year 6	Year 7	Year 8	Year 9
Construction:									
Demolition and clearing	100,000		100,000						
Land development cost	100,000		75,000						
Construction costs	2,000,000	$5,500,000	4,000,000	$3,500,000					
On-site improvements	150,000	100,000	150,000	100,000					
Project administration	20,000	50,000	60,000	45,000					
Engineering architectural fees, and insurance	200,000	125,000	75,000	50,000					
Total	2,570,000	5,775,000	4,460,000	3,695,000					
Rental income:									
Old office building	197,000	197,000							
New office building #1			761,000	1,627,000	$1,689,000	$1,689,000	$1,689,000	$1,689,000	$1,689,000
New office building #2					761,000	1,627,000	1,689,000	1,689,000	1,689,000
Total	197,000	197,000	761,000	1,627,000	2,450,000	3,316,000	3,378,000	3,378,000	3,378,000
Expenses (cash):									
Ground rent	256,000	256,000	256,000	256,000	256,000	256,000	256,000	256,000	256,000
Real estate taxes	144,000	275,000	438,000	564,000	628,000	628,000	628,000	628,000	628,000
Mortgage interest	167,000	709,000	1,375,000	1,905,000	1,643,000	1,627,000	1,608,000	1,588,000	1,567,000
Mortgage fees	330,000		330,000		495,000				
Leasing costs		198,000	247,000	247,000	247,000	50,000			
Total	897,000	1,438,000	2,646,000	2,972,000	3,269,000	2,561,000	2,492,000	2,472,000	2,451,000
Amortization					156,000	172,000	191,000	211,000	232,000
Total expenses and amortization	897,000	1,438,000	2,646,000	2,972,000	3,425,000	2,733,000	2,683,000	2,683,000	2,683,000
Cash flow	(700,000)	(1,241,000)	(1,885,000)	(1,345,000)	(975,000)	583,000	695,000	695,000	695,000
Accumulated cash flow	(700,000)	(1,941,000)	(3,826,000)	(5,171,000)	(6,146,000)	(5,563,000)	(4,868,000)	(4,173,000)	(3,478,000)
Expenses (tax deduction)									
Ground rent	256,000	256,000	256,000	256,000	256,000	256,000	256,000	256,000	256,000
Real estate taxes	144,000	275,000	438,000	564,000	628,000	628,000	628,000	628,000	628,000
Mortgage interest	167,000	709,000	1,375,000	1,905,000	1,643,000	1,627,000	1,608,000	1,588,000	1,567,000
Mortgage fees	82,000	82,000	248,000	248,000	50,000	50,000	50,000	50,000	50,000
Leasing costs		10,000	22,000	35,000	47,000	49,000	49,000	49,000	49,000
Depreciation			275,000	266,000	532,000	514,000	497,000	480,000	464,000
Total	649,000	1,332,000	2,614,000	3,274,000	3,156,000	3,124,000	3,088,000	3,051,000	3,014,000
Taxable income	(452,000)	(1,135,000)	(1,853,000)	(1,647,000)	(706,000)	192,000	290,000	327,000	364,000
Income tax (50%)	(226,000)	(568,000)	(927,000)	(824,000)	(353,000)	96,000	145,000	164,000	182,000
Refinancing surplus									
After-tax cash and benefits	(474,000)	(673,000)	(958,000)	(521,000)	(622,000)	487,000	550,000	531,000	513,000
Construction loan advance	2,570,000	5,775,000	4,460,000	3,695,000					
Construction loan balance	$2,570,000	$8,345,000	$12,805,000	16,500,000					
Permanent loan balance				$16,500,000	$16,344,000	$16,172,000	$15,981,000	$15,770,000	$15,538,000

Note: IRRAT means Internal Rate of Return After Taxes

The net cash flow after debt service payment and federal income taxes is calculated as follows:

Net cash flow before debt service and taxes
— Mortgage payment (interest and mortgage amortization)
— Federal income tax payment (or add tax savings)
After-tax cash flow (total cash benefits to equity)

Pro Forma Statements and the System for Deriving Cash Flow to Equity. In the process of analyzing real estate investment returns, the analyst usually sets up pro forma statements of forecasted investment results. Several years may be covered by the projected statements. Exhibit 15-1 shows a five-year pro forma statement of income and cash flow for a two-bedroom townhouse development to be financed by a limited partnership. The net cash flow before debt service and taxes is indicated on the bottom line. A 22-year pro forma statement for proposed redevelopment of an office building complex may be seen in Exhibit 15-2. This pro forma statement includes construction and demolition costs, taxable income, after-tax benefits, the construction loan balance per period, and the permanent loan balance per period.

The overall system for cash flow analysis may be described by the following hierarchy of accounts:

	Year 10	Year 11	Year 12	Year 13	Year 14	Year 15	Year 16	Year 17	Year 18	Year 19	Year 20	Year 21	Year 22
	$ 1,689,000	$ 1,689,000	$ 1,689,000	$ 2,278,000	$ 2,531,000	$ 2,531,000	$ 2,531,000	$ 2,531,000	$ 2,531,000	$ 2,531,000	$ 2,531,000	$ 2,531,000	$ 2,531,000
	1,689,000	1,689,000	1,689,000	1,689,000	1,689,000	2,278,000	2,531,000	2,531,000	2,531,000	2,531,000	2,531,000	2,531,000	2,531,000
	3,378,000	3,378,000	3,378,000	3,967,000	4,220,000	4,809,000	5,062,000	5,062,000	5,062,000	5,062,000	5,062,000	5,062,000	5,062,000
	256,000	384,000	384,000	384,000	384,000	384,000	384,000	384,000	384,000	384,000	384,000	512,000	512,000
	628,000	628,000	628,000	628,000	628,000	628,000	628,000	628,000	628,000	628,000	628,000	628,000	628,000
	1,542,000	1,515,000	1,485,000	1,452,000	1,416,000	2,639,000	2,612,000	2,583,000	2,551,000	2,516,000	2,477,000	2,433,000	2,386,000
	2,426,000	2,527,000	2,497,000	2,464,000	2,428,000	4,446,000	3,624,000	3,595,000	3,563,000	3,528,000	3,489,000	3,573,000	3,526,000
	257,000	284,000	314,000	347,000	383,000	250,000	277,000	306,000	338,000	373,000	412,000	456,000	503,000
	2,683,000	2,811,000	2,811,000	2,811,000	2,811,000	4,696,000	3,901,000	3,901,000	3,901,000	3,901,000	3,901,000	4,029,000	4,029,000
	695,000	567,000	567,000	1,156,000	1,409,000	113,000	1,161,000	1,161,000	1,161,000	1,161,000	1,161,000	1,033,000	1,033,000
	(2,783,000)	(2,216,000)	(1,649,000)	(493,000)	916,000	1,029,000	2,190,000	3,351,000	4,512,000	5,673,000	6,834,000	7,867,000	8,900,000
	256,000	384,000	384,000	384,000	384,000	384,000	384,000	384,000	384,000	384,000	384,000	512,000	512,000
	628,000	628,000	628,000	628,000	628,000	628,000	628,-00	628,000	628,000	628,000	628,000	628,000	628,000
	1,542,000	1,515,000	1,485,000	1,452,000	1,416,000	2,639,000	2,612,000	2,583,000	2,551,000	2,516,000	2,477,000	2,433,000	2,386,000
	50,000	50,000	50,000	50,000	50,000	79,000	79,000	79,000	79,000	79,000	79,000	79,000	79,000
	49,000	49,000	49,000	49,000	49,000	49,000	49,000	49,000	49,000	49,000	49,000	49,000	49,000
	449,000	434,000	420,000	406,000	392,000	379,000	366,000	354,000	342,000	336,000	330,000	330,000	330,000
	2,974,000	3,060,000	3,016,000	2,969,000	2,919,000	4,158,000	4,118,000	4,077,000	4,033,000	3,992,000	3,947,000	4,031,000	3,984,000
	404,000	318,000	362,000	998,000	1,301,000	651,000	944,000	985,000	1,029,000	1,070,000	1,115,000	1,031,000	1,078,000
	202,000	159,000	181,000	499,000	651,000	326,000	472,000	493,000	515,000	535,000	558,000	516,000	539,000
						12,547,000							
	493,000	408,000	386,000	657,000	758,000	12,334,000	689,000	668,000	646,000	626,000	603,000	517,000	494,000
	5,281,000	$14,997,000	$14,683,000	$14,336,000	$13,953,000	$26,250,000	$25,973,000	$25,667,000	$25,329,000	$24,956,000	$25,544,000	$24,088,000	$23,585,000

$IRR^{AT} = 21\%$

Gross potential income
- Estimated vacancy and bad-debt expense

Effective gross income
- Operating expenses
  Fixed expenses
  Variable expenses
  Repair and maintenance
  Reserves for replacement

Net operating income
- Depreciation
- Mortgage interest

Taxable income (net profit)

Net operating income (cash flow before debt service and taxes)
- Debt service (interest and principal)

Cash throw-off (cash flow before taxes or cash flow to equity before taxes)
- Federal income tax payment

Spendable income (cash flow to equity after taxes)
+ Tax savings (from taxable loss)

After-tax cash benefits to equity

These balances may be used in real estate investment return analysis. The selected balance may be compared against the equity investment or the total capital invest-

Cash Flow and Profit Planning   253

ment. If the cash flow results for more than one year are considered, present value techniques may be useful.

FORECASTING CASH INFLOWS AND OUTFLOWS

Most cash inflows and outflows related to real estate investment vary with time. Two of the most important factors affecting the level and certainty of the cash flows are (1) the pattern of continuing inflation and (2) the movement of the general business and real estate cycles.

The Impact of Inflation. Inflation affects real estate cash flows with an uneven distribution. During most of the 1970s, revenues, particularly from apartment space, rose, but they rose less than operating and financial costs. Inflation has also had an uneven impact on operating costs. Utility costs during the 1970s rose far more rapidly than repair, maintenance, and management costs. The energy crisis forced fuel and other energy costs relatively high over a short period of years.

The Impact of the General Economic and Real Estate Cycles. When the recession of 1974-1975 occurred as a result of high interest rates and the scarcity of funds, high levels of unemployment persisted; rents were maintained at the already high levels, but a relatively high level of building vacancy occurred. The financial costs on a relatively high level caused investor costs to rise a great deal; values of properties went down somewhat, because of the relatively low level of cash flows and high capitalization rates. During the prosperity of 1975-1978 rents increased as vacant space disappeared. Increasing personal incomes and business profits caused a higher demand for space. Higher rents could be paid. Construction costs continued to rise, whereas mortgage monies became more available at a more reasonable cost. Utility costs continued to climb, and management expenses remained relatively steady.

The Complexities of Forecasting Future Cash Flows. If the investor wants to estimate realistically the future cash flows from a property, the impact of future inflation trends and future rises and declines in the general economic and real estate cycles must be taken into account. The investor must predict realistically how much rents can be raised over the projection period. The increase in rents, of course, has a close relationship with the general income levels of the community residents and the profits of local business and industry. The rent levels will also depend on the swings in the business and real estate cycles that will be felt locally. Construction costs are closely related to the pattern of inflation and to the availability of construction materials. Labor costs associated with construction rose with inflation, but they did not surpass the rate of inflation the way that building material costs did during the 1970s. Will utility costs continue to rise slowly as they have during the latter 1970s, as Mideast oil prices have stabilized? Will the abundance of Alaskan crude oil stabilize U.S. oil prices, or will the building of the trans-Canadian oil and natural gas pipelines toward the Middle West and East force fuel prices even higher? What will be the pattern of repair and maintenance costs? Will the mortgage rates continue to rise with continued deficit spending by the federal government and pressure on the money and capital markets by business and consumers?

The complexities of forecasting future cash flows can be controlled through sensitivity analysis and the application of probabilities to expense and revenue estimates. Sensitivity analysis is concerned with the analysis of end results by changing one variable or expense-revenue account balance at a time. Sensitivity analysis might also apply to the change of the pattern of costs while the pattern of revenues is held constant. Alternatively, the pattern of revenues might be changed in different patterns while the cost structure is held steady. The end results, or the final cash flows, could be observed as the changes in one factor were made while the other factors were held constant. For example, rents might be permitted to rise 3 percent a year while operating costs were held steady, or the rents might be held at one level while the operating costs were permitted to rise 3 percent a year over the holding period. Perhaps a pattern of annual rent increases of 5 percent might be forecasted along with annual cost increases of 3 percent over the same projected investment period (Exhibit 15-3). The ending cash flow figures could be examined to see if the investor's objectives could be met realistically.

Expected values for each investment variable could be figured. The values for each important variable could be selected on the basis of an optimistic projection, most probable projection, and pessimistic projection. Each projected value could be assigned a probability of occurrence. The sum of the projected values times their probability of occurrence would give the expected value of an investment variable for the

Exhibit 15-3. *After-Tax Cash Flow from Four Different Assumptions, Apartment Building Yield Analysis*

Years	3% Annual Increase in Rent and Expense	3% Annual Increase in Expense and After Year 5 in Rent	6% Annual Increase in Rent; 3% Annual Increase In Expense	"Worst Case" Scenario: 3% Annual Increase in Rent and Expenses for Years 1-7; Stable Rents and 10% Expense Increase Thereafter
1	$110,474	$110,474	$110,474	$110,474
2	112,298	103,064	121,442	112,298
3	114,289	95,544	133,588	114,289
4	116,439	87,897	146,692	116,439
5	118,738	80,106	160,896	118,738
6	121,176	81,386	176,257	121,176
7	123,742	82,758	192,833	123,742
8	127,123	84,908	211,384	105,806
9	131,978	88,499	232,654	87,677
10	136,844	92,059	255,257	67,736

Source: Reprinted by permission from *The Real Estate Review*, Vol. 6, No. 2, Summer 1976, p. 51. Copyright 1976 by Warren, Gorham, and Lamont, Inc.; 210 South Street; Boston, Mass. All rights reserved.

Exhibit 15-4. *Utility Cost Estimation Using Probability Analysis*

Type of Projection	Estimated Annual Cost	Probability of Occurrence	Product
Pessimistic projection: (Highest possible annual utility cost)	$1,000	.35	$350
Most probable projection: (Most likely annual utility cost)	700	.50	350
Optimistic projection: (Lowest possible annual utility cost)	300	.15	45
		1.00	
Expected value of annual utility cost			$745

projected time interval. For example, utility costs might be estimated through calculation of expected values (Exhibit 15-4).

CASH FLOW DIFFERENCES IN TERMS OF THE BASIC INVESTMENT FORMS

The three basic investment forms have distinctive cash flow patterns. Acreage investment, the first basic investment form, involves land purchase at one time or in installment payments, tax deductibility of loan interest and property taxes, and taxation of possible capital gains at the time of property sale. The second basic investment form, land subdivision, involves land purchase at one time or in installment payments, land surveying expense, subdivision of the land into marketable parcels, cash flows from land sales taxable at the investor's ordinary income tax rate, and tax-deductible loan interest and property taxes spread over the time of the land holding.

Land development and improvement, the third basic investment form, involves payment and receipt of developer fees that are subject to taxation at the ordinary income tax rate of the developer. This investment form also involves equity investment, perhaps contributed by a number of investors, and mortgage financing for the remaining amount of the needed funds. Cash flows proceed from income property operations, mortgage financing, refinancing at a later time in the investment period, and sales proceeds at the end of the investment period. To summarize, the table below gives a capsule view.

Basic Investment Form	Distinctive Cash Flow Patterns
Acreage investment	Land purchase—outright or installment payments Tax-deductible loan interest and property taxes Capital-gains taxation at the time of property sale
Land subdivision investment	Land purchase Land surveying expense Subdivision of land for marketability Sales of land taxed at ordinary tax rate of investor Tax deductible loan interest and property taxes
Land development and improvement	Developer fee taxed at ordinary tax rate Equity contributed by one or more investors Cash flow from operations, mortgage financing, and refinancing Capital gains taxation at the time of property sale

CASH FLOWS BY THE STAGE OF REAL ESTATE INVESTMENT AND DEVELOPMENT

Cash flows differ according to the current stage of real estate investment and development. During the three stages of real estate investment, ratios using various cash flows measure the adequacy of these cash flows for successful financing and investment return. Cash inflows and outflows associated with the planning, operating, and termination stages of investment may be utilized in ratio analysis (Exhibit 15-5).

Exhibit 15-5. The Overall Cash Flow Picture

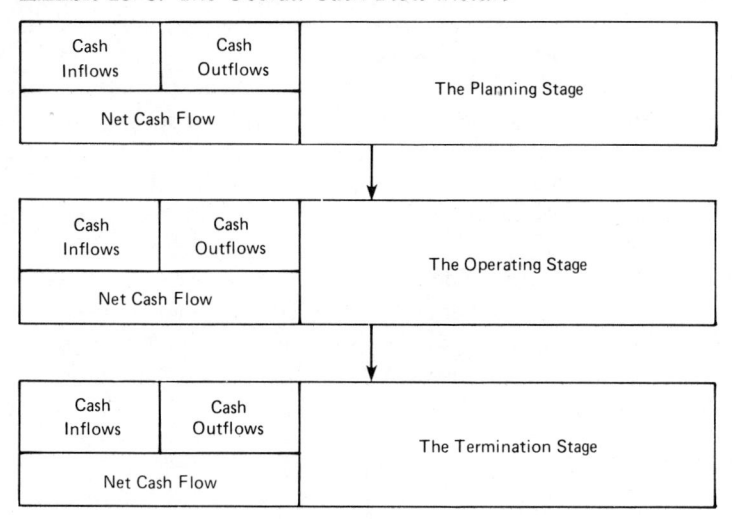

Cash Inflows	Cash Outflows	The Planning Stage
Net Cash Flow		

Cash Inflows	Cash Outflows	The Operating Stage
Net Cash Flow		

Cash Inflows	Cash Outflows	The Termination Stage
Net Cash Flow		

Cash Flows of the Planning Stage

The planning stage of real estate investment and development involves financing, organizational, architectural, demolition, construction, and management costs. There is little revenue and mainly outlays. The financing of the investment includes the raising of sufficient equity from the necessary number of investors; the acquisition of mortgage monies; the payment of the initial fees for insurance and development services; and the payment of fees for market, feasibility, and environmental studies. The closing costs on the necessary loans include the surveying fee, title insurance charge, prepaid interest, loan origination fees, recording fees, real estate commissions, and prorated financial and operating costs. Attorneys' fees must be paid for organizational expense. Architects' fees must be paid for the design of the new or remodeled structure and for the inspection services as construction progresses. If structures require demolition, the demolition costs must be paid. Construction costs must be paid from the equity and mortgage funds. Management costs in the form of developer fees and supervisory fees must be met before the investment reaches the operational stage.

The Use of Leverage. If the investor wishes to increase her or his return on equity investment through the use of mortgage funds, the investor may seek to *lever* the equity investment. As long as the total investment generates a return greater than the cost of the borrowed funds, the use of leverage or borrowed funds will inflate the return on the investor's equity contribution. Leverage can work in reverse, however. If the cost of borrowed funds exceeds the return on the total investment, the negative leverage will force a rapid decline in the owner's return on equity investment.

The Loan-to-Value Ratio. The cash flow from mortgage financing may be compared to the appraised value of the investment. The mortgage lender scrutinizes the loan-to-value ratio before advancing new or additional mortgage money. The investor should always consider the viewpoint of the lender if the investor seeks to employ positive leverage.

$$\text{Loan-to-value ratio} = \frac{\text{Loan amount}}{\text{Appraised value of property}}$$

The lender wants to know what portion of the appraised value has not previously been pledged for other mortgage loans. The remaining unpledged appraised value is the lender's security for the prospective loan.

Usually the first mortgage on income-producing property covers 66 2/3 to 80 percent of the appraised value of the property. The other subordinated mortgage loans cover much smaller portions of the appraised value. The lender usually wants to assure himself or his financial organization that a buffer of equity investment insulates the mortgage debt from rapid default if business or economic conditions quickly turn unfavorable.

The Debt Coverage Ratio. For financial protection, the lender usually wants to see a reasonable debt coverage ratio reflected from the cash flow statement. For an apartment project, the lender may want to see a minimum debt coverage ratio of 1.3; for a relatively risky motel mortgage, the lender may require a minimum ratio of 1.5. The ratio is calculated in the following way:

$$\text{Debt coverage ratio} = \frac{\text{Net operating income available for debt service}}{\text{Debt service}}$$

The protracted cash flow statement covering five to ten years shows the lender what financial protection is afforded by the debt coverage ratio maintained over time.

Cash Flows of the Operating Stage

The operation of an income property involves revenues, operating costs, tax payments, additional capital expenditures for additional phases of the land development, and refinancing proceeds. During the operating stage of the investment property, operating cash flows permit periodic payment to the sources of funds established in the planning stage. Cash outflows may take the form of mortgage payments, stockholder dividends, or cash distributions to the partners (Exhibit 15-6).

The profitability of the operation of an investment property is partly determined by the examination of two strategic ratios: the operating ratio and the breakeven ratio. The investor and the investor's lenders are aware of ratios being generated in the marketplace that are associated with reasonable profitability from the type of investment property.

The Operating Ratio. Cash flow statements provide the ingredients for the computation of operating ratios. From the pro forma statements, the investor and the lender can view the operating expense totals and the effective gross income projections. The operating ratio is calculated in the following manner:

$$\text{Operating ratio} = \frac{\text{Operating expenses for the time period}}{\text{Effective gross income for the same time period}}$$

If the property is a rental apartment project, the investors with profitable rental apartment projects may disclose successful operation with operating ratios from 35 to 45 percent.

The Breakeven Ratio. The investor and the lender both examine the breakeven ratio to see how close the total expected operating expenses and mortgage debt service are to the gross potential income. The higher the breakeven ratio, the less the buffer of profit for the mortgage lender in case real estate and economic conditions change in an

Exhibit 15-6. The Profit Picture of the Planning and Operating Stages of Real Estate Investment

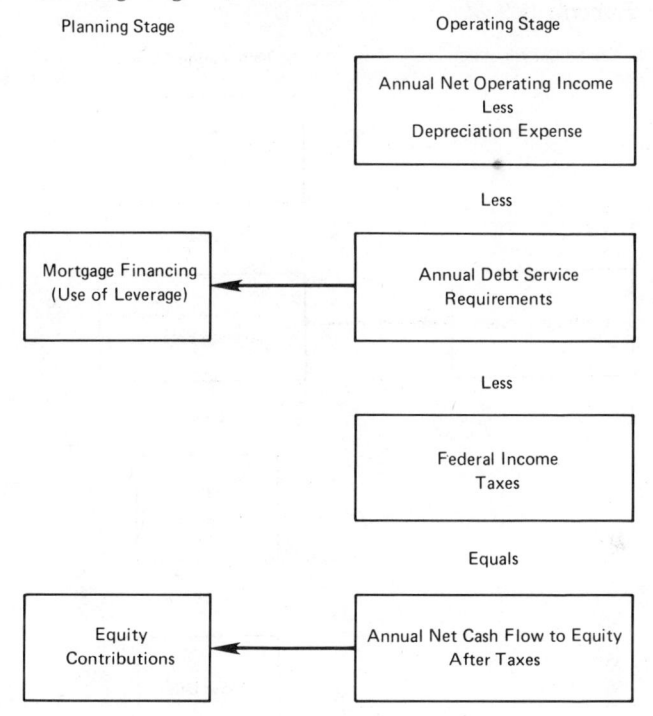

```
        Planning Stage                          Operating Stage

                                         ┌─────────────────────────┐
                                         │ Annual Net Operating Income │
                                         │          Less           │
                                         │   Depreciation Expense  │
                                         └─────────────────────────┘

                                                    Less

   ┌─────────────────────┐             ┌─────────────────────────┐
   │  Mortgage Financing │ ◄───────────│   Annual Debt Service   │
   │  (Use of Leverage)  │             │      Requirements       │
   └─────────────────────┘             └─────────────────────────┘

                                                    Less

                                         ┌─────────────────────────┐
                                         │     Federal Income      │
                                         │         Taxes           │
                                         └─────────────────────────┘

                                                   Equals

   ┌─────────────────────┐             ┌─────────────────────────┐
   │       Equity        │ ◄───────────│ Annual Net Cash Flow to Equity │
   │    Contributions    │             │       After Taxes       │
   └─────────────────────┘             └─────────────────────────┘
```

unfavorable direction. The lower the breakeven ratio, the higher the portion of gross income that will remain to the investor in profit. The formula for the breakeven ratio is

$$\text{Breakeven ratio} = \frac{\text{Operating expenses and debt service}}{\text{Gross potential income}}$$

An acceptable breakeven ratio for an income property may be 82 to 85 percent of gross potential income. The investor sees that 15 to 18 percent of gross potential income may remain for profit at the end of the operating period. The lender may approve a loan with this realistically projected breakeven ratio.

Cash Flows of the Termination Stage

When the investment has run its course and the investor decides to sell the income property, certain cash inflows and outflows are expected. The outflows involve the payment of existing mortgage balances, selling expenses, and federal income taxes. If a cash flow is generated for the owners, a distribution of the cash is made on the agreed-upon settlement basis. The cash inflow stems mainly from the sale proceeds (Exhibit 15-7). The capital contributors receive their final payments at the end of the investment holding period.

Ratio analysis is also important at the termination stage of the investment. The commonly used ratios and evaluation methods for determining investment yield are covered in Chapter 17.

Exhibit 15-7. The Profit Picture of the Termination Stage When the Investment Property Is Sold

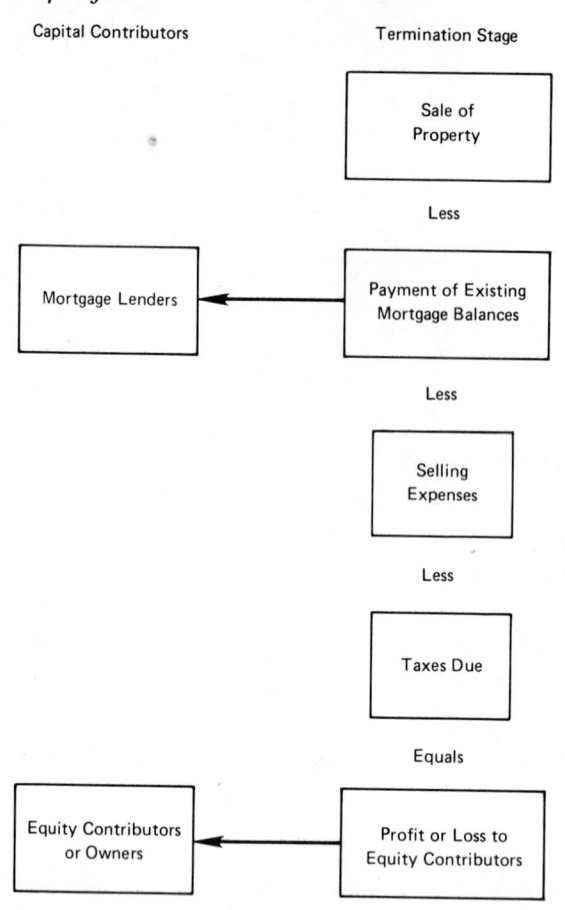

```
Capital Contributors              Termination Stage

                              ┌──────────────┐
                              │   Sale of    │
                              │   Property   │
                              └──────────────┘
                                    Less
┌──────────────────┐          ┌──────────────────┐
│ Mortgage Lenders │ ◄─────── │ Payment of Existing │
│                  │          │ Mortgage Balances │
└──────────────────┘          └──────────────────┘
                                    Less
                              ┌──────────────┐
                              │   Selling    │
                              │   Expenses   │
                              └──────────────┘
                                    Less
                              ┌──────────────┐
                              │  Taxes Due   │
                              └──────────────┘
                                   Equals
┌──────────────────┐          ┌──────────────────┐
│ Equity Contributors│ ◄──── │ Profit or Loss to │
│   or Owners     │          │ Equity Contributors│
└──────────────────┘          └──────────────────┘
```

SUMMARY

The real estate investor is usually very concerned with the net cash flow position and the taxable income for each time period of his or her investment. A negative net cash flow projected for a time period means that the investor must find the cash somewhere else to pay obligations incurred. A positive net cash position for a time period means money in the pocket of the investor. If a net profit is generated, the real estate investor immediately thinks about the federal income taxes that will be payable. Pro forma statements for five to ten years provide a means for the investor to project the cash positions for that time period.

Forecasting cash inflows and outflows involves consideration of future inflation patterns and future trends in the general business and real estate cycle. The complexities of this forecasting job may be controlled through the use of sensitivity analysis and probability analysis for determination of expected values of strategic expenses and incomes.

Cash flow distributions differ in terms of the basic investment forms and in terms of the three stages of real estate investment and development. Acreage investment involves different cash flow distributions than land subdivision or land development and improvement. Cash flows of the planning stage are quite different from those of the operating and termination stages; each stage's cash distribution is different. Cash flows of the planning stage involve the use of leverage and may be analyzed by means of loan-to-value and debt coverage ratios. Cash flows of the operating stage may be partly scrutinized in terms of operating and breakeven ratios. Cash flows of the termination stage, similar to those of the operating stage, deal with cash payments to the capital contributors from the net operating income generated per time period and from the net proceeds at the time of sale. Mortgage debt must be repaid, selling expenses met, and tax payments made. The investment yield may be computed in a number of ways. Chapter 17 covers the commonly used methods of yield measurement.

Key Terms and Concepts

Cash throw-off to equity after taxes
Tax savings
Noncash expense
Net cash flow before taxes
Expected value
Equity contributors

Net cash flow before debt service and taxes
Spendable income
After-tax cash benefits to equity
Sensitivity analysis
Probability of occurrence

Questions for Student Self-examination

Multiple-Choice Questions

1. In real estate investment analysis, taxable income arises from the surplus of effective gross income over _____.
    a. operating expenses
    b. mortgage interest
    c. depreciation expense
    d. all of the above

2. What is the difference between spendable income and after-tax cash benefits to equity?
    a. depreciation
    b. federal income tax payment
    c. tax savings
    d. mortgage interest

3. What is the difference between net operating income and cash throw-off?
    a. tax savings
    b. debt service
    c. federal income tax payment
    d. depreciation

4. Usually the first mortgage loan on income-producing property covers _____ percent of the appraised value of the property.
    a. 50 to 60
    b. 40 to 45
    c. 66 2/3 to 80
    d. 60 to 70

5. If the property is a rental apartment project, the typical investor with a profitable project will disclose successful operation with operating ratios from _____ percent.
   a. 10 to 15
   b. 60 to 70
   c. 80 to 85
   d. 35 to 45

True-False Questions

T F 1. Profit projections enable the investor to estimate the cash return on the cash invested and how much cash is needed at specific intervals to cover net outlays.

T F 2. Profit, generally speaking, means the dollar difference between the cash inflows and the cash outflows associated with a real estate investment.

T F 3. If revenues exceed costs, the investment generates a profit.

T F 4. If the real estate investor realizes a tax loss from the investment and, at the same time, receives taxable income from other sources, the loss from the real estate investment may be applied to the other taxable income.

T F 5. Noncash expenses are deducted from cash inflows in order to derive net cash flow.

T F 6. During the 1970s, revenues, particularly from apartment space, rose, but less than operating and financial costs rose.

T F 7. Sensitivity analysis refers to the analysis of end results by changing one variable or expense-revenue account balance at a time.

T F 8. Construction costs must be paid from the equity and mortgage funds.

T F 9. Management costs, in the form of developer fees and supervisory fees, must be met before the real estate investment reaches the operational stage.

T F 10. As long as the total investment generates a return less than the cost of the borrowed funds, the use of leverage or borrowed funds will inflate the return on the investor's equity contribution.

Answers
Multiple-Choice: 1d, 2c, 3b, 4c, 5d.
True-False: 1F, 2F, 3T, 4T, 5F, 6T, 7T, 8T, 9T, 10F.

Problems

1. If in the first year of its operation, a small apartment building generates rental income of $20,000 a year, cash operating expenses of $5,000, depreciation of $1,000, mortgage interest of $5,000, and mortgage amortization of $1,000, what is the taxable income? the net cash flow before federal income taxes?

2. If the gross rental income is $10,000, the vacancy rate is 10 percent, and the coin-operated laundry income is $500, what is the effective gross income?

3. If the property generates a net operating income of $10,000, a debt service of $1,500, and a required federal income tax payment of $1,000, what is the cash throw-off? the spendable income?

4. If the income property operation results in a tax loss of $5,000 for the owner and the owner's marginal federal income tax rate is 60 percent, what is the owner's tax savings, assuming that the owner has taxable income from other sources to which the tax loss may be applied?

5. What are the after-tax cash benefits to the owner if the tax savings from a tax loss on the building are $500, the federal income tax payment required is $2,000, the debt service payment is $1,000, and the net operating income is $15,000?

6. If a young savings and loan mortgage loan officer buys five acres of land on the outskirts of her home town for $10,000, what holding costs, tax-deductible items, and favorable tax circumstances may she anticipate?

7. If the owner realizes a net operating income of $30,000 from her investment property, operating expenses of $10,000, and effective gross income for the same time period of $45,000, what is the operating ratio for the property for that time period?

Chapter 16

Mathematics of Investment Analysis

Introduction
The Relationship of This Chapter to Other Chapters of the Text
The Components of Real Estate Investment Returns
 Amount of Equity Funds Invested   Amount of Borrowed Funds and Their Related Loan Terms   Net Operating Income and Sale Proceeds
Some Fundamental Concepts
 Mortgage Payment   The Mortgage Constant   The Mortgage Balance Due
Real Estate Investment as a Dynamic Process
The Use of Sensitivity Analysis
The Time Value of Money in Real Estate Investment Analysis
 The Future Worth of a Single Sum   The Future Worth of an Annuity   The Present Value of a Single Sum   The Present Value of an Annuity
Summary
Key Terms and Concepts
Questions for Student Self-examination

LEARNING OBJECTIVES After studying this chapter, you should be familiar with

The components of real estate investment returns
The analysis of the amount of equity and borrowed funds
The analysis of net operating income components
The contribution of sale proceeds to investment return
The nature of the mortgage payment
The use of the mortgage constant
Real estate investment as a dynamic process, not a static phenomenon
The use of sensitivity analysis
The time value of money in real estate investment analysis

Cash flow and profit planning, presented in the last chapter, are important to successful real estate investment. The future flows of funds must be accounted for. If an investment return is to be gained, the cash inflows must adequately surpass the cash outflows. Since the three stages of an investment involve different overall balances of the net cash flow picture, the cash flows of each of the stages and each of the time intervals of the expected holding period need to be studied closely. The investor may find, for one thing, that an equity investment, that will supplement the initial equity investment, is required well into the expected investment holding period. The investor must have the additional funds ready at the needed time.

INTRODUCTION

In this chapter, the four components of investment yield are studied in some depth. Those components include (1) the amount of equity funds invested, (2) the amount of borrowed funds and their related loan terms, (3) the net operating income for each investment period, and (4) the sale proceeds, including the change in property value and equity buildup.

Some fundamental investment concepts directly related to return measurement are analyzed. The distribution of funds between equity and mortgage investment and between the various types of equity contributors is examined first. The distribution of cash flows to general and limited partners and to syndicate members and the syndicator is part of the discussion. The forms of return to the real estate developer are also considered briefly. The nature of the mortgage payment is studied in light of possible mortgagee participation in the equity. The importance of the mortgage constant is pointed out. The reader finds that the mortgage balance currently due may be estimated from precomputed mortgage tables, sometimes labeled *loan progress* tables.

It is pointed out that real estate investment is a dynamic process and not a static phenomenon. Examples of interest rate or yield changes over time are taken from the money and capital markets. Since variability of investment factors is of prime importance, sensitivity analysis may be employed to forecast the possible impact on net cash flow and overall yield of the possible range in strategic investment variables.

The time value of money is associated with real estate investment analysis. The relationship of future and present values to investment yield analysis is pointed out.

The use of four different sets of interest tables is illustrated. These tables are used to find (1) the future worth of a single sum, (2) the future worth of an annuity, (3) the present value of a single sum, and (4) the present value of an annuity.

THE RELATIONSHIP OF THIS CHAPTER TO OTHER CHAPTERS OF THE TEXT

This chapter adds detail to the mathematics of investment analysis and introduces the reader to the usefulness of the compound interest and present value tables. The first section discusses in detail the components of real estate investment returns. The second section discusses some fundamental concepts related to the mathematics of real estate investment yield analysis. This chapter provides the reader with a suitable background for continued study of investment yield measurement. It bridges the gap between cash flow and profit planning and investment yield measurement.

THE COMPONENTS OF REAL ESTATE INVESTMENT RETURNS

The investment analyst examines several components of investment return. One is the amount of equity funds invested. Then the amount of borrowed funds and the related loan terms are investigated. The net operating income for each year or shorter segment of a year for the expected investment holding period is derived. The fourth component is the sale proceeds, including capital appreciation, capital depreciation, and equity buildup through mortgage repayment. To summarize, the four investment components are

Amount of equity funds invested.
Amount of borrowed funds and their related loan terms.
Net operating income for each period of analysis of the expected investment holding period.
Sale proceeds, including change in property value and equity buildup.

Amount of Equity Funds Invested. The purchase or development of a property requires one or more sources of capital. If borrowed funds contribute to the investment, the remaining portion of the purchase price or development cost is covered with equity funds from the owner or ownership group. Front-end costs, which are paid by the owner or ownership groups, also represent contributions of equity. The *front-end costs*, or the costs encountered during the planning and financing stages of real estate development, include prepaid interest, architectural fees, surveying costs, organizational legal expense, loan origination fees, environmental impact report fees, fees for market and feasibility reports, and other such expenses. The amount of equity invested in the project may be considered on a before-tax or an after-tax basis. Some front-end costs may be expensed immediately for federal income tax purposes; others must be capitalized (Table 16-1). If the front-end costs may be deducted immediately, the equity invested is significantly less than the nominal cost. The effective cost of the planning and financing expense depends on the tax bracket of the taxpayer.

The various concepts of the amount of equity funds invested may be summarized in the following way:

Total purchase price or development cost less borrowed funds.

Downpayment toward development cost or purchase, plus front-end costs.
   Before taxes.
   After taxes.

The amount most frequently used to represent equity funds invested is total purchase price less borrowed funds, or total development cost less borrowed funds.

Amount of Borrowed Funds and Their Related Loan Terms. In cash flow analysis, the amount of the debt service each year is usually needed in order to derive the cash flow available for equity. Often income property mortgages have three- to five-year interest-only clauses. This clause means lower debt service charges during the first years of the operation of a real estate project. The lower expense occurs as other start-up outlays are high and the project is being rented. Once the full debt service goes into effect, it is anticipated that the full rental revenue will be rolling off the project.

Since most income properties are sold before the maturity of the usual mortgages, often the mortgage will require a balloon payment at maturity. The amortization that starts after the interest-only period may be based on a loan period substantially in excess of the actual loan maturity. The amortization during the operation of the property is lower than it would have been if the amortization schedule had spanned only the actual loan period. Most lenders realize that the loan will probably be paid off entirely by the sale proceeds long in advance of the loan maturity date.

Participations are frequently built into income property mortgages. The borrower must pay the established debt service amounts plus a portion of the gross revenue generated by the income property. The lender often participates in the equity of the project being financed by means of a mortgage. The equity participation of the lender usually applies to the gross revenue received in excess of a specified amount. This clause tends to give the lender inflation protection.

The interest rate of the income property or home mortgage often *floats* with the changes in a specified money and capital market index. In other words, the interest

Table 16-1. Tax treatment of front-end costs

Type of Front-End Cost	Tax Treatment
Preliminary economic and engineering studies	Immediately deductible
Organizational legal expense	Capitalized and amortized over 60 months or more
Syndication sales fees	Capitalized and amortized over 60 months or more
Advertising and sales promotion costs	Immediately deductible
Recording costs	Immediately deductible
Income property appraisal fees, transfer taxes, insurance premiums, loan origination fees	Immediately deductible
Prepaid interest	
Home financing	Deductible when paid
Income property financing	Deductible in the year to which the interest relates, not when paid
Property taxes incurred during construction	
Taxpayer's personal residence	Immediately deductible
Income property	Capitalized and amortized over a specified period of time
Construction loan interest	Capitalized and amortized

rate on the income property or home mortgage may be fixed or variable. If the interest rate is fixed, the amount of the debt service payments is established at the closing of the loan. If the interest rate varies with the changes in an index observed at the end of a specific period of time, the amount of the debt service is recalculated in each time period when the index indicates a change is needed. Therefore, the periodic debt service covering interest payment and principal repayment may vary on the basis of a variable interest rate and/or on the basis of an equity participation.

Possible loan terms related to income property debt service are summarized below:

Interest-only period at the opening of the mortgage.
Balloon payment at loan maturity.
Equity participation.
Variable interest rate.

Net Operating Income and Sale Proceeds. The derivation of net operating income for each period of analysis of the expected investment holding period was covered in depth in Chapter 15 on cash flow and profit planning. Net operating income is one of the four components of investment yield.

Sale proceeds, which were derived for tax purposes in Part III, include two components not previously considered in detail. The possible change in property value between the time of initial investment and the end of the holding period is one of the components. The other component of equity yield is the *equity buildup* at the end of the holding period from the repayment of the mortgage loan over the holding period. The mortgage balance does not remain constant over the holding period. The balance owed the lender declines as mortgage payments are made and the balance attributed to equity accumulation increases.

The three possible alternatives with respect to property value change are decrease of value, increase of value, and stability of value. In our inflationary era, many properties increase in current dollar value as the American dollar depreciates. Property values, whether home or income property values, often increase during periods of economic prosperity. Many income property values decline during periods of economic recession, even though house values may not reflect the depressed economic conditions if inflation persists.

The investor may receive investment return from an increase in property value over the holding period and from equity buildup from the mortgage repayment. The full or partial equity buildup will be realized at the sale of the property if the property value surpasses the mortgage balance at the time of the sale.

SOME FUNDAMENTAL CONCEPTS

Before we proceed to measure investment returns in Chapter 17, let us observe some fundamental investment concepts that are related to mathematical analysis of investment returns. First, in most property investments, there are investments by owners and by lenders—equity and mortgage investments. Second, real estate investment usually involves mortgage payment and knowledge of the mortgage balance due at any one time. Third, real estate investment is a dynamic process, not a static process. As a dynamic process, the yields of competing investments are always undergoing scrutiny. The trends of strategic investment ratios are always being observed. Sensitivity analysis is often used to identify the impact on strategic ratios of the possible change of various investment factors. Last, the time value of money is significant in investment analysis.

Table 16-2. *Distribution of cash flows to general and limited partners of a limited partnership*

	Year 1	Year 2	Year 3	Year 4	Year 5
Net cash generated	$6,800	$8,050	$9,250	$10,500	$11,500
General partner's share (15%)	1,020	1,208	1,388	1,575	1,725
Limited partner's share (85%)	5,780	6,842	7,862	8,925	9,775
Five-share interest ($5,000— $\frac{1}{10}$ interest of limited partner's share)	$ 578	$ 684	$ 786	$ 893	$ 978

It is usually considered wise to obtain cash receipts as early as possible and to delay payment of cash expenditures as long as possible within the discount or full payment period. This type of cash budgeting policy promotes the greatest yield on an investment. In addition, discounted cash flows and future values from the compounding of amounts are important to investment decision making.

A real estate investment is usually supported by both equity and mortgage monies. The owner or owner group invests equity capital. The lenders invest personal or institutional capital in mortgages on the property. If only one mortgage is acquired for an investment property, the financing may be described in the following way:

Total appraised value of the property	$1,000,000
First and only mortgage (75% of appraised value)	750,000
Equity investment	250,000

The returns to the two types of investments are different. The owners, stockholders, syndicate members, or partners receive cash flows from operations each year and distributions from the sale proceeds of the investment properties at the end of the holding period. The method of distributing cash flows to general and limited partners of a limited partnership is illustrated in Table 16-2. Exhibit 16-1 shows, by means of an apartment case, a method of distribution of cash flows to syndicate members and the sponsor-syndicator over the life of the investment. The time value of money is not taken into account in this illustration.

The mortgage lenders receive the fixed and variable periodic debt service payments plus the cash proceeds from early mortgage repayment. Part of the cash proceeds from early mortgage repayment may be prepayment penalties. The lenders may receive fixed periodic mortgage payments at the established interest rate. The other periodic income may vary with the variable interest rate on the indexed mortgage and the lender's participation in the owner's equity.

In contrast, the cash returns to syndicators may take the form of commissions or profits on the purchase of syndicate properties, fees for syndicate management, and a share of the resale proceeds (Exhibit 16-1). The developer's return takes similar forms plus mortgage banking fees, property management fees, and participation in the gross income from the continuing operation of the development.

The Mortgage Payment. The loan payment to the mortgagee may be a fixed amount, or it may vary with a changing mortgage rate and/or participation in the equity of the financed property, as was stated previously. Lender participation in the owner's equity may take several forms:

1. Mortgagee participation in gross income.
2. Mortgagee participation in net operating income.
3. Mortgagee participation in the cash throw-off (net operating income less debt service).
4. Mortgagee participation in the net cash reversion.

Exhibit 16-1. An Apartment Case Illustrating a Method of Cash Flow Distribution to Syndicate Investors and the Syndicator

---

A 20-unit apartment complex is available for purchase at a price of $255,000. After thorough investigation you conclude that the apartment complex should produce the following results:

10 one-bedroom units @ $185 per month	$22,200
10 two-bedroom units @ $225 per month	27,000
Gross annual income at 100% occupancy	49,200
Deduct vacancy expense of 5%	2,460
Effective gross income (EGI)	46,740
Deduct operating expenses (40% of EGI)	18,696
Net annual operating income	28,044
Deduct mortgage payments	20,000
Annual cash flow	$ 8,044

Through your investigation you have determined that in the general investment market a return of 10 percent is acceptable. Based on that rate, the value of the equity for this project would be $80,440 ($8,044 divided by .10).

The price for the property requires a $55,000 equity, so if you can sell the equity to the syndicate members for $80,400, there will be a profit of $25,440. This $25,440 profit could be paid as a development syndication fee.

In addition to this fee, the apartment will require management. If the management fee is 7 percent of gross income per year, the management fee would be $3,444 per year.

A further possible fee could be based on an incentive basis, as far as the resale of the property is concerned. The syndicator could earn 20 percent of the net resale proceeds after the other investors have had all of their equity returned.

Assume the apartments are held for five years and the value increases at 5 percent per year.

Sale at the end of year five	$325,452
Less mortgage balance	190,000
Equity	135,452
Less transaction costs	15,000
Net equity on resale	120,452
Less original equity invested	80,440
Amount in excess of the original investment	40,012
Distribution of resale proceeds:	
80% to syndicate investors	32,010
20% to sponsor–syndicator	8,002
Benefits to investors:	
Invested (value of the equity)	80,440
Received from resale proceeds	32,010
Annual cash flow received for five years	40,220
Total benefits to investors	152,670
Benefits to syndicator:	
Received on the original purchase	25,440
Received by means of management fees	17,220
Received from resale proceeds	8,002
Total benefits to the syndicator	$ 50,662

Real Estate Investment Analysis

The most common forms of lender participation are percentage participants in gross income and net resale proceeds. Regardless of the form of mortgagee participation, the mortgagor must pay the regular debt service, figured on a fixed or variable mortgage rate, plus the amount for the lender's participation in the equity.

Here is an example of the mortgagee's participation in the gross income and the mortgagor's total obligation to the lender:

Gross income	$300,000
Less mortgagee participation (5%)	15,000
Gross income to mortgagor	285,000
Less operating expenses (40% of total gross income)	120,000
Net operating income to mortgagor	165,000
Less debt service	140,000
Cash throw-off	$ 25,000

The lender receives the debt service payment ($140,000) plus percentage participation in the gross income ($15,000), which totals $155,000 for the year.

If the lender participates in the net cash reversion when the property is sold, the borrower or mortgagor receives the amount of the net cash reversion after the mortgagee's percentage participation. For example:

Net cash reversion at property resale	$1,500,000
Less mortgagee participation (20%)	500,000
Net cash reversion to the mortgagor-owner	$1,000,000

The lender in the year of property sale would receive the regular debt service payment plus the amount representing participation in the net cash reversion.

The Mortgage Constant. The *mortgage constant,* or the *constant annual percent,* is that portion of the original loan amount that the mortgagor pays periodically in debt service. The debt service payments cover the amortization of the principal and the interest payments. Usually the mortgage constant for monthly debt service payments is used although some income property mortgages require quarterly, semiannual, or annual payments instead of monthly payments.

Any one mortgage constant or constant annual percent covers a number of combinations of mortgage interest rates and loan maturities. For example, .12 as a constant annual multiplier, based on monthly debt service payments, is used for the repayment of the following loans:

Interest Rate (Percent)	Full Term to Maturity	
	Years	Months
7	12	7
8	13	10
9⅝	16	11
10½	19	11
10⅞	21	11
11	22	9
11½	27	10

The lender knows what debt service coverage is necessary. As the lender looks over the cash flow statement of the prospective borrower, he or she can ascertain what debt service amount would fulfill the required debt service coverage.

$$\text{Debt service coverage} = \frac{\text{Net operating income}}{\text{Debt service}}$$

For example, if the required coverage is 1.25 and the net operating income of the property is $125,000, the debt service can be $100,000 a year. If $833,333 is needed, a debt service of $100,000 a year would mean the use of a .12 mortgage constant. Using the .12 constant, the lender could set up the loan with any of the above interest and maturity combinations, or the lender could set the loan up with a *hangout,* or a balloon payment required at the loan maturity. If the lender wanted to charge 10⅞ percent interest and was agreeable to a balloon payment of 20 percent of the loan principal at maturity, the loan term might be set at 20 years. If the lender wanted to charge only 9⅝ percent interest with a hangout of 21 percent, this loan could be written for 15 years (Exhibit 16-2).

The Mortgage Balance Due. In order to calculate the net cash proceeds from a financed property, it is necessary for the analyst or investor to know the mortgage balance at the time of actual or anticipated property sale. The mortgage lender has the current balance available from the computer or hand-accounting system. The lender can estimate the balance that will be due—assuming regular, full mortgage payments in the future—at the estimated time of property sale. Without inquiring of the lender, the investor or analyst can estimate the mortgage balance at any time with the use of loan progress charts of various interest rates. All the investor needs to know is (1) the original term of the loan in years, (2) the age of the loan at the time of property sale, and (3) the nominal interest rate on the loan. For example, if the loan rate is 11½ percent, the loan term was originally 20 years, and the age of the loan at property sale will be 14 years, $553 of a $1,000 loan will remain due to the lender, or 55 percent of the original loan amount will remain outstanding (Exhibit 16-3).

Real Estate Investment as a Dynamic Process

The variables associated with real estate investment keep changing, so that real estate investment is a dynamic phenomenon, not a static process. The levels of cash inflows and outflows keep changing. The competitive yields in the marketplace also change. This dynamic relationship keeps the investor constantly alert for changes in competitive investments.

The knowledgeable investor keeps abreast of the changes in money market and capital market yields, as well as the changes in the yields on competing investment properties. For example, the bank prime rate was 11½ percent in May 1979, whereas in April 1977 it was only 6¼ percent (Exhibit 16-4). Money market securities were yielding 9½-10½ percent in May 1979 and 4-5½ percent in April 1977. Bond yields in May 1979 ranged from approximately 9½ to 10 percent; in April 1977, they were 6¼-8½ percent (Exhibit 16-5). During the same months, IBM's dividend yield was 3.8 percent in 1977 and 4.3 percent in 1979; the closing price was lower in 1979 (Exhibit 16-5). In like manner, on a lower closing price, General Motors' dividend yield was 8.7 percent in 1977 and 10.2 percent in 1979.

Exhibit 16-2. Constant Annual Percent

12.00% Interest Rate	2 Years	3 Years	4 Years	5 Years	7 Years	10 Years	Monthly Payments Years	Full Term Months
			Percent Paid Off					
7	10.7	16.6	23.0	29.8	45.0	72.1	12	7
1/4	10.2	15.9	22.0	28.5	43.1	69.5	12	10
1/2	9.7	15.1	20.9	27.2	41.3	66.7	13	2
3/4	9.2	14.3	19.9	25.9	39.3	63.9	13	6
8	8.6	13.5	18.8	24.5	37.4	61.0	13	10
1/8	8.4	13.1	18.2	23.8	36.4	59.5	14	0
1/4	8.1	12.7	17.7	23.1	35.4	58.0	14	2
3/8	7.9	12.3	17.2	22.4	34.3	56.4	14	5
1/2	7.6	11.9	16.6	21.7	33.3	54.9	14	7
5/8	7.3	11.5	16.1	21.0	32.3	53.3	14	10
3/4	7.1	11.1	15.5	20.3	31.2	51.7	15	0
7/8	6.8	10.7	14.9	19.6	30.2	50.0	15	3

	5 Years	10 Years	15 Years	20 Years	25 Years	30 Years		
9	18.9	48.4	94.6				15	6
1/8	18.1	46.7	91.7				15	9
1/4	17.4	45.0	88.7				16	0
3/8	16.7	43.2	85.6				16	4
1/2	15.9	41.5	82.5				16	7
5/8	15.2	39.7	79.3				16	11
3/4	14.4	37.9	76.0				17	3
7/8	13.7	36.0	72.6				17	8
10	12.9	34.1	69.1				18	0
1/8	12.1	32.2	65.5				18	5
1/4	11.4	30.3	61.9				18	11
3/8	10.6	28.3	58.1				19	5
1/2	9.8	26.4	54.3				19	11
5/8	9.0	24.3	50.3	94.4			20	6
3/4	8.2	22.3	46.3	87.2			21	2
7/8	7.4	20.2	42.1	79.8			21	11
11	6.6	18.1	37.9	72.1			22	9
1/8	5.8	15.9	33.5	64.2			23	8
1/4	5.0	13.8	29.1	55.9			24	10
3/8	4.2	11.6	24.5	47.4	87.6		26	2
1/2	3.4	9.3	19.9	38.5	71.7		27	10
5/8	2.5	7.0	15.1	29.4	54.9		30	0
3/4	1.7	4.7	10.2	19.9	37.4	68.9	33	2
7/8	.8	2.4	5.1	10.1	19.1	35.4	38	8

Source: *Financial Constant Percent Amortization Tables*, Publication No. 287 (Boston: Financial Publishing Company, 1975), p. 42. Reprinted with permission.

The Use of Sensitivity Analysis

When the investor wishes to consider more than one amount for a strategic investment variable, sensitivity analysis may be employed to analyze the impact of the different amounts. All other variables must remain at the original amounts while the investment yield is figured for each possible amount of the single strategic variable. For example, the prospective operating expense ratio might turn out to be 50 percent rather than 40 percent. Through sensitivity analysis, the cash flow statement and the investment yield calculation could be carried out using an operating expense ratio of 50 percent. The same calculations may have been made earlier using a 40 percent ratio. For a similar

Exhibit 16-3. Loan Progress Chart

Age of Loan	5	10	11	12	13	14	15	16	17	18	19	Age of Loan
1	843	943	952	959	965	969	973	977	980	982	984	1
2	667	880	898	913	925	935	944	951	957	962	967	2
3	470	809	838	861	880	897	910	922	932	940	947	3
4	248	729	770	803	831	854	873	889	903	915	926	4
5		639	694	738	775	805	831	853	871	887	901	5
6		539	609	665	712	751	784	812	835	856	873	6
7		426	513	584	642	690	731	766	795	821	843	7
8		300	406	492	563	622	672	714	750	781	808	8
9		159	286	389	474	546	606	656	700	737	769	9
10			151	274	375	460	531	592	643	687	725	10
11				145	264	364	448	519	580	632	677	11
12					140	256	354	437	508	569	622	12
13						135	249	346	429	499	560	13
14							132	244	339	421	492	14
15								129	239	333	414	15
16									126	234	328	16
17										124	231	17
18											122	18

Age of Loan	20	21	22	23	24	25	26	27	28	29	30	Age of Loan
1	986	988	989	991	992	993	993	994	995	995	996	1
2	971	974	977	980	982	984	986	988	989	990	991	2
3	954	959	964	968	972	975	978	980	983	985	986	3
4	935	942	949	955	960	965	969	972	975	978	981	4
5	913	923	932	940	947	953	958	963	967	971	974	5
6	889	902	913	924	932	940	947	953	958	963	967	6
7	861	878	892	905	916	925	934	941	948	954	959	7
8	831	851	869	884	897	909	919	929	937	944	950	8
9	797	821	842	860	877	891	903	914	924	932	940	9
10	759	782	812	834	853	870	885	898	909	920	929	10
11	716	749	779	805	827	847	864	880	893	905	916	11
12	667	707	741	772	798	821	841	859	875	889	902	12
13	613	659	699	734	765	792	816	837	855	871	886	13
14	553	606	652	693	728	759	787	811	832	851	868	14
15	485	546	600	646	687	723	755	782	807	829	848	15
16	409	479	540	594	641	682	718	750	778	803	825	16
17	323	404	474	535	589	636	678	714	746	775	800	17
18	228	319	400	470	531	585	632	674	710	743	772	18
19	120	225	316	396	466	527	581	628	670	707	740	19
20		119	223	313	393	462	523	577	625	667	704	20
21			118	220	311	390	459	520	575	622	664	21
22				117	219	308	387	457	518	572	620	22
23					116	216	306	385	454	515	570	23
24						115	216	304	383	452	513	24
25							114	214	303	381	450	25
26								113	213	302	380	26
27									113	212	300	27
28										112	211	28
29											112	29

Source: *Financial Constant Percent Amortization Tables,* Publication No. 287 (Boston: Financial Publishing Company, 1975), p. 128. Reprinted with permission.

Exhibit 16-4. Short-Term Money Market Yields

	May 3, 1979	July 14, 1978	April, 1977
Bank prime rate	11 1/2-11 3/4%	9%	6 1/4%
Treasury bill rate			
9/14/78	9.5	7.45	4.54
10/19/78	9.57	7.77	4.80
Federal funds in the open market, closing bid	10 1/2	7 3/4	4.73
Dealers' commercial paper	9.8	7.88	4.80
Commercial paper placed directly by major finance companies	9.5	7 3/4	4.81
Bankers acceptances			
30 days	9.8	7.8	NA
90 days	9.9	NA	4.78
180 days	10.05	8.2	—
Certificates of depsoit ($100,000 or more)			
One month	9 5/8	7.7	NA
Three months	10.10	NA	4.75
One year	10	8.75	NA
Eurodollar rates			
One month	10-9 15/15	8 1/4	NA
Three months	10 5/8-10 9/16	NA	5.16
Six months	11 1/16-10 31/32	9 1/8	NA

reason, the investor might hold all other variables constant in the calculations and use a 35 percent operating expense ratio. The cash flow returns using the three different operating expense ratios would show the investor the risk-return relationship surrounding the eventual operating expense ratio.

Other results from changes in various investment factors may be examined with sensitivity analysis. For example, while all other factors are held constant, different levels of utility costs might be incorporated into the cash flow analysis. Most investors today have observed the upward trend in utility costs and expect future increases in these costs. They would like to know the impact on investment yields from various size increases in utility costs that might be experienced in the future. The rent structure might also be examined. Various possible levels of property tax expenditures might be examined in light of their impact on yields. The possible financing methods for the investment could be scrutinized in terms of equity yields. In all, sensitivity analysis can be very enlightening to the investor. Computer equipment may be well used for this purpose.

The Time Value of Money in Real Estate Investment Analysis

Many investors are aware that dollars received today are worth more than dollars received in the future. The logic is that if you receive money today, it can be invested, and it will bring a return over a period of time. The investment may accumulate to a sizable future sum. If, on the other hand, you are offered money that will be paid in the future rather than at present, you will not have the money to invest for the additional return. That money received in the future is worth less than the money you receive

Exhibit 16-5. Capital Market Yields

	May 3, 1979	July 14, 1978	April 1977
Common Stock Yields			
International Business Machines			
Closing price	$318	$259 3/8	NA
Dividend yield	4.3%	4.4%	3.8%
General Motors			
Closing price	58 1/2	60 1/8	NA
Dividend yield	10.2%	11.0%	8.7%
Bond Yields (Yield to Maturity)			
Utilities			
NY Tel 8 7/8 2018, Aaa	NA	9.06%	8.22
Pac G&E 9 3/8 2011, Aa	NA	9.50%	NA
Detroit Edison 9 7/8 2008, Baa	NA	10.03	NA
Utilities:			
Aaa	9.76		
A	10.6		
Industrials			
GMAC (new listing) 8 7/8 1985, Aaa	NA	9.00	NA
Household Finance 8 1/2 1983, Aa	NA	8.87	NA
McDonald 8 5/8 1988, A	NA	8.94	NA
Industrials:			
Aaa	9.75		8.04
Aa	9.6		8.28
A	9.58		8.55
U.S. Government			
U.S. Treas. bond 7 5/8 Aug. 1981	NA	8.50	6.31
U.S. Treas. bond 8 1/2 May 1999	NA	8.65	7.67
U.S. Treas. bond 9 1/4 May 1989	9.34	NA	NA

now. In other words, $100 received a year from now is worth less than $100 received now. You could earn over 5 percent per year on the $100 received now if it were placed in a passbook savings account of a local commercial bank or savings and loan association.

Therefore, the present worth of future cash flows is important to the real estate investor. Sometimes the future cash flow takes the form of a single sum; sometimes it takes the form of an annuity or a periodic cash flow received in specific intervals over time. An example of a single sum to be received in the future by a real estate investor is the expected net cash proceeds from the future sale of a property or the reversion. An example of an annuity to be received in the future is a series of established lease payments to be received in quarterly, semiannual, or annual intervals.

The future worth of expected cash flows may also be important to the investor. For example, the real estate investor's purpose may be to accumulate money for his or her children's college education. The investor may buy bonds of a real estate company or a real estate-oriented financial institution, or he may place a sum of money in a long-term money market certificate of deposit of a thrift institution or a commercial bank in order to accumulate savings for a future real estate investment that requires substantial equity. In these illustrations only a single sum is invested at the market rate of interest for an accumulated future amount.

In other situations, repeated cash amounts are invested at the going rate of interest until an amount is accumulated for a previously planned purpose of the investor. An example would be the investment of a portion of the cash flow of an investment in a savings medium that in the future would return the equity investment in the real estate project.

Let us proceed to the use of the compound interest and present value tables. Tables are handy for our needed calculations of current or future value. Furthermore, in the next chapter, we find use for the tables in the calculation of investment yields. This material is germane to the more complicated calculations of the succeeding chapter.

Most investors use hand calculators of varying degrees of sophistication and precomputed tables. Some investors have access to computers, and the compound interest and present value tables are callable on a subroutine basis.

The Future Worth of a Single Sum. When the investor wants to know the future worth of a sum of money deposited at interest today, he or she may calculate the amount with the appropriate formula or with the appropriate precalculated table. The compound interest tables for a single sum or the "Amount of 1 at Compound Interest" tables are usually employed by the real estate investor.

The general formula for the future value of 1 compounded annually is

$$S^n = (1 + i)^n$$

where S^n = the compound interest factor
i = the annual rate of interest and
n = the number of years in the compounding period.

If the interest compounds at intervals less than a year, the formula changes to

$$S^n = \left(1 + \frac{i}{m}\right)^{nm}$$

where m = the number of compounding intervals per year.

Therefore, the investor must note the number of compounding periods per year and adjust the interest rate and the total number of compounding periods. The correct tables to fit the specific situation must be selected. Widely distributed compound interest tables exist for monthly, quarterly, semiannual, and annual compounding periods.

If the investor has deposited $100 at 8 percent annual interest compounded annually for 10 years, the future value of the accumulated sum will be

$$\$100 \times 2.159 = \$215.90$$

$P \times S^n$ = Future value of the single sum, where P = amount of the principal invested at interest (Exhibit 16-6).

The Future Worth of an Annuity. When the investor wants to know the future worth of an annuity that receives a specified rate of interest, she or he may calculate the amount by hand or with precomputed tables. The appropriate tables may be labeled "Accumulation of 1 per Period," "Future Value of 1 per Period," or "Sum of an Annuity of $1 for n Years." Similar to the compound interest tables for a single sum, some of the precalculated tables cover monthly, quarterly, semiannual, and annual compounding periods. Most of the precalculated tables cover only annual compounding periods.

The general formula for the future value of 1 per period compounded annually is

$$S_n = \frac{S^n - 1}{i} \text{ or } \frac{(1 + i)^n - 1}{i}$$

Exhibit 16-6. Amount of $1 Table (the amount of $1, with interest, at the end of a given time)

Years	7%	7 1/4%	7 1/2%	7 3/4%	8%	8 1/8%	8 1/4%
1	1.070	1.073	1.075	1.078	1.080	1.081	1.083
2	1.145	1.150	1.156	1.161	1.166	1.169	1.172
3	1.225	1.234	1.242	1.251	1.260	1.264	1.268
4	1.311	1.323	1.335	1.348	1.360	1.367	1.373
5	1.403	1.419	1.436	1.452	1.469	1.478	1.486
6	1.501	1.522	1.543	1.565	1.587	1.598	1.609
7	1.606	1.632	1.659	1.686	1.714	1.728	1.742
8	1.718	1.751	1.783	1.817	1.851	1.868	1.885
9	1.838	1.877	1.917	1.958	1.999	2.020	2.041
10	1.967	2.014	2.061	2.109	2.159	2.184	2.209
11	2.105	2.160	2.216	2.273	2.332	2.361	2.392
12	2.252	2.316	2.382	2.449	2.518	2.553	2.589
13	2.410	2.484	2.560	2.639	2.720	2.761	2.803
14	2.579	2.664	2.752	2.843	2.937	2.985	3.034
15	2.759	2.857	2.959	3.064	3.172	3.228	3.284
16	2.952	3.064	3.181	3.301	3.426	3.490	3.555
17	3.159	3.287	3.419	3.557	3.700	3.773	3.848
18	3.380	3.525	3.676	3.833	3.996	4.080	4.166
19	3.617	3.780	3.951	4.130	4.316	4.412	4.510
20	3.870	4.055	4.248	4.450	4.661	4.770	4.882
21	4.141	4.349	4.566	4.795	5.034	5.158	5.284
22	4.430	4.664	4.909	5.166	5.437	5.577	5.720
23	4.741	5.002	5.277	5.567	5.871	6.030	6.192
24	5.072	5.365	5.673	5.998	6.341	6.520	6.703
25	5.427	5.754	6.098	6.463	6.848	7.049	7.256
26	5.807	6.171	6.556	6.964	7.396	7.622	7.855
27	6.214	6.618	7.047	7.504	7.988	8.241	8.503
28	6.649	7.098	7.576	8.085	8.627	8.911	9.204
29	7.114	7.612	8.144	8.712	9.317	9.635	9.963
30	7.612	8.164	8.755	9.387	10.063	10.418	10.785
31	8.145	8.756	9.412	10.114	10.868	11.264	11.675
32	8.715	9.391	10.117	10.898	11.737	12.180	12.638
33	9.325	10.072	10.876	11.743	12.676	13.169	13.681
34	9.978	10.802	11.692	12.653	13.690	14.239	14.810
35	10.677	11.585	12.569	13.633	14.785	15.396	16.032
36	11.424	12.425	13.512	14.690	15.968	16.647	17.354
37	12.224	13.326	14.525	15.828	17.246	18.000	18.786
38	13.079	14.292	15.614	17.055	18.625	19.462	20.336
39	13.995	15.328	16.785	18.377	20.115	21.044	22.013
40	14.974	16.440	18.044	19.801	21.725	22.753	23.830
41	16.023	17.632	19.398	21.336	23.462	24.602	25.796
42	17.144	18.910	20.852	22.989	25.339	26.601	27.924
43	18.344	20.281	22.416	24.771	27.367	28.762	30.227
44	19.628	21.751	24.098	26.691	29.556	31.099	32.721
45	21.002	23.328	25.905	28.759	31.920	33.626	35.421
46	22.473	25.019	27.848	30.988	34.474	36.358	38.343
47	24.046	26.833	29.936	33.390	37.232	39.312	41.506
48	25.729	28.779	32.182	35.977	40.211	42.506	44.910
49	27.530	30.865	34.595	38.766	43.427	45.960	48.637
50	29.457	33.103	37.190	41.770	46.902	49.694	52.650

Source: *Financial Constant Percent Amortization Tables,* Publication No. 287 (Boston: Financial Publishing Company, 1975), p. 234. Reprinted with permission.

If the interest compounds at intervals less than a year, the interest rate, i, and the compounding period, n, would have to be adjusted. The annual rate, i, would have to be divided by the number of compounding periods per year, m, and the number of compounding periods, n, would have to be multiplied by m, the number of compounding periods per year.

To find the future value of an annuity earning interest at a given rate, the investor would use the following formula:

$$P \times S_n = \text{Future value of an annuity}$$

If the annual investment were $100 for 10 years compounded at a 10 percent rate of interest, the future value of the annuity would be

$$\$100 \times 15.9374 = \$1{,}593.74 \text{ (Exhibit 16-7)}$$

The Present Value of a Single Sum. When the investor wants to calculate the present value of a single sum, such as a reversion, she or he uses the appropriate formula to work it by hand or uses present value tables for the compound interest period and the interest rate. The tables may be labeled the "Present Worth of $1," "Present Value, Reversion of 1," or simply the "Present Value of 1." Quite often the present value tables cover only annual compounding periods.

The general formula for the present value of 1 compounded annually is

$$V^n = \frac{i}{S^n} \text{ or } \frac{1}{(1+i)^n}$$

If the investment occurs more often than once a year, or the compounding of interest occurs more than once a year, the interest rate, i, and the compounding period, n, must be adjusted, as mentioned above.

To find the present value of a single sum earning interest at a given rate, the investor uses the following formula:

$$P \times V^n = \text{Present value of a single sum}$$

If the reversion expected from the sale of an investment property five years hence is $1,000 and the appropriate interest or discount rate is 10 percent, the present value of the reversion would be

$$\$1{,}000 \times .620921 = \$620.92, \text{ present value of the reversion expected}$$

The Present Value of an Annuity. Real estate investment often involves the need for the present value of a future stream of income, such as a future series of lease payments. If a lease is being purchased, the prospective purchaser and seller will both decide independently on the present value of the stream of lease payments. Tables are often used for the calculation. Most of the tables are based on annual compounding of interest. If the compounding period is less than a year, the rate and the compounding period must be adjusted.

The general formula for the present value of an annuity compounded annually for a specified period of time is

$$a_n = \frac{1 - V^n}{i} \text{ or } \frac{1 - [1/(1+i)^n]}{I}$$

Exhibit 16-7. Sum of an Annuity of $1 for n Years

n	8%	9%	10%	11%	12%	13%	14%	15%
1	1.000000	1.000000	1.000000	1.000000	1.000000	1.000000	1.000000	1.000000
2	2.080000	2.090000	2.100000	2.110000	2.120000	2.130000	2.140000	2.150000
3	3.246400	3.278100	3.310000	3.342100	3.374400	3.406900	3.439600	3.472500
4	4.506112	4.573129	4.641000	4.709731	4.779328	4.849797	4.921144	4.993375
5	5.866601	5.984711	6.105100	6.227801	6.352847	6.480271	6.610104	6.742381
6	7.335929	7.523335	7.715610	7.912860	8.115189	8.322706	8.535519	8.753738
7	8.922803	9.200435	9.487171	9.783274	10.089012	10.404658	10.730491	11.066799
8	10.636628	11.028474	11.435888	11.859434	12.299693	12.757263	13.232760	13.726819
9	12.487558	13.021036	13.579477	14.163972	14.775656	15.415707	16.085347	16.785842
10	14.486562	15.192930	15.937425	16.722009	17.548735	18.419749	19.337295	20.303718
11	16.645487	17.560293	18.531167	19.561430	20.654583	21.814317	23.044516	24.349276
12	18.977126	20.140720	21.384284	22.713187	24.133133	25.650178	27.270749	29.001667
13	21.495297	22.953385	24.522712	26.211638	28.029109	29.984701	32.088654	34.351917
14	24.214920	26.019189	27.974983	30.094918	32.392602	34.883712	37.581065	40.504705
15	27.152114	29.360916	31.772482	34.405359	37.279715	40.417464	43.842414	47.580411
16	30.324283	33.003399	35.949730	39.189948	42.753280	46.671735	50.980352	55.717472
17	33.750226	36.973705	40.544703	44.500843	48.883674	53.739060	59.117601	65.075093
18	37.450244	41.301338	45.599173	50.395936	55.749715	61.725138	68.394066	75.836357
19	41.446263	46.018458	51.159090	56.939488	63.439681	70.749406	78.969235	88.211811
20	45.761964	51.160120	57.274999	64.202832	75.052442	80.946829	91.024928	102.443583
21	50.422921	56.764530	64.003499	72.265144	81.698736	92.469917	104.768418	118.810120
22	55.456755	62.873338	71.402749	81.214309	92.502584	105.491006	120.435996	137.631638
23	60.893296	69.531939	79.543024	91.147884	104.602894	120.204837	138.297035	159.276384
24	66.764759	76.789813	88.497327	102.174151	118.155241	136.831465	158.658620	184.167841
25	73.105940	84.700896	98.347059	114.413307	133.333870	155.619556	181.870827	212.793017
26	79.954415	93.323977	109.181765	127.998771	150.333934	176.850098	208.332743	245.711970
27	87.350768	102.723135	121.099942	143.078636	169.374007	200.840611	238.499327	283.568766
28	95.338830	112.968217	134.209936	159.817286	190.698887	227.949890	272.889233	327.104080
29	103.965936	124.135356	148.630930	178.397187	214.582754	258.583376	312.093725	377.169693
30	113.283211	136.307539	164.494023	199.020878	241.332684	293.199215	356.786847	434.745146
31	123.345868	149.575217	181.943425	221.913174	271.292606	332.315113	407.737006	500.956918
32	134.213537	164.036987	201.137767	247.323624	304.847719	376.516078	465.820186	577.100456
33	145.950620	179.800315	222.251544	275.529222	342.429446	426.463168	532.035012	644.665525
34	158.626670	196.982344	245.476699	306.837437	384.520979	482.903380	607.519914	765.365353
35	172.316804	215.710755	271.024368	341.589555	431.663496	546.680819	693.572702	881.170156
36	187.102149	236.124723	299.126805	380.164406	484.463116	618.749325	791.672881	1014.345680
37	203.070320	258.375948	330.039486	422.982490	543.598690	700.186738	903.507084	1167.497532
38	220.315945	282.629783	364.043434	470.510564	609.830533	792.211014	1030.998076	1343.622161
39	238.941221	309.066463	401.447778	523.266726	684.010197	896.198445	1176.337806	1546.165485
40	259.056519	337.882445	442.592556	581.826066	767.091420	1013.704243	1342.025009	1779.090308
41	280.781040	369.291865	487.851811	646.826934	860.142391	1146.485795	1530.908613	2046.953854
42	304.243523	403.528133	537.636992	718.977896	964.359478	1296.528948	1746.235819	2354.996933
43	329.583005	440.845665	592.400692	799.065465	1081.082615	1466.077712	1991.708833	2709.246473
44	356.949646	481.521775	652.640761	887.962666	1211.812529	1657.667814	2271.548070	3116.633443
45	386.505617	525.858734	718.904837	986.638559	1358.230032	1874.164630	2590.564800	3585.128460
46	418.426067	574.186021	791.795321	1096.168801	1522.217636	2118.806032	2954.243872	4123.897729
47	452.900152	626.862762	871.974853	1217.747369	1705.883752	2395.250816	3368.838014	2743.482388
48	490.132164	684.280411	960.172338	1352.699580	1911.589803	2707.633422	3841.475336	5466.004746
49	530.342737	746.865648	1057.189572	1502.496534	2141.980579	3060.625767	4380.281883	6275.405458
50	573.770156	815.083556	1163.908529	1669.771152	2400.018249	3459.507117	4994.521346	7217.716277

Source: Mary Alice Hines, *Real Estate Finance* (Englewood Cliffs, N.J.: Prentice-Hall, 1978), p. 365. © 1978 by Prentice-Hall, Inc. Reprinted by permission of Prentice-Hall.

To find the present value of an annuity to be received a specified number of periods into the future, using a given interest or discount rate, the investor uses the following formula:

$P \times a_n$ = Present value of an annuity

As an example, if the annual lease payment expected over the next 10 years is $1,000, and the appropriate rate of interest, or the discount rate, is 10 percent, the present value of the annuity is

$1,000 × 6.145 (Exhibit 16-9)

Exhibit 16-8. Present Worth of $1 Table (for computing the value of a reversion)

Years	9 1/4%	9 3/8%	9 1/2%	9 5/8%	9 3/4%	9 7/8 %	10%
1	.915332	.914286	.913242	.912201	.911162	.910125	.909091
2	.837832	.835918	.834011	.832110	.830216	.828328	.826446
3	.766895	.764268	.761654	.759051	.756461	.753882	.751315
4	.701963	.698760	.695574	.692407	.689258	.686127	.683013
5	.642529	.638866	.635228	.631614	.628026	.624461	.620921
6	.588127	.584106	.580117	.576159	.572233	.568338	.564474
7	.538332	.534040	.529787	.525573	.521397	.517259	.513158
8	.492752	.488265	.483824	.479428	.475077	.470770	.466507
9	.451032	.446414	.441848	.437334	.432872	.428460	.424098
10	.412844	.408150	.403514	.398937	.394416	.389952	.385543
11	.377889	.373165	.368506	.363910	.359377	.354905	.350494
12	.345894	.341180	.336535	.331959	.327450	.323008	.318631
13	.316608	.311916	.307338	.302813	.298360	.293978	.289664
14	.289801	.285198	.280674	.276227	.271885	.267557	.263331
15	.265264	.260753	.256323	.251974	.247703	.243510	.239392
16	.242805	.238403	.234085	.229851	.225698	.221625	.217629
17	.222247	.217968	.213777	.209670	.205647	.201706	.197845
18	.203430	.199285	.195230	.191261	.187378	.183578	.179859
19	.186206	.182204	.178292	.174469	.170732	.167079	.163508
20	.170440	.166586	.162824	.159150	.155564	.152063	.148644
21	.156009	.152307	.148697	.145177	.141744	.138396	.135131
22	.142800	.139252	.135797	.132431	.129152	.125958	.122846
23	.130709	.127336	.124015	.120803	.117678	.114637	.111678
24	.119642	.116404	.113256	.110197	.107224	.104334	.101526
25	.109513	.106426	.103430	.100522	.097698	.094957	.092296
26	.100240	.097304	.094457	.091696	.089019	.086423	.083905
27	.091753	.088964	.086262	.083645	.081111	.078656	.076278
28	.083985	.081338	.078778	.076301	.073905	.071587	.069343
29	.076874	.074366	.071943	.069602	.067339	.065153	.063039
30	.070365	.067992	.065702	.063491	.061357	.059297	.057309
31	.064407	.062164	.060002	.057916	.055906	.063968	.052099
32	.058954	.056836	.054796	.052831	.050940	.049117	.047362
33	.053963	.051964	.050042	.048193	.046414	.044703	.043057
34	.049394	.047510	.045700	.043962	.042291	.040685	.039143
35	.045212	.043438	.041736	.040102	.038534	.037029	.035584
36	.041384	.039715	.038115	.036581	.035110	.033701	.032349
37	.037880	.036310	.034808	.033369	.031991	.030672	.029408
38	.034672	.033198	.031788	.030439	.029149	.027915	.026735
39	.031737	.030353	.029030	.027767	.026560	.025406	.024304
40	.029050	.027751	.026512	.025329	.024200	.023123	.022095
41	.026590	.025372	.024211	.023105	.022050	.021045	.020086
42	.024339	.023198	.022111	.021076	.020091	.019153	.018260
43	.022278	.021209	.020193	.019226	.018306	.017432	.016600
44	.020392	.019391	.018441	.017538	.016680	.015865	.015091
45	.018665	.017729	.016841	.015998	.015198	.014439	.013719
46	.017085	.016209	.015380	.014593	.013848	.013142	.012472
47	.015638	.014820	.014045	.013312	.012618	.011961	.011338
48	.014314	.013550	.012827	.012143	.011497	.010886	.010307
49	.013102	.012388	.011714	.011077	.010476	.009907	.009370
50	.011993	.011327	.010698	.010105	.009545	.009017	.008519

Source: *Financial Constant Percent Amortization Tables,* Publication No. 287 (Boston: Financial Publishing Company, 1975), p. 220. Reprinted with permission.

Exhibit 16-9. Present Worth of $1 per Year (Inwood coefficient)

Years	9 1/4%	9 3/8%	9 1/2%	9 5/8%	9 3/4%	9 7/8%	10%
1	.915	.914	.913	.912	.911	.910	.909
2	1.753	1.750	1.747	1.744	1.741	1.738	1.736
3	2.520	2.514	2.509	2.503	2.498	2.492	2.487
4	3.222	3.213	3.204	3.196	3.187	3.178	3.170
5	3.865	3.852	3.840	3.827	3.815	3.803	3.791
6	4.453	4.436	4.420	4.404	4.387	4.371	4.355
7	4.991	4.970	4.950	4.929	4.909	4.889	4.868
8	5.484	5.459	5.433	5.409	5.384	5.359	5.335
9	5.935	5.905	5.875	5.846	5.817	5.788	5.759
10	6.348	6.313	6.279	6.245	6.211	6.178	6.145
11	6.726	6.686	6.647	6.609	6.570	6.533	6.495
12	7.071	7.027	6.984	6.941	6.898	6.856	6.814
13	7.388	7.339	7.291	7.243	7.196	7.150	7.103
14	7.678	7.625	7.572	7.520	7.468	7.417	7.367
15	7.943	7.885	7.828	7.772	7.716	7.661	7.606
16	8.186	8.124	8.062	8.002	7.942	7.882	7.824
17	8.408	8.342	8.276	8.211	8.147	8.084	8.022
18	8.612	8.541	8.471	8.402	8.335	8.268	8.201
19	8.798	8.723	8.650	8.577	8.505	8.435	8.365
20	8.968	8.890	8.812	8.736	8.661	8.587	8.514
21	9.124	9.042	8.961	8.881	8.803	8.725	8.649
22	9.267	9.181	9.097	9.014	8.932	8.851	8.772
23	9.398	9.309	9.221	9.135	9.049	8.966	8.883
24	9.517	9.425	9.334	9.245	9.157	9.070	8.985
25	9.627	9.531	9.438	9.345	9.254	9.165	9.077
26	9.727	9.629	9.532	9.437	9.343	9.251	9.161
27	9.819	9.718	9.618	9.521	9.425	9.330	9.237
28	9.903	9.799	9.697	9.597	9.498	9.402	9.307
29	9.980	9.873	9.769	9.666	9.566	9.467	9.370
30	10.050	9.941	9.835	9.730	9.627	9.526	9.427
31	10.115	10.004	9.895	9.788	9.683	9.580	9.479
32	10.173	10.060	9.950	9.841	9.734	9.629	9.526
33	10.227	10.112	10.000	9.889	9.780	9.674	9.569
34	10.277	10.160	10.045	9.933	9.823	9.715	9.609
35	10.322	10.203	10.087	9.973	9.861	9.752	9.644
36	10.363	10.243	10.125	10.010	9.896	9.785	9.677
37	10.401	10.279	10.160	10.043	9.928	9.816	9.706
38	10.436	10.313	10.192	10.073	9.957	9.844	9.733
39	10.468	10.343	10.221	10.101	9.984	9.869	9.757
40	10.497	10.371	10.247	10.126	10.008	9.892	9.779
41	10.523	10.396	10.271	10.150	10.030	9.913	9.799
42	10.548	10.419	10.294	10.171	10.050	9.933	9.817
43	10.570	10.440	10.314	10.190	10.069	9.950	9.834
44	10.590	10.460	10.332	10.207	10.085	9.966	9.849
45	10.609	10.478	10.349	10.223	10.101	9.980	9.863
46	10.626	10.494	10.364	10.238	10.114	9.994	9.875
47	10.642	10.509	10.378	10.251	10.127	10.005	9.887
48	10.656	10.522	10.391	10.263	10.138	10.016	9.897
49	10.669	10.535	10.403	10.275	10.149	10.026	9.906
50	10.681	10.546	10.414	10.285	10.159	10.035	9.915

Source: *Financial Constant Percent Amortization Tables,* Publication No. 287 (Boston: Financial Publishing Company, 1975), p. 228. Reprinted with permission.

SUMMARY

After studying cash flow and profit planning, we learn that there are four basic components affecting real estate investment returns: the amount of equity funds invested, the amount of borrowed funds, the net operating income per interval of the expected holding period, and sale proceeds. Sale proceeds include the change in property value over the holding period and the equity buildup from mortgage repayment over the holding period.

Some fundamental concepts related to mathematical analysis are associated closely with investment return measurement, the topic taken up in chapter 17. Equity investment usually supplements mortgage investment. Equity funds may be derived from such sources as general and limited partners or syndicate members. Their returns are subject to prearranged and approved distribution systems. The amount of the mortgage payment and the remaining mortgage balance are needed in order to calculate the property investment yield. Variable factors, such as interest rates and mortgagee participation in gross income, may render an estimate of the future mortgage payments difficult. The use of the mortgage constant is important to the investor's and the lender's return. A single mortgage constant may fit many financing agreements, but the debt service requirement each year is a known amount. Tables may be used to calculate the mortgage payment and the mortgage balance due.

Since real estate investment is a dynamic process and competing investment yields are significant, the investor must always be aware of current yields and the trend in yields in the money and capital markets. The change in market yields was illustrated with data from the 1977 and 1979 markets. Since investment yields are subject to volatility from the impact of many changing variables, it was suggested that sensitivity analysis might be used to forecast the impact on yield and net cash flow, as changes in one strategic variable are made and the other investment variables are held constant.

The time value of money is very significant in real estate investment analysis. Therefore, the future worth of a single sum and an annuity and the present worth of a single sum and an annuity were studied in light of their real estate investment applications.

Key Terms and Concepts

Compound interest
Present value
Investment yield measurement
Capital depreciation
Constant annual percent (mortgage constant)
Eurodollar rates
Loan progress tables
Mortgagee participation in equity

Cash budgeting policy
Money market yields
Bankers acceptances
Future worth of a single sum
Future worth of an annuity
Present value of an annuity
Sponsor-syndicator
Dealers' commercial paper
Certificates of deposit

Questions for Student Self-examination

Multiple-Choice Questions

1. Often income property mortgages have _____ interest-only clauses.
   a. 2-year
   b. 3- to 5-year
   c. 10- to 13-year
   d. 20- to 25-year

2. The equity participation of the lender usually applies to the _____ received in excess of a specified amount.
   a. gross revenue
   b. net income
   c. net cash flow
   d. none of the above

3. The mortgage balance _____ over the investment holding period.
   a. increases
   b. does not remain constant
   c. remains constant
   d. none of the above

4. The cash return to the syndicator takes the form of
   a. commissions
   b. fees for syndicate management
   c. a share of the resale proceeds
   d. all of the above

5. The developer's return from a real estate development takes the form of
   a. participation in the gross income from the operation of the development
   b. fixed debt service payments
   c. profits on the purchase of syndicate properties
   d. cash from early mortgage repayment

True-False Questions

T F 1. The purchase or development of a property requires at least two sources of capital.
T F 2. Front-end costs that are paid by the owner or by ownership groups represent contributions of creditor capital.
T F 3. All front-end costs may be immediately expensed for federal income tax purposes.
T F 4. The effective cost of the planning and financing expense depends on the tax bracket of the taxpayer.
T F 5. Most income properties are sold before the maturity of the usual mortgages.
T F 6. Income property mortgages always have a balloon payment at maturity.
T F 7. The income property mortgage has a fixed interest rate.
T F 8. The interest rate on a home mortgage may be variable.
T F 9. Property value never declines over the investment holding period.
T F 10. The investor may receive a return from equity buildup from the mortgage repayment.

Answers
Multiple-choice: 1b, 2a, 3b, 4d, 5a.
True–False: 1F, 2F, 3F, 4T, 5T, 6F, 7F, 8T, 9F, 10T.

Problems

1. If an income project costs $1,000,000, the borrowed funds amount to $750,000, and the front-end costs outside of construction costs amount to $20,000, how much equity is contributed by the owner?

2. As the Rainier Apartments are being developed, the following costs are encountered:

Prepaid interest	$ 3,000
Architectural fees	12,000
Surveying costs	1,000
Organizational expense	5,000
Annual management fee	7,500

   What do the front-end costs total?

3. What total cost would have to be capitalized and amortized for the development of the Rainer Apartment project? Costs are enumerated below.

Preliminary economic and engineering studies	$ 1,000
Organizational legal expense	5,000
Syndication sales fees	6,000
Recording costs	200
Appraisal fees	2,500
Construction loan interest	10,000

4. If the shopping center generates a gross revenue of $20,000,000 and the mortgage lender participates in the gross revenue above the amount of $15,000,000 at the rate of 5 percent, how much money would be paid the lender on the basis of the participation clause in the shopping center mortgage?

5. If the income property mortgage interest rate floats above the prime rate two points, what would be the current mortgage rate if the prime rate were 11 percent?

6. If the income property mortgagee participates in the cash throw-off from the shopping center on the basis of a 50–50 split with the owner, how much would the mortgagee receive if the gross receipts from the center were $10,000,000 and the cash throw-off from the year's operations were $30,000?

Chapter 17

Investment Return Measurement

Introduction
The Relationship of This Chapter to Other Chapters of the Text
Some Indications of Recent Real Estate Investment Yields
    Real Estate Values Versus Competing Asset Values   Rates of Return on Equity of Various Types of Real Property
Methods of Measuring Investment Yields
    Total Dollar Return   Broker's Method, or the Cash-on-Cash Return   Cash Payback   Net Present Value   Internal Rate of Return   Financial Management Rate of Return
Summary
Key Terms and Concepts
Questions for Student Self-examination

> **LEARNING OBJECTIVES** After studying this chapter, you should be familiar with
>
> The comparative performance of real estate values versus other competing asset values
> Rates of return on equity of various types of real property
> The methods of measuring investment yields, including
> - Total dollar return
> - Broker's method, or the cash-on-cash return
> - Cash payback
> - Net present value
> - Internal rate of return
> - Financial management rate of return

Real estate investors have always sought to measure their returns from property ownership. The measurement techniques have changed over time, but the desire to measure the total investment return has always prevailed. Today some rather sophisticated investment measurement methods exist. Some real estate investors use the newer methods of analysis; some investors prefer to use the older, less sophisticated methods. In this chapter, a summary of the most commonly used methods of analysis is presented, along with research results concerning real estate investment returns over recent years.

INTRODUCTION

The first portion of the chapter covers some indications of recent real estate investment yields on various types of properties. Value trends of real estate and competing investments, as disclosed by the National Association of Realtors, are first presented. Then Ricks' research findings concerning returns on equity after tax and after financing over the period since World War II are discussed. Finally, the information from Kelleher's 1976 study of annual returns from Standard & Poor's 500 stocks and multiple-tenant income properties is given. The trends in the Standard and Poor 500 Stock Price Index, the Standard and Poor 500 Stock Dividend Yield Index, the net operating income index for multiple-tenant income property, and the operating income ratio for multiple-tenant income property are observed and compared. Kelleher also offers the reader study results of the internal rate of return of Standard and Poor's 500 stocks and multiple-tenant income properties from 1960 through 1973. The investor can observe the differences between the calculated internal rates of return for each category and across the years.

The second portion of the chapter deals with the most commonly used methods of investment yield analysis. The methods reviewed include (1) total dollar return, (2) average annual return on equity, or cash-on-cash, (3) cash payback, (4) net present value, (5) internal or discounted rate of return, and (6) financial management rate of return.

THE RELATIONSHIP OF THIS CHAPTER TO OTHER CHAPTERS OF THE TEXT

This chapter concludes Part IV, "Real Estate Investment Analysis." The prior chapters of the section presented the needed preliminary discussion of cash flow and profit analysis and the time value of money, which make this chapter easier to comprehend and appreciate. The next part deals with investment returns from various specific types of properties. The current chapter covers investment yield measurement in general without regard to the special investment characteristics, returns, and risks of specific types of properties.

SOME INDICATIONS OF RECENT REAL ESTATE INVESTMENT YIELDS

Considerable speculation and little well-founded research exists about recent real estate investment yields. There are several reasons for this situation. The government collects data on some real estate areas such as housing starts, construction costs, nominal interest rates on residential mortgages, terms to maturity and loan-to-value ratios for residential mortgages, total mortgage amounts by type of residential mortgages, and bid and asked prices for GNMA-guaranteed mortgage-backed securities. The government on its various levels does not usually collect data on income property investments and their financing methods. The government also does not usually collect data on real property values and value trends. Any data on investment yields is available from private sources who do not consistently collect value and investment data. Therefore, mystery surrounds real estate investment yields to a large extent.

Real estate investment yields and property values differ by locality, according to our limited knowledge. One area with balanced industry representation that is not subject to periodic recessions in business activity may promote real estate investment yields that are quite different from another area with industry concentrated in cyclical businesses, where declines in business activity occur periodically. The same thing is true of areas of the country that are subject to different degrees of expansion. For example, business in the Northeast tends to be rather stagnant overall, while economies in the West, Southwest, and Southeast tend to be expanding rapidly. Property value levels and patterns of increase tend to follow the pattern of economic expansion or contraction of the area of the country in which they are located. Therefore, evidence of real estate investment yields may fit only one locality, rather than the region or the nation as a whole.

Real Estate Values Versus Competing Assets Values. Several recent articles in the public media have compared real estate values with values associated with other types of investments. Often the articles have dealt with house values from an owner-occupied point of view. A few articles have dealt with the values of rental houses. Most of the articles have cited the increase in house values in selected locations, such as southern or northern California, the Boston area, the New York City area, or small towns in the Midwest. These articles on the rise in house values have pointed out that this area of investment has yielded higher returns in the latter 1970s than other traditional forms of investment, such as stocks and bonds.

A recent study by the National Association of Realtors confirms the conclusions of the many articles mentioned above. The economist for the National Association of Realtors collected data on value changes from 1967 to 1977 for cash, common stock

Exhibit 17-1. *Performance of Small Investments in Real Estate*

Change in Value 1967-77, Adjusted for Inflation

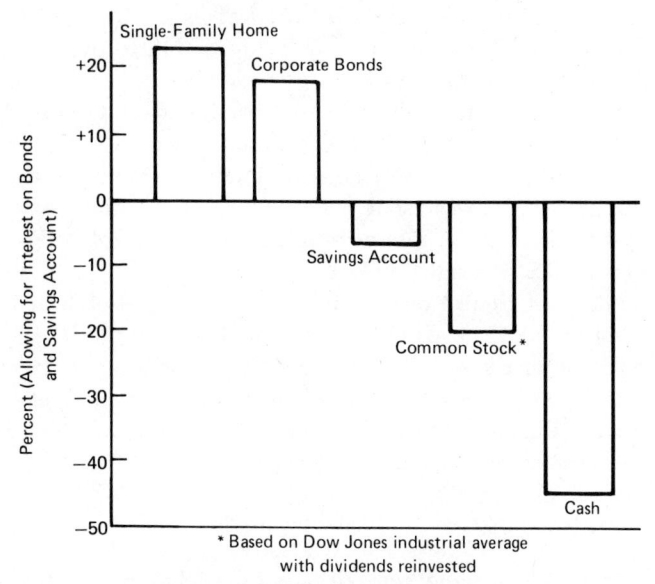

[Bar chart showing percent change (allowing for interest on bonds and savings account):
- Single-Family Home: approximately +22
- Corporate Bonds: approximately +18
- Savings Account: approximately -7
- Common Stock*: approximately -20
- Cash: approximately -45]

*Based on Dow Jones industrial average with dividends reinvested

Data: National Association of Real Estate Boards

Adapted by *Business Week*, in "The Stellar Performance of Small Investments in Real Estate," Personal Business Supplement, May 15, 1978. Reprinted by special permission. © 1978 by McGraw-Hill, Inc. All rights reserved.

Table 17-1. *Comparison of annual returns for Standard and Poor's 500 stocks and real estate properties*

| | Standard & Poor's 500 Stocks || Multiple-Tenant Real Estate ||
Year	Price Index on December 31	Annual Dividend as Percent of Price	Net Operating Income Index	Annual Yield Income as Percent of Price
1960	58.11	3.35	77.6	8.9
1961	71.55	2.86	84.9	8.8
1962	63.10	3.38	81.0	8.6
1963	75.02	3.11	82.0	8.4
1964	84.75	3.03	93.4	8.4
1965	92.43	3.04	96.7	8.5
1966	80.44	3.64	97.8	8.4
1967	96.47	3.06	100.0	8.6
1968	103.86	2.99	103.3	9.0
1969	92.06	3.48	111.1	9.6
1970	92.15	3.36	121.3	10.8
1971	102.10	2.99	121.5	10.0
1972	118.10	2.71	132.1	9.6
1973	97.55	3.64	140.1	9.5

Source: Dennis G. Kelleher, "How Real Estate Stacks Up to the S&P 500," *Real Estate Review* (Summer 1976), p. 63.

included in the Dow Jones Industrial Average, savings accounts, corporate bonds, and single-family homes. The change in value from 1967 to 1977, adjusted for inflation, for single-family homes had the greatest positive percentage (Exhibit 17-1).

In a study of annual returns for Standard and Poor's 500 stocks and multiple-tenant real estate from 1960 through 1973, Kelleher found that (1) the Standard and Poor 500 Stock Index fluctuated from 58.11 up to 118.10 over the time period, (2) the stock dividend yield approximated 3 percent, (3) the net operating income index for the real estate sample gradually increased from 77.6 in 1960 to 140.1 in 1973, and (4) the stabilized annual yield for the real estate (income as a percent on price) approximated 9 percent (Table 17-1). The same study indicated that the internal rate of return for multiple-tenant real estate over the 1960-1973 time period came close to being twice that of the internal rate of return for the Standard & Poor's 500 stocks (7.2 percent versus 13.2 percent) (Table 17-2).

Rates of Return on Equity of Various Types of Real Property. The stability and level of equity yields after taxes was shown by the Ricks study of rates of return on equity after tax and after financing of various property types from 1954 through 1966. For the eleven types of real properties, the average equity yield over the 13-year time span approximated 8 to 9 percent (Table 17-3). During each sample period, the equity yield for hotel and motel investment was the highest—10.4 percent in 1959 to 12.8 percent in 1965.

Table 17-2. Internal rates of return for Standard and Poor's 500 stocks and multiple-tenant real estate*

Time Period for Which Investment Is Held	Standard & Poor's 500 Stocks	Multiple-Tenant Real Estate
1960 through 1966		
Jan. 1960–Dec. 1960	0.3	11.4
Jan. 1960–Dec. 1961	12.5	15.6
Jan. 1960–Dec. 1962	5.1	12.6
Jan. 1960–Dec. 1963	9.0	12.5
Jan. 1960–Dec. 1964	10.4	14.3
Jan. 1960–Dec. 1965	10.7	13.9
Jan. 1960–Dec. 1966	7.8	13.5
1967 through 1973		
Jan. 1967–Dec. 1967	23.6	8.5
Jan. 1967–Dec. 1968	17.2	8.0
Jan. 1967–Dec. 1969	8.3	8.8
Jan. 1967–Dec. 1970	7.1	8.5
Jan. 1967–Dec. 1971	8.4	10.2
Jan. 1967–Dec. 1972	9.9	11.9
Jan. 1967–Dec. 1973	6.4	12.5
Summary		
Jan. 1960–Dec. 1973	7.2	13.2

Source: Dennis G. Kelleher, "How Real Estate Stacks Up to the S&P 500," *Real Estate Review* (Summer 1976), p. 63.
* Assume a single investment on January 1, 1960.

Table 17-3. Rate of return on equity after tax, after financing

Property Type	Quarter and Year				
	3rd, '54	4th, '59	3rd, '63	1st, '65	4th, '66
Apartments—elevator	8.32	8.58	8.81	9.55	9.53
Apartments—nonelevator	8.67	8.00	8.58	9.35	9.34
Hotels and Motels	10.99	10.43	12.12	12.82	11.42
Retail stores	7.42	7.23	7.65	7.87	8.63
Shopping centers	7.14	7.26	7.99	8.74	8.71
Office buildings	7.35	7.88	8.42	9.18	8.90
Medical office buildings	8.65	8.78	8.34	9.56	8.65
Warehouses	7.33	7.56	7.61	8.21	7.66
Industrial	7.84	7.60	8.10	8.92	8.32
Miscellaneous commercial	8.28	7.22	7.81	8.16	8.55
Institutional	6.75	7.92	8.73	8.18	6.96
All loans	7.98	8.01	8.27	9.07	8.87

Source: R. Bruce Ricks, "Imputed Equity Returns on Real Estate Financed with Life Insurance Company Loans," *Journal of Finance* (December 1969), Vol. 24, No. 5, p. 933. Reprinted by permission.

METHODS OF MEASURING INVESTMENT YIELDS

Investigation of investor practices indicates that the principal methods of measuring real estate investment yields are

- Total dollar return
- Broker's method, or cash-on-cash return
- Cash payback
- Net present value
- Internal or discounted rate of return
- Financial management rate of return

The previous two chapters of this section have given the student the background for the derivation of the amounts required in the investment yield formulas and the usefulness of the compound interest and present value tables. In the following part of the chapter, each of the yield measurement methods will be presented in terms of its benefits and weaknesses.

Total Dollar Return. This method of ascertaining real estate investment yield is easy to understand and calculate. The total net cash flows available to the equity investor after taxes would be the most meaningful dollar amounts for the equity investor to study. If taxable income is significant to an investor with a high tax bracket, some notice will probably be given by this investor to the total taxable income per year in the holding period. Most investors want to observe a high volume of net cash flow after taxes, a high volume of tax-sheltered income from noncash depreciation write-off, and a low volume of taxable income.

Suppose the after-tax annual cash flows for years 1–5 for alternative investments A and B were

	After-Tax Annual Cash Flows	
Year	Investment A	Investment B
1	$ 1,000	$ 25,000
2	2,500	33,500
3	3,200	36,250
4	3,800	52,500
5	4,500	63,250
Total dollar return	$15,000	$210,500

In this case, the investor, on the basis of the total dollar return method of calculating yield, would select investment B, which yielded $210,500, rather than investment A, which yielded only $15,000. This method of investment return analysis does not consider the investment requirement or initial cash outlay.

Broker's Method, or the Cash-on-Cash Return. The cash-on-cash return is figured by a general formula whose components vary with the user of the formula. The general formula is

$$\text{Cash-on-cash return} = \frac{\text{Cash return}}{\text{Cash investment}}$$

The numerator takes on various definitions. *Cash return* can be defined as

Cash flow (net operating income less debt service)
Cash flow before reserves
Cash flow plus after-tax effects
Cash flow plus after-tax effects plus equity buildup
Cash flow plus after-tax effects plus equity buildup plus appreciation

The denominator also has various definitions, depending on the user of the formula. *Equity investment* may mean

The difference between the purchase price and the original mortgage balance.
The initial equity, including discount points paid, loan origination fees, and legal fees.
Downpayment plus prepaid interest or discount points paid before or after taxes.

Commonly used definitions for the numerator and denominator of the equation are

$$\text{Cash-on-cash return} = \frac{\text{Stabilized annual cash flow}}{\text{Initial equity required}}$$

If the initial equity requirement for investment A were $50,000, and for investment B, $200,000, the cash-on-cash return could be figured. The stabilized annual cash flow might be defined as the average annual cash flow after taxes.

Investment Alternative	Calculation	Stabilized Annual Cash Flow After Taxes
A	$ 15,000 divided by 5	$ 3,000
B	$210,500 divided by 5	$42,100

Therefore, the cash-on-cash return would be

Investment Alternative	Calculation	Cash-on-Cash Return
A	$\dfrac{\$3,000}{\$50,000}$	6%
B	$\dfrac{\$42,100}{\$200,000}$	21%

The investor would prefer investment B, since its cash-on-cash yield was 21 percent, a far superior yield in comparison with the 6 percent yield on investment A.

Cash Payback. The cash payback method of investment yield analysis is also popular. The investor is essentially analyzing her or his liquidity position when the payback period is examined. The more quickly the cash commitment is recouped or returned to the investor, the greater the liquidity and near-term profitability of the real estate investment.

As illustrations of the use of the payback method, let us again turn to alternative investments A and B. The cash equity investment for A was $50,000, and for B, $200,000. Over the five-year investment period, the after-tax annual cash flows of investment A never returned the initial capital investment to the owner. In the case of investment B, the investor gets back his or her initial cash investment in four years and nine and a half months from the expected after-tax annual cash flows.

Year	Investment B Annual Cash Flows After Tax
1	$ 25,000
2	33,500
3	36,250
4	52,500
Four-year total	$147,250

Initial cash equity investment	$200,000
Less four-year total	147,250
Portion of the fifth year cash flow needed	$ 52,750

$$\dfrac{\$52,750}{\$63,250} = 0.8$$

0.8×12 months $= 9.6$, or $9\frac{1}{2}$ months

The investor would select investment B if he or she wanted the return of the initial cash investment from the annual cash flows after taxes within the holding period. The return of the equity investment in investment A ($50,000) would have to come from the $15,000 of periodic cash flows and $35,000 from the net sale proceeds of the property.

Net Present Value. Some investors are using present using present value methods for calculating investment returns. There are three methods of yield analysis that employ present value and compound interest tables: (1) net present value, (2) internal rate of return, and (3) financial management rate of return. The net present value method assumes that the investor has a required rate of return that may be used for a discount rate in finding the present value of the net cash flows. The other two methods seek the rate of return generated by the investment cash flows in relation to the cash investment. Their assumptions are different, but they both lead to an internal rate of return.

In calculating the net present value, or the *internal* rate of return of a real estate investment, the analyst needs the expected net cash inflows and outflows for each equal-length interval of the investment holding period. Let us examine the cash flow distributions of investments C and D. The investor's required rate of return for each of the investments is 10 percent.

Year	Cash Flow Distribution (Net Cash Flows, Negative or Positive) C	D
0	− $50,000	− $120,000
1	2,000	5,000
2	5,000	13,500
3	20,500	− 10,000
4	− 15,000	52,000
5	90,000	145,000

The negative cash flows of year 0 represent the initial cash investment for the real property. The fifth-year cash flows include the net cash inflows or outflows from the year's operations, as well as the net cash proceeds from the sale of the investment property.

The general formulas for finding the net present value are

Net present value = Present value of the annual net cash inflows or outflows, using as a discount rate the investor's required rate of return.

Net present value = Present value of the annual net cash flows from operations and property sale less the cost of the real property.

If we assume that the investor's required rate of return is 10 percent, the net present values of investments C and D can be calculated. Since the annual cash flows are both positive and negative through the holding period, the present value of the negative flows must be subtracted from the present value of the positive cash flows to find the net present value.

	Investment C			Investment D		
Year	Net Cash Flow	Present Value Factor at 10%	Present Value	Net Cash Flow	Present Value Factor at 10%	Present Value
0	− $50,000	———	− $50,000	− $120,000	———	− $120,000
1	2,000	0.909	1,818	5,000	0.909	4,545
2	5,000	0.826	4,130	13,500	0.826	11,151
3	20,500	0.751	15,396	− 10,000	0.751	7,510
4	− 15,000	0.683	− 10,245	52,000	0.683	35,516
5	90,000	0.621	55,890	145,000	0.621	90,045
			Net present value $16,989			Net present value $13,747

Real Estate Investment Analysis

On a net present value basis, the investor would select investment C, whose net present value of $16,989 exceeds the net present value of investment D, $13,747. The investor, fortunately, would need only $50,000 for the initial cash outlay to purchase investment property C; investment property D requires a much larger initial capital amount, $120,000.

Internal Rate of Return. The internal rate of return method is a procedure for finding the rate of interest that equates the investment cash outlays to the net cash operating revenues over the investment holding period. Trial-and-error search is usually employed to find the single or multiple internal rates of return. There is only one internal rate of return if, during the holding period, net cash outflows change in the subsequent year to net cash inflows only once. There may be more than one internal rate of return if the sign of the net cash flows in succeeding years changes more than once. For example, there may be more than one internal rate of return for investments C and D, since the cash flow signs change more than once during the five-year holding period. In investment C, the sign of the cash flows changes from year 0 to year 1, from year 3 to year 4, and from year 4 to year 5. In investment D, the sign of the cash flows changes from year 0 to year 1, from year 2 to year 3, and from year 3 to year 4.

One of the internal rates of return for investments C and D is calculated in the following example.

Investment C

Year	Net Cash Flow	Present Value Factor at 15%	Present Value
0	− $50,000	―	− $50,000
1	2,000	0.870	1,740
2	5,000	0.756	3,780
3	20,500	0.658	13,489
4	− 15,000	0.572	− 8,580
5	90,000	0.497	44,730
		Net present value	$ 5,159

Investment D

Year	Net Cash Flow	Present Value Factor at 15%	Present Value
0	− $120,000	―	− $120,000
1	5,000	0.870	4,350
2	13,500	0.756	10,206
3	− 10,000	0.658	− 6,580
4	52,000	0.572	29,744
5	145,000	0.497	72,065
		Net present value	− $10,215

Investment C

Year	Net Cash Flow	Present Value Factor at 20%	Present Value
0	− $50,000	―	− $50,000
1	2,000	0.833	1,666
2	5,000	0.694	3,470
3	20,500	0.579	11,870
4	− 15,000	0.482	− 7,230
5	90,000	0.402	36,180
		Net present value	− $ 4,044

Interpolation:

Investment C			Investment D		
Trial Rates	Net Present Value	Goal versus a Trial NPV	Trial Rates	Net Present Value	Goal versus a Trial NPV
0.15	$5,159	0	0.10	$13,747	0
0.20	− 4,044	− 4,044	0.15	− 10,215	$10,215
0.05 Difference	9,203 Difference	4,044 Difference	0.05 Difference	$23,962 Difference	$10,215 Difference
0.20 Rate used for a base	− 0.05 Difference in trial rates	× 4,044 / 9,203 Small difference divided by total difference in NPV	0.15 Rate used for a base	− 0.05 Difference in trial rates	× 10,215 / 23,962 Small difference divided by total difference in NPV
= 0.20 − (0.05 × 0.439) = 0.20 − 0.022 = 0.178 = Internal rate of return for C			= 0.15 − (0.05 × 0.43) = 0.15 − 0.0215 = 0.1285 = Internal rate of return for D		

The investor, on the basis of internal rate of return, would select investment property C over investment property D. The internal rate of return of C of 18 percent is five percentage points higher than the internal rate of return of D, 13 percent. Luckily, the initial capital investment for investment C is substantially less than that for investment D, whereas C has a much higher internal rate of return. The internal rate of return computation could have resulted in the opposite situation. The higher rate of return might have been generated by the project having the highest initial capital commitment.

Financial Management Rate of Return. The financial management rate of return is another method of deriving the internal rate of return of a real estate investment. The time value of money is taken into account, just as it was in the internal rate of return and the net present value methods of analysis. This method, though, is based on the terminal value rate of return concept. Only one internal rate of return is possible. Multiple rates of return—like those that are possible when the internal rate of return method is used—are not possible using the financial management rate of return method.

Assumptions of the financial management rate of return model:

1. When the initial cash outflows over the first few years of the investment are evaluated by means of present value tables to find the value of the cash outflows at time 0, the discount rate used is the current safe rate of interest, or the bank passbook savings rate.
2. If a negative net cash flow is expected for any year during the holding period, a portion of the positive cash flow in the previous year or previous few years is set aside to accumulate interest at the safe rate of interest to cover the eventual negative net cash outflow.
3. Any remaining positive net cash flows—once the net cash outflows are accounted for—are assumed to accumulate interest to the end of the holding period at the rate of return on comparable real estate investments at the present time.

4. Once the present value of the initial cash outflows and the terminal value of the positive net cash inflows from operations are determined, the financial management rate of return generated by the investment may be calculated.

Since the assumptions for the financial management rate of return are different from the assumptions of the internal rate of return, the two measures of investment yield may be significantly different. The financial management rate of return accounts for time disparities, size of investment disparities, and rates for reinvestment for the various cash flow circumstances.

Let us proceed to measure the financial management rate of return for investments C and D. We can then observe any differences between the internal rates of return and the financial management rates of return. As investors we may prefer to use one of the measures over the other, or we may observe each of the measures for each of the competing investment alternatives for the information each gives.

In calculating the financial management rates of return for investments C and D, let us assume that the safe rate of interest is 7 percent and the rate of return for real estate investments of comparable risk is 10 percent.

Investment C

Year	Net Cash Flow	Revised Net Cash Flow I	Revised Net Cash Flow II
0	− $50,000	− $50,000	− $ 50,000
1	2,000	2,000	
2	5,000	5,000	
3	20,500	6,550	
		(20,500 − 13,950°)	
4	− 15,000	——	
5	90,000	90,000	107,509
			(90,000 + 17,509†)

°Calculations:

15,000 × 0.93 (present value of 1 discounted for 1 year at 7%) = 13,950
20,500 − 13,950 = 6,550

†Calculations:

2,000 × 1.464 (the value of 1 receiving compound interest at 10% for four years) = 2,928
5,000 × 1.331 (the value of 1 receiving compound interest at 10% for three years) = 6,655
6,550 × 1.21 (the value of 1 receiving compound interest at 10% for two years) = 7,926
Terminal value = 17,509
90,000 + 17,509 = 107,509 = Total terminal value

The financial management rate of return may be found by calculating the internal rate of return for the revised net cash flow II.

To estimate the financial management rate of return, the total terminal value may be divided by the initial cash outlay, or $107,509/$50,000. The trial number that may be used to find the correct rate of return in the "Amount of 1 at Compound Interest" tables is 2.150. The tables indicate that the rate of return lies between 13 and 14 percent.

Interpolation:

Investment C

Trial Rates	Net Present Value	Goal versus a Trial NPV
0.14	2.194973	
		2.1500
0.13	2.081952	2.0820
0.01 Difference	0.113021 Difference	0.0680 Difference

0.13   +   0.10   ×   0.068
Rate used   Difference in   0.113
for a base   trial rates   Small difference
                                         divided by total
                                         difference in NPV

= 0.13 + 0.006
= 0.136 = FMRR = Financial management rate of return for investment C

Investment D

Year	Net Cash Flow	Revised Net Cash Flow I	Revised Net Cash Flow II
0	− $120,000	− $120,000	− $120,000
1	5,000	5,000	
2	13,500	4,200 (13,500 − 9,300*)	
3	− 10,000	—	
4	52,000	52,000	
5	145,000	145,000	215,110 (145,000 + 70,110†)

*Calculations:

10,000 × 0.93 = 9,300
13,500 − 9,300 = 4,200

†Calculations:

5,000 × 1.464 (the value of 1 receiving compound interest at 10% for four years) = 7,320
4,200 × 1.331 (the value of 1 receiving compound interest at 10% for three years) = 5,590
52,000 × 1.10 (the value of 1 receiving compound interest at 10% for one year) = 57,200
Terminal value = 70,110

145,000 + 70,110 = 215,110 = Total terminal value

To find the financial management rate of return, interpolation is needed. To find the approximate rate, the total terminal value may be divided by the initial cash outlay, or $215,110/$120,000. The trial number that may be used in scanning the "Amount of 1 at Compound Interest" tables is 1.7926. The rate of return lies between 10.25 percent and 10 percent.

Interpolation:

Investment D

Trial Rates	Net Present Value	Goal versus a Trial NPV
0.1025	1.7959	
		1.7926
0.10	1.7716	1.7716
0.0025	0.0243	0.0210
Difference	Difference	Difference

0.10   +   0.0025   ×   0.0210
Rate used   Difference in   0.0243
for a base   trial rates   Small difference
                                     divided by total
                                     difference in NPV

= 0.10 + 0.0025 × 0.86
= 0.10 + 0.0022 = 0.1022
               = FMRR = Financial
                       management rate of
                       return for
                       investment D

If the investor observed only the financial management rate of return for investments C and D, she or he would invest in C, since its FMRR is 13.6 percent, in comparison with the FMRR for D of 10.2 percent. All three methods of yield measurement that are based on the time value of money—net present value, internal rate of return, and financial management rate of return—indicate the highest yield for investment C.

SUMMARY

This chapter concludes Part IV, "Real Estate Investment Analysis." Earlier in the part we studied cash flow and profit planning and the mathematics of yield analysis. In this final chapter we looked over some studies of rates of return on various types of assets and the six chief methods of investment yield analysis, including real estate.

Little research has been conducted on real estate yields in which the prospective investor could reliably base his or her judgment and proceed to invest cash. The government does not systematically collect real estate investment yield data and publish it for popular consumption. Therefore, the data needed by the investor are usually collected by private agencies and organizations and analyzed for personal use. Limited amounts of good, reliable research on yields are made available to the typical investor. Even the limited amount of good information indicates that real estate investment yields and property values differ by locality.

A study of yields of competing investment alternatives from 1967 to 1977, conducted by the National Association of Realtors, shows that the single-family home yielded the greatest change in value, in comparison with corporate bonds, savings accounts, common stock, and cash. A study by Kelleher, covering 1960 through 1973, reported by *Real Estate Review*, indicates that the internal rate of return for multiple-tenant real estate far surpassed the internal rate of return for Standard and Poor 500 stocks over the same period. The Ricks study of life insurance company loans on the books between 1954 and 1966 showed the rate of return on equity after financing and after taxes was quite stable—between 8 and 9 percent. There was some variation in the yields, based on the nature of the risk of the particular type of property. The highest risk properties—hotels and motels—yielded the highest equity returns.

The most often used measurements of investment yields still seem to be the methods not employing the time value of money—total dollar return, cash-on-cash return, and cash payback. Some use is made of the measurement methods based on the time value of money—net present value, internal or discounted rate of return, and financial management rate of return.

Key Terms and Concepts

Standard & Poor's 500 Stock Price Index
Standard & Poor's 500 Stock Dividend Yield Index
Cash payback
Internal or discounted rate of return method
Broker's method

Total dollar return method
Average annual return on equity method
Cash-on-cash method
Net present value method
Bid and asked prices
Dow Jones Industrial Average
Financial management rate of return

Questions for Student Self-examination

Multiple-Choice Questions

1. When 11 types of real properties were studied over the period 1954–1966, the average equity yield was the highest for
   a. hotel and motel investment
   b. elevator apartments
   c. shopping centers
   d. office buildings

2. Which method of real estate investment yield analysis does not consider the investment requirement or the initial cash outlay?
   a. cash-on-cash return
   b. net present value
   c. total dollar return
   d. none of the above

3. What numerator is used for the cash-on-cash return formula?
   a. cash flow before reserves
   b. cash flow plus after-tax effects
   c. cash flow plus after-tax effects plus equity buildup
   d. all of the above

4. Which method of calculating investment return does not employ present value methods?
   a. cash payback
   b. net present value
   c. internal rate of return
   d. financial management rate of return

5. Present value of the annual net cash flows from operations and property sale less the cost of the real property equals
   a. cash payback period
   b. internal rate of return
   c. financial management rate of return
   d. net present value

True-False Questions

T F 1. Real estate investment yields and property values differ by locality.
T F 2. Business in the West tends to be rather stagnant overall, whereas Northeast, Southwest, and Southeast economies tend to be rapidly expanding.
T F 3. The rise in house values in the latter 1970s has yielded higher returns than other traditional forms of investment, such as stocks and bonds.
T F 4. Over the period 1960-1973, the internal rate of return for Standard and Poor's 500 stocks came close to being twice that of multiple-tenant real estate.
T F 5. The more quickly the cash commitment is recouped or returned to the investor, the less the liquidity and near-term profitability of the real estate investment.
T F 6. The net present value method assumes that the investor has a required rate of return, which may be used for a discount rate.
T F 7. The net present value method is a procedure for finding the rate of interest that equates the investment cash outlays to the net cash operating revenues over the investment holding period.
T F 8. The cash flow distribution of a real estate investment may create multiple internal rates of return.
T F 9. The internal rate of return method is based on the terminal value rate of return concept.
T F 10. The financial management rate of return accounts for time disparities, and rates for reinvestment for the various cash flow circumstances.

Answers
Multiple-Choice: 1a, 2c, 3d, 4a, 5d.
True-False: 1T, 2F, 3T, 4F, 5F, 6T, 7F, 8T, 9F, 10T.

Problems

1. If a small apartment building yields the following cash flows, what total dollar return will the owner receive?

Investment Year	Annual Cash Flow
1	$3,000
2	2,500
3	1,250
4	2,750

2. If the owner had to put $10,000 into the above apartment investment and the above annual cash flows did result, what is the cash-on-cash return?

3. If the owner of the small apartment building discussed in Problem 1 put $7,000 of equity into the investment, what is the cash payback period?

4. Based on the circumstances of Problem 3, what would be the net present value if the appropriate discount rate were 10 percent?

5. If the investor put $40,000 into the income property that generated the following cash flows, what was the investor's internal rate of return?

Year	Net Cash Flow
1	$ 2,000
2	5,000
3	10,000
4	22,000
5	25,000

6. Based on the annual net cash flows of Problem 1, what would be the internal rate of return if the owner invested a total of $7,500?

Part Five

Analysis of Investment in Specific Types of Property

Chapter 18

Home Ownership for Occupancy and Rental Income

Introduction
The Relationship of This Chapter to Other Chapters of the Text
General House Investment Factors
The Demand for Houses
    The Balance of Sales Between Existing and New Houses   The Trend in the Home-Buying Age Group   Regional Patterns of Home Sales   The Trend in Personal Incomes and Family Expenditures for Housing   Mortgage Assumption   Home Financing Programs
The Supply of Houses
    Housing Starts   The Availability of Loans   Methods of Construction   Cost of Construction
Owner-Occupied Housing
The Traditional Single-Family Detached Dwelling
    Purchase and Investment Motivations   Construction-Cost Trends   The Demand for the Owner-Occupied Single-Family House   The Characteristics of the Traditional Single-Family House   The Investment Yield
Owner-Occupied Condominium and Cooperative Housing
Owner-Occupied Mobile Homes
Rental Housing
    The Rented Single-Family Detached Dwelling   The Rented Condominium or Cooperative Unit   Rental Mobile Homes
Summary
Key Terms and Concepts
Questions for Student Self-examination

LEARNING OBJECTIVES After studying this chapter, you should be familiar with

General house investment factors
The demand for houses
The balance of sales between existing and new houses
The trend in the home-buying age group
Regional patterns of home sales
The trend in personal incomes and family expenditures for housing
Possibilities for mortgage assumption
Advantageous home financing programs
The supply of houses
The trend in housing starts
The availability of loans
Permitted methods of construction
Costs of construction
Purchase and investment motivations associated with the traditional house
Construction-cost trends related to the traditional single-family detached dwelling
The demand for the owner-occupied single-family house
Characteristics of the traditional single-family house
Condominium and cooperative housing that is owner-occupied
Owner-occupied mobile homes
Rented single-family detached dwellings
Rented condominium or cooperative units
Rental mobile homes

Two-thirds of American households live in owner-occupied structures. Since the portion has increased over the years, it may continue to increase in our affluent society. The majority of these households live in single-family detached houses with fee simple ownership. The other households living in owner-occupied structures occupy condominium and cooperative apartments, single-family detached condominium houses, mobile homes, and houseboats.

The remaining one-third of American households live in rented homes. Many of these homes are single-family detached houses owned in fee simple by the landlord. Some of these households live in rented condominium and cooperative apartments, rented single-family detached condominium houses, rented mobile homes, and rented houseboats.

INTRODUCTION

The chapter deals with housing investment and trends. Both owner-occupied and rental housing are covered. Three forms of owner-occupied housing are primarily considered: single-family detached houses owned in fee simple, condominium and cooperative housing units, and mobile homes. The same three forms of housing are studied from a rental investment standpoint.

Several key factors are studied in detail with regard to single-family detached housing, owner-occupied and rented: purchase and investment motivations, construction cost trends, the demand for the space, the characteristics of the houses purchased or constructed, and the comparative yield on the house investment. These factors are also considered briefly in the purchase and investment of the condominium and cooperative housing units and mobile homes.

THE RELATIONSHIP OF THIS CHAPTER TO OTHER CHAPTERS OF THE TEXT

This chapter on home ownership begins Part V, on the analysis of investment in specific types of properties. This is the lowest density land-use form. It carries the highest quality zoning classification. All American consumers must have shelter for themselves and their families. The owner-occupied home is usually the largest investment made by a household, family, or individual. The other forms of real estate investment generally involve higher land-use density, lower-quality zoning regulations, and less popular investment appeal. Later chapters cover the other forms of real estate investment, such as apartment projects, shopping centers, office buildings, and industrial buildings.

GENERAL HOUSE INVESTMENT FACTORS

Regardless of whether the house is owner-occupied or is rental property, the investment in the house is related to the demand and supply of houses in general. The demand for houses is associated with the balance of sales between existing and new houses, the trend of the home-buying age group, regional patterns of home sales, the trend in personal incomes and family expenditures for housing, the possibilities for mortgage assumption, and the existence of advantageous home financing programs. The supply of houses is associated with the availability of loans, the permitted methods of construction, and the trend in construction costs.

The Demand for Houses

The Balance of Sales Between Existing and New Houses. The demand for existing single-family houses continues to be about five times greater than the demand for new single-family houses in the United States (Exhibits 18-1 and 18-2). The multiple is not always as high as 5. In the spring of 1977, the multiple was a little less than 4 in favor of sales of existing single-family houses. Combined sales of existing (3.88 million) and new (0.82 million) single-family units surpassed 4.7 million houses in April 1978.

One reason that existing single-family houses sell better, or, in other words, in higher volume, is that the median prices of existing houses are substantially lower than the median prices of new houses. The continued inflation in construction material prices and labor costs force new-house prices relatively high. Exhibit 18-3 shows the 1977 and 1978 price relationships between existing and new-house prices and the extent of median price increase within each category of house price. From April 1977, to April 1978, the median price of existing single-family houses rose 15 percent, and the median price of new single-family houses rose 10 percent.

Exhibit 18-1. Existing Single-Family Home Sales for the United States *(Seasonally Adjusted Annual Rate)*

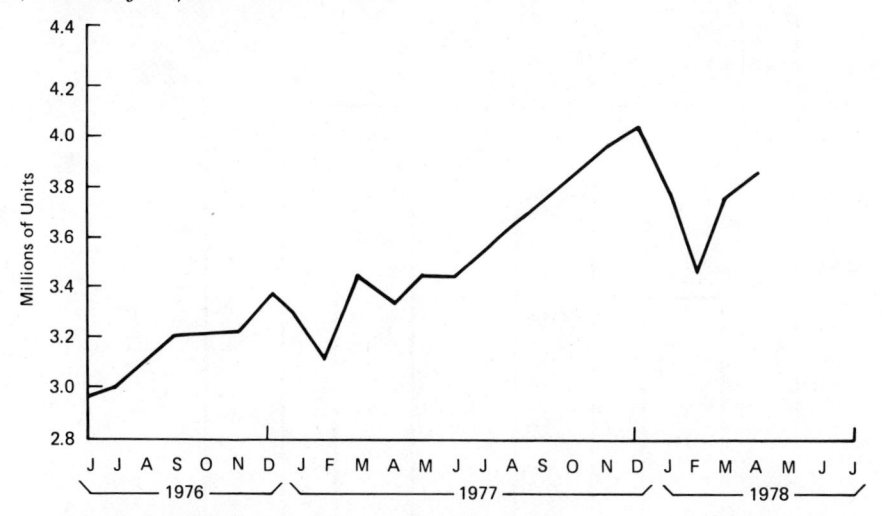

Source: *Spring 1978 Real Estate Market Report* (Chicago: Department of Economics and Research, National Association of Realtors, 1978), p. 5. Reprinted with permission.

The Trend in the Home-Buying Age Group. The "war babies" born between 1945 and 1955 are coming into the home-buying age group. In the early and mid-1980s these war babies will be 25 to 40 years of age, a prime home-buying age group. These are the ages of family formation and house purchase. The older age groups who also prefer ownership of primary and vacation homes will be expanding in size because of better health care, early retirement, higher social security and pension payments, and longer life expectancy.

Exhibit 18-2. New Single-Family Home Sales for the United States *(Seasonally Adjusted Annual Rate)*

Source: *Spring 1978 Real Estate Market Report* (Chicago: Department of Economics and Research, National Association of Realtors, 1978), p. 5. Reprinted with permission.

Exhibit 18-3. Median Sales Price of Single-Family Homes

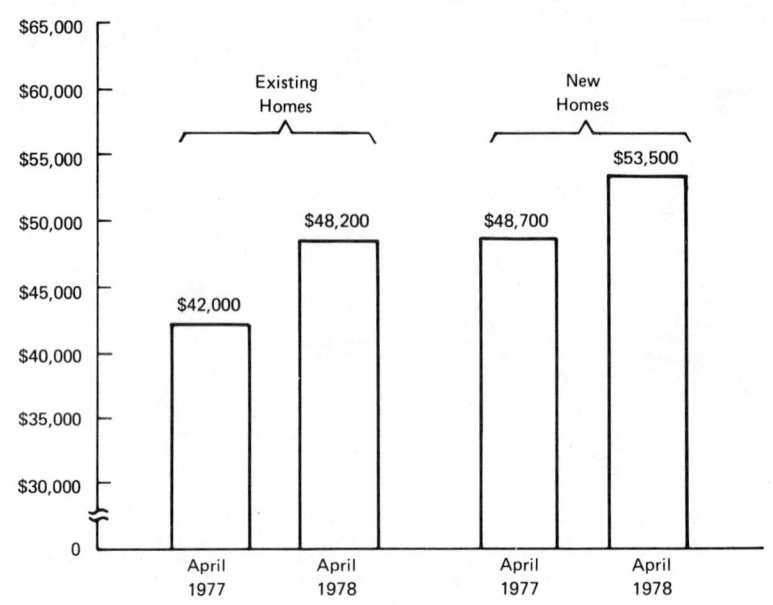

[Bar chart showing:
- Existing Homes: April 1977 = $42,000; April 1978 = $48,200
- New Homes: April 1977 = $48,700; April 1978 = $53,500]

Source: *Spring 1978 Real Estate Market Report* (Chicago: Department of Economics and Research, National Association of Realtors, 1978), p. 6. Reprinted with permission.

Regional Patterns of Home Sales. All regions of the United States contribute to the increasing level of home sales. In the latter 1970s, the heaviest increase in sales volume and housing starts was realized in the South. The lowest increase in house sales volume was in the West; the lowest increase in private housing starts was in the North Central region. The lowest level of private housing starts was in the Northeast.

In 1977, the median sales prices of houses differed widely among the regions, according to the National Association of Realtors. The 1977 median house sales prices, with the percentage increases over 1976 in parentheses, were:

West, $57,300 (24.3 percent).
Northeast, $44,400 (6.2 percent).
South, $39,800 (9.0 percent).
North Central, $36,700 (11.6 percent).[1]

The Trend in Personal Incomes and Family Expenditures for Housing. According to Federal Reserve statistics, personal incomes rose 10 to 11 percent per year from 1975 through 1978. During this time, the personal savings rate ranged from 5 to 7 percent. As the savings rate indicates, personal consumption expenditures described a relatively high volume. The previously mentioned trend in house sales indicates that part of the personal consumption expenditures were committed to house purchases.

Family spending on housing differs by the income level of the family. As researchers have known for years, housing expenditures as a portion of family income decrease as the family income level increases (Table 18-1). According to a report of the National Association of Realtors, "the rise in the price of single-family homes during the past 15

[1] "Existing Home Sales Record Set," *Alabama Realtor* (May 1978), p. 4.

Table 18-1. Family spending by income

Spending Category	All Families	$12,000–14,999	$15,000–19,999	$20,000–24,999	$25,000– and Up°
Food	$1,568	$1,750	$2,010	$2,293	$2,651
Housing	2,468	2,591	3,027	3,495	4,682
Clothing	671	692	867	1,082	1,564
Transport	1,639	1,956	2,257	2,712	3,234

Source: Adapted from "*Consumer Views*" (April 1977), Citibank, 399 Park Avenue, New York, N.Y. 10022. Reprinted by permission.
° Average income about $38,500; families average 3.8 people.

years has been matched by the increase in median family income, leaving the relationship between home prices and family income virtually unchanged."[2]

Mortgage Assumption. Mortgage assumption becomes very important to housing demand when interest rates are rising rapidly. Existing houses gain more interest from the prospective buyers when the lenders are permitting mortgage assumption by the new owners. When lenders no longer permit mortgage assumption or charge high fees for mortgage assumption, housing demand tends to dry up. As the home mortgage market of the late 1970s created 9 5/8 to 10 percent home mortgages, the lenders were permitting mortgage assumption. Therefore, the high volume of sales of existing houses persisted. Many buyers gained 7 to 8 percent home mortgages by buying the equity of the previous owners.

Home Financing Programs. House investment is encouraged by advantageous financing programs. Five graduated-payment mortgage programs are available. FHA 245 graduated-payment mortgage insurance may be offered by any FHA-approved lender or mortgage banker in the country to any qualifying mortgagor. As of December 1978, federally chartered savings and loan associations may offer conventional loans with graduated mortgage payments. The graduated-payment mortgages offer initial monthly mortgage payments that are lower than the standard-level annuity mortgage payments, but they may require substantial downpayments to compensate for the negative amortization during the first years of the loan.

Variable-rate mortgages are available in California and a few other places in the country. The lender whose mortgage monies are scarce may make a variable-rate loan where standard loans with fixed rates and maturities would be unacceptable. Low- or no-downpayment loans may be acquired from HUD under the FHA 203(b) program and from the Veterans Administration if the credit and real estate requirements are met.

The Supply of Houses

Housing Starts. Housing starts on an annualized basis slightly surpassed two million units in 1978. The uptrend in housing starts through 1978 started from the trough of approximately one million units in early 1975. The last peak in housing starts, 2.5 million units, was reached in early 1973. According to Federal Reserve statistics, usually three-fourths of the housing starts are represented by single-family houses. There-

[2] Ibid.

fore, in 1977 and 1978, construction commenced for approximately 1.5 million single-family houses per year.

The Availability of Loans. Mortgage debt for one- to four-family dwellings keeps rising, partly because of inflation in house prices (Exhibit 18-4). This type of mortgage debt reached ⅔ of $1 trillion, or $671 billion, by 1978, from $416 billion in 1973. In the latter part of the 1970s, total mortgage debt, covering residential, commercial, and farm structures, totaled more than $1 trillion. Therefore, we might say that mortgage loans have been available to qualified borrowers in recent years.

High interest periods have historically been associated with a lack of home mortgage money. Disintermediation may take place, as it did during the 1973-1974 period of recession. Mortgage monies may dry up at the typical mortgage-lending institutions. During recent high-interest periods, when home mortgage loan rates have approximated 10 percent, significant disintermediation has not occurred. Home mortgage funds have continued to be available, partly because investors have been locked into high-yielding certificates of deposit with relatively long maturities at commercial banks and at thrift institutions. To gain the high investment yields from the savings certificates, the investors must not transfer the funds from the accounts until the certificates mature. Therefore, savings have not been as freely transferable between investment media as they have been in the past. In particular, savings and loan associations and mutual savings banks have not realized major outflows of savings during recent high-interest periods.

Methods of Construction. Less costly methods and materials of construction foster home construction. For example, many local building departments have permitted the use of plastic pipe for house water pipes. The use of plastic pipe tends to hold down

Exhibit 18-4. Mortgage Banking Single-Family Lending

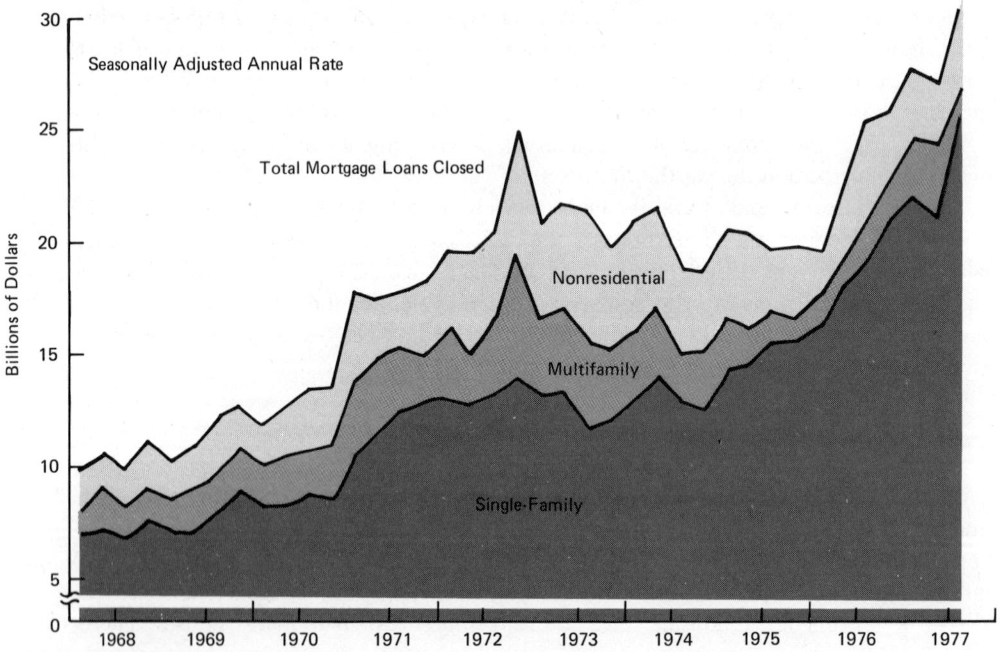

Source: *The Mortgage Banker* (January 1978), p. 32. Reprinted with permission.

the cost of construction. Manufactured houses have been encouraged for the housing of low- and moderate-income families. Mobile home shipments are again increasing. In 1977 and 1978, mobile home shipments reached approximately 300,000 units. The peak in shipments was reached in 1972, when the volume was 576,000 units. As recently as 1975, only 217,000 units were shipped. Mobile homes have been needed to house the families and households earning less than $15,000 a year. The young and the elderly comprise a major portion of this earnings group.

Cost of Construction. As the value of construction contracts more than doubled from 1975 to mid-1978—a rate of growth approximating 25 percent per annum—the construction-cost index was rising at a rate of approximately 7.5 percent per annum. At the time, the Consumer Price Index was rising at a little slower rate than the construction-cost index (Table 18-2). As construction costs continue to rise at such a rapid pace, the prices of the finished structures must rise just as rapidly to permit a reasonable profit to the builder. We can more fully understand the recent increase in new house prices as we observe the pattern of the indices and the growth rates.

Construction costs have risen more for some materials than for others. Lumber, asphalt roofing, and gypsum wallboard have increased the most in price since 1972 (Table 18-3).

Table 18-2. Percentage change in residential construction costs and consumer prices

Year	Residential Construction	Consumer Prices
1950	5.5%	1.0%
1955	3.0	− 0.4
1960	1.6	1.6
1965	3.2	1.7
1966	4.4	2.9
1967	6.0	2.9
1968	7.3	4.2
1969	8.3	5.4
1970	5.4	5.9
1971	8.5	4.3
1972	9.8	3.4
1973	9.2	6.2
1974	8.1	11.0
1975	6.7	9.1
1976	8.2	5.8
1977	9.2	6.5

Source: *1978 Savings and Loan Fact Book* (Chicago: U.S. League of Savings Associations, 1978), p. 21. Reprinted with permission.

Table 18-3. Percentage change in cost of selected building materials

Material	1972	1973	1974	1975	1976	1977°
Southern pine	10.1%	28.6%	− 18.5%	− 10.1%	27.8%	27.3%
Gypsum wallboard	0.4	7.5	14.2	− 3.4	10.8	26.7
Building board	2.5	12.0	1.0	8.6	9.5	19.6
Plywood	12.3	25.5	− 10.3	13.9	20.9	16.5
Douglas fir	17.3	29.4	− 15.3	19.6	26.1	14.9
Asphalt roofing	0.0	6.6	47.7	5.0	2.5	13.6
Hardwood lumber	14.5	69.3	− 22.7	− 12.9	36.4	11.8
Millwork	5.1	15.1	2.0	7.4	11.0	9.6
Concrete products	3.7	5.5	20.3	7.0	5.7	7.5
Plumbing fixtures	2.0	7.8	24.0	1.3	9.6	6.7
Heating equipment	2.5	2.0	22.1	4.5	4.3	4.9
Paint	2.0	8.8	25.8	5.2	4.2	4.6
All materials	5.0	11.7	16.5	6.0	9.9	9.4

Source: *1978 Savings and Loan Fact Book* (Chicago: U.S. League of Savings Associations, 1978), p. 21. Reprinted with permission.
° 12 months ending October.

OWNER-OCCUPIED HOUSING

The investment in owner-occupied housing takes three forms: single-family detached houses owned in fee simple, condominium and cooperative housing units, and mobile homes. Each has its own investment characteristics.

The Traditional Single-Family Detached Dwelling

The traditional single-family dwelling stands alone as a separate residential building, which accommodates one household or family and has been constructed by traditional on-site construction methods. A portion of this type of housing unit may have been constructed at a distant assembly-manufacturing plant. For example, roof trusses are often produced at a distant manufacturing plant and transported to the construction site.

Purchase and Investment Motivations. The dwelling is normally purchased for the occupancy of the owner and the owner's family. The house provides shelter and facilitates the lifestyles of the family or the household members. The structure may be the primary home of the household, or it may be a weekend or vacation home. Most households do not maintain more than two homes.

Most home investors expect price appreciation and tax shelter from the federal tax exemption of mortgage interest and property taxes. Buildup in the owner's equity through periodic mortgage payments is also expected.

Second homes are often purchased for weekend and vacation living by middle- to high-income households. Recent research from Texas indicated that the head of the household of the second home was usually a white, middle-aged male whose children had already left home for separate living accommodations. Most of the second homes were located 100 to 200 miles from the principal residence, were owned by families with median incomes of $35,000 or more, and accommodated two bedrooms and two baths in a little over 1,200 square feet of space.

Construction-Cost Trends. The cost to construct a single-family detached house generally varies from $20 to $30 a square foot, depending on the area of the country and the amenities and equipment built into the house. Most families pay more for their principal residences than they do for their second homes. While the median new-home price for a principal residence currently approximates $53,500 on a national basis, the Texas research showed a median new second-home price of $35,000. The range for the second homes in the Texas research study was $4,000 to $150,000.[3]

The Demand for the Owner-Occupied Single-Family House. The single-family detached dwelling owned in fee simple and built by conventional on-site methods is still greatly preferred by the homeowner over other forms of housing accommodation. The preferred sites for these traditional single-family houses are still the suburban areas rather than the central business district or any other area of the crowded central city. The educational programs of the suburban schools and the shopping and recreational facilities of the suburban areas are preferred by the majority of homeowners.

The Characteristics of the Traditional Single-Family House. The three-bedroom, two-bath home is preferred. "Since 1968, there has been a slight increase in the market share of homes with four or more bedrooms—from 22.4 percent to 26.0 percent, and a corresponding drop in the share of those with two or fewer bedrooms from 21.1 percent to 18.3 percent."[4] The formal living room combined with a family room or den is being replaced by a great room or a single, all-purpose living room. One-story homes account for approximately 60 percent of all houses built for sale; two-story or more, approximately 25 percent of the market; and split levels, the remaining 15 percent. More than half of the homes have a two-car garage. About 80 percent of the homes in the North Central area of the country had basements; in the Northeast, about 70 percent; in the West, about 30 percent; and in the South, approximately 20 percent.

The Investment Yield. The investment yield on an owner-occupied house must include the owner's profit on its sale after taxes are paid, the tax savings afforded by the tax deductibility of the mortgage interest payments and property taxes, the interest foregone on the money put up as the equity investment on an after-tax basis, and perhaps the imputed rental value of the home to the owner and the associated home maintenance costs. A cash flow analysis leading to an adjusted average annual return of 12.5 percent after taxes on ownership of a home with the specified assumptions is shown in Table 18–4. If the analyst were to calculate the investment yield on any particular owner-occupied single-family home, the format of the cash flow analysis could be used and the appropriate financial variables inserted. Some of the key factors are the imputed annual rental income, the annual operating expenses, the mortgage terms, the mortgage interest and principal amortization per year, the expected change in the selling price over time, the owner's other income, the expected change in the owner's other or outside income, and the tax bracket of the homeowner. The reader may find useful the amortization schedule presented in Table 18–5 for a $50,000 mortgage loan that has 10 percent interest, a 25-year term, and level monthly payments.

---

[3] Bart Eleveld and Roger P. Sindt, "The Leisure Home," *Tierra Grande*, Second Quarter, No. 3 (College Station, Texas: Texas A&M University, 1978), pp. 7–9.

[4] "Existing Home Sales Record Set," *Alabama Realtor* (May 1978), p. 4. The article quotes the results of a recent survey by the National Association of Realtors.

Table 18-4. *Pro forma cash-flow analysis: home ownership, 1967-1976*

Section III: Cash flow schedules

Year	Effective Gross Income	Operating Expenses	Net Income	Depreciation	Interest	Principal Amortization	Before-Tax Cash Flow	Taxable Income	Taxes	After-Tax Cash Flow	Before-Tax Cash on Cash	After-Tax Cash on Cash
1	$3,000	$1,200	$1,800	0	$1,229	$315	$256	$571	$171	$85	4.04	1.34
2	3,112	1,200	1,852	0	1,208	336	309	645	193	116	4.86	1.82
3	3,229	1,323	1,906	0	1,185	358	363	721	216	146	5.71	2.31
4	3,350	1,389	1,961	0	1,162	382	418	800	240	178	6.58	2.80
5	3,476	1,459	2,017	0	1,136	408	474	881	264	209	7.46	3.30
6	3,606	1,532	2,075	0	1,109	435	531	966	290	241	8.36	3.80
7	3,742	1,608	2,133	0	1,079	464	590	1,054	316	274	9.29	4.31
8	3,882	1,689	2,193	0	1,048	495	650	1,145	343	306	10.23	4.82
9	4,027	1,773	2,254	0	1,015	528	711	1,239	372	339	11.19	5.34
10	4,178	1,862	2,317	0	980	564	773	1,337	401	372	12.18	5.80

Section IV: Sale schedules

Year	Selling Price	Selling Expenses	Prepayment Penalty	Amount Realized	Unpaid Mortgage	Before-Tax Residual	Adjusted Basis	Gain	Depreciation Recapture	Capital Gain	Taxes	After-tax Residual
1	$27,178	$1,631	0	$25,547	$18,735	$6,812	$25,400	$147	0	$147	$22	$6,790
2	29,080	1,745	0	27,336	18,400	8,936	25,400	1,936	0	1,936	290	8,645
3	31,116	1,867	0	29,249	18,042	11,207	25,400	3,849	0	3,849	577	10,630
4	33,294	1,998	0	31,297	17,660	13,637	25,400	5,897	0	5,897	884	12,752
5	35,625	2,137	0	33,487	17,252	16,235	25,400	8,087	0	8,087	1,213	15,022
6	38,118	2,287	0	35,831	16,817	19,014	25,400	10,431	0	10,431	1,565	17,450
7	40,787	2,447	0	38,340	16,353	21,987	25,400	12,940	0	12,940	1,941	20,046
8	43,642	2,619	0	41,023	15,858	25,166	25,400	15,623	0	15,623	2,343	22,822
9	46,697	2,802	0	43,895	15,329	28,566	25,400	18,495	0	18,495	2,774	25,791
10	49,965	2,998	0	46,968	14,766	32,202	25,400	21,568	0	21,568	3,235	28,967

Section V: Rates of return*

Year	Equity	Before-Tax Cash Flow	Before-Tax Residual	Rate of Return	After-Tax Cash Flow	After-Tax Residual	Rate of Return
1	$6,350	$256	$ 6,812	11.52	$ 85	$ 6,790	8.32
2	0	309	8,936	23.11	116	8,645	18.25
3	0	363	11,207	25.29	146	10,630	20.37
4	0	418	13,637	25.41	178	12,752	20.72
5	0	474	16,235	24.94	209	15,022	20.50
6	0	531	19,014	24.28	241	17,450	20.08
7	0	590	21,987	23.58	274	20,046	19.59
8	0	650	25,166	22.91	306	22,822	19.10
9	0	711	28,566	22.27	339	25,791	18.62
10	0	773	32,202	21.69	372	28,967	18.16

Source: Real III Computer Program, University of Georgia, calculations by author; Paul F. Wendt, MAI, CRE, "Inflation and the Real Estate Investor," *The Appraisal Journal* (July 1977), p. 351, with the permission of *The Appraisal Journal* and the American Institute of Real Estate Appraisers. The opinions and statements set forth herein do not necessarily reflect the viewpoint of the American Institute of Real Estate Appraisers or its individual members, and neither the institute nor its editors and staff assume responsibility for such expression of opinion or statements.

* PRESUMPTIONS: Purchase price in 1967: $25,400. Original equity in 1967: $6,350. Mortgage of $19,050, 6½%, 25 years, monthly payment. Selling price increases annually by 7%, 10-year holding. Imputed rental income of $3,000 per year, increasing 3.75% per year. Operating expenses of $1,200 per year, increasing 5% per year. Outside taxable income of $25,000, increasing 5% per year; 30% tax bracket. No depreciation—owner-occupied.

Table 18-5. Amortization schedule for a $50,000 mortgage at 10 percent for 25 years with level monthly payments

Payment Number	Payment Amount	Interest Charge Per Period	Total	Principal Paid	Mortgage Amount Paid	Seller's Equity	Buyer's Equity
1	$454.35	$416.67	$ 416.67	$ 37.68	$ 454.35	$49,962.32	$ 37.68
2	454.35	416.35	833.02	38.00	908.70	49,924.32	75.68
3	454.35	416.04	1,249.06	38.31	1,363.05	49,886.01	113.99
4	454.35	415.72	1,664.78	38.63	1,817.40	49,847.38	152.62
5	454.35	415.39	2,080.17	38.96	2,271.75	49,808.42	191.58
6	454.35	415.07	2,495.24	39.28	2,726.10	49,769.14	230.86
7	454.35	414.74	2,909.98	39.61	3,180.45	49,729.53	270.47
8	454.35	414.41	3,324.39	39.94	3,634.80	49,689.59	310.41
9	454.35	414.08	3,738.47	40.27	4,089.15	49,649.32	350.68
10	454.35	413.74	4,152.21	40.61	4,543.50	49,608.71	391.29
11	454.35	413.41	4,565.62	40.94	4,997.85	49,567.77	432.23
12	454.35	413.06	4,978.68	41.29	5,452.20	49,526.48	473.52
24	454.35	408.74	9,907.78	45.61	10,904.40	49,003.38	996.62
36	454.35	403.97	14,782.09	50.38	16,356.60	48,425.49	1,574.51
48	454.35	398.69	19,595.91	55.66	21,808.80	47,787.11	2,212.89
60	454.35	392.86	24,342.88	61.49	27,261.00	47,081.88	2,918.12
120	454.35	353.18	46,802.65	101.17	54,522.00	42,280.65	7,719.35
180	454.35	287.90	66,164.20	166.45	81,783.00	34,381.20	15,618.80
240	454.35	180.48	80,428.15	273.87	109,044.00	21,384.15	28,615.85
300	454.35	3.76	86,305.03	450.62	136,305.03	0.00	50,000.00

Owner-Occupied Condominium and Cooperative Housing

The owner-occupant of condominium and cooperative housing may seek care-free home maintenance, seasonal housing, a home in a strategic location of a city or recreational area, and adequate living space with tax-deductible mortgage interest and property tax payments. Condominium and cooperative housing space may be acquired at a price that is more reasonable than that for similar space in a single-family detached house that is owned in fee simple. One probable reason for this is the lesser amount of costly land that is required. The condominium or cooperative single-family detached home may easily be as expensive as a single-family detached home owned in fee simple. The land and building costs may be essentially the same for equally good locations. Instead of the homeowner paying exterior maintenance expense directly out of his or her pocket, the homeowners' association of the condominium or cooperative project collects maintenance allowances each month from each owner, so that funds will be accumulated for required maintenance costs.

The demand for condominium and cooperative housing has continued to be strong in major cities, along beaches, and beside golf courses and ski slopes. In other areas of the country and in smaller metropolitan areas, the demand for multifamily condominium and cooperative housing is growing, because of the higher cost of single-family detached housing.

Owner-Occupied Mobile Homes

The mobile home owner may seek reasonable housing expense that can be financed with a lower income than that required to finance the single-family detached housing that is traditionally constructed on the house lot. The cost per square foot of a mobile home is usually approximately half the cost per square foot of a traditional single-family house. The mobile home—single- or double-wide—is usually priced between $8,000 and $25,000, which is considerably less than the average or median price of a traditional single-family house. The terms are more stringent and costly for mobile home financing than for traditional site-built home financing. Usually the mobile home escapes property taxes, since most local governments consider mobile homes personal property for tax purposes. Mobile home licenses and personal property taxes must often be paid in lieu of real property taxes.

The average mobile home today is a single-wide home, 14 feet wide and perhaps 70 feet long. Double-wide mobile homes comprise 25 to 30 percent of the market. The median square footage of living space approximates 1,600 square feet.

RENTAL HOUSING

The three basic forms of single-family housing—single-family detached housing owned in fee simple, condominium and cooperative housing, and mobile homes—are also subject to rental by the owner for investment income. In some cases, the owner expects to occupy the unit for two to four weeks of the year, during vacation periods, and expects to rent out the unit the remaining 48 to 50 weeks of the year. Overall, the house owner expects to generate a profit over the investment holding periods.

The Rented Single-Family Detached Dwelling. The owner may expect investment return from periodic net cash flows after financing and after taxes and from capital gains at the sale of the property at the end of the investment holding period. Often the rented dwelling is financed with the maximum amount of funds that can be obtained from mortgage lenders under the appropriate programs of the U.S. Department of Housing and Urban Development, the Veterans Administration, and conventional lending institutions. Usually the returns are levered in order to increase the return to the equity investor. (The term *levered* refers to the borrowing of money at a cost less than the overall return on the property so that the return to the investor is increased.)

The property owner works within tax and financing constraints. The owner may deduct from otherwise taxable net income the operating and maintenance expenses, the mortgage interest on the loans acquired to purchase the property, the property taxes, and depreciation by the permitted methods. The space must usually be rented at the current monthly amount set by the marketplace. The monthly rent should cover the monthly mortgage debt service, operating and maintenance expenses, accrued property taxes and insurance premiums, and a reasonable cash return to the owner as profit.

If the investor purchased a house for future rental for $30,000, a 75 percent loan at 10 percent for 20 years might be acquired from a local lender. The loan would require monthly debt service of $217.35. The annual property taxes might amount to $360 or, in other words, $30 a month. The annual property insurance premium might amount to $240, or $20 a month. Maintenance costs and replacement reserves per month might be estimated at $20. The investor would probably manage and rent the property personally so that no property management fees would have to be paid. Rental house property management fees often total 10 percent of the gross rental receipts. Therefore, the monthly rent should cover the anticipated cash expenses plus a return to the owner.

Estimated monthly expenses:

Mortgage debt service	$217.35
Accrued property taxes	30.00
Accrued insurance premiums	20.00
Maintenance costs and replacement reserves	20.00
	$287.35

Therefore, the monthly rent must surpass $287.35 in order for the owner to reap a profit. Since the owner has $7,500 in equity in the property, he or she might want an 8 percent cash-on-cash return. Eight percent of $7,500 would be $600 a year, or $50 a month. Therefore, the rent would have to be $337.35 a month. Recently, rents for houses have not risen as rapidly as have financing and other ownership costs. In many areas, for example, a $30,000 rental house would not command a rent of $337.35 a month. The market rents might fall in a range of $175 to $200 a month. Therefore, the rental house owner has had to look to future capital gains for the overall return on the property. The capital gains would be taxed on a capital-gains basis rather than at the higher ordinary tax rates of the property owner. Investment and owner-occupied house prices have risen in some areas in recent years at a rate of 8 to 12 percent a year. The investor does not know how long the inflationary pattern in house prices will persist.

The Rented Condominium or Cooperative Unit. As condominium and cooperative housing demand remains strong, an investor may purchase a condo or co-op unit for rental. The homeowners' association usually must approve the rental of the condo or co-op space by its owner as part of the association agreement with the building owners. The investor would either seek to rent the space for the whole year or for that part of the year that he or she will not be occupying the space. The rental amount should exceed the owner's financing and maintenance costs and permit the owner a return on the equity investment in the space.

The owner may speculate on the rise in condominium or cooperative unit prices in the local market. If the demand for the space is strong and inflation continues, the owner may realize a substantial capital gain, taxed on a capital-gains basis when the investment holding period ends. After the oversupply of condo space occurred in the mid-1970s, prices of condo units in many markets declined sharply. In those markets construction stopped for a number of months to permit the sale of vacant space; now construction has again commenced in many of those markets as reasonable vacancy rates have been attained once more. The condo market tends to flourish with the rise in personal incomes, the income tax provisions currently in effect, and the pressure of demand for well-located residential space where land costs are relatively high.

Rental Mobile Homes. Many mobile homes in areas of warm winter climates are rented while the owner is away from the space. Other mobile homes in mobile home parks and isolated locations are rented for investment income. The economic life of a mobile home is relatively short, since the construction is not as indestructible as that of traditional site-built homes. Therefore, the rental period is relatively short—perhaps eight to ten years if the mobile home is well cared for. Again, the owner, in order to derive an investment return, must look to periodic residual cash flows and capital gains at the sale of the mobile home. The usual income property tax provisions apply.

SUMMARY

To begin the section on investment in specific types of properties, we considered the pros and cons of house investment for occupancy or rental. First, the demand for and the supply of houses was considered. As the demand for houses was examined, the reader observed the balance of real estate sales between existing and new houses. The trend in home-buying age groups was studied, as were the regional patterns of home sales. Another aspect of the subject—the trend in personal incomes and family expenditures for housing—was brought into the discussion. Advantageous financing, including mortgage assumption, also was considered as a powerful force behind the demand for houses.

Key Terms and Concepts

Single-family detached condominium house
Houseboat
Regional patterns
Median new second-home price
Single-wide mobile home
Maintenance costs
War babies
Personal savings rate

Personal consumption expenditures
Tax bracket
Square footage of living space
Construction Cost Index
Consumer Price Index
Roof trusses
Plastic pipe
Double-wide mobile home
Replacement reserves

Questions for Student Self-examination

Multiple-Choice Questions

1. Rented homes are lived in by _____ of American households.
   a. one-half
   b. one-third
   c. one-fourth
   d. one-fifth

2. The demand for existing single-family houses continues to be about _____ times greater than the demand for new single-family houses in the United States.
   a. two
   b. ten
   c. eight
   d. five

3. In the latter 1970s, the lowest level of private housing starts was in the _____.
   a. South
   b. Northeast
   c. West
   d. Southeast

4. Which building material has not increased significantly in price recently?
   a. lumber
   b. paint
   c. asphalt roofing
   d. gypsum wallboard

5. Which economic factor is not usually anticipated by most home investors?
   a. equity buildup through mortgage repayment
   b. tax shelter
   c. household shelter
   d. price depreciation

True–False Questions

T F 1. Single-family detached housing is the highest density land-use form.
T F 2. The largest investment made by a household, family, or individual is usually the private automobile.
T F 3. The median prices of new houses are substantially lower than the median prices of existing houses.
T F 4. Housing expenditures as a portion of family income decrease as the family income level increases.
T F 5. Mortgage assumption becomes less important to housing demand when interest rates are rapidly rising.
T F 6. The graduated-payment mortgages offer initial monthly mortgage payments that are higher than the standard-level annuity mortgage payments and may require substantial downpayments.
T F 7. The graduated-payment mortgages exhibit negative amortization during the first years of the loan.
T F 8. According to Federal Reserve statistics, usually three-fourths of the housing starts are represented by single-family houses.
T F 9. The young and the elderly comprise a major portion of mobile home demand.
T F 10. Most second homes are located 500 to 600 miles from the principal residence.

Answers
Multiple-Choice: 1b, 2d, 3b, 4b, 5d.
True–False: 1F, 2F, 3F, 4T, 5F, 6F, 7T, 8T, 9T, 10F.

Problems

1. If a young couple desires a house price at $50,000 but has only enough savings for a downpayment of 5 percent or less, plus 3 percent closing costs, what kind of house financing might they consider?

2. If the population age distribution of the United States changed so that 40 percent of the population was 50 years of age or older, what implications would there be for the housing market? How would this phenomenon affect housing demand?

3. How could a general business recession in the United States affect the demand and supply of housing?

4. If a family owns its own home, currently valued at $75,000, how can the family figure its yield on its house investment? What elements should be considered in calculating the investment yield?

5. A businessman in his thirties, who is married and has five children, is considering the purchase of a $30,000 house that may be remodeled and repaired and rented for investment income. What investment characteristics would such a rental house have for this family?

6. If you buy a $70,000 condominium unit in Florida for an investment and plan to rent it, what should you consider in terms of unit location, building location, and tax shelter?

Chapter 19
Apartment Building Investment

Introduction
The Relationship of This Chapter to Other Chapters of the Text
Some Factors Creating the Momentum for Increased Apartment Investment
    The Affordability of One-Family Homes   Second-Home and Condominium Demand   Vacancy Rates for Rental Apartment Buildings   Gradual Rise in Apartment Rents   Stable Mortgage Financing Terms   Rise in the Number of Households   Environmental Regulations

The Market Survey and Feasibility Analysis

Apartment Construction Costs

Trends in Apartment Building Income and Expenses

The Appraisal of Apartment Projects

The Financing of Apartment Buildings

Investment Yield Analysis for Apartments

Summary

Key Terms and Concepts

Questions for Student Self-examination

LEARNING OBJECTIVES After studying this chapter, you should be familiar with

Factors creating the momentum for increased apartment investment
Demand factors behind increased investment in apartment buildings
The demand for second-home and condominium units
Supply factors behind increased investment in apartment buildings
Vacancy rate trends for rental apartment buildings
Apartment rent increases
The stability of mortgage financing terms
The rise in the number of households
The impact on apartment supply of environmental regulations
Benefits of a market survey and feasibility analysis
The content of the market survey
The content of the feasibility analysis
Apartment construction costs
Trends in apartment building income and expenses
Appraising apartment projects
Financing apartment buildings
Investment yield analysis for apartments

Apartment building investment and construction is expanding, after hitting a low point in 1976. In 1976, only 336,000 residential units with two or more units per building were completed; in 1973, 840,000 apartment units were completely constructed for rental or sale. More than one million multifamily units were started in 1972. Half that number were started in 1977. In the latter part of the 1970s, multifamily construction and investment were again expanding. Multifamily mortgage debt outstanding surpassed $110 billion. At the same time, contract rates on apartment permanent mortgages exceeded 10 percent.

INTRODUCTION

The chapter begins with an explanation of some factors creating the momentum for increased apartment investment. Some demand and supply factors are examined. The benefits of a market study and a feasibility analysis are then studied from the prospective investor's point of view. Then the following topics are discussed: construction costs for various types of apartments, appraised valuation of apartments, apartment building and project financing, and investment yield analysis. The reader observes the overall investment picture associated with apartment projects. The recent investment situation for apartment development and ownership is observed, as well as the investment circumstances where a reasonable yield is realized by the owner.

THE RELATIONSHIP OF THIS CHAPTER TO OTHER CHAPTERS OF THE TEXT

This chapter is the second of a six-chapter sequence, making up Part V, devoted to analysis of investment in specific types of property. Chapter 18 dealt with home ownership for occupancy and rental income. This chapter follows up the topic of home ownership with information about investment in multifamily residential buildings and projects. Subsequent chapters deal with nonresidential investment—investment in commercial and industrial properties.

SOME FACTORS CREATING THE MOMENTUM FOR INCREASED APARTMENT INVESTMENT

There are demand and supply factors that are promoting expansion in apartment investment. The demand factors are related to high home mortgage financing; increased lot and house prices; higher personal incomes, which create the need for tax shelters among potential real estate investors; second-home preferences; and the preference for condominium homes. The supply factors are related to lower vacancy rates, the rise in apartment rents, the stability of apartment mortgage financing, the rise in the number of households, and the reduced supply of new apartment buildings as a result of environmental protection regulations.

The Affordability of One-Family Homes. Home financing costs are relatively high, as home mortgage interest rates approximate 10 percent. Median family incomes are increasing, but in the 1970s they did not increase as rapidly as did the average house sale price (Table 19-1). The ratio of average house sale price to median family income is gradually increasing to a factor over 3.0 (Table 19-2). Therefore, families are being squeezed out of the one-family residential market and into the multifamily residential market to some extent. The apartment building investor seeks to satisfy this demand and acquire a reasonable yield on his or her investment at the same time.

Second-Home and Condominium Demand. Many in our affluent society want second homes for vacation and weekend use. The apartment project investor may anticipate the nature of the demand for multifamily space. Part of the second-home demand is associated with time-sharing rental or condominium space. Some second homes are wholly owned and unshared condominium apartments in investment properties. The investor may gain a return from the construction and development of the condominium or rental apartment project. The investment may be rather short-term if the condominium apartment building units are rapidly sold out. The rental apartment building may be sold during construction, while it is being rented, after it is completely rented, or after an extensive operating period of the totally rented project. In other words, the length of the investment period for the rental apartment building, in contrast to that for the condominium apartment building, may be relatively long.

Vacancy Rates for Rental Apartment Buildings. As house prices and home mortgage financing terms remain relatively high, the household or family unit may rent apartments. The overbuilt apartment condition of the mid-1970s is evaporating with the increased rental of apartments, as the general population and households expand. The low level of rents, high construction costs, and high financing costs have held down apartment building until the latter part of the 1970s. Rental apartment vacancy rates have declined from over 6 percent in 1975 to 5 percent in 1978, for example.

Table 19-1. Cooperative increases of average sale prices of new homes, new home price index, and median family income, 1963-1976

Year	Average Sale Price of Houses Sold in 1974° Price	Percent of Change	Price Index of New One-Family Houses Sold	Median Family Income Yearly Average	Percent of Change
1963	$22,600	—	69.2	$ 6,249	—
1964	22,700	+ 0.6	69.6	6,569	+ 5.1
1965	23,300	+ 2.3	71.2	6,957	+ 5.9
1966	24,200	+ 4.2	74.2	7,532	+ 8.3
1967	25,000	+ 3.0	76.4	7,933	+ 5.3
1968	26,200	+ 5.1	80.3	8,632	+ 8.8
1969	28,300	+ 7.7	86.5	9,433	+ 9.3
1970	29,100	+ 3.0	89.1	9,867	+ 4.6
1971	30,700	+ 5.4	93.9	10,285	+ 4.2
1972	32,700	+ 6.5	100.0	11,116	+ 8.1
1973	35,600	+ 8.9	108.9	12,051	+ 8.4
1974	38,900	+ 9.4	119.1	12,836	+ 6.5
1975	42,800	+ 10.0	131.0	13,719	+ 6.9
1976	46,400	+ 8.4	142.0	15,130†	+ 8.3

Source: Charles Lee Thiemann, "Homeownership—No Longer Affordable?" *Federal Home Loan Bank Board Journal* (August 1978), p. 2. Reprinted with permission.
° Average sale price of homes sold adjusted for quality of units sold, using price index of new one-family houses sold.
† Estimated.

Gradual Rise in Apartment Rents. During the last half of the 1970s, rents finally began to rise with the tightness in the market for rental apartments. The Consumer Price Index, until that time, had been rising at a faster rate than the Rent Index (Table 19-3).

Stable Mortgage Financing Terms. The mortgage financing terms for apartment investment have been relatively stable on a high level in the latter 1970s. These con-

Table 19-2. The ratio of average house sale price to median family income, 1970-1976

Year	Average House Sale Price	Median Family Income	Ratio of Average House Sale Price to Median Family Income
1970	$29,100	$ 9,867	2.95
1971	30,700	10,285	2.90
1972	32,700	11,116	2.99
1973	35,600	12,051	2.95
1974	38,900	12,836	3.03
1975	42,800	13,719	3.12
1976	46,400	15,130	3.07

Source: Adapted from "Homeownership—No Longer Affordable?" *Federal Home Loan Bank Board Journal* (August 1978), p. 2. Reprinted with permission.

Table 19-3. Movements in the consumer price index and rent index

Month/Year	Consumer Price Index; 1967 = 100	Percent Change, One Year Ago	Rent Index; 1967 = 100	Percent Change, One Year Ago
April 1976	168.2	6.1	143.2	5.4
April 1977	179.6	6.8	151.6	5.9
April 1978	191.3	6.5	161.4	6.5

Source: *Spring Real Estate Market Report 1978* (Chicago: Department of Economics and Research, The National Association of Realtors, 1978), p. 10. Reprinted with permission.

tract rates have been stable along with the other long-term capital market rates. Apartment projects have been financed on a 75 percent of appraised value basis, at a 9½ to 10¼ percent contract rate during 1977 and 1978. Until the excessive vacancy rates disappeared, a reasonable profit could not be acquired at this level of financing cost.

Rise in the Number of Households. The number of households has increased with the number of family members who have been separately housed during the affluent period of the 1970s, with the advent of a relatively high divorce rate, and with the continued increase in longevity among elderly persons. Many young adults, many divorced persons, and many retired persons prefer apartment living. The single-family home may require too much of a financial or maintenance burden.

Environmental Regulations. State and federal environmental programs have reduced the construction of apartment buildings in general, and in many advantageous locations, because of their possible environmental effects. The investment in existing apartment buildings in good locations has meant, in some cases, windfall profits to the owners because of the impact of environmental protection regulation on continued apartment development. This has particularly been the case regarding investment in apartment buildings located at the edge of sea coasts or shorelines.

THE MARKET SURVEY AND FEASIBILITY ANALYSIS

Before income property investment takes place, a market survey should be conducted and a feasibility analysis prepared. The investor may survey the market and prepare the feasibility analysis, or an outside analyst may be employed.

The market survey for the prospective apartment project should include population, income, transportation, and neighborhood factors. These questions might be addressed:

Population trends—municipality, metropolitan area, neighborhood.
    Total population count and projected trend.
    Age distribution and trends.
    Household formation.
Income trends.
    Average personal income.
    Bases for employment in the area.
    Unemployment rate.
    Household income.

Transportation trends
    Current city transportation systems in the area of the project site.
    Transportation arteries serving the project site.
    Rider cost for the appropriate transportation media serving the project area.
    Future plans for transportation in the area.
Neighborhood trends.
    Planning and zoning practices.
    Tax policies and trends.
    Cultural and recreational facilities provided.
    Climatic conditions.
    Average family size and trends.
    City service, such as fire and police protection and garbage pickup.
    Proximity of churches, synagogues, and other places of worship.
    Shopping facilities and trends.

Questions need to be answered about the present and future competing apartment space. The prospective apartment project investor needs to know the complete competitive situation. These factors should be recognized:

The rental structure for each present and future planned apartment project that is competitive with the proposed development or investment property.
The vacancy rate, current and projected.
Absorption rate (time required for space rent-up), according to the current building owner or manager.
Amenities currently provided the apartment tenants by the building owners and the utilization of the amenities.
    Swimming pools.
    Sauna baths.
    Tennis courts.
    Bicycle rental.
    Covered and outside parking space.
        Rental rates if rented.
        Number of parking spaces per apartment unit.
    Superette (food store on the premises)—financial position and tenant utilization.
    Drugstore (on the premises)—financial position and tenant utilization.
Apartment unit characteristics
    Livable square footage per type of apartment unit.
    Appliances and other furnishings included in the rent.
    Lease provisions, such as length of typical lease, unusual provisions.

The resulting tenancy profile drawn from these factors and others included in the market survey might resemble information given in Table 19-4.

Since the feasibility analysis seeks to ascertain the economic viability and investor profitability from the proposed investment, it should incorporate the market study results and add other financial factors, such as probable mortgage financing, present and future gross revenues, present and future operating expenses, probable depreciation schedule for tax purposes, probable construction or renovation cost, and probable appraised value over the holding period. The investor's return on equity, the payback period, the net present value, and the expected internal rate of return can be

Apartment Building Investment

Table 19-4. Tenancy profile, based on a market survey

Element	Conclusion
Average family	2.3 persons 45% require one-bedroom units 30% require two-bedroom units 25% require three-bedroom units
Average age of family head	35 years of age 65% are 35 to 65 years of age
Families with children	35%
Occupational activity	25% professional 40% executive 25% retired 10% other
Places of work	55% downtown business core 20% north side of city 15% south side 10% local
Shopping, schools, beaches, churches, and recreation	Close by and within bus and driving distance
Commutation to work	55% automobile 20% bus 25% train
Commutation time to work	70% less than 30 minutes 30% less than one hour
Former domicile	55% from nearby communities
Type of former dwelling	60% single-family 40% apartment
Average anticipated tenancy	Three to five years
Attainable rent per room	$100 to $110 per room per month
Conclusions and recommendations	Location is ideal for apartments of 3½, 4½, 5, and 5½ rooms, up to a total of 75 units

figured from the feasibility study. The feasibility analysis should be studied closely before the potential investor commits money to the venture. The risks and potential returns should be analyzed in detail in advance of purchase or construction, whichever the investment may require.

APARTMENT CONSTRUCTION COSTS

Construction costs for apartment buildings have been rising rapidly. For example, over the two-and-a-half-year period from May 1974 to May 1978, apartment house construction costs rose 50 to 110 percent, depending on the type of apartment building, according to the Southern Building Code Congress International (Table 19-5a). At the end of the 1970s, the cost per square foot of apartment buildings approximated $25 to

$35. These building costs are higher in some parts of the country than in other parts. The highest construction costs for apartment building may be found in Alaska and Hawaii and the lowest costs in South Carolina, Mississippi, North Carolina, and Arkansas (Table 19-5b).

Table 19-5a. Apartment house construction costs per square foot (average)

Type of Apartment House	May 1974	Dec. 1976–Jan. 1977	June–July 1979
Type I	$19.70	$31.50	$35.20
Type II	19.70	31.50	33.10
Type III	NA	NA	31.00
Type IV—1 hour	NA	NA	30.90
Unprotected	NA	NA	29.10
Type V—1 Hour	18.30	27.00	29.70
Unprotected	15.40	24.60	27.10
Basement	6.50	13.70	NA
Type VI—1 Hour	14.00	23.00	25.80
Unprotected	12.25	21.80	24.00

Reprinted by permission from *Southern Building*. Birmingham, Ala.: Southern Building Code Congress International, Inc. December/January 1976/1977, p. 6; May 1974, p. 29; advance copy for June/July 1979 issue. NA means "not available."

Table 19-5b. Regional modifiers, April–May 1978

Central United States	Modifier	Eastern United States	Modifier	Western United States	Modifier
Alabama	1.00	Connecticut	1.10	Alaska	1.76
Arkansas	0.97	Delaware	1.04	Arizona	1.10
Illinois	1.13	District of Columbia	1.12	California	1.16
Indiana	1.08	Florida	1.03	Colorado	1.09
Iowa	1.10	Georgia	1.00	Hawaii	1.40
Kansas	1.04	Maine	1.05	Idaho	1.07
Kentucky	1.02	Maryland	1.06	Montana	1.06
Louisiana	1.02	Massachusetts	1.12	Nevada	1.15
Michigan	1.12	New Hampshire	1.05	New Mexico	1.01
Minnesota	1.10	New Jersey	1.14	Oregon	1.13
Mississippi	0.94	New York	1.16	Utah	1.06
Missouri	1.07	North Carolina	0.96	Washington	1.15
Nebraska	1.07	Pennsylvania	1.02	Wyoming	1.09
North Dakota	1.10	Rhode Island	1.10		
Ohio	1.12	South Carolina	0.93		
Oklahoma	1.10	Vermont	1.05		
South Dakota	1.08	Virginia	1.02		
Tennessee	1.02	West Virginia	1.10		
Texas	1.00				
Wisconsin	1.10				

Source: *Southern Building* (April–May 1978), p. 8; (May 1974), p. 29. Reprinted with permission.

As the builder increases the density of the acreage, the construction cost per unit declines (Table 19-6). Table 19-6 shows that the unit development cost for four detached houses per acre is close to double the unit development cost for fourplexes, where eight and a quarter units on the average are placed on an acre of land.

Table 19-6. Development costs for detached houses, duplexes, triplexes, and fourplexes

Detached houses at four per acre

Net density—12 units on 3 acres = 4.0 units/acre
Gross density—12 units on 3.1 acres = 3.87 units/acre
Average lot size—9,611 sq. ft.

Development costs:

Clearing and grubbing	$ 350
Grading streets	276
Street pavement	498
Storm drainage	611
Sanitary sewer	827
Water distribution	468
Curbs and gutter	701
Driveways	700
Sidewalks	208
Street trees	306
Grading/seeding	741
Total	$5,686

Duplexes at five per acre

Net density—16 units on 3.2 acres = 5 units/acre
Gross density—16 units on 3.37 acres = 4.75 units/acre
Average lot size—7,854 sq. ft. (min. 5,060 sq. ft.)

Development costs:

Clearing and grubbing	$ 330
Grading streets	198
Street pavement	356
Storm drainage	471
Sanitary sewer	711
Water distribution	375
Curbs and gutter	496
Driveways	370
Sidewalks	156
Street trees	216
Grading/seeding	594
Total	$4,275

Duplexes at 7¼ per acre

Net density—20 units on 2.75 acres = 7.27 units/acre
Gross density—20 units on 2.99 acres = 6.69 units/acre
Average lot size—4,888 sq. ft. (min. 4,000 sq. ft.)

Development costs:

Clearing and grubbing	$ 253
Grading streets	160
Street pavement	287
Storm drainage	426
Sanitary sewer	633
Water distribution	321
Curbs and gutter	402
Driveways	320
Sidewalks	120
Street trees	180
Grading/seeding	331
Total	$3,433

Triplexes at six per acre

Net density—18 units on 3.0 acres = 6.0 units/acre
Gross density—18 units on 3.14 acres = 5.73 units/acre
Average lot size—6,375 sq. ft. (min. 4,700 sq. ft.)

Development costs:

Clearing and grubbing	$ 296
Grading streets	183
Street pavement	333
Storm drainage	421
Sanitary sewer	669
Water distribution	348
Curbs and gutter	460
Driveways	320
Sidewalks	144
Street trees	204
Grading/seeding	486
Total	$3,864

Source: *Cost Effective Site Planning* (Washington, D.C.: National Association of Home Builders). Reprinted with permission.

Table 19-6. (Continued)

Fourplexes at 8¼ per acre

Net density—24 units on 2.91 acres = 8.25 units/acre

Gross density—24 units on 3.05 acres = 7.87 units/acre

Average lot size—4,628 sq. ft. (min. 2,940 sq. ft.)

Development costs:

Clearing and grubbing	$ 215
Grading streets	137
Street pavement	250
Storm drainage	322
Sanitary sewer	607
Water distribution	300
Curbs and gutter	343
Driveways	398
Sidewalks	104
Street trees	150
Grading/seeding	312
Total	$3,138

TRENDS IN APARTMENT BUILDING INCOME AND EXPENSES

If the analyst is attempting to appraise the value of an apartment building or project or attempting to determine the investment yield, the cash flow analysis needs to reflect the trend in operating income and expenses. The trends are important, regardless of whether the cash flow analysis is based on a stabilized statement for a single time period or a statement covering estimated income and expenses for many time periods.

Looking at the median net operating income on a dollars per room per annum basis for various types of apartment buildings, we observe that the greatest increase from 1976 to 1977 was reflected in the statistics for low-rise 12-24-unit buildings. The second best profit picture was exhibited by the increase in median net operating income for garden apartment buildings (Table 19-7). These operating profits have been achieved even though total operating expense for all types of apartment buildings

Table 19-7. Median and average net operating income in terms of dollars per room per annum of unfurnished buildings

	Average			Median	
Building Type	1974	1975	1976	1977	% Change 1976-1977
Elevator	$367.43	$372.67	$393.67	$341.85	− 13.2
Low-rise 12-24 units	218.13	243.56	257.37	265.05	+ 3.0
Low-rise 25 units and over	261.00	256.54	287.76	287.65	− 0.04
Garden	243.37	252.23	272.03	276.49	+ 1.6

Reprinted by permission from *Income/Expense Analysis: Apartments* (Chicago: Institute of Real Estate Management, National Association of Realtors, 1978), pp. 66, 90, 122, and 178.

increased on a basis of dollars per square foot of rentable area at approximately a 5 percent rate between 1976 and 1977 (Table 19-8). Rents in 1977 rose approximately 6 percent (Table 19-8).

Between 1975 and 1976, the greatest increases in operating expenses for all types of apartments were experienced in maintenance and repairs, heating fuel, and utilities excluding heating fuel. These annual increases approximated 8½ to 9 percent (Table 19-9). Purchased steam was the most costly heating fuel while oil cost per rentable square foot increased the most from 1972 to 1976 (Table 19-10). Payroll expense only increased 3 percent over the same time period (Table 19-9).

In 1977 the highest vacancy and bad debt expense per rentable square foot was realized by owners of apartment projects in the South, mountain states, and Northwest. The Northeast achieved generally the highest gross rental income per square foot of rentable area. Total expenses were definitely the highest in the Northeast in 1977; the lowest, in the South (Table 19-11). On a square footage basis, the highest net operating incomes generated from all types of apartments were realized in the West and Southwest (Table 19-11)

The investor may wish to compare her or his projected cash flow analysis to standardized cash flow analyses offered by the Institute of Real Estate Management. An industry-standardized cash flow analysis for low-rise 12-24-unit unfurnished buildings constructed from 1969 to 1977 is shown in Table 19-12. Comparison can be made on the following bases:

Table 19-8. Trends in apartment income-expense data in terms of dollars per square foot of rentable area by building type

Building Type	Average Gross Possible Rental Income 1976	1977	% Change	Average Total Expenses 1976	1977	% Change	Average Vacancies and Bad Debts 1976	1977
Elevator	$3.66	$3.92	+ 7.1	$1.94	$2.13	+ 9.8	$0.04	$0.05
Low-rise 12-24 units	2.92	3.11	+ 6.5	1.43	1.49	+ 4.2	0.03	0.05
Low-rise 25 units or more	3.17	3.38	+ 6.6	1.57	1.65	+ 5.1	0.05	0.06
Garden	2.71	2.89	+ 6.6	1.31	1.34	+ 2.3	0.07	0.08

Reprinted by permission from *Income/Expense Analysis: Apartments* (Chicago: Institute of Real Estate Management, National Association of Realtors, 1978), pp. 10, 12-15.

Table 19-9. Average expense per room in dollars per annum°

Expense Item	1973	1974	1975	1976	Percent Change 1975-1976
Heating fuel	$ 20.14	$ 25.43	$ 31.28	$ 34.00	8.7
Utilities (excluding heating fuel)	41.74	46.66	54.65	59.19	8.3
Payroll	44.33	44.94	48.56	49.94	2.8
Maintenance and repairs	28.38	31.85	33.53	36.54	9.0
Total expense	280.77	298.86	319.30	340.12	6.5

Reprinted by permission from *Income/Expense Analysis: Apartments, Condominiums & Cooperatives* (Chicago: Institute of Real Estate Management, National Association of Realtors, 1977), p. 7.
° Based on weighted average.

Table 19-10. Heating fuel costs, in dollars per rentable square foot

Fuel	1972	1976	Percent Change
Oil	$0.10	$0.26	160.0
Electricity	0.09	0.16	77.8
Coal	0.20	0.34	70.0
Gas	0.07	0.11	57.1
Purchased steam	0.35	0.44	25.7

Reprinted by permission from *Income/Expense Analysis: Apartments, Condominiums & Cooperatives* (Chicago: Institute of Real Estate Management, National Association of Realtors, 1977), p. 8.

Table 19-11. Regional 1977 income-expense data in terms of dollars per square foot of rentable area of unfurnished buildings

Region	Elevator	Low-Rise 12-24 Units	Low-Rise 25 or More Units	Garden
I. Median value of gross possible rental income				
Northeast	$4.15	$3.22	$3.50	$3.22
Middle Atlantic	3.94	3.12	3.50	2.97
North-Central, Great Lakes	3.79	3.34	3.17	3.05
South	3.51	2.33	2.70	2.67
West, Southwest	4.03	3.27	3.41	3.29
Upper North Central, mountain states, Northwest	3.36	3.02	3.04	2.92
II. Median value of total all expenses				
Northeast	$2.43	1.87	1.94	1.83
Middle Atlantic	2.20	1.64	1.91	1.64
North-Central, Great Lakes	2.12	1.79	1.67	1.50
South	1.81	.97	1.22	1.35
West, Southwest	1.78	1.45	1.55	1.49
Upper North Central, mountain states, Northwest	1.59	1.40	1.41	1.38
III. Median value of net operating income				
Northeast	$1.38	1.28	1.53	1.37
Middle Atlantic	1.54	1.54	1.56	1.26
North-Central, Great Lakes	1.52	1.23	1.33	1.23
South	1.58	1.29	1.41	1.44
West, Southwest	1.88	1.60	1.85	1.48
Upper North Central, mountain states, Northwest	1.53	1.52	1.62	1.72

Reprinted by permission from *Income/Expense Analysis: Apartments* (Chicago: Institute of Real Estate Management, National Association of Realtors, 1978), pp. 11, 53-55, 78-80, 109-111, 160-162.

1. Dollars per room per annum.
2. Percentage of gross possible total income per room.
3. Dollars per square foot gross per annum.
4. Dollars per square foot rentable.

Table 19-12. Median income and operating costs: low-rise apartment buildings, 12-24 units unfurnished, built between 1969 and 1977

Income and Operating Costs	Percentage of Gross Possible Total Income	Dollars per Square Feet of Rentable Area
Income		
Rents—apartments	98.9	$3.14
Rents—garage/parking	1.8	0.06
Rents—stores/offices	6.0	0.10
Gross possible rents	99.2	3.23
Vacancies/rent loss	3.2	0.09
Total rents collected	95.9	3.09
Other income	1.1	0.03
Gross possible income	100.0	3.26
Total collections	97.1	3.19
Expenses		
Management costs	6.0	0.21
Other administrative costs	1.0	0.04
Subtotal administrative costs	6.6	0.25
Supplies	0.6	0.02
Heating fuel	1.1	0.10
Electricity	1.7	0.05
Water/sewer	1.8	0.07
Gas	1.1	0.04
Building services	1.1	0.04
Other operating expenses	0.8	0.03
Subtotal operating expenses	8.3	0.28
Security	1.6	0.06
Grounds maintenance	0.9	0.04
Maintenance—repairs	3.9	0.13
Painting/decorating	1.6	0.05
Subtotal maintenance	6.7	0.23
Real estate taxes	15.6	0.43
Other tax/fee/permit	0.2	0.01
Insurance	2.4	0.07
Subtotal tax-insurance	18.0	0.50
Recreational/amenities	1.1	0.03
Other payroll expense	3.1	0.10
Total all expenses	42.6	1.41
Net operating income	54.9	1.73

Reprinted by permission from *Income/Expense Analysis: Apartments* (Chicago: Institute of Real Estate Management, National Association of Realtors, 1978), p. 84.

The operating expense ratio—total operating expenses divided by effective gross income—varies widely for apartment investment. The Institute of Real Estate Management says that nationwide apartment operating-expense ratios currently approximate 50 percent. Many mortgage lenders want to see at least a ratio of 32 percent. Many building owners who are subject to relatively low property taxation may say that, including reserves for replacement, their operating expense ratios run 20 to 25 percent of effective gross income. According to the Institute of Real Estate Management, operating ratios do vary according to the section of the country. In 1976, for example, the Northeast apartment operating ratios approximated 60 percent, regardless of the type of apartment building. The lowest ratios—approximately 25 to 50 percent—originated in the South.

THE APPRAISAL OF APARTMENT PROJECTS

In recent years, values of apartment projects have often been determined primarily on the basis of cost, since the value of the project from the cost approach has, in many instances, far surpassed the value of the project from the income approach. The market in many areas has not permitted rents to rise as rapidly as did operating expenses and construction costs. If operating expenses approximate 40 percent, the capitalized net operating income will result in a relatively low value from the income approach. The derivation of the capitalization rate includes, of course, the current relatively high mortgage rate. The enclosed abstract of an appraisal of a four-unit apartment building shows the dilemma of the appraiser (Exhibits 19-1 and 19-2). Of course, other apartment projects in the marketplace may generate rents and net operating incomes that will permit the normal situation where the value from the income approach surpasses the value from the cost approach.

Exhibit 19-1. *Estimated Cost of a New Four-Unit Apartment Building*

First floor, 2,310 sq. ft. @ $15.00		$34,650
Second floor, 2,310 sq. ft. @ $14.00		32,340
Deck, 264 sq. ft. @ $10.00		2,640
Parking area, 1,180 sq. ft. @ $0.75		885
Dividers, 48 sq. ft. @ $12.00		576
Patios, 408 sq. ft. @ $1.00		408
Value of building and site improvements		$71,499
Extras:		
4 dishwashers	$1,200	
4 ranges	1,400	
4 hood vents	160	
4 refrigerators	2,000	
4 disposals	260	
4 smoke detectors	120	5,140
		76,639
Add land by cost (verified by seller)		9,200
Estimated value by cost approach		$85,839

Exhibit 19-2. Estimated Value of a New Four-Unit Apartment Building by the Income Approach

Estimated annual income, rent $210		$10,080
Vacancy @ 7%		705
Effective gross income		$ 9,375
Operating expenses:		
Tax @ 80,000 × .15 = $12,000 × 3.60%	$432	
Insurance 75,000 × 1.05	788	
Yard maintenance	300	
Painting and decorating (One month rent per annum)	440	
Roof reserve for replacement	200	
Ranges, refrigerators, dish washers, and disposals reserve for replacement	514	
Carpet and draperies reserve for replacement	300	
Air conditioning equipment reserve for replacement	600	
Management fee @ 6%	562	4,136
Net income to land and improvements		$ 5,239
Income to land @ 10.20% × $9,200		938
Residual income to the improvements		$ 4,301
Capitalized income to the improvements $4,301/.102*		42,167
Add land estimated by market value		9,200
Estimated value by the income approach		$51,367

*Band of Investment Approach to Derivation of the Capitalization Rate:

1st Mortgage	.80 @ .1051 =	0.0840
Equity	.20 @ .09 =	0.0180
Capitalization rate		0.1020

THE FINANCING OF APARTMENT BUILDINGS

Apartment buildings and projects can be financed through Veterans Administration-guaranteed mortgage loans, Federal Housing Administration-insured mortgage loans, and conventional mortgage loans. With conventional financing, 65 to 75 percent of appraised value may be borrowed by the investor. If the apartment structure does not exceed four units and the owner resides in one of the units, nearly 100 percent of appraised value may be borrowed from a lender with a Veterans Administration loan guaranteed, depending on the amount of the appraised value. If the apartment structure is financed with FHA mortgage insurance, approximately 90 percent of the appraised value may be borrowed from a lender if the owner resides in the building; approximately 85 percent of the appraised value may be borrowed if the owner does *not* reside in the building.

The contract rate of multifamily mortgages approximated 10 percent in 1978. Some mortgage loans have provided for participation in the equity by the lender, which has raised the effective yield to the lender. The contract mortgage rates for apartments through the latter 1970s have approximated 9½ to 10½ percent (Table 19-13). The capitalization rate, based on the loan constant and the equity yield requirement, has generally slightly exceeded 10 percent, as the loan constant has exceeded 10 percent (Table 19-13). In contrast, the usual length of the conventional apartment loan has declined to 22 or 23 years; many FHA-insured and VA-guaranteed apartment loans have run for 30 years.

Table 19-13. Mortgage terms for conventionally financed apartments

Quarter/Year	Average Loan Amount ($000)	Average Interest Rate	Average Loan-to-Value Ratio	Average Capitalization Rate	Average Debt Coverage Factor	Average Percentage Constant	Average Term (Yr./Mo.)
Second quarter 1977	$2,417	9.33%	73.5%	10.0%	1.32	10.2%	24/2
Third quarter 1977	NA	9.31	NA	10.0	NA	10.1	24/5
Third quarter 1978	NA	9.49	NA	10.1	NA	10.4	22/7
Fourth quarter 1978	3,519	9.90	74.8	10.2	1.24	10.9	21/9

Source: *Investment Bulletin*, No. 769, November 29, 1977, Table M; No. 788, April 20, 1979, Table M (Washington, D.C.: American Council of Life Insurance). Reprinted with permission.
NA means "not available."

Most lenders have required an ample debt service coverage factor on multifamily mortgage loans in the 1970s. On conventional multifamily loans, for example, major life insurance companies have required a 1.27 to 1.34 coverage factor for the lending of their money.

As of September 1978, new residential rental building owners have been qualified to take 200 percent declining balance or sum-of-the-years'-digits depreciation on their buildings. Investment in existing rental apartment buildings has not qualified for the fastest accelerated depreciation. Therefore, the construction of new rental apartment buildings has been encouraged by the tax laws through allowed depreciation methods.

INVESTMENT YIELD ANALYSIS FOR APARTMENTS

The investment yields from apartment buildings and projects can be sizable. The owner may not receive a reasonable yield, as Exhibits 19-1 and 19-2 indicated. The income and expense structure may not permit a reasonable yield on the owner's investment. Just because an apartment building is constructed or purchased does not mean that the investor will receive a reasonable yield on the money committed. The investor may be more optimistic about inflationary trends than the investment climate and the property actually justify.

There is some research evidence from the 1970s about yields from multifamily real estate. A Coldwell Banker publication issued in 1974, *Using the Discounted Yield to Compare Real Estate Alternatives*, projected after-tax returns of 10 to 15 percent on residential income property for taxpayers in a 50 percent tax bracket. The projection did not presume any appreciation or depreciation in selling prices. Projected yields were higher for properties with first-owner depreciation and favorable long-term financing. The Coldwell Banker study projected the yields in a range of 12.5 to 17 percent when a 20 percent increase in the selling price over a 10-year holding period was assumed. The net operating income was assumed to be constant over the 10-year holding period.

Since the level of construction costs and interest rates was favorable in the mid- and late 1960s, the after-tax returns on equity investment in apartment buildings constructed in most large metropolitan areas "probably have averaged annual returns of 15% or better."[1] In 1975 Mader estimated that an investor in new residential income

---

[1] Paul F. Wendt, MAI, CRE, "Inflation and the Real Estate Investor," *The Appraisal Journal* (July 1977), p. 352.

property might earn a return of 14.7 percent for a 10-year holding period. He assumed a 5 percent annual inflationary increase in sale prices and expenses, a 60 percent loan for 25 years at 8 percent, an ordinary income tax rate for the taxpayer of 40 percent, and a 20 percent capital-gains tax rate for the taxpayer. He also assumed double declining balance depreciation for tax purposes. He figured that, if the loan amount were raised to 75 percent of appraised value, the estimated rate of return would rise to 18.6 percent.[2] Blazar and Hilton, in their 1976 article, "Investment Opportunities in Existing Apartment Buildings," forecasted an after-tax return for apartment investment for a 10-year holding period of 15.1 percent (see Supplementary Tables 19-14 through 19-20 for the case study).

SUMMARY

The apartment investment chapter very appropriately follows the house investment chapter in Part V. There is a natural flow from house investment, with minimal financial requirements and responsibilities, to investment in more complicated, multiunit residential structures.

Certain demand and supply factors of the latter 1970s impel increased apartment investment. Some households are financially crowded out of the single-family ownership market and are forced to rent residential space in multifamily and single-family buildings. The second-home market also tends to favor multifamily residential space. Condominium space in multifamily buildings is often an attractive residential alternative. The builders and developers see the relatively low apartment vacancy rates, the permitted depreciation methods, the gradually rising rents, the rather stable mortgage financing terms, and the overall rise in the number of households over recent years and tend to move toward apartment construction and development. Owners of existing apartment buildings also note the increase in building values resulting from restrictions on new apartment building construction in some desirable locations, because of environmental protection regulations.

The prospective income property investor should survey the market for comparable space characteristics and housing needs, as well as conduct a feasibility analysis in advance of investment. If the investor does not have the time or the inclination, an outside analyst may be employed to conduct the market and feasibility studies. The risk and return position of the investment should be analyzed well before funds are committed.

Apartment construction costs are rapidly rising. Apartment incomes are gradually rising, whereas some operating expenses are outrunning the income sources on a percentage basis. Operating ratios on a national, stabilized basis tend to range around 40 to 50 percent for apartment buildings of various types in many areas. Investors in some areas may turn in operating ratios lower than this because of lower property tax and utility expense.

A variety of types of financing may be acquired for apartment building investment. Conventional, FHA, and VA financing is available for many types of multifamily projects. Conventional financing tends to be more readily available from local lenders, because of less administrative paperwork, but the terms tend to be less liberal than those of VA and FHA financing.

[2] Chris Mader, *The Dow-Jones-Irwin Guide to Real Estate Investing* (Homewood, Ill.: Dow-Jones-Irwin, 1975), pp. 176, 178.

Some apartment investments yield reasonable returns to their owners; some have not done so in the decade of the 1970s. Capital gains may or may not "bail out" the investor and give a reasonable overall yield. Research shows that apartment investments in the 1970s have yielded returns ranging from 14 to 18 percent after taxes.

Key Terms and Concepts

Time-sharing rental or condominium space
Household formation trend
Tenancy profile
Southern Building Code Congress International
Dollars per square foot gross per annum
Market survey
Area employment base
Unemployment rate trends
Domicile
Purchased steam
Garden apartment
Percent of gross possible total income per room
Absorption rate
Amenities
Superette
Renovation cost
Rentable square footage
Institute of Real Estate Management
First-owner depreciation

Supplementary Tables

Table 19-14. Summary of purchase

Land	$ 500,000	
Building	3,500,000	
Purchase price		$4,000,000
Mortgage (30 years, 9.5% interest)		3,000,000
Equity requirement		$1,000,000

Reprinted by permission from Sheldon M. Blazar and Hugh G. Hilton, "Investment Opportunities in Apartment Buildings," *Real Estate Review* (Summer 1976), p. 49.

Table 19-15. Assumptions of apartment building yield analysis

Income tax bracket of investor: 55% (combined federal, state, and city income tax)
Investor has other sources of taxable income
The investment: 200-unit apartment building, which cost $20,000 per unit, or $4 million
Land cost: $500,000
Mortgage financing available: $3 million mortgage (75% loan-to-value);
 30-year term at 9.5 percent interest
Equity required: $1 million

Reprinted by permission from Sheldon M. Blazar and Hugh G. Hilton, "Investment Opportunities in Apartment Buildings," *Real Estate Review* (Summer 1976), p. 49.

Table 19-16. Summary of cash flow (year 1)

200 units at $300 per month		$720.000
Less 5% vacancy factor		36,000
		684,000
Operating expenses at 25%	$171,000	
Real estate taxes at 15%	102,600	
Total expenses 40%		273,600
Income after cash expenses		410,400
Debt service on $3 million mortgage (10.10% constant)		302,708
Cash flow (10.8% of equity investment)		$107,692

Reprinted by permission from Sheldon M. Blazar and Hugh G. Hilton, "Investment Opportunities in Apartment Buildings," *Real Estate Review* (Summer 1976), p. 49.

Table 19-17. Annual cash flow, assuming rent and expenses increase 3 percent per year

	Year 1	Year 2	Year 3	Year 4	Year 5	Year 6	Year 7	Year 8	Year 9	Year 10
Annual revenue										
200 units at $300/month; 3% annual increase	$720,000	$741,600	$763,848	$786,763	$810,366	$834,677	$859,718	$885,509	$912,074	$939,437
Less 5% vacancy factor	36,000	37,080	38,192	39,338	40,518	41,734	42,986	44,275	45,604	46,972
Net rental revenue (reflects 3% annual increase)	684,000	704,520	725,656	747,425	769,848	792,943	816,732	841,234	866,470	892,465
Operating expenses at 25%	171,000	176,130	181,414	186,856	192,462	198,236	204,183	210,308	216,617	223,117
Real estate taxes at 15%	102,600	105,678	108,848	112,114	115,477	118,941	122,510	126,186	129,971	133,869
Total expense 40%	273,600	281,808	290,262	298,970	307,939	317,177	326,693	336,494	346,588	356,986
Net operating income	410,400	422,712	435,394	448,455	461,909	475,766	490,039	504,740	519,882	535,479
Debt service on $3 million mortgage (10.10% constant)	302,708	302,708	302,708	302,708	302,708	302,708	302,708	302,708	302,708	302,708
Cash flow	107,692	120,004	132,686	145,747	159,201	173,058	187,331	202,032	217,174	232,771
Tax analysis										
Cash flow	107,692	120,004	132,686	145,747	159,201	173,058	187,331	202,032	217,174	232,771
Plus loan amortization	18,499	20,335	22,353	24,572	27,011	29,691	32,638	35,878	39,438	43,352
Less depreciation (125% declining balance)	131,250	126,328	121,591	117,031	112,642	108,418	104,353	101,711	101,711	101,711
Taxable income (loss)	(5,059)	13,011	33,448	53,288	73,570	94,331	115,616	136,199	154,901	174,412
Taxable savings (55% bracket)	(2,782)									
Tax payable		7,706	18,397	29,308	40,463	51,882	63,598	74,909	85,196	95,927
After-tax cash flow	$110,474	$112,298	$114,289	$116,439	$118,738	$121,176	$123,742	$127,123	$131,978	$136,844

Reprinted by permission from Sheldon M. Blazar and Hugh G. Hilton, "Investment Opportunities in Existing Apartment Buildings," *Real Estate Review* (Summer, 1976), p. 49.

Table 19-18. Tax on sale of property after ten years: apartment building yield analysis

1975 to 1984	
Cash flow from property (cumulative)	$1,677,696
Less portion reported as taxable income	844,717
Untaxed balance of cash flow	832,979
Plus net proceeds of sale	2,327,710
Total	3,160,689
Less investment in property	1,000,000
Taxable gain	2,160,689
Ordinary portion ($61,397), taxed at 55%	33,768
Capital gain portion ($2,099,292), taxed at 30%	629,788
Total tax	663,556
Net proceeds of sale	2,327,710
Less total tax	663,556
Net cash proceeds after tax	1,664,154
After-tax return on investment	15.1%

Reprinted by permission from Sheldon M. Blazar and Hugh G. Hilton, "Investment Opportunities in Existing Apartment Buildings," *Real Estate Review* (Summer 1976), p. 52.

Table 19-19. Refinancing proceeds after ten years: apartment building yield analysis

Net rental revenue in year 11	$ 967,619
Operating costs	378,750
Net operating income	588,869
Capitalized at 10 times	$5,888,690
Mortgage value at 75%	4,416,518
Existing balance at end of year 11	2,706,233
Additional tax-free financing	$1,710,285

Reprinted by permission from Sheldon M. Blazar and Hugh G. Hilton, "Investment Opportunities in Existing Apartment Buildings," *Real Estate Review* (Summer 1976), p. 52.

Table 19-20. After-tax cash flow from four different assumptions: apartment building yield analysis

Years	3% Annual Increase in Rent and Expense	3% Annual Increase in Expense and, After Year 5, in Rent	6% Annual Increase in Rent; 3% Annual Increase in Expense	"Worst Case" Scenario: 3% Annual Increase in Rent and Expenses for Years 1-7; Stable Rents and 10% Expense Increase Thereafter.
1	$110,474	$110,474	$110,474	$110,474
2	112,298	103,064	121,442	112,298
3	114,289	95,544	133,588	114,289
4	116,439	87,897	146,692	116,439
5	118,738	80,106	160,896	118,738
6	121,176	81,386	176,257	121,176
7	123,742	82,758	192,833	123,742
8	127,123	84,908	211,384	105,806
9	131,978	88,499	232,654	87,677
10	136,844	92,059	255,257	67,736

Reprinted by permission from Sheldon M. Blazar and Hugh G. Hilton, "Investment Opportunities in Existing Apartment Buildings," *Real Estate Review* (Summer 1976), p. 51.

Questions for Student Self-examination

Multiple-Choice Questions

1. The highest construction costs for apartment buildings may be found in
   a. Alaska and Hawaii
   b. South Carolina and Mississippi
   c. North Carolina and Arkansas
   d. Ohio and Indiana

2. Which is not a typical basis of comparison for apartment investment?
   a. dollars per unit per annum
   b. percent of gross possible total income per room
   c. dollars per rentable square foot
   d. dollars per square foot gross per annum

3. The operating expense ratio is defined as
   a. total operating income divided by effective gross income
   b. effective gross income divided by total operating income
   c. total operating expenses divided by effective gross income
   d. total operating income divided by total gross income

4. Apartment buildings and projects can be financed through
   a. conventional mortgage loans
   b. Veterans Administration-guaranteed mortgage loans
   c. Federal Housing Administration-insured mortgage loans
   d. all of the above

5. If an apartment structure is financed with FHA mortgage insurance and the owner does not reside in the building, approximately _____ percent of the appraised value may be borrowed.
   a. 65 to 75
   b. 90
   c. 85
   d. 95 to 100

True-False Questions

T F 1. The ratio of average house sales price to median family income is gradually increasing to a factor of over 3.0.

T F 2. Median family incomes increased in the 1970s, but not as rapidly as the average house sale price.

T F 3. The market study for an apartment project seeks to ascertain the economic viability and investor profitability from the proposed investment.

T F 4. As the builder increases the density of the acreage, the construction cost per unit tends to increase.

T F 5. According to the Institute of Real Estate Management, operating ratios do vary according to the section of the country.

T F 6. Under normal market conditions, the value of an apartment project from the cost approach surpasses the value from the income approach.

T F 7. The usual length of the conventional apartment loan has been 35 years.

T F 8. On conventional multifamily loans, major life insurance companies may require a 1.27 to 1.34 debt service coverage factor for the lending of their money.
T F 9. The second-home market tends to favor multifamily residential space.
T F 10. Research shows that apartment investments in the 1970s yielded returns ranging from 14 to 18 percent after taxes.

Answers
Multiple-Choice: 1a, 2a, 3c, 4d, 5c.
True–False: 1T, 2T, 3F, 4F, 5T, 6F, 7F, 8T, 9T, 10T.

Problems

1. If a family of four wants a second home and wants no yard or maintenance work associated with that vacation home, what alternatives are available?

2. If a shopping center developer must pay $3,000 for a market and feasibility analysis, how might he recoup this expenditure?

3. If an apartment building has produced a 10 percent vacancy rate, based on your knowledge of national trends in apartment building vacancy rates, is this rate reasonable, low, or high?

4. What shows on the bottom line of a feasibility analysis for a proposed income property?

5. How can one use a tenancy profile to forecast future apartment building income and expenses?

6. If an elevator apartment building generates $390 of average net operating income per room per annum, would a knowledgeable property manager or investor consider this amount reasonable? Would an amount of $290 be reasonable for the elevator building?

Chapter 20

Shopping Center Investment

Introduction
The Relationship of This Chapter to Other Chapters of the Text
The Shopping Center
    Neighborhood Shopping Center   Community Shopping Center   Specialty Shopping Center
    Regional Shopping Center   Super-regional Shopping Center
The Trend in Shopping Center Development
Shopping Center Construction Costs
Cash Flow Analysis
    Revenue Sources   Expense Sources   Components of Cash Flow Analysis
Financing the Shopping Center
Shopping Center Investment Yields
    Shopping Center Investment as Inflation Protection   Return on Equity Realized
Summary
Key Terms and Concepts
Questions for Student Self-examination

LEARNING OBJECTIVES After studying this chapter, you should be familiar with

The nature of the shopping center
The relationship of the shopping center to the central business district
Categories of shopping centers and their characteristics
The trend in shopping center development
Shopping center construction costs
Cash flow analysis and the individual components of revenue and expense
Financing the shopping center
Shopping center investment yields
Shopping center investment as inflation protection

Investment in shopping centers, particularly regional shopping centers, reached a peak of importance in the latter 1970s. American investors particularly noticed the pervasive profitability of shopping centers in the United States as foreign investors have sought and bought shopping centers. One of the strongest motivations behind the foreign investment in shopping centers has been their inflation protection through percentage net leases. When foreign businesspeople started to invest in American shopping centers, there may have been more yield from the investments than the yields that have been acquired in recent years. The good yields of earlier years drew the investors into the market. The press has reported the payment of exorbitant prices by the foreign investors, which has forced down the equity yields on the investments. In their anxiety to buy up profitable shopping centers, the foreign investors have bid up the prices, to their own and their competitors' dismay.

This chapter summarizes the key factors that contribute to the profitability of the shopping center investment.

INTRODUCTION

The characteristics of a shopping center are surveyed, as the sources of revenue and cost are examined. As the discussion progresses, the operating differences among the various types of shopping centers are observed. The differences in construction costs are also encountered.

Since the financing of the center depends on the types of tenants and their respective lease terms, the alternate methods of financing the land and the improvements, which depend on the tenancy, the development group, and the investment group, are outlined. Once the operating and financial characteristics of the shopping center are examined, the possible yields from such an investment are introduced.

THE RELATIONSHIP OF THIS CHAPTER TO OTHER CHAPTERS OF THE TEXT

Shopping centers in the United States are familiar income-producing properties. The small investor would have a difficult time investing alone in such a huge financial venture, but the small investor might join with others in a general or limited partnership to acquire the land and the necessary loans for such a venture.

In earlier chapters, the possibilities of an individual investing directly in a house or in an apartment building of only a few units, with only a limited amount of funds, were presented. Now we discover that the small investor can develop or buy the equity in a neighborhood shopping center, but that the community, regional, and super-regional centers might be out of financial range. The same relationship tends to be true in the topic covered Chapter 21. The small investor might develop or buy the equity in a small office building, but he or she would need additional financial support from partners to invest in a mid-rise or high-rise office building with substantial square footage of rentable space.

The financing of shopping centers, like the financing of office buildings and many other types of income properties, depends on the preleasing of space by high-credit-rated tenants. Shopping center tenants are a little different, for financing purposes, from office building and industrial building tenants. Their retailing and service orientation leads to a unique set of storeroom leases.

THE SHOPPING CENTER

A shopping center is a group of retail and service establishments located in one area that together attract more customers and clients than the same establishments would in independent locations or in smaller groups. The center has free parking on the surface or in convenient parking garages for all potential customers.

A retail and service center in the middle of an urban area—the central business district—is one type of shopping center. The central business district is different from the neighborhood or community shopping center, in that many government offices, financial offices, and transient housing facilities are also located in this area. The central business district closely approximates what has been labeled recently as a super-regional shopping center. The new super-regional centers are normally located on the outskirts of a major metropolitan area or in less densely developed areas between two or more major population centers.

Shopping centers may be categorized as

Neighborhood shopping centers.
Community shopping centers.
Specialty shopping centers.
Regional shopping centers.
Super-regional shopping centers.

Neighborhood Shopping Center. The neighborhood shopping center may consist of five to ten storeroom tenants offering convenience goods and services to potential customers in the area of the center—perhaps within three to five minutes' driving time. Many customers walk to the center to purchase their goods and services. The key tenants are often supermarkets and drugstores. A small variety store may also be located in the one-story retail center. The stores may be located in a single line, or in an *L*- or *U*-shaped design, with parking in front and at the rear of the stores.

Community Shopping Center. The community shopping center may consist of 10 to 15 stores, which offer convenience and shopping goods and services to a potential customer radius of approximately 10 minutes' driving time. The key tenants are usually supermarkets, drugstores, and variety stores or junior department stores. Other smaller tenants enjoy the customer drawing power of the larger stores. An *L-* or *U-*, or *I-* shaped design often accommodates the numerous storerooms.

Specialty Shopping Center. The specialty shopping center flourished during the late-1970s. It may continue to flourish in the more affluent sections of metropolitan areas of the United States. No key chain tenant may be located in the center. Small specialty chains and independent stores are represented by small boutiques, specialty food stores, and specialty restaurants. If the specialty goods are greatly in demand, customers may drive for hours to reach the specialty center.

Regional Shopping Center. The regional shopping center located in suburban areas of major cities offers a variety of specialty and shopping goods and services, plus a variety of convenience goods and services to a trading radius of 25 to 30 minutes' driving time. The key tenants are primarily high-credit-rated chain stores, including one or two major department stores. The department store chains that are often found in regional shopping center locations include Federated Department Stores, Associated Dry Goods, City Stores, Sears Roebuck, Montgomery Ward, and J. C. Penney. The design of the center may involve one or two stories of rentable space under a single roof, with a weather-controlled interior space. The layout of the mall and the department stores accommodates generous free customer parking within easy walking distance of the entrances and shielded loading docks for delivery trucks. The mall may house 30 to 50 storeroom tenants.

Super-regional Shopping Center. The super-regional shopping center accommodates chain and independent store tenants on multiple levels of retail and service space, which is usually enclosed under a single roof for weather protection and temperature control. Three to four department stores may be directly linked to a mall of 50 to 100 tenants. The customer radius, in terms of driving time, may be 30 to 40 minutes. Multiple movie theaters, motels, and office buildings may be located in the vicinity.

THE TREND IN SHOPPING CENTER DEVELOPMENT

While the construction of super-regional shopping centers is declining, the construction of regional and community centers in medium- and small-sized urban communities is continuing. Generally, the gross and net leasable space is contracting to more profitable dimensions in terms of today's markets. Developers are realizing more competition for new space in urban areas, which are already ringed once or twice by regional shopping centers. In 1976 and 1977, shopping center developers started cutting back their previous plans for a high level of expansion. They became more optimistic in 1978 about shopping center expansion, as they observed a high level of a single-family house construction in the suburbs of most cities of any size.

SHOPPING CENTER CONSTRUCTION COSTS

The cost of construction of a shopping center is rising rapidly. Table 20-1 shows that construction costs for the three principal types of shopping centers rose approximately 18 percent from 1975 to 1978. If the same percentage increases in construction costs persist, in 1982 costs per square foot of gross leasable area will approximate $40 to $50, depending on the type of center. With higher future rates of inflation, this would be a conservative projection.

Community shopping centers usually cost somewhat more to construct than convenience or neighborhood shopping centers (Table 20-1). Regional and super-regional centers cost significantly more to build than the other, smaller types of centers.

CASH FLOW ANALYSIS

Cash flow analysis is tailored to the revenue and cost sources of the particular type of income property. Since the shopping center investor usually does not own the major department store buildings, the cash flow analysis covers the expense and income factors associated with the mall, the parking lot, and the other land improvements.

Revenue Sources. The mall tenants usually sign net percentage leases, but they may sign leases providing for only a flat rent for a period of time. The percentage lease usually establishes a basic rent per square foot for the storeroom space, plus a percentage of gross receipts over a basic amount. The lease is *net*, in that the tenant pays all of the property taxes, insurance premiums, and maintenance costs allocated to the storeroom space, or the amount of such expense over that basic amount assumed by the landlord at the opening of the lease. The mall tenants usually pay their proportionate share of the common area maintenance expense associated with the enclosed walkway and mall furniture and furnishings.

According to the Urban Land Institute's *Dollars and Cents of Shopping Centers*, the median mall tenant sales per square foot of mall gross leasable area ranged from $89 and $110 in 1977 (Table 20-2). The mall tenant sales per square foot of GLA were substantially higher for neighborhood and super-regional centers in 1977 than for community and regional centers.

The higher the credit rating of the storeroom tenant, usually the lower the square footage and percentage lease requirement. The higher the markup on the merchandise and the higher the merchandise turnover, usually the higher the square footage and percentage rents. Table 20-3 shows the range in national percentage leases for selected store categories in 1976. The range in percentage lease terms varies by the market area of the country (Table 20-4). Because the shopping center lease involves storeroom rent and tax and common area maintenance costs during the initial and subsequent lease renewal periods, a summary of lease provisions for a sample shopping center is shown in Table 20-5.

Table 20-1. Shopping center construction costs

Shopping Center Type	Dollars per Square Foot of Gross Leasable Area (Median Total Capital Cost) 1978	1975	Percentage Change 1975-1978
Regional and super-regional	$45.25	$42.87	5.6%
Community	36.39	28.20	29.0%
Neighborhood	31.06	26.20	18.5%

Reprinted by permission from Urban Land Institute, *Dollars and Cents of Shopping Centers* (Washington, D.C.: Urban Land Institute, 1975 and 1978), p. 7 (in both books).

Table 20-2. 1977 Mall tenant sales of U.S. shopping centers

Shopping Center Type	Dollars per Square Foot of Mall Gross Leasable Area		
	Median	Lower Decile	Upper Decile
Super-regional	$100.07	$73.39	$145.34
Regional	88.91	57.18	121.17
Community	91.74	51.50	131.23
Neighborhood	110.76	51.08	191.45

Source: Urban Land Institute, *Dollars and Cents of Shopping Centers*. Washington, D.C.: Urban Land Institute, 1978, p. 6. Reprinted with permission.

Expense Sources. The mall owner usually encounters operating expenses of the following types: maintenance and repairs, utilities, management fees, general and administrative costs, advertising and promotion costs, association dues, insurance premiums, and real estate taxes. Replacement reserves are usually set aside for assets with economic lives beyond one year (Table 20-6).

Components of Cash Flow Analysis. After taking into account the typical income and expense sources, the cash flow analysis indicates the taxable income and the net cash flow accruing to the owner (Table 20-6). Continued cash flow analysis may show the net worth of the investment per year of the expected holding period and the gain that would be realized on the sale of the property at the end of any year of the expected holding period (Table 20-7). The excess depreciation and capital gain at the end of each year of the holding period may be calculated.

The percentage of the cash flow after debt service to total receipts may be calculated and compared against the statistics compiled by the Urban Land Institute in *Dollars and Cents of Shopping Centers* for various types of shopping centers (Table 20-8). The Urban Land Institute also compiles data on the median revenue, expense, and net cash flow per square foot for a variety of shopping center types. "According to ULI's 1978 report, the median net cash flow per sq. ft. for the sample of super regional malls was $2.09 compared to net operating income of $1.60.... Moreover, the 1977 net cash flow per sq. ft. for super regionals was significantly higher than that for regionals and was nearly three times greater than that for neighborhood and community centers."[1] In spite of the probability of the existing super-regional centers, most analysts forecast a decline in the construction of super-regional centers, because of the costs and planning difficulties of putting such new centers together.

FINANCING THE SHOPPING CENTER

Mortgage financing is usually employed for the shopping center buildings and the other land improvements. The lender may finance on a leasehold basis if the land is leased; otherwise, the lender finances on the basis of a fee estate. The land may be acquired as a contribution from one of the partners. Otherwise, the land may be purchased

[1] Maureen A. O'Leary, Patricia A. Cousineau, and Nancy N. Robinson, "Some Findings on the Profitability of Real Estate Investments," *REITs Quarterly* (1977: IV), p. 11.

Table 20-3. National percentage lease ranges for selected store categories, 1976

Store Category	Percentage Lease Range
Art shops	6-10
Auto accessories stores	3- 6
Barber shops	5-10
Beauty shops	5-10
Book and stationery stores	5- 8
Candy stores	6-12
Department stores	1.5-3.5
Discount department stores (over 75,000 sq. ft.)	1- 2.5
Discount department stores (under 75,000 sq. ft.)	1- 4
Drugstores—independent	2.5-6
Drugstores—chain	2.5-5
Drugstores—prescription (medical buildings)	5-10
Electrical appliance stores	3- 6
Five-and-dime stores	3- 5
Fabric (yard goods) stores	4- 6
Florists	6-10
Furniture stores	3- 6
Gas stations (costs per gallon sold)	1- 2 cents
Gift shops	6-10
Supermarkets	1- 2
Convenience food stores	2- 3.5
Hardware stores	4- 6
Hosiery and knit goods stores	6-10
Jewelry stores	4-10
Luggage/leather goods stores	5-10
Liquor and wine stores	2- 6
Men's clothing stores	4- 8
Men's furnishings (haberdashery) stores	5- 8
Motion-picture theaters	7-15
Radio, TV, and hi-fi stores	3- 8
Record shops	5- 7
Restaurants	5- 9
Restaurants—liquor	6-10
Sporting goods stores	3.5-8
Women's ready-to-wear stores—chain	3- 6
Women's ready-to-wear stores—independent	4- 8
Women's furnishings/accessories stores	5- 8
Women's shoe stores	5- 7

Reprinted by permission from Nathan Schloss, "Inflation-Proofing Retail Investments with Percentage Leases," *Real Estate Review* (Winter 1978), p. 37.

Table 20-4. Percentage lease ranges in selected market areas for selected store categories, 1976

Store Category	National	Chicago	Dallas	Los Angeles
Hosiery and knit goods stores	6-10	6-8	6-7	7-10
Luggage/leather goods stores	5-10	6-8	5-7	7-10
Radio, TV, hi-fi stores	3- 8	4-5	5-6	5- 8
Women's furnishings/accessories stores	5- 8	6-7	4.5-6.5	5- 7

Reprinted by permission from Nathan Schloss, "Inflation-Proofing Retail Investments with Percentage Leases," *Real Estate Review* (Winter 1978), p. 38.

through a land contract, a purchase-money mortgage, or an institutional land loan. After land acquisition, the owner may sell the land to an investor or investor group and lease the land back for shopping center improvements. Sale-leasebacks are common in shopping center development.

The mortgage financing of the mall buildings usually owned by the shopping center investor-developer is dependent on the fixed lease revenue derived from the Aaa credit rated tenants. The mortgage debt service usually should be covered by the square footage rentals paid monthly by this class of tenants in the mall space. The main portion of the percentage lease income from all tenants covers the operating expenses and profit to the owner. The major department stores usually build and finance their separate buildings, which are attached to the mall, through their own financing efforts. Individually, the department store structures and the land beneath may be financed through sale-leaseback arrangements, or the title may be held by a real estate subsidiary of the department store chain and the property leased to the operating department store company.

The lender often protects his or her financial position from inflation erosion by asking the shopping center owner-borrower for variable mortgage interest and/or participation in the equity of the shopping center. Often the shopping center permanent first mortgage will have its interest rate indexed to a floating index or bank interest rate. Perhaps every six months the required debt service payment is adjusted to reflect a rate adjusted to a money and capital market index or a rate that floats two to three points above the bank prime or commercial paper rate. The lender may also wish a percentage of the gross revenues received by the owner-mortgagor above a base amount. The term of the loan may be as long as 25 years, and the loan-to-value ratio may range from 70 to 80 percent. The debt coverage requirement normally ranges from 1.2 to 1.4. In loan analysis and evaluation, the lender may consider no need for a vacancy and bad debt allowance for the prime tenants; only a 5 percent allowance, perhaps, for the tenants with good credit ratings; and perhaps a 10 percent allowance for unrated or local tenants. The lessor of land or shopping center buildings may require a return competitive with the yields on high-rated corporate industrial bonds if the cash flow analysis of the shopping center shows a stability and profitability.

SHOPPING CENTER INVESTMENT YIELDS

The methods of calculating real estate investment yields mentioned earlier can be applied to all income property evaluation. Generally, no matter how the investment

Table 20-5. Summary of lease provisions; estimates of sales and sales growth, sample shopping center

No.	Tenant	Gross Leasable Area (Sq. Ft.)	Gross Sales Dollars	$/Sq. Ft.	Annual Rent Dollars	$/Sq. Ft.	Percent Rent	Tax/ Sq. Ft.	Prorated	Common Area Maintenance/ Sq. Ft.	Prorated	Lease Term
1	1	30,000	$3,900,000	$130	$75,000	$2.50	1.50%	0.30	No	0.10	No	75/95
2	2	5,000	425,000	85	25,000	5.00	5.00	0.25	Yes	0.15	Yes	75/80
3	2A	0	0	0	30,000	6.00	5.00	0.30	Yes	0.15	Yes	81/90
4	3	4,000	280,000	70	26,000	6.50	8.00	0.00	Yes	0.18	Yes	75/80
5	4	3,000	360,000	120	24,000	8.00	6.00	0.00	No	0.20	Yes	75/78
6	4A	0	0	0	24,000	8.00	8.00	0.00	No	0.20	Yes	79/85

Source: Jared Shlaes, MAI, CRE, and Michael S. Young, "Evaluating Major Investment Properties," *The Appraisal Journal* (January 1978), p. 107, with permission of *The Appraisal Journal* and The American Institute of Real Estate Appraisers. The opinions and statements set forth herein do not necessarily reflect the viewpoint of the American Institute of Real Estate Appraisers or its individual members, and neither the institute nor its editors and staff assume responsibility for such expressions of opinion or statement.

Table 20-6. Sample shopping center, cash flow projection

Income	1977	1978	1979	1980	1981
Fixed rent	$150,000	$150,000	$150,000	$150,000	$129,000
Percent rent	233	2,617	6,077	15,846	21,412
Real estate taxes	10,964	11,227	11,533	11,848	9,000
Common area	14,285	14,821	13,014	13,712	4,350
Total°	$175,483	$178,665	$180,625	$191,407	$163,762
Expenses					
Maintenance and repairs	$ 12,000	$ 11,864	$ 12,075	$ 12,274	$ 13,255
Utilities	15,000	16,850	18,710	21,125	24,134
Management fee	7,019	7,146	7,225	7,656	6,550
General and administrative	750	717	765	679	767
Advertising and promotion	2,500	2,433	2,268	2,529	2,436
Association dues	1,000	1,000	1,000	1,000	1,000
Replacement reserves	8,000	8,000	8,000	8,000	8,000
Insurance	9,000	9,226	9,878	10,261	10,645
Real estate taxes	15,000	16,227	17,657	19,127	20,589
Total°	$ 70,269	$ 73,466	$ 77,582	$ 82,655	$ 87,380
Debt service					
Interest	$ 63,488	$ 62,885	$ 62,228	$ 61,513	$ 60,736
Principal	6,824	7,427	8,083	8,798	9,576
Total°	$ 70,312	$ 70,312	$ 70,312	$ 70,312	$ 70,312
Taxable income					
Net cash flow	$ 34,901	$ 34,886	$ 32,730	$ 38,440	$ 6,069
+Amortization	6,824	7,427	8,083	8,798	9,576
−Depreciation	34,666	33,164	33,229	33,226	33,226
Total°	$ 7,058	$ 9,149	$ 7,584	$ 14,011	17,581
Ratio analysis					
Coverage ratio	1.4963	1.4961	1.4655	1.5467	1.0863
Breakeven ratio	0.8011	0.8047	0.8187	0.7991	0.9629
Operating ratio	0.4004	0.4111	0.4295	0.4318	0.5335

Source: Jared Shlaes, MAI, CRE, and Michael S. Young, "Evaluating Major Investment Properties," *The Appraisal Journal* (January 1978), p. 109, with permission of *The Appraisal Journal* and The American Institute of Real Estate Appraisers. The opinions and statements set forth herein do not necessarily reflect the viewpoint of the American Institute of Real Estate Appraisers or its individual members, and neither the institute nor its editors and staff assume responsibility for such expressions of opinions or statement.
° Errors in summation due to rounding.

yield of a successful shopping center is calculated, the return on investment will surpass the recent rate of inflation.

Shopping Center Investment as Inflation Protection. The sales of goods and services of shopping centers of various kinds increased on a per capita basis generally faster than the rise in the Consumer Price Index from 1966 through 1976. Personal consumption expenditures and disposable personal income on a per capita basis also increased generally more than the Consumer Price Index over the same period.

Further experience showing the inflation protection given by shopping center investment comes from the recent operating histories of super-regional malls. In 1977, according to the Urban Land Institute, the median net cash flow per square foot for a sample of super-regional malls was $2.09. Net operating income that year was $1.60

Table 20-7. Summary of estimated equity reversions, sample shopping center

	1977	1978	1979	1980	1981
Sale price	$1,002,036	$1,001,896	$981,361	$1,035,739	$727,441
Less Commission	48,097	48,091	47,105	49,715	34,917
Less Loan balance	743,175	735,748	727,664	718,866	709,290
Net worth°	210,762	218,056	206,591	267,157	– 16,766
Sale price	1,002,036	1,001,896	981,361	1,035,739	727,441
Less Commission	48,097	48,091	47,105	49,715	34,917
Less Adjusted basis	765,333	732,168	698,939	665,712	632,485
Gain on sale°	188,605	221,636	235,317	320,311	60,038
Excess depreciation	8,000	14,497	21,060	27,620	34,180
Capital gain	$ 180,605	$ 207,138	$214,256	$ 292,690	$ 25,857

Net operating income capitalization rate = 10.50%   Sales commission rate = 4.80%

Source: Jared Shlaes, MAI, CRE, and Michael S. Young, "Evaluating Major Investment Properties," *The Appraisal Journal* (January 1978), p. 109, with permission of *The Appraisal Journal* and The American Institute of Real Estate Appraisers. The opinions and statements set forth herein do not necessarily reflect the viewpoint of the American Institute of Real Estate Appraisers or its individual members, and neither the institute nor its editors and staff assume responsibility for such expressions of opinion or statement.
° Errors in summation a result of rounding.

Table 20-8. 1978 Operating results and cash flow after debt service, four types of shopping centers

	Median Percent of Total Receipts			
	Super-regional	Regional	Community	Neighborhood
Operating expenses	33.6%	38.1%	32.3%	27.1%
Net operating income	14.7	16.6	20.6	20.1
Depreciation and amortization of deferred costs	14.1	16.4	19.5	18.2
Mortgage and other loan principal payments	5.5	9.7	14.9	12.6
Funds after debt service (net cash flow)	21.5	21.0	24.9	23.7

Reprinted by persmission from *Dollars & Cents of Shopping Centers: 1978* (Washington, D.C.: Urban Land Institute, 1978), pp. 15, 53, 101, 149.

per square foot. The net cash flow had increased 36 percent from the 1974 data published in a 1975 ULI survey.[2] Over the same period of time, the Consumer Price Index increased 25 percent. The implication is made that the cash earnings of super-regional malls more than kept pace with inflation.

Return on Equity Realized. Life insurance company data shows that the rate of return on equity after taxes and after financing during the mid-1960s approximated 8.7 percent (Table 20-9). A 1975 shopping center financial analysis of Peachtree Square in Columbia, Georgia, shows a return on investment of 30 percent. The last analytical portion of the investment summary concerning the sample shopping center shows the derivation of the net proceeds of a shopping center sale, the derivation of net spendable cash, and the derivation of net present value per year of the expected holding period (Table 20-10). The net present value calculations show that the investor re-

[2] Ibid.

Table 20-9. *Rate of return on equity after tax, after financing*

	Quarter and Year				
Property Type	3rd, '54	4th, '59	3rd, '63	1st, '65	4th '66
Shopping centers	7.14	7.26	7.99	8.74	8.71
Retail stores	7.42	7.23	7.65	7.87	8.63
Apartments—elevator	8.32	8.58	8.81	9.55	9.53
Apartments—nonelevator	8.67	8.00	8.58	9.35	9.34

Reprinted by permission from R. Bruce Ricks, "Imputed Equity Returns on Real Estate Financed with Life Insurance Company Loans," *Journal of Finance* (December 1969), p. 933.

Table 20-10. *Investment summary and calculation of net present value*°

	1977	1978	1979	1980	1981
Net worth of share	$ 210,762	$ 218,056	$206,591	$ 267,157	$−16,766
Annual reversion					
Gain on sale	$ 188,605	$ 221,636	$235,317	$ 320,311	$ 60,038
Less tax, total gain	39,379	73,313	81,008	99,519	26,759
Less tax, preference	12,045	13,929	14,278	19,954	0
Net proceeds of sale†	$ 117,179	$ 134,393	$140,030	$ 200,837	$ 33,279
Annual performance					
Taxable income	$ 7,058	$ 9,149	$ 7,584	$ 14,011	$−17,581
Cash distribution	34,901	34,886	32,730	38,440	6,069
Less income tax	3,741	4,918	4,151	7,887	0
Net cash distribution†	$ 31,160	$ 29,968	$ 28,579	$ 30,552	$ 6,069
Plus tax savings	0	0	0	0	9,507
Net spendable cash (NSC)	$ 31,160	$ 29,968	$ 28,579	$ 30,552	$ 15,576
Present value (PV)					
Summary					
Cumulative PV of NSC	$ 28,587	$ 53,810	$ 75,879	$ 97,523	$ 107,647
PV of net proceeds	107,504	113,116	108,129	142,278	21,629
PV including sale	$ 136,091	$ 166,927	$184,008	$ 239,801	$ 129,276
Net present value	$ 36,091	$ 66,927	$ 84,008	$ 139,801	$ 29,276
Sale price comparison					
Estimated sale price	$1,002,036	$1,001,896	$981,361	$1,035,739	$ 727,441
Required sale price to give 9% return	888,524	803,278	751,714	670,474	622,303

Source: Jared Shlaes, MAI, CRE, and Michael S. Young, "Evaluating Major Investment Properties," *The Appraisal Journal*, 46:1 (January, 1978), p. 110, with permission of *The Appraisal Journal* and The American Institute of Real Estate Appraisers. The opinions and statements set forth herein do not necessarily reflect the viewpoint of the American Institute of Real Estate Appraisers or its individual members, and neither the institute nor its editors and staff assume responsibility for such expressions of opinion or statement.

† Errors in summation due to rounding.

° Assumptions:

Taxable income	$ 50,000
Cash contribution	$100,000
Method of tax filing	Married
Rate of change of taxpayer's income	8%
Discount rate—investor's required return	9%

ceives the greatest return in 1980. The analysis suggests that the investor sell the project at the end of that year before the low-yield year of 1981 sets in. The investor's required yield of 9 percent will be surpassed by the cash flow yield of the shopping center.

SUMMARY

The shopping center has been such a good inflation hedge that domestic and foreign investors have eyed and gone on to purchase shopping centers of various types in the United States. In fact, the competition for the purchase of profitable shopping centers has forced the investment yield of many shopping centers down because of unreasonably high purchase prices.

The categories of shopping centers are neighborhood, community, specialty, regional, and super-regional centers. Shopping center development continues at a slower pace than during the mid-1970s. Centers are getting smaller, and good locations are becoming scarce in major metropolitan areas. Many malls are being built now in medium and relatively small urban areas, which are not yet ringed once or twice by regional centers.

Shopping center construction costs are rapidly climbing with inflation. The increasing revenues, operating costs, and construction costs find their way into the analyst's cash flow projections and investment yield measurements. The shopping center may be financed through fee and leasehold mortgage loans, sale-leasebacks, land loans, and land contracts. The loans may carry variable yields by means of variable interest rates and equity participation.

Shopping center investment yields are often substantial, as is shown in the Peachtree Square analysis. Historical evidence pointed at least to reasonably good yields over the long pull. The increases in net cash flows from shopping centers have tended to surpass, in terms of percentage, the increases in the Consumer Price Index, which is the prime indicator of the progress of inflation in the United States.

Supplementary Exhibits

Exhibit 1. *Proposed Community Shopping Center Site, Columbia, Ga., ABC Development Corporation*

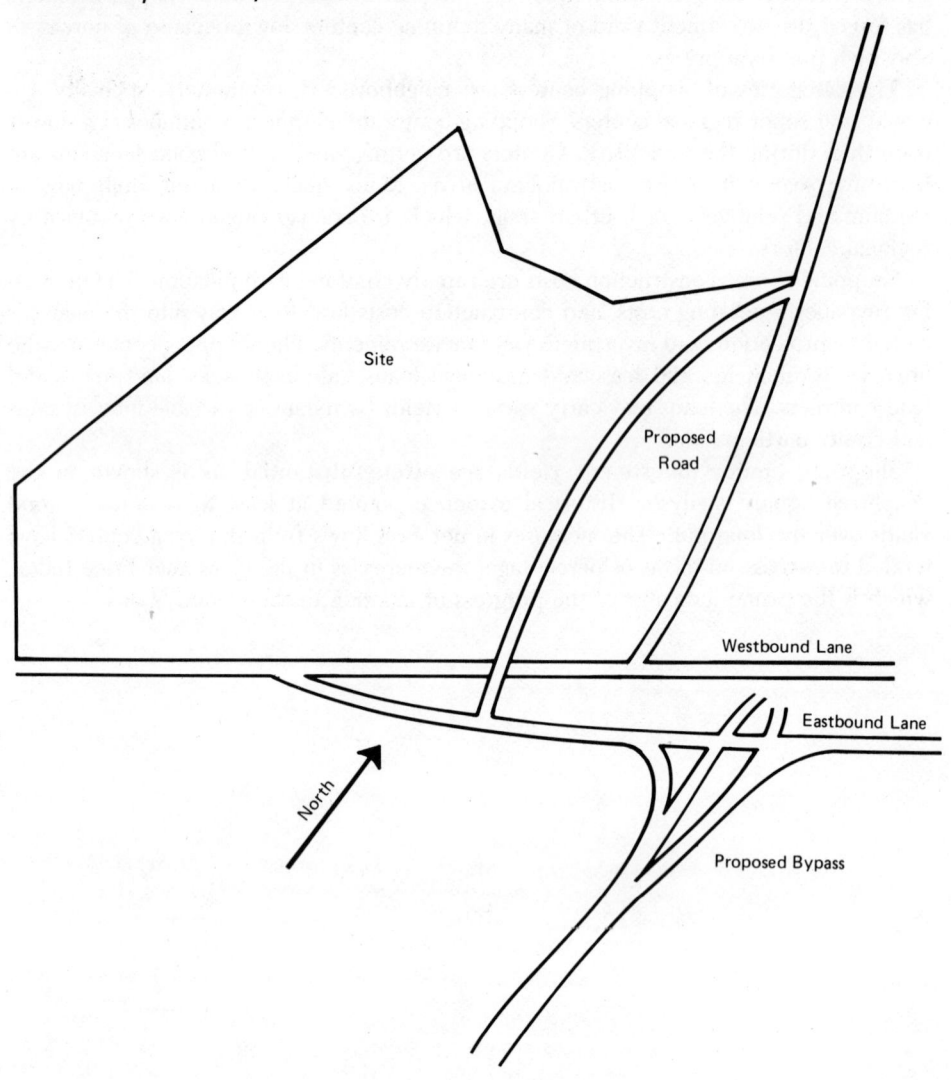

Exhibit 2. *Proposed Development Plan, Community Shopping Center; Peachtree Square, Columbia, Ga.*

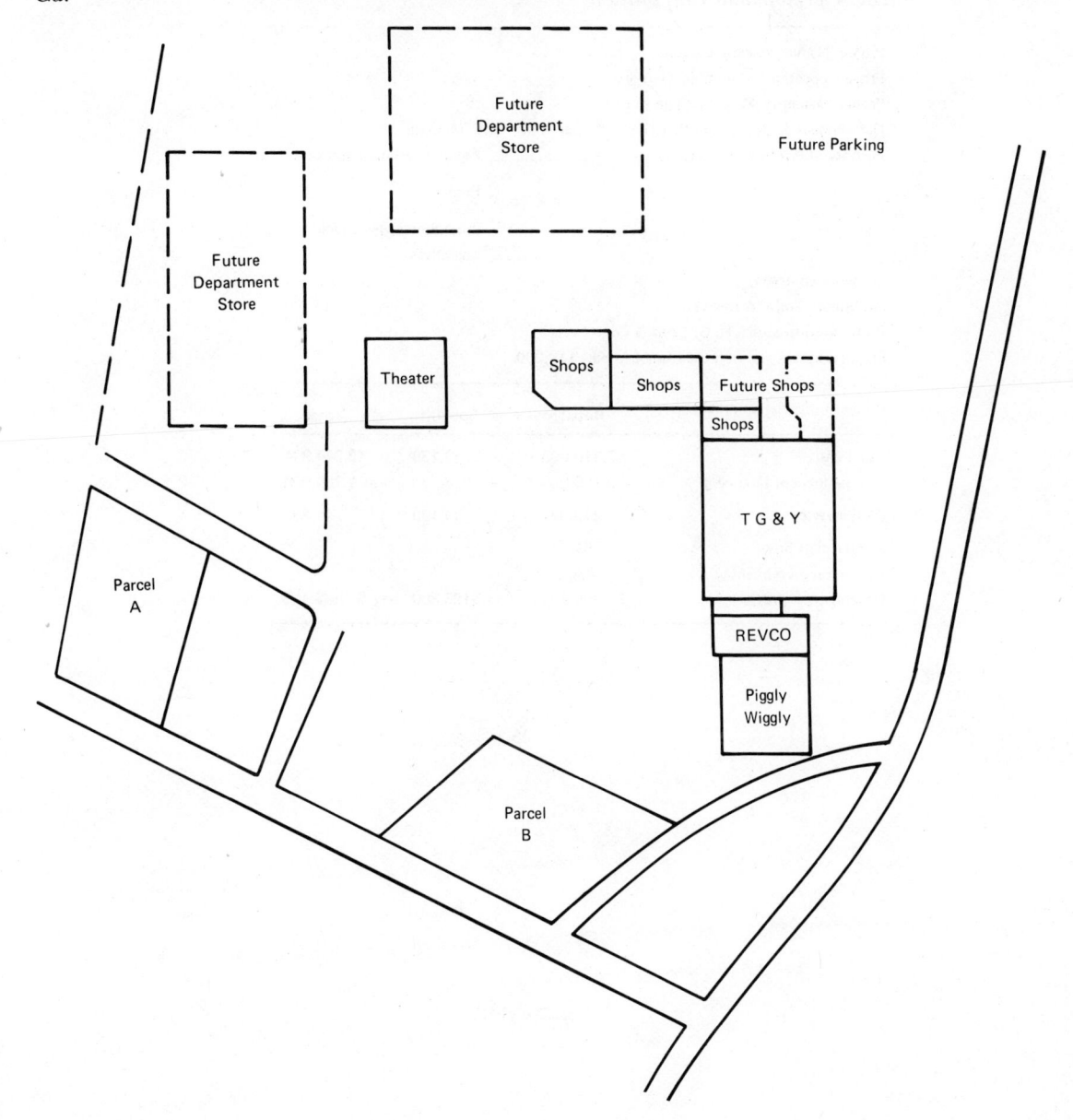

Shopping Center Investment

Exhibit 3. *Community Shopping Center Pro-Forma Analysis of ABC Development Corporation*

Project Name: Peachtree Square
Project Location: Columbia, Georgia
Project Manager: M. C. McClain
Date Prepared: September 9, 1975   Prepared by: M.C. McClain
Purpose of Pro Forma Analysis: _____ Feasibility/board approval
                                 _____ Financing
                                 _____ Project manager budget objectives

Sitework contractor:
Architect: Smith & Blackburn
Building contractor: H. G. Laws & Co.
Planned square feet of gross leasable area: 112,200

Project Financial Summary	Retail	+	Spin-off	=	Total
Total cost	$2,310,095		$ 34,139		$2,344,234
Less permanent financing	2,100,000				2,100,000
Cash invested	210,095		34,139		244,234
Annual cash flow	61,679				
Return on investment	30%				
Development profit	$ 396,695	+	$165,800	=	$ 562,495

Exhibit 4. *Shopping Center Financial Analysis; September, 1975*

1. Annual net income: $2.60 per sq. ft. — $291,789
2. Appraised value:
   Capitalized net income @ 10.5% — 2,778,940
3. Permanent loan:
   Appraised value @ 75.5% — 2,100,000
4. Total project cost — 2,310,095
5. Cash invested:
   Total project cost—permanent loan — 210,095
6. Annual debt service:
   a. Conventional terms:
   _____ % _____ yrs. 10.9 Loan constant %
   b. Kicker terms:
   c. Total annual debt service — 229,110
7. Annual cash flow: $0.56 per sq. ft.
   Net income — total debt service — 62,679
8. Development profit:
   a. Capitalized cash flow @ 10% — 626,790
   b. Less cash invested — 210,095
   c. Gross development profit — 416,695
   d. Less selling expense — 20,000
   e. Net development profit — 396,695
9. ROI = $\dfrac{\text{Annual cash flow}}{\text{Cash invested}} = \dfrac{62,679}{210,095} = 30\%$
10. Market value:
    Capitalized cash flow + permanent loan — 2,726,790
11. Ratio of: $\dfrac{\text{permanent loan}}{\text{market value}} = \dfrac{2,100,000}{2,726,790} = 77\%$
12. Effective debt service constant: $\dfrac{\text{total annual debt service}}{\text{permanent loan amount}} = 10.91\%$
13. Coverage: $\dfrac{\text{annual net income}}{\text{total annual debt service}} = \dfrac{291,789}{\$\,229,110} = 1.27$

Exhibit 5. *Land Acquisition, Improved Land Cost Allocation, and Spin-off Land Development Profit, Community Shopping Center; Peachtree Square, Columbia, Ga.*

Land Acquisition

	Property Owners	Acres	X	Cost/Acre	=	Total Cost	Terms of Land Purchase
1	James Johnson, Inc.	19.985	X	$14,230.22		$284,391	Cash
2							
	Totals					284,391	

Improved Land Cost Allocation

Parcel	Acres	Cost/Ac.	Parcel Cost	Cost/sq. ft.-GLA	Sitework	Cost/sq. ft.-GLA	Total Cost	Cost/sq. ft.-GLA
Retail I	12.63	$14,230	$179,700	$1.60	$322,797	$2.87	$502,497	$4.47
Retail II	6.03	14,230	85,800		51,958		137,758	
Parcel "A"	0.64	14,230	9,100		6,067		15,167	
Parcel "B"	0.69	14,230	9,800		6,067		15,867	
Totals	19.99		$284,400		$386,887		$671,287	

Spin-off Land Development Profit

Parcel Land + SW Cost	(%)	(yrs.)	=	$ Hold Cost	Total Cost	Est. Mkt. Value @ Date	Dvlpmt. Profit
Retail II $(137,759)	(10%)	(2 yrs.)	=	$27,559	$165,318		
Parcel "A" (15,167)	(10%)	(1 yr.)	=	1,517	16,684	$100,000	$83,316
Parcel "B" (15,867)	(10%)	(1 yr.)	=	1,588	17,455	100,000	82,545
Totals $				$	$	$	$

Exhibit 6. *Sitework Cost Allocation Schedule for Community Shopping Center; Peachtree Square, Columbia, Ga.*

	Acreage	19.99	=	12.63	+	6.03	+	.64	+	.69
	Percent of Acreage	100	=	63	+	30	+	3.5	+	3.5

	Total Cost	Retail Center I	Retail Center II	Parcel "A"	Parcel "B"
Engineering services	$ 4,000	$ 2,520	$ 1,200	$ 140	$ 140
Demolition/clearing/grading%fill	83,358	52,515	25,000	2,922	2,922
Electrical power	--				
Natural gas lines	--				
Water system	33,062	20,829	9,918	1,158	1,158
Sanitary sewer	20,459	12,890	6,138	715	715
Storm sewer	23,840	15,020	7,152	834	834
Curbs and gutters	2,000	2,000			
Parking lot paving and striping	167,128	167,128			
Lighting	24,540	24,540			
Sidewalks/misc. concrete					
Banks and walls					
Erosion control					
Landscaping	20,000	20,000			
Performance bond	8,500	5,355	2,550	298	298
Field supervision					
Gen. contractor overhead and profit					
Contingency					
Subtotal sitework	$386,887	$322,797 +	$51,958 +	$6,067 +	$6,067
Cost/sq. ft.-GLA		$2.87			

362 *Analysis of Investment in Specific Types of Property*

Exhibit 7. *Predevelopment Costs for Community Shopping Center; Peachtree Square, Columbia, Ga.*

Predevelopment Costs	Sq. Ft.-GLA	Total Cost
Legal and closing		$ 7,000
Market/traffic study		1,000
Rezoning and use permits		
Ground lease—preconstruction		
Interest expense—land loan		25,000
Liability coverage—undeveloped property		
Boundary/topo surveys		
Preliminary engineering study (soil tests, etc.)		5,000
Preliminary architectural study		10,000
General management expense		20,000
Advertising and promotion		3,000
Travel and entertainment		5,000
Aerial photography		1,000
Miscellaneous		2,000
Subtotal predevelopment costs	0.73	82,000
Raw land—purchase price		179,700
Total land and predevelopment	$2.33	$261,700

Exhibit 8. Construction Costs and Indirect Cost For Community Shopping Center; Peachtree Square, Columbia, Ga.

		Sq. Ft.	$/sq. ft.–GLA	Total Cost
Construction Costs				
1.	TG&Y	40,000	$10.66	$ 426,400
2.	Piggly Wiggly	27,720	17.35	480,942
3.	Revco	8,400	12.25	102,900
4.	Cobb Theatre	6,800	20.00	136,000
5.	Shops	25,800	11.70	301,776
6.	Restaurant	3,500	17.00	59,500
7.	Canopy and fronts			60,000
8.	Shop extras (40-feet-deep shops)			10,000
	Subtotal—BBC			1,507,598
	Tenant construction allowance			20,000
	Retail center pylons			5,000
	Subtotal construction			1,532,598
	Contingency allowance			10,000
	Escalation: ($___) (___%)			
	Subtotal construction costs			1,533,598
	Architectural fees under contract			23,000
	Architectural reimbursements			
	Subtotal architectural costs			1,556,598
	Subtotal construction and architectural costs			

Indirect Costs
  Legal and title policy:
    Construction loan @ $_____   10,000
    Permanent loan @ $_____   15,000
  Fees on loans (points):
  Fees on loans (points):
    Construction (___ %) ($___)   1,000
    Permanent procurement fee (___%) ($___)   21,000
  Mortgage fee (refundable)
  Interest (retail center only):
    Construction loan (10%) ($2,100,000) (0.75 yr.) (75% draw)   118,000
  Taxes:
    Land ($ Appraised) (Percent assmnts) (Tax rate) (Years)
      (_____) (_____) (_____) (____)   1,000
    Construction
      ($ Appraised) (Percent assmnts) (Tax rate) (Years) (Percent completed)
      (_____) (_____) (_____) (____) (_____)
  Insurance (liability and builder's risk supplement)   3,000
  Performance bond ($___) (___Percent rate) ($___) (___Percent rate)
  Ground lease during construction ($___/mo.)
  Operating fund (capitalize losses to break even)

Subtotal indirect costs	$1.50	$169,000

Exhibit 9. *Summary of Retail Center Costs; Peachtree Square, Columbia, Ga.*

Summary of Retail Center Costs	Sq. Ft.-GLA	Total Cost
Land	$ 1.60	$ 179,700
Predevelopment	0.73	82,000
Subtotal	2.33	261,700
Sitework	2.87	322,797
Construction	13.66	1,533,598
Architectural work	0.20	23,000
Indirect	1.50	169,000
Subtotal	15.37	1,725,598
Total retail center costs	$20.58	$2,310,095

Exhibit 10. *Income and Expenses for Community Shopping Center; Peachtree Square, Columbia, Ga.*

	Tenant	Term	Sq. Ft.	Common Area Maintenance	Rent/Sq. Ft.*	Rental
	Income and Expenses					
1	Piggly Wiggly	20	27,740	0.10	$2.65	$ 73,458
2	TG&Y	20	40,000	0.10	2.25	90,000
3	Revco	15	8,400	0.10	2.95	24,780
4	Theater	20	6,800	--	3.50	23,800
5	Restaurant	10	3,500	0.15	4.90	17,150
6	Local shops	5-10	25,800	0.15	4.52	116,520
	Subtotal—gross income					345,708
	Vacancy on locals (5 percent)					(6,684)
	Subtotal					
	Effective Gross Income Including Common Area Maintenance					

	$/Sq. Ft.-GLA	Total Cost
General and Administrative Expense		
Management fee (3%)	0.09	10,100
Repairs—buildings and parking lot	0.06	6,733
Ground rent		
Real estate taxes (105,420 sq. ft.)	0.15	15,813
Other taxes		
Insurance (exclusive of common area)	0.04	4,489
Leasing commissions		
Subtotal general and administrative expense	0.34	37,135
Common Area Expense		
Grounds maintenance (labor and materials, cleaning and landscaping)	0.06	6,733
Electricity (parking and security lights)	0.03	3,367
Insurance (common area maintenance liability only)		
Parking lot repairs and striping		
Other		
Subtotal common area expense	0.09	10,100

*Base rent plus common area maintenance.

Exhibit 11. Summary of Operations for Community Shopping Center; Peachtree Square, Columbia, Ga.

	Sq. Ft.-GLA	Total Cost
Effective gross income including common area maintenance		$339,024
Less general and administrative expense	(0.34)	(37,135)
Less common area expense	(0.09)	(10,100)
Net income from operations		$291,789

Key Terms and Concepts

Regional shopping center
Super-regional center
Central business district
Specialty chains
High-credit-rated stores
Gross and net leaseable space
Common area maintenance allowance
Indirect costs
Specialty shopping center
Customer driving time
Variety store
Independent store
Department store chain

Shopping center mall
Aaa credit
Department store real estate subsidiary
Junior department store
Store drawing power
Key chain tenant
Boutiques
Loading docks
Net percentage lease
Operating department store company
Development corporation
Predevelopment costs

Questions for Student Self-examination

Multiple-Choice Questions

1. The new super-regional shopping centers are not usually located
   a. in the center of a major population center
   b. on the outskirts of a major metropolitan area
   c. in less densely developed areas between two or more major population centers
   d. all of the above

2. Which shopping center label is not commonly used?
   a. community shopping center
   b. village shopping center
   c. regional shopping center
   d. specialty shopping center

3. The _____ shopping center may consist of 10 to 15 stores that offer convenience and shopping goods and services to a potential customer radius described by approximately 10 minutes' driving time.
   a. super-regional
   b. community
   c. specialty
   d. neighborhood

4. No key chain tenant may be located in the _____ shopping center.
   a. neighborhood
   b. community
   c. regional
   d. specialty

5. Which is not a familiar department store chain that frequently has an outlet in a regional shopping center?
   a. Consolidated Department Stores
   b. Associated Dry Goods
   c. Federated Department Stores
   d. City Stores

True-False Questions

T F 1. One of the strongest motivations behind foreign investment in shopping centers has been inflation protection through percentage net leases.
T F 2. The financing of shopping centers depends on the preleasing of space by high-credit-rated tenants.
T F 3. In a specialty shopping center, three to four department stores may be directly linked to a mall of 50 to 100 tenants.
T F 4. An analyst could forecast the construction cost for regional and super-regional centers in 1980 to approximately $20 to $25 a square foot, depending on the characteristics of the construction.
T F 5. The shopping center developer-owner usually owns the major department store buildings.
T F 6. Shopping center mall tenants usually sign net percentage leases.
T F 7. The developer usually pays the common area maintenance expense associated with the enclosed walkway and mall furniture and furnishings.
T F 8. The higher the credit rating of the shopping center storeroom tenants, usually the higher the square footage and percentage lease requirement.
T F 9. The higher the markup on the merchandise and the higher the merchandise turnover, usually the higher the square footage and percentage shopping center storeroom rents.
T F 10. The Federal Reserve compiles data on the median revenue, expense, and net cash flow per square foot for a variety of shopping center types.

Answers
Multiple-Choice: 1a, 2b, 3b, 4d, 5a.
True-False: 1T, 2T, 3F, 4F, 5F, 6T, 7F, 8F, 9T, 10F.

Problems

1. Which type of shopping center classification could be assigned to the traditional central business district?

2. What is the difference between the typical driving times for the customer radius of the neighborhood and the regional shopping centers? What is the difference in the number of stores integrated into these two types of centers?

3. If a regional shopping center generates an average of $250 of gross revenues per square foot of gross leasable area, how does this compare with the median total construction cost per square foot of gross leasable area?

4. Would a major department store that might wish to be in a regional shopping center pay $8 a square foot and 8 percent of gross revenues over a base amount? Would a supermarket pay that annual rent?

5. Would a breakeven ratio for a shopping center typically be 0.55? 0.80? Would an operating ratio typically be 0.85? 0.42?

6. If the sale price of a shopping center were $1,000,000, the selling commission $50,000, and the adjusted basis $750,000, what would be the gain on the sale?

Chapter 21

Office Building Investment

Introduction
The Relationship of This Chapter to Other Chapters of the Text
Recent Trends in Office Building Investment
The Future Trend in Office Space
    Demand Factors Related to Office Building Development   Supply Factors Related to Office Building Development
The Cost Trend in Office Building Construction
Income-Expense Relationships for Office Buildings
    Income Relationships   Expense Relationships
The Financing of the Office Building
Office Building Leasing and Management
Investment Yields on Office Buildings
Summary
Key Terms and Concepts
Questions for Student Self-examination

LEARNING OBJECTIVES After studying this chapter, you should be familiar with

Recent trends in office building investment
The future trend in office space
Principal demand factors related to office building development
Principal supply factors related to office building development
The cost trend in office building construction
Income-expense relationships for office buildings
Financing office buildings
Office building leasing and management
Office building investment yields

Special attention has recently been given office building investment, as foreign investors have purchased office buildings in various sections of the United States. According to the press, the first preference of foreign investors has been profitable shopping centers. Their second preference has appeared to be profitable office buildings. The question has been asked: Why do foreign investors prefer these two forms of real estate investment in the United States? This chapter presents information that will help answer that question. If foreign investors are interested in these two forms of investment properties, what attractions do shopping centers and office buildings have for domestic American real estate investors?

INTRODUCTION

This chapter covers the recent and future economic trend in office building investment. The chapter content explores the strategic demand and supply factors and the operation of these market forces in the recent marketplace. Then the income and expense picture of typical office buildings is presented to the reader. The coverage of the typical office building lease is surveyed. The financing characteristics of office building development and investment are summarized before office building yields are discussed.

THE RELATIONSHIP OF THIS CHAPTER TO OTHER CHAPTERS OF THE TEXT

Since office building investment is very common among investments in income-producing properties, this chapter is part of Part V, "Analysis of Investment in Specific Types of Property." House investment is the most prevalent form of personal real estate investment for owner occupancy or investment return, but apartment building, shopping center, and office building investment come next in the hierarchy of commonly conceived income property alternatives. From these common investment property types, we move on to industrial building investment and other miscellaneous forms of real estate investment. In a six-chapter sequence we get the feel of investment in the principal types of properties that have unique investment characteristics.

RECENT TRENDS IN OFFICE BUILDING INVESTMENT

During the early 1970s, the nation experienced an office building boom. Millions of square feet of office space were constructed in many urban areas of the country. The owners had every reason to be optimistic about their investment future. As the recession of 1974 and 1975 took its toll, many buildings changed ownership, including office buildings. The excess capacity and the resulting vacant space spelled investment failure in many situations.

Toward the latter 1970s, the vacant office space began to fill up with the expansion of business during a period of prosperity. Office building again resumed. Instead of excess space in such cities as Houston and Chicago, many areas were cramped for space, and company real estate officers were seeking more space. Even the excess office space in Manhattan was reported to be disappearing.

THE FUTURE TREND IN OFFICE SPACE

Since the government sector actively moved into new buildings in the mid-1970s, their period of high demand for building space has subsided. The private sector still needs more office space, because of the continued business prosperity. The number of permits for the future construction of nonresidential structures, including private office buildings, that are issued indicates the construction pattern for the near term. The building permits issued in 1977 and 1978 indicate a new high in office building construction and development at the turn of the decade.

Demand Factors Related to Office Building Development. One factor determining the demand for office space is the trend in the profitability of business. Profitable companies that anticipate continued financial success tend to seek more office building space for expansion of operations. Any business may expand into numerous office buildings until the time for consolidation of office operations into a single office building arrives. Therefore, office expansion is interpreted as two types of office demand—temporary branch space and consolidated space under a single roof.

Another factor is the amount of space utilized by the average office tenant and the average store tenant of the office building. During the 1970s, the space of the average office tenant expanded from 2,693 square feet to 3,933 square feet (Table 21-1). By mid-1970, approximately 4,000 square feet were desired by the average office tenant. The average office tenant in a skyscraper demand over 8,000 square feet (Table 21-2). At the same time, the average store tenant of the office building wanted less space than earlier. The average store tenant wanted only approximately 2,000 square feet rather than the approximately 4,000 square feet of earlier years (Table 21-1).

Another factor related to office space demand is the trend in the office building rentable area per employed person. The area per person was expanding in the mid-1970s (Table 21-1). In 1975, the average square footage of office space per person was the greatest in office buildings under a height of five stories (Table 21-2). The least amount of square footage per person was reflected in statistics for office buildings of 10 to 20 stories (Table 21-2).

The decentralization of business is another factor in the demand for office space. Most businesses now are fully decentralized, with headquarters offices in major urban areas. The branch, district, and divisional offices of a company seek space in selected cities outside the headquarters area because of market, production, financing, and

Table 21-1. Comparative space usage in office buildings: 1969, 1975, and 1977

	Square Footage of Occupancy		
Type of Occupant	1969	1975	1977
Average office tenant	2,693 sq. ft.	3,933 sq. ft.	4,347 sq. ft.
Average store tenant	4,377	1,948	1,800
Area per person (based on office rentable area)	147	164	197

Reprinted by permission from *Downtown and Suburban Office Building Experience Exchange Report*, 1970, 1976, and 1978 editions, published annually by Building Owners and Managers Association International, Washington, D.C.

Table 21-2. 1975 Operating factors on a square footage basis and key ratios for various heights of office buildings

	Under 5 Stories	10 to 20 Stories	20 to 30 Stories	50 Stories and Higher
I. Operating factors on a square footage basis				
Total operating income (cents/sq. ft.)	$388.9	$580.8	$644.4	$814.2
Average office tenant sq. ft.	2227 sq. ft.	2992 sq. ft.	3658 sq. ft.	8097 sq. ft.
Average sq. ft. per person	345.2 sq. ft.	197.0 sq. ft.	202.5 sq. ft.	211.6 sq. ft.
II. Key ratios				
Operating ratio	136.5%	76.4%	84.7%	78.3%
Management ratio	50.8%	46.3%	47.5%	40.7%
Average office occupancy	89.2%	92.1%	94.0%	92.0%

Source: Reprinted by permission from the *Experience Exchange Report for Downtown and Suburban Office Buildings, 1976*. Published by Building Owners and Managers Association International, 1221 Massachusetts Avenue NW, Washington, D.C. 20005. Current copies available at $95.00.

other considerations. Therefore, the regional and district offices must be accommodated.

The headquarters office may or may not be in the central business district of a major urban center. Some headquarters office buildings are constructed in suburbs and outlying rural areas beyond the suburbs.

Supply Factors Related to Office Building Development. Office building development depends on the current and near-term vacancy rates of competing office buildings, the availability of mortgage money for office building financing, operating and financial costs, the differential of expected rental rates above operating and financial costs, the cost of office building construction, the tax benefits associated with office building investment, and the trend in office building values in the marketplace. These are all key considerations of the office building investor. The building developer may be the sole investor, one of the building investors, or merely an entrepreneur looking for development fees and other such returns.

THE COST TREND IN OFFICE BUILDING CONSTRUCTION

Construction costs in general are rising rapidly—faster than inflation, as measured by the Consumer Price Index. According to a recognized building cost service that surveys office building construction costs across the United States, square footage costs have recently been rising approximately 10 percent a year (Table 21-3). Construction of high-quality high-rise office buildings requires $40 to $70 a square foot. Lesser-quality construction requires $25 to $40 a square foot.

INCOME-EXPENSE RELATIONSHIPS FOR OFFICE BUILDINGS

The income-expense relationships for office buildings may be categorized by all office buildings, suburban office buildings, and downtown office buildings. For income-expenses purposes, office buildings may also be classified on the basis of height, regional location, and general type of building.

Income Relationships. Office rental prices per square foot tend to be a little higher in the central business district, in comparison with building locations four to eight miles from the central business district. Inner-city office space prices tend to be lower than central business district or suburban prices. Average office rental rates and total net income have been trending upward (Table 21-4). Total operating income per square foot has been the highest for skyscrapers (office buildings 50 stories and higher) and lowest for office buildings under five stories (Table 21-2). Since the operating ratio for suburban buildings has run lower than for downtown buildings, net operating income has been higher for suburban buildings (Table 21-5).

Expense Relationships. Operating costs for office buildings have been rising, primarily as a result of the rise in energy costs (Table 21-4). The three general categories of operating expenses that represent the greatest proportions of total actual rent collections have been (1) utilities; (2) janitorial, maintenance, and repair; and (3) taxes (Tables 21-6). On the basis of building height, the operating ratio in 1975 was the highest—85 percent—for office buildings with 20 to 30 stories (Table 21-2). Buildings with

Table 21-3. Average construction cost per square foot for various types of office buildings

Type of Office Building	May 1974	April-May 1978	June-July 1979
Type I	$24.65	$39.20	$41.40
Type II	24.65	39.20	39.20
Type III	18.20	30.20	33.20
Type IV—One hour	NA	27.00	30.40
unprotected	NA	25.50	28.60
Type V—One hour	18.20	30.20	29.90
unprotected	16.90	28.70	28.10
Type VI—One hour	15.10	27.00	29.80
unprotected	13.70	25.50	28.00

Source: *Southern Building* (May 1974), p. 29; (April-May 1978), p. 8; (June-July 1979), advance copy for the issue, no page number assigned. Reprinted with permission.
NA means "not available."

Table 21-4. *1974-1975 changes in income, costs, and ratios for U.S. office buildings*°

	1974	1975	%/$ Change
Average Rental Rate	$6.40	$7.00	+$0.60
Operating Costs	$2.49	$2.75	+$0.26
Construction Costs	$0.19	$0.14	−$0.05
Fixed Charges	$2.28	$2.23	−$0.05
Total Income	$5.93	$6.43	+$0.50
Operating Ratio	79.9%	80.0%	+0.1%
Management Ratio	42.5%	44.3%	+1.8%
Real Estate Taxes	$1.21	$1.20	−$0.01
Depreciation	$1.04	$0.99	−$0.05
Energy Costs	$0.69	$0.85	+$0.16

Source: Reprinted from the *Experience Exchange Report for Downtown and Suburban Office Buildings, 1976.* Published by Building Owners and Managers Association International, 1221 Massachusetts Avenue NW, Washington, D.C. 20005. Current copies available at $95.00.
°Revenues and costs on a square footage basis.

Table 21-5. *Comparison of downtown and suburban office building operations for 1977, key operating factors and ratios*

Factors/Ratios	Downtown Buildings	Suburban Buildings
Operating ratio	79.4%	71.9%
Management ratio	45.2%	41.0%
Average office vacancy	6.8%	5.9%
Average office occupancy	93.5%	94.1%
Labor cost—cents per sq. ft.	85.4%	49.2%
Average office tenant sq. ft.	5110	2631
Average store tenant sq. ft.	1826	2143
Average sq. ft. per employee of building company	11,742	17,085

Source: Reprinted from *Downtown and Suburban Office Building Experience Exchange Report,* 1978 edition, published annually by Building Owners and Managers Association International, Washington, D.C.

10 to 20 stories showed an operating ratio of only 76 percent. Sample data for office buildings under five stories was insufficient in 1975 to make reliable estimates about the operating ratio. Downtown buildings showed higher operating ratios than suburban buildings (Table 21-5). In contrast, the office building operating ratio approximated 50 percent of total actual collections in 1977 (Table 21-6). The management ratio ran 40 to 50 percent of total actual collections in 1975 (Table 21-2). Skyscrapers exhibited management ratios at the lowest end of the scale, around 40 percent. According to 1975 data, downtown buildings were inclined to show 45 percent management ratios, as compared to 41 percent ratios for suburban buildings (Table 21-5).

The higher occupancy ratios have been generated by suburban office buildings rather than downtown office buildings (Table 21-5). Office buildings of 20 to 30 stories

Table 21-6. *1977 median annual income and operating costs versus total actual collections,° total USA*

Account	Dollars per Net Rentable Office Area	Percentage of Total Actual Collections
Utilities	$0.98	17.0
Janitorial, maintenance, and repair	0.86	15.0
Administration	0.34	6.0
Miscellaneous fees, insurance, and services	0.20	3.5
Taxes	0.68	11.5
Net operating income	2.78	47.0
Total actual collections	5.80	100.0

Reprinted by permission from *1978 Income/Expense Analysis: Suburban Office Buildings* (Chicago: Institute of Real Estate Management, National Assn. of Realtors, 1978), p. 136.
°Based on dollars per net rentable office area.

tended to have the highest occupancy ratios of all office buildings of any height categories (Table 21-2). Overall, the lowest occupancy ratios—or, in other words, the highest vacancy ratios—were realized by office buildings under five stories.

The chart of accounts for office buildings has been standardized by the Institute of Real Estate Management of the National Association of Realtors. The investor can compare her or his projected or actual operating results on the basis of dollars per gross area of entire building, dollars per gross rentable office area, or dollars per net office area with standardized national income and expense amounts. The 1977 statistical analysis for suburban office buildings is shown in Table 21-7.

THE FINANCING OF THE OFFICE BUILDING

The land and the office building may be financed independently. The investor may own or lease the land. The office building may comprise a leasehold estate for the investor, or it may be owned in fee simple. One investor or an investor group may own the land and another investor or investor group may own the building or the leasehold estate on which the building is constructed.

The land, perhaps held under option earlier, may be purchased by means of a land contract, a purchase-money mortgage from the previous owner, a land loan, or outright cash. The previous owner, who may wish to construct an office building on the site, may sell the land to a life insurance company, an endowment fund, or a pension fund and lease the land back. The owner's money is thereby released from the land, and the lease payments become a fully tax-deductible amount over the term of the ground lease.

If the land underneath the proposed office building is leased, leasehold financing for the building usually requires subordination of the landowner's interest in the ground

Table 21-7. Suburban office buildings, 1977 statistical analysis, total USA

Chart of Accounts	Median $/Gross Area of Entire Building	Median $/Gross Rentable Office Area	Median $/Net Office Area
Income			
Offices	$5.28	$6.00	$6.35
Retail	0.40	0.48	0.53
Parking	0.25	0.33	0.30
Escalation	0.16	0.19	0.17
Retail % income	0.06	0.06	0.07
Miscellaneous income	0.03	0.03	0.04
Vacancy/delinquent rents	0.47	0.52	0.62
Total collections	4.79	5.45	5.80
Expenses			
Electricity	same	0.65	0.61
Water	0.02	0.03	0.03
Sewer	0.01	0.02	0.02
Heating fuel			
Gas	0.11	0.11	0.13
Fuel oil	0.08	0.14	0.11
Electricity	0.42	0.47	0.49
Steam	0.28	0.65	0.72
Other	0.08	0.59	0.07
Combination electric	0.74	0.86	0.89
Total energy plant	0.10	1.09	0.13
Subtotal utilities	0.80	0.94	0.98
Janitorial			
Payroll/contract	0.34	0.38	0.41
Cleaning supplies	0.03	0.03	0.04
Miscellaneous	0.01	0.01	0.02
Maintenance and repair			
Payroll	0.13	0.14	0.16
Supplies	0.03	0.03	0.03
Heating/ventilation and air conditioning repairs	0.07	0.08	0.08
Electric repairs	0.01	0.01	0.01
Plumbing repairs	0.01	0.01	0.01
Elevator repair maintenance	0.04	0.05	0.06
Exterior repairs	0.02	0.03	0.02
Roof repairs	0.01	0.02	0.02
Parking lot repairs	0.01	0.01	0.01
Decorating—tenant	0.04	0.04	0.05
Decorating—public	0.02	0.02	0.02
Miscellaneous repairs	0.03	0.03	0.04
Subtotal Janitorial/maintenance/repairs	0.69	0.79	0.86

Reprinted by permission from *1978 Income/Expense Analysis: Suburban Office Buildings* (Chicago: Institute of Real Estate Management, National Association of Realtors, 1978), p. 136.

lease. Leasehold lenders who provide financing for income properties usually require first-mortgage interests. The ground lease usually must be subordinated.

When the term of the ground lease ends, the ownership of the building accrues to the landowner unless other provisions are made. To safeguard the unwanted transfer-

Table 21-7. (Continued)

Chart of Accounts	Median $/Gross Area of Entire Building	Median $/Gross Rentable Office Area	Median $/Net Office Area
Administrative			
Payroll—administrative	0.13	0.14	0.17
Advertising	0.01	0.01	0.01
Management fee	0.20	0.23	0.25
Other administrative	0.03	0.03	0.04
Other payroll costs			
Payroll taxes	0.01	0.02	0.02
Employee benefits	0.01	0.02	0.02
Subtotal Administrative/payroll	0.28	0.31	0.34
Insurance	0.07	0.08	0.08
Services			
Landscape	0.03	0.04	0.04
Trash removal	0.02	0.02	0.03
Security—payroll	0.06	0.07	0.08
Security—contracted	0.02	0.03	0.03
Window washing	0.01	0.01	0.01
Snow removal	0.02	0.02	0.02
Miscellaneous	0.01	0.01	0.02
Subtotal insurance/services	0.17	0.20	0.20
Net operating costs	2.01	2.22	2.43
Real estate taxes	0.53	0.63	0.64
Other tax/fee/permit	0.01	0.01	0.01
Total operating costs	2.55	2.89	3.13
Occupancy level 91%			
Vacancy level 9%			

ral of the ownership of the building to the landowner at the end of the lease, the ground lease is usually negotiated on renewal terms, which may mean indefinite duration of the lease.

Recent office building mortgage loans have been described by approximately 22-year terms, a contract interest rate of approximately $9\frac{1}{2}$ to 10 percent, and mortgage debt service constants of 10 to 11 percent (Table 21-8). The first-mortgage loan-to-value ratio usually ranges from 70 to 80 percent. The required debt service coverage ratio usually ranges from 1.25 to 1.30. Life insurance companies, pension funds, and endowment funds are often associated with office building long-term financing.

OFFICE BUILDING LEASING AND MANAGEMENT

Professional managers are often employed by office building owners to maintain, advertise, and lease the building space. In fact, today many office buildings in the United States are owned by foreign investors and investor groups. American property managers are hired for the daily operation and leasing of the office buildings. In return for the

Table 21-8. Terms of office building mortgage loans made by 15 life insurance companies

Quarter/Year	Average Loan Amount ($000)	Average Interest Rate	Average Loan-to-Value Ratio	Average Capitalization Rate	Average Debt Coverage Factor	Average Percentage Constant	Average Term (Yr./Mo.)
Second Quarter 1977	$3,962	9.15%	73.5%	9.7%	1.31	10.1	21/4
Third Quarter 1977	NA	9.19	NA	9.8	NA	10.0	22/5
Third Quarter 1978	NA	9.73	NA	9.9	NA	10.8	20/7
Fourth Quarter 1978	$4,695	9.81	74.4	10.1	1.25	10.9	22/6

Source: *Investment Bulletin*, No. 769, November 29, 1977, Table M; No. 788, April 20, 1979, Table M (Washington, D.C.: American Council of Life Insurance). Reprinted with permission.
NA means "not available."

contracted services, the management companies usually require approximately 5 percent of the gross income from the sizable structure as their compensation.

When the building manager leases the office space, he or she negotiates the lease terms with the prospective lessee. On the resulting lease contract, the lessee may or may not plan to occupy the space. Many buildings have many layers of sublessees superimposed on the actual occupant-lessee of the space. Once the lease terms have been negotiated, the lessee is usually bound to a certain number of dollars per square foot of leased space per year in rental payments. If the leased space totals 20,000 square feet and the negotiated rate is $10 per square foot, the lessee must pay $200,000 a year in rent to the lessor. For the $200,000 a year, the lessee generally receives the air space confined by the rough flooring, the unfinished ceiling, and the inside of the exterior walls. The office space usually has the minimal provisions for basic utility services built into the flooring. Additional utility services and special furnishings and equipment are the lessee's responsibility, as are the office partitions.

In order to protect the investor's yield in an inflationary economic climate, the office building leases tend to be short. Some of the space may be leased on a relatively long-term basis—perhaps 15 to 20 years—to high-credit-rated tenants, but the majority of the space will be rented on a short-term basis—three- to five-year terms. The lower the credit rating of the tenant, usually the shorter the term of the lease.

If the term of the lease exceeds three years, it usually is suggested that an *escalator* clause be inserted into the lease by the landlord. The clause may state that the tenant will pay a share of the increase in operating costs and taxes, based on the ratio of the tenant's net rentable area to the total net rentable area of the building. Alternatively, the tenant may agree to pay increases in the landlord's expenses that are beyond the control of the landlord, such as an increase in union pay scales for building maintenance workers. The tenant may agree to an *index* lease, in which lease payments are tied to a consumer price index. As the index increases as a result of inflation, the rent requirement for the tenant increases on a proportional basis.

INVESTMENT YIELDS ON OFFICE BUILDINGS

There is little research evidence concerning investment yields on office buildings. Many appraisers have been heard to say that many single-tenant, owner-occupied office buildings do not produce a reasonable yield for the owner. These buildings may

Table 21-9. Computer investment analysis

Sample High-Rise Office Building—Base Case ($000 omitted)

Key factors are:

Total invested	Mortgage Terms Amount	% Intr.	Life	Operating and Inflation Assumptions Net sale price	Gross income	Operating expense	% Annual inflation	Depreciation Amount	Life	Type	Tax Rates Income	Cap gain
30000	22500	10.00	30	29100	5000	2400	5.0	24000	40	150%	50%	30%

Completed summary:

Equity amount	Mortgage Terms % Debt	Monthly	Yearly		% Net sale to total	% Income to total	% Expense to income		% Net to total	% Deprec. to total
7500	75.0	197.45	2369		97.0	16.7	48.0		8.7	80.0

Computed Results:

Yr.	Gross income	Operating expense	Mortgage intr.	Mortgage amort.	Cash flow	% Return	Depreciation	Taxable income	Taxes due	Cash flow	% Return	Sale price	Debt repay.	Taxes due	Cash flow	Total profit	% Return
1	5000	2400	2244	125	231	3.1	900	−544	−272	503	6.7	30555	22375	496	7684	686	9.2
2	5250	2520	2231	138	361	4.8	866	−368	−184	544	7.3	32083	22237	1268	8578	2125	13.7
3	5512	2646	2217	153	497	6.6	834	−184	−92	589	7.9	33687	22084	2046	9557	3693	15.1
4	5788	2778	2201	169	640	8.5	802	6	3	637	8.5	35371	21916	2833	10623	5396	15.7
5	6078	2917	2183	186	791	10.5	772	205	102	689	9.2	37140	21729	3629	11781	7243	16.0
6	6381	3063	2164	206	949	12.7	743	411	206	743	9.9	38997	21524	4438	13035	9240	16.1
7	6700	3216	2142	227	1115	14.9	716	627	313	802	10.7	40946	21296	5261	14389	11396	16.2
8	7035	3377	2118	251	1289	17.2	689	851	426	863	11.5	42994	21045	6099	15849	13719	16.2
9	7387	3546	2092	277	1472	19.6	663	1086	543	929	12.4	45143	20768	6956	17420	16219	16.2
10	7757	3723	2063	306	1664	22.2	638	1332	666	998	13.3	47400	20461	7832	19107	18904	16.1

Reprinted by permission from Chris Mader, *The Dow Jones-Irwin Guide to Real Estate Investing* (Homewood, Ill.: Dow Jones-Irwin, 1975). © 1975 by Dow Jones-Irwin.

Table 21-10. Rate of return on equity after tax, after financing: office buildings and apartment buildings

Property Type	Quarter and Year				
	3rd, '54	4th, '59	3rd, '63	1st, '65	4th, '66
Office buildings	7.35	7.88	8.42	9.18	8.90
Medical office buildings	8.65	8.78	8.34	9.56	8.65
Apartments—elevator	8.32	8.58	8.81	9.55	9.53
Apartments—nonelevator	8.67	8.00	8.58	9.35	9.34

Reprinted by permission from R. Bruce Ricks, "Imputed Equity Returns on Real Estate Financed with Life Insurance Company Loans," *Journal of Finance* (December 1969), p. 933.

serve a public relations function, in that they are community showplaces. They are primarily objects of prestige and image building. Many bank and utility company buildings fall into this investment category.

Many investors analyze potential income property yields with the use of the computer. A one-page summary of the possible yield from a high-rise office building may be split into (1) the key assumptions, (2) the yield on equity from building operations before income tax payments, (3) the yield on equity from building operations after income tax payments, and (4) the overall yield, assuming sale of the investment property at the end of each year analyzed (Table 21-9). Computer simulation of possible investment returns saves the investor a great deal of anguish and anxiety later. Without making the investment, the investor can see what the future may hold.

Investment research of the 1950s and 1960s indicates that in the mid-1960s investors in office buildings of all kinds were receiving approximately 9 percent on their investments after taxes and financing (Table 21-10). In earlier years, these same investors would have received a yield ranging from approximately 7½ to 8½ percent. Medical office buildings have generally prompted higher investment returns; 1963 and 1966 were exceptions to the rule. In 1978, high returns on equity from high-rise medical office buildings were possible, as the abstracted office building appraisal in the Appendix indicates. The lender or owner group might observe from the appraisal that a 50 percent cash-on-cash before-tax return on equity might be gained in the first year of the investment.

In contrast, owners of elevator apartment buildings were earning 9½ percent on their investments in the mid-1960s. In the 1950s, their returns approximated only 8½ percent. From 1959 through 1966 nonelevator apartment buildings earned lesser returns on investment for their owners than did elevator apartment buildings. The differential in favor of the elevator buildings was ¼ to ½ percent.

SUMMARY

After an overbuilt period of office building investment, the construction of new office buildings has begun once again in earnest. The high occupancy rates, the relatively stable cost of money, the trend toward higher space rates, and the availability of mortgage money have prompted new investment in office buildings in various urban areas and with various physical characteristics.

Most revenues and costs related to office buildings have been rising with inflation. Some increases in costs have outpaced the increases in the Consumer Price Index or indices of inflation in the United States. For example, the increases in construction costs for office buildings have surpassed the rate of inflation. Utility costs have also risen strategically. The operating ratio for many office buildings remains around 50 percent of effective gross income. The management ratio is approximately $2/3$ to $3/4$ of the operating ratio. Therefore, the management ratio is compiled regularly by the office building statistical services.

The land and the office building may be financed independently or together, in a single transaction. The land may be owned outright or financed by a land contract, a purchase-money mortgage, or a land loan. The building financing depends on the financing of the land beneath it. A leasehold mortgage loan or a mortgage loan on the fee interest may provide the funds for the building construction and permanent financing. A leasehold lender usually requires the subordination of the ground lease.

The building management maintains, operates, and leases the owner's premises. The lease usually covers only the bare essentials of the office space. The lessee must furnish the space to suit the functions of the office, the number and type of personnel, and the social image of the firm. The lease may have an escalator clause, so that the lessee participates in the rising costs of the building operation.

Investment yields from office building ownership are difficult to obtain. A research effort by Ricks uncovered investment yields after taxes and financing during the mid-1960s of $8\frac{1}{2}$ to $9\frac{1}{2}$ percent for office buildings. In contrast, yields from apartment buildings hovered around $9\frac{1}{2}$ percent.

Supplementary Exhibits

Exhibit 1. Description of Improvements

The site will be improved with a nine-story elevatored office building containing a total of 108,500 square feet of gross air-conditioned area and 91,900 square feet of net rentable area. There will be landscaping and plaza areas separating the building from the parking areas. A covered walkway will connect the professional building with the hospital.

Foundation:	Prestressed concrete piling with poured-in-place pile cap.
Ground floor:	4-inch concrete slab, poured in place.
Structural:	Prestressed concrete structural wall panels on building exterior and around building core.
Curtain wall:	Aluminum frame with brick finish.
Windows:	1-inch thermal insulating glass.
Floors:	Carpet or vinyl tile or wood base.
Interior walls:	1/2-inch gypsum board on metal studs with paint finish.
Ceilings:	Suspended 2 x 4 acoustical lay-in ceiling.
Light fixtures:	Trotter type fluorescent.
Mechanical:	Central electro-hydro system supplying water to the central core on all floors. Tenants shall have their own airhandling unit sized to their individual space.

Exhibit 2. Cost Approach

Building Calculations

    Commercial buildings—gross

A. 100'8" x 60'	=	6,040
B. 55'4" x 60'	=	3,320
Total gross rentable area		9,360 sq. ft.

    Commercial buildings—net

A. 56' x 39'4"	=	2,202
57'4" x 59'4"	=	3,401
B. 56' x 19'4"	=	1,082
58'8" x 34'	=	1,995
Total net rentable area		8,680 sq. ft.

Office tower—gross

105 x 105 = 11,025 sq. ft. x 9 floors = 99,225 sq. ft.
                      Total gross rentable area

Office tower—net

102 X 102 = 10,404 sq. ft. x 9 floors = 93,636 sq. ft.
Less: 34 x 34 = 1156 sq. ft. x 9 floors = 10,404 sq. ft.

Total net rentable area = 83,232 sq. ft.

Asphalt paving—194,950 sq. ft.

Concrete walks and patios—13,080 sq. ft.

Covered walkways—4,183 sq. ft.

Exhibit 3. Cost Approach to Value

The following is an estimate of value, taking into consideration the reproduction or replacement cost of the proposed improvements and adding the final value estimate of the land. Factors used in computing this estimate were the Dodge Building Cost Calculator and Valuation Guide, statement of cost given by the developer's representative, and discussions with area general contractors active in the building of projects of this type.

Gross building area—office tower (99,225 sq. ft. @ $33.00)	$3,274,425
Gross building areas—commercial bldgs. (9.360 sq. ft. @ $30.00)	280,800
Asphalt parking area (194,950 sq. ft. @ $0.50)	97,475
Concrete walks and plazas (13,080 sq. ft. @ $2.00)	26,160
Covered walkways (4,183 sq. ft. @ $7.00)	29,281
Site preparation	125,000
Landscaping	50,000
Construction contingency	25,000
Subtotal building costs	3,908,141
Architect and engineering	175,000
Interim financing ($4,875,000 x 60% x 9% x 18 months)	394,875
Commitment and brokerage fees	121,875
Legal fees, permits, closing, etc.	150,000
Miscellaneous	25,000
Subtotal indirect costs	866,750
Total improvement costs	4,774,891
Add land value	360,000
Total value by cost approach	5,134,891
Rounded off,	5,135,000

Exhibit 4. Comparable Office Buildings

Office Building	Sq. Ft.	Occupancy	Rent/Sq. Ft.	Gross/Net	Adjusted Rent
1. Forwood Professional Bldg.	16,000	100%	$7.50	Gross	$7.50
2. Coker Building	4,800	100%	$7.50	Gross	$7.50
3. Roberts Bros. Building	7,000	100%	$7.00	Gross	$7.00
4. Pediatrics Associates	15,000	100%	$8.00	Gross	$8.00
5. 813 Building	19,800	85%	$6.00	Net	$8.15
6. Winthrop Square	20,000	100%	$6.00	Net	$8.15
7. Woodall-Hynson	5,700	100%	$6.00	Net	$8.15
8. Children's Medical	13,000	100%	$7.00	Net	$9.15
9. McMurphy Building	5,500	100%	$7.00	Net	$9.15

Exhibit 5. Market Data for Rental and Occupancy

Considering the comparable office buildings as shown on the previous pages, the indicated rental range on a gross basis is from $7.00 to $9.15 per square foot. While many of the comparable properties are leased on a net basis, adjustments were made to the comparables to reflect a gross equivalent rent. It is important to note that the majority of the city's medical buildings are leased to doctors on a net basis. On a net basis, medical leases currently are in the $6.00-$7.00 range. The subject property is master leased to Capitol Hill Professional Associates, Ltd. for a period of thirty years for $640,000 per annum. This equates to $6.96 per square foot on a net basis. It is the appraiser's opinion that the subject property, leased on the open market, would have to be rented on a gross basis. This is because the building is over one story and it is extremely difficult to allocate expenses for net rentals. Thus, a gross rent equivalent was derived to convert the comparables to accurately compare with the subject.

The subject property will be the city's first major high-rise professional building adjoining a hospital. Based on our survey of the market rental conditions, continued expected demand for well-located medical facilities, and projected completion in 18 months to two years, it is believed that a fair and reasonable rental of $9.25 per square foot for office space and $10.00 per square foot for commercial space, on a gross lease basis, is the economic rent set forth in the market for the subject property.

Gross rental income—Office Tower—83,232 sq. ft. @ $9.25 =	$769,896
Commercial space—8,680 sq. ft. @ $10.00 =	86,800
Gross annual rental income	$856,696

Exhibit 6. Capitalization Rate

There are many methods of deriving a capitalization rate in order to illustrate the risk, quantity, quality, and durability of the net income stream. In this appraisal the mortgage equity band of investment technique has been selected to derive the capitalization rate to be used to convert the anticipated net annual income into the projection of value. The rate obtained by the use of this technique represents a weighted average, the weighting being for the percentage of value occupied by the mortgage and equity positions. In this regard, it is important to note that tax-free bond-type financing is available for this type project under the Medical Clinic Board Act of 1955. The most favorable loan obtainable on today's market, for a project qualifying under this act, is an 8-3/4 percent interest rate for thirty years. Considering the strength of ownership, prospective tenants, and location factors, the appraiser feels the equity position could currently be sold on an 8 percent "cash-on-cash" basis. Using these factors, the overall capitalization rate can be computed as follows:

	Percent of Value	Rate	Weighted Rate
First mortgage	75	.0945	.0709
Equity	25	.08	.0200
		Overall weighted rate	.0909
		Round to	.09

Exhibit 7. Income Approach to Value

Office tower rental income—83,232 sq. ft. @ $9.25		$769,896
Commercial building rental income—8,680 sq. ft. @ $10.00		86,800
Total gross rental income		856,696
Less 5% vacancy allowance		42,835
Effective gross income		813,861
Less expenses:		
Fixed:		
Taxes	22,000	
Insurance	7,350	
Total fixed expenses	29,350	
Operating:		
Management	40,700	
Janitorial	41,350	
Utilities	92,000	
Maintenance/repairs	9,190	
Elevators	7,500	
Supplies	4,600	
Miscellaneous	2,500	
Total operating expenses	197,840	
Total estimated expenses ($2.47)		227,190
Net income before debt service		586,671
Capitalized at overall rate of .0900		6,518,667
Rounded off,		$6,515,000

Exhibit 8. *Correlation and Final Estimate of Value*

Cost approach	$5,135,000
Income approach	$6,515,000

Preliminary value indication from the cost approach was $5,135,000; that from the income approach was $6,515,000.

Since this is primarily an investment property, principal weight was given to the income approach as an indication of value, with the cost approach figure being considered merely as a supporting preliminary estimate.

Estimate of market value of subject property as of August 30, 1978, assuming completion of improvements as proposed:

Six million five hundred fifteen thousand dollars
($6,515,000)

John Graves
Assistant Vice President

August 30, 1978

Key Terms and Concepts

Investment by foreign investors
Consolidation of office space
Headquarters office buildings
Office Building Experience Exchange Report
Total actual rent collections
Dollars per net office area
Index lease
Computer simulation
Average office tenant space
Average store tenant space
Management ratio
Building Owners and Managers Association International
Dollars per gross area of entire building
Escalator clause
Office space demand
Business decentralization
Average office occupancy
Suburban office buildings
Dollars per gross rentable office area
Occupant-lessee
Total net rentable area

Questions for Student Self-examination

Multiple-Choice Questions

1. The most prevalent form of personal real estate investment for owner occupancy or investment return is
    a. shopping center investment
    b. apartment building investment
    c. house investment
    d. office building investment

2. Where are headquarters corporate office buildings located?
   a. central business district of a major urban center
   b. suburbs
   c. outlying rural areas beyond the suburbs
   d. all of the above

3. Which is a factor that determines the demand for office space rather than the supply of office space?
   a. the trend in the profitability of business
   b. the availability of mortgage money for office building financing
   c. operating and financial costs
   d. the cost of office building construction

4. Construction of a high-quality high-rise office building at the end of the 1970s approximated _____ a square foot.
   a. $5 to $10
   b. $100 to $110
   c. $20 to $50
   d. $40 to $70

5. Which category of office building data is not organized by the Institute of Real Estate Management in common income-expense patterns?
   a. all office buildings
   b. outlying central city office buildings
   c. suburban office buildings
   d. downtown office buildings

True-False Questions

T F 1. According to the press, the first preference of foreign investors has been profitable office buildings.
T F 2. The space for the average office tenant in the office building has been tending to decline during the past decade.
T F 3. During the last decade, the average store tenant of the office building wanted more space than in the past.
T F 4. Inflation, as measured by the Consumer Price Index, has been rising more rapidly than construction costs in general.
T F 5. Square footage costs of office buildings have recently been rising more than 20 percent a year.
T F 6. Inner-city office space prices tend to be lower than central business district prices or suburban prices.
T F 7. Lately, total operating income per square foot has been the highest for office buildings under five stories in height.
T F 8. The operating ratios for downtown office buildings have been running lower than operating ratios for suburban office buildings.
T F 9. Operating costs for office buildings have been rising, primarily because of the rise in management costs.
T F 10. The land and the office building may be financed independently.

Answers
Multiple-Choice: 1c, 2d, 3a, 4d, 5b.
True-False: 1F, 2F, 3F, 4F, 5T, 6T, 7T, 8F, 9F, 10T.

Problems

1. If one floor of a 20-story, 1,000,000-square-foot office building—that one floor containing 50,000 square feet of leasable area—were vacant six months of the year, what would you say was the vacancy rate for that year?

2. If 1,000,000 square feet of office building space were vacant for most of the year in the Chicago Loop (downtown), and you knew the total square feet of office building space in that area was 50,000,000, would you be alarmed at this situation?

3. If your company had to pay $12 a square foot for downtown office space, totaling 5,000 square feet in the 40-story Standard Oil Building, would this be reasonable? Would $8 a square foot be more reasonable for such space?

4. If an owner of an office building paid 50 cents a square foot of net rentable office area, would the owner consider this exorbitant, reasonable, or relatively low? What if it were 25 cents a square foot of net rentable office area?

5. If you owned an office building, what would you consider to be the typical income sources?

6. If the required debt service coverage for an office building mortgage were 1.5, what would you as an analyst infer from this knowledge?

Chapter 22

Industrial Building Investment

Introduction
The Relationship of This Chapter to Other Chapters of the Text
The Trends in Industrial Building Expansion
Locational Preferences of Industrial Land Users
    An Overview of Site Selection Factors   The Principal Site Selection Factors and Their Relative Importance in the Various States
The Trend in Construction Costs and Land Prices
    Construction Costs of Industrial Plants and Warehouses   Industrial Land Prices   Acreage Prices in Industrial Parks
Financing Industrial Development
    The Three Basic Methods of Financing Industrial Development   State Tax Incentive and Financing Programs for Pollution Control
Investment Yields on Industrial Buildings
Summary
Key Terms and Concepts
Questions for Student Self-examination

> **LEARNING OBJECTIVES** After studying this chapter, you should be familiar with
>
> The trends in industrial building expansion
> Locational preferences of industrial land users
> Significant site selection factors
> Trend in construction costs and land prices
> Acreage prices in industrial parks
> Three basic methods of financing industrial development
> State tax incentives and financing programs for pollution control

As investment in commercial and residential buildings has increased during the 1970s, so has investment in industrial buildings. Economic expansion during the 1970s has occurred as a result of the expansion of the economic base; basic industry has also expanded. The expansion of industry calls for greater expenditures for plant and equipment.

INTRODUCTION

This chapter first looks over the trends in industrial building or plant expansion. The trend in the value of new industrial construction is observed. Then the locational preferences of industrial land users is examined. Stemming from the locational preferences is the range in industrial land prices. A study is made of the trend toward new locations in industrial parks and the range in site prices in industrial parks.

The emphasis then changes to financing and investment returns. State government incentives for industrial development and pollution control are surveyed. The functions of the individual state pollution-regulation agencies are also surveyed, as well as the state tax incentive and financing programs for pollution control. Industry often tends to pollute the water, the air, and the tranquillity of the environment. Industry also seeks continuous, reasonably priced power sources. The state agencies then tend to regulate the site selection and operation of the new power plants serving new and existing industries.

The evidence of investment yields from industrial building investment is then presented. The evidence stems from loan data of life insurance companies and from the knowledge of institutional investment practices and competing yields where sale-leasebacks to industry are involved.

THE RELATIONSHIP OF THIS CHAPTER TO OTHER CHAPTERS OF THE TEXT

In Part V, devoted to analysis of investment in specific types of property, we have previously studied investment in residential and selected types of commercial buildings. Now is the time to explore investment in industrial buildings. Industrial buildings house the industries that propel the continued expansion of our economy. Our economy must continue to expand to accommodate the needs and desires of our expanding population. The number of people who are of working age continues to grow, and the work force participation of females and the elderly continues to increase.

The last chapter of the text, Chapter 23, gives a quick survey of investment in the more specialized types of development, such as hotels and motels, planned unit developments, and new towns.

THE TRENDS IN INDUSTRIAL BUILDING EXPANSION

The value of new industrial construction in the United States is advancing rapidly. Many new buildings and inflation are the primary factors behind this growth in values. Between 1969 and 1979, approximately $6 billion was added to the value of new industrial construction (evidence of the trend shown in Table 22-1). In 1979, the estimated value was $12-13 billion.

During the last half of the 1970s, plant and equipment expenditures of manufacturing plants exhibited the strongest trend upward. The trend of nonmanufacturing plant and equipment expenditures was upward but not in so pronounced a pattern.

Research shows that more companies are choosing office and industrial parks over single sites for their company locations. Some estimates indicate that about two thirds of all new industrial facilities are going into planned industrial parks. There were approximately 100 planned industrial parks at the end of World War II, and it is now estimated that we have 4,000 parks or more. These industrial parks involve 25 acres or more and are controlled and owned by a single body, and permitted land uses are regulated by protective covenants. These parks are spread unevenly across the various states. The states with the greatest concentrations of planned parks are California, Texas, Florida, North Carolina, Illinois, Minnesota, Ohio, Pennsylvania, and New York.

Table 22-1. Value of new industrial construction in millions of dollars

Date	Dollars
January 1979	$12,719
1978	10,763
1977	7,713
1976	7,182
1975	8,017
1974	7,902
1973	6,243
1972	4,676
1971	5,423
1970	6,538
1969	6,783
1968	6,021
1967	6,131
1966	6,679

Source: Federal Reserve Bulletin (March 1979), p. A50 (December 1975), p. A51.

LOCATIONAL PREFERENCES OF INDUSTRIAL LAND USERS

When an industrial company officer seeks a site for a new plant or warehouse, certain factors are usually considered. Some factors in site selection tend to be more important than others, but there is a general consensus about which factors are high on the list. There is also a consensus about the relative importance of certain plant location factors on a state-by-state basis.

An Overview of Site Selection Factors. In selection a plant location, first the responsible officer should review the company organization and the current company strategy in meeting the established goals. The criteria for the site and the facility should fit into company strategy already established. Then the basic economic factors related to each possible site should be examined. Government policies and tax programs should be ascertained as they affect each possible location. The amenities and environmental factors associated with the location should be surveyed. All specific factors—economic, physical, and financial—related to each alternative site should be reviewed. Perhaps international factors and company strategy are important in the decision making. The decision making should involve project feasibility analysis, construction planning, and provision for property management (Table 22-2).

The Principal Site Selection Factors and Their Relative Importance in the Various States. The general consensus is that certain factors are strategic in site selection for industrial development, no matter where the site is (Table 22-3). Labor, resources, energy, transportation, taxes, land availability, environmental controls, and the quality of life are in that list. On a state-by-state basis, the general consensus ranks these various factors in various orders. In most states the first factor is labor availability (Table 22-3).

Data are compiled by a number of organizations for the site selection officer, who must screen possible locations in various states. Whether a state agency, the state Chamber of Commerce, or the local Industrial Development Board prepares the locational study for the company that is considering relocation or a new plant, the following data are covered: population, personal income, wage rates, labor force, union membership, unemployment, construction trends, and production information for the city, county, section of the state, and state.

THE TREND IN CONSTRUCTION COSTS AND LAND PRICES

Construction Costs of Industrial Plants and Warehouses. Conservative estimates of construction costs of industrial plants and warehouses show square footage costs rising rapidly. As was mentioned earlier, construction costs in general have outpaced inflation. Conservative estimates of construction costs for industrial plants indicate square footage costs at $30 or more by 1980 (Table 22-4). By 1980 warehouse square footage costs, conservatively estimated, will exceed $25.

Industrial Land Prices. Industrial land prices tend to be the highest in the Northeast and West. The real estate "bargains" tend to be in the South and Midwest. Recent studies tend to show that

1. Higher industrial land prices prevail in metropolitan areas than in small towns.
2. The larger the metropolitan area, the higher the cost for industrial land.
3. Sites with many amenities in planned unit developments cost more than tracts zoned for industrial use but are not located in a planned park.

Table 22-2. Major considerations in site selection

Review of company goals and strategy
    Markets to be served
    Current profitability and future profit goals
    Decentralization policies
Economic factors strategic to company profitability
    Acquisition of skilled and unskilled labor
    Location with respect to company markets
    Transportation media needed and its availability
    Dependence on public utilities and cost control
    Acquisition of capital and borrowed funds
    Availability of materials and services for production and auxiliary support of production
Governmental considerations related to the site
    Taxation by local, state, and federal government
        Payroll taxes
        Income taxes
        Inventory taxes
        Sales taxes
    Industrial development assistance
Environmental considerations
    Control of waste water discharge
    Control of smokestack emission
    Noise abatement policies
    Climate
    Recreational opportunities for employee leisure time
    Quality of life of the community and area
Specific site requirements
    Sufficient acreage available at a reasonable price
    Level ground for widespread assembly or production plant
    Sufficient space adjacent to the plant for housing and recreation
    Location near low-cost power source
    The proximity of prospective worker homes
    Opportunities for sale-leaseback financing
Preliminary studies needed
    Feasibility analysis
    Environmental impact study
    Cost estimation for projected improvements and land development

Table 22-3. Key factors in site selection for industrial development

Availability of appropriate labor and its cost
Access to raw materials and semifinished goods
Energy sources and cost
Transportation facilities and cost
Land availability
Taxation of profits, property, and inventory
Extent of the environmental controls
Quality of life for company employees

Table 22-4. The trend in construction costs of industrial plants and warehouses (average cost per square foot)

Type of Structure	May 1974	April-May 1978	June-July 1979
Industrial plants			
Type I	$13.80	$22.00	$24.20
Type II	13.80	22.00	22.00
Type III	10.10	16.10	17.70
Type IV—1 hour	9.15	14.00	18.10
Unprotected	7.60	12.20	16.30
Type V—1 hour	10.10	16.10	17.70
Unprotected	9.10	14.40	15.80
Type VI—1 hour	9.20	14.40	15.80
Unprotected	7.60	12.20	14.00
Tilt up	7.00	10.30	NA
Warehouses			
Type I	11.10	17.80	19.60
Type II	11.10	17.80	17.80
Type III	8.80	14.10	15.50
Type IV—1 hour	7.75	12.40	15.60
Unprotected	6.40	10.20	13.20
Type V—1 hour	8.80	14.10	15.50
Unprotected	7.65	11.90	13.10
Type VI—1 hour	7.75	12.40	14.80
Unprotected	6.40	10.20	13.00

Source: *Southern Building* (May 1974), p. 29; (April-May 1978), p. 8; (June-July 1979); advance copy with no assigned page number. Reprinted with permission. NA means "not available."

4. The more natural and man-made amenities a site has, the higher the cost of the land.
5. The greater the percent occupancy in an industrial park, the higher the cost of the land.
6. Access to interstate or limited access highways increases the cost of industrial land.
7. The availability of rail service at an industrial site does not necessarily have an impact on land prices.

In a survey of 1,400 industrial park developers in 1975 it was discovered that an industrial company could pay anywhere from $200 to $260,000 an acre for sites in industrial parks in the United States. The highest acreage prices tended to be found in California and the Northeast, according to the survey results.

FINANCING INDUSTRIAL DEVELOPMENT

The Three Basic Methods of Financing Industrial Development. There are three basic ways in which industrial development is financed. The first way consists of industrial company financing of the new plant or warehouse by the sale of a bond and/or stock issue. No property is pledged for the loan of debt capital. The stockholder becomes an owner of the overall corporation.

The second way of financing is the mortgaging of the new industrial plant or existing company property to obtain loan funds. The lender receives a pledge of real property collateral in case the mortgagor defaults on the loan terms. In 1978, industrial mortgage loans made by life insurance companies carried interest rates of approximately 10 percent and terms to maturity of approximately 20 years (Table 22-5). The lender required a debt-service coverage ratio of 1.24.

The third way of financing industrial development is the sale-leaseback. The company usually builds the structure that meets their industrial or warehouse requirements and immediately sells the property to an outside investor. The sale-leaseback is usually arranged far in advance of the construction and development of the industrial property. The industrial company does not have to meet a substantial equity commitment in order to acquire a traditional mortgage loan. The leasing of the specially built property from the outside owner permits the release of the otherwise committed downpayment and permits the full tax deductibility of the lease payments that cover the use of the land and the buildings.

The sale-leaseback for industrial development can be financed by private enterprise or government organizations. State-sponsored industrial development authorities or privately sponsored and state-approved development credit corporations may finance the development with tax-exempt municipal bond financing. State or local government revenue or general obligation bonds may be sold to raise the funds to purchase and lease back the industrial facility. The state government may loan money for building construction and equipment purchase. The state government may also guarantee loans for construction and equipment acquisition. As well as financing new industrial development, the state or local government may finance the expansion of existing facilities.

Tax incentives may also be offered industry for new plant location or plant expansion within the tax jurisdiction. Common tax incentives are inventory tax exemption on goods in transit, tax exemption on manufacturers' inventories, sales- or use-tax exemption on new equipment, tax exemption on raw materials used in manufacturing, and accelerated depreciation of industrial equipment.

State Tax Incentive and Financing Programs for Pollution Control. Industrial development is often associated with environmental pollution of various types. Industry

Table 22-5. Terms of industrial mortgage loans made by 15 life insurance companies

	Second Quarter 1976	First Quarter 1977	Second Quarter 1977	Fourth Quarter 1978
Average loan amount ($000)	NA	NA	$1,081	$1,560
Average interest rate	9.83%	9.83%	9.34%	9.83%
Average loan-to-value ratio	NA	NA	73.1%	73.2%
Average capitalization rate	10.3%	10.2%	9.9%	10.2%
Average debt coverage factor	NA	NA	1.30	1.24
Average percent constant	11.0	10.8	10.7	11.3
Average term (Yr./Mo.)	18/0	NA	19/3	19/3

Source: *Investment Bulletin* No. 769, November 29, 1977, Table M. No. 788, April 20, 1979, Table M. (Washington, D.C.: American Council of Life Insurance). Reprinted with permission.
NA means "not available."

does tend to pollute the air and water as an offshoot of their industrial processes. Noise may be generated by industrial operations. If industry discharges solid wastes into nearby streams, rivers, lakes, or oceans, water pollution results. Many states regulate the various forms of pollution. Most states have actively functioning air- and water-pollution and solid wastes control agencies. Some states have agencies that deal with land-use control, occupational safety and health, coastal resources, noise-control, hazardous waste control, and power plant siting. Industry new to an area and industries expanding existing plants must acquire permits and licenses to build and operate industrial plants and warehouses that may violate the environmental standards set forth by the agencies.

Many states have tax incentive and financing programs for industrial pollution control. The most common tax incentives are real property tax exemption, personal property tax exemption, sales or use tax exemption on the purchase of pollution-control facilities, and accelerated depreciation of pollution-control equipment. Most states have financing programs for the purchase and installation of pollution-control facilities by industrial firms.

INVESTMENT YIELDS ON INDUSTRIAL BUILDINGS

Investment yields on industrial buildings may be different, depending on the source of ownership of the industrial building or warehouse. If the industrial firm owns its own plant or warehouse and finances the assets with a life insurance company loan, evidence from the mid-1960s shows 7.7 to 8.9 percent yields on equity after tax and after financing (Table 22-6). Yields on equity associated with warehouse and industrial building loans were lower than the average equity yields on all the life insurance loans in the income property sample from the 1960s.

If the investor in an industrial sale-leaseback is a state or local government development agency, that investor is usually getting a yield from the lease which approximates the long-term municipal bond rate at the time the lease was negotiated. In 1978, that tax-exempt bond rate approximated 5½ percent. If the lessor is a tax-exempt pension fund or endowment fund or a taxable life insurance company, the lessor may accept the long-term bond yield at the time of lease negotiation. Currently, that yield would approximate 8½ percent.

Table 22-6. Rate of return on equity, after tax, after financing

Property Type	Quarter and Year				
	3rd '54	4th '59	3rd '63	1st '65	4th '66
Warehouses	7.33	7.56	7.61	8.21	7.66
Industrial	7.84	7.60	8.10	8.92	8.32
All loans in sample (commercial, industrial, and institutional)	7.98	8.01	8.27	9.07	8.87

Source: Reprinted by permission from R. Bruce Ricks, "Imputed Equity Returns on Real Estate Financed with Life Insurance Company Loans," *Journal of Finance* (December 1969), p. 933.

SUMMARY

The trend in the value of new industrial construction in the United States is rapidly upward. Industrial park sites are often being selected over single sites for industrial development, particularly because of the time and money required for environmental permits and licenses required for single-site development. Industrial park developers have already spent the time and money to qualify the park sites available for sale or lease.

Industrial land users generally concentrate on a few factors as they proceed to select sites for new plants and warehouses. These factors include labor availability, resource availability, energy availability, transportation, taxes on business and industry, availability of land, lack of red tape in obtaining environmental permits, and the quality of life of the community. Many other factors are included in the overall site selection checklist appropriate for industrial company officers. Regardless of the state in which the prospective site is located, the prime factor for plant location is labor availability.

Construction costs and land prices continue to move upward. The trend in construction costs tends even to surpass the rise of inflation. Industrial land prices tend to be the highest in the Northeast and West and the lowest in the South and Midwest.

Industrial development may be financed by means of corporate stock and bond issues, mortgage financing, and sale-leasebacks. Private or government organizations may finance the sale-leaseback for industry. The state or local government may loan money or guarantee loans for building construction and equipment purchase or expansion of existing facilities. Tax incentives and financing programs for plant development and pollution control may be offered by state or local governments. Most states regulate air and water pollution through state agencies. Some states have land-use control, occupational safety and health, coastal resources, noise-control, hazardous waste control, and power plant siting agencies. Industrial development must conform to the standards set by the federal, state, and local agencies.

The yields to investors in industrial sale-leasebacks tend to range from $5\frac{1}{2}$ to $8\frac{1}{2}$ percent in today's market. In the mid-1960s, equity investors in warehouses and industrial buildings received returns after taxes and financing approximating $7\frac{1}{2}$ to 9 percent, where life insurance companies held the loans.

Key Terms and Concepts

Economic base
Industrial land
Industrial development
Pollution control
Company strategy
Labor availability
Privately sponsored development credit corporations
Inventory tax exemption on goods in transit
State tax-incentive and financing programs for pollution control
Site selection
International factors
Warehouse requirements
State-approved development credit corporations
Revenue or general obligation bonds
Tax exemption on manufacturers' inventories
Plant and equipment expenditures
Planned industrial parks
Planned office parks
Quality-of-life factors
State-sponsored industrial development authorities

Tax-exempt municipal bond financing
Sales or use tax exemption on new equipment
Tax exemption on raw materials used in manufacturing

Questions for Student Self-examination

Multiple-Choice Questions

1. About _____ of all new industrial facilities are going into planned industrial parks.
   a. one-half
   b. one-quarter
   c. two-thirds
   d. three-fourths

2. Which factor ranks first in industrial site selection?
   a. resource availability
   b. energy
   c. labor availability
   d. transportation

3. Conservative estimates of construction costs for industrial plants indicate square footage costs at _____ or more by 1980.
   a. $50
   b. $72
   c. $12
   d. $30

4. Industrial land prices tend to be the highest in the _____.
   a. Northeast
   b. Southeast
   c. Midwest
   d. Southwest

5. In which state is there a great concentration of planned industrial parks?
   a. Arizona
   b. Wyoming
   c. California
   d. Utah

True-False Questions

T F 1. Those of working age continue to decline in number.
T F 2. The work force participation of females and the elderly continues to increase.
T F 3. The value of new industrial construction in the United States is declining significantly.
T F 4. More companies are choosing office and industrial parks over single sites for their company locations.
T F 5. By 1980, warehouse square footage costs, conservatively estimated, will exceed $55.
T F 6. Industrial mortgage loans made by life insurance companies run approximately 20 years.

T F 7. On an industrial sale-leaseback, the lessee completely deducts the lease payments made to the lessor for tax purposes.
T F 8. A state-sponsored industrial development authority may finance a sale-leaseback with tax-exempt municipal bond financing.
T F 9. The state government may loan money for industrial building construction and equipment purchase.
T F 10. The state or local government cannot finance the expansion of existing industrial facilities.

Answers
Multiple-Choice: 1c, 2c, 3d, 4a, 5c.
True-False: 1F, 2T, 3F, 4T, 5F, 6T, 7T, 8T, 9T, 10F.

Problems

1. Why would National Cash Register pay 10 percent over the acreage price that they would pay for a location outside an industrial park for their distribution center in a planned industrial park?

2. If you needed more office space in office parks of the West, Southwest, North Central region and the South, what states would have the most planned office park developments, where you would have the greatest variety of locations and facilities from which to select?

3. If you were a typical site selection officer for a major company and were considering the following factors in site selection, which one would you typically place first in importance: transportation, land availability, quality of life, resource availability, labor availability?

4. Which construction costs are typically higher on the average—warehouse construction costs or industrial plant construction costs? Why would your conclusion be reasonable?

5. According to recent data on industrial land prices, in which area of the country would you expect to find the highest acreage costs? the lowest? Why?

6. What are the usual characteristics of state tax-incentive and financing programs for pollution control?

Chapter 23

Other Income Property Investment

Introduction
The Relationship of This Chapter to Other Chapters of the Text
Investment in Hotels and Motels
Construction Costs and Their Trend
Operating and Financing Characteristics of Hotels and Motels
    The Management Organization   Operating Statistics for the Lodging Industry   Financing Characteristics of the Hotel–Motel Structures, Equipment, and Furnishings
Yields for Investors in Hotel and Motel Properties
Investment in Mobile Home Parks
    The Economies of Scale of the Mobile Home Park   Overall Construction Costs   Typical Sources of Operating and Financial Expenses and Revenues   Investment Yields on Mobile Home Parks
Investment in Planned Unit Developments and New Towns
    Current Types of Planned, Large-Scale Developments   The Corporate and Institutional Investment Opportunities   The HUD-Sponsored New Town Program
Summary
Key Terms and Concepts
Questions for Student Self-examination

LEARNING OBJECTIVES After studying this chapter, you should be familiar with

The general investment characteristics of hotels and motels
Demand factors affecting hotel and motel occupancy and profitability
Construction costs and their trends
Operating and financing characteristics of hotels and motels
Investment yields in hotel and motel properties
Investment characteristics of mobile home parks
The types of mobile home parks
The economies of scale of mobile home parks
Typical sources of operating and financial expenses and revenues
Investment yields on mobile home parks
Current types of planned, large-scale developments
Corporate and institutional investment opportunities in planned developments
The HUD-sponsored new-town program

The real estate investor has a wide variety of alternative investment opportunities. Income properties, large and small, surround the investor. Many businesses occupy premises for their sole operation. Other businesses occupy multitenant or owner space, such as shopping centers and office buildings. This chapter winds up the income property investment part of the book, covering a few significant types of large-scale developments—hotels and motels, mobile home parks, and planned unit developments and new towns.

INTRODUCTION

This chapter deals with transient housing, permanent housing facilities for mobile homes, and the development of new communities. Motels and hotels have long been our organized, large-scale forms of transient housing accommodation. This lodging industry experiences its ebbs and flows of business, since it is affected significantly by the economic cycle of the United States. The demand factors, the trend in construction costs, the financing patterns, and the investment yields associated with the hotel–motel business are explored.

Next, mobile home parks are analyzed. The various types of mobile home parks, categorized by length of park occupancy, the predominant resident population, and the type of mobile home pad ownership or rental, are described. The evidence of economies of scale of the mobile home park is then observed. Since the overall construction costs of mobile home parks have been rising rapidly, 1970 and 1975 cost data are scrutinized. Possible investment yields from mobile home parks and the typical sources of operating and financial expenses and revenues are studied.

At the end of the chapter, a brief history of the new-town and planned unit development movement is given. The current types of planned. large-scale developments are then enumerated. The argument for corporate and institutional investment in new towns is offered. Finally, the current status of the HUD-sponsored new-town program and the location of the publicly and privately developed new towns of the United States are given.

THE RELATIONSHIP OF THIS CHAPTER TO OTHER CHAPTERS OF THE TEXT

Earlier chapters of Part V cover home ownership, multifamily building and project ownership, shopping center investment, office building investment, and industrial building investment. Each of these real estate investment phenomena has its own investment characteristics and investment trends. The last chapter of the text summarizes the current status of hotel and motel investment, mobile home park investment, and investment in planned unit developments and new towns. The six chapters of Part V give a balanced outlook on income property investment. The chapters cover possibilities for real estate investment by a single investor and by groups of investors, where major sums of money are required. Subjects ranging from house investement by a single family to new-town development by major corporations and financial institutions are covered. The building of the house may require three to four months, while the new-town construction and development may take ten years or more.

INVESTMENT IN HOTELS AND MOTELS

Investment in hotels and motels involves the strategic factors of demand, construction costs, financing, and investment yields. Hotels and motels have not been covered in prior chapters because they are transient housing accommodations, which are not investment alternatives for the general public. Hotels are differentiated from motels in that they are usually full-service hostelries, whereas motels are limited-service hostelries. The vast majority of the rooms is devoted to transient housing regardless of the label *hotel* or *motel*. A few of the rooms may be utilized for permanent or relatively permanent housing accommodations. For example, seasonally employed construction workers may be housed for a relatively long period in a motel near the construction site. Many single people, some of whom are elderly, make their permanent homes in hotel suites or hotel apartments.

Some of the most strategic demand factors affecting the hotel and motel business are listed below:

- Profitability of the business sector in general.
- Importance of personal sales forces to corporate business.
- Expansion of government offices and the affiliated suppliers, clients, and professional associates.
- General level of fuel costs.
- General level of plane fares, including rising fuel, financing, and construction costs.
- Relative level of the convention, conference, and seminar trade.

When business is profitable, executives and middle management are "on the road," stimulating more profitable business and managing real estate and office operations in widespread areas of the United States. Hotels and motels must be utilized as "homes away from home." When business is profitable, personal selling usually complements impersonal selling done by corporate business. Personal selling implies housing large salesforces in the markets in which the business wants profitable trade. The expansion of government offices implies many visitors to those expanded offices to carry on government and private business. Government agencies are served by private business and industry, whose representatives must be housed temporarily near the government offices for the transaction of business. Government offices attract clients, suppliers of goods and services, and professional people in different vocations.

When fuel costs are high, many companies restrict their travel expense allowances to only the most necessary travel by personal sales representatives. Automobile travel expenses are reduced. As fuel costs rise, airline fares usually rise, because of the cost component related to airplane fuel. Companies may have to reduce representative travel when their travel budgets are more quickly depleted by the rising airline fares and rising ground transportation costs. Plane fares also tend to reflect rising financial costs and rising construction costs of the airline business.

Much of the hotel and motel business is derived from the convention, conference, and seminar trade. This trade is closely associated with the profitability of business and industry and the good financial positions of government agencies, educational institutions, and other organizations. When money is plentiful and personal incomes reach a relatively high level, more conventions, conferences, and seminars are attended at the expense of the organization or the affluent individual. Many downtown and suburban hotels and motels cater to this lucrative trade. Meeting rooms of all sizes attract the convention and conference trade on a regular basis.

CONSTRUCTION COSTS AND THEIR TREND

Like the construction costs of other types of income properties, those of hotels and motels are rising rapidly. The normally conservative estimates of *Southern Building* show that 1979 construction cost per square foot for the highest quality hotel or motel was $38; only five years earlier, the square footage cost was estimated at approximately $23 (Table 23-1). In contrast, low-quality hotels and motels could be built for approximately $29 a foot in 1979.

OPERATING AND FINANCING CHARACTERISTICS OF HOTELS AND MOTELS

The operating characteristics of a transient housing operation have much to do with the value of the hotel-motel property. The financing, of course, depends greatly on the value of the property as an operating hostelry.

The Management Organization. The prime factor in the hotel-motel business is the management. Certain management firms are known worldwide for their professional, profitable hotel-motel management. Hilton International, Holiday Inns, Inc., Sheraton Corp., Marriott Corp., and Hyatt Hotels keep their national and international reputations for excellence by operating managing schools in various places of the United States and abroad. When one of these organizations manages a hotel or motel, the

Table 23-1. Construction costs per square foot for hotels and motels

Type of Hotel/Motel	May 1974	April–May 1978	June–July 1979
Type I	$22.60	$36.10	$38.30
Type II	22.60	36.10	36.10
Type III	NA	NA	31.50
Type IV—One hour	NA	NA	31.00
unprotected	NA	NA	29.20
Type V—One hour	19.50	31.20	30.50
unprotected	18.20	28.90	28.70
Type VI—One hour	17.75	28.20	30.40
unprotected	16.35	26.00	28.60

Source: *Southern Building* (May 1974), p. 29; (April–May 1978), p. 8; (June–July 1979), advance copy for the issue with no page number assigned. Reprinted with permission. NA means "not available."

value of the business may reach peak amounts. The value of the structure depends on the value of the business it houses.

Operating Statistics for the Lodging Industry. A few organizations make public operating statistics for the lodging industry. These statistics may cover the occupancy rate and the average room rate by age of the structure, the size of the lodging operation, the area of the country, the sales volume category, and the type of restaurant operation. Sales and expenses of various types may be distributed on the basis of selected years and urban location (Supplementary Table I). The following ratios may be compiled for various years and various lodging locations: the number of times the average rate was earned, the ratio of house income to room sales, the ratio of house income to total sales, the productivity index, and the net income before income taxes to total sales (Supplementary Table II).

Financing Characteristics of the Hotel-Motel Structures, Equipment, and Furnishings. The equipment and furnishings may be financed by means of a chattel mortgage or they may be leased over a relatively long period. The building may be owned by the hotel chain and mortgaged, or it may be owned by an individual, a group of individuals, or an institution and leased to the hotel management company on a sale-leaseback basis. If the building is mortgaged, the loan will probably run 20 to 25 years and perhaps have an interest rate of approximately 10 percent (Table 23-2). The lender, based on historical evidence from life insurance company loans, may require a debt coverage ratio of 1.4 to 1.9. Lenders generally consider motel and hotel mortgage loans relatively risky and usually require more stringent mortgage terms than the terms for other types of income property loans.

YIELDS FOR INVESTORS IN HOTEL AND MOTEL PROPERTIES

As lenders generally consider hotel and motel loans relatively risky, investors require higher rates of return from their hotel and motel investments to compensate for the relatively high financial risk. Based on life insurance company data from the mid-1960s, the investor may acquire an 11 to 13 perent return on equity after taxes and financing (Tables 23-3 and 23-4).

Table 23-2. 1977-1978 Life insurance company loan terms for hotels and motels

	Second Quarter 1977	Second Quarter 1978	Third Quarter 1978	Fourth Quarter 1978
Average Loan Amount ($000)	$9,356	$8,406	$9,520	$7,296
Average Interest Rate	9.56%	9.97%	10.08%	10.29%
Average Loan-to-Value Ratio	73.8%	71.1%	71.6%	71.6%
Average Capitalization Rate	11.2%	11.5%	11.5%	11.8%
Average Debt Coverage Factor	1.44	1.38	1.41	1.68
Average Percent Constant	10.4%	10.8%	11.2%	11.1%
Average Term (Yrs./Mos.)	20/6	20/5	19/8	17/5

Source: American Council of Life Insurance (Washington, D.C.), various *Investment Bulletins* entitled "Mortgage Commitments on Multifamily and Nonresidential Properties Reported by 15 Life Insurance Companies." Reprinted by permission.

Table 23-3. Rate of return on equity after taxes and financing for hotels and motels

Property Type	Quarter and Year				
	3rd '54	4th '59	3rd '63	1st '65	4th '66
Hotels and motels	10.99%	10.43%	12.12%	12.82%	11.42%
All income property loans in sample	7.98	8.01	8.27	9.07	8.87

Source: R. Bruce Ricks, "Imputed Equity Returns on Real Estate Financed with Life Insurance Company Loans," *Journal of Finance*, 24:5 (December, 1969), p. 933. Reprinted with permission.

INVESTMENT IN MOBILE HOME PARKS

The prospective investor in a mobile home park may consider the park an investment that will yield a reasonable return on his or her money, or the investor may consider the mobile home park only a temporary investment vehicle while waiting for the economic and market conditions for land development to improve. Many mobile home parks in outlying areas become apartment and commercial developments with the passage of time and as a result of population pressures on outlying metropolitan areas. A request for a change in zoning is made. When the city or county commissioners grant the zoning request, the land use is changed from a mobile home park to one requiring higher density.

Mobile home parks may be classified by the length of park occupancy, the predominant resident population, and type of mobile home pad ownership or rental.

1. *Length of park occupancy.* Three kinds of mobile home parks exist: overnight accommodation for travel trailers, permanent home sites for mobile homes, and a combination arrangement of the previous two kinds. In resort or vacation areas, mobile home park owners find a demand for overnight travel trailer accommodations. The overnight stay may be extended to a few days, but the park or that portion of the park is set aside for transient accommodations only. Permanent home sites are desired by those living in a mobile home in one location the year round or for a long season of the year. For example, Northerners flock to their mobile homes in warm winter climates during the cold months of the year. These mobile home owners or renters may reside

in the home the full season in the one location every year. Many mobile home parks for permanent residents or transient residents exist. A few mobile home parks accommodate both types of residents in segregated areas of the same development.

2. *The predominant resident population.* The mobile home park usually caters either to adults only or to family units. If both clienteles are served, the adults without children may occupy one area of the park, while the families occupy another area separated from the first group by recreational areas, lakes, driveways, or other natural or artificial barriers. The adults may be permitted to house their children over 16 years of age, or only visitation rights for children may be permitted. In the reserved family section, a limit of two children per couple per mobile home may be permitted. The limit on children for a single-wide home may be a single child.

3. *Type of mobile home pad ownership or rental.* The mobile home pad may be rented from the park owner on a monthly basis, or the park owner may sell the mobile home lots on a condominium basis. Direct sale of pads by the original owner without a condominium contract is often done in mobile home subdivisions. The pad ownership in today's market may be on a time-sharing basis, in that the ownership interest may cover fee title for perhaps only four weeks of the calendar year. The other owners of the same mobile home pad may exercise their ownership rights during other weeks of the year. The manager of the park hired by the pad owners aids in determination of the weeks of residency allocated to each time-sharing pad owner. The time-sharing programs are particularly prevalent in resort and vacation areas.

The Economies of Scale of the Mobile Home Park. There are economies of scale for the mobile home park owner in the construction and operations arenas. Generally, economies of scale are found in construction costs when the park reaches 150 to 200 pads.

Typical construction costs are

Land cost
Land improvement cost
   Grading
   Landscaping
Land development cost
   Laying of underground utility lines
      Electric lines

Table 23-4. Return on sales, total assets, and investment, hotels and motels

	1977	1976
Earnings ratio (ratio of net income before income tax or loss to total sales)	4.5%	N/A
Rate of return on total assets, median, all establishments	3.8%	3.2%
Return on invested capital (average ratio of net income after income tax, but before interest, to total interest-bearing debt and equity)	11.3%	8.2%
Return on equity (average ratio of net income after income taxes to stockholders' equity)	13.2%	8.1%

Reprinted by permission from *U.S. Lodging Industry 1978.* Philadelphia, Pennsylvania: Laventhol & Horwath, 1978, p. 22, Exhibits 4 and 5.
NA means "not available."

      Water lines
      Gas lines
      Storm and sanitary sewer lines
      Cable television lines
      Telephone lines
   Lake construction
   Road construction
      Laying of the road bed
      Surfacing of the road
Concrete mobile home pads with tie-down capacity
Clubhouse and laundry building construction

Economies of scale in park operations may also be reached when the park accommodates 150 to 200 pads. Such economies may result from spreading the management, security, and utility costs over a relatively large number of pads. For example, if a separate sewerage plant must be built for the mobile home park, economies of scale in plant operating costs may be reached by larger numbers of occupied pads.

Overall Construction Costs. The total investment required for the development of a mobile home park is rising rapidly. Exclusive of land, a typical 150-pad park in 1970 cost from $450,000 to $600,000. In 1975, the total cost for the same size park had jumped to a range of $700,000 to $1.4 million.[1] in 1975, developers were predicting a cost increase of 3 to 5 percent per quarter.

Typical Sources of Operating and Financial Expenses and Revenues. Mobile home park owners may receive revenues from (1) monthly pad rentals from permanent residents; (2) travel trailer overnight charges; (3) coin-operated machines in the recreation building, clubhouse, and laundries; (4) rental of bicycles, boats, and other recreational equipment; and (5) profits from mobile home sales and brokerage.

Typical mobile home park expenses payable by the owner are

Utility bills for common areas
Payroll for property management and direction of recreational programs
Road and common area maintenance
   Landscaping service around the clubhouse and entrances
   Swimming pool maintenance
   Road repair
   Clubhouse maintenance
Interest on floor plan loans for maintaining mobile home sales inventory
Interest on the mobile home park mortgage loan as well as principal repayment
Taxes—local property and federal and state income

Investment Yields on Mobile Home Parks. A mobile home park can be a lucrative venture. To reach the highest possible investment yields, the owner or the ownership group should have mobile home park construction expertise, management skills, and sales ability. In the latter case, the owners or their park managers must market the pads and the mobile homes available in inventory for sale or rental. With these considerations in mind, we observe from a Bank of America mobile home parks report that the average net profit in California in 1975 ran between 10 and 12 percent.[2]

---

[1] "Mobile Home Parks Offer Equal Potential for Feast or Famine," *Mortgage Banker* (1977), p. 74.
[2] Ibid.

INVESTMENT IN PLANNED UNIT DEVELOPMENTS AND NEW TOWNS

Planned unit developments and new towns have been built around the world since World War II. The devastation of military campaigns across the countryside of many nations called for the rebuilding of cities and the construction of totally new cities in the aftermath of World War II. In some developing countries, new capital cities were planned and developed, such as Brasilia, the capital of Brazil in South America. As a part of the American urban renewal program of the 1960s, many mixed-use developments, called *towns in town*, were developed on the property acquired for redevelopment in the inner cities and bulldozed for the change in land use. Then, as the costs of expanding city services reached new highs, as middle- and upper-income residents fled the central cities for the suburbs and sought city services in the suburbs, many city planners encouraged the establishments of new towns, where the cost of the infrastructure would be less per city resident served. When developers observed the high front-end costs of building totally new towns, they tended to reduce their scale of development to planned unit developments, which could become profitable in a shorter period of time with less capital expenditure.

Current Types of Planned, Large-Scale Developments. Some classify our current planned developments in the following way:

Industrial or office park or apartment complex.
Planned unit development (PUD) or mixed use development.
New town within a town or minicity or microcity.
Satellite new town.
Free-standing new town.

The Corporate and Institutional Investment Opportunities. Because the front-end costs for land acquisition, land improvement, and public building construction for new towns—HUD sponsored or otherwise—total perhaps $50 billion or more, new town investment is often delegated to the corporation or financial institution that has long-term financial holding power. The capital requirements of planned unit developments also require corporate and financial institution investment. The investor must have ample risk capital for the development of the land and for the long-term sell-off and leasing of the developed land. Research of new town developments show; that positive cash flows from new towns may not appear for five to ten years, and perhaps not even within that period of time. Table 23-5 shows the financial commitment, development plans, and the corporate and institutional sponsors of nine new towns planned in the late 1960s and early 1970s. By the end of the 1970s, Reston, Virginia, and Columbia, Maryland, for example, had encountered major financial problems. The corporate and institutional investors had found the cash flow situation disastrous.

The HUD-Sponsored New Town Program. The U.S. Department of Housing and Urban Development financially sponsored and guaranteed loans for 13 projects in 1968. Ten years later, all 13 new towns were in such bad financial straits that HUD closed down the new town program and tried to protect the federal government investment from further losses. HUD-sponsored new towns include

Maumelle, Arkansas
Shenandoah, Georgia
Park Forest South, Illinois
St. Charles, Maryland
Cedar-Riverside, Minnesota

Table 23-5. Profile of nine significant new towns

New Town	Year Land Acquired Initially	Expected Completion	Projected Population	Acreage	Residential	Commercial	Industrial	Open Space
Clear Lake City, Bayport, Texas	1962	About 1985	125,000	23,210	5,600 (24)	90 (4)	13,050 (56)	3,660 (16)
Columbia, Maryland	1963	1980	110,000	14,000	8,150 (56)	200 (1)	2,550 (17)	3,000 (20)
Coral Spring, Florida	1963	About 1985	112,000	10,400	3,600 (34.8)	1,100 (10.5)	560 (5.4)	1,000 (10)
Irvine, California	1966[†]	About 2000	430,000	32,000	21,450 (66)	4,000 (13)	4,150 (13)	2,500 (8)
Lake Havasu City, Arizona	1963	1973 or 1974	100,000	16,520	11,800 (71)	400 (2)	320 (2)	1,200 (7)[‡]
Mission Viejo, California	1964	1990	97,000	About 11,000	8,243 (75)	504 (5)	315 (3)	504 (5)
Rancho Bernardo, California	1961	1980	50,000	5,800	4,500 (77)	1,135 (20)	63 (1)	[§]
Reston, Virginia	1961	1980	80,000	7,400	4,300 (58)	300 (4)	1,300 (18)	1,200 (16)
Westlake Village, California	1965	1980 to 1995	70,000	12,000	Specific land-use categories not designated			

Size / Land Use Acreage° (Percentage)

Source: Mahlon Apgar, "New Business from New Towns?" *Harvard Business Review*, IV (January–February 1971). Copyright 1970, by the President and Fellows of Harvard College. All rights reserved.

° Figures do not always add up to 100%.
† Planning and development in process 1964–1970.
‡ Institutions assigned 2,800 acres (17%).
§ Many housing areas oriented toward open-space uses.

New Town	Land Acquisition Cost ($ million)	Housing (per dwelling unit)	Commercial (per acre)	Industrial Sites (per acre)	Developer	Other Corporate Participant Name	Role
Clear Lake City, Bayport, Texas	Not Available	$21,000 to over $65,000	$22,000 to $150,000	$8,000 to $25,000	Friendswood Development Co.	Humble Oil (parent)	Owner/Investor
Columbia, Md.	$25.0	$14,000 to $60,000	$60,000	$25,000 to $30,000	The Rouse Company	Connecticut General Life	Joint Venture
Coral Springs, Florida	$10.0	$30,000 to $150,000	$30,000 to $40,000	$10,000 to $15,000	Coral Ridge Properties	Westinghouse Electric (parent)	Owner/Investor, Product Showcase
Irvine, California	Not Available	$27,500 and up	$4,160 to $11,400	$32,000	The Irvine Company	None	None
Lake Havasu City, Ariz.	Not Available	$6,600 to $20,000 per site	$9,000 to $25,000 per site	About $25,000	McCulloch Properties, Inc.	McCulloch Oil (parent)	Owner plans
Mission Viejo, California	Not Available	$22,000 to $70,000	$50,000 to $60,000	$15,000 to $25,000	Mission Viejo Development Co.	Philip Morris	Owner
Rancho Bernardo, Calif.	Not Available	$24,700 to $60,000	$92,000 to $200,000	$13,500 to $34,500	Avco Community Developers, Inc.	Avco Corporation (parent)	Owner/Investor
Reston, Va.	$13.2	$32,000 to $100,000	Lease only	$25,000 to $45,000	Gulf-Reston, Inc.	Gulf Oil (parent)	Owner/Investor, Product Showcase
Westlake Village, California	$32.0	$31,000 to $85,000	$100,000 to $125,000	$40,000 to $65,000	Westlake Village	American-Hawaiian Steamship Company, Prudential Life Insurance Company	Joint Venture‖

‖ American-Hawaiian subsidiary began the project, Prudential is investor.

Jonathan, Minnesota
Gananda, New York
Radisson, New York
Riverton, New York
Roosevelt Island, New York
Soul City, North Carolina
Newfields, Ohio
Harbison, South Carolina
Flower Mound, Texas

From the listing, we can see that HUD-sponsored new towns were concentrated in New York. Two were near Minneapolis–St. Paul, Minnesota; one was near Chicago; one was near Atlanta; and one was near Washington, D.C.

SUMMARY

Miscellaneous income property investment topics were brought up in Chapter 23. Hotels, motels, mobile home parks, PUDs, and new towns are significant income property investments, but they tend to be less widely known real estate investments. All of these forms of investment require sizable sums of money from one or more investors, but the new towns take, in addition to millions of dollars of front-end money, unusually extended holding power. Corporations and financial institutions often take equity positions in planned unit developments and new towns. Financial institutions merely finance loans associated with hotels, motels, and mobile home parks.

Lodging industry business fluctuates with the general economy. Relatively high corporate profitability usually means relatively high profitability of hotels and motels. Usually the hotel or motel structures are financed on the basis of the efficiency and profitability of the hotel management organization. The mortgage lender will observe whether or not the owners of the building have a binding contract with a major hotel–motel management group, such as Hilton International, Sheraton, Marriott, Hyatt, or Holiday Inns, Inc. The hotel equipment and furnishings may be leased. The buildings may be financed through a sale-leaseback arrangement with a major financial institution or corporation. Investment yields from hotel–motel properties may be substantial, according to limited research evidence.

As mobile home living becomes more pervasive in our society for lower income citizens and citizens who migrate for seasons from one area of the country to another, mobile home park investment becomes more generally considered as an investment alternative. Good temporary or long-term yields may be gained from mobile home park investment. Expertise in mobile home park construction and management is required for financially successful operations. Economies of scale from operations and construction may be realized.

Corporations and large financial institutions may take substantial equity and lender positions in planned unit development and new-town development. Several types of planned developments are currently in investment vogue. Various types of land uses are involved in the large-scale developments, including residential, commercial, industrial, and institutional land uses. Some privately financed new towns have been successful, according to the press, but the HUD-sponsored new towns have had such phenomenal losses that the new-towns program has been dismantled.

Key Terms and Concepts

Lodging industry
Mobile home pad ownership or rental
Mobile home park
Economies of scale
Clubhouse
Security cost
Planned unit development
New town
Hostelries
Hotel-motel management
Average room rate
Ratio of house income to room sales
Travel trailer charges
Corporate participants
Ratio of house income to total sales
Productivity index
Time-sharing pad owner
Concrete mobile home pads with tie-down capacity
Mobile home floor-plan loans

Supplementary Table I. Lodging industry statistics

Category	Percentage of Occupancy 1977	1976	Average Room Rate 1977	1976
Age				
Built Prior to 1940	58.0%	57.7%	$34.09	$27.45
1940–1959	69.7	65.6	27.11	23.46
1960–1969	69.0	69.8	22.71	21.28
1970s	69.2	67.5	25.33	21.88
Size				
Under 150 Rooms	66.4%	69.7%	$22.20	$19.91
150–299	70.6	67.7	22.75	21.44
300–599	69.2	64.3	28.57	25.42
Over 600	68.2	64.9	35.93	33.02
Area				
Northeast	71.1%	70.5%	$26.09	$24.11
Southeast	63.7	64.1	24.74	24.79
North Central	69.2	68.1	24.48	21.58
South Central	64.4	63.3	22.63	19.91
West	74.4	70.0	25.54	21.73
Total sales				
Less than $750,000	58.5%	60.2%	$18.50	$17.33
$750,000–$1,499,999	65.6	67.8	21.50	19.64
$1,500,000–$2,999,999	70.9	68.2	23.41	21.86
$3,000,000–$4,999,999	72.5	67.5	27.36	25.79
$5,000,000 and over	72.8	68.5	32.41	32.54
Restaurant not operated	67.2%	64.7%	$21.56	$19.54
Restaurant operated—total food and beverage sales ratio to room sales				
Under 50% of room sales	69.2%	69.4%	$23.55	$23.10
50–74%	66.1	65.5	25.33	23.16
75–99%	70.8	67.1	25.93	21.84
100–124%	71.8	68.1	26.92	21.13
125% and over	67.2	67.8	31.95	22.45
Median, all establishments	68.6%	67.4%	$24.90	$22.15

Reprinted by permission from *U.S. Lodging Industry 1978* (Philadelphia: Laventhol & Horwath, 1978), p. 28.

Supplementary Table II. Lodging industry statistics: comparison of data by location

	Center City 1977	Center City 1976	Airport 1977	Airport 1976	Suburban 1977	Suburban 1976	Highway 1977	Highway 1976	Resort 1977	Resort 1976
Occupancy	64.9%	63.3%	77.4%	68.4%	70.0%	71.5%	69.4%	68.1%	61.5%	64.6%
Double occupancy	47.6	37.0	29.3	26.0	46.8	38.0	42.3	49.5	113.9	110.8
Average rate	$29.13	$25.54	$23.87	$22.36	$22.79	$22.96	$20.70	$18.76	$30.52	$28.14
Amount per available room										
Room Sales	$ 6657	$ 5891	$ 6907	$ 5609	$ 6141	$ 5919	$ 5479	$ 4800	$6658	$ 6425
Food Sales	3163	2935	2294	2193	2435	2219	2210	2684	3108	3074
Beverage	1215	1169	1482	1103	1199	1142	835	1090	1135	874
Other	633	557	539	448	421	421	379	348	544	445
Total Sales	$12510	$10588	$10624	$ 9005	$10563	$ 9544	$ 8105	$ 8102	$11134	$10729
Payroll and related expenses	4774	4327	3537	3011	3097	3022	2773	2952	3747	3690
Administrative and general expenses	734	650	757	687	674	771	591	637	755	699
Energy costs	600	529	507	404	532	495	463	416	581	530
Fixed charges	$ 2125	$ 2146	$ 2605	$ 2075	$ 2396	$ 2537	$ 1855	$ 1772	$ 2550	$ 2378
Net income before income tax	$ 352	$ 59	$ 961	$ 501	$ 888	$ 490	$ 380	$ 430	$ 379	$ 314
No. of times rate earned	96	92	135	116	128	124	116	125	100	104
Ratio of total sales to total assets	107.6%	111.1%	90.8%	86.2%	80.2%	88.4%	85.4%	80.1%	73.4%	81.2%
Ratio of net income before income taxes to total sales	3.2%	.6%	7.6%	4.9%	7.5%	3.5%	5.1%	4.7%	3.7%	2.5%
Return on total assets	3.4%	.7%	6.9%	4.2%	6.0%	3.1%	4.4%	3.8%	2.7%	2.0%

Reprinted by permission from *U.S. Lodging Industry 1978* (Philadelphia: Laventhol & Horwath, 1978), pp. 24-25.
All figures are medians.

Questions for Student Self-examination

Multiple-Choice Questions

1. The building of a single-family house usually requires _____.
   a. ten to twelve months
   b. one to two years
   c. eight to nine months
   d. three to four months

2. Airline fares often reflect
   a. the rise in fuel costs
   b. rising financial costs
   c. rising construction costs
   d. all of the above

3. The normally conservative estimates of *Southern Building* show 1978 construction cost per square foot for the highest quality hotel or motel to be _____.
   a. $12
   b. $53
   c. $76
   d. $36

4. The prime factor in the hotel-motel business is
   a. the building facilities
   b. the beverage service
   c. the total number of rooms
   d. the management

5. Which is not a world-renowned hotel-motel management firm?
   a. Hilton International
   b. Travel Inns, Inc.
   c. Sheraton Corp.
   d. Marriott Corp.

True-False Questions

T F   1. The lodging industry is a very stable business because it is unaffected by the economic cycle.
T F   2. New-town construction and development may take ten years or more.
T F   3. When business is profitable, impersonal selling usually takes the place of personal selling.
T F   4. The financing of a hotel-motel property depends greatly on the value of the property as an operating hostelry.
T F   5. The hotel building may be owned by the hotel chain.
T F   6. Lenders generally consider motel and hotel mortgage loans relatively safe.
T F   7. The mobile home park usually caters either to adults only or to family units.
T F   8. Mobile home park owners may sell mobile home lots on a condominium basis.
T F   9. We observe from a Bank of America mobile home parks report that the average net profit in California in 1975 was between 10 and 12 percent.

T F 10. Research of new-town developments shows that positive cash flows from new towns may not appear for five to ten years.

Answers
Multiple-Choice: 1d, 2d, 3d, 4d, 5b.
True-False: 1F, 2T, 3F, 4T, 5T, 6F, 7T, 8T, 9T, 10T.

Problems

1. How does a general business recession tend to affect the hotel and motel industry? At the other extreme, how does general business prosperity tend to affect the industry?

2. How significant is the major hotel-motel management company in the hotel-motel business? What influence does such a company have on operations and financing?

3. Why may a life insurance company require a debt coverage ratio of 1.9 on a hotel or motel mortgage loan?

4. On a comparative basis, considering the many types of income property investments, what relative level of return of equity is required by investors in hotels and motels? For example, does the apartment building investor require the same relative equity yield as the hotel-motel investor?

5. Would you expect the term to maturity of a new hotel-motel mortgage to be 10 to 12 years? Why?

6. What could a mobile home park operator-investor gain from offering both transient traveler space and permanent mobile home space? How could she or he lose by doing this?

Appendix

Value of $1 Compounded at 5-20%

Rate	Periods	Amount of 1: How $1 Left at Compounded Interest Will Grow	Amount of 1 Per Period: How $1 Deposited Periodically Will Grow	Sinking Fund: Periodic Deposit That Will Grow to $1 at Future Date	Present Worth of 1: What $1 Due in the Future is Worth Today	Present Worth of 1 Per Period: What $1 Payable Periodically Is Worth Today	Partial Payment: Annuity Worth $1 Today— Periodic Payment Necessary to Pay a Loan of $1	Periods
5%								
	1	1.050 000 0000	1.000 000 0000	1.000 000 0000	.952 380 9524	.952 380 9524	1.050 000 0000	1
	2	1.102 500 0000	2.050 000 0000	.487 804 8780	.907 029 4785	1.859 410 4308	.537 804 8780	2
	3	1.157 625 0000	3.152 500 0000	.317 208 5646	.863 837 5985	2.723 248 0294	.367 208 5646	3
.05 Per Period	4	1.215 506 2500	4.310 125 0000	.232 011 8326	.822 702 4748	3.545 950 5042	.282 011 8326	4
	5	1.276 281 5625	5.525 631 2500	.180 974 7981	.783 526 1665	4.329 476 6706	.230 974 7981	5
	6	1.340 095 6406	6.801 912 8125	.147 017 4681	.746 215 3966	5.075 692 0673	.197 017 4681	6
	7	1.407 100 4227	8.142 008 4531	.122 819 8184	.710 681 3301	5.786 373 3974	.172 819 8184	7
	8	1.477 455 4438	9.549 108 8758	.104 721 8136	.676 839 3620	6.463 212 7594	.154 721 8136	8
	9	1.551 328 2160	11.026 564 3196	.090 690 0800	.644 608 9162	7.107 821 6756	.140 690 0800	9
	10	1.628 894 6268	12.577 892 5355	.079 504 5750	.613 913 2535	7.721 734 9292	.129 504 5750	10
	11	1.710 339 3581	14.206 787 1623	.070 388 8915	.584 679 2891	8.306 414 2183	.120 388 8915	11
	12	1.795 856 3260	15.917 126 5204	.062 825 4100	.556 837 4182	8.863 251 6364	.112 825 4100	12
	13	1.885 649 1423	17.712 982 8465	.056 455 7652	.530 321 3506	9.393 572 9871	.106 455 7652	13
	14	1.979 931 5994	19.598 631 9888	.051 023 9698	.505 067 9530	9.898 640 9401	.101 023 9695	14
	15	2.076 928 1794	21.578 563 5882	.046 342 2876	.481 017 0981	10.379 658 0382	.096 342 2876	15
	16	2.182 874 5884	23.657 491 7676	.042 269 9080	.458 111 5220	10.837 769 5602	.092 269 9080	16
	17	2.292 018 3178	25.840 366 3560	.038 699 1417	.436 296 6876	11.274 066 2478	.088 699 1417	17
	18	2.406 619 2337	28.132 284 6738	.035 546 2223	.415 520 6549	11.689 586 9027	.085 546 2223	18
	19	2.526 950 1954	30.539 003 9075	.032 745 0104	.395 733 9570	12.085 320 8597	.082 745 0104	19
	20	2.653 297 7051	33.065 954 1029	.030 242 5872	.376 889 4829	12.462 210 3425	.080 242 5872	20
ANNUALLY If compounded annually nominal annual rate is 5%	21	2.785 962 5904	35.719 251 8080	.027 996 1071	.358 942 3646	12.821 152 7072	.077 996 1071	21
	22	2.925 260 7199	38.505 214 3984	.025 970 5086	.341 849 8711	13.163 002 5783	.075 970 5086	22
	23	3.071 523 7559	41.430 475 1184	.024 136 8219	.325 571 3058	13.488 573 8841	.074 136 8219	23
	24	3.225 099 9437	44.501 998 8743	.022 470 9008	.310 067 9103	13.798 641 7943	.072 470 9008	24
	25	3.386 354 9409	47.727 098 8180	.020 952 4573	.295 302 7717	14.093 944 5660	.070 952 4573	25
	26	3.555 672 6879	51.113 453 7589	.019 564 3207	.281 240 7350	14.375 185 3010	.069 564 3207	26
	27	3.733 456 3223	54.669 126 4468	.018 291 8598	.267 848 3190	14.643 033 6200	.068 291 8599	27
	28	3.920 129 1385	58.402 582 7692	.017 122 5304	.255 093 6371	14.898 127 2571	.067 122 5304	28
	29	4.116 135 5954	62.322 711 9076	.016 045 5149	.242 946 3211	15.141 073 5782	.066 045 5149	29
	30	4.321 942 3752	66.438 847 5030	.015 051 4351	.231 377 4487	15.372 451 0269	.065 051 4351	30
SEMIANNUALLY If compounded semiannually nominal annual rate is 10%	31	4.538 039 4939	70.760 789 8782	.014 132 1204	.220 359 4749	15.592 810 5018	.064 132 1204	31
	32	4.764 941 4686	75.198 829 3721	.013 280 4189	.209 866 1666	15.802 676 6684	.063 280 4189	32
	33	5.003 188 5420	80.063 770 8407	.012 490 0437	.199 872 5396	16.002 549 2080	.062 490 0437	33
	34	5.253 347 9691	85.066 959 3827	.011 755 4454	.190 354 7996	16.192 904 0076	.061 755 4454	34
	35	5.516 015 3676	90.320 207 3518	.011 071 7072	.181 290 2854	16.374 194 2929	.061 071 7072	35
	36	5.791 816 1360	95.836 322 7194	.010 434 4571	.172 657 4146	16.546 851 7076	.060 434 4571	36
	37	6.081 406 9428	101.628 138 8554	.009 839 7945	.164 435 6330	16.711 287 3405	.059 839 7945	37
	38	6.385 477 2899	107.709 545 7982	.009 284 2282	.156 605 3647	16.867 892 7053	.059 284 2282	38
	39	6.704 751 1544	114.095 023 0881	.008 764 6242	.149 147 9664	17.017 040 6717	.058 764 6242	39
	40	7.039 988 7121	120.799 774 2425	.008 278 1612	.142 045 6823	17.159 086 3540	.058 278 1612	40
QUARTERLY If compounded quarterly nominal annual rate is 20%	41	7.391 988 1477	127.839 762 9546	.007 822 2924	.135 281 6022	17.294 367 9562	.057 822 2924	41
	42	7.761 587 5551	135.231 751 1023	.007 394 7131	.128 839 6211	17.423 207 5773	.057 394 7131	42
	43	8.149 666 9329	142.993 338 6575	.006 993 3328	.122 704 4011	17.545 911 9784	.056 993 3328	43
	44	8.557 150 2795	151.143 005 5903	.006 616 2504	.116 861 3344	17.662 773 3128	.056 616 2506	44
	45	8.985 007 7935	159.700 155 8699	.006 261 7347	.111 296 5089	17.774 069 8217	.056 261 7347	45
	46	9.434 258 1832	168.685 163 6633	.005 928 2036	.105 996 6752	17.880 066 4968	.055 928 2036	46
	47	9.905 971 0923	178.119 421 8465	.005 614 2109	.100 949 2144	17.981 015 7113	.055 614 2109	47
	48	10.401 269 6469	188.025 392 9388	.005 318 4306	.096 142 1090	18.077 157 8203	.055 318 4306	48
	49	10.921 333 1293	198.426 662 5858	.005 039 6453	.091 563 9133	18.168 721 7336	.055 039 6453	49
	50	11.467 399 7858	209.347 995 7151	.004 776 7355	.087 203 7270	18.255 925 4606	.054 776 7355	50
MONTHLY If compounded monthly nominal annual rate is 60%	51	12.040 769 7750	220.815 395 5008	.004 528 6697	.083 051 1685	18.338 976 6291	.054 528 6697	51
	52	12.642 808 2638	232.856 165 2759	.004 294 4966	.079 096 3510	18.418 072 9801	.054 294 4966	52
	53	13.274 948 6770	245.498 973 5397	.004 073 3368	.075 329 8581	18.493 402 8382	.054 073 3368	53
	54	13.938 696 1108	258.773 922 2166	.003 864 3770	.071 742 7220	18.565 145 5602	.053 864 3770	54
	55	14.635 630 9164	272.712 618 3275	.003 666 8637	.068 326 4019	18.633 471 9621	.053 666 8637	55
	56	15.367 412 4622	287.348 249 2439	.003 480 0978	.065 072 7637	18.698 544 7258	.053 480 0978	56
	57	16.135 783 0853	302.715 661 7060	.003 303 4300	.061 974 0607	18.760 518 7865	.053 303 4300	57
	58	16.942 572 2396	318.851 444 7913	.003 136 2568	.059 022 9149	18.819 541 7014	.053 136 2568	58
	59	17.789 700 8515	335.794 017 0309	.002 978 0161	.056 212 2999	18.875 754 0013	.052 978 0161	59
	60	18.679 185 8941	353.583 717 8825	.002 828 1845	.053 535 5237	18.929 289 5251	.052 828 1845	60

Reproduced from *Financial Compound Interest & Annuity Tables*, Publication #376, 5-20% by 1% increments, annual compounding, 1-60 years. Copyright 1978, Financial Publishing Company, Boston, MA.

Tables 417

Value of $1 Compounded at 5-20%

Rate 6%

Rate	Periods	Amount of 1: How $1 Left at Compounded Interest Will Grow	Amount of 1 Per Period: How $1 Deposited Periodically Will Grow	Sinking Fund: Periodic Deposit That Will Grow to $1 at Future Date	Present Worth of 1: What $1 Due in the Future is Worth Today	Present Worth of 1 Per Period: What $1 Payable Periodically Is Worth Today	Partial Payment: Annuity Worth $1 Today— Periodic Payment Necessary to Pay a Loan of $1	Periods
.06 Per Period	1	1.060 000 0000	1.000 000 0000	1.000 000 0000	.943 396 2264	.943 396 2264	1.060 000 0000	1
	2	1.123 600 0000	2.060 000 0000	.485 436 8932	.889 996 4400	1.833 392 6664	.545 436 8932	2
	3	1.191 016 0000	3.183 600 0000	.314 109 8128	.839 619 2830	2.673 011 9495	.374 109 8128	3
	4	1.262 476 9600	4.374 616 0000	.228 591 4924	.792 092 6632	3.465 105 6127	.288 591 4924	4
	5	1.338 225 5776	5.637 092 9600	.177 396 4004	.747 258 1729	4.212 363 7856	.237 396 4004	5
	6	1.418 519 1123	6.975 318 5376	.143 362 6285	.704 960 5404	4.917 324 3260	.203 362 6285	6
	7	1.503 630 2590	8.393 837 6499	.119 135 0181	.665 057 1136	5.582 381 4396	.179 135 0181	7
	8	1.593 848 0745	9.897 467 9088	.101 035 9426	.627 412 3713	6.209 793 8110	.161 035 9426	8
	9	1.689 478 9590	11.491 315 9834	.087 022 2350	.591 898 4635	6.801 692 2745	.147 022 2350	9
	10	1.790 847 6965	13.180 794 9424	.075 867 9582	.558 394 7769	7.360 087 0514	.135 867 9582	10
	11	1.898 298 5583	14.971 642 6389	.066 792 9381	.526 787 5254	7.886 874 5768	.126 792 9381	11
	12	2.012 196 4718	16.869 941 1975	.059 277 0294	.496 969 3636	8.383 843 9404	.119 277 0294	12
	13	2.132 928 2601	18.882 137 6691	.052 960 1053	.468 839 0222	8.852 682 9626	.112 960 1053	13
	14	2.260 903 9558	21.015 065 9292	.047 584 9090	.442 300 9644	9.294 983 9270	.107 584 9090	14
	15	2.396 558 1931	23.275 969 8850	.042 962 7640	.417 265 0607	9.712 248 9877	.102 962 7640	15
	16	2.540 351 6847	25.672 528 0781	.038 952 1436	.393 646 2837	10.105 895 2715	.098 952 1436	16
	17	2.692 772 7858	28.212 879 7628	.035 444 8042	.371 364 4186	10.477 259 6901	.095 444 8042	17
	18	2.854 339 1529	30.905 652 5485	.032 356 5406	.350 343 7911	10.827 603 4812	.092 356 5406	18
	19	3.025 599 5021	33.759 991 7015	.029 620 8604	.330 513 0105	11.158 116 4917	.089 620 8604	19
	20	3.207 135 4722	36.785 591 2035	.027 184 5570	.311 804 7269	11.469 921 2186	.087 184 5570	20
ANNUALLY If compounded annually nominal annual rate is 6%	21	3.399 563 6005	39.992 726 6758	.025 004 5467	.294 155 4027	11.764 076 6213	.085 004 5467	21
	22	3.603 537 4166	43.392 290 2763	.023 045 5685	.277 505 0969	12.041 581 7182	.083 045 5685	22
	23	3.819 749 6616	46.995 827 6929	.021 278 4847	.261 797 2612	12.303 378 9794	.081 278 4847	23
	24	4.048 934 6413	50.815 577 3545	.019 679 0050	.246 978 5483	12.550 357 5278	.079 679 0050	24
	25	4.291 870 7197	54.864 511 9957	.018 226 7182	.232 998 6305	12.783 356 1583	.078 226 7182	25
	26	4.549 382 9629	59.156 382 7155	.016 904 3467	.219 810 0288	13.003 166 1870	.076 904 3467	26
	27	4.822 345 9407	63.705 765 6784	.015 697 1663	.207 367 9517	13.210 534 1387	.075 697 1663	27
	28	5.111 686 6971	68.528 111 6191	.014 592 5515	.195 630 1431	13.406 164 2818	.074 592 5515	28
	29	5.418 387 8990	73.639 798 3162	.013 579 6135	.184 556 7388	13.590 721 0206	.073 579 6135	29
	30	5.743 491 1729	79.058 186 2152	.012 648 9115	.174 110 1309	13.764 831 1515	.072 648 9115	30
SEMIANNUALLY If compounded semiannually nominal annual rate is 12%	31	6.088 100 6433	84.801 677 3881	.011 792 2196	.164 254 8405	13.929 085 9920	.071 792 2196	31
	32	6.453 386 6819	90.889 778 0314	.011 002 3374	.154 957 3967	14.084 043 3887	.071 002 3374	32
	33	6.840 589 8828	97.343 164 7133	.010 272 9350	.146 186 2233	14.230 229 6119	.070 272 9350	33
	34	7.251 025 2758	104.183 754 5961	.009 598 4254	.137 911 5314	14.368 141 1433	.069 598 4254	34
	35	7.686 086 7923	111.434 779 8719	.008 973 8590	.130 105 2183	14.498 246 3616	.068 973 8590	35
	36	8.147 251 9999	119.120 866 6642	.008 394 8348	.122 740 7720	14.620 987 1336	.068 394 8348	36
	37	8.636 087 1198	127.268 118 6640	.007 857 4274	.115 793 1811	14.736 780 3147	.067 857 4274	37
	38	9.154 252 3470	135.904 205 7839	.007 358 1240	.109 238 8501	14.846 019 1648	.067 358 1240	38
	39	9.703 507 4879	145.058 458 1309	.006 893 7724	.103 055 5190	14.949 074 6838	.066 893 7724	39
	40	10.285 717 9371	154.761 965 6188	.006 461 5359	.097 222 1877	15.046 296 8715	.066 461 5359	40
QUARTERLY If compounded quarterly nominal annual rate is 24%	41	10.902 861 0134	165.047 683 5559	.006 058 8551	.091 719 0450	15.138 015 9165	.066 058 8551	41
	42	11.557 032 6742	175.950 544 5692	.005 683 4152	.086 527 4010	15.224 543 3175	.065 683 4152	42
	43	12.250 454 6346	187.507 577 6434	.005 333 1178	.081 629 6235	15.306 172 9410	.065 333 1178	43
	44	12.985 481 9127	199.758 031 8780	.005 006 0565	.077 009 0788	15.383 182 0198	.065 006 0565	44
	45	13.764 610 8274	212.743 513 7907	.004 700 4958	.072 650 0743	15.455 832 0942	.064 700 4958	45
	46	14.590 487 4771	226.508 124 6181	.004 414 8527	.068 537 8060	15.524 369 9002	.064 414 8527	46
	47	15.465 916 7257	241.098 612 0952	.004 147 6805	.064 658 3075	15.589 028 2077	.064 147 6805	47
	48	16.393 871 7293	256.564 528 8209	.003 897 6549	.060 998 4033	15.650 026 6110	.063 897 6549	48
	49	17.377 504 0330	272.958 400 5502	.003 663 5619	.057 545 6635	15.707 572 2746	.063 663 5619	49
	50	18.420 154 2750	290.335 904 5832	.003 444 2864	.054 288 3618	15.761 860 6364	.063 444 2864	50
MONTHLY If compounded monthly nominal annual rate is 72%	51	19.525 363 5315	308.756 058 8582	.003 238 8028	.051 215 4357	15.813 076 0721	.063 238 8028	51
	52	20.696 885 3434	328.281 422 3897	.003 046 1669	.048 316 4488	15.861 392 5208	.063 046 1669	52
	53	21.938 698 4640	348.978 307 7331	.002 865 5076	.045 581 5554	15.906 974 0762	.062 865 5076	53
	54	23.255 020 3718	370.917 006 1970	.002 696 0209	.043 001 4674	15.949 975 5436	.062 696 0209	54
	55	24.650 321 5941	394.172 026 5689	.002 536 9634	.040 567 4221	15.990 542 9657	.062 536 9634	55
	56	26.129 340 8898	418.822 348 1630	.002 387 6472	.038 271 1529	16.028 814 1186	.062 387 6472	56
	57	27.697 101 3432	444.951 689 0528	.002 247 4350	.036 104 8612	16.064 918 9798	.062 247 4350	57
	58	29.358 927 4238	472.648 790 3959	.002 115 7359	.034 061 1898	16.098 980 1696	.062 115 7359	58
	59	31.120 463 0692	502.007 717 8197	.001 992 0012	.032 133 1979	16.131 113 3676	.061 992 0012	59
	60	32.987 690 8533	533.128 180 8889	.001 875 7215	.030 314 3377	16.161 427 7052	.061 875 7215	60

Value of $1 Compounded at 5-20%

Rate 7%	Periods	Amount of 1: How $1 Left at Compounded Interest Will Grow	Amount of 1 Per Period: How $1 Deposited Periodically Will Grow	Sinking Fund: Periodic Deposit That Will Grow to $1 at Future Date	Present Worth of 1: What $1 Due in the Future is Worth Today	Present Worth of 1 Per Period: What $1 Payable Periodically Is Worth Today	Partial Payment: Annuity Worth $1 Today— Periodic Payment Necessary to Pay a Loan of $1	Periods
	1	1.070 000 0000	1.000 000 0000	1.000 000 0000	.934 579 4393	.934 579 4393	1.070 000 0000	1
	2	1.144 900 0000	2.070 000 0000	.483 091 7874	.873 438 7283	1.808 018 1675	.553 091 7874	2
	3	1.225 043 0000	3.214 900 0000	.311 051 6657	.816 297 8769	2.624 316 0444	.381 051 6657	3
.07 Per Period	4	1.310 796 0100	4.439 943 0000	.225 228 1167	.726 895 2120	3.387 211 2565	.295 228 1167	4
	5	1.402 551 7307	5.750 739 0100	.173 890 6944	.712 986 1795	4.100 197 4359	.243 890 6944	5
	6	1.500 730 3518	7.153 290 7407	.139 795 7998	.666 342 2238	4.766 539 6598	.209 795 7998	6
	7	1.605 781 4765	8.654 021 0925	.115 553 2196	.622 749 7419	5.389 289 4016	.185 553 2196	7
	8	1.718 186 1798	10.259 802 5690	.097 467 7625	.582 009 1046	5.971 298 5062	.167 467 7625	8
	9	1.838 459 2124	11.977 988 7489	.083 486 4701	.543 933 7426	6.515 232 2488	.153 486 4701	9
	10	1.967 151 3573	13.816 447 9613	.072 377 5027	.508 349 2921	7.023 581 5409	.142 377 5027	10
	11	2.104 851 9523	15.783 599 3186	.063 356 9048	.475 092 7964	7.498 674 3373	.133 356 9048	11
	12	2.252 191 5890	17.888 451 2709	.055 901 9887	.444 011 9592	7.942 686 2966	.125 901 9887	12
	13	2.409 845 0002	20.140 642 8598	.049 650 8481	.414 964 4479	9.357 650 7444	.119 650 8481	13
	14	2.578 534 1502	22.550 487 8600	.044 344 9386	.387 817 2410	8.745 467 9855	.114 344 9386	14
	15	2.759 031 5407	25.129 022 0102	.039 794 6247	.362 446 0196	9.107 914 0051	.109 794 6247	15
	16	2.952 163 7486	27.888 053 5509	.035 857 6477	.338 734 5978	9.446 648 6029	.105 857 6477	16
	17	3.158 815 2110	30.840 217 2995	.032 425 1931	.316 574 3905	9.763 222 9934	.102 425 1931	17
	18	3.379 932 2757	33.999 032 5105	.029 412 6017	.295 863 9163	10.059 086 9097	.099 412 6017	18
	19	3.616 527 5350	37.378 964 7862	.026 753 0148	.276 508 3330	10.335 595 2427	.096 753 0148	19
	20	3.869 684 4625	40.995 492 3212	.024 392 9257	.258 419 0028	10.594 014 2455	.094 392 9257	20
ANNUALLY If compounded annually nominal annual rate is 7%	21	4.140 562 3749	44.865 176 7837	.022 289 0017	.241 513 0867	10.835 527 2323	.092 289 0017	21
	22	4.430 401 7411	49.005 739 1586	.020 405 7732	.225 713 1652	11.061 240 4974	.090 405 7732	22
	23	4.740 529 8630	53.436 140 8997	.018 713 9263	.210 946 8833	11.272 187 3808	.088 713 9263	23
	24	5.072 366 9534	58.176 670 7627	.017 189 0207	.197 146 6199	11.469 334 0007	.087 189 0207	24
	25	5.427 432 6401	63.249 037 7160	.015 810 5172	.184 249 1775	11.653 583 1783	.085 810 5172	25
	26	5.807 352 9249	68.676 470 3562	.014 561 0279	.172 195 4930	11.825 778 6713	.084 561 0279	26
	27	6.213 867 6297	74.483 823 2811	.013 425 7340	.160 930 3673	11.986 709 0386	.083 425 7340	27
	28	6.648 838 3638	80.697 690 9108	.012 391 9283	.150 402 2124	12.137 111 2510	.082 391 9283	28
	29	7.114 257 0492	87.346 529 2745	.011 448 6518	.140 562 8154	12.277 674 0664	.081 448 6518	29
	30	7.612 255 0427	94.460 786 3237	.010 586 4035	.131 367 1172	12.409 041 1835	.080 586 4035	30
SEMIANNUALLY If compounded semiannually nominal annual rate is 14%	31	8.145 112 8956	102.073 041 3664	.009 796 9061	.122 773 0067	12.531 814 1902	.079 796 9061	31
	32	8.715 270 7983	110.218 154 2621	.009 072 9155	.114 741 1277	12.646 555 3179	.079 072 9155	32
	33	9.325 339 7542	118.933 425 0604	.008 408 0653	.107 234 6988	12.753 790 0168	.078 408 0653	33
	34	9.978 113 5370	128.258 764 8146	.007 796 7381	.100 219 3447	12.854 009 3615	.077 796 7381	34
	35	10.676 581 4846	138.236 878 3516	.007 233 9596	.093 662 9390	12.947 672 3004	.077 233 9596	35
	36	11.423 942 1885	148.913 459 8363	.006 715 3097	.087 535 4570	13.035 207 7574	.076 715 3097	36
	37	12.223 618 1417	160.337 402 0248	.006 236 8480	.081 808 8383	13.117 016 5957	.076 236 8480	37
	38	13.079 271 4117	172.561 020 1665	.005 795 0515	.076 456 8582	13.193 473 4539	.075 795 0515	38
	39	13.994 820 4105	185.640 291 5782	.005 386 7616	.071 455 0077	13.264 928 4616	.075 386 7616	39
	40	14.974 457 8392	199.635 111 9887	.005 009 1389	.066 780 3810	13.331 708 8426	.075 009 1389	40
QUARTERLY If compounded quarterly nominal annual rate is 28%	41	16.022 669 8880	214.609 569 8279	.004 659 6245	.062 411 5710	13.394 120 4137	.074 659 6245	41
	42	17.144 256 7801	230.632 239 7158	.004 335 9072	.058 328 5711	13.452 448 9847	.074 335 9072	42
	43	18.344 354 7547	247.776 496 4959	.004 035 8953	.054 512 6832	13.506 961 6680	.074 035 8953	43
	44	19.628 459 5875	266.120 851 2507	.003 757 6913	.050 946 4329	13.557 908 1009	.073 757 6913	44
	45	21.002 451 7587	285.749 310 8382	.003 499 5710	.047 613 4887	13.605 521 5896	.073 499 5710	45
	46	22.472 623 3818	306.751 762 5969	.003 259 9650	.044 498 5876	13.650 020 1772	.073 259 9650	46
	47	24.045 707 0185	329.224 385 9787	.003 037 4421	.041 587 4650	13.691 607 6423	.073 037 4421	47
	48	25.728 906 5098	353.270 092 9972	.002 830 6953	.038 866 7898	13.730 474 4320	.072 830 6953	48
	49	27.529 929 9655	378.998 999 5070	.002 638 5294	.036 324 1026	13.766 798 5346	.072 638 5294	49
	50	29.457 025 0631	406.528 929 4724	.002 459 8495	.033 947 7594	13.800 746 2940	.072 459 8495	50
MONTHLY If compounded monthly nominal annual rate is 84%	51	31.519 016 8175	435.985 954 5355	.002 293 6519	.031 726 8780	13.832 473 1720	.072 293 6519	51
	52	33.725 347 9947	467.504 971 3530	.002 139 0147	.029 651 2878	13.862 124 4598	.072 139 0147	52
	53	36.086 122 3543	501.230 319 3477	.001 995 0908	.027 711 4839	13.889 835 9437	.071 997 0908	53
	54	38.612 150 9191	537.316 441 7021	.001 861 1007	.025 898 5831	13.915 734 5269	.071 861 1007	54
	55	41.315 001 4835	575.928 592 6212	.001 736 3264	.024 204 2833	13.939 938 8102	.071 736 3264	55
	56	44.207 051 5873	617.243 594 1047	.001 620 1059	.022 620 8255	13.962 559 6357	.071 620 1059	56
	57	47.301 545 1984	661.450 645 6920	.001 511 8286	.021 140 9584	13.983 700 5941	.071 511 8286	57
	58	50.612 653 3623	708.752 190 8905	.001 410 9304	.019 757 9051	14.003 458 4991	.071 410 9304	58
	59	54.155 539 0977	759.364 844 2528	.001 316 8900	.018 465 3318	14.021 923 8310	.071 316 8900	59
	60	57.946 426 8345	813.520 383 3505	.001 229 2255	.017 257 3195	14.039 181 1504	.071 229 2255	60

Tables 419

Value of $1 Compounded at 5-20%

Rate 8%

Period	Amount of 1: How $1 Left at Compounded Interest Will Grow	Amount of 1 Per Period: How $1 Deposited Periodically Will Grow	Sinking Fund: Periodic Deposit That Will Grow to $1 at Future Date	Present Worth of 1: What $1 Due in the Future is Worth Today	Present Worth of 1 Per Period: What $1 Payable Periodically Is Worth Today	Partial Payment: Annuity Worth $1 Today— Periodic Payment Necessary to Pay a Loan of $1	Period
	.08 Per Period						
1	1.080 000 0000	1.000 000 0000	1.000 000 0000	.925 925 9259	.925 925 9259	1.080 000 0000	1
2	1.166 400 0000	2.080 000 0000	.480 769 2308	.857 338 8203	1.783 264 7462	.560 769 2308	2
3	1.259 712 0000	3.246 400 0000	.308 033 5140	.793 832 2410	2.577 096 9872	.388 033 5140	3
4	1.360 488 9600	4.506 112 0000	.221 920 8045	.735 029 8528	3.312 126 8400	.301 920 8045	4
5	1.469 328 0768	5.866 600 9600	.170 456 4546	.680 583 1970	3.992 710 0371	.250 456 4546	5
6	1.586 874 3229	7.335 929 0368	.136 315 3862	.620 169 6269	4.622 879 6640	.216 315 3862	6
7	1.713 824 2688	8.922 803 3597	.112 072 4014	.583 490 3953	5.206 370 0592	.192 072 4014	7
8	1.850 930 2103	10.636 627 6285	.094 014 7606	.540 268 8845	5.746 638 9437	.174 014 7606	8
9	1.999 004 6271	12.487 557 8388	.080 079 7092	.500 248 9671	6.246 887 9109	.160 079 7092	9
10	2.158 924 9973	14.486 562 4659	.069 029 4887	.463 193 4881	6.710 081 3989	.149 029 4887	10
11	2.331 638 9971	16.645 487 4632	.060 076 3421	.428 882 8593	7.138 964 2583	.140 076 3421	11
12	2.518 170 1168	18.977 126 4602	.052 695 0169	.397 113 7586	7.536 078 0169	.132 695 0169	12
13	2.719 623 7262	21.495 296 5771	.046 521 8052	.367 697 9247	7.903 775 9416	.126 521 8052	13
14	2.937 193 6243	24.214 920 3032	.041 296 8528	.340 461 0414	8.244 236 9830	.121 296 8528	14
15	3.172 169 1142	27.152 113 9275	.036 829 5449	.315 241 7050	8.559 478 6879	.116 829 5449	15
16	3.425 942 6433	30.324 283 0417	.032 976 8720	.291 890 4676	8.851 369 1555	.112 976 8720	16
17	3.700 018 0548	33.750 225 6850	.029 629 4315	.270 268 9514	9.121 638 1069	.109 629 4315	17
18	3.996 019 4992	37.450 243 7398	.026 702 0959	.250 249 0291	9.371 887 1360	.106 702 0959	18
19	4.315 701 0591	41.446 263 2390	.024 127 6275	.231 712 0640	9.603 599 2000	.104 127 6275	19
20	4.660 957 1438	45.761 964 2981	.021 852 2088	.214 548 2074	9.818 147 4074	.101 852 2088	20
	ANNUALLY If compounded annually nominal annual rate is 8%						
21	5.033 833 7154	50.442 921 4420	.019 832 2503	.198 655 7476	10.016 803 1550	.099 832 2503	21
22	5.436 540 4126	55.456 755 1573	.018 032 0684	.183 940 5070	10.200 743 6621	.098 032 0684	22
23	5.871 463 6456	60.893 295 5699	.016 422 1692	.170 315 2843	10.371 058 9464	.096 422 1692	23
24	6.341 180 7372	66.764 759 2155	.014 977 9616	.157 699 3373	10.528 758 2837	.094 977 9616	24
25	6.848 475 1962	73.105 939 9527	.013 678 7791	.146 017 9049	10.674 776 1886	.093 678 7791	25
26	7.396 353 2119	79.954 415 1490	.012 507 1267	.135 201 7638	10.809 977 9524	.092 507 1267	26
27	7.988 061 4689	87.350 768 3609	.011 448 0962	.125 186 8183	10.935 164 7077	.091 448 0962	27
28	8.627 106 3864	95.338 829 8297	.010 488 9057	.115 913 7207	11.051 078 4914	.090 488 9057	28
29	9.317 274 8973	103.965 936 2161	.009 618 5350	.107 327 5192	11.158 406 0106	.089 618 5350	29
30	10.062 656 8891	113.283 211 1134	.008 827 4334	.099 377 3325	11.257 783 3431	.088 827 4334	30
	SEMIANNUALLY If compounded semiannually nominal annual rate is 16%						
31	10.867 669 4402	123.345 868 0025	.008 107 2841	.092 016 0487	11.349 799 3918	.088 107 2841	31
32	11.737 082 9954	134.213 537 4429	.007 450 8132	.085 200 0451	11.434 999 4368	.087 450 8132	32
33	12.676 049 6350	145.950 620 4381	.006 851 6324	.078 888 9304	11.513 888 3674	.085 851 6324	33
34	13.690 133 6059	158.626 670 0732	.006 304 1101	.073 045 3061	11.586 933 6736	.086 304 1101	34
35	14.785 344 2943	172.316 803 6790	.005 803 2646	.067 634 5427	11.654 568 2163	.085 803 2646	35
36	15.968 171 8379	187.102 147 9733	.005 344 6741	.062 624 5766	11.717 192 7928	.085 344 6741	36
37	17.245 625 5849	203.070 319 8112	.004 924 4025	.057 985 7190	11.775 178 5119	.084 924 4025	37
38	18.625 275 6317	220.315 945 3961	.004 538 9361	.053 690 4806	11.828 868 9925	.084 538 9361	38
39	20.115 297 6822	238.941 221 0278	.004 185 1297	.049 713 4080	11.878 582 4004	.084 185 1297	39
40	21.724 521 4968	259.056 518 7100	.003 860 1615	.046 030 9333	11.924 613 3337	.083 860 1615	40
	QUARTERLY If compounded quarterly nominal annual rate is 32%						
41	23.462 483 2165	280.781 040 2068	.003 561 4940	.042 621 2345	11.967 234 5683	.083 561 4940	41
42	25.339 481 8739	304.243 523 4233	.003 286 8407	.039 464 1061	12.006 698 6743	.083 286 8407	42
43	27.366 640 4238	329.583 005 2972	.003 034 1370	.036 540 8389	12.043 239 5133	.083 034 1370	43
44	29.555 971 6577	356.949 645 7210	.002 801 5156	.033 834 1101	12.077 073 6234	.082 801 5156	44
45	31.920 449 3903	386.505 617 3787	.002 587 2845	.031 327 8797	12.108 401 5032	.082 587 2845	45
46	34.474 085 3415	418.426 066 7690	.002 389 9085	.029 007 2961	12.137 408 7992	.082 389 9085	46
47	37.232 012 1688	452.900 152 1105	.002 207 9922	.026 858 6075	12.164 267 4067	.082 207 9922	47
48	40.210 573 1423	490.132 164 2793	.002 040 2660	.024 869 0810	12.189 136 4877	.082 040 2660	48
49	43.427 418 9937	530.342 737 4217	.001 885 5731	.023 026 9268	12.212 163 4145	.081 885 5731	49
50	46.901 612 5132	573.770 156 4154	.001 742 8582	.021 321 2286	12.233 484 6431	.081 742 8582	50
	MONTHLY If compounded monthly nominal annual rate is 96%						
51	50.653 741 5143	620.671 768 9286	.001 611 1575	.019 741 8783	12.253 226 5214	.081 611 1575	51
52	54.706 040 8354	671.325 510 4429	.001 489 5903	.018 279 5169	12.271 506 0383	.081 489 5903	52
53	59.082 524 1023	726.031 551 2783	.001 377 3506	.016 925 4786	12.288 431 5169	.081 377 3506	53
54	63.809 126 0304	785.114 075 3806	.001 273 7003	.015 671 7395	12.304 103 2564	.081 273 7003	54
55	68.913 856 1129	848.923 201 4111	.001 177 9629	.014 510 8699	12.318 614 1263	.081 177 9629	55
56	74.426 964 6019	917.837 057 5239	.001 089 5180	.013 435 9906	12.332 050 1170	.081 089 5180	56
57	80.381 121 7701	992.264 022 1259	.001 007 7963	.012 440 7321	12.344 490 8490	.081 007 7963	57
58	86.811 611 5117	1072.645 143 8959	.000 932 2748	.011 519 1964	12.356 010 0454	.080 932 2748	58
59	93.756 540 4326	1159.456 755 4076	.000 862 4729	.010 665 9226	12.366 675 9680	.080 862 4729	59
60	101.257 063 6672	1253.213 295 8402	.000 797 9488	.009 875 8542	12.376 551 8222	.080 797 9488	60

420 Tables

Value of $1 Compounded at 5-20%

Rate 9%	Periods	Amount of 1: How $1 Left at Compounded Interest Will Grow	Amount of 1 Per Period: How $1 Deposited Periodically Will Grow	Sinking Fund: Periodic Deposit That Will Grow to $1 at Future Date	Present Worth of 1: What $1 Due in the Future is Worth Today	Present Worth of 1 Per Period: What $1 Payable Periodically Is Worth Today	Partial Payment: Annuity Worth $1 Today— Periodic Payment Necessary to Pay a Loan of $1	Periods
.09 Period	1	1.090 000 0000	1.000 000 0000	1.000 000 0000	.917 431 1927	.917 431 1927	1.090 000 0000	1
	2	1.188 100 0000	2.090 000 0000	.478 468 8995	.841 679 9933	1.759 111 1859	.568 468 8995	2
	3	1.295 029 0000	3.278 100 0000	.305 054 7573	.772 183 4801	2.531 294 6660	.395 054 7573	3
	4	1.411 581 6100	4.573 129 0000	.218 668 6621	.708 425 2111	3.239 719 8771	.308 668 6621	4
	5	1.538 623 9549	5.984 710 6100	.167 092 4570	.649 931 3863	3.889 651 2634	.257 092 4570	5
	6	1.677 100 1108	7.523 334 5649	.132 919 7833	.596 267 3269	4.485 918 5902	.222 919 7833	6
	7	1.828 039 1208	9.200 434 6757	.108 690 5168	.547 034 2448	5.032 952 8351	.198 690 5168	7
	8	1.992 562 6417	11.028 473 7966	.090 674 3778	.501 866 2797	5.534 819 1147	.180 674 3778	8
	9	2.171 893 2794	13.021 036 4382	.076 798 8021	.460 427 7795	5.995 246 8943	.166 798 8021	9
	10	2.367 363 6746	15.192 929 7177	.065 820 0899	.422 410 8069	6.417 657 7012	.155 820 0899	10
	11	2.580 426 4053	17.560 293 3923	.056 946 6567	.387 532 8504	6.805 190 5515	.146 946 6567	11
	12	2.812 664 7818	20.140 719 7976	.049 650 5585	.355 534 7251	7.160 725 2766	.139 650 5585	12
	13	3.065 804 6121	22.953 384 5794	.043 566 5597	.326 178 6469	7.486 902 9235	.133 566 5597	13
	14	3.341 727 0272	26.019 189 1915	.038 433 1730	.299 246 4650	7.786 150 3885	.128 433 1730	14
	15	3.642 482 4597	29.360 916 2188	.034 058 8827	.274 538 0413	8.060 688 4299	.124 058 8827	15
	16	3.970 305 8811	33.003 398 6784	.030 299 9097	.251 869 7627	8.312 558 1925	.120 299 9097	16
	17	4.327 633 4104	36.973 704 5595	.027 046 2485	.231 073 1768	8.543 631 3693	.117 046 2485	17
	18	4.717 120 4173	41.301 337 9699	.024 212 2907	.211 993 7402	8.755 625 1094	.114 212 2907	18
	19	5.141 661 2548	46.018 458 3871	.021 730 4107	.194 489 6699	8.950 114 7793	.111 730 4107	19
	20	5.604 410 7678	51.160 119 6420	.019 546 4750	.178 430 8898	9.128 545 6691	.109 546 4750	20
ANNUALLY If compounded annually nominal annual rate is 9%	21	6.108 807 7369	56.764 530 4098	.017 615 6348	.163 698 0640	9.292 243 7331	.107 616 6348	21
	22	6.658 600 4332	62.873 338 1466	.015 904 9930	.150 181 7101	9.442 425 4432	.105 904 9930	22
	23	7.257 874 4722	69.531 938 5798	.014 381 8800	.137 781 3854	9.580 206 8286	.104 381 8800	23
	24	7.911 083 1747	76.789 813 0520	.013 022 5607	.126 404 9408	9.706 611 7694	.103 022 5607	24
	25	8.623 080 6604	84.700 896 2267	.011 806 2505	.115 967 8356	9.822 579 6049	.101 806 2505	25
	26	9.399 157 9198	93.323 976 8871	.010 715 3599	.106 932 5097	9.928 972 1146	.100 715 3599	26
	27	10.245 082 1326	102.723 134 8069	.009 734 9054	.097 607 8070	10.026 579 9217	.099 734 9054	27
	28	11.167 139 5246	112.968 216 9396	.008 852 0473	.089 548 4468	10.116 128 3685	.098 852 0473	28
	29	12.172 182 0818	124.135 356 4641	.008 055 7226	.082 154 5384	10.198 282 9069	.098 055 7226	29
	30	13.267 678 4691	136.307 538 5459	.007 336 3514	.075 371 1361	10.273 654 0430	.097 336 3514	30
SEMIANNUALLY If compounded semiannually nominal annual rate is 18%	31	14.461 769 5314	149.575 217 0150	.006 685 5995	.069 147 8313	10.342 801 8743	.096 685 5995	31
	32	15.763 328 7892	164.036 986 5464	.006 096 1861	.063 438 3773	10.406 240 2517	.096 096 1861	32
	33	17.182 028 3802	179.800 315 3356	.005 561 7255	.058 200 3462	10.464 440 5979	.095 561 7255	33
	34	18.728 410 9344	196.982 343 7158	.005 076 5971	.053 394 8130	10.517 335 4109	.095 076 5971	34
	35.	20.413 967 9185	215.710 754 6502	.004 635 8375	.048 986 0670	10.566 821 4779	.094 635 8375	35
	36	22.251 225 0312	236.124 722 5687	.004 235 0500	.044 941 3459	10.611 762 8237	.094 235 0500	36
	37	24.253 835 2840	258.375 947 5999	.003 870 3293	.041 230 5925	10.652 993 4163	.093 870 3293	37
	38	26.436 680 4595	282.629 782 8839	.003 538 1975	.037 826 2317	10.690 819 6480	.093 538 1975	38
	39	28.815 981 7009	309.066 463 3434	.003 235 5500	.034 702 9648	10.725 522 6128	.093 235 5500	39
	40	31.409 420 0540	357.882 445 0443	.002 959 6092	.031 837 5824	10.757 360 1952	.092 959 6092	40
QUARTERLY If compounded quarterly nominal annual rate is 36%	41	34.236 267 8588	369.291 865 0983	.002 707 8853	.029 208 7912	10.786 568 9865	.092 707 8853	41
	42	37.317 531 9661	403.528 132 9572	.002 478 1420	.026 797 0562	10.813 366 0426	.092 478 1420	42
	43	40.676 109 8431	440.845 664 9233	.002 263 3675	.024 584 4552	10.837 950 4978	.092 268 3675	43
	44	44.336 959 7290	481.521 774 7664	.002 076 7493	.022 554 5461	10.860 505 0439	.092 076 7493	44
	45	48.327 286 1046	525.858 734 4954	.001 901 6514	.020 692 2441	10.881 197 2880	.091 901 6514	45
	46	52.676 741 8540	574.186 020 6000	.001 741 5959	.018 983 7102	10.900 180 9981	.091 741 5959	46
	47	57.417 648 6209	626.862 762 4540	.001 595 2455	.017 416 2479	10.917 597 2460	.091 595 2455	47
	48	62.585 236 9967	684.280 411 0748	.001 461 3892	.015 978 2090	10.933 575 4550	.091 461 3892	48
	49	68.217 908 3264	746.865 648 0716	.001 338 9289	.014 658 9074	10.948 234 3624	.091 338 9289	49
	50	74.357 520 0758	815.083 556 3980	.001 226 8681	.013 448 5389	10.961 682 9013	.091 226 8681	50
MONTHLY If compounded monthly nominal annual rate is 108%	51	81.049 696 8826	889.441 076 4738	.001 124 3016	.012 338 1091	10.974 021 0104	.091 124 3016	51
	52	88.344 169 6021	970.490 773 3565	.001 030 4065	.011 319 3661	10.985 340 3765	.091 030 4065	52
	53	96.295 144 8663	1058.834 942 9585	.000 944 4343	.010 384 7396	10.995 725 1160	.090 944 4343	53
	54	104.961 707 9042	1155.130 087 8248	.000 865 7034	.008 527 2840	11.005 252 4000	.090 865 7034	54
	55	114.408 261 6156	1260.091 795 7290	.000 793 5930	.008 740 6275	11.013 993 0276	.090 793 5930	55
	56	124.705 005 1610	1374.500 057 3447	.000 727 5373	.008 018 9243	11.022 011 9519	.090 727 5373	56
	57	135.928 455 6255	1499.205 062 5057	.000 667 0202	.007 356 8113	11.029 368 7632	.090 667 0202	57
	58	148.162 016 6318	1635.133 518 1312	.000 611 5709	.006 749 3682	11.036 118 1314	.090 611 6709	58
	59	161.496 598 1287	1783.295 534 7630	.000 560 7595	.006 192 0809	11.042 310 2123	.090 560 7595	59
	60	176.031 291 9602	1944.792 132 8917	.000 514 1938	.006 680 8082	11.047 991 0204	.090 514 1938	60

Tables 421

Value of $1 Compounded at 5-20%

Rate: 10%

	Periods	Amount of 1: How $1 Left at Compounded Interest Will Grow	Amount of 1 Per Period: How $1 Deposited Periodically Will Grow	Sinking Fund: Periodic Deposit That Will Grow to $1 at Future Date	Present Worth of 1: What $1 Due in the Future is Worth Today	Present Worth of 1 Per Period: What $1 Payable Periodically Is Worth Today	Partial Payment: Annuity Worth $1 Today— Periodic Payment Necessary to Pay a Loan of $1	Periods
	1	1.100 000 0000	1.000 000 0000	1.000 000 0000	.909 090 9091	.909 090 9091	1.100 000 0000	1
	2	1.210 000 0000	2.100 000 0000	.476 190 4762	.826 446 2810	1.735 537 1901	.576 190 4762	2
	3	1.331 000 0000	3.310 000 0000	.302 114 8036	.751 314 8009	2.486 851 9910	.402 114 8036	3
.1 Per Period	4	1.464 100 0000	4.641 000 0000	.215 470 8037	.683 013 4554	3.169 865 4463	.315 470 8037	4
	5	1.610 510 0000	6.105 100 0000	.163 797 4808	.620 921 3231	3.790 786 7694	.263 797 4808	5
	6	1.771 561 0000	7.715 610 0000	.129 607 3804	.564 473 9301	4.355 260 6995	.229 607 3804	6
	7	1.948 717 1000	9.487 171 0000	.105 405 4997	.513 158 1182	4.868 418 8177	.205 405 4997	7
	8	2.143 588 8100	11.435 888 1000	.087 444 0176	.466 507 3802	5.334 926 1979	.187 444 0176	8
	9	2.357 947 6910	13.579 476 9100	.073 640 5391	.424 097 6184	5.759 023 8163	.173 640 5391	9
	10	2.593 742 4601	15.937 424 6010	.062 745 3949	.385 543 2894	6.144 567 1057	.162 745 3949	10
	11	2.853 116 7061	18.531 167 0611	.053 963 1420	.350 493 8995	6.495 061 0052	.153 963 1420	11
	12	3.138 428 3767	21.384 283 7672	.046 763 3151	.318 630 8177	6.813 691 8229	.146 763 3151	12
	13	3.452 271 2144	24.522 712 1439	.040 778 5238	.289 664 3797	7.103 356 2026	.140 778 5238	13
	14	3.797 498 3358	27.974 983 3583	.035 746 2232	.263 331 2543	7.366 687 4569	.135 746 2232	14
	15	4.177 248 1694	31.772 481 6942	.031 473 7769	.239 392 0494	7.606 079 5063	.131 473 7769	15
	16	4.594 972 9864	35.949 729 8636	.027 816 6207	.217 629 1358	7.823 708 6421	.127 816 6207	16
	17	5.054 470 2850	40.544 702 8499	.024 664 1344	.197 844 6689	8.021 553 3110	.124 664 1344	17
	18	5.559 917 3135	45.599 173 1349	.021 930 2222	.179 858 7899	8.201 412 1009	.121 930 2222	18
	19	6.115 909 0448	51.159 090 4484	.019 546 8682	.163 507 9908	8.364 920 0917	.119 546 8682	19
	20	6.727 499 9493	57.274 999 4933	.017 459 6248	.148 643 6280	8.513 563 7198	.117 459 6248	20
ANNUALLY If compounded annually nominal annual rate is 10%	21	7.400 249 9443	64.002 499 4426	.015 624 3898	.135 130 5709	8.648 694 2907	.115 624 3898	21
	22	8.140 274 9387	71.402 749 3868	.014 005 0630	.122 845 9736	8.771 540 2643	.114 005 0630	22
	23	9.954 302 4326	79.543 024 3255	.012 571 8127	.111 678 1578	8.883 218 4221	.112 571 8127	23
	24	9.849 732 6758	88.497 326 7581	.011 299 7764	.101 525 5980	8.984 744 0201	.111 299 7764	24
	25	10.834 705 9434	98.347 059 4339	.010 168 0722	.092 295 9982	9.077 040 0182	.110 168 0722	25
	26	11.918 176 5377	109.181 765 3773	.009 159 0386	.083 905 4529	9.160 945 4711	.109 159 0386	26
	27	13.109 994 1915	121.099 941 9150	.008 257 6423	.076 277 6844	9.237 223 1556	.108 257 6423	27
	28	14.420 993 6106	134.209 936 1065	.007 451 0132	.069 343 3495	9.306 566 5051	.107 451 0132	28
	29	15.863 092 9717	148.630 929 7171	.006 728 0747	.063 039 4086	9.369 605 9137	.106 728 0747	29
	30	17.449 402 2689	164.494 022 6889	.006 079 2483	.057 308 5533	9.426 914 4670	.106 079 2483	30
SEMIANNUALLY If compounded semiannually nominal annual rate is 20%	31	19.194 342 4958	181.943 424 9578	.005 496 2140	.052 098 6848	9.479 013 1518	.105 496 2140	31
	32	21.113 776 7454	201.137 767 4535	.004 971 7167	.047 362 4407	9.526 375 5926	.104 971 7167	32
	33	23.225 154 4199	222.251 544 1989	.004 499 4063	.043 056 7643	9.569 432 3569	.104 499 4063	33
	34	25.547 669 8619	245.476 698 6188	.004 073 7064	.039 142 5139	9.608 574 8699	.104 073 7064	34
	35	28.102 436 8481	271.024 368 4806	.003 689 7051	.035 584 1027	9.644 158 9726	.103 689 7051	35
	36	30.912 680 5329	299.126 805 3287	.003 343 0638	.032 349 1843	9.676 508 1569	.103 343 0638	36
	37	34.003 948 5862	330.039 485 8616	.003 029 9405	.029 408 3494	9.705 916 5063	.103 029 9405	37
	38	37.404 343 4448	364.043 434 4477	.002 746 9250	.026 734 8631	9.732 651 3694	.102 746 9250	38
	39	41.144 777 7893	401.447 777 8925	.002 490 9840	.024 304 4210	9.756 955 7903	.102 490 9840	39
	40	45.259 255 5682	442.592 555 6818	.002 259 4144	.022 094 9282	9.779 050 7185	.102 259 4144	40
QUARTERLY If compounded quarterly nominal annual rate is 40%	41	49.785 181 1250	487.851 811 2499	.002 049 8028	.020 086 2983	9.799 137 0168	.102 049 8028	41
	42	54.763 699 2375	537.636 992 3749	.001 859 9911	.018 260 2712	9.817 397 2880	.101 859 9911	42
	43	60.240 069 1612	592.400 691 6124	.001 688 0466	.016 600 2465	9.833 997 5345	.101 688 0466	43
	44	66.264 076 0774	652.640 760 7737	.001 532 2365	.015 091 1332	9.849 088 6678	.101 532 2365	44
	45	72.890 483 6851	718.904 836 8510	.001 391 0347	.013 719 2120	9.862 807 8798	.101 391 0347	45
	46	80.179 532 0536	791.795 320 5361	.001 262 9527	.012 472 0109	9.875 279 8907	.101 263 9527	46
	47	88.197 485 2590	871.974 852 5897	.001 146 8221	.011 338 1918	9.886 618 0825	.101 146 8221	47
	48	97.017 233 7849	960.172 337 8487	.001 041 4797	.010 307 4470	9.896 925 5295	.101 041 4797	48
	49	106.718 957 1634	1057.189 571 6336	.000 945 9041	.009 370 4064	9.906 295 9359	.100 945 9041	49
	50	117.390 952 8797	1163.908 528 7970	.000 859 1740	.008 518 5513	9.914 814 4872	.100 859 1740	50
MONTHLY If compounded monthly nominal annual rate is 120%	51	129.129 938 1677	1281.299 381 6766	.000 780 4577	.007 744 1375	9.922 558 6247	.100 780 4577	51
	52	142.042 931 9844	1410.429 319 8443	.000 709 0040	.007 040 1250	9.929 598 7498	.100 709 0040	52
	53	156.247 225 1829	1552.472 251 8287	.000 644 1339	.006 400 1137	9.935 998 8634	.100 644 1339	53
	54	171.871 947 7012	1708.719 477 0116	.000 585 2336	.005 818 2851	9.941 817 1486	.100 585 2336	54
	55	189.059 142 4713	1880.591 424 7128	.000 531 7476	.005 289 3501	9.947 106 4987	.100 531 7476	55
	56	207.965 056 7184	2069.650 567 1841	.000 483 1734	.004 808 5001	9.951 914 9988	.100 483 1734	56
	57	228.761 562 3902	2277.615 623 9025	.000 439 0556	.004 371 3637	9.956 286 3626	.100 439 0556	57
	58	251.637 718 6293	2506.377 186 2927	.000 398 9822	.003 973 9670	9.960 260 3296	.100 398 9822	58
	59	276.801 490 4922	2758.014 904 9220	.000 362 5796	.003 612 6973	9.963 873 0269	.100 362 5796	59
	60	304.481 639 5414	3034.816 395 4142	.000 329 5092	.003 284 2703	9.967 157 2972	.100 329 5092	60

Value of $1 Compounded at 5-20%

11%

.11 Per Period

ANNUALLY
If compounded annually
nominal annual rate is
11%

SEMIANNUALLY
If compounded semiannually
nominal annual rate is
22%

QUARTERLY
If compounded quarterly
nominal annual rate is
44%

MONTHLY
If compounded monthly
nominal annual rate is
132%

Periods	Amount of 1: How $1 Left at Compounded Interest Will Grow	Amount of 1 Per Period: How $1 Deposited Periodically Will Grow	Sinking Fund: Periodic Deposit That Will Grow to $1 at Future Date	Present Worth of 1: What $1 Due in the Future is Worth Today	Present Worth of 1 Per Period: What $1 Payable Periodically Is Worth Today	Partial Payment: Annuity Worth $1 Today— Periodic Payment Necessary to Pay a Loan of $1	Periods
1	1.110 000 0000	1.000 000 0000	1.000 000 0000	.900 900 9009	.900 900 9009	1.110 000 0000	1
2	1.232 100 0000	2.110 000 0000	.473 933 6493	.811 622 4332	1.712 523 3341	.583 933 6493	2
3	1.367 631 0000	3.342 100 0000	.299 213 0696	.731 191 3813	2.443 714 7154	.409 213 0696	3
4	1.518 070 4100	4.709 731 0000	.212 326 3515	.658 730 9741	3.102 445 6896	.322 326 3515	4
5	1.685 058 1551	6.227 801 4100	.160 570 3095	.593 451 3281	3.695 897 0176	.270 570 3095	5
6	1.870 414 5522	7.912 859 5651	.126 376 5636	.534 640 8361	4.230 537 8537	.236376 5636	6
7	2.076 160 1529	9.783 274 1173	.102 215 2695	.481 658 4109	4.712 196 2646	.212 215 2695	7
8	2.304 537 7697	11.859 434 2702	.084 321 0542	.433 926 4963	5.146 122 7609	.194 321 0542	8
9	2.558 036 9244	14.163 972 0399	.070 601 6644	.390 924 7714	5.537 047 5324	.180 601 6644	9
10	2.839 420 9861	16.722 008 9643	.059 801 4271	.352 184 4788	5.889 232 0111	.169 801 4271	10
11	3.151 757 2945	19.561 429 9503	.051 121 0071	.317 283 3142	6.206 515 3254	.161 121 0071	11
12	3.498 450 5969	22.713 187 2449	.044 027 2864	.285 840 8236	6.492 356 1490	.154 027 2864	12
13	3.883 280 1626	26.211 637 8418	.038 150 9925	.257 514 2555	6.749 870 4045	.148 150 9925	13
14	4.310 440 9805	30.094 918 0044	.033 228 2015	.231 994 8248	6.981 865 2293	.143 228 2015	14
15	4.784 589 4883	34.405 358 9849	.029 065 2395	.209 004 3467	7.190 869 5759	.139 065 2395	15
16	5.310 894 3321	39.189 948 4732	.025 516 7470	.188 292 2042	7.379 161 7801	.135 516 7470	16
17	5.895 092 7086	44.500 842 8053	.022 471 4845	.169 632 6164	7.548 794 3965	.132 471 4845	17
18	6.543 552 9065	50.895 935 5139	.019 842 8701	.152 822 1769	7.701 616 5734	.129 842 8701	18
19	7.263 343 7262	56.939 488 4204	.017 562 5041	.137 677 6369	7.839 294 2103	.127 562 5041	19
20	8.062 311 5361	64.202 832 1466	.015 575 6369	.124 033 9071	7.963 328 1174	.125 575 6369	20
21	8.949 165 8051	72.265 143 6828	.013 837 9300	.111 742 2586	8.075 070 3760	.123 837 9300	21
22	9.933 574 0437	81.214 309 4879	.012 313 1011	.100 668 7015	8.175 739 0775	.122 313 1011	22
23	11.026 267 1885	91.147 883 5315	.010 971 1818	.090 692 5239	8.266 431 6013	.120 971 1818	23
24	12.239 156 5792	102.174 150 7200	.009 787 2113	.081 704 9764	8.348 136 5778	.119 787 2113	24
25	13.585 463 8029	114.413 307 2992	.008 740 2421	.073 608 0869	8.421 744 6647	.118 740 2421	25
26	15.079 864 8212	127.998 771 1021	.007 812 5750	.066 313 5918	8.488 058 2565	.117 812 5750	26
27	16.738 649 9516	143.078 635 9233	.006 989 1636	.059 741 9746	8.547 800 2310	.116 989 1636	27
28	18.579 901 4462	159.817 285 8749	.006 257 1454	.053 821 5987	8.601 621 8298	.116 257 1454	28
29	20.623 690 6053	178.397 187 3211	.005 605 4695	.048 487 9268	8.650 109 7565	.115 605 4695	29
30	22.892 296 5719	199.020 877 9265	.005 024 5985	.043 682 8169	8.693 792 5735	.115 024 5985	30
31	25.410 449 1948	221.913 174 4984	.004 506 2669	.039 353 8891	8.733 146 4626	.114 506 2669	31
32	28.205 598 6063	247.323 623 6932	.004 043 2854	.035 453 9542	8.768 600 4167	.114 043 2854	32
33	31.308 214 4529	275.529 222 2995	.003 629 3791	.031 940 4992	8.800 540 9160	.113 629 3791	33
34	34.752 118 0428	306.837 436 7524	.003 259 0547	.028 775 2245	8.829 316 1405	.113 259 0547	34
35	38.574 851 0275	341,589 554 7952	.002 927 4900	.025 923 6257	8.855 239 7662	.112 927 4900	35
36	42.818 084 6405	380.164 405 8226	.002 630 4409	.023 354 6178	8.878 594 3840	.112 630 4409	36
37	47.528 073 9509	422.982 490 4631	.002 364 1641	.021 040 1962	8.899 634 5802	.112 364 1641	37
38	52.756 162 0855	470.510 564 4141	.002 125 3508	.018 955 1317	8.918 589 7119	.112 125 3508	38
39	58.559 339 9150	523.266 726 4996	.001 911 0713	.017 076 6952	8.935 666 4071	.111 911 0713	39
40	65.000 867 3056	581.826 066 4146	.001 718 7267	.015 384 4101	8.951 050 8172	.111 718 7267	40
41	72.150 962 7092	646.826 933 7202	.001 546 0086	.013 859 8289	8.964 910 6461	.111 546 0086	41
42	80.087 568 6072	718.977 896 4294	.001 390 8633	.012 486 3324	8.977 396 9785	.111 390 8633	42
43	88.897 201 1540	799.065 465 0366	.001 251 4619	.011 248 9481	8.988 645 9266	.111 251 4619	43
44	98.675 893 2810	887.962 666 1906	.001 126 1735	.010 134 1875	8.998 780 1140	.111 126 1735	44
45	109.530 241 5419	986.638 559 4716	.001 013 5424	.009 129 8986	9.007 910 0126	.111 013 5424	45
46	121.578 568 1115	1096.168 801 0135	.000 912 2683	.008 225 1339	9.016 135 1465	.110 912 2683	46
47	134.952 210 6037	1217.747 369 1250	.000 821 1884	.007 410 0305	9.023 545 1770	.110 821 1884	47
48	149.796 953 7702	1352.699 579 7287	.000 739 2624	.006 675 7032	9.030 220 8802	.110 739 2624	48
49	166.274 618 6849	1502.496 533 4989	.000 665 5589	.006 014 1470	9.036 235 0272	.110 665 5589	49
50	184.564 826 7402	1668.771 152 1837	.000 599 2433	.005 418 1505	9.041 653 1777	.110 599 2433	50
51	204.866 957 6816	1853.335 978 9239	.000 539 5676	.004 881 2166	9.046 534 3943	.110 539 5676	51
52	227.402 323 0266	2058.202 936 6056	.000 485 8607	.004 397 4925	9.050 931 8868	.110 485 8607	52
53	252.416 578 5595	2285.605 259 6322	.000 437 5209	.003 961 7049	9.054 893 5917	.110 437 5209	53
54	280.182 402 2011	2538.021 838 1917	.000 394 0076	.003 569 1035	9.058 462 6952	.110 394 0076	54
55	311.002 466 4432	2818.204 240 3928	.000 354 8359	.003 215 4086	9.061 678 1038	.110 354 8359	55
56	345.212 737 7520	3129.206 706 8360	.000 319 5698	.002 896 7645	9.064 574 8683	.110 319 5698	56
57	383.186 138 9047	3474.419 444 5880	.000 287 8179	.002 609 6977	9.067 184 5660	.110 287 8179	57
58	425.336 614 1842	3857.605 583 4927	.000 259 2282	.002 351 0790	9.069 535 6451	.110 259 2282	58
50	472.123 641 7445	4282.942 197 6769	.000 233 4844	.002 118 0892	9.071 653 7343	.110 233 4844	59
60	524.057 242 3363	4755.065 839 4213	.000 210 3020	.001 908 1885	9.073 561 9228	.110 210 3020	60

Tables 423

Value of $1 Compounded at 5-20%

Rate 12%

.12 Per Period

ANNUALLY
If compounded annually nominal annual rate is
12%

SEMIANNUALLY
If compounded semiannually nominal annual rate is
24%

QUARTERLY
If compounded quarterly nominal annual rate is
48%

MONTHLY
If compounded monthly nominal annual rate is
144%

Periods	Amount of 1: How $1 Left at Compounded Interest Will Grow	Amount of 1 Per Period: How $1 Deposited Periodically Will Grow	Sinking Fund: Periodic Deposit That Will Grow to $1 at Future Date	Present Worth of 1: What $1 Due in the Future is Worth Today	Present Worth of 1 Per Period: What $1 Payable Periodically Is Worth Today	Partial Payment: Annuity Worth $1 Today— Periodic Payment Necessary to Pay a Loan of $1	Periods
1	1.120 000 0000	1.000 000 0000	1.000 000 0000	.892 857 1429	.892 857 1429	1.120 000 0000	1
2	1.254 400 0000	2.120 000 0000	.471 698 1132	.797 193 8776	1.690 051 0204	.591 698 1132	2
3	1.404 928 0000	3.374 400 0000	.296 349 9806	.711 780 2478	2.401 831 2682	.416 348 9806	3
4	1.573 519 3600	4.779 328 0000	.209 234 4363	.635 518 0784	3.037 349 3466	.329 234 4363	4
5	1.762 341 6832	6.352 847 3600	.157 409 7319	.567 426 8557	3.604 776 2023	.277 409 7319	5
6	1.973 822 6852	8.115 189 0432	.123 225 7184	.506 631 1212	4.111 407 3235	.243 225 7184	6
7	2.210 681 4074	10.089 011 7284	.099 117 7359	.452 349 2153	4.563 756 5389	.219 117 7359	7
8	2.475 963 1763	12.299 693 1358	.081 302 8414	.403 883 2280	4.967 639 7668	.201 302 8414	8
9	2.773 078 7575	14.775 656 3121	.067 678 8888	.360 610 0250	5.328 249 7918	.187 678 8888	9
10	3.105 848 2083	17.548 735 0695	.056 984 1642	.321 973 2366	5.650 223 0284	.176 984 1642	10
11	3.478 549 9933	20.654 583 2779	.048 415 4043	.287 476 1041	5.937 699 1325	.168 415 4043	11
12	3.895 975 9925	24.133 133 2712	.041 436 8076	.256 675 0929	6.194 374 2255	.161 436 8076	12
13	4.363 493 1117	28.029 109 2638	.035 677 1951	.229 174 1901	6.423 548 4156	.155 677 1951	13
14	4.887 112 2851	32.392 602 3754	.030 871 2461	.204 619 8126	6.628 168 2282	.150 871 2461	14
15	5.473 565 7593	37.279 714 6605	.026 824 2396	.182 696 2613	6.810 864 4895	.146 824 2396	15
16	6.130 393 6504	42.753 280 4197	.023 390 0180	.163 121 6618	6.973 986 1513	.143 390 0180	16
17	6.866 040 8884	48.883 674 0701	.020 456 7275	.145 644 3409	7.119 630 4922	.140 456 7275	17
18	7.689 965 7950	55.749 714 9585	.017 937 3114	.130 039 5901	7.249 670 0824	.137 937 3114	18
19	8.612 761 6904	63.439 680 7535	.015 763 0049	.116 106 7769	7.365 776 8592	.135 763 0049	19
20	9.646 293 0933	72.052 442 4440	.013 878 7800	.103 666 7651	7.469 443 6243	.133 878 7800	20
21	10.803 848 2645	81.698 735 5372	.012 240 0915	.092 559 6117	7.562 003 2360	.132 240 0915	21
22	12.100 310 0562	92.502 583 8017	.010 810 5088	.082 642 5104	7.644 645 7464	.130 810 5088	22
23	13.552 347 2629	104.602 893 8579	.009 559 9650	.073 787 9557	7.718 433 7022	.129 559 9650	23
24	15.178 628 9345	118.155 241 1209	.008 463 4417	.065 882 1033	7.784 315 8055	.128 463 4417	24
25	17.000 064 4066	133.333 870 0554	.007 499 9698	.058 823 3066	7.843 139 1121	.127 499 9698	25
26	19.040 072 1354	150.333 934 4620	.006 651 8581	.052 520 8094	7.895 659 9215	.126 651 8581	26
27	21.324 880 7917	169.374 006 5974	.005 904 0937	.046 893 5798	7.942 553 5013	.125 904 0937	27
28	23.883 866 4867	190.698 887 3891	.005 243 8691	.041 869 2677	7.984 422 7690	.125 243 8691	28
29	26.749 930 4651	214.582 753 8758	.004 660 2068	.037 383 2747	8.021 806 0438	.124 660 2068	29
30	29.959 922 1209	241.332 684 3409	.004 143 6576	.033 377 9239	8.055 183 9677	.124 143 6576	30
31	33.555 112 7754	271.292 606 4618	.003 686 0570	.029 801 7177	8.084 985 6854	.123 686 0570	31
32	37.581 726 3085	304.847 719 2373	.003 280 3263	.026 608 6766	8.111 594 3620	.123 280 3263	32
33	42.091 533 4655	342.429 445 5457	.002 920 3096	.023 757 7469	8.135 352 1089	.122 920 3096	33
34	47.142 517 4813	384.520 979 0112	.002 600 6383	.021 212 2740	8.156 564 3830	.122 600 6383	34
35	52.799 619 5791	431.663 496 4926	.002 316 6193	.018 939 5304	8.175 503 9134	.122 316 6193	35
36	59.135 573 9286	484.463 116 0717	.002 064 1406	.016 910 2950	8.192 414 2084	.122 064 1406	36
37	66.231 842 8000	543.598 690 0003	.001 839 5924	.015 098 4777	8.207 512 6860	.121 839 5924	37
38	74.179 663 9360	609.830 532 8003	.001 639 7998	.013 480 7836	8.220 993 4697	.121 639 7998	38
39	83.081 223 6084	684.010 196 7363	.001 461 9665	.012 036 4140	8.233 029 8836	.121 461 9665	39
40	93.050 970 4414	767.091 420 3447	.001 303 6256	.010 746 7982	8.243 776 6818	.121 303 6256	40
41	104.217 086 8943	860.142 390 7861	.001 162 5982	.009 595 3555	8.253 372 0373	.121 162 5982	41
42	116.723 137 3216	964.359 477 6804	.001 036 9577	.008 567 2817	8.261 939 3190	.121 036 9577	42
43	130.729 913 8002	1081.082 615 0020	.000 924 9987	.007 649 3587	8.269 588 6777	.120 924 9987	43
44	146.417 503 4563	1211.812 528 8023	.000 825 2102	.006 829 7845	8.276 418 4623	.120 825 2102	44
45	163.987 603 8710	1358.230 032 2586	.000 736 2523	.006 098 0219	8.282 516 4842	.120 736 2523	45
46	183.666 116 3355	1522.217 636 1296	.000 656 9363	.005 444 6624	8.287 961 1466	.120 656 9363	46
47	205.706 050 2958	1705.883 752 4651	.000 586 2064	.004 861 3057	8.292 822 4523	.120 586 2064	47
48	230.390 776 3313	1911.589 802 7609	.000 523 1248	.004 340 4515	8.297 162 9038	.120 523 1248	48
49	258.037 669 4911	2141.980 579 0923	.000 466 8576	.003 874 4032	8.301 038 3070	.120 466 8576	49
50	289.002 189 8300	2400.018 248 5833	.000 416 8635	.003 460 1814	8.304 498 4884	.120 416 6635	50
51	323.682 452 6096	2689.020 438 4133	.000 371 8826	.003 089 4477	8.307 587 9361	.120 371 8826	51
52	362.524 346 9228	3012.702 891 0229	.000 331 9279	.002 758 4354	8.310 346 3715	.120 331 9279	52
53	406.027 268 5535	3375.227 237 9457	.000 296 2763	.002 462 8888	8.312 809 2603	.120 296 2763	53
54	454.750 540 7799	3781.254 506 4992	.000 264 4625	.002 199 0078	8.315 008 2681	.120 264 4625	54
55	509.320 605 6735	4236.005 047 2791	.000 236 0715	.001 963 3998	8.316 971 6679	.120 236 0715	55
56	570.439 078 3543	4745.325 652 9525	.000 210 7337	.001 753 0356	8.318 724 7035	.120 210 7337	56
57	638.891 767 7568	5315.764 731 3069	.000 188 1197	.001 565 2103	8.320 289 9138	.120 188 1197	57
58	715.558 779 8876	5954.656 499 0637	.000 167 9358	.001 397 5092	8.321 687 4231	.120 167 9358	58
59	801.425 833 4742	6670.215 278 9513	.000 149 9202	.001 247 7761	8.322 935 1992	.120 149 9202	59
60	897.596 933 4911	7471.641 112 4255	.000 133 8394	.001 114 0858	8.324 049 2850	.120 133 8394	60

424 Tables

Value of $1 Compounded at 5-20%

Rate 13%	Periods	Amount of 1: How $1 Left at Compounded Interest Will Grow	Amount of 1 Per Period: How $1 Deposited Periodically Will Grow	Sinking Fund: Periodic Deposit That Will Grow to $1 at Future Date	Present Worth of 1: What $1 Due in the Future is Worth Today	Present Worth of 1 Per Period: What $1 Payable Periodically Is Worth Today	Partial Payment: Annuity Worth $1 Today— Periodic Payment Necessary to Pay a Loan of $1	Periods
.13 Per Period	1	1.130 000 0000	1.000 000 0000	1.000 000 0000	.884 955 7522	.884 955 7522	1.130 000 0000	1
	2	1.276 900 0000	2.130 000 0000	.469 483 5681	.783 146 6834	1.668 102 4356	.599 483 5681	2
	3	1.442 897 0000	3.406 900 0000	.293 521 9701	.693 050 1623	2.361 152 5979	.423 521 9701	3
	4	1.630 473 6100	4.849 797 0000	.206 194 1974	.613 318 7277	2.974 471 3255	.336 194 1974	4
	5	1.842 435 1793	6.480 270 6100	.154 314 5434	.542 759 9360	3.517 231 2615	.284 314 5434	5
	6	2.081 951 7526	8.322 705 7893	.120 153 2321	.480 318 5274	3.997 549 7890	.250 153 2321	6
	7	2.352 605 4804	10.404 657 5419	.096 110 8038	.425 060 6437	4.422 610 4327	.226 110 8038	7
	8	2.658 444 1929	12.757 263 0224	.078 386 7196	.376 159 8617	4.798 770 2944	.208 386 7196	8
	9	3.004 041 9380	15.415 707 2153	.064 868 9020	.332 884 8834	5.131 655 1278	.194 868 9020	9
	10	3.394 567 3899	18.419 749 1532	.054 289 5558	.294 588 3481	5.426 243 4760	.184 289 5558	10
	11	3.835 861 1506	21.814 316 5432	.045 841 4545	.260 697 6532	5.686 941 1292	.175 841 4545	11
	12	4.334 521 1002	25.650 177 6938	.038 986 0847	.230 705 8878	5.917 647 0170	.168 986 0847	12
	13	4.898 011 1032	29.984 700 7940	.033 350 3411	.204 164 5025	6.121 811 5194	.163 350 3411	13
	14	5.534 752 5466	34.882 711 8972	.028 667 4959	.180 676 5509	6.302 488 0703	.158 667 4959	14
	15	6.254 270 3777	40.417 464 4438	.024 741 7797	.159 890 7530	6.462 378 8233	.154 741 7797	15
	16	7.067 325 5268	46.671 734 8215	.021 426 2445	.141 496 2416	6.603 875 0648	.151 426 2445	16
	17	7.986 077 8453	53.739 060 3483	.018 608 4385	.125 217 9129	6.729 092 9777	.148 608 4385	17
	18	9.024 267 9652	61.725 138 1936	.016 200 8548	.110 812 3123	6.839 905 2900	.146 200 8548	18
	19	10.197 422 8006	70.749 406 1588	.014 134 3943	.098 063 9932	6.937 969 2832	.144 134 3943	19
	20	11.523 087 7647	80.946 828 9594	.012 353 7884	.086 782 2949	7.024 751 5781	.142 353 7884	20
ANNUALLY If compounded annually nominal annual rate is 13%	21	13.021 089 1741	92.469 916 7241	.010 814 3279	.076 798 4910	7.101 550 0691	.140 814 3279	21
	22	14.713 830 7668	105.491 005 8983	.009 479 4811	.067 963 2664	7.169 513 3355	.139 479 4811	22
	23	16.626 628 7665	120.204 836 6650	.008 319 1328	.060 144 4835	7.229 657.8190	.138 319 1328	23
	24	18.788 090 5061	136.831 465 4315	.007 308 2605	.053 225 2067	7.282 883 0257	.137 308 2605	24
	25	21.230 542 2719	155.619 555 9376	.006 425 9276	.047 101 9528	7.329 984 9785	.136 425 9276	25
	26	23.990 512 7672	176.850 098 2095	.005 654 5063	.041 683 1441	7.371 668 1225	.135 654 5063	26
	27	27.109 279 4270	200.840 610 9767	.004 979 0727	.036 887 7381	7.408 555 8607	.134 979 0727	27
	28	30.633 485 7525	227.949 890 4037	.004 386 9291	.032 644 0160	7.441 199 8767	.134 386 9291	28
	29	34.615 838 9003	258.583 376 1562	.003 867 2246	.028 888 5098	7.470 088 3864	.133 867 2246	29
	30	39.115 897 9573	293.199 215 0565	.003 410 6503	.025 565 0529	7.495 653 4393	.133 410 6503	30
SEMIANNUALLY If compounded semiannually nominal annual rate is 26%	31	44.200 964 6918	332.315 113 0138	.003 009 1921	.022 623 9406	7.518 277 3799	.133 009 1921	31
	32	49.947 090 1017	376.516 077 7056	.002 655 9291	.020 021 1864	7.538 298 5663	.132 655 9291	32
	33	56.440 211 8150	426.463 167 8073	.002 344 8684	.017 717 8641	7.556 016 4304	.132 344 8684	33
	34	63.777 439 3509	482.903 379 6223	.002 070 8076	.015 679 5257	7.571 695 9561	.132 070 8076	34
	35	72.068 506 4665	546.680 818 9732	.001 829 2209	.013 875 6865	7.585 571 6425	.131 829 2209	35
	36	81.437 412 3072	618.749 325 4397	.001 616 1634	.012 279 3686	7.597 851 0111	.131 616 1634	36
	37	92.024 275 9071	700.186 737 7469	.001 428 1904	.010 866 6978	7.608 717 7089	.131 428 1904	37
	38	103.987 431 7750	792.211 013 6540	.001 262 2899	.009 616 5468	7.618 334 2557	.131 262 2899	38
	39	117.505 797 9058	896.198 445 4290	.001 115 8243	.008 510 2184	7.626 844 4741	.131 115 8243	39
	40	132.781 551 6335	1013.704 243 3348	.000 986 4810	.007 531 1667	7.634 375 6408	.130 986 4810	40
QUARTERLY If compounded quarterly nominal annual rate is 52%	41	150.043 153 3459	1146.485 794 9683	.000 872 2306	.006 664 7493	7.641 040 3901	.130 872 2306	41
	42	169.548 763 2808	1296.528 948 3141	.000 771 2901	.005 898 0082	7.646 938 3983	.130 771 2901	42
	43	191.590 102 5073	1466.077 711 5950	.000 682 0921	.005 219 4763	7.652 157 8746	.130 682 0921	43
	44	216.496 815 8333	1657.667 814 1023	.000 603 2572	.004 619 0056	7.656 776 8802	.130 603 2572	44
	45	244.641 401 8916	1874.164 629 9356	.000 533 5711	.004 087 6156	7.660 864 4957	.130 533 5711	45
	46	276.444 784 1375	2118.806 031 8273	.000 471 9639	.003 617 3589	7.664 481 8546	.130 471 9639	46
	47	312.382 606 0754	2395.250 815 9648	.000 417 4928	.003 201 2026	7.667 683 0572	.130 417 4928	47
	48	352.992 344 8652	2707.633 422 0402	.000 369 3262	.002 832 9226	7.670 515 9798	.130 369 3262	48
	49	398.881 349 6977	3060.625 766 9055	.000 326 7306	.002 507 0112	7.673 022 9910	.130 326 7306	49
	50	450.735 925 1584	3459.507 116 6032	.000 289 0585	.002 218 5940	7.675 241 5849	.130 289 0585	50
MONTHLY If compounded monthly nominal annual rate is 156%	51	509.331 595 4290	3910.243 041 7616	.000 255 7386	.001 963 3575	7.677 204 9424	.130 255 7386	51
	52	575.544 702 8348	4419.574 637 1906	.000 226 2661	.001 737 4845	7.678 942 4269	.130 226 2661	52
	53	650.365 514 2033	4995.119 340 0254	.000 200 1954	.001 537 5969	7.680 480 0238	.130 200 1954	53
	54	734.913 031 0497	5645.484 854 2287	.000 177 1327	.001 360 7052	7.681 840 7291	.130 177 1327	54
	55	830.451 725 0862	6380.397 885 2784	.000 156 7300	.001 204 1639	7.683 044 8930	.130 156 7300	55
	56	938.410 449 3474	7210.849 610 3646	.000 138 6799	.001 065 6318	7.684 110 5247	.130 138 6799	56
	57	1060.403 807 7626	8149.260 059 7120	.000 122 7105	.000 943 0370	7.685 053 5617	.130 122 7105	57
	58	1198.256 302 7717	9209.663 867 4745	.000 108 5816	.000 834 5460	7.685 888 1077	.130 108 5816	58
	59	1354.029 622 1320	10407.920 170 2462	.000 096 0807	.000 738 5363	7.686 626 6440	.130 096 0807	59
	60	1530.053 473 0092	11763.949 792 3782	.000 085 0199	.000 653 5719	7.687 280 2159	.130 085 0199	60

Tables 425

Value of $1 Compounded at 5-20%

Rate 14%

Periods	Amount of 1: How $1 Left at Compounded Interest Will Grow	Amount of 1 Per Period: How $1 Deposited Periodically Will Grow	Sinking Fund: Periodic Deposit That Will Grow to $1 at Future Date	Present Worth of 1: What $1 Due in the Future is Worth Today	Present Worth of 1 Per Period: What $1 Payable Periodically Is Worth Today	Partial Payment: Annuity Worth $1 Today— Periodic Payment Necessary to Pay a Loan of $1	Periods
1	1.140 000 0000	1.000 000 0000	1.000 000 0000	.877 192 9825	.877 192 9825	1.140 000 0000	1
2	1.299 600 0000	2.140 000 0000	.467 289 7196	.769 467 5285	1.646 660 5109	.607 289 7196	2
3	1.481 544 0000	3.429 600 0000	.290 731 4804	.674 971 5162	2.321 632 0271	.430 731 4804	3
4	1.688 960 1600	4.921 144 0000	.203 204 7833	.592 080 2774	2.913 712 3045	.343 204 7833	4
5	1.925 414 5824	6.610 104 1600	.151 283 5465	.519 368 6644	3.433 080 9689	.291 283 5465	5
6	2.194 972 6239	8.535 518 7424	.117 157 4957	.455 586 5477	3.888 667 5165	.257 157 4957	6
7	2.502 268 7913	10.730 491 3663	.093 192 3773	.399 637 3225	4.288 304 8391	.233 192 3773	7
8	2.852 586 4221	13.332 760 1576	.075 570 0288	.350 559 0549	4.638 863 8939	.215 570 0238	8
9	3.251 948 5212	16.085 346 5797	.062 168 3838	.307 507 9429	4.946 371 8368	.202 168 3838	9
10	3.707 221 3141	19.337 295 1008	.051 713 5408	.269 743 8095	5.216 115 6463	.191 713 5408	10
11	4.226 232 2981	23.044 516 4150	.043 394 2714	.236 617 3768	5.452 733 0231	.183 394 2714	11
12	4.817 904 8198	27.270 748 7131	.036 669 3269	.207 559 1024	5.660 292 1255	.176 669 3269	12
13	5.492 411 4946	32.088 653 5329	.031 163 6635	.182 069 3881	5.842 361 5136	.171 163 6635	13
14	6.261 349 1038	37.581 065 0275	.026 609 1448	.159 709 9896	6.002 071 5032	.166 609 1448	14
15	7.137 937 9784	43.842 414 1313	.022 808 9630	.140 096 4821	6.142 167 9852	.162 808 9630	15
16	8.137 249 2954	50.980 352 1097	.019 615 4000	.122 891 6509	6.265 059 6362	.159 615 4000	16
17	9.276 464 1967	59.117 601 4051	.016 915 4359	.107 799 6938	6.372 859 3300	.156 915 4359	17
18	10.575 169 1843	68.394 065 6018	.014 621 1516	.094 561 1349	6.467 420 4649	.154 621 1516	18
19	12.055 692 8700	78.969 234 7861	.012 663 1593	.082 948 3640	6.550 368 8288	.152 663 1593	19
20	13.743 489 8719	91.024 927 6561	.010 986 0016	.072 761 7228	6.623 130 5516	.150 986 0016	20
21	15.667 578 4539	104.768 417 5280	.009 544 8612	.063 826 0726	6.686 956 6242	.149 544 8612	21
22	17.861 039 4375	120.435 995 9819	.008 303 1654	.055 987 7830	6.742 944 4072	.148 303 1654	22
23	20.361 584 9587	138.297 035 4193	.007 230 8130	.049 112 0903	6.792 056 4976	.147 230 8130	23
24	23.212 206 8529	158.658 620 3780	.006 302 8406	.043 080 7810	6.835 137 2786	.146 302 8406	24
25	26.461 915 8123	181.870 827 2310	.005 498 4079	.037 790 1588	6.872 927 4373	.145 498 4079	25
26	30.166 584 0261	208.332 743 0433	.004 800 0136	.033 149 2621	6.906 076 6994	.144 800 0136	26
27	34.389 905 7897	238.499 327 0694	.004 192 8839	.029 078 3001	6.935 154 9995	.144 192 8839	27
28	39.204 492 6003	272.889 232 8591	.003 664 4905	.025 507 2808	6.960 662 2803	.143 664 4905	28
29	44.693 121 5643	312.093 725 4594	.003 204 1657	.022 374 8077	6.933 037 0879	.143 204 1657	29
30	50.950 158 5833	356.786 847 0237	.002 802 7939	.019 627 0243	7.002 664 1122	.142 802 7939	30
31	58.083 180 7850	407.737 005 6070	.002 452 5613	.017 216 6880	7.019 880 8002	.142 452 5613	31
32	66.214 826 0949	465.820 186 3920	.002 146 7511	.015 102 3579	7.034 983 1581	.142 146 7511	32
33	75.484 901 7482	532.035 012 4868	.001 879 5755	.013 247 6823	7.048 230 8404	.141 879 5755	33
34	86.052 787 9929	607.519 914 2350	.001 646 0366	.011 620 7740	7.059 851 6144	.141 646 0366	34
35	98.100 178 3119	693.572 702 2279	.001 441 8099	.010 193 6614	7.070 045 2758	.141 441 8099	35
36	111.834 203 2756	791.672 880 5398	.001 263 1480	.008 941 8032	7.078 987 0340	.141 263 1480	36
37	127.490 991 7342	903.507 083 8154	.001 106 7982	.007 843 6914	7.086 830 7755	.141 106 7982	37
38	145.339 730 5769	1030.998 075 5495	.000 969 9339	.006 880 4311	7.093 711 2065	.140 969 9339	38
39	165.687 292 8577	1176.337 806 1465	.000 850 0959	.006 035 4659	7.099 746 6724	.140 850 0959	39
40	188.883 513 8578	1342.025 098 9841	.000 745 1425	.005 294 2683	7.105 040 9407	.140 745 1425	40
41	215.327 205 7979	1530.908 612 8419	.000 653 2069	.004 644 0950	7.109 685 0357	.140 653 2069	41
42	245.473 014 6098	1746.235 818 6398	.000 572 6603	.004 073 7675	7.113 758 8033	.140 572 6603	42
43	279.839 236 6549	1991.708 833 2494	.000 502 0814	.003 573 4003	7.117 332 2836	.140 502 0814	43
44	319.016 729 7866	2271.548 069 9043	.000 440 2284	.003 134 6318	7.120 466 9154	.140 440 2284	44
45	363.679 071 9567	2590.564 799 6909	.000 386 0162	.002 749 6771	7.123 216 5925	.140 386 0162	45
46	414.594 142 0307	2954.243 871 6476	.000 338 4951	.002 411 9974	7.125 628 5899	.140 338 4961	46
47	472.637 321 9150	3368.838 013 6783	.000 296 8383	.002 115 7872	7.127 744 3771	.140 296 8383	47
48	538.806 546 9831	3841.475 335 5932	.000 260 3167	.001 855 9537	7.129 600 8308	.140 260 3167	48
49	614.239 463 5607	4380.281 882 5763	.000 228 2958	.001 628 0296	7.131 228 3603	.140 228 2958	49
50	700.232 988 4592	4994.521 346 1370	.000 200 2194	.001 428 0961	7.132 656 4564	.140 200 2194	50
51	798.265 606 8435	5694.754 334 5961	.000 175 6002	.001 252 7159	7.133 909 1723	.140 175 6002	51
52	910.022 791 8015	6493.019 941 4396	.000 154 0115	.001 098 8736	7.135 008 0459	.140 154 0115	52
53	1037.425 982 6538	7403.042 733 2411	.000 135 0796	.000 963 9242	7.135 971 9701	.140 135 0796	53
54	1182.665 620 2253	8440.468 715 8949	.000 118 4768	.000 845 5475	7.136 817 5176	.140 118 4768	54
55	1348.238 807 0568	9623.134 336 1202	.000 103 9162	.000 741 7084	7.137 559 2260	.140 103 9162	55
56	1536.992 240 0448	10971.373 143 1770	.000 091 1463	.000 650 6214	7.138 209 8473	.140 091 1463	56
57	1752.171 153 6510	12508.365 383 2218	.000 079 1264	.000 570 7205	7.138 780 5678	.140 079 9465	57
58	1997.475 115 1622	14260.536 536 8728	.000 070 1236	.000 500 6320	7.139 281 1999	.140 070 1236	58
59	2277.121 631 2849	16258.011 652 0350	.000 061 5081	.000 439 1509	7.139 720 3508	.140 061 5081	59
60	2595.918 659 6648	18535.133 283 3199	.000 053 9516	.000 385 2201	7.140 105 5708	.140 053 9516	60

.14 Per Period

ANNUALLY
If compounded annually nominal annual rate is

14%

SEMIANNUALLY
If compounded semiannually nominal annual rate is

28%

QUARTERLY
If compounded quarterly nominal annual rate is

56%

MONTHLY
If compounded monthly nominal annual rate is

168%

Value of $1 Compounded at 5-20%

Rate	Periods	Amount of 1: How $1 Left at Compounded Interest Will Grow	Amount of 1 Per Period: How $1 Deposited Periodically Will Grow	Sinking Fund: Periodic Deposit That Will Grow to $1 at Future Date	Present Worth of 1: What $1 Due in the Future is Worth Today	Present Worth of 1 Per Period: What $1 Payable Periodically Is Worth Today	Partial Payment: Annuity Worth $1 Today— Periodic Payment Necessary to Pay a Loan of $1	Periods
15%								
	1	1.150 000 0000	1.000 000 0000	1.000 000 0000	.869 565 2174	.869 565 2174	1.150 000 0000	1
	2	1.322 500 0000	2.150 000 0000	.465 116 2791	.756 143 6673	1.625 708 8847	.615 116 2791	2
	3	1.520 875 0000	3.472 500 0000	.287 976 9618	.657 516 2324	2.283 225 1171	.437 976 9618	3
.15	4	1.749 006 2500	4.993 375 0000	.200 265 3516	.571 753 2456	2.854 978 3627	.350 265 3516	4
Per Period	5	2.011 357 1875	6.742 381 2500	.148 315 5525	.497 176 7353	3.352 155 0980	.298 315 5525	5
	6	2.313 060 7656	8.753 738 4375	.114 236 9066	.432 327 5959	3.784 482 6939	.264 236 9066	6
	7	2.660 019 8805	11.066 799 2031	.090 360 3636	.375 937 0399	4.160 419 7338	.240 360 3636	7
	8	3.059 022 8625	13.726 819 0836	.072 850 0896	.326 901 7738	4.487 321 5077	.222 850 0896	8
	9	3.517 876 2919	16.785 841 9461	.059 574 0150	.284 262 4120	4.771 583 9197	.209 574 0150	9
	10	4.045 557 7357	20.303 718 2381	.049 252 0625	.247 184 7061	5.108 768 6259	.199 252 0625	10
	11	4.652 391 3961	24.349 275 9738	.041 068 9830	.214 943 2227	5.233 711 8486	.191 068 9830	11
	12	5.350 250 1055	29.001 667 3698	.034 480 7761	.186 907 1502	5.420 618 9988	.184 480 7761	12
	13	6.152 787 6213	34.351 917 4753	.029 110 4565	.162 527 9567	5.583 146 9554	.179 110 4565	13
	14	7.075 705 7645	40.504 705 0966	.024 688 4898	.141 328 6580	5.724 475 6134	.174 688 4898	14
	15	8.137 061 6292	47.580 410 8611	.021 017 0526	.122 894 4852	5.847 370 0986	.171 017 0526	15
	16	9.357 620 8735	55.717 472 4902	.017 947 6914	.106 864 7697	5.954 234 8684	.167 947 6914	16
	17	10.761 264 0046	65.075 093 3638	.015 366 8623	.092 925 8867	6.047 160 7551	.165 366 8623	17
	18	12.375 453 6053	75.836 357 3683	.013 186 2874	.080 805 1189	6.127 965 8740	.163 186 2874	18
	19	14.231 771 6460	88.211 810 9736	.011 336 3504	.070 265 3208	6.198 231 1948	.161 336 3504	19
	20	16.366 537 3929	102.443 582 6196	.009 761 4704	.061 100 2789	6.259 331 4737	.159 761 4704	20
ANNUALLY If compounded annually nominal annual rate is	21	18.821 518 0019	118.810 120 0126	.008 416 7914	.053 130 6773	6.312 462 1511	.158 416 7914	21
	22	21.644 745 7022	137.631 638 0145	.007 265 7713	.046 200 5890	6.358 662 7401	.157 265 7713	22
	23	24.891 457 5575	159.276 383 7166	.006 278 3947	.040 174 4252	6.398 837 1653	.156 278 3947	23
	24	28.625 176 1911	184.167 841 2741	.005 429 8296	.034 934 2828	6.433 771 4481	.155 429 8296	24
15%	25	32.918 952 6198	212.793 017 4653	.004 699 4023	.030 377 6372	6.464 149 0853	.154 699 4023	25
	26	37.856 795 5128	245.711 970 0851	.004 069 8058	.026 415 3367	6.490 564 4220	.154 069 8058	26
	27	43.535 314 8397	283.568 765 5978	.003 526 4815	.022 969 8580	6.513 534 2800	.153 526 4815	27
	28	50.065 612 0656	327.104 080 4375	.003 057 1309	.019 973 7896	6.533 508 0695	.153 057 1309	28
	29	57.575 453 8755	377.169 692 5031	.002 651 3265	.017 368 5127	6.550 876 5822	.152 651 3265	29
	30	66.211 771 9568	434.745 146 3786	.002 300 1982	.015 103 0545	6.565 979 6367	.152 300 1982	30
SEMIANNUALLY If compounded semiannually nominal annual rate is	31	76.143 537 7503	500.956 918 3354	.001 996 1796	.013 133 0909	6.579 112 7276	.151 996 1796	31
	32	87.565 068 4128	577.100 456 0857	.001 732 8006	.011 420 0790	6.590 532 8066	.151 732 8006	32
	33	100.699 828 6748	664.665 524 4985	.001 504 5161	.009 930 5035	6.600 463 3101	.151 504 5161	33
	34	115.804 802 9760	765.365 353 1733	.001 306 5655	.008 635 2204	6.609 098 5305	.151 306 5655	34
30%	35	133.175 523 4224	881.170 156 1493	.001 134 8546	.007 508 8873	6.616 607 4178	.151 134 8546	35
	36	153.151 851 9358	1014.345 679 5717	.000 985 8572	.006 522 4672	6.623 136 8851	.150 985 8572	36
	37	176.124 629 7261	1167.497 531 5074	.000 856 5329	.005 677 7976	6.628 814 6827	.150 856 5329	37
	38	202.543 324 1850	1343.622 161 2335	.000 744 2569	.004 937 2153	6.633 751 8980	.150 744 2569	38
	39	232.924 822 8128	1546.165 485 4186	.000 646 7613	.004 293 2307	6.638 045 1287	.150 646 7613	39
	40	267.863 546 2347	1779.090 308 2314	.000 562 0850	.003 733 2441	6.641 778 3728	.150 562 0850	40
QUARTERLY If compounded quarterly nominal annual rate is	41	308.043 078 1699	2046.953 854 4661	.000 488 5308	.003 246 2992	6.645 024 6720	.150 488 5308	41
	42	354.249 539 8954	2354.996 932 6360	.000 424 6290	.002 822 8689	6.647 847 5408	.150 424 6290	42
	43	407.386 970 8797	2709.246 472 5314	.000 369 1063	.002 454 6686	6.650 302 2094	.150 369 1063	43
	44	468.495 016 5117	3116.633 443 4111	.000 320 8590	.002 134 4944	6.652 436 7038	.150 320 8590	44
60%	45	538.769 268 9884	3585.128 459 9227	.000 278 9300	.001 856 8821	6.654 292 7860	.150 278 9300	45
	46	619.584 659 3367	4123.897 728 9111	.000 242 4890	.001 613 9844	6.655 906 7704	.150 242 4890	46
	47	712.522 358 2372	4743.482 388 2478	.000 210 8156	.001 403 4647	6.657 310 2351	.150 210 8156	47
	48	819.400 711 9727	5456.004 746 4850	.000 183 2843	.001 220 4041	6.658 530 6392	.150 183 2843	48
	49	942.310 818 7687	6275.405 458 4577	.000 159 3523	.001 061 2210	6.659 591 8602	.150 159 3523	49
	50	1083.657 441 5840	7217.716 277 2264	.000 138 5480	.000 922 8008	6.660 514 6611	.150 138 5480	50
MONTHLY If compounded monthly nominal annual rate is	51	1246.206 057 8216	8301.373 718 8103	.000 120 4620	.000 802 4355	6.661 317 0966	.150 120 4620	51
	52	1433.136 966 4948	9547.579 776 6319	.000 104 7386	.000 697 7700	6.662 014 8666	.150 104 7386	52
	53	1648.107 511 4690	10980.716 743 1267	.000 091 0687	.000 606 7565	6.662 621 6231	.150 091 0687	53
	54	1895.323 638 1894	12628.824 254 5957	.000 079 1839	.000 527 6144	6.663 149 2375	.150 079 1839	54
180%	55	2179.622 183 9178	14524.147 892 7850	.000 068 8509	.000 458 7971	6.663 608 0326	.150 068 8509	55
	56	2506.565 511 5054	16703.770 076 7028	.000 059 8667	.000 398 9523	6.664 006 9849	.150 059 8667	56
	57	2882.550 338 2312	19210.335 588 2082	.000 052 0553	.000 346 9150	6.664 353 8999	.150 052 0553	57
	58	3314.932 888 9659	22092.885 926 4394	.000 045 2634	.000 301 6652	6.664 655 5651	.150 045 2634	58
	59	3812.172 822 3108	25407.818 815 4053	.000 039 3580	.000 262 3176	6.664 917 8827	.150 039 3580	59
	60	4383.998 745 6574	29219.991 637 7161	.000 034 2231	.000 228 1023	6.665 145 9850	.150 034 2231	60

Tables 427

Value of $1 Compounded at 5-20%

Rate 16%	Periods	Amount of 1: How $1 Left at Compounded Interest Will Grow	Amount of 1 Per Period: How $1 Deposited Periodically Will Grow	Sinking Fund: Periodic Deposit That Will Grow to $1 at Future Date	Present Worth of 1: What $1 Due in the Future is Worth Today	Present Worth of 1 Per Period: What $1 Payable Periodically Is Worth Today	Partial Payment: Annuity Worth $1 Today— Periodic Payment Necessary to Pay a Loan of $1	Periods
	1	1.160 000 0000	1.000 000 0000	1.000 000 0000	.862 068 9655	.862 068 9655	1.160 000 0000	1
	2	1.345 600 0000	2.160 000 0000	.462 962 9630	.743 162 9013	1.605 231 8668	.622 962 9630	2
.16 Per Period	3	1.560 896 0000	3.505 600 0000	.285 257 8731	.640 657 6735	2.245 889 5404	.445 257 8731	3
	4	1.810 639 3600	5.066 496 0000	.197 375 0695	.552 291 0979	2.798 180 6382	.357 375 0695	4
	5	2.100 341 6576	6.877 135 3600	.145 409 3816	.476 113 0154	3.274 293 6537	.305 409 3816	5
	6	2.436 396 1228	8.977 477 0176	.111 389 8702	.410 442 2547	3.684 735 9083	.271 389 8702	6
	7	2.826 219 7345	11.413 873 3404	.087 612 6771	.353 829 5299	4.038 565 4382	.247 612 6771	7
	8	3.278 414 8920	14.240 093 0749	.070 224 2601	.305 025 4568	4.343 590 8950	.230 224 2601	8
	9	3.802 961 2747	17.518 507 9669	.057 082 4868	.262 952 9800	4.606 543 8750	.217 082 4868	9
	10	4.411 435 0786	21.321 469 2416	.046 901 0831	.226 683 6034	4.833 227 4785	.206 901 0831	10
	11	5.117 264 6912	25.732 904 3202	.038 860 7515	.195 416 8995	5.028 644 3780	.198 860 7515	11
	12	5.936 027 0418	30.850 169 0114	.032 414 7333	.168 462 8444	5.197 107 2224	.192 414 7333	12
	13	6.885 791 3685	36.786 196 0533	.027 184 1100	.145 226 5900	5.342 333 8124	.187 184 1100	13
	14	7.987 517 9875	43.671 987 4218	.022 897 9733	.125 195 3362	5.467 529 1486	.182 897 9733	14
	15	9.265 520 8655	51.659 505 4093	.019 357 5218	.107 927 0140	5.575 456 1626	.179 357 5218	15
	16	10.748 004 2040	60.925 026 2748	.016 413 6162	.093 040 5293	5.668 496 6919	.176 413 6162	16
	17	12.467 684 8766	71.673 030 4787	.013 952 2494	.080 207 3528	5.748 704 0447	.173 952 2494	17
	18	14.462 514 4569	84.140 715 3553	.011 884 8526	.069 144 2697	5.817 848 3144	.171 884 8526	18
	19	16.776 516 7700	98.603 229 8122	.010 141 6556	.059 607 1290	5.877 455 4435	.170 141 6556	19
	20	19.460 759 4531	115.379 746 5821	.008 667 0324	.051 385 4561	5.928 840 8996	.168 667 0324	20
ANNUALLY If compounded annually nominal annual rate is 16%	21	22.574 480 9656	134.840 506 0353	.007 416 1691	.044 297 8070	5.973 138 7065	.167 416 1691	21
	22	26.186 397 9201	157.414 987 0009	.006 352 6353	.038 187 7646	6.011 326 4711	.166 352 6353	22
	23	30.376 221 5874	183.601 384 9211	.005 446 5820	.032 920 4867	6.044 246 9579	.165 446 5820	23
	24	35.236 417 0414	213.977 606 5085	.004 673 3862	.028 379 7299	6.072 626 6878	.164 673 3862	24
	25	40.874 243 7680	249.214 023 5498	.004 012 6153	.024 465 2844	6.097 091 9723	.164 012 6153	25
	26	47.414 122 7708	290.088 267 3178	.003 447 2266	.021 090 7624	6.118 182 7347	.163 447 2266	26
	27	55.000 382 4142	337.502 390 0886	.002 962 9420	.018 181 6918	6.136 364 4265	.162 962 9420	27
	28	63.800 443 6004	392.502 772 5028	.002 547 7527	.015 673 8722	6.152 038 2987	.162 547 7527	28
	29	74.008 514 5765	456.303 216 1032	.002 191 5252	.013 511 9588	6.165 550 2575	.162 191 5252	29
	30	85.849 876 9088	530.311 730 6798	.001 885 6833	.011 648 2403	6.177 198 4978	.161 885 6833	30
SEMIANNUALLY If compounded semiannually nominal annual rate is 32%	31	99.585 857 2142	616.161 607 5885	.001 622 9508	.010 041 5865	6.187 240 0843	.161 622 9508	31
	32	115.519 594 3684	715.747 464 8027	.001 397 1408	.008 656 5401	6.195 896 6244	.161 397 1408	32
	33	134.002 729 4674	831.267 059 1711	.001 202 9828	.007 462 5346	6.203 359 1590	.161 202 9828	33
	34	155.443 166 1822	965.269 788 6385	.001 035 9798	.006 433 2194	6.209 792 3784	.161 035 9798	34
	35	180.314 072 7713	1120.712 954 8207	.000 892 2891	.005 545 8788	6.215 338 2573	.160 892 2891	35
	36	209.164 324 4147	1301.027 027 5920	.000 768 6235	.004 780 9300	6.220 119 1873	.160 768 6235	36
	37	242.630 616 3211	1510.191 352 0067	.000 662 1677	.004 121 4914	6.224 240 6787	.160 662 1677	37
	38	281.451 514 9324	1752.821 968 3278	.000 570 5086	.003 553 0098	6.227 793 6885	.160 570 5086	38
	39	326.483 757 3216	2034.273 483 2602	.000 491 5760	.003 062 9395	6.230 856 6281	.160 491 5760	39
	40	378.721 158 4931	2360.757 240 5818	.000 423 5929	.002 640 4651	6.233 497 0932	.160 423 5929	40
QUARTERLY If compounded quarterly nominal annual rate is 64%	41	439.316 543 8520	2739.478 399 0749	.000 365 0330	.002 276 2630	6.235 775 3562	.160 365 0330	41
	42	509.607 190 8883	3178.794 942 9269	.000 314 5846	.001 962 2957	6.237 735 6519	.160 314 5846	42
	43	591.144 341 4072	3688.402 133 7952	.000 271 1201	.001 691 6342	6.239 427 2861	.160 271 1201	43
	44	685.727 436 0324	4279.546 475 2025	.000 233 6696	.001 458 3054	6.240 885 5915	.160 233 6696	44
	45	795.443 825 7976	4965.273 911 2349	.000 201 3988	.001 257 1598	6.242 142 7513	.160 201 3988	45
	46	922.714 837 9252	5760.717 737 0324	.000 173 5895	.001 083 7584	6.243 226 5097	.160 173 5895	46
	47	1070.349 211 9932	6683.432 574 9576	.000 149 6237	.000 934 2715	6.244 160 7842	.160 149 6237	47
	48	1241.605 085 9121	7753.781 786 9508	.000 128 9693	.000 805 4091	6.244 966 1933	.160 128 9693	48
	49	1440.261 899 6581	8995.386 872 8630	.000 111 1681	.000 694 3182	6.245 660 5115	.160 111 1681	49
	50	1670.703 803 6034	10435.648 772 5211	.000 095 8254	.000 598 5501	6.246 259 0616	.160 095 8254	50
MONTHLY If compounded monthly nominal annual rate is 192%	51	1938.016 412 1799	12106.352 576 1244	.000 082 6013	.000 515 9915	6.246 775 0531	.160 082 6013	51
	52	2248.099 038 1287	14044.369 988 3043	.000 071 2029	.000 444 8203	6.247 219 8734	.160 071 3781	52
	53	2607.794 884 2293	16292.468 026 4330	.000 061 3781	.000 383 4657	6.247 603 3391	.160 061 3781	53
	54	3025.042 065 7060	18900.262 910 6623	.000 052 9093	.000 330 5739	6.247 933 9130	.160 052 9093	54
	55	3509.048 796 2189	21925.304 976 3683	.000 045 6094	.000 284 9775	6.248 218 8905	.160 045 6094	55
	56	4070.496 603 6140	25434.353 772 5872	.000 039 3169	.000 245 6703	6.248 464 5608	.160 039 3169	56
	57	4721.776 060 1922	29504.850 376 2012	.000 033 8927	.000 211 7847	6.248 676 3455	.160 033 6927	57
	58	5477.260 229 8229	34226.626 436 3934	.000 029 2170	.000 182 5730	6.248 858 9186	.160 029 2170	58
	59	6353.621 866 5946	39703.886 666 2163	.000 025 1865	.000 157 3905	6.249 016 3091	.160 025 1865	59
	60	7370.201 365 2497	46057.508 532 8109	.000 021 7120	.000 135 6815	6.249 151 9906	.160 021 7120	60

Value of $1 Compounded at 5-20%

Rate 17%

	Periods	Amount of 1: How $1 Left at Compounded Interest Will Grow	Amount of 1 Per Period: How $1 Deposited Periodically Will Grow	Sinking Fund: Periodic Deposit That Will Grow to $1 at Future Date	Present Worth of 1: What $1 Due in the Future is Worth Today	Present Worth of 1 Per Period: What $1 Payable Periodically Is Worth Today	Partial Payment: Annuity Worth $1 Today— Periodic Payment Necessary to Pay a Loan of $1	Periods
	1	1.170 000 0000	1.000 000 0000	1.000 000 0000	.854 700 8547	.854 700 8547	1.170 000 0000	1
	2	1.368 900 0000	2.170 000 0000	.460 829 4931	.730 513 5510	1.585 214 4057	.630 829 4931	2
	3	1.601 613 0000	3.538 900 0000	.282 573 6811	.624 370 5564	2.209 584 9622	.452 573 6811	3
.17 Per Period	4	1.873 887 2100	5.140 513 0000	.194 533 1137	.533 650 0482	2.743 235 0104	.364 533 1137	4
	5	2.192 448 0357	7.014 400 2100	.142 563 8643	.456 111 1523	3.199 346 1627	.312 563 8643	5
	6	2.565 1642018	9.206 848 2457	.108 614 8021	.389 838 5917	3.589 184 7545	.278 614 8021	6
	7	3.001 242 1161	11.772 012 4475	.084 947 2428	.333 195 3776	3.922 380 1320	.254 947 2428	7
	8	3.511 453 2758	14.773 254 5635	.067 689 8916	.284 782 3740	4.207 162 5060	.237 689 8916	8
	9	4.108 400 3327	18.284 707 8393	.054 690 5102	.243 403 7384	4.450 566 2444	.224 690 6102	9
	10	4.806 828 3892	22.393 108 1720	.044 656 5967	.208 037 3833	4.658 603 6277	.214 656 5967	10
	11	5.623 989 2154	27.199 936 5613	.036 764 7916	.177 809 7293	4.836 413 3570	.206 764 7916	11
	12	6.580 067 3820	32.823 925 7767	.030 465 5819	.151 974 1276	4.988 387 4846	.200 465 5819	12
	13	7.698 678 8370	39.403 993 1587	.025 378 1386	.129 892 4168	5.118 279 9014	.195 378 1386	13
	14	9.007 454 2393	47.102 671 9957	.021 230 2181	.111 019 1596	5.229 299 0610	.191 230 2181	14
	15	10.530 721 4599	56.110 126 2350	.017 822 0950	.094 888 1706	5.324 187 2317	.187 822 0950	15
	16	12.330 304 1081	66.648 847 6949	.015 004 0103	.081 101 0005	5.405 288 2322	.185 004 0103	16
	17	14.426 455 8065	78.979 151 8031	.012 661 5693	.069 317 0945	5.474 605 3267	.182 661 5693	17
	18	16.878 953 2936	93.405 607 6096	.010 705 9953	.059 245 3799	5.533 850 7065	.180 705 9953	18
	19	19.748 375 3535	110.284 560 9032	.009 067 4523	.050 637 0768	5.584 487 7834	.179 067 4523	19
	20	23.105 599 1636	130.032 936 2568	.007 690 3593	.043 279 5528	5.627 767 3362	.177 690 3593	20
ANNUALLY If compounded annually nominal annual rate is 17%	21	27.033 551 0215	153.138 535 4204	.006 530 0350	.036 991 0708	5.664 758 4070	.176 530 0350	21
	22	31.629 254 6951	180.172 086 4419	.005 550 2493	.031 616 2998	5.696 374.7069	.175 550 2493	22
	23	37.006 227 9933	211.801 341 1370	.004 721 4054	.027 022 4785	5.723 397 1853	.174 721 4054	23
	24	43.297 286 7521	248.807 569 1303	.004 019 1703	.023 096 1355	5.746 493 3208	.174 019 1703	24
	25	50.657 825 5000	292.104 855 8824	.003 423 4282	.019 740 2867	5.766 233 6075	.173 423 4282	25
	26	59.269 655 8350	342.762 681 3825	.002 917 4705	.016 872 0399	5.783 105 6475	.172 917 4705	26
	27	69.345 497 3270	402.032 337 2175	.002 487 3621	.014 420 5470	5.797 526 1944	.172 487 3621	27
	28	81.134 231 8726	471.377 834 5444	.002 121 4404	.012 325 2538	5.809 851 4482	.172 121 4404	28
	29	94.927 051 2909	552.512 066 4170	.001 809 9152	.010 534 4050	5.820 385 8532	.171 809 9152	29
	30	111.064 650 0103	647.439 117 7079	.001 544 5468	.009 003 7649	5.829 389 6181	.171 544 5468	30
SEMIANNUALLY If compounded semiannually nominal annual rate is 34%	31	129.945 640 5121	758.503 767 7182	.001 318 3850	.007 695 5256	5.837 085 1437	.171 318 3850	31
	32	152.036 399 3992	888.449 408 2303	.001 125 5565	.006 577 3723	5.843 662 5160	.171 125 5565	32
	33	177.882 587 2970	1040.485 807 6295	.000 961 0895	.005 621 6857	5.849 284 2017	.170 961 0895	33
	34	208.122 627 1375	1218.368 394 9265	.000 820 7698	.004 804 8596	5.854 089 0613	.170 820 7698	34
	35	243.503 473 7509	1426.491 022 0640	.000 701 0209	.004 106 7176	5.858 195 7789	.170 701 0209	35
	36	284.899 064 2885	1669.994 495 8149	.000 598 8044	.003 510 0150	5.861 705 7939	.170 598 8044	36
	37	333.331 905 2176	1954.893 560 1034	.000 511 5368	.003 000 0129	5.864 705 8067	.170 511 5368	37
	38	389.998 329 1046	2288.225 465 3210	.000 437 0199	.002 564 1135	5.867 269 9203	.170 437 0199	38
	39	456.298 045 0523	2678.223 794 4256	.000 373 3818	.002 191 5500	5.869 461 4703	.170 373 3818	39
	40	533.868 712 7112	3134.521 839 4779	.000 319 0279	.001 873 1197	5.871 334 5900	.170 319 0279	40
QUARTERLY If compounded quarterly nominal annual rate is 68%	41	624.626 393 8722	3668.390 552 1892	.000 272 5991	.001 600 9570	5.872 935 5470	.170 272 5991	41
	42	730.812 880 8304	4293.016 946 0613	.000 232 9364	.001 368 3393	5.874 303 8864	.170 232 9364	42
	43	855.051 070 5716	5023.829 826 8918	.000 199 0513	.001 169 5208	5.875 473 4071	.170 199 0513	43
	44	1000.409 752 5688	5878.880 897 4634	.000 170 1004	.000 999 5904	5.876 472 9976	.170 170 1004	44
	45	1170.479 410 5055	6879.290 650 0321	.000 145 3638	.000 854 3508	5.877 327 3483	.170 145 3638	45
	46	1369.460 910 2914	8049.770 060 5376	.000 124 2272	.000 730 2143	5.878 057 5627	.170 124 2272	46
	47	1602.269 265 0409	9419.230 970 8290	.000 106 1658	.000 624 1148	5.878 681 6775	.170 106 1658	47
	48	1874.655 040 0979	11021.500 235 8699	.000 090 7317	.000 533 4315	5.879 215 1090	.170 090 7317	48
	49	2193.346 396 9145	12896.155 275 9678	.000 077 5425	.000 455 9243	5.879 671 0333	.170 077 5425	49
	50	2566.215 284 3900	15089.501 672 8823	.000 066 2712	.000 389 6789	5.880 060 7122	.170 066 2712	50
MONTHLY If compounded monthly nominal annual rate is 204%	51	3002.471 882 7363	17655.716 957 2723	.000 056 6389	.000 333 0589	5.880 393 7711	.170 056 6389	51
	52	3512.892 102 8015	20658.188 840 0086	.000 048 4070	.000 284 6657	5.880 678 4369	.170 048 4070	52
	53	4110.083 760 2777	24171.080 942 8101	.000 041 3718	.000 243 3040	5.880 921 7409	.170 041 3718	53
	54	4808.797 999 5249	28281.164 703 0878	.000 035 3592	.000 207 9522	5.881 129 6931	.170 035 3592	54
	55	5626.293 659 4442	33089.962 702 6127	.000 030 2206	.000 177 7369	5.881 307 4300	.170 030 2206	55
	56	6582.763 581 5497	38716.256 362 0569	.000 025 8289	.000 151 9119	5.881 459 3419	.170 025 8289	56
	57	7701.833 390 4131	45299.019 943 6065	.000 022 0755	.000 129 8392	5.881 589 1811	.170 022 0755	57
	58	9011.145 066 7833	53000.853 334 0196	.000 018 8676	.000 110 9737	5.881 700 1548	.170 018 8676	58
	59	10543.039 728 1365	62011.998 400 8030	.000 016 1259	.000 094 8493	5.881 795 0041	.170 016 1259	59
	60	12335.356 481 9197	72555.038 128 9395	.000 013 7826	.000 081 0678	5.881 876 0719	.170 013 7826	60

Tables 429

Value of $1 Compounded at 5-20%

Rate 18%	Periods	Amount of 1: How $1 Left at Compounded Interest Will Grow	Amount of 1 Per Period: How $1 Deposited Periodically Will Grow	Sinking Fund: Periodic Deposit That Will Grow to $1 at Future Date	Present Worth of 1: What $1 Due in the Future is Worth Today	Present Worth of 1 Per Period: What $1 Payable Periodically Is Worth Today	Partial Payment: Annuity Worth $1 Today— Periodic Payment Necessary to Pay a Loan of $1	Periods
	1	1.180 000 0000	1.000 000 0000	1.000 000 0000	.847 457 6271	.847 457 6271	1.180 000 0000	1
.18 Per Period	2	1.392 400 0000	2.180 000 0000	.458 715 5963	.718 184 4298	1.565 642 0569	.638 715 5963	2
	3	1.643 032 0000	3.572 400 0000	.279 923 8607	.608 630 8727	2.174 272 9296	.459 923 8607	3
	4	1.938 777 7600	5.215 432 0000	.191 738 6709	.515 788 8752	2.690 061 8047	.371 738 6709	4
	5	2.287 757 7568	7.154 209 7600	.139 777 8418	.437 109 2162	3.127 171 0209	.319 777 8418	5
	6	2.699 554 1530	9.441 967 5168	.105 910 1292	.370 431 5392	3.497 602 5601	.285 910 1292	6
	7	3.185 473 9006	12.141 521 6698	.082 361 9994	.313 925 0332	3.811 527 5933	.262 361 9994	7
	8	3.758 859 2027	15.326 995 5704	.065 244 3589	.266 038 1637	4.077 565 7571	.245 244 3589	8
	9	4.435 453 8592	19.085 854 7731	.052 394 8239	.225 456 0710	4.303 021 8280	.232 394 8239	9
	10	5.233 835 5538	23.521 308 6322	.042 514 6413	.191 064 4669	4.494 086 2949	.222 514 6413	10
	11	6.175 925 9535	28.755 144 1860	.034 776 3862	.161 919 0398	4.656 005 3347	.214 776 3862	11
	12	7.287 592 6251	34.931 070 1395	.028 627 8089	.137 219 5252	4.793 224 8599	.208 627 8089	12
	13	8.599 359 2976	42.218 662 7646	.023 686 2073	.116 287 7332	4.909 512 5931	.203 686 2073	13
	14	10.147 243 9712	50.818 022 0622	.019 678 0583	.098 548 9265	5.008 061 5196	.199 678 0583	14
	15	11.973 747 8860	60.965 266 0334	.016 402 7825	.083 516 0394	5.091 577 5590	.196 402 7825	15
	16	14.129 022 5055	72.939 013 9195	.013 710 0839	.070 776 3046	5.162 353 8635	.193 710 0839	16
	17	16.672 246 5565	87.068 036 4250	.011 485 2711	.059 979 9191	5.222 333 7827	.191 485 2711	17
	18	19.673 250 8167	103.740 282 9814	.009 639 4570	.050 830 4399	5.273 164 2226	.189 639 4570	18
	19	23.214 436 1053	123.413 533 9181	.008 102 8390	.043 076 6440	5.316 240 8666	.188 102 8390	19
	20	27.393 034 6042	146.627 970 0234	.006 819 9812	.036 505 6305	5.352 746 4971	.186 819 9812	20
ANNUALLY If compounded annually nominal annual rate is 18%	21	32.323 780 8330	174.021 004 6276	.005 746 4327	.030 936 9750	5.383 683 4721	.185 746 4327	21
	22	38.142 061 3829	206.344 785 4605	.004 846 2577	.026 217 7754	5.409 901 2476	.184 846 2577	22
	23	45.007 632 4318	244.486 846 8434	.004 090 1996	.022 218 4538	5.432 119 7013	.184 090 1996	23
	24	53.109 006 2695	289.494 479 2752	.003 454 2973	.018 829 1981	5.450 948 8994	.183 454 2973	24
	25	62.668 627 3981	342.603 485 5448	.002 918 8261	.015 956 9475	5.466 905 8470	.182 918 8261	25
	26	73.948 980 3297	405.272 112 9429	.002 467 4779	.013 522 8369	5.480 428 6839	.182 467 4779	26
	27	87.259 796 7891	479.221 093 2726	.002 086 7195	.011 460 0313	5.491 888 7152	.182 086 7195	27
	28	102.966 560 2111	566.480 890 0616	.001 765 2846	.009 711 8909	5.501 600 6061	.181 765 2846	28
	29	121.500 541 0491	669.447 450 2727	.001 493 7692	.008 230 4160	5.509 831 0221	.181 493 7692	29
	30	143.370 638 4379	790.947 991 3218	.001 264 3056	.006 974 9288	5.516 805 9509	.181 264 3056	30
SEMIANNUALLY If compounded semiannually nominal annual rate is 36%	31	169.177 353 3568	934.318 629 7597	.001 070 2987	.005 910 9566	5.522 716 9076	.181 070 2987	31
	32	199.629 276 9610	1103.495 983 1165	.000 906 2108	.005 009 2853	5.527 726 1928	.180 906 2108	32
	33	235.562 546 8139	1303.125 260 0775	.000 767 3859	.004 245 1570	5.531 971 3499	.180 767 3859	33
	34	277.963 805 2405	1538.687 806 8914	.000 649 9044	.003 597 5907	5.535 568 9406	.180 649 9044	34
	35	327.997 290 1837	1816.651 612 1319	.000 550 4633	.003 048 8057	5.538 617 7462	.180 550 4633	35
	36	387.036 802 4168	2144.648 902 3156	.000 466 2768	.002 583 7336	5.541 201 4799	.180 466 2768	36
	37	456.703 426 8518	2531.685 704 7324	.000 394 9937	.002 189 6048	5.543 391 0846	.180 394 9937	37
	38	538.910 043 6852	2988.389 131 5843	.000 334 6284	.001 855 5973	5.545 246 6819	.180 334 6284	38
	39	635.913 851 5485	3527.299 175 2694	.000 283 5030	.001 572 5401	5.546 819 2219	.180 283 5030	39
	40	750.378 344 8272	4163.213 026 8179	.000 240 1991	.001 332 6611	5.548 151 8830	.180 240 1991	40
QUARTERLY If compounded quarterly nominal annual rate is 72%	41	885.446 446 8961	4913.591 371 6451	.000 203 5171	.001 129 3738	5.549 281 2568	.180 203 5171	41
	42	1044.826 807 3374	5799.037 818 5413	.000 172 4424	.000 957 0964	5.550 238 3532	.180 172 4424	42
	43	1232.895 632 6582	6843.864 625 8787	.000 146 1163	.000 811 0987	5.551 049 4519	.180 146 1163	43
	44	1454.816 846 5366	8076.760 258 5369	.000 123 8120	.000 687 3717	5.551 736 8236	.180 123 8120	44
	45	1716.683 878 9132	9531.577 105 0735	.000 104 9144	.000 582 5184	5.552 319 3420	.180 104 9144	45
	46	2025.686 977 1176	11248.260 983 9867	.000 088 9026	.000 493 6597	5.552 813 0017	.180 088 9026	46
	47	2390.310 632 9988	13273.947 961 1043	.000 075 3355	.000 418 3557	5.553 231 3574	.180 075 3355	47
	48	2820.566 546 9386	15664.258 594 1031	.000 063 8396	.000 354 5387	5.553 585 8961	.180 063 8396	48
	49	3328.268 525 3875	18484.825 141 0417	.000 054 0984	.000 300 4565	5.553 886 3526	.180 054 0984	49
	50	3927.356 859 9573	21813.093 666 4292	.000 045 8440	.000 254 6242	5.554 140 9768	.180 045 8440	50
MONTHLY If compounded monthly nominal annual rate is 216%	51	4634.281 094 7496	25740.450 526 3864	.000 038 8494	.000 215 7832	5.554 356 7600	.180 038 8494	51
	52	5468.451 691 8045	30374.731 621 1360	.000 032 9221	.000 182 8671	5.554 539 6271	.180 032 9221	52
	53	6452.772 996 3293	35843.183 312 9405	.000 027 8993	.000 154 9721	5.554 694 5993	.180 027 8993	53
	54	7614.272 135 6686	42295.956 309 2698	.000 023 6429	.000 131 3323	5.554 825 9316	.180 023 6429	54
	55	8984.841 120 0889	49910.228 444 9383	.000 020 0360	.000 111 2986	5.554 937 2301	.180 020 0360	55
	56	10602.112 521 7049	58895.069 565 0272	.000 016 9794	.000 094 3208	5.555 031 5510	.180 016 9794	56
	57	12510.492 775 6118	69497.182 086 7321	.000 014 3891	.000 079 9329	5.555 111 4839	.180 014 3891	57
	58	14762.381 475 2219	82007.674 862 3439	.000 012 1940	.000 067 7397	5.555 179 2236	.180 012 1940	58
	59	17419.610 140 7618	96770.056 337 5658	.000 010 3338	.000 057 4066	5.555 236 6302	.180 010 3338	59
	60	20555.139 966 0990	114189.666 478 3276	.000 008 7574	.000 048 6496	5.555 285 2798	.180 008 7574	60

430 *Tables*

Value of $1 Compounded at 5-20%

Rate 19%	Periods	Amount of 1: How $1 Left at Compounded Interest Will Grow	Amount of 1 Per Period: How $1 Deposited Periodically Will Grow	Sinking Fund: Periodic Deposit That Will Grow to $1 at Future Date	Present Worth of 1: What $1 Due in the Future is Worth Today	Present Worth of 1 Per Period: What $1 Payable Periodically Is Worth Today	Partial Payment: Annuity Worth $1 Today— Periodic Payment Necessary to Pay a Loan of $1	Periods
.19 Per Period	1	1.190 000 0000	1.000 000 0000	1.000 000 0000	.840 336 1345	.840 336 1345	1.190 000 0000	1
	2	1.416 100 0000	2.190 000 0000	.456 621 0046	.706 164 8189	1.546 500 9533	.646 621 0046	2
	3	1.685 159 0000	3.606 100 0000	.277 307 8950	.593 415 8142	2.139 916 7675	.467 307 8950	3
	4	2.005 339 2100	5.291 259 0000	.188 990 9377	.498 668 7514	2.638 585 5189	.378 990 9377	4
	5	2.386 353 6599	7.296 598 2100	.137 050 1666	.419 049 3709	3.057 634 8898	.327 050 1666	5
	6	2.839 760 8553	9.682 951 8699	.103 274 2921	.352 142 3285	3.409 777 2184	.293 274 2921	6
	7	3.379 315 4178	12.522 712 7252	.079 854 9022	.295 917 9231	3.705 695 1415	.269 854 9022	7
	8	4.021 385 3472	15.902 028 1430	.062 885 0604	.248 670 5236	3.954 365 6651	.252 885 0604	8
	9	4.785 448 5631	19.923 413 4901	.050 192 2023	.208 966 8266	4.163 332 4917	.240 192 2023	9
	10	5.694 683 7901	24.708 862 0533	.040 471 3094	.175 602 3753	4.338 934 8670	.230 471 3094	10
	11	6.776 673 7102	30.403 545 8434	.032 890 9005	.147 565 0212	4.486 499 8882	.222 890 9005	11
	12	8.064 241 7152	37.180 219 5536	.026 896 0219	.124 004 2195	4.610 504 1077	.216 896 0219	12
	13	9.596 447 6411	45.244 461 2688	.022 102 1529	.104 205 2265	4.714 709 3342	.212 102 1529	13
	14	11.419 772 6929	54.840 908 9099	.018 234 5628	.087 567 4172	4.802 276 7515	.208 234 5628	14
	15	13.589 529 5045	66.260 681 6027	.015 091 9063	.073 586 0649	4.875 862 8163	.205 091 9063	15
	16	16.171 540 1104	79.850 211 1073	.012 523 4484	.061 837 0293	4.937 699 8457	.202 523 4484	16
	17	19.244 132 7314	96.021 751 2176	.010 414 3070	.051 963 8902	4.989 663 7359	.200 414 3070	17
	18	22.900 517 9503	115.265 883 9490	.008 675 5939	.043 667 1346	5.033 330 8705	.198 675 5939	18
	19	27.251 616 3609	138.166 401 8993	.007 237 6496	.036 695 0711	5.070 025 9416	.197 237 6496	19
	20	32.429 423 4694	165.418 018 2602	.006 045 2907	.030 836 1942	5.100 862 1358	.196 045 2907	20
ANNUALLY If compounded annually nominal annual rate is 19%	21	38.591 013 9286	197.847 441 7296	.005 054 3994	.025 912 7682	5.126 774 9040	.195 054 3994	21
	22	45.923 306 5751	236.438 455 6582	.004 229 4304	.021 775 4355	5.148 550 3395	.194 229 4304	22
	23	54.648 734 8243	282.361 762 2333	.003 541 5560	.018 298 6853	5.166 849 0248	.193 541 5560	23
	24	65.031 994 4410	337.010 497 0576	.002 967 2666	.015 377 0465	5.182 226 0713	.192 967 2666	24
	25	77.388 073 3847	402.042 491 4986	.002 487 2993	.012 921 8878	5.195 147 9590	.192 487 2993	25
	26	92.091 807 3278	479.430 564 8833	.002 085 8078	.010 858 7292	5.206 006 6883	.192 085 8078	26
	27	109.589 250 7201	571.522 372 2111	.001 749 7128	.009 124 9825	5.215 131 6708	.191 749 7128	27
	28	130.411 208 3569	681.111 622 9313	.001 468 1881	.007 668 0526	5.222 799 7234	.191 468 1881	28
	29	155.189 337 9448	811.522 831 2882	.001 232 2512	.006 443 7416	5.229 243 4650	.191 232 2512	29
	30	184.675 312 1543	966.712 169 2330	.001 034 4341	.005 414 9089	5.234 658 3740	.191 034 4341	30
SEMIANNUALLY If compounded semiannually nominal annual rate is 38%	31	219.763 621 4636	1151.387 481 3872	.000 868 5173	.004 550 3437	5.239 208 7176	.190 868 5173	31
	32	261.518 709 5417	1371.151 102 8508	.000 729 3142	.003 823 8182	5.243 032 5358	.190 729 3142	32
	33	311.207.264 3546	1632.669 812 3924	.000 612 4937	.003 213 2926	5.246 245 8284	.190 612 4937	33
	34	370.336 644 5819	1943.877 076 7470	.000 514 4358	.002 700 2459	5.248 946 0743	.190 514 4358	34
	35	440.700 607 0525	2314.213 721 3289	.000 432 1122	.002 269 1142	5.251 215 1885	.190 432 1122	35
	36	524.433 722 3925	2754.914 328 3814	.000 362 9877	.001 906 8186	5.253 122 0071	.190 362 9877	36
	37	624.076 129 6470	3279.348 050 7739	.000 304 9387	.001 602 3686	5.254 724 3757	.190 304 9387	37
	38	742.650 594 2800	3903.424 180 4210	.000 256 1853	.001 346 5282	5.256 070 9040	.190 256 1853	38
	39	883.754 207 1932	4646.074 774 7010	.000 215 2355	.001 131 5363	5.257 202 4403	.190 215 2355	39
	40	1051.667 506 5599	5529.828 981 8941	.000 180 8374	.000 950 8709	5.258 153 3112	.190 180 8374	40
QUARTERLY If compounded quarterly nominal annual rate is 76%	41	1251.434 332 8063	6531.496 488 4540	.000 151 9411	.000 799 0512	5.258 952 3623	.190 151 9411	41
	42	1489.266 356 0395	7832.930 821 2603	.000 127 6653	.000 671 4716	5.259 623 8339	.190 127 6653	42
	43	1772.226 963 6869	9322.247 177 2997	.000 107 2703	.000 564 2618	5.260 188 0957	.190 107 2703	43
	44	2108.950 036 7875	11094.474 140 9867	.000 090 1350	.000 474 1696	5.260 662 2653	.190 090 1350	44
	45	2509.650 603 2771	13203.424 227 7742	.000 075 7379	.000 398 4618	5.261 060 7272	.190 075 7379	45
	46	2986.484 217 8997	15713.074 831 0512	.000 063 6413	.000 334 8419	5.261 395 5690	.190 063 6413	46
	47	3553.916 219 3007	18699.559 048 9510	.000 053 4772	.000 281 3797	5.261 676 9488	.190 053 4772	47
	48	4229.160 300 9678	22253.475 268 2517	.000 044 9368	.000 236 4536	5.261 913 4023	.190 044 9368	48
	49	5032.700 758 1517	26482.635 569 2195	.000 037 7606	.000 198 7005	5.262 112 1028	.190 037 7606	49
	50	5988.913 902 2005	31515.336 327 3712	.000 031 7306	.000 166 9752	5.262 279 0780	.190 031 7306	50
MONTHLY If compounded monthly nominal annual rate is 228%	51	7126.807 543 6186	37504.250 229 5717	.000 026 6636	.000 140 3153	5.262 419 3933	.190 026 6636	51
	52	8480.900 976 9062	44631.057 773 1903	.000 022 4059	.000 117 9120	5.262 537 3053	.190 022 4059	52
	53	10092.272 162 5183	53111.958 750 0965	.000 018 8282	.000 099 0857	5.262 636 3910	.190 018 8282	53
	54	12009.803 873 3968	63204.230 912 6148	.000 015 8217	.000 083 2653	5.262 719 6563	.190 015 8217	54
	55	14291.666 609 3422	75214.034 786 0117	.000 013 2954	.000 069 9708	5.262 789 6271	.190 013 2954	55
	56	17007.083 265 1172	89505.701 395 3539	.000 011 1725	.000 058 7990	5.262 848 4262	.190 011 1725	56
	57	20238.429 085 4895	106512.784 660 4711	.000 009 3885	.000 049 4109	5.262 897 8371	.190 009 3885	57
	58	24083.730 611 7325	126751.213 745 9606	.000 007 8895	.000 041 5218	5.262 939 3589	.190 007 8895	58
	59	28659.639 427 9617	150834.944 357 6931	.000 006 6298	.000 034 8923	5.262 974 2512	.190 006 6298	59
	60	34104.970 919 2744	179494.583 785 6548	.000 005 5712	.000 029 3212	5.263 003 5724	.190 005 5712	60

Tables

Value of $1 Compounded at 5-20%

Rate 20%	Periods	Amount of 1: How $1 Left at Compounded Interest Will Grow	Amount of 1 Per Period: How $1 Deposited Periodically Will Grow	Sinking Fund: Periodic Deposit That Will Grow to $1 at Future Date	Present Worth of 1: What $1 Due in the Future is Worth Today	Present Worth of 1 Per Period: What $1 Payable Periodically Is Worth Today	Partial Payment: Annuity Worth $1 Today— Periodic Payment Necessary to Pay a Loan of $1	Periods
	1	1.200 000 0000	1.000 000 0000	1.000 000 0000	.833 333 3333	.833 333 3333	1.200 000 0000	1
	2	1.440 000 0000	2.200 000 0000	.454 545 4545	.694 444 4444	1.527 777 7778	.654 545 4545	2
	3	1.728 000 0000	3.640 000 0000	.274 725 2747	.578 703 7037	2.106 481 4815	.474 725 2747	3
.20 Per Period	4	2.073 600 0000	5.368 000 0000	.186 289 1207	.482 253 0864	2.588 734 5679	.386 289 1207	4
	5	2.488 320 0000	7.441 600 0000	.134 379 7033	.401 877 5720	2.990 612 1399	.334 379 7033	5
	6	2.985 984 0000	9.929 920 0000	.100 705 7459	.334 897 9767	3.325 510 1166	.300 705 7459	6
	7	3.583 180 8000	12.915 904 0000	.077 423 9263	.279 081 6472	3.604 591 7638	.277 423 9263	7
	8	4.299 816 9600	16.499 084 8000	.060 609 4224	.232 568 0394	3.837 159 8032	.260 609 4224	8
	9	5.159 780 3520	20.798 901 7600	.048 079 4617	.193 806 6995	4.030 966 5027	.248 079 4617	9
	10	6.191 736 4224	25.958 682 1120	.038 522 7569	.161 505 5829	4.192 472 0856	.238 522 7569	10
	11	7.430 083 7069	32.150 418 5344	.031 103 7942	.134 587 9857	4.327 060 0713	.231 103 7942	11
	12	8.916 100 4483	39.580 502 2413	.025 264 9649	.112 156 6548	4.439 216 7261	.225 264 9649	12
	13	10.699 320 5379	48.496 602 6895	.020 620 0011	.093 463 8790	4.532 680 6051	.220 620 0011	13
	14	12.839 184 6455	59.195 923 2274	.016 893 0552	.077 886 5658	4.610 567 1709	.216 893 0552	14
	15	15.407 021 5746	72.035 107 8729	.013 882 1198	.064 905 4715	4.675 472 6424	.213 882 1198	15
	16.	18.488 425 8895	87.442 129 4475	.011 436 1350	.054 087 8929	4.729 560 5353	.211 436 1350	16
	17	22.186 111 0674	105.930 555 3370	.009 440 1469	.045 073 2441	4.774 633 7794	.209 440 1469	17
	18	26.623 333 2809	128.116 666 4044	.007 805 3857	.037 561 0368	4.812 194 8162	.207 805 3857	18
	19	31.947 999 9371	154.739 999 6853	.006 462 4532	.031 300 8640	4.843 495 6802	.206 462 4532	19
	20	38.337 599 9245	186.687 999 6224	.005 356 5307	.026 084 0533	4.869 579 7335	.205 356 5307	20
ANNUALLY If compounded annually nominal annual rate is 20%	21	46.005 119 9094	225.025 599 5468	.004 443 9388	.021 736 7111	4.891 316 4446	.204 443 9388	21
	22	55.206 143 8912	271.030 719 4562	.003 689 6187	.018 113 9259	4.909 430 3705	.203 689 6187	22
	23	66.247 372 6695	326.236 863 3475	.003 065 2575	.015 094 9383	4.924 525 3087	.203 065 2575	23
	24	79.496 847 2034	392.484 236 0170	.002 547 8730	.012 579 1152	4.937 104 4239	.202 547 8730	24
	25	95.398 216 6441	471.981 083 2203	.002 118 7290	.010 482 5960	4.947 587 0199	.202 118 7290	25
	26	114.475 459 9729	567.377 299 8644	.001 762 4956	.008 735 4967	4.956 322 5166	.201 762 4956	26
	27	137.370 551 9675	681.852 759 8373	.001 466 5923	.007 279 5806	4.963 602 0962	.201 466 5923	27
	28	164.844 662 3610	819.223 311 8048	.001 220 6684	.006 066 3171	4.969 668 4143	.201 220 6684	28
	29	197.813 594 8331	984.067 974 1657	.001 016 1900	.005 055 2643	4.974 723 6786	.201 016 1900	20
	30	237.376 313 7998	1181.881 568 9988	.000 846 1085	.004 212 7202	4.978 936 3988	.200 846 1085	30
SEMIANNUALLY If compounded semiannually nominal annual rate is 40%	31	284.851 576 6597	1419.257 882 7986	.000 704 5936	.003 510 6002	4.982 446 9990	.200 704 5936	31
	32	341.821 891 8717	1704.109 459 3583	.000 586 8168	.002 925 5002	4.985 372 4992	.200 586 8168	32
	33	410.186 270 2460	2045.931 351 2300	.000 488 7750	.002 437 9168	4.987 810 4160	.200 488 7750	33
	34	492.223 524 2952	2456.117 621 4760	.000 407 1466	.002 031 5973	4.989 842 0133	.200 407 1466	34
	35	590.668 229 1542	2948.341 145 7712	.000 339 1738	.001 692 9978	4.991 535 0111	.200 339 1738	35
	36	708.801 874 9851	3539.009 374 9255	.000 232 5649	.001 410 8315	4.992 945 8426	.200 282 5649	36
	37	850.562 249 9821	4247.811 249 9106	.000 235 4154	.001 175 6929	4.994 121 5355	.200 235 4154	37
	38	1020.674 699 9785	5098.373 499 8927	.000 196 1410	.000 979 7441	4.995 101 2796	.200 196 1410	38
	39	1224.809 639 9742	6119.048 199 8712	.000 163 4241	.000 816 4534	4.995 917 7330	.200 163 4241	39
	40	1469.771 567 9691	7343.857 839 8454	.000 136 1682	.000 680 3778	4.996 598 1108	.200 136 1682	40
QUARTERLY If compounded quarterly nominal annual rate is 80%	41	1763.726 881 5629	8813.629 407 8145	.000 113 4606	.000 566 9815	4.997 165 0923	.200 113 4606	41
	42	2116.471 057 8755	10577.355 289 3774	.000 094 5416	.000 472 4846	4.997 637 5770	.200 094 5416	42
	43	2539.765 269 4506	12693.826 347 2529	.000 078 7785	.000 393 7372	4.998 031 3141	.200 078 7785	43
	44	3047.718 323 3407	15233.591 616 7035	.000 065 6444	.000 328 1143	4.998 359 4284	.200 065 6444	44
	45	3657.261 988 0088	18281.309 940 0442	.000 054 7007	.000 273 4286	4.998 632 8570	.200 054 7007	45
	46	4388.714 385 6106	21938.571 928 0530	.000 045 5818	.000 227 8572	4.998 860 7142	.200 045 5818	46
	47	5266.457 262 7327	26327.286 313 6636	.000 037 9834	.000 189 8810	4.999 050 5952	.200 037 9834	47
	48	6319.748 715 2793	31593.743 576 3964	.000 031 6518	.000 158 2341	4.999 208 8293	.200 031 6518	48
	49	7583.698 458 3351	37913.492 291 6756	.000 026 3758	.000 131 8618	4.999 340 6911	.200 026 3758	49
	50	9100.438 150 0021	45497.190 750 0107	.000 021 9794	.000 109 8848	4.999 450 5759	.200 021 9794	50
MONTHLY If compounded monthly nominal annual rate is 240%	51	10920.525 780 0026	54597.628 900 0129	.000 018 3158	.000 091 5707	4.999 542 1466	.200 018 3158	51
	52	13104.630 936 0031	65518.154 680 0155	.000 015 2629	.000 076 3089	4.999 618 4555	.200 015 2629	52
	53	15725.557 123 2037	78622.785 616 0186	.000 012 7190	.000 063 5908	4.999 682 0462	.200 012 7190	53
	54	18870.668 547 8445	94348.342 739 2223	.000 010 5990	.000 052 9923	4.999 735 0385	.200 010 5990	54
	55	22644.802 257 4133	113219.011 287 0667	.000 008 8324	.000 044 1602	4.999 779 1988	.200 008 8324	55
	56	27173.762 708 8960	135863.813 544 4801	.000 007 3603	.000 036 8002	4.999 815 9990	.200 007 3603	56
	57	32608.515 250 6752	163037.576 253 3761	.000 006 1336	.000 030 6668	4.999 846 6658	.200 006 1336	57
	58	39130.218 300 8103	195646.091 504 0513	.000 005 1113	.000 025 5557	4.999 872 2215	.200 005 1113	58
	59	46956.261 960 9723	234776.309 804 8616	.000 004 2594	.000 021 2984	4.999 893 5179	.200 004 2594	59
	60	56347.514 353 1668	281732.571 765 8339	.000 003 5495	.000 017 7470	4.999 911 2649	.200 003 5495	60

Glossary

Aaa Credit. The highest credit rating that can be received by a business corporation.

Absorption Rate. The portion of the units rented or sold within the first, second, and subsequent years after the opening of an income property to tenants. The absorption rate is also indicated in terms of how long it took to rent completely or sell all the units available.

Accelerated Depreciation. A method of figuring depreciation expense that permits greater tax deductions in the early life of the asset than those deductions permitted by the use of the straight-line method of depreciation. Methods of accelerated depreciation include sum-of-the-years' digits, double declining balance, 150 percent declining balance, and 125 percent declining balance methods.

Accrued Depreciation. The loss in value of an asset as a result of physical deterioration, functional obsolescence, and perhaps environmental obsolescence.

Accrual Method of Accounting. The method of accounting in which revenues and expenses are accounted for as they are encountered. If the expense is incurred today, but will be paid later, an accrued expense will be recorded.

Acid-test Ratio. A ratio, similar to the current ratio, that shows the extent of liquidity of the corporation at a given time. Current assets, less inventory, are divided by current liabilities in order to derive the acid-test ratio.

Adjusted Basis. The cost of an improvement, plus renovation and remodeling costs during the time of ownership, less depreciation deductions for the improvement.

Adverse Environmental Effects. The detrimental effects on the living and working environment of actions taken by land developers, public and private.

Adverse Possession. The illegal possession of a property by an occupant who is not the legal owner, which may develop into ownership rights after the statutory requirements for title transferral are met by the illegal tenant. If the owner gives no sign of approval to the illegal occupant and the requirements for adverse possession rights are met, the courts may permit the transfer of title from the owner of record to the current occupant.

Advertising Cost. The expense incurred in publicly promoting the favorable features about a good or service. The media are paid and the advertiser is usually identified.

After-tax Cash Benefits to Equity. Spendable income plus tax savings resulting from a tax loss.

After-tax Net Cash Proceeds. The net cash reversion before tax, less the tax liability.

Age Distribution. The distribution according to age of the given population at the time of the analysis.

Allodial System. The property ownership system in which private property ownership is respected and protected by law. The system permits public and private ownership of property within the boundaries of the state or nation.

Alternative Minimum Tax. The tax that is applicable to taxable income, plus capital-gains preference items and adjusted itemized deductions preferences, less a $20,000 exemption. The alternative minimum tax rates are 10 percent on the first $40,000; 20 percent on the next $40,000; and 25 percent above $80,000, which went into effect with the tax year 1979. The taxpayer figures his or her regular tax liabilities, including any regular minimum tax, less all nonrefundable credits, including the foreign tax credit. Then the taxpayer figures the alternative minimum tax and pays the higher of the two amounts.

Amenities. The landscaping, entertainment facilities, and other development features that make a residential development conducive to good living conditions beyond the structural accommodations of each individual building unit.

AMMINET Market Service. A commercial mortgage market service maintained by a subsidiary of the Federal Home Loan Mortgage Corporation, where recent sale, bid, and asked prices on mortgages are broadcast by private wire service.

Annuity Payments. Payments received or made at equal intervals, usually for equal amounts, over an extended period of time.

Annuity Recapture. Annuity recapture assumes that the equal amounts set aside for investment recapture each year are invested as they are periodically set aside at the rate of interest reflecting the investor's yield requirement.

Appraisal Fee. The fee required by the preparer of an estimated market value of a real or personal property.

Appraisal Methods. The three methods of appraising real property; the systems for evaluation of assets; methods for estimating the dollar value of specific assets.

Appraisal Principles. Some generalities about real property appraising, which tend to hold in most instances. A well-known real estate appraisal trade association tends to subscribe to ten appraisal principles.

Appraisal Process. The system of analysis that amounts to an orderly progression of steps taken to estimate professionally the value of an asset.

Appraisal Trade Associations. The private organizations that promote professional standards and provide continuing professional education to members who are real estate appraisers and those who are related in functional activity or general interest. Numerous real estate appraisal trade associations exist in the United States to serve their individual memberships.

Appropriate Capitalization Rate. A rate for the conversion of annual net operating income into total value for an asset from the income approach. The appropriate capitalization rate may reflect mortgage financing terms, anticipated property appreciation or depreciation, expected yield on the investor's investment, and the equity buildup through the mortgage repayment.

Area Employment Base. The basic employment sources of an area of the country.

Arm's-length Transaction. A transaction that is free of influences that might distort the sale price. Influences that may result in sale prices under or above a free market price include transactions between family members, transactions involving atypical tax influences, and distress sales.

Asset Lifetime. The economic life of an asset. The period for which the asset will be functionally useful to the typical occupant.

Asset Turnover. The commonly used business credit ratio, which is derived from the division of total company sales for the year by the total assets of the company at a given point in the year—usually the year-end asset volume.

Assignment of Rents. A clause in an income property mortgage or a separate contractual agreement wherein the mortgagor agrees to assign the rents from the mortgaged income property to the lender in the event of mortgagor default on the loan terms. At loan default, the mortgagee becomes the legal owner of the rent receipts issuing from the property tenants.

Availability of Funds. The extent to which the lenders are inclined to commit funds to loans.

Average Annual Return on Equity Method. The stabilized annual average net profit is divided by the initial equity required in order to find the average annual return on equity.

Average Office Occupancy. The average portion of the business days of the year that the office space is occupied.

Average Office Tenant Space. The average amount of space occupied by the office tenant in an office building.

Average Room Rate. The room rate that represents the average paid by the motel or hotel residents over the given period of time.

Average Store Tenant Space. The average amount of space occupied by the retail store tenant in an office building.

Avocation. Use of time that usually does not provide the primary financial support for an individual or household. The avocation may be a hobby that may or may not provide a form of income.

Balance Sheet. The financial condition of a corporation's assets, liabilities, and net worth, shown in one financial statement, which represents the corporation position on a given date.

Balloon Payment. The unusually high principal amount still due on a mortgage loan when the last payment is required. The balloon payment usually arises from the amortization of the loan over a longer period than the actual loan period.

Band-of-Investment Method. The method of determining the weighted cost of the sources of funds for the real estate investment. The product of the percentage amount of mortgage funds and the loan constant plus the product of the percentage amount of equity funds and the owner's yield requirement gives the appropriate captilization rate using the band-of-investment method.

Bank. The financial intermediary, in the form of a commercial bank or a mutual savings bank. Sometimes the layperson uses the term to describe any mortgage-lending institution.

Bank Prime Rate. The interest rate offered by a commercial bank to its prime commercial loan customers. These prime commercial loan customers exhibit the highest credit ratings for bank commercial loan purposes.

Bank Trust Department. The section of the commercial bank that contracts with clients who establish trust accounts to manage their assets. The trust officer assumes a fiduciary relationship with the client establishing the trust account.

Banker's Acceptance. A short-term negotiable instrument that reflects the bank guarantee of the payment of an obligation of a depositor to another party.

Basic Lending Patterns. The usual lending patterns of a financial institution when typical borrowers with adequate credit request loans.

Beneficiary Payments. The annuity or lump-sum payments to those named as beneficiaries in life insurance policies.

Bid and Asked Prices. The market activity in a given stock, which is reflected in bid prices and asking prices.

Bond-type Mortgage-backed Security. The indenture agreement backed by a pool of mortgages that pays interest and principal to investors every six months in the same way that a corporate or Treasury bond does.

Boot. The money or property that is not of like kind to the property exchanged. Boot may be paid by one of the exchangers and received by one of the other exchangers.

Boutique. A speciality shop selling ladies' apparel, household goods, or some such merchandise in a limited amount of space.

Breakeven Ratio. The portion of gross revenue represented by operating expenses and the debt service requirement for the specified time interval.

Brokerage Cost. The expense of the seller who engages a broker to sell his or her property, where a buyer who is ready, willing, and able to do business is located by that broker or his sales associate.

Broker's Method. See *Cash-on-cash return method.*

Builder's or Trade Breakdown Method. A method of estimating construction cost of a building that utilizes the cost estimates of each of the subcontractors and the estimates of overhead and profit. These three sets of costs are added together to arrive at the estimated cost of constructing a building when the builder's or trade breakdown method is used.

Building Code. Regulations associated with building construction that promote the health, safety, and sanitary conditions of the community.

Building Code Enforcement. The local government enforcement of building codes that have been established for existing or proposed structures of the local community.

Building Construction. The building one step at a time of a permanent improvement to land, which requires on-site specialized construction labor and delivery of materials and services. The completion of the construction project is assured by the supervision and management of the builder (general contractor) and architect.

Building Owners and Managers Association International. The trade association of owners and managers of income properties, who benefit from exchange of information and management techniques, partly in the form of the periodically published *Office Building Experience Exchange Report.*

Building Trades. The groups of construction workers who specialize in a certain area of building construction, such as the bricklayers and electricians.

Business Decentralization. The location of employees and offices in various areas of the country that are close to important markets, prime sources of raw materials, prime financial centers, or expanding markets. The headquarters office in a financial center remains a small operation.

"By Operation of Law." A change in the owner's property rights through the exercise of the established law. Transfer of title may take place through the operation of law. For example, condemnation causes the involuntary transfer of title through operation.

Capital Appreciation. The increase in value of a capital asset with time.

Capital Asset. An asset, such as stock or bonds, that is held for investment return.

Capital Constraints. The restrictions on the employment of capital that often originate from institutional regulations and investment conventions.

Capital Depreciation. The loss in value of an asset with time.

Capital Gain. A gain in value of an asset held more than 12 months from the time of purchase. This type of realized financial gain is usually taxed by the Internal Revenue Service on a more favorable basis than the ordinary rates payable on ordinary earned income of individuals or businesses.

Capitalized Versus Expensed Cost. To *capitalize* means to spread incurred cost over an appropriate number of time periods; to *expense* means to take incurred cost as a current operating expense, rather than spreading it over a number of time periods.

Cash Budgeting Policy. A policy in cash planning, such as delaying cash outflows as long as possible to still qualify for discounts and increasing the speed at which cash inflows are received.

Cash Flow. The cash amount represented by net operating income less mortgage interest and principal payment before federal income taxes. This amount is called *cash flow before taxes*. If federal income taxes are deducted from the residual amount, the resulting amount is called *cash flow after taxes* or *spendable cash flow*.

Cash Flow Analysis. The detailed study of actual or estimated cash inflows and outflows associated with specific time periods of property ownership by an investor. Cash flow analysis is usually expected to reveal total net cash benefits to the investor by time period, tax savings per time period, and the investor's total cash return on cash investment by time period.

Cash Flow Ratio. A ratio for financial analysis that is based on cash flows from an investment rather than account profits.

Cash Flow Yield. The yield on investment that results from the comparison of the net cash flow on a stabilized, periodic basis to the cash investment. Cash flow instead of net profit is compared to the cash investment.

Cash-on-Cash Return Method. The method of calculating return on investment in which the cash return is compared to the cash investment. Often the stabilized annual cash flow is divided by the initial equity required in order to find the cash-on-cash return.

Cash Payback. The time in which the net cash flows from an investment pay back or return to the investor the original cash investment.

Cash Throw-off to Equity After Taxes. Net operating income after debt service and federal income taxes.

Central Business District. The retail-service-government center in the middle of an urban area. This is one type of super-regional shopping center without interconnected walkways sheltered from the weather.

Certificates of Deposit. Evidence of deposits that are negotiable instruments whereby the full interest will be paid by the issuing financial institution, if the full deposit remains with the institution for a given period of time.

Citizenship Rights. Those legal, social, and economic rights held by residents of a country who have voting rights.

Civil Rights Laws. The many acts of Congress providing all American citizens with the freedom to buy or rent a home of their preference; the freedom to use any public services or accommodations, regardless of age, race, ethnic origin, color, religion, or sex; the freedom to vote for representatives to be elected without payment of poll taxes or satisfying property ownership requirements; and the freedom to finance their purchases with federally regulated lenders without threat of discrimination.

Class Life Basis. A group of assets may be considered in the same class of asset for depreciation purposes. An economic life is assigned to that class of asset for tax purposes.

Clubhouse. The structure that houses the dining rooms, locker rooms, meeting rooms, and management offices associated with recreational activities of the membership.

Commercial Paper. The form of short-term debt obligation often issued by a business organization in order to raise funds at a reasonably low rate. Short-term debt sold by commercial paper dealers or by the issuers themselves, who are usually high-credit-rated corporations.

Common-area Maintenance Allowance. The expense required for the maintenance of common areas of an income property, which is shared on some equitable basis among the tenants of the building.

Common Stock. The shares of ownership of a corporation that receive dividends after prior claims on the corporation are paid.

Community Master Plan. A comprehensive plan for the future development of the land within the general boundaries of a community. The master plan is the established land-use goal to which the city government officials have agreed to adhere. The plan, usually designed by the city planning officers, is subject to change, but the general land-use plan remains the community goal for development.

Community Property. The form of joint ownership of assets, including real property, that exists between a husband and wife in a state whose statutes provide for community property. The husband and wife hold the assets acquired during the marriage under an undivided interest.

Community Service. Volunteer work that serves the general community.

Company Strategy. The strategy implemented by a company after thoughtful deliberation by the management group.

Comparable Property. A property that has sold recently that is very similar in physical, functional, and environmental characteristics to the subject.

Component Depreciation. Depreciation calculation by building component and its estimated economic life, rather than the improvement and its furnishings as a whole.

Composition of Investment Returns. Estimation of investment returns from various sources to arrive at the expected overall investment return.

Compound Interest. The interest paid on interest and principal when a deposit remains in a financial institution for two or more interest-paying periods.

Comptroller of the Currency. The federal government office that charters national banks and approves or disapproves proposed bank mergers and consolidations.

Computer Simulation. The representation of the operating and financial characteristics of an economic phenomenon through computer programming techniques.

Computer System. The system of hardware and "software" required to effectively utilize the computer capabilities.

Concrete Mobile Home Pads with Tie-Down Capacity. Mobile home lots with concrete slabs that permit the mobile home to be tied down to concrete platform to protect the mobile home from heavy wind damage.

Condemnation. Acquisition of real property interests by an organization that will develop the land for the public good. The property owners must involuntarily sell their interests in the land to the organization holding the approved right of eminent domain for reasonable and equitable compensation from the condemning organization.

Condominium. A housing unit whose air space may be purchased. Common-area maintenance allowances are paid by the condominium purchaser periodically in order to maintain the areas of the condominium development that are used in common by the condominium owners. The condominium may be a single-unit structure or a multiple-tenant structure used for residential, commercial, institutional, or industrial purposes.

Conformity. The similarity between assets. A high degree of conformity means a high degree of similarity between the assets. A low degree of conformity may mean widely divergent assets.

Consolidation of Office Space. The rearrangement of office space so that all, or at least part, of the offices maintained by a company in a metropolitan area are brought under a single roof.

Constant Annual Percent (Mortgage Constant). The percent of the original loan amount that must be paid each year or each time in order that the lender will receive at the end of the payment intervals the total repayment of principal and interest required on the outstanding loan balances over the loan period.

Construction Cost Index. A index of prices paid for many types of commonly used construction materials.

Construction Loan. A loan given by a lender for the construction of land improvements, which usually requires an existing commitment or permanent loan commitment from lender.

Construction Loan Interest. The interest payable to the construction lender by the mortgagor.

Consumer Loan. A loan made by a financial institution to a consumer, who may propose to use the money for a private automobile, a family vacation, or home improvement.

Consumer Price Index. The index maintained by the Bureau of Labor Statistics of the U.S. Department of Commerce, which shows the overall change in the price of an established group of goods and services over time. The group of goods and services represents those commodities and services that are usually required during a year's time by a typical middle-class household with an employed head of household.

Consummate Right. An inchoate right that became an exercisable, active right.

Contingencies. Events that may possibly take place but whose occurrence is uncertain.

Convertible Debenture. An unsecured debt obligation that is converitible to common stock or shares of beneficial interest of the business organization.

Convertible Debenture Bond. The long-term debt instrument that is convertible to the common stock of the issuer. The issuer of the bond is borrowing on an unsecured basis; no real property collateral is pledged for the loan.

Cooperative Association. An association of individuals and households who join together to finance a cooperative apartment building or apartment project. The association finances the development as one entity; association members who own individual apartment units share their proportionate amounts of the master mortgage and the common-area maintenance expense.

Corporate Employee Relocation. The transfer from one area to another of the employees of a corporation. As the need arises, the corporation transfers any employee from one company location to another.

Corporate Participants. The corporations involved in a real estate development.

Corporation. A form of business organization that has an infinite life, at least one type of stockholders—common stockholders—a board of directors, and a management group. The single entity is subject to federal and state income taxation on its net profits. When dividends are distributed to its shareholders, the amount is taxed as part of the personal incomes of the stockholders. Therefore, the corporate stockholders are subject to double taxation. The financial liability of the stockholders is limited to their individual investments in the corporate stock.

Cost. The dollar amount required for the acquisition of a property or the construction of an improvement.

Cost Approach. One of the three general approaches to the estimation of real property interests. In using the cost approach, the appraiser seeks the depreciated cost new of the subject property.

Cost of New Residence. The amount paid plus the sales commissions and other purchasing expenses.

Credit Bureau. The local private organization that keeps records concerning the credit standing of active business men and women and business firms.

Credit Check. See *Credit investigation*.

Credit Guidelines for Home Loans. Minimum credit requirements set by mortgage lenders for the funding or acceptance of a specified type of home loan.

Credit Investigation. The acquisition and analysis of credit information regarding a person or business entity.

Credit Rating Report. The report showing the credit history of the person or business. A credit rating on the report shows the overall credit standing of the party.

Credit Union. A financial institution supported by the deposits or share purchases of a group of individuals who are associated by their place of employment or other common interest.

Credit Union Shares. The ownership interests of a credit union. These ownership interests are usually entitled to dividends as the credit union receives a profit from its operation.

Cumulative Charges. Expenses that are accumulated to reach a total of all expenses for a time period.

Curable Depreciation. A situation in which the cost of curing the defect that is causing a loss in value is less than the rise in value of the asset following the cure of the defect.

Current Ratio. The ratio that shows the extent of liquidity of the corporation at the given point in time. Current assets are divided by current liability in order to derive the current ratio.

Curtesy Right. The right of the surviving widower in a full or partial life estate in the real property owned by the married couple at the time of death of the spouse and the property sold during the marriage where the curtesy right was not released by the spouse.

Customer Driving Time. The time required for a customer to drive from home to a certain destination, such as a shopping center.

Dealers' Commercial Paper. The specialized commercial paper dealers who often act as selling agents for issuers of commercial paper, such as industrial corporations.

Debenture. A long-term debt that is based on the good faith and credit of the issuer. Assets are not pledged as collateral for the debt.

Debenture Bond. A long-term indenture agreement in which the loan is unsecured by collateral and secured in general by the general credit rating and financial status of the borrower-issuer.

Debt Financing. The financing of an asset through the borrowing of money rather than the sale of stock or shares of beneficial interest.

Debt Ratio. The portion of total assets represented by total debt.

Debt Service Coverage. The factor calculated by dividing the annual debt service requirement into the earnings available to meet the annual debt service requirement. The debt service factor usually ranges from barely in excess of 1.0 to approximately 1.5.

Debt Service Payments. Periodic payments required by the mortgage contract, which are made by the mortgagor and represent payment of interest and repayment of the loan principal.

Declining Neighborhood. If the property of a neighborhood deteriorates because of a lack of proper maintenence to counteract the decline in physical and/or functional characteristics, the property values of the neighborhood decline. The decline in property values may be associated with decline in city services, decline in private property maintenance, or decline in public property maintenance.

Deed Recording Fee. The fee required by the appropriate county, parish, or township office where the property is located for the office's recording of the deed.

Default Risk. The risk of financial loss derived from the possibility of not meeting the terms of a contract totally.

Defeasible Fee Estate. The fee estate rests with an owner on a conditional basis. If the specified condition occurs, the fee estate may transfer from the possessor of the title to the subsequent party, as stated in the original agreement.

Deferred Luxuries. The anticipation of luxury goods and services in the future rather than receipt of them at present. Luxury goods and services are not essential to living, but they add to comfort, prestige, personal image, and lifestyle of the recipient.

Department Store Chain. A series of department stores, all owned or operated by a national or regional department store holding company. Examples of such national chain operations are Federated Department Stores, Allied Department Stores, and Associated Dry Goods.

Department Store Real Estate Subsidiary. The subsidiary corporation of a major department store, which is financed by the main store so that it may deal in and invest in real estate required by the main store.

Depletion. The loss of value resulting from using up of a fixed supply of natural resources.

Depositor Funds. The money deposited in financial institutions by individuals, government entities, or business organizations.

Depreciation Expense. The tax-deductible expense that is calculated by a method approved by the Internal Revenue Service for the particular asset class.

Designated Appraiser. An appraiser who has been granted one or more professional appraisal designations, since the appraiser met all the educational and experience requirements for each of those designations.

Development Corporation. The corporate entity established for the development and perhaps permanent investment in a development project.

Discount Note. A short-term debt obligation that is sold on a discount basis. At the maturity date, the issuer pays the investor par value. The return on the investment is the difference between par value at the discount price as related to the discount price paid by the investor.

Discount Point. One percent of the original mortgage loan amount describes one discount point. The lender considers that one discount point paid by the mortgagor at the closing of the loan represents approximately one-eighth of a percent in effective mortgage yield.

Discount Window Operations. The lending of money by the Federal Reserve District Banks to member banks of the Federal Reserve District.

Discounted Cash Flow Analysis. The analysis of the present cash value of an income property, taking into account the expected cash inflows and outflows for each time period involved in the analysis. The net cash flows from all of the time intervals are discounted to present value by an appropriate discount rate.

Disintermediation. The financial setting in which the usual depositors of funds in the thrift institutions and commercial banks and the usual purchasers of life insurance remove their deposited funds or borrow on their equity in their life insurance policies and invest directly in relatively high-yielding, short-term securities, such as Treasury bills, bankers' acceptances, commercial paper, and Eurodollar securities. The short-term market yields usually must exceed the yields to the investors on their deposits with the traditional financial institutions before disintermediation occurs.

Diversified Real Estate Holding Companies. The companies whose operations cover a wide range of real estate activities and investment.

Divident Payout Ratio. The ratio between annual dividends paid and annual earnings available for dividend payout.

Dividend Yield. The return, in the form of a dividend, on invested capital. The dividend yield is derived by dividing the value of the investment into the annual dividend on the investment.

Dollar and Percentage Adjustments. The types of adjustments made to the recent selling prices of comparable properties, which reflect the current market value of the subject. The adjustments may be made in dollars or in percentages for each of the relevant factors of comparison.

Dollars per Gross Area of Entire Building. The standardized dimension upon which the revenue and expenses are calculated for an office building.

Dollars per Gross Rentable Office Area. A basis upon which revenue and expenses are figured for standardized accounting control and year-to-year financial comparisions.

Dollars per Net Office Area. A standardized dimension for the calculation of revenue and expense amounts for an income property.

Dollar per Square Foot Gross per Annum. One dimension used for display of standard costs for an income property.

Double-wide Mobile Home. A manufactured house that is delivered on wheels in half sections from the factory to the site and measures approximately 24 feet in depth and 65 feet in width when completely installed at the site.

Dow Jones Industrial Average. The stock price index continuously maintained by Dow Jones & Co., which includes prices from 30 industrial corporation stocks listed on the New York Stock Exchange and actively traded. The 30 companies are usually labelled *blue chip* companies because of their long earnings histories and high credit ratings.

Dower Right. The right of the surviving widow to a partial life estate in the real property owned jointly by the married couple at the time of death and the real property transferred earlier without the release of the dower right.

Dun & Bradstreet Report. The financial report issued by the Dun & Bradstreet Corporation of New York, which shows the financial history and current overall credit standing of a company or person.

Economically Obsolete Building. A building with functional features that are outmoded, according to the functional requirements of its typical tenants. The cash flow remaining from gross revenue after cash operating expenses and the debt service payments are met does not permit a reasonable return on the owner's investment.

Economies of Scale. Decreased unit costs resulting from the spreading of fixed costs over a sufficient number of units.

Effective Gross Income. The vacancy and bad-debt allowance is subtracted from gross income in order to derive effective gross income.

Ellwood Formula. The mathematical formula used to derive the capitalization rate. The investor's yield requirement, the mortgage financing terms, the percentage of the mortgage paid off at a given time, the appropriate sinking fund rate, and the expected property appreciation or depreciation are elements of the following Ellwood formula:

$$R = Y - M \times C \; \genfrac{}{}{0pt}{}{+ \text{Dep}}{- \text{App}} \; \frac{1}{S_n}$$

Employment History. The successive positions of employment held by an individual.

Energy Conservation. The deliberate steps taken by business, industry, and households to conserve or lessen the consumption of energy.

English Common Law. The law of England which was developed over the centuries according to custom and convention. The law was effective with or without written documentation or statutory approval.

Entrepreneurial Position of the Investor. The investor is assuming the owner's risk associated with an investment. If the investment yields a loss, the equity of the investor declines. If the investment yields a profit or net cash flow, the investor's equity increases.

Environmental Controls. The environmental regulations promulgated for the restriction of private and public land development so that the public may be assured of healthy, safe, and sanitary living and working conditions. Environmental controls are issued by federal, state, and local government agencies and affect all land developers who are covered by the specific regulations.

Environmental Impact Study Fee. The fee required by the preparer of an environmental impact study, which is a requirement of the local or federal environmental agency before the project development proceeds.

Environmental Protection. Preservation of healthful and safe environmental conditions through private actions and public regulations.

Environmental Protection Agency. The federal agency established by the Council of Environmental Quality for the protection of the environment through the passage of regulations by federal agency.

Equilibrium. A leveling off or a period of stability of a economic phenomenon, when demand and supply of goods and services are generally equal. Neither overall expansion nor overall contraction of the phenomenon prevails. The state of equilibrium will be followed by either a state of growth or a state of decline.

Equity. Ownership interest; perhaps the owner's financial contribution as a downpayment when an asset is being purchased partly with borrowed funds.

Equity Buildup. The increase in investor's equity brought about by the periodic payment of mortgage debt service, which includes in each payment an amount toward principal repayment.

Equity Contributors. The owners of an asset who individually invested money.

Equity Ratio. The portion of total assets represented by net worth or equity.

Equity Trust. A type of tax-exempt real estate investment trust that primarily invests directly in real property. Only a minor portion of the assets of the trust may be invested in mortgages.

Escalator Clause. A clause that increases the tenant's lease payment when property taxes assigned to the tenant unit, insurance premiums, or maintenance costs rise.

Escrow Account. A demand deposit account maintained with a commercial bank for the deposit of money held by a fiduciary agent for its owner. The monies deposited in the escrow account may represent the earnest money deposit on a purchase agreement.

Estate in Fee. The real property estate that grants the complete package of ownership rights and privileges to the current property owner.

Estate Settlement. The distribution of the assets of an estate at the death of the owner.

Estimated Useful Life. The useful life of an asset, which is estimated by an appraiser, an Internal Revenue Service representative, or other such informed person. The term *useful life* applies to the period of time in which the asset is economically useful to the typical occupant of the property.

Eurodollar Rates. The rates on the debt obligations that are bought and sold in the international money market. Usually the rates are quoted in U.S. dollars.

Excess Depreciation. The surplus depreciation expense, found by subtracting the straight-line depreciation over a certain time period from the depreciation amount actually taken for tax purposes, by means of accelerated depreciation methods.

Existing Home Prices. The market prices of houses that already exist.

Expansionary Phase. The stage of general business activity in which sales volume and net profits are continuing to increase as a whole in the business sector. This is one phase of the general business or real estate cycle that continually reoccurs, though not at equal intervals.

Expected Value. The estimated future value of each investment variable. The sum of the projected values times their probability of occurrence would give the expected value of an investment variable for the projected time interval. For example, utility costs might be estimated through calculation of expected values.

Factors of Production. Factors defined by the economists to be labor, capital, land, and entrepreneurship.

Family Size. The number of family members within a single household.

Feasibility Study Fee. The fee required by the preparer of a feasibility study, which will show the prospective investor the estimated cash flow and associated tax benefits that may be realized from the subject investment.

Federal Agency Security. A debt obligation—short or long-term—of an agency of the federal government. The investor may consider that the full faith and credit of the U.S. government is behind the principal and interest repayment of the federal agency.

Federal Deposit Insurance Corporation. The subsidiary corporation of the Federal Reserve that insures deposits of commercial banks and mutual savings banks.

Federal Home Loan Mortgage Corporation. A corporate subsidiary of the Federal Home Loan Bank Board, which was established as a secondary mortgage market facility for the member savings and loan associations. The organization buys and sells mortgages, mortgage participations, mortgage-backed securities, and other short and long-term debt obligations.

Federal National Mortgage Association. A private corporation whose board of directors is partially appointed by the President of the United States, with the consent of the U.S. Senate, and whose establishment was predicated on its operation as a secondary mortgage market institution to stabilize mortgage flows and the construction business. Its debt ceiling is regulated by the U.S. Department of Housing and Urban Development; its stockholders are both private investors from the general public and mortgage seller-servicers.

Federal Reserve. The federal agency charged with the control of the United States money supply, the establishment and administration of current monetary policy, the regulation and financial assistance to the member national banks, and the coordination of monetary policy with current fiscal policy of the Treasury Department.

Fee Simple Absolute. The real property estate that grants to the possessor the complete bundle of property ownership rights. Only the government may restrict these rights and only on condition that the public good is benefited.

Fee Simple Determinable. An estate in property that automatically terminates on the happening of a stated event and reverts to the grantor.

Fee Simple Subject to a Condition Subsequent. A fee simple estate that is subject to termination upon the happening of a stated event if the grantor or party who has succeeded to his or her interest decides to exercise the power of termination.

Fee Simple Subject to an Executory Limitation. A fee simple estate that can be terminated at the happening of a stated event. When the stated event occurs, the title vests in a third party.

Feudal System. The property ownership system in which the sovereign power owns all land. Tenant rights to the land are given by the sovereign power to subordinates.

FHA Housing Programs. Housing programs established and supported by the U.S. Department of Housing and Urban Development with the use of Federal Housing Administration mortgage insurance.

FHA 203(b) Program. The mortgage insurance program of the U.S. Department of Housing and Urban Development, which helps finance buyers of middle income, unsubsidized housing units that conform to the requirements set forth in the Federal Housing Administration Minimum Property Standards manual.

FHA 245 Graduated Payment Mortgage Insurance. The mortgage insurance program of the U.S. Department of Housing and Urban Development, which helps finance buyers of housing units qualified for the FHA graduated payment plan.

FHA-VA Interest Rate. The interest rate set by the U.S. Department of Housing and Urban Development in cooperation with the United States Congress, which establishes the nominal rate on any FHA-insured or VA-guaranteed mortgage loan negotiated at that time. The administered interest rate is changed from time to time in an effort to keep the FHA-VA rate relatively close to the current mortgage market rate on permanent mortgage loans.

Financial Capacity. The innate capability of a party to finance assets, which is derived from current earning power, accumulated wealth, and credit standing.

Financial Foundation for Investment. Before investment in real property, negotiable instruments, and other assets, it is often suggested that the investor have investments for personal and family protection, shelter, transportation, and emergencies. This basic financial position suggested for the prospective investor is often called the financial foundation for investment.

Financial Institutions. The privately owned organizations that receive deposits, insurance premiums, or pension fund contributions from individuals, businesses, and government agencies and, after paying the operating costs of the organization, invest the remaining funds in loans and negotiable securities subject to reserve requirements set by the appropriate regulators.

Financial Management Rate of Return. A method of calculating return on investment that is based on the terminal value rate-of-return concept. In using present value methods, only one internal rate of return is possible using this particular method.

Financial Risk. The risk of default on the contract; the risk of bankruptcy of the borrower; the risk of loss of principal invested.

First-owner Depreciation. The particularly favorable depreciation methods that can be utilized by the owner of a new commercial or industrial property.

Fixed-income Security. An indenture agreement with a fixed income, payable at given, equal intervals, usually six-month intervals.

Flow of Funds Statement. The financial statement for a corporation that shows the sources and uses of funds for a given time period of company operation.

Flower Bond. A Treasury debt obligation specifically designed for payment of estate taxes at par value at the death of the investor.

Foreclosure. The legal action taken by the mortgage lender to acquire the property title—if the title is not already held by the mortgage lender—and to attain the legal right to sell the real estate collateral for the reimbursement of the mortgage lender for the mortgage debt outstanding.

Foreign Tax Credit. A tax credit that is a deduction from the taxes otherwise due. This is a deduction off the top of the taxes, calculated before the consideration of this expense. Usually the foreign tax credit is permitted for those American companies that must pay various types of taxes to the foreign governments of the countries where their plants and distribution outlets are located.

Foreign Versus Domestic Real Estate Investors. In contrast to domestic real estate investors who are permanent residents of the United States, foreign real estate investors live permanently beyond the bounds of the United States.

Form Report. An appraisal report made on the form prescribed by the client or on a form usually employed by the appraiser for the particular type of property.

Foundations and Endowments. Organizations established by profitable companies or well-to-do persons for philanthropic endeavors. When an institution receives generous contributions from profitable companies and well-to-do individuals, the institution may invest this endowment fund and use the proceeds or income from the invested funds to support various of its activities and functions. Universities often maintain their personnel, plant, and equipment on the income from endowment funds.

Fourplex. A multifamily structure housing four residential units.

Franchise, Small-Business. The small business agreement whereby the franchisee agrees to operating and financing regulations set by the franchisor, in order to do business under the franchise name.

Freehold Estate. An estate in real property, such as fee simple, that endures indefinitely with no specified termination date.

Front-end Cost. Expenses encountered by the developer in the planning stage of a project.

Fully Amortized Loan. The loan whose total principal repayment and interest payments are scheduled through level-payment periodic mortgage payments.

Functional Obsolescence. The loss in value of an asset from its outmoded functional characteristics. If real property is involved, the room layout, room sizes, electrical outlets and voltage, storage space, and garage space may be outmoded and functionally out of date, according to current lifestyles, family size, and occupant preferences.

Future Worth of a Single Sum. The estimated future value of a single sum that receives compound interest payments over a future time period.

Future Worth of an Annuity. The estimated future value of periodically received annuity payments that receive compound interest as they are reinvested, up to the established time in the future.

Gap Loan. The loan that bridges the gap between the construction loan maturity and the funding of the permanent loan.

Garden Apartment. The apartment unit in a two-or three-story walkup multifamily building. Often several garden-apartment buildings will be clustered in an apartment project so that green space may be left between the buildings for the visual and outside entertainment of the building occupants.

General Business Cycle. The fluctuating pattern of general business activity over a number of years within a given country. The four phases of the general business cycle are sometimes called expansion, prosperity, recession, and depression.

General Contractor. The person specializing in building construction, who contracts with the owner to construct a building or a number of buildings in a real estate project. The general contractor subcontracts the specialized areas of construction work that need to be performed in order to complete the structure.

General Obligation Bond. A long-term debt obligation of the state or local government, whose principal and interest repayment is dependent on the general taxing power and credit standing of the issuer.

GNMA-guaranteed Mortgage-backed Securities. The long-term debt obligations that are each backed by a pool of mortgages, where the Government National Mortgage Association guarantees the payment of the interest and the repayment of the principal to the investors in these securities.

Goals for Integration. Objectives set by government agencies and Congress for the integration of racial groups in their social and economic endeavors.

Government Housing Programs. The mortgage insurance and financial programs related to housing that are promulgated and administratively supported by government agencies on the federal, state, and local levels. Government housing programs usually concern housing for low- and moderate-income people.

Government National Mortgage Association. The government agency that manages and maintains properties acquired by the federal government in foreclosure actions, guarantees mortgage-backed securities that meet its requirements, and subsidizes mortgagors and building tenants through special mortgage purchases and rent supplements.

Graduated-payment Mortgage. The mortgage contract in which the mortgagor pays less than the traditional monthly level payment during the first few years of the mortgage. Then, after the seventh or tenth year, as monthly payments progressively increase in a step-up pattern, the mortgagor pays monthly payments in excess of the traditional level monthly payments. Negative amortization, from the lender's viewpoint, takes place in the early years of the mortgage, since the mortgagor does not pay the complete interest and principal required for full amortization of the mortgage that should be paid in the first few years of the mortgage.

Gross Allowable Income. The gross income from the members of a household that is approved or allowed for mortgage financing purposes. The temporary income of minor children from sporadic summer employment or the sporadic and temporary income of the wife may not be allowed for mortgage financing purposes.

Gross Contract Price. The total sale price on the purchase agreement or other such sales contract.

Gross Income Multiplier. This multiplier is found by dividing annual estimated income at the time of sale into the sale price. When several recent sales of comparable properties are examined in order to determine their gross income multiplier, the resulting factor is multiplied by the subject's gross income in order to arrive at total value from the income approach.

Gross Leasable Space. The total space, from the middle of one wall to the middle of the opposite wall and from the middle of the ceiling to the middle of the final flooring, that is available for lease. The areas consumed by columns, stairways, and cleaning and storage closets are also included in the total gross leasable space.

Gross Monthly Income. The total monthly income without any deductions that is generated by the members of the prospective mortgagor's household.

Gross National Product. The final sales value of all the goods and services produced in the United States during one year's time, as estimated by the U.S. Department of Commerce. Often the value is referred to as the GNP.

Gross Potential Income. The gross income that is potentially available from a property, as compared with gross income derived from comparable properties.

Gross Private Domestic Investment in Structures. The financial investment in structures made by private individuals or organizations, where depreciation of existing structures is not accounted for.

Gross Rent Multiplier. The factor derived from recent comparable sale data, which is multiplied by the monthly estimated rent for the subject in order to find the value of the subject from the income approach. The multiplier for each of the recent comparable property sales is found by dividing the gross monthly income for the comparable property at the time of sale into the sale price. An appraiser may use annual rent estimates instead of monthly rent estimates.

Ground Lease. The agreement between the landowner and the tenant, which grants land use to the tenant in return for periodic rental or lease payments to the landowner.

Growth-inducing Impact. The possible results that may occur from growth in land or economic development that may favorably or unfavorably affect the environment and community.

Hand-held Calculator. A small calculator that is easily transportable and can easily be held in the hand.

Hazard Insurance Premium. The payment made periodically to the insurance company for hazard insurance coverage. The hazards usually covered include fire damage, water damage, theft, vandalism, bodily injury to a visitor on the premises, and tornado damage.

Headquarters Office Building. An office building that caters to the headquarters office operations of numerous companies.

Hierarchy of Investment Risks in Real Estate Investment. The ranking, from high to low, of real estate investments, in terms of their overall risk statures.

High-credit-rated Stores. Retail stores that have received the highest credit ratings from Dun & Bradstreet, Robert Morris & Associates, Standard & Poor, and other credit-rating agencies.

Highest and Best Use. The use of an asset so that it will reach its highest possible appraised value.

Highest Present Value. The use of property in order to gain the highest present value for the land and the structures.

Hostelries. Motels and hotels where transient housing accommodations are provided.

Hotel-Motel Management. The management of transient housing facilities by local firms or internationally renowned firms such as Sheraton, Hilton, and Holiday Inn.

Houseboat. A house on a floating boat platform. The houseboat is often a residential accommodation along a major river, along a ocean shoreline, or in a wide-ranging bayou region of the country.

Household Formation Trend. The trend in the number of households that depend on the rate of househole formation. Household formation is dependent on relative levels of personal incomes, the divorce rate, the marriage rate, the current stage of the general business cycle, general population increase or decrease, and other such factors.

House's Basis. The original cost of the house, less the accumulated depreciation taken.

Housing Manufacturer. The manufacturer of housing units by the factory assembly-line method under the manufacturing plant roof.

Housing Starts. This term is used by the federal government in statistical compilations of results from the sampling of initial house and apartment construction across the United States. Any area may be sampled to determine the current level of housing starts extrapolated for the current fiscal year.

HUD Special Assistance Programs. The Special Assistance Programs of the U.S. Department of Housing and Urban Development permit rent supplements to be paid to low- and moderate-income apartment tenants, mortgage subsidies to be paid to low- and moderate-income mortgagors, and mortgage subsidies to be paid to mortgagees of low- and moderate-income housing projects. Usually the special assistance takes the form of payments of tax monies, which the Treasury funnels into the Government National Mortgage Association through its purchases of specially designed, nonnegotiable GNMA bonds.

Hybrid Mortgage Trust. The real estate investment trust that invests in a balanced portfolio of long-term mortgages and real properties.

Inchoate Right. A property right that is dormant. If the appropriate condition were to exist, the inchocate right would be an active, effective right. For example, the inchoate right to property distributed by will becomes an exercisable right when the person who drew up the will dies.

Income Approach. The approach to real estate appraising that focuses on the capitalization of net operating income with the appropriate capitalization rate and the right capitalization method.

Income Capitalization Method. A method of converting annual operating income into overall present value of the income property.

Income Property Valuation. The appraisal of real property that produces income for its owner.

Incurable Depreciation. The defect in a structure or its environment that causes loss in property value that cannot be cured or, at least, cannot be cured on an economic basis. The term *incurable*, as applied to depreciation, often means that the cost required to cure the defect surpasses the resulting rise in the market value of the property.

Indenture Agreement. A written agreement that obligates the lender to provide funds for a return on the investment and the borrower or issuer to receive the funds and repay them by the contract terms with interest. For example, a mortgage with its two parts is an indenture agreement that is secured with real estate collateral. A mortgage bond and commercial paper are also forms of indenture agreements.

Independent Store. A retail store owned by its proprietor, not a chain store holding company. The independent store may be affiliated with a wholesale chain or a national or regional merchandising service, but it retains its individual ownership and independent managerial control.

Index Lease. A lease whose periodic payments depend on the current level of the base index. The index may be the Consumer Price Index or any weighted combination of money and capital market interest rates.

Indirect Costs. The costs not directly associated with the construction or operation of a building or an enterprise. Indirect costs include provisions for coverage of overhead and profit for the subcontractor and contractor.

Industrial Development. The development of land for the construction of industrial buildings, which occurs when the land is prepared.

Industrial Land. Land zoned for industrial use, since it is suited for industrial development.

Inflation Protection. A form of financial protection in which the decline of the dollar from inflation is ameliorated or neutralized.

Inflationary Risk. The risk of loss resulting from inadequate financial protection against inflation. Inflation protection or a lessening of the inflationary risk may be derived from a mortgage yield based at least partially on a percentage of gross revenue from the income property.

Inflationary Trend. The pattern over time of increasing inflation or declining value of the United States dollar.

Inheritance Right. The right to inherit property from a parent or other natural ancestor.

Installment Sale. A sale of a property that results in payments by the buyer over a period of time to the seller.

Institute of Real Estate Management. The trade association devoted to professionalism in real property management, which is an affiliated organization of the National Association of Realtors.

Institutional Lender. A lender who adheres to the regulations and investment conventions of her or his employer, a traditional financial intermediary.

Institutional Lending Policies and Practices. The lending policies and practices influenced by the regulators and officers of the particular lending institution. These lending policies and practices change over time.

Institutional Portfolio. The total investment holdings of a private financial company.

Institutional Purchase or Sale. The purchase or sale of an asset by a financial institution. It could also mean the purchase or sale of the financial institution itself.

Intangible Drilling Cost. Expenses related to the drilling of oil and gas wells that are deductible but are not necessarily current costs of drilling. Deductible costs related to the rapidly depleted oil and gas deposits.

Interest Accrued. The interest expense that has been incurred but that need not be paid for at present.

Interest only Amortization. During the early portion of loan repayment, the borrower may be permitted to pay only the interest due and make no contribution toward the principal retirement. When only interest is being paid, the lender is permitting at that time interest-only amortization.

Interest Rate Ceilings. Regulation Q, administered by the Federal Reserve and the Federal Home Loan Bank Board, establishes and changes periodically the maximum interest rates that may be paid by thrift institutions and commercial banks on their various types of deposits.

Interest Rate Risk. The investor's risk, associated with the rise or fall of interest rates while an investment is being held. The value of the investment may be subject to significant rise or fall because of the change in the relevant interest rates during the investment holding period.

Internal or Discounted Rate of Return Method. The method of figuring yield on investment where the rate of interest is found that equates the net cash outlay to the net cash inflows of future time periods. The rate of interest obtained is called the internal rate of return or the return on investment.

Internal Revenue Service. The federal agency that devises, administers, and enforces the tax code of the United States. The agency collects federal income taxes from individuals, households, and businesses.

International Factors. Factors of supply and demand related to the international scene.

Inventory Tax Exemption on Goods in Transit. The exemption of a company from taxation on inventories of goods in transit.

Investible Funds. Funds of individuals or organizations that are available for short- or long-term investment.

Investment Banking House. A financial institution that buys or deals in issues of stock and bonds or mortgages that must be sold to appropriate investors at the market yields.

Investment by Foreign Investors. Investment in the United States by investors based outside the United States, or investment in any country by investors based outside that country.

Investment Goals. The objectives that an investor has set for his or her investment returns, in terms of the risks that may be assumed.

Investment Management. The managerial control of the various assets of an investor's portfolio.

Investment Managers. Those who agree to manage the assets or investments of others.

Investment Objectives. The goals of an investor, which are usually financial goals related to return on investment and assumption of risk.

Investment Yield Measurement. The methods used in measuring the investor's yield on the investment.

Investor's Equity. The investor's cash commitment

to an investment. The investor's downpayment is ofter called the investor's equity.

Investor's Psychological Makeup. The stability or instability of the investor's psychological outlook with regard to investment preferences.

Investor's Yield Requirement. The yield requirement of the investor, which includes return from operating net cash flows, equity buildup, and property appreciation or depreciation.

Joint Investment. An investment owned by two or more parties.

Joint Ownership of Property. The ownership of a single property by two or more parties, who may be individual persons or business entities.

Joint Tenancy. The joint ownership form in which two or more partners hold an undivided interest in a property and agree to survivorship rights for the remaining partners at the death of a partner. Four unities are also required for the establishment of a joint tenancy agreement: the unities of time, possession, interest, and title.

Junior Department Store. A retail store of many departments—some leased and some not—which tends to sell to the public lower-priced—perhaps discount-priced—consumer durable and nondurable goods. Examples are K-Mart, Woolco, and Woolworth.

Junior Mortgage. A mortgage subordinate in priority to the first-mortgage loan. The junior mortgage may be a second mortgage, a third mortgage, or any subsequent lien.

Key Chain Tenant. A chain-store tenant that maintains an Aaa credit rating.

Labor Availability. The availability of labor of the desired kind and skill in the area of the proposed industrial or commercial development.

Land Contract. The financing of a real property purchaser by the present property owner, where the title is transferred to the buyer when all or a sufficient portion of the borrowed money is repaid. The seller is called the *vendor*, and the buyer is labeled the *vendee*.

Land Contract Financing. The financing of real property by the seller. The title remains with the vendor (seller) until the vendee (buyer) completes the agreed payment.

Land-coverage Ratio. The portion of the total land that is covered by permanent, substantial improvements.

Land Development. The preparation of land for the impending construction of buildings and other permanent improvements. Land development usually entails street, curb and gutter construction; the laying of utility lines; and the landscaping of the raw land for the construction of the planned buildings.

Land Development Loan. A loan to prepare the land for permanent structures. With the loan the developer installs the necessary utility lines; constructs the streets, curbs, and gutters; and landscapes and grades the land for further construction.

Land Loan. Money borrowed for the acquisition of land.

Land-use Zones. Zoning ordinances passed by local government officials that prescribe permitted land use in designated zones or areas.

Large-lot Zoning. Zoning ordinances associated with residential areas that require an unusually large lot for each single-family dwelling.

Lease. The contract in oral or written form, recorded or unrecorded, that specifies the approval of the landlord to the possession of the landlord's property by the tenant for a specific or indefinite period of time. For the rights of property possession, the tenant or lessee usually pays the landlord—the lessor—rent on an established, periodic basis.

Lease Deductions. The expense deductible for federal income tax purposes that is derived from the lease payment. The complete lease payment is tax deductible.

Lease Renewal. The extension of a lease for a stated period of time. After a lease has run for the initial period and the lease payments have been paid the lessor by the lessee according to the terms of the lease, the lessor may grant an extension of the lease period.

Leasehold Estate from Period to Period. The real property estate that conveys the right of possession of property that spans the initial contract time period and may be extended automatically to an additional time period of the same duration as the original lease period. Any number of extensions of the contract may be approved, but the additional time period is the same as the original time period.

Leasehold Estate at Sufferance. The possession of real property by a tenant who is not currently under lease, where the landlord permits the tenancy until the landowner desires to terminate the rights of possession. The landlord "suffers" the tenancy of the occupant until vacancy of the premises is demanded by the landlord.

Leasehold Estate at Will. The right of property possession that may be terminated at the will of the tenant or the landlord with reasonable notice to the other party of the proposed vacancy of the premises.

Leasehold Estate for Years. The real property estate that conveys the right of possession of the property to the tenant by the landlord for an extended period of time. The period of time covered by the leasehold estate may be 5 years, 10 years, 40 years, or a longer period of time. A 50-year ground lease is a good example of a leasehold estate for years.

Leasehold Financing. The financing of improvements on leased land by the land lessee.

Leasehold Mortgage Loan. A mortgage loan made by a lender for the permanent financing of the improvements resting on leased land. The landowner usually must subordinate his ownership interest in the land to the first-mortgage leasehold mortgage loan.

Lender-borrower Negotiation. The interplay between the prospective lender and the prospective borrower, which results in the fixing of the loan amount and terms for repayment.

Lender Participation. The extent to which the lender receives a portion of the cash flow, the gross revenue, or other such financial sum that the owner generates as return from the investment.

Less-than-freehold Estate. The real property estate that permits occupancy by the estate holder of another party's real property. Only leasehold rights are held, not fee simple rights.

Leverage. The use of borrowed money to supplement equity in the purchase of an asset.

Liabilities. The debts of the person or the company. These debts may be short- or long-term.

Life Estate. A real property estate given by a grantor to a grantee on the basis that the grantee's estate runs only during the lifetime of a specified person. The life indicated by the grantor may or may not be that of the grantee. At the death of the specified person, the title to the real property may revert to the grantor or the grantor's estate, or it may be transferred to another person who is specified in the life estate by the grantor.

Life Style. The living patterns of an individual that are influenced by the individual's social and economic preferences.

Like-kind Property. A term that applies to tax-free exchanges. A property held for productive use in a trade or business or for investment can be exchanged tax free for another property held for productive use in a trade or business or for investment. Property held for productive use in a trade or business can be exchanged tax free for a property held for investment; the reverse is also true. The properties subject to tax-free exchange must be of like kind with regard to their nature or character but not with regard to their grade or quality. City real estate may be exchanged for ranch or farm property. Real property may be exchanged for a leasehold estate with 30 years or more to run. Improved real estate may be exchanged for unimproved real estate and vice versa.

Limited Partner of a Limited Partnership. The partner of a limited partnership who does not actively engage in the management of the organization but contributes money or other assets to the limited partnership. The limited partner's financial liability is usually limited to her or his financial contribution to the partnership.

Limited Partnership. The form of business organization in which two or more owners assume either general-partner of limited-partner status.

Linear Foot. The horizontal measurement of 12 inches. For cost-estimation purposes, the linear foot measures 12 inches in length, the height depends on the height of the wall or other construction component, and the depth or thickness depends on the thickness of the wall or other construction component. Wall costs are only one of the costs measured by cost estimators on the basis of linear feet.

Liquidity. The conversion of nonliquid assets into cash equal to, less than, or more than the par value of the assets. The degree of liquidity relates to the relative speed of conversion of an asset into cash. A high degree of liquidity of an asset implies that it usually can be converted to cash quickly (within a few hours or days).

Liquidity Risk. The risk of not being able to convert an asset at par value into cash immediately.

Loading Dock. The rear of a store, where merchandise and fixtures are delivered and carried out on trucks.

Loan-acquisition Process. The solicitation of loans by loan officers and other officers of lending institutions. The term may also apply to the process by which a prospective borrower procures a loan. Phone calls to competing lending institutions may start the loan-shopping process. The rendering of credit and financial information to the interested loan officers also furthers the loan-acquisition process. The loan is finalized after loan officer and borrower negotiation of the income property loan terms.

Loan Application. The form filled in by the loan applicant, the loan officer, or both parties jointly in order for the financial institution to make a decision about funding or not funding the offered mortgage. Many lenders design their own loan application forms.

Loan Closing Costs. The total costs that must be borne by the seller and buyer in the finalization of the loan, which is required to transfer the title from the seller to the buyer.

Loan Constant. The decimal percentage of the total original loan amount, which is multiplied by the original loan amount to find the annual level loan payment, which includes the payment of interest and the repayment of principal.

Loan Default. The failure to observe all the loan requirements as agreed upon by the borrower and the lender at the time of loan origination. For example, if the borrower does not meet a scheduled loan payment at the time and on the day specified in the loan contract, the loan may be declared in default by the lender.

Loan Negotitation. The bargaining over the loan amount and repayment terms that takes place between the prospective borrower and the prospective lender. The negotiation may amount to substantial bargaining in the case of the income property mortgage loan, but the bargaining may be insignificant with respect to house mortgage loans.

Loan Origination Fee. The 2 to 3 percent of the original loan amount that is paid as a fee to the lender or lender representative for the underwriting of the loan.

Loan Progress Tables. Tables that show the loan balance on a $1,000 loan at the beginning of any stated year in the loan payment period, when the original term of the loan and the nominal interest rate on the loan are known.

Loan Rediscount Rate. The rate that the Federal Reserve charges its member banks for borrowed money.

Loan-to-value Ratio. The quotient calculated from dividing the appraised value or sale price into the loan amount. Lenders often determine the loan amount that they will extend to a prospective borrower by multiplying the typical loan-to-value ratio for the particular credit and real estate situation by the appraised value or sale price, whichever is lower.

Loan Warehousing Costs. The interest and administrative costs associated with a bank loan for the warehousing of mortgage loans.

Lodging Industry. The service industry grouping that includes motels and hotels.

Long-term Capital Loss. A capital loss that is realized on an asset held more than 12 months.

Long-term Investment Yields. The investment yields on long-term investment securities or other assets.

Low-density Standards. Zoning ordinances that specify relatively low-density development for a zoned area.

Maintenance Costs. The expenses incurred in the repair and upkeep of a real property.

Management Ratio. The portion of the revenue from an office building that is consumed by the management fees.

Margin Requirement. The Federal Reserve requirement that specifies the percentage of the purchase price of a stock or bond that must be paid by the investor. The rest of the purchase price of the stock or bond may be borrowed from the brokerage house and interest paid for the use of the money.

Marginal Tax Rate. The percentage of federal income taxes due on the last part of taxable income received, as noted on the appropriate federal income tax tables.

Marital Rights. The rights of each of the spouses of the marriage contract.

Market Approach. The approach to the appraised value of the subject property that requires the adjustment of recent sale prices of comparable properties. An estimate of the subject may be derived from the adjusted prices of each comparable property.

Market Comparison Method. A method of deriving value using current market data on comparable properties that have sold recently. The real-property characteristics of the comparable properties are adjusted according to knowledge from the current marketplace, so that the value for the subject will be derived.

Market Rental Rates. The rental rates currently being paid by the tenants of competing structures.

Market Study Fee. The fee required by the preparer of a market study for a prospective investment.

Market Value. The value of an asset in the marketplace. This value is usually determined by taking the recent selling prices of comparable properties and adjusting the price of each of them to reflect the estimated value of the subject property.

Marketability. The ability to convert an asset into

cash at, below, or above par value within a reasonably short period of time. ***Degree of marketability*** is the relative degree of capability of turning an asset's par value into cash within a reasonably short period of time. If the typical conversion period is short, the asset exhibits a high degree of marketability. If the typical conversion period is long, the asset exhibits a relatively low degree of marketability.

Master Tax Guide. A paperback, thoroughly comprehensive guide to tax regulations of the Internal Revenue Service, published by Prentice-Hall, Inc. In one comprehensive source, abbreviated treatment of the federal income tax provisions for business and individuals may be found.

Median New Second-home Price. The median price of a new second home. The median value is usually the middle value of a range that extends from high to low values.

Mergers and Consolidations. The purchase of the assets or stock of one business by another business (merger), or the trading of securities by existing business for the securities of a comprehensive business entity and then the dissolution of the original business entities (consolidation). A larger organization in terms of asset or stock dollar volume usually results from the merger or consolidation of two or more companies into a single company.

Minimum Investment Requirement. The minimum amount that may be invested in a security or non-negotiable certificate of deposit.

Mobile Home. A single-family housing unit that is manufactured at an assembly plant and delivered in finished form from the plant to the house site. The mobile home may rest on a long, flat bed device with wheels. It is transported to the house site by means of this wheeled platform. Usually, once the mobile home is installed at the intended site, it is never again moved.

Mobile Home Floor-plan Loans. The loans made to mobile home sales companies to floor-plan their inventories. As the mobile homes are individually sold, the financial institution releases the title of the mobile home to the new owner, as the operator of the mobile home sales company pays back part of the floor-plan loan with the sales receipts.

Mobile Home Shipments. The volume of shipments of mobile homes from their manufacturing plants to the place of purchase or installation.

Mobility. The facility to move from place to place. A high degree of mobility is marked by the inclination to move frequently and the actual incidence of frequent moves from place to place.

Modified Legal List. The term *legal list* refers to the list of investments eligible for financial institution investment, which is established by the regulatory authority. Quite often the term *legal list* is used synonymously with *New York legal list* which is set by the New York Insurance Commission for the investment of life insurance companies doing business in New York State. Since the New York legal list has been modified in recent years, that list is now often called the *modified legal list.*

Money and Capital Market Indices. Statistical amounts that reflect the weighted current yields from selected money and capital market securities. The statistical series or index is maintained over an extended period of time to show the general increase, decrease, or stability in interest rates in general or in the interest rates that significantly affect the mortgage market.

Money Costs. Costs of goods and services in terms of U.S. dollars.

Money Market Certificates. The certificates of deposit approved by the Federal Reserve, the Federal Home Loan Bank Board, and the National Credit Union Administration for member sale, where the interest rate on a minimum deposit of $10,000 is based on the average discount yield on the newly issued six-month Treasury bills at the time of deposit. The money market certificates authorized in June of 1978 by the Federal Reserve and the Federal Home Loan Bank Board and in November of 1978 by the National Credit Union Administration mature six months from the date of deposit.

Money Market Yields. The current yields on short-term negotiable instruments in the money market.

Monthly Fixed Payments. Total monthly housing expense, state tax and social security figured monthly, and installment debts of one year or longer that are due on a monthly basis—definition formulated by FHA for their credit analysis for mortgage insurance purposes. The length of the installment debt may vary according to the interpreter of monthly fixed payments.

Moody's Investment Services. The financial investment services provided by Moody's Corporation to the general investing public. Investors may rely on the published corporate financial statements and the credit ratings given by Moody's to the various corporations they analyze.

Mortgage. The financing agreement whereby the mortgagor pledges collateral to the lender in return for funds. The mortgage or mortgage deed is also one part of the two-part security called the mortgage; this part of the two-part security is a pledge of real property for the repayment of the borrowed funds. The other part is the promissory note.

Mortgage Amortization. The repayment of principal that has been borrowed from a lender.

Mortgage Assumption. The assumption of the mortgage obligation of the seller by the buyer with the permission of the mortgage lender.

Mortgage-backed Securities. Indenture agreements that are collateralized by a pool of mortgage loans whose mortgagors are currently repaying their mortgage debt. The repayment of security principal and interest may be guaranteed by an agency of the federal government—the Government National Mortgage Association—or it may be *guaranteed* by the issuer of the security. The guarantee of an issuer stems from the overall credit standing of the issuer and the extent to which mortgage income is pledged for the repayment of the security principal and interest. Most mortgage-backed securities resemble pass-through securities rather than bond-type securities.

Mortgage Bankers. The financial middlemen who originate mortgages, sell them to lender-correspondents, and retain the loan servicing for a fee. Mortgages bankers also may issue mortgage-backed securities of the pass-through type, which may or may not be guaranteed as to interest and principal payment by the Government National Mortgage Association.

Mortgage Bond. A long-term debt obligation of the issuer, in which mortgaged property is pledged as collateral for the repayment of the bond principal and interest. In a way, the mortgage debt is merely divided into portions—bonds—that the current investor clientele prefer.

Mortgage Brokers. The financial middlemen who place mortgages with investors without retaining the loan servicing. The broker may or may not have originated the loan.

Mortgage Coefficient. The factor *C* in the Ellwood capitalization rate formula is derived by adding the expected equity yield rate to the product of the percentage of mortgage paid off at the end of the projection period and the sinking-fund factor and then by subtracting the loan constant or loan factor.

The Mortgage Corporation. A label for the Federal Home Loan Mortgage Corporation, which is a corporate subsidiary of the Federal Home Loan Bank Board.

Mortgage Debt. The debt of a borrower, the mortgagor, in which real property is pledged for the repayment of the loan. The mortgagor gives a mortgage to the lender, the mortgagee, in order to borrow money for a legal purpose.

Mortgage-equity Method. A method of deriving the capitalization rate in which substantial information about the expected equity return and about the mortgage financing is required for formula purposes. One mortgage-equity method utilizes the Ellwood formula.

Mortgage Market Conditions. The absence or presence of mortgage money, the level of the mortgage rates, the number of discount points payable at closing, the prevailing loan-to-value ratios, and the interest of lenders in particular types of property loans make up some of the variables that are analyzed in assessment of mortgage market conditions. The condition of the mortgage market is dependent on the current status of these and other related variables.

Mortgage Money. An amount of dollars invested or to be invested in a mortgage obligation or in many mortgages.

Mortgage Originator-sellers. The financial intermediaries who originate mortgages and sell them to secondary mortgage market participants.

Mortgage Payment. The periodic payment to the mortgage lender by the borrower of monies toward the amount due in mortgage interest and mortgage principal repayment.

Mortgage Pool. A group of mortgages (1) that may be pledged for collateral behind a mortgage-backed security or (2) that may be sold as an entity in the secondary mortgage market to a private investor or government institution.

Mortgage Recording Fee. The cost of recording a mortgage at the appropriate county, parish, or township office where the real property is located.

Mortgage Yield. The effective yield on a mortgage to an investor. The yield may include the contract rate, the prepaid interest, the amortized discount on the discount price paid, and the variable returns from the mortgagor in the form of equity participation over the term of the mortgage.

Mortgagee Participation in Equity. The lender's receipt of a percentage of the gross or net receipts rendered by the income property tenants to the owner or ownership group. The profits that would otherwise accrue to the owner are shared with the mortgage lender in order to obtain mortgage monies from that lender.

Mortgaging Out. The acquisition of mortgage financing that covers total developmental costs or even more. No equity may be required from the owner.

Mortgagor's Personal Wealth. The personal net worth of the mortgagor without considering the net worth of the businesses in which the mortgagor is a principal investor.

Multifamily Mortgage Debt. Mortgage debt that is associated with multiple-unit dwelling structures. The mortgage debt may be associated with the financing of a multiunit building of two or more apartment units. In some statistical series compiled and reported by the government, multifamily mortgage debt applies only to financing of apartment buildings with five or more dwelling units.

Municipal Security. The debt obligation issued by the state or local government instrumentality whose interest payment is tax free for federal income tax purposes. In investor conversation, the debt obligation may be called a *tax-exempt muny*.

Municipal Tax-exempt Security. A debt obligation of any length sold or issued by a state or local government or affiliated agency whose interest is exempt from federal income taxation.

Mutual Savings Bank. The financial intermediary that is labeled a thrift institution because it, like the savings and loan association, accepts deposits for institutional investment in a large volume of residential mortgage loans. Unlike the other thrift institutions, the mutual savings bank also invests heavily in corporate bonds. The mutual savings bank usually insures its deposits through the FDIC or a state insurance association. Therefore, the mutual savings bank is usually regulated by the FDIC.

Narrative Report. The lengthy, comprehensive report that involves discussion in paragraph form rather than the filling in of a blank form.

National Credit Union Administration. The federal agency that regulates the federally chartered credit unions.

National Environmental Policy Act. The statute passed by the United States Congress in 1969 that provided for the formation of a Council of Environmental Quality, which in turn created, through executive action, the Environmental Protection Agency.

National and Regional Stock Exchanges. The organized, privately owned stock and bond security exchanges that function on a national or regional basis.

Negative Leverage. When the effective rate of interest on borrowed money exceeds the rate of return on the total investment, negative leverage results.

Negative Taxable Income. When a business or investment generates a loss and does not pay federal income taxes that fiscal year, it is sometimes said that a negative taxable income resulted from business operation or investment management.

Net Cash Flow Before Debt Service and Taxes. Taxable income plus depreciation and mortgage interest before debt service and federal income taxes are deducted. Net operating income before debt service and taxes are deducted.

Net Cash Flow Before Taxes. Rental income, less cash operating expenses and mortgage debt service.

Net Cash Reversion Before Tax. The sales price, less selling expenses, less the balance outstanding on the mortgage.

Net Effective Monthly Income. Gross monthly income, less monthly federal income tax.

Net Gain on a Sale. Adjusted sale price, less the adjusted basis.

Net Leasable Space. The gross leasable space, less the space unusable for business activities of the typical occupant.

Net Operating Income. The income remaining after the operating expenses are subtracted from the effective gross income.

Net Percentage Lease. The tenant lease that specifies that the tenant pay at least part of the landlord's usual expense for property taxes, insurance premiums, and outside maintenance costs and a percentage of the gross revenue generated by the tenant in the rented space.

Net Present Value Method. The method of figuring return on investment that requires that the present value of the net cash outlays be subtracted from the present value of the net cash inflows, where an appropriate discount rate is used.

Net Profit. Gross revenue, less bad-debt loss, vacancy allowance, operating expenses, depreciation expense, and mortgage interest. It may be expressed on a before- or after-tax basis.

New Town. A planned urban community that is self-sufficient with regard to city social and municipal services and employment sources.

News Releases. Promotional literature prepared by the benefiting party that is transmitted to the news media.

1974 Employment Retirement Income Security Act. The first statute passed by the U.S. Congress about the vesting of retirement benefits even though a worker moves from one company to another.

Noncash Expense. Those expenses that are deducted from operating income for federal income tax purposes but that are actually expenses for which no cash in spent. For example, depreciation expense is often a noncash expense, since the tax deduction may be taken but no property depreciation may be experienced. No cash may be expended to maintain, repair, or modernize the property.

Nonrecourse Debt. Debt the payment of principal and interest of which must come from the borrowing entity and not from shareholders' personal assets.

Nonrefundable Credits. Payments made in advance and not refunded when the benefits from the payments cannot be realized. These amounts may be tax deductible under certain circumstances.

Nonresidental Structures. Structures that do not provide transient or permanent dwelling space for their occupants. The space is usually utilized for administration of business; wholesaling activities; retailing activities; storage of goods; supply of business or personal services; or manufacturing, processing, or assembly activities.

Nonstandard Home Mortgage. The home mortgage contract that is not the traditional contract with level-payment, fully amortized monthly debt service with fixed interest rate and maturity date. At present, nonstandard home mortgages encompass the reverse annuity, the graduated-payment, and the variable-rate types of mortgages.

Notorious Possession. The possession of property in such a manner that any bystander, neighbor, or visitor to the community may observe that occupancy. The occupancy or possession of the property is not hidden from normal observation. No attempt is made to conceal the occupancy by the tenants or owners.

Obsolescence. The decline in value from functional or environmental characteristics of property that are not presently favored by the typical property occupant because of recent changes in the standard of living, development of new appliances and fixtures, and the general life or business style of the typical property occupant.

Occupant-lessee. The occupant of space who leases that space from the landlord, the lessor.

Office Building Experience Exchange Report. Reports on office building operations and leasing that separate suburban buildings from downtown buildings and specialized office buildings from general-purpose office buildings. The range of dollar amounts for the buildings sampled is established for the many standard accounts for an office building. This report is a regular publication of the Building Owners and Managers Association International, which is based in Washington, D.C.

Office-space Demand. The demand for office space that comes from business centralization or decentralization, business expansion, consolidation of local offices, and other such fundamental reasons.

Open Market Committee Functions. The Open Market Committee of the Federal Reserve Board decides how the current monetary policy established by the Board should be carried out. U.S. Treasury securities of various maturities are bought and sold by the New York Federal Reserve Bank's trading desk and the New York dealers in Treasury securities to move the monetary system of the United States toward established targets.

Operating Department Store Company. An individual department store owned and operated by a major department store chain.

Operating Ratio. The ratio derived by dividing effective gross income or total gross income into total operating expenses. The resulting fraction shows how much of gross income is absorbed by operating expenses. The remaining portion will be used to meet the required debt service payments and income tax payments and to pay dividends to stockholders.

Operating Stage. The second phase of a project, which involves investment of capital and day-to-day operation and management of the investment.

Ordinary and Necessary Business Expense. The normal operating and financial expense related to a specific type of investment.

Organizational Legal Expense. The attorney's fee for establishing the necessary business entity for the holding, managing, and financing of an investment.

Overall Risk. The overall status of the risk of an asset after the extent of financial, liquidity, inflationary, and interest rate risk inherent in the asset has been recognized.

Overbuilt Market. Market conditions that reflect an oversupply of building space in comparison with the demand for that building space.

Over-the-counter Transactions. Transactions in bonds, stocks, and other negotiable instruments that are traded by specialized dealers in metropolitan offices not associated with the national or regional stock and bond exchanges.

Overtime Payment. The extra compensation required or paid for work beyond the normal working hours.

Owner-occupied House. The single-family detached house that is owned by the occupant of that house.

Participation Certificate. The negotiable instrument that indicates that a portion of a mortgage may be bought and sold in the marketplace. Each investor in a participation certificate owns a specific portion of the total mortgage loan.

Partnership. A form of joint ownership in which two or more parties agree to contract jointly in the operation of a business or in the ownership of assets. This group of partners may organize as a general or as a limited partnership.

Partnership Allocations. The allocations of cash flow, depreciation, and other types of income from a partnership property that are made to the individual partners from time to time.

Partitioning of an Undivided Interest. The splitting up of an undivided interest into separate interests for each of the co-owners by the court with jurisdictional authority.

Pass-through-type Mortgage-backed Security. A type of mortgage-backed security that promises repayment of security principal and interest from the repayments of principal and interest associated with the mortgages in the pool behind the pass-through security. The yield to the security investor may be uneven over the established payment periods because of the diversity of the mortgages in the mortgage pool, the extent to which the mortgagor payments are slow, the extent to which the mortgage contracts in the pool are in default, and the extent to which the issuer takes financial responsibility for level security payments.

Pension Fund. A fund accumulated and invested by a company, which may contribute sums for each individual employee covered and may receive contributions from the employees covered by the fund. At retirement time, the employee covered by the fund receives the appropriate retirement income.

Pension Fund Counselors. The managers of the assets of pension funds.

Pension Plan. The plan for financial investment for future retirement income. Pension plans often involve employee and employer contributions. Some plans only involve employee contributions; some plans involve only employer contributions.

Percent of Gross Possible Total Income per Room. A standard measure of expenditures associated with an income property, such as an apartment building.

Permanent Loan Commitment. The written letter of intent issued by a lender, which guarantees the borrower permanent mortgage money at a certain time or when construction of the improvements is completed.

Personal Consumption Expenditures. The dollar portion of personal disposable income that is consumed by expenditures of various kinds.

Personal Property. Assets that are not real properties, but are mobile and sometimes intangible. Examples: furniture, other furnishings, office equipment, livestock, farm equipment, and stock and bond market securities.

Personal Savings Rate. The ratio of average individual personal savings to average individual disposable personal income for the 12-month period.

Physical Deterioration. The loss in value of an asset from wear and tear and the natural elements, such as rain, snow, and ice.

Planned Industrial Parks. Industrial parks that are developed and leased under the control of a single developer. The park is planned specifically for the occupancy requirements of the industrial land user.

Planned Office Parks. Office buildings constructed as one development by a single developer who planned the structures and amenities specifically for the typical office occupants.

Planned Unit Development. A development that is primarily residential and was planned in advance and developed by a single business entity. Commercial development is often integrated into the development as a minor land use. This commercial space tends to be occupied by those who serve the residential clientele of the planned unit development, as well as by persons living and working nearby.

Planning Stage. The initial phase of a project, which involves planning and organizing.

Plant and Equipment Expenditures. Company expenditures for new buildings and equipment.

Plastic Pipe. Water and other pipes made of plastic.

Policy Loans. The loans made by a life insurance company on the policies held by company policyholders. The policy cash value is borrowed by the policyholder in return for a promise to repay the loan principal plus a stated rate of interest on the loan amount.

Pollution. The detrimental saturation of the air with harmful particles, spillage of chemicals and other waste materials into public water sources, emission of noise into the air, emission of vehicular exhaust fumes into the air, and other such harmful states of the environment.

Pollution Control. The control of polluting sources of the environment.

Pollution-control Facilities. The equipment needed for control of pollution from smokestacks, automotive exhaust systems, water cooling systems, and other sources.

Pool of Mortgages. A group of mortgages gathered

together for a reason, such as use of the pool for collateral for a mortgage-backed security.

Portfolio. The accumulated investment holdings of the investor.

Portfolio Managers. Those persons who manage the assets in individual, business, or institutional portfolios.

Portfolio Planning. The planning of the total investment of an individual or organization, where numerous investments are considered in a portfolio context.

Portfolio Strategy. The intelligent management of an investor's various assets, which leads to the investor's financial goals.

Positive Leverage. A condition in which the effective rate of interest on the borrowed money is less than the rate of return on the invested money.

Power of Eminent Domain. The power given by the federal government to the state and local governments and their agencies, utility companies, and other such organizations to acquire title involuntarily from private and public owners of land and improvements in order to pass the title to parties who develop the subject land in a manner beneficial to the public and in a manner approved by the local governing body.

Predevelopment Costs. The expenses related to legal organizational costs, feasibility study preparation, environmental impact study preparation, and architectural drawings. These are expenses incurred before any land development or financing takes place.

Preferred Stock. The shares of ownership of a corporation that receive dividends after prior claims of the corporation are paid but before dividends are paid to the common stockholders. This type of stock has prior claim to any corporation funds available for shareholder dividends before the common stock.

Preliminary Prospectus. The "red herring" that has not been approved officially by the Securities and Exchange Commission. The Securities and Exchange Commission must approve the printed offerings of securities to be sold to the general public that are issued by certain types of companies.

Prepaid Interest. Interest expense paid in advance on a loan that extends for a period of time.

Prepayment Penalty. The financial amount required of the borrower by the lender when the mortgage obligation is paid in its entirety before the scheduled date of total loan repayment. When a mortgage loan is negotiated, the lender may or may not require this penalty for possible early payment of the total obligation.

Prepayment Plan. A plan by a borrower to pay the loan requirements earlier than scheduled in order to pay off the loan more rapidly and lessen the interest payment requirement.

Present Value. The discounted cash flow from an investment, where an appropriate discount rate reflects the investor's required rate of return. The present value of expected future net cash flows.

Present Value of an Annuity. The discounted present worth of annuity payments received in the future, discounted at the appropriate discount rate.

Price. The dollar amount paid to the previous owner by the new owner for the acquisition of title.

Price-earnings Ratio. The factor calculated by dividing annual net profit per share of stock into the current market price of the share of stock.

Primary Mortgage Market. The market in which the prospective borrower and the prospective lender or the lender's representative negotiate the terms of the resulting mortgage loan.

Primary Reserves. See *Required Reserves.*

Principal Investment Motivations. The chief motivations or inducements that attract potential investors into an investment. Often in real estate these investment motivations include tax shelter, capital gains taxable on a more favorable basis than ordinary earnings, shelter for a household or business, and a reasonable cash flow yield on the cash investment.

Principal Repayment. The repayment of loan principal, usually in installments, along with the periodic payments toward interest. Also called *amortization.*

Printed Security Offering. The SEC-approved prospectus, or the "red herring", which is an unapproved, preliminary prospectus showing the characteristics of the security offering in print for the use of prospective investors.

Private Mortgage Insurance. Insurance for the protection of the mortgage lender in case the mortgagor defaults on the insured mortgage loan that is provided by a private mortgage insurance company.

Private Property Rights. Those property rights reserved for private citizens and organizations, as compared to public entities and organizations. Private individual property rights include rights of inheritance, rights of legal protection, and rights against confiscation by the state without just compensation.

Privately Held Stock. Corporate common and preferred stock that is held by the principal owner-investors of a corporation. The stock is not held by the public at large.

Privately Sponsored Development Credit Corporations. Corporations who finance industrial development with private sources of funds.

Probability of Occurrence. The estimated possibility of occurrence of an event when the possibility is seen to lie between 1.0 and 0. If the assigned probability were 0.9, there would be a 90 percent probability of the occurrence of the event. If the assigned probability were 0.1, there would be a 10 percent probability of the occurrence of the event. The factor 1.0 implies that there is no question about the occurrence of the event; it will occur. The factor of zero implies that there is no possibility of the event occurring.

Productivity Index. An index that shows the efficiency in the use of capital to produce goods and services.

Professional Appraisal Organization. An association predominantly for professional appraisers.

Profit. Taxable income or net profit.

Profit-and-loss Statement. The basic type of corporate financial statement, which shows the net result from the operation of the enterprise for a given time period. The bottom line on the statement is usually the net profit after taxes.

Profitability. The generation of profit from the employment of assets or the owner's equity.

Promotional Literature. Published information that advertises and promotes a product.

Property Exchange. The swapping of one property for another. If there is a difference in the property values, the difference may be made up by payment of cash or notes.

Property Law. The body of law associated with the rights and privileges of owners of property interests.

Property Productivity. The extent to which a property yields a return on investment. A high vacancy rate for an income property usually means relatively low productivity and a relatively low return on investment.

Property Tax Appraisal. The estimation of property value for property taxation purposes.

Purchase-money Mortgage. The mortgage financing provided by the property seller, another individual, or a financial institution in order to complete the sale of the property. Often the purchase money mortgage is financed by the property seller.

Purchase of Mortgage Loans. The payment of money for an existing mortgage loan, which prompts the transfer of its title from the original investor to the present investor. Many persons, businesses, and financial institutions purchase mortgage loans as investments.

Purchased Steam. Steam heat purchased from a utility company that generates such energy.

Purchasing Power of the Dollar. The amount of goods and services that may be bought with the United States dollar at a stated time. Inflation usually erodes the purchasing power of the dollar; as the dollar declines in value, it purchases fewer goods and services.

Qualified Investment. Assets whose characteristics fit the requirements for tax credits.

Qualified Tax-exempt Retirement Plans. Retirement programs that qualify with the Internal Revenue Service as tax-exempt pension funds.

Quality-of-life Factors. Factors related to a location that help determine the quality of life of the building occupants.

Quantity Survey Method. The method of estimating the cost of constructing a building at the present time, based on the cost per construction component and the number of each construction component. Each component cost includes the builder's overhead and profit per component. Examples of construction components are bricks, two-by-four lumber and sheets of drywall.

Railroad Rolling Stock. The assets of a railroad company that roll down railroad tracks.

Range of Value. The spread between the highest possible value and the lowest possible value.

Rate of Inflation. The rate of increase in the money supply over the increase in productivity. This is the rate at which the United States dollar declines in value with the continuance of inflation.

Ratio Analysis. The analysis of financial data that utilizes relationships between any two financial factors. A ratio shows the proportionate relationship of one factor to another.

Ratio of House Income to Room Sales. The ratio of motel or hotel income from sources other than room sales to receipts from room rentals.

Ratio of House Income to Total Sales. The portion of motel-hotel income other than room sales, as compared to total motel-hotel sales.

Real Estate. The land and everything attached to the land and everything under and over the earth's surface; the physical aspects of the earth's surface, site improvements such as utility lines and landscaping, and buildings resting on the earth's surface.

Real Estate Appraisal. The report of estimated value for a real property as of a given date.

Real Estate Collateral. The real property of the borrower that is pledged for a loan.

Real Estate Cycle. The fluctuating pattern of the overall real estate business resulting from periodic increases and decreases in the total value of real estate transactions. Four stages in the real estate cycle are expansion, peak of prosperity, recession or contraction, and depression. If only three stages are defined, they are growth, equilibrium, and decline.

Real Estate Industry. The industry comprised of persons who work in areas directly related to real estate transactions.

Real Estate Investment. The purchase of real property with the intent to receive a return or yield from the investment, as well as the return of the purchase price.

Real Estate Investment Trust. The form of trust that was devised by Congress and the Internal Revenue Service in 1960 as a tax-exempt investment vehicle for the small investors who wish to invest with others in real estate and mortgage interests.

Real Estate License Requirements. Requirements set by the state real estate licensing agency, commission, or other government body, which must be satisfied by the license examination applicant before the real estate license examination may be taken. The real estate license requirements often involve:

The age of the applicant.
The previous full-time real estate experience.
The educational preparation of the applicant.
The moral character and honesty of the applicant.
The previous criminal and legal history of the applicant.

Real Estate Tax Burden. The tax burden for a parcel of real estate is usually interpreted as the percent of market value represented by property taxes payable on the property. If the analyst multiplies the assessment ratio by the applicable tax rate, this percent may be derived. For example, the typical range for the tax burden for single-family houses in the United States is 1 to 3 percent.

Real Property. The interests, benefits, and rights inherent in the ownership of real estate. The bundle of rights with which the ownership of real estate is endowed.

Real Estate Stocks. The corporate common and preferred stock that is sold by companies who provide goods and services primarily associated with the real estate industry.

Realized Gain. In a tax-free exchange, the realized gain is the difference between the total amount received and the total amount given.

Recession. A significant decline in the level of industrial production, reflected in a decrease in economic activity. A recession is a mild but significant decline in general economic activity, while a depression is a major decline in industrial production and economic activity.

Recognized Gain. The amount of gain recognized for tax purposes in a tax-free exchange is the lesser of (1) the gain realized or (2) the total value of the unlike property received in the exchange.

Refinancing. The financing of an investment after the original financing has occurred. Refinancing may occur when the property owner wishes to free up tax-free capital with a higher loan on the property. The owner may wish to refinance the original loan to acquire a lower interest rate, a longer term, or lower mortgage payments.

Regional Patterns. Patterns of business or social activity that tend to occur on a regional basis.

Regional Shopping Center. The shopping center located in a suburban area of a major metropolitan area that offers a variety of specialty and shopping goods and services, plus a variety of convenience goods and services, to a trading radius of 20 to 30 minutes' driving time. The key tenants are primarily high-credit-rated chain stores, including one or two major department stores.

Regular Savings Account. The passbook savings account of the commercial bank, mutual savings bank, or savings and loan association in which the funds may be withdrawn at any time after the deposit without any obligation of advance notice to the financial institution.

Regular Treasury Bills. Short-term obligations of the U.S. Treasury that usually do not exceed 180 days in maturity and that are sold at a discount and do not mature at a tax payment time.

Regulatory Agencies. The federal agencies that regulate the activities and procedures of the financial institutions under their individual controls.

Rehabilitated Properties. Real properties that have been remodeled, repaired, and prepared for continued use and subsequent sale by the owner.

Relative Yield. The yield of an investment in comparison with yields of competing investments.

Remainderman. The party to whom the fee simple

estate passes when the specified lifetime associated with the life estate ends.

Renovation Cost. The total expense incurred in modernizing a building to satisfy current space needs.

Rentable Square Footage. The total square footage of the building, less the common areas of the halls and lobby, the space set aside for maintenance supplies and equipment, and the elevator shafts and stairwells.

Rental Income. The periodic income that a property owner derives from his building rental tenants.

Replacement Reserves. The accounting reserves set aside for the periodic, needed replacement of short-lived equipment, furnishings, and construction components of an income property. The replacement reserves cover replacement of the roof, the carpeting, the kitchen appliances, the draperies, and other such short-lived assets.

Replacement Value. The cost of replacing the functional utility of an existing house in today's market.

Reproduction Value. The cost of constructing a physical structure like the subject property at the present time.

Required Reserves. The portion of the various types of deposits received by a commercial bank that must be held at the bank because of Federal Reserve regulatory restrictions. The other portion of the various types of bank deposits may be loaned out or invested in approved securities.

Residential Private Investment. The investment by private individuals and organizations in residential structures.

Restraints on Investment Maximization. The maximum return from an investment if often impossible to achieve because of zoning regulations, Internal Revenue Service regulations concerning depreciation expense, building code enforcement, limitations on loan-to-value ratios from lenders and their regulators, and other government and private section regulations and conventions.

Return on Investment. The income derived from an investment that provides for the investor's recoupment of capital and a financial profit on the investment. There are several possible sources of income or cash flow from an investment. The term *investment* may refer to total investment of all owners and lenders, or only to the cash investment of the owners. Several formulas have been derived for calculation of return on investment.

Return on Sales. The before- or after-tax yield on total sales of a business enterprise.

Return on Stockholders' Equity. The ratio of net profit before or after taxes to stockholders' equity or net worth. The ratio shows the relative amount of profit generated with the equity of the investors.

Return on Total Assets. The before- or after-tax yield on total assets generated by an investment.

Revenue Act of 1978. The significant piece of tax legislation that Congress passed in the fall of 1978.

Revenue Bond. A long-term debt obligation of the state or local government whose principal and interest repayment is made from the revenue generated from the property occupant and paid to the issuer.

Reverse Annuity Mortgage. The mortgage loan in which a mortgagor with considerable equity in her or his house may receive periodic cash payments from the lender in exchange for the agreement to pay the outstanding loan from the sale proceeds or the value of the property after the death of the mortgagor.

Reversion. The value of the owner's real property at the end of the investment holding period.

Reversionary Interest. The interest held by a party to whom a property title may pass upon the occurrence of an event. The grantor of a life estate, for example, may have a reversionary interest that may be actuated by the death of the specified person on whom the life estate rests or by the death of the remainderman specified in the life estate agreement.

Risk Assumption. The recognition of risk inherent in a contractual agreement and the decision to accept the recognized risk.

Risk Dimensions. The varying degrees of risk of a particular asset or classification of assets. The degree of risk may range from high to low.

Risk-return Analysis of Real Estate Investment. Real estate investment alternatives are considered in light of both overall estimated risk and yield characteristics. Often it is assumed that relatively high-risk characteristics should be matched by relatively high-yield characteristics of the particular investment. In like manner, it is often assumed that relatively low-risk characteristics should be matched by relatively low-yield characteristics of the particular investment.

Robert Morris & Associates. A Philadelphia-based organization that maintains financial data on various lines of business involved in bank commercial loans. Standard ratios are maintained for the successful operation of businessess associated primarily with the established lines of trade.

Roof Trusses. Roof supports manufactured at an industrial plant and delivered as finished units to the construction site.

Royalties. Periodic payments for creators of copywritten assets that are sold in the marketplace. A portion of the gross or net revenues after expenses may be payable to the creator of the salable assets.

Rules of Thumb. Lending or investment rules that may not be formally adopted but that are operating conventions within the lending or investment community. Often these informal rules apply to the loan amount or purchase price per unit, the suggested land price per unit or square foot, the appropriate construction cost per unit or square foot, the desirable breakeven point on a particular type of income property, the desirable operating ratio, and other such investment and financing dimensions.

Safety of Principal. The extent to which the principal or investment amount is safe from decline in value or from loss.

Sale of Construction Services. Marketing the capabilities of a construction company.

Sale of Existing Loans. The transfer of title of an existing loan to another investor. Mortgage originating institutions often sell their loans to other primary and secondary mortgage market investors.

Sale-leaseback Agreement. A real estate contract that provides for the sale of real property to an investor and then the lease of the property from the new owner by the seller.

Sales or Use Tax Exemption on New Equipment. The exemption of a company from taxation on the purchase or use of new equipment.

Salomon Brothers. A New York investment banking firm that maintains data on the supply and demand for credit in the United States.

Salvage Value. The estimated value of the property at the end of its normal economic life.

Sandwich Lessee. The lessee who sublets to the sublessee and who gets a return on his or her investment in the lease by paying less to the lessor than the amount received from the sublessee.

Savings and Checking Deposit Verification. The investigation of the current balance of the prospective mortgagor's savings and checking account deposits by special form or by telephone call to reliable sources at the appropriate depository institutions.

Savings Rate. The portion of personal disposable income that is saved, on the average, over a year's time.

Secondary Income. The source of income that supplements the primary source of income. A secondary income, for example, may be derived from rents from income property, dividends from stockholders, interest from bond holdings, and profits from tenant farmers.

Secondary Mortgage Market. The market within which existing mortgages are traded among market participants. Traditional mortgage lenders and specially designed secondary mortgage market institutions trade mortgages and mortgage interests in this market.

Secondary Mortgage Market Institutions. The specially designed financial intermediaries who buy and sell mortgages as government or government-related organizations. This group of intermediaries includes the Federal National Mortgage Association, the Government National Mortgage Association, and the Federal Home Loan Mortgage Corporation.

Secondary Mortgage Market Organization. An organization—publicly or privately sponsored—that buys and sells mortgages on the secondary market level of business.

Secondary Reserves. The reserves set aside by commercial banks that supplement the primary reserves. These reserves are needed for unexpected withdrawals of funds, the appearance of unusually good investment opportunities, or other favorable or unfavorable circumstances that might arise at the bank.

Second-home Community. A community of residential and commercial land use—perhaps industrial land use—where households maintain second homes, not their principal places of residence. The second home is usually maintained as a recreational residence for leisure-time activities.

Security Cost. The expense of assuring physical and financial protection for the occupants of a building.

Selling Expenses. The costs associated with the marketing of an asset.

Sell-out or Termination Stage. The final phase of the real estate investment, in which the investor sells the project to another investor or investor group and receives net proceeds from the sale after taxes are deducted.

Sensitivity Analysis. The analysis of end results by changing one variable or expense-revenue account balance at a time.

Share of Beneficial Interest. The individual ownership interest of a trust, for example, the single share of stock of a real estate investment trust.

Share Price Index. The index showing the current relative level of the share price in terms of a base year, which is represented by an index of 100.

Shelter Production. The construction or manufacture of single-family or multi-family housing units by traditional on-site construction or by manufacturing plant methods.

Shopping Center Mall. The customer walking and lounging space between the various buildings housing the shopping-center storeroom tenants.

Shopping the Market for a Loan. The investigation for the best loan amount and terms available among the competing lenders handling the types of loans that are available in the relevant market.

Short-term Investment Yields. The investment yields from short-term investments.

Short-term Mortgage Trust. A real estate investment that invests primarily in short-term development and construction loans.

Single-family Detached Condominium House. The single-family detached house that may be owned as a condominium. Monthly common-area maintenance fees normally are required by the homeowners' association.

Single-wide Mobile Home. A manufactured house, approximately 12 feet in width by 65 feet in length, that is delivered on wheels from the factory to the site.

Sinking-fund Factor. The discount factor that reflects the use of a safe rate of interest for reinvestment of periodic amounts set aside and the length of the expected economic life of the asset or the term of the mortgage.

Sinking-fund Recapture. Sinking-fund recapture assumes that the equal amounts set aside for investment recapture each year are invested as they are periodically set aside at a safe rate of interest.

Site Selection. The selection of a site for a business, which involves investigation of such factors as the labor supply, transportation facilities, sources of raw materials and semifinished goods, power sources and adequacy, and proximity to the market.

Socioeconomic Groups. Groups of a society that are classified by their general social and economic characteristics.

Soft Costs. Costs that do not directly contribute to the construction of permanent improvements but cover such things as environmental impact studies, feasibility studies, soil test borings, and organizational legal costs.

Solar Heating System. The heating system that operates partially or wholly on solar energy sources. Special solar heating panels and heat pumps are usually required as part of the installation of this type of heating system.

Sole Investment. The party's single investment. No other investments have been made by the investor.

Southern Building Code Congress International. A trade association based in Birmingham, Alabama, which codifies the Southern Building Code and publishes literature on construction topics for their membership.

Special First-year Depreciation Allowance. Extra depreciation that may be permitted by the taxing authorities and the tax code for the first year of the economic life of a depreciable asset.

Specialty Chains. Chain stores that offer specialty goods and services for which customers will travel some distance and search diligently. Examples are furniture chain stores and fireplace chain stores.

Specialty Shopping Center. Merchants of specialty retail goods and services are located in a shopping center that attracts customers from a 30- to 40-minute driving radius of the center. No key chain tenant may be located in the center. Small specialty chains and independent stores are represented by the small boutiques, specialty food stores, and specialty restaurants.

Speculative Income Property. An investment in an income property for the purpose of recognizing a capital gain and perhaps a good cash-on-cash return within a reasonable period of time. If the owner-developer does not adequately prelease an income property so that mortgage financing may rest on the established leases, the owner has developed a speculative income property.

Speculative Land Purchase. Purchase of land with the intention of selling to another party in the near or relatively near future for a capital gain.

Spendable Income. Cash flow to equity after taxes. Net operating income, less debt service and federal income tax payment.

Sponsor-syndicator. The syndicate manager. This manager may have sold the syndicate shares as a sponsor of the syndication agreement.

Spouse. The marriage partner. The term *spouse* may apply to either the husband or the wife. The legal term has no sex connotation.

Square Footage of Living Space. The number of

square feet under the roof of the structure that is heated and air conditioned.

Squatter. The residential occupant of another's property without the owner's permission.

Stabilized Annual Income. A representative income is selected for the recent fluctuating annual incomes from an investment. The stabilized annual income may be an average of the recently generated annual incomes.

Stage of Real Estate Development. One of the phases of real estate development. Three phases or stages of real estate development may be identified as (1) the planning phase, (2) the operating phase, and (3) the termination or sell-out phase.

Standard Mortgage. The mortgage contract with fixed interest rate and fixed maturity, which has been widely used in the United States since the development of the FHA-insured mortgage in 1934.

Standard & Poor. A company that publishes financial statements of many American and foreign companies and constantly revised credit ratings for these companies.

Standard & Poor's 500 Stock Dividend Yield Index. The continuously maintained stock dividend yield index of Standard & Poor's Corporation, which includes the dividend yields of 500 stocks.

Standard & Poor's 500 Stock Price Index. The continously maintained stock price index of Standard & Poor's Corporation, which includes 500 stocks from various industries.

Standard Ratios. Some ratios are considered as standards for the business community. For example, the first-mortgage loan usually reflects 75 to 80 percent of appraised value or sale price, whichever is less. A standard ratio at this time for an apartment project operating ratio is 45 percent.

State-approved Development Credit Corporations. Corporations set up with the approval of the state government for the financing of industrial and commercial development within the state.

State-chartered Life Insurance Company. The life insurance company can only be chartered by a state and not by a federal government entity. The company is usually charged with the taking of insurance premiums for investment in assets that assure timely payments to the insured and the insured's beneficiaries, current coverage of the operating expenses of the company, and payment of a reasonable amount of dividends to the mutual shareholders or the stockholders.

State Insurance Commission. The commission set up by the state government for the chartering and regulating of the life insurance companies doing business within the state boundaries.

State and Local Retirement Funds. The retirement funds associated with state and local government agencies and their employees. Contributions may be made periodically by both the appropriate government agency and the employee for the accumulation of the retirement fund, for withdrawal in later years by the employee.

State-sponsored Industrial Development Authorities. State agencies that compile data on industrial development factors viewed favorably by companies that might locate within the state. The agencies may also sell tax-exempt industrial development bonds to finance a sale-leaseback for an industrial corporation selecting a new site within the state.

State Tax Incentive and Financing Programs for Pollution Control. Programs of state government that provide tax incentives and financing sources for company installation of pollution-control devices.

Statement of Changes in Net Worth. The financial statement that shows the changes in net worth of a corporation over a given period of time.

Step-up Amortization Plan. A plan whereby mortgage payments gradually increase over time. Mortgage payments are established at an initial level for a period of time. Once that period of time passes, mortgage payments are raised in dollar amount for a given period of time. At the end of that period of time, the mortgage payments may again rise in dollar amount. At some point in the mortgage term, the mortgage payments may stabilize, so that the mortgagor pays the same periodic amounts for the remainder of the mortgage periods.

Store Drawing Power. The attraction that the retail store has for customers. The variety of goods and services usually determines the degree of its drawing power.

Straight-line Depreciation. The method of depreciation that amounts to an equal depreciation expense every year of the asset economic life, assumed for income tax purposes. The amount of annual straight-line depreciation expense is found by dividing 1.0 by the number of years of economic life for tax purposes and then multiplying this decimal percentage by the original cost of the asset, less salvage value.

Straight-line Recapture. The equal amount of dollars set aside each year for accumulation of the total investment outlay over the economic life of the depreciable property where the amounts are not assumed to be invested by the property owner. No interest accumulates on the amounts set aside.

Subcontractor. One who contracts with the general contractor to perform part of the work of the owner-developer, which was contracted to be done by the general contractor.

Subdivision Developer. The person who subdivides raw land and improves it for residential construction. This person may also construct houses on a speculative basis on the improved, subdivided land.

Subject Property. The property to be appraised. The property chiefly under consideration.

Subjective Judgment. The judgment made on the basis of intuition, personal preference, or personal opinion.

Sublessee. The contracting tenant who leases from the primary lessee. The primary lessee has contracted for the use of the space with the lessor, the owner.

Subletting. The renting of leased space by the lessee, who rented the space from the lessor, who is usually the owner of the building or the land.

Subordinated Financing. Financing of the investment in an asset that requires the establishment of priority rights among the numerous financial interests involved. For example, if the developer requires leasehold financing, the mortgage lender usually requires the subordination of the landowner's interest to the interest of the leasehold mortgagee.

Subsidized Housing. Housing that is provided for low- and moderate-income occupants on a rental or ownership basis, where the government provides mortgage interest supplements, rent supplements, or other payments from government tax sources to permit ownership by a private investor who will receive a market yield on the investment.

Subsidized Interest Payments. If the mortgagor pays only part of the interest payments required by the mortgagee, who must obtain a market yield on the investment, the remainder of the required payments may be paid by a government agency from tax revenue sources. When the governmental unit supplements the individual mortgagor's payments, so that the lender will be satisfied, the interest payments are said to be subsidized.

Subsidized Rent. If a government agency pays the landlord part of the required rent and the tenant pays part of the rent, the required rent payment is said to be subsidized.

Substantial Economic Impact. The effect of real estate development that materializes in substantial economic changes.

Substitution. The replacement of one thing for another.

Suburban Office Buildings. Office buildings located in the outlying areas of metropolitan areas.

Sum of the Years' Digits Depreciation. The depreciation method in which the first year's depreciation is found by taking the fraction of the number of years of the economic life, divided by the sum of the digits of the economic life of the asset, times the depreciable amount. The second year's depreciation is calculated by taking the fraction of the economic life, minus one, divided by the sum of the years' digits of the economic life of the asset, times the depreciable dollar amount. The depreciation expense of subsequent years is found in a similar manner.

Sum of the Years' Digits. Add the numerals that individually make up a total number of years. If the economic life of an asset is five years, add $1 + 2 + 3 + 4 + 5$ and get the total sum of 15.

Superette. A limited goods and services food store, often found in the ground-floor or first-floor space of an apartment building, which caters to the needs of the building tenants and the apartment tenants in other buildings in the vicinity.

Super-regional Shopping Center. The type of shopping center that accommodates chain and independent store tenants on multiple levels of retail and service space, usually enclosed under a single roof for weather protection and temperature control. Three or four department stores may be directly linked to a mall of 50 to 100 tenants. The customer radius in terms of driving time may be 30 to 45 minutes.

Supervisory Personnel. Employees of a company who supervise on a managerial basis other employees of the company.

Syndicate Manager. The person in charge of the sale of syndicate shares, the acquisition of the syndicate property, the management of that property, and the record-keeping and periodic disbursement of cash flow and other benefits on a proportional basis to the syndicate members.

Syndication Sales Fee. The fee charged by the syndicate manager for the sales expenses associated with the marketing of the syndication shares to individual investors.

Syndicate Share. One share of the ownership of a syndicate.

Tangible Personal Property. Personal property that may be touched and used.

Tax Bracket. The marginal tax bracket found in the Internal Revenue Service tables that apply to the taxable income of the taxpayer.

Tax Code. The tax legislation passed by the Congress of the United States.

Tax Credit. The tax provisions that approve the deduction of certain tax-deductible expenses from the tax payment due within the consideration of the subject expense. The tax credit permits deduction "off the top" of the otherwise payable taxes. A very favorable type of tax deduction.

Tax Deductibility. The provision for reduction of otherwise taxable income by expenses that the Internal Revenue Service and other income-taxing authorities approve for deduction. For example, the income property investor may deduct for income tax purposes depreciation expense, mortgage interest payments, and property tax payments.

Tax Deferral. The avoidance of current payment of taxes in favor of payment of taxes in the future.

Tax-exempt Municipal Bond Financing. Financing by means of municipal bonds whose interest is not considered income for federal income tax purposes. The bond interest received by the investor is exempt from federal income taxation.

Tax Exemption on Manufacturers' Inventories. Exemption of certain manufacturers from taxation on company inventories.

Tax Exemption on Raw Materials Used in Manufacturing. The exemption of a company from taxation on raw materials used in manufacturing.

Tax-free Exchange. An exchange or swapping of real property, where the payment of taxes is avoided at the present time.

Tax Rate Schedules. The tables of tax rates prepared by the Internal Revenue Service and other taxing agencies of the local, state, and federal governments.

Tax Reform Acts of 1976 and 1977. Major tax legislation of the latter part of the decade of the 1970s.

Tax Savings. Tax loss, multiplied by the investor's marginal federal income tax rate.

Tax Shelter. A financial technique of charging noncash expenses against otherwise taxable income so that federal income taxes are reduced and overall cash flow is increased.

Tax Shelter Loophole. Those who are normally taxed in the upper part of the tax rate schedule may find tax shelter in provisions of the tax code. Accelerated depreciation permitted for certain types of improvements may be considered one of the "tax shelter" loopholes of the Internal Revenue tax code.

Tax Shield. The tax-deductible expense or the tax loss which can be used to reduce otherwise taxable income. As the deduction is made, the required tax payment is reduced.

Tax Surcharge. The additional tax levied on top of the ordinary taxation of income or property value.

Tax-anticipation Treasury Bills. Short-term obligations of the U.S. Treasury that usually do not exceed 180 days in maturity and that are sold at a discount and mature at a tax payment time. For tax payment, the par value of the bills is accepted by the Internal Revenue Service.

Tenancy by the Entireties. The type of joint ownership of property for husbands and wives that is utilized within a particular state. Otherwise, a state may provide community property rights or joint tenancy ownership for husbands and wives who jointly own property.

Tenancy in Common. The joint ownership form that permits ownership of an undivided interest in the asset, unequal contributions to the partnership venture, and the right of inheritance of the heirs and friends of the individual partners in the event of death. Survivorship rights between the partners are not permitted.

Tenancy Profile. The general social and economic characteristics of the tenants of an income property.

Tenant-claimant. The unlawful tenant who, after meeting the statutory requirements of adverse possession, asks the court to transfer the property title from the owner of record to the tenant.

Termination Stage. The phase of a project in which the project is sold and the net proceeds after taxes collected by the investor or investor group.

Tertiary Reserves. The reserves that supplement the primary and secondary reserves of a business entity, such as a commercial bank. These reserves act as a buffer against unforeseen losses and as a source of funds for exceptionally profitable ventures that cannot be predicted in advance.

Thrift Institution. A mutual savings bank or a savings and loan association that receives deposits and invests those funds primarily in residential mortgage loans.

Time Deposit. The savings account of the commercial bank, mutual savings bank, or savings and loan association, in which the funds receive a higher-than-passbook rate of interest for the extended deposit time of the funds. The regulatory agency establishes the maximum rate of interest that may be paid on a deposit left in the financial institution for the contractual period of time.

Time-sharing Pad Owner. The owner for a given period of the year of a mobile home site, who shares the ownership of the site with other owners.

Time-sharing Rental or Condominium Space. The sharing of rental or condominium space, in terms of usage by certain occupants during certain time periods and usage by other occupants during other time periods of the year. The occupants may be renters or condominium owners, but they share the same space on a time-assignment and preference basis.

Times Interest Earned Before Taxes. The factor that shows how much protection is available for the full payment or required interest in case the earnings available for interest fluctuate with the level of financial success of the company. The factor is calculated by dividing the required interest amount into the net profit of the company available for the payment of interest federal income taxes are deducted.

Title Insurance Premium. The premium paid at the time of underwriting of title insurance on real property, which benefits the mortgagee, mortgagor, or both.

Total Actual Rent Collections. The total of the dollars of rent collected during one time period. This amount may differ from the contractual amount due.

Total Dollar Return Method. The method of figuring the return on investment by merely observing the total dollar return over the investment period.

Total Monthly Housing Expense. The total monthly house mortgage payment, utility expenses, and maintenance expenses.

Total Net Rentable Area. The total building area that is usable and rentable.

Travel Trailer Charges. Charges associated with mobile homes that are constantly used for highway travel.

Treasury Bond. An obligation of the U.S. Treasury which matures beyond five years into the future.

Treasury Note. Obligations of the U.S. Treasury that usually mature beyond 180 days in the future but within five years; intermediate-term U.S. Treasury obligations. Usually, shorter term Treasury obligations are called *bills* and longer term obligations are called *bonds*.

Treasury Securities. The short- and long-term debt obligations issued by the U.S. Treasury to cover the costs of running the United States government.

Trespasser. An occupant of real property, temporarily or permanently, who has not received permission from the landowner for the occupancy.

Triplex. A multifamily structure housing three residential units.

Trough. The lowest point in the curve. In economics, the trough is represented by the lowest level in the contraction or depression phase of the economic cycle.

Trust. A legal device for the holding of assets by a trustee for the joint owners or single owner of the assets, where the trustee may hold the right to maintain or manage the assets in a fiduciary capacity for the owners. Business trusts, land trusts, and real estate investment trusts are widely used specific forms of a trust.

200 Percent Declining Balance. Twice the straight-line rate, figured on a declining balance as current payments are subtracted from the balance owed.

Undivided Interest. An interest in property held jointly by two or more parties, where the property interest is not divided among the joint owners. The co-owners together own an undivided interest in the real property.

Unemployment Rate Trends. The increasing or decreasing pattern of unemployment rates over time for an area.

Unit-in-place Method. The method of cost estimation where the costs of the separate units of a building, including direct and indirect costs, are added together to derive total building cost.

Unrealized Capital Gain. The capital gain recognized on paper through computations but not realized in cash because the asset has not been sold.

Urban Land Institute. A private research and publication group supported by its membership, who encourage improvements in real estate development. The organization publishes monographs and newsletters about the recent changes in various areas of real estate development.

U.S. Department of Housing and Urban Development. The Cabinet department of the Executive Branch of the United States government that is concerned principally with housing programs involving federal mortgage insurance.

V.A. Loan Eligibility. The eligibility requirements for a Veterans Administration-guaranteed loan. Generally the veteran of a military conflict involving the United States must show proof of his or her military service, the service must have occured within approved intervals, and the service must have continued for an approved period of time.

Vacancy Rate. The portion of the rentable or salable units that was not rented or sold over the year's time.

Value in Exchange. The value placed on a property as a result of the forces of supply and demand. Strangers to the property may be bidding for the property against other strangers to the property.

Value in Use. The subjective value placed on an asset from the owner's use and familiarity with the asset. For example, a long-term owner of a single-family dwelling may attach more value to the family homestead, because of the long-term use and familiarity with the house, than a stranger would.

Value Indicators. The principal factors that determine the value of an asset.

Variable Rate of Interest. A rate of interest that changes with an index or a base rate, such as the New York bank commercial paper or prime rate.

Variable Rate Mortgage. The mortgage whose interest rate changes, usually every six months, based on the movement up or down of a money and capital market index or the movement up or down of the New York bank commercial paper or bank prime rate. Notice is given the mortgagor by the mortgage lender sufficiently in advance of the periodic mortgage payment.

Variety Store. The retail store that specializes in lower priced items related to home equipment and maintenance, such as toys, gifts, clothing, and other consumer nondurable goods.

Veterans Administration Home Mortgage Guarantee. The guarantee of the top $25,000 of the Veterans Administration-guaranteed home mortgage, which guarantees the lender against any loss of $25,000 or less when the loan goes into default and the mortgaged property is sold. Any loss incurred by the lender up to and including $25,000 will be met from federal tax monies in the possession of the Veterans Administration, a federal government agency.

Victorian-style House. The style of house that flourished at the turn of the twentieth century in the United States. The building style features high-ceiled rooms, frame exterior, lattice work around the veranda roof line, turrets from the upper floors, leaded glass windows, wide and long verandas, and two and three stories of living space. The newly rich built these ostentacious houses for public display of their newly acquired wealth.

War Babies. The babies born during and after a period U.S. military involvement.

Warehouse Requirements. The structural, equipment, and shelving requirements for a warehouse.

Warehousing. Storage of assets anticipating their sale at a future date.

Wholesale Price Index. The index of prices paid for an established group of wholesale goods and services by retailers, wholesalers, manufacturers, and other processors, which shows increases or decreases in price levels over time. The index is maintained by the Bureau of Labor Statistics of the U.S. Department of Commerce for the measurement of wholesale price changes.

Windfall Profits. The unexpected profits that accrue to a company or individual experiencing a favorable piece of luck with respect to an investment.

Working Capital. The surplus of current asset value over the value of current liabilities. This capital is used to meet expenses and operating requirements of the business enterprise.

Wraparound Loan. A loan that is extended by a mortgage lender when a prior mortgage loan on the same property remains intact. The wraparound lender receives the mortgagor's payment, which is designed to cover both loans. The wraparound lender agrees to pay the established mortgagee and to keep the balance of the mortgage loan payment as a yield on his investment.

Yield-recapture Method. The investor's yield requirement is added to the recapture rate to find the appropriate capitalization rate. Straight-line, annuity, or sinking-fund recapture rates may be used.

Yield to Maturity. The annual expected percentage yield on a security investment, taking into account the expected dividends and the amortized discount or premium.

Zoning Ordinances. Land-use regulations passed by local government officials, which designate the areas for residential, commercial, industrial, and institutional improvements. Zoning ordinances usually promote the community adherence to the adopted master plan for the community.

Index

Ability to pay, concept, 113
Accrued depreciation, 122-124
   economic obsolescence, 123-124
   functional obsolescence, 123
   physical deterioration, 123
Acid test ratio, 86
Adjusted basis, 241
Adverse possession, 39
   characteristics, 47
   usual statutory period, 48
Allodial system, 3
American stock exchange, 32
AMMINET market service, 30
Amortization plan, 61, 267-268
   balloon payment, 267
   floating interest, variable interest, 267-268
   interest-only period, 267
   mortgage balance due, 272
   mortgage constant, 271
   partial amortization, 62
   step-up amortization plan, 62
Annuity recapture, 139-140
Anticipation, principle of, 114
Apartment investment
   appraisal, 335
      cost approach, 335
      income approach, 336
      construction costs, 328-331
      development costs, 330-331
      feasibility analysis, 327-328
      financing, 336-337
      income and expense trend, 331-335
      investment yield analysis, 337-338
      market survey, 326-327
      reasons for the increase in, 324
Appraisal
   approaches, 110
   estimate of value, 111
   principles, 110
   process, 110
   report, 111
Appraisal principles
   ten principles, 110, 113
      anticipation, 114
      balance, 114
      change, 114
      competition, 114
      conformity, 114
      contribution, 115
      highest and best use, 116
      increasing and decreasing returns, 115-116
      substitution, 115
      supply and demand, 115
Appraisal process, 110
   steps in, 116-118
Assignment of rents, 62

Balance, principle of, 115
   principle applied in income property appraising, 136
Balance sheet, 84
Balloon payment, 61-62
   example of use, 272
   See Hangout, 272
Band of investment method, 140-141
Bank, definition of commonly used term, 14
Bank loan, short term, finance company use, 100
Basis, 238
   adjusted, 241
Black home ownership, 7
Bond, real estate, 168
   investment risks, 187
   purchase of, 177
   types of, 169
Bond purchase, investment risks, 187
Bond yields, competition from income property loan yields, 98
Boot, 239-240
Breakeven ratio, 60
   cash flows, operating stage, 258-259
Broker's method of investment yield measurement, 292-293

Index   467

Builder's method of cost estimating, 119
  See Trade Breakdown Method
Building codes, 21, 38, 46
Building construction, 170-171
  stock of a company, 173-174
Building-loan agreement, 63
Business cycle, 26
  four phases, 26
Business trust
  a special type, a REIT, 100
  general characteristics, 159
By operation of law, 41

Capital constraints, 63
Capital gain, 28
  definition, 177
Capital gains
  calculation of gain or loss, 231
  installment sale, 236-237
  nature of gain, 232
  taxation, 233-236
    corporate, 234
    debt obligations, 177
    individual, 233
Capital markets, flow of monies, 30
Capitalization rate
  derivation of, 137-143
    band of investment method, 140
    market comparison method, 138-139
    mortgage-equity method, 141-143
    theoretical method, 138
    yield-recapture method, 139
      annuity recapture, 139-140
      sinking fund recapture, 140
      straight line recapture, 139
  need for, 137
  use in general formula, 137
Cash budgeting policy, 269
Cash flow
  cash throw-off, 250
  definition, 251
  differences among basic investment forms, 256
  forecasting flows, 254
  net cash flow calculation, 251-254
  stages of investment and development, 256-260
    operating stage, 258-259
    planning stage, 257-258
    termination stage, 259-260

Cash flow distribution
  developer fees and equity participation, 269
  mortgage repayment, 269
  syndicator commissions, fees, profits, 269
  time value of money, 269
  to partners, 269
  to syndicate members, 269-270
Cash-on-cash return measurement, 292-293
Cash payback, 293
Change, principle of, 114
Civil rights act of 1968, 21
  bases of prohibited discrimination, 21
  purchase and rental application, 21
Commercial bank, 97-98
  construction loans, 94, 97
  financing construction loans, 63, 68
  financing development loans, 68
  financing land loans, 68
  financing permanent loans, 63
  general characteristics, 97-98
  mortgage lender, 92, 97
Commercial paper, 168
  definition, 177-178
  finance company sale, 100
Common stock, 31
Community master plan, 46
Community property, 49
  community-property rates, 49
  the overall marital rights, 49
Community shopping center, 347
  construction costs and indirect cost, 364
  development plan, 359
  financial analysis, 361
  income and expenses for the center, 365
  land cost/profit analysis, 362
  prodevelopment costs, 363
  pro forma analysis, 360
  retail center costs, 365
  site layout, 358
  sitework cost allocation schedule, 362
  summary of operations, 366
Comparative investment yields, 288
  internal rate of return, 290
  return on equity, real property, 290-291
Competition, principle of, 114
Comptroller of the currency, 97
Condemnation, power of, 47

Condominium, favorable aspects of ownership, 23
Condominium housing
  owner-occupied, 316
  rental, 318
Conformity, principle of, 114
Constant annual percent, 271
  definition, 271
  table, 273
  See Mortgage constant or loan constant
Construction
  cost trend, 23, 26, 28, 29
  value trends, 12
    private industrial and commercial, 12
    public, 12
Construction, building, 170-171
Construction company investment
  risks of investment, 186
Construction costs
  apartments, 328-331
  houses, 311-312
Construction loan, 63
  general loan terms, 68
  release of funds, 68
  sources of funds, 63, 68
Construction methods, houses, 310
Construction period interest, capitalization and amortization, 222-223
Construction period taxes, capitalization and amortization, 222-223
Consumer price index, 28
Consummate right, 43
Contribution
  principle of, 115
  principle applied in income property appraising, 136
Conventional home loan
  definition, 66
  graduated payment, 66
  insured by private mortgage insurance, 66
  loan-to-value ratios, 66
  reverse annuity, 66
  usual loan term range, 66
  variable rate loans, 66
Conventional loan, 64
Cooperative housing
  owner-occupied, 316
  rental, 318
Corporate bonds, 98
Corporation
  general characteristics, 156
  tax status, 157
Cost, 111-112

Cost approach, income property appraising, 135
Cost estimation methods
  builder's or trade breakdown, 119
  four methods, 118-122
  market comparison, 119
  quantity survey, 119
  unit in place, 119
Credit analysis, 74, 78
  ratio analysis, 79-86
Credit investigation, 74, 78-79
  credit rating, 79
  employment, 79
  ratio analysis, 79-80
  regulation by NCUA, 101
  savings and checking deposits, 79
Credit union
  general characteristics, 101
  mortgage lender, 92
  shares, 101
Crime insurance, 21
Culture, American, 32
Current ratio, 86
Curtesy rights, 43-44
  divorce terminates the right, 43

Debentures, REIT issuance, 100
Debt coverage ratio, cash flow, planning stage, 258
Debt ratio, 86
Debt service, 267
  balloon payment, hangout, 272
  fixed or variable payments, 269
  lender participation, 269-271
  mortgage balance due, 272
Debt service coverage formula, 272
Debt service coverage requirement, 60-61
Debt service requirements, 61
Defeasible fee, 40
Demand and supply, 113
Depreciable asset, 139
Depreciation
  change in methods, 220
  comparison of three methods, 218-219
  declining balance depreciation calculation, 216-217
  guidelines and regulations, 214
  personal property, 214-215
  real property, 215
    allowable methods, 216
    asset lifetimes, 215
  recapture of excess depreciation, 220

significance for tax purposes, 220
straight line depreciation calculation, 216
sum-of-the-years digits depreciation, 218
tax deductibility, 214
Developer compensation, 269
Development loans
  general loan terms, 68
  loan repayment, 68
  sources of funds, 68
Developments, large-scale, 407-410
  current types, 407
  HUD new town program, 407
  investment opportunities, 407
Disaster relief grants, 21
Discount points
  closing requirement, 97
  definition, 65
  seller payment, 64
Discount rate, need for, 137
Discounted cash flow
  income stream of even cash flows, 144
  income stream of uneven cash flows, 144
  method of use, 143-145
Discounted cash flow analysis, method of income approach to value, 137
Disintermediation, 27
  money-market certificates, 27
Dollars per square foot of rental area, 332
Dower rights, 42-43
  divorce terminates the right, 43
Dun and Bradstreet reports, 76

Economic cycle, 26
Economic obsolescence, 123-124
Ellwood formula, mortgage-equity method, 141-143
Ellwood tables for real estate appraising and financing, 142
Eminent domain, power of, 39
  characteristics, 46
  use of, 46-47
Employee retirement income security act, 1974, 99
Endowment fund
  general characteristics, 101
  mortgage lender, 92
English common law, 3

Environmental controls, 44
  federal and state controls, 44-46
Environmental impact study, 45
  statement, 46
Environmental protection agency, 45
Equity
  funds invested, 266
  participation, 267
Equity participation, 267, 271
Equity ratio, 86
Equity trust, 100
Escrow expense, 81-82

Fannie Mae, 81
Feasibility analysis, apartment investment, 327-328
Federal agencies
  apartment project loans, 94
  mortgage lenders, 94
Federal Deposit Insurance Corporation, 97
Federal environmental controls, 45
  summary of laws, 1899-1976, 45
Federal Home Loan Bank Board
  portfolio constraints, 97
  regulations, 96
Federal Home Loan Mortgage Corporation, 102-104, 30
Federal housing administration insured mortgage loans, 63
  annual insurance premium, 65
  discount points, 65
  graduated payment amortization schedules, 65 (FHA 245)
  many insurance programs, 64
  section 203(b) characteristics, 65
  subsidized rent and interest payments, 64
Federal income taxation
  corporation, 207
  individual, 205
Federal National Mortgage Association, 30
  institutional lender, 104
Federal Reserve
  bank requirements, 97
  regulation by, 97
Federal Savings and Loan Insurance Corp., regulations, 96

Index 469

Federally chartered financial institutions, 66
Fee simple determinable estate, 40
Fee simple estate, 39
  defeasible fee, 40
    fee simple determinable estate, 40
    fee simple estate subject to a condition subsequent, 40
    fee simple estate subject to an executory limitation, 40
  distinguishing features, 39
  subject to a condition subsequent, 40
  subject to an executory limitation, 40
Feudal system, 3
FHA housing programs, 20
  insurance on institutional purchases, 30
  regular underwriting requirements, 30
  section 203(b) program, 20
FHA-VA interest rate, 64
Finance company
  general characteristics, 100
  mortgage lender, 92
Financial foundation for real estate investment, suggested foundation, 191–192
Financial management rate of return, 296–299
Financial risk, 184
Financial standards, 79
Financial statements, 83
  balance sheet, 83–84
  changes in net worth, 85–86
  flow of funds statement, 84–85
  profit and loss statement, 84
Financing methods
  apartments, 336–337
  hotels and motels, 403
  industrial buildings, 393–395
  office buildings, 375–378
  shopping centers, 350
Flood insurance, 21
Flow of funds statement, 84–85
FNMA stock, 174
Forecasting cash flows, 254
  complexities of, 254–255
    sensitivity analysis, 254–255
  general economic and real estate cycles, 254
  inflation impact, 254
Foreclosure, 26

Foreclosure counseling assistance, 21
Foreign real estate investors, 39
Foundation
  general characteristics, 101
  mortgage lender, 92
Freehold estate
  definition, 39
  fee simple estate, 39
    defeasible fee, 40
  life estate, 40
Front end costs, 267
  tax treatment of the various types, 267
  types of costs, 267
Functional obsolescence, 123
Future worth of a single sum, 277
Future worth of an annuity, 277

Gap loan, 68
  loan terms, 68–69
  reasons for, 68
General partnership
  general characteristics, 154
  legal nature, 154
  liability status, 155
  tax status, 155
GNMA-guaranteed mortgage-backed securities, 130
  bond-type, 103
  pass-through type, 104
  sample yields, 179
Government housing programs, 20
  federal programs, 32
  groups assisted, 20
  methods of housing policy implementation, 21
  special assistance programs, 30
Government National Mortgage Association, 30, 101
  general characteristics, 102, 104
  GNMA-guaranteed mortgage-backed securities, 103
Graduated payment mortgage, 30
  conventional, 66
  FHA 245 program, 65–66
  five plans, 65–66
  income requirements, 66
Grantee, 40–41
Grantor, 40–41
Gross income multiplier, 127
  formula, 143
  method of use, 143
Gross income multiplier analysis, method of income approach to value, 136–137

Gross national product, per cent invested in structures, 24
Gross private domestic investment in structures, 24
Gross rent multiplier, 126
  derivation, 129
  GRM analysis, 129
  use of, 135
Gross stabilized income of prospective mortgagor, 76
Ground lease, 98
Growth-inducing impact, 45

Hangout
  definition, 272
  See Balloon Payment, 272
Highest and Best Use
  principle of, 116
  income property appraising, 136
Home ownership, 7
  black home ownership, 7
  capital gains, 28
  government goals and programs, 20
  recent room changes, 23
  sale price trends, 7, 23
  second-home ownership, 26
  social acceptance, 19
  trends in, 30
  vacancy rates, rental versus owner occupied units, 24
Home ownership trends
  age groups, 30
  ethnic groups, 30
  geographic locations, 31
  income groups, 30
  urban-suburban locations, 31
Homestead exemption, 21
Hotel and motel investment, 401
  construction cost trends, 402
  lodging industry statistics, 411–412
  operating and financing, 402–403
  yields, 403–404
House financing programs, 309
House investment
  general factors, 306
  demand, 306–309
  supply, 309–312
  owner-occupied housing, 312–317
  rental housing, 317–319
House sales patterns, 306–308
Houses, demand for, 306–309
  home financing programs, 309

mortgage assumption, 309
regional sale patterns, 308
sales, existing versus new, 306-307
trend, home-buying age group, 307
trend, personal incomes and expenditures, 308-309
Houses, 309-312
  availability of loans, 310
  construction costs, 311-312
  construction methods, 310
  housing starts, 309-310
Housing management counseling, 21
Housing manufacturer companies, 173, 175
Housing policies, 20-21
  federal housing subsidies, 30
  government methods of implementation, 21
  mortgage interest subsidies, 30
  rent supplement programs, 30
Housing starts, 7, 309-310
  subsidized, 7
Housing tenure, 24
Housing values, 31
Hybrid trust, 100

Income approach
  house appraising, 126-129
  income property appraising, 135-145
Income capitalization, a method of finding present value, 136-137
Income property financing, 67
  financing land development and construction, 68
  financing the land, 68
  gap loans, 68
  permanent financing, 69
  wraparound loans, 69
Income property mortgage lenders, 94
Income property values, 31
Income trends, personal and family, 23
Increasing and decreasing returns, principle of, 115
Indirect source of pollution, 46
Individuals and households as mortgage lenders, 92, 94
Industrial bonds, 31
Industrial building investment financing, 393-395
  government incentives, 394-395

investment yields, 395
locational preferences, 391-392
trend, construction costs and land prices, 391-393
trends in general, 390
Inflation, price, 28
Inflation risk, 184
Inheritance laws, 43
Installment sale, real property, 236-237
Institute of real estate management, 331-335
  office building analysis, suburban, 375
Institutional lenders, 30
Insurance policies, types, 98
Integration
  congressional goals, 21
  U.S. department of housing and urban development goals, 21
Interest, variable, 267-268
  floating interest, 267-268
  money and capital market index, 267-268
Interest rate risk, 184
Interest subsidies, 21
Internal rate of return
  interpolation, 296
  yield measurement, 295-296
Internal Revenue Service
  organizational forms, 152
  REIT regulations, 100
Interpolation, 296, 298-299
Interstate land sales, 21
Investible funds, 27
Investment goals, 187, 189-191
  liquidity, 189-190
  profitability, 190
  safety of principal, 190
  tax shelter, 190
Investment growth
  mortgage debt, multifamily, 11
  nonresidential structure, 9, 11
  residential structures, 9, 11
  total growth, 9
Investment holding period, needed in mortgage-equity method, 138, 142-143
Investment interest, deduction, limitation on, 223
Investment recapture, 139
Investment risks
  degrees of risk, 188
  financial, 184
  inflationary, 184

interest rate, 184
liquidity, 184
risk hierarchy, 189
Investment tax credit, 221-222
Investment yield measurement, 291-299
  broker's method or cash-on-cash return, 292-293
  cash payback, 293
  financial management rate of return, 296-299
  internal rate of return, 295-296
  net present value, 293-295
  total dollar return, 291-292
Investor case illustrations, 190-191, 193
Investor's yield requirement
  income approach requirement, 138-142

Joint ownership
  community property, 49
  joint tenancy, 49
  rights and limitations, 48
  tenancy by the entireties, 48
  tenancy in common, 48
Joint property ownership, 22
  condominium, 22
  cooperative, 22
  corporate, 22
  joint tenancy, 22
  partnership, 22
  tenancy in common, 22
  trust, 22
Joint tenancy, 49
  partitioning, 49
Joint venture, general characteristics, 158
Junior mortgage loan
  finance company lending, 92
  life insurance companies, 94
  pension funds, 94

Land contract, 63
Land coverage ratio, 44
Land development, investment risks, 186
Land loan, 63
Land price subsidies, 21
Land trust, general characteristics, 159
Land use, 44
Lease purchase for subletting, 171
Leasehold estate, 41
  characteristics, 41

Leasehold estate (cont.)
  leasehold estate at sufferance, 42
  leasehold estate at will, 42
  leasehold estate for years, 42
  leasehold estate from period to period, 41
Leases
  index, 378
  office building, 377-378
  percentage, shopping centers, 351-352
  shopping center examples, 353
Leasing
  lessee, 185
  lessor, 185
  sublessee, 185
Leasing for subletting, risks of investing, 185
Legal list, 98
Lender participation in income, 61-62
Lenders
  home mortgage money, 92
  other types of mortgage money, 92
Lessee, 185
Lessor, 185
Leverage
  definition, 58
  effect of favorable leverage, 32
  effect on investor's return on investment, 58
Life estate, 40
  curtesy rights, 43-44
  dower rights, 42
Life insurance company
  general characteristics, 98
  mortgage lender, 92, 98
Limited partnership, real estate
  fund raising ability, 155
  general characteristics, 155
  legal organization, 156
  liability status, 156
  property holdings, 156
  shares of, 176
  tax status, 156
Linear foot, use of, 119
Liquidity risk, 184
Loan amount per unit, 60
Loan constant, 61-62
  definition of, 140
  use with band of investment method, 140
Loan money availability, 310
Loan progress chart
  discussion of its use, 272
  table, 274

Loan-to-value ratio, 60
  cash flows, planning stage, 257-258
Location, 112-113

Marital rights
  curtesy rights, 43-44
  dower rights, 42
  general characteristics, 42
  importance in property ownership, 38
Market comparison approach to value, 124-126
  adjustment of comparables, 125-126
  apartment building, 125
  income property appraising, 135
  single-family dwelling, 124-125
  types of adjustments to value, 126
Market comparison cost estimating method, 119
Market comparison method, 138-139
Market survey, apartment investment, 326-327
Market value, 111-112
Marketability, degree of, 31
Master plan, community, 46
Minimum taxes
  alternative minimum tax, 224
  regular 15 per cent add-on, 224
  tax preference items, 224
Mobile home parks
  construction costs, 406
  economies of scale, 405
  investment characteristics, 404
  investment yields, 406
  operating and financing expenses and revenues, 406
Mobile home shipments, 7
Mobile homes
  owner-occupied, 316
  rental, 318-319
Money cost, 28, 32
Money-market certificates, 27-28
Monthly fixed payments, 81
Mortgage
  applying for a mortgage loan, 75
  definition, 14
  nonstandard home, 30
  rising cost of, 23
  standard home, 30
Mortgage amortization, 32
Mortgage assumption, house purchase, 309

Mortgage-backed securities, 178
  bond-type, 178
  GNMA-guaranteed, 103, 178
  pass-through type, 178
Mortgage bankers, 30
Mortgage bonds, 178
Mortgage companies
  financing construction loans, 63
  financing permanent loans, 63
Mortgage equity method using the Ellwood formula, 141-143
Mortgage financing
  effect of leverage on investor's return on investment, 58-59
  effect on lender rules of thumb, 60
  importance to the investor, 56-58
  subordinated, 61
  tax effects of mortgage interest, 59
Mortgage insurance, 21
  government housing policy, 21
Mortgage interest
  tax effects, 59
  tax savings, 60
Mortgage interest subsidies, 30
Mortgage lenders
  income property, 94
  residential, 94
Mortgage loan application
  nature of the application, 76
  personal interview, 75
  property appraisal, 79
  ratio analysis, 79-86
    home loan application, 80
      credit guidelines, 81-82
    income property application, 82-86
    common ratios, 85
  shopping the market, 75
  system for applying, 75
Mortgage loan correspondent, 63
  endowment funds, 64
  life insurance companies, 64
  mutual savings banks, 64
  pension funds, 64
Mortgage market net flow of funds, 94
  commercial mortgages
  home mortgages
  multifamily mortgages
Mortgage money, 27
  cost related to leverage, 32
  movement of, 29
  trend in the supply, 27

472   Index

Mortgage out, 58
Mortgage participation
  definition, 177
  issuers, 177
Mortgage pool, 92
Mortgage terms, conventionally financed apartments, 337
Mortgage terms
  in general, 55-56
    strategic terms, 61
      possible lender participation in income, 61-62
      prepayment penalty, 62
      reasonable interest rate, 61
      relatively long mortgage term, 61
Mortgage default, 62-63
Motel investment, 401
Municipal tax-exempt bonds, 28
Mutual fund, tax-exempt real estate, 100
Mutual savings bank
  general characteristics, 98-99
  mortgage lender, 92, 94

National Credit Union Administration, 101
National Environmental Policy Act, 45
Neighborhood shopping center, 347
Net cash flow, estimates needed, 137
Net effective monthly income, 81
Net operating income
  derivation of, 137
  numerator of general formula, 137
Net present value
  yield measurement, 293-295
New town loan guarantees, 21
New towns
  HUD new town program, 407, 410
  listing of new towns, 408-409
  See Developments, Large Scale, 407
New York State Insurance Commission, 98
New York Stock Exchange, 32
Noncash expenses, 251
Nonstandard home mortgage, 30
  graduated payment, 30
  reverse annuity, 30
  variable rate, 30
Note, real estate, 168
Notorious possession, 47

Office building investment
  appraisal illustration, 381-385
  cost trend, 373
  financing, 375-378
  future trend, 371
    demand factors, 371-372
    supply factors, 372-373
  investment yields, 378-380
  leasing and management, 377
  recent trends, 371
Operating ratio, cash flows, operating stage, 258
Organization, legal, 152
  business trust, 159
  corporation, 156-157
  general partnership, 154-155
  joint venture, 158
  land trust, 159
  limited partnership, 155-156
  proprietorship, 152
  real estate investment trust, 159
  real estate syndicate, 158
Overbuilt condition, 26
Owner-occupied housing, 312-317
  condominium and cooperative housing, 316
  mobile homes, 317
  traditional detached dwelling, 312-316

Participation, income property mortgages, 267
  equity participation, 267
Partnership
  general, 154-155
  limited, 155-156
Partnership, special allocation to partners, 225
Pension fund, 94
  general characteristics, 99
  private noninsured pension fund, 92
  state and local, 92
Percentage leases, shopping centers, 351
Permanent loan, 63
  Conventional loan, 64
  FHA insured loan, 64
  interest rate change, 69
  lender participation, 69
  loan terms, 69
  VA guaranteed loan, 64
Permits, construction and operating, 46
  environmental control, 46
Personal incomes and expenditures trends, 308-309

Personal interview, mortgage loan application, 75
  borrower's capacity and intention to repay the loan, 76
  borrower's objectives, 75
  general format, 75
  nature of the application, 76-78
    home loan application, 76-77
    income property loan application, 78
Personal property, definition, 13
Physical deterioration, 123
Planned unit developments
  See Developments, large-scale, 407
Planning costs
  construction loan interest, 204
  fees, 202
  financing, 203
  insurance premiums, 204
  organizational legal expense, 202
  property taxes, 203-204
  recording, 203
Planning stage
  costs, tax implications, 201-205
    construction-related, 203-205
    financing, 203
    planning, 202
    recording, 203
    other taxation, 214-225
Policy loans, 98
Population trends, 22
  family size trends, 23
  mobility trends, 23
  trends in the age distribution, 23
Portfolio analysis, 6
Portfolio strategy, 191-193
  investments for selected objectives, 192
  possible portfolio items, 193
Prepaid interest, tax deductibility, 223
Prepayment penalty, 62
Present value of a single sum, 279
Present value of an annuity, 279
Price, 111-112
Primary mortgage market
  definition of, 14, 91
  institutional lending patterns, 96
Principles, appraising
  used in income property appraising, 135
  balance, 136
  contribution, 136

Index 473

Principles, appraising (cont.)
　used in income property
　　appraising (cont.)
　　　highest and best use, 135
　　　substitution, 136
Private housing investment, 7
　versus the gross national
　　product, 7, 9, 24
Private mortgage insurance,
　premium schedule, 66
Private property rights, history of,
　3
Pro forma statement of income
　and cash flow, 251-253
Profit
　calculation of net income, 250
　definition, 14, 250
　termination stage, 260
Profit-and-loss statement, 84
Property appreciation, needed for
　mortgage-equity method,
　138
Property depreciation, needed for
　mortgage-equity method,
　138
Property ownership
　government restrictions, 40
　history, 3
　　Babylonian empire, 3
　　Egyptian empire, 3
　　Greek empire, 3
　　Roman, 3
Property sale, 231
　calculation of after-tax net cash
　　proceeds, 234
　computation of gain or loss,
　　231-233
　excess depreciation, 235
　installment sale, 236-237
　nature of gain or loss, 232-233
　tax-free exchange, 237-240
　tax-free home sale, 240-241
　taxation of gain or loss, 233, 235
　　individual, 233
　　corporate, 234
Property taxes, urban locations, 31
Proprietorship organization
　fund raising ability, 154
　general characteristics, 152-153
　liability status, 153
　tax status, 153
Purchase-money mortgage, 63
Purchasing power of the dollar, 28
　consumer price index, 28
　wholesale price index, 28

Quantity survey cost, estimating
　method, 119-120

Ratio analysis, 79-86
　home price and mortgage ratios,
　　80-82
　　FHA credit guidelines, 81
　　FHLMC credit guidelines, 81
　　FNMA credit guidelines, 82
　income property ratios, 82
　　American Homes, Inc.,
　　　illustration, 86
　　common ratios, 85
　　financial statements, 83-86
Ratios, commonly used financial
　and credit, 85-86
　acid test, 85
　current ratio, 85
　debt ratio, 85
　equity ratio, 85
　return on sales, 85
　return on stockholders equity,
　　85
　return on total assets, 85
　times interest earned before
　　taxes, 85
Real estate, definition, 13
Real estate appraisal, definition,
　14
Real estate appraising, definition,
　111
Real estate cycle, 26
　four phases, 26-27
　overbuilt condition, 26
　relationship to business cycle,
　　26
Real estate investment
　approaches to, 5
　attributes of, 31
　definition, 14
　economic aspects of, 24
　economic cycle impact, 26
　financing, 100
　growth in, 9
　inflation, 28
　investment alternatives, 11-13
　population characteristics, 22
　portfolio analysis, 6
　property prices, 28
　reasons for studying, 4
　relative yield on real estate, 32
　risk-return analysis, 6
　significance of, 7
　versus the gross national
　　product, 7, 9
　views on, 5
Real estate investment attributes
　inflation protection, 31
　leverage, 32
　marketability, 31

　relative yield on real estate, 32
　tax shelter, 32
Real estate investment
　　opportunities, 167-170
　selected alternatives, 170
　　characteristics of, 170
　selected yields, 169
Real estate investment returns,
　266-268
　a dynamic process, 268, 272
　competing investment yields,
　　268, 272, 275-276,
　　288-291
　components, equity funds
　　invested, 266, 268
　　borrowed funds and their
　　　terms, 267-268
　　net operating income, 268
　　sale proceeds, 268
　time value of money, 275-282
Real estate investment trust
　financing construction loans, 68
　financing development loans, 68
　financing land loans, 68
　general characteristics, 100
　mortgage lender, 92
Real estate license requirements,
　4
Real estate loans
　financing residential property,
　　63
　　financing the lot, 63
　　financing house construction,
　　　63
Real estate purchase, risks of
　investment, 185
Real estate recessions, 27
Real estate stock, 167-168
　types of, 168
Real property, definition, 13
Real property rights
　establishment, 3
　freehold estates, 39-41
　legal framework for protection
　　of, 6
　marital rights, dower and
　　curtesy, 41
Reasons for studying real estate
　investment, 4
　employment opportunities, 4, 5
　field of study, 4, 5
　general area of business activity,
　　4
　general interest in individual
　　shelter, 4
　personal investment success, 4,
　　5

474　Index

real estate license exam
  preparation, 4
Reconciliation, value, 118
Refinancing, 62
Regional shopping center, 348
Remainderman
  vested, 40
  inchoate, 40, 43
Rent supplements, 21
Rental housing, 317-319
  condominium or cooperative
    unit, 318
  mobile homes, 318-319
  single-family detached dwelling,
    317
Rental income, American, 26
Replacement value, 112
Reproduction value, 112
Residential mortgage debt
  growth in, 9, 11
  less than market interest rates,
    30
  multifamily, 11
Residential mortgage lenders, 94
Restrictive housing devices, 22
Return on sales, ratio, 86
Return on stockholders' equity,
  ratio, 86
Return on total assets, ratio, 86
Reverse annuity mortgage
  financing, 30
Reversion, 41
  net cash, 271
Riot insurance, 21
Rules of thumb in real estate
  financing, 55
  breakeven ratio, 55, 60
  debt service coverage, 55, 60
  loan amount per unit, 55, 60
  loan-to-value ratio, 55, 60
  return on investment, 55, 58-60

Sale-leaseback agreements, 98
Sale price trends
  average, one-family homes, 7
  average prices, new and existing
    units, trends, 29
  property price trends, 28
Sale proceeds, 266
  change in property value, 266,
    268
  equity buildup, 266, 268
  net cash reversion, 271
Savings, trend, 24
Savings and loan associations
  Federal Home Loan Bank
    Board regulations, 96

Federal Savings and Loan
  Insurance Corporation,
  96
investments, 94
lending patterns, 96-97
mortgage lender, 92
stock, 174
Savings rate, trend, 24
Scarcity, 113
Second-home ownership, 23, 26
  rationale for, 23
  trend toward, 23
Secondary income, 82
Secondary mortgage market
  definition of, 14, 91
  institutional lending patterns,
    96, 101
    Federal Home Loan
      Mortgage Corporation,
      102
    Federal National Mortgage
      Association, 101-102
    Government National
      Mortgage Association,
      102-103
  maintenance of, 21
  system, 30
Security yields, real estate,
  selected, 169
Sensitivity analysis
  computer use, 275
  use of, 273, 275
Shares of beneficial interest
  real estate investment trust, 172
  recent financial data, 172
  share price index, 172
Shopping center
  definition, 347
  financing, 350
  investment yields, 352-356
  types, 347
    community, 347
    neighborhood, 347
    regional, 348
    specialty, 348
    super-regional, 348
Shopping center development
  cash flow analysis, 349-354
    components, 350
    expense sources, 350
    projection, 354
    revenue sources, 349-351
  construction costs, 348-349
  financing, 350
  investment yields, 352-356
  trend, 348

Short-term mortgage trust, 100
Sinking fund factor, 140
Sinking fund rate, 140
Sinking fund recapture, 140
Socioeconomic groups, 20
Solar heating system, 55
Sources of mortgage funds, 92-95
Special partnership allocations,
  225
Specialty shopping center, 348
Spouses, 42
Squatter, 47
Stabilized gross annual revenue,
  need for, 137
Stable monthly income, 82
Stages of investment and
  development, cash flows,
  256-260
Stages of real estate development,
  199
  planning and construction,
    199-200
  operation, 200
  sell-off or termination, 200
  timing, 200-201
Standard home mortgage, 30
State and local retirement fund,
  mortgage lender, 92
State-chartered financial
  institutions, 66
State department of banking or
  financial institutions, 96
State department of revenue,
  organizational forms, 152
State environmental controls, 46
State insurance commission, 98
Statement of changes in net
  worth, 85-86
Stock
  investment risks, 186-187
  purchase, 171-177
  real estate, 167-168
    types of, 168
      common and preferred, 98
Straight line recapture, 139
  rate, 139
Subordinated financing, 61, 63
Sublessee, 185
Subletting, 185
Substitution, principle applied to
  income property
  appraising, 136
  principle of, 115
Super-regional shopping center,
  348
Supply and demand, principle of,
  115

Index 475

Syndicate, real estate
  general characteristics, 159
  shares, 175
Syndicator compensation, 269-270

Tax abatement, 21
Tax credit, 21
Tax deductibility
  interest, 222
  mortgage prepayment penalty, 222
  repair expense, 222
  taxes, 222
Tax environment for real estate investment, 202
Tax-free exchange, 237-240
  basis, 238
  exchange of mortgaged properties, 238-239
  general characteristics, 237-238
  holding period, 238
  like-kind property, 238
  tax consequences of boot and mortgages, 239-240
Tax-free home sales
  calculation of adjusted basis of the new residence, 241
  calculation of gain, 241
  sale of a principal residence and its replacement, 240
  terminology and conditions, 240-241
Tax savings
  calculation, 60, 250
  circumstances of, 250
Tax shelter
  definition and discussion, 32
  depreciation expense, 32
  federal income tax deductions, 32
  for consolidated income, 21
Tax shields, 76
Taxation, federal income
  corporation, 207
  single and married individuals, 205
Tenancy by the entireties, 48

Tenancy in common, 48
Tenancy profile, 328
Tenant-claimant, 48
Thrift institution, definition, 98
Time value of money
  future worth of a single sum, 277
  future worth of an annuity, 277
  in real estate investment analysis, 275-282
  present value of a single sum, 279
  present value of an annuity, 279
Times interest earned (before taxes) ratio, 86
Total dollar return, 291-292
Total monthly housing expense, 81
Trade breakdown method of cost estimating, 119, 122
Treasury bonds, 28
  taxable bonds, 28
Trust, forms of
  business, 159
  land, 159
  real estate investment, 159

Unit in place cost estimating method, 119, 121
U. S. Housing and Urban Development Department
  new towns program, 407, 410
Urban Land Institute
  Dollars and Cents of Shopping Centers, 349
Utility, concept of, 113

Vacancy rate, 24
Value in exchange, 112
Value in use, 112
Variable-rate home loan, 66
  index, 66
  institutional offerings, 66
  variable elements, 66

Variable rate mortgage, 30
  inflation hedge, 62
Veterans Administration home mortgage program, 20
  loan guarantees, 21
Veterans Administration guaranteed mortgage loans, 63
  assumption, 64
  loan guarantee, 64
  loan term, 64
  monthly escrow payments, 65
  no VA loan limit, 64
  purchase of more than one home, 64
  seller payment of points, 64

Wholesale price index, 28
Wraparound loan
  debt service payment, 69
  definition, 69
  reasons for, 69

Yield measurement
  apartment investment, 337-338
  hotels and motels, 403-404
  industrial buildings, 395
  mobile home parks, 406
  office buildings, 378-380
  shopping centers, 352-356
  See Investment Yield Measurement, 291-299
Yield recapture method, 139
Yields, competitive investment, 288
  internal rate of return, 290
  return on equity, 290-291

Zoning, 21
Zoning ordinances, 38
  coverage, 44
  description, 44
  relationship to the community master plan, 44